BRIEF THERAPY

with Individuals and Couples

BRIEF
THERAPY

with Individuals and Couples

EDITED BY

Jon Carlson

& Len Sperry

ZEIG, TUCKER & THEISEN, INC., PUBLISHERS
PHOENIX, ARIZONA

Library of Congress Cataloging-in-Publication Data

Brief therapy with individuals and couples / edited by Jon Carlson and Len Sperry.
    p. cm.
Includes bibliographical references and index.
ISBN 1-891944-43-6
    1. Brief psychotherapy.   I. Carlson, Jon. II. Sperry, Len.

RC480.55 .B77 2000
616.89'14—dc21

                                                00-028969

Published by

ZEIG, TUCKER & THEISEN, INC.
3618 North 24th Street
Phoenix, AZ 85016

Manufactured in the United States of America

10 9 8 7 6 5 4 3 2 1

Contents

Part III   287

Introduction

———— ∞∞∞ ————

In 1946 Franz Alexander and Thomas French, two Chicago psychoanalysts, made the observation that not all patients need years of treatment and that some actually improve after only a few consultations. It was at this point that the search for more flexible, briefer, and time-efficient treatment was launched. Now, more than 50 years later (with the assistance of a health care upheaval), brief or short-term treatment is the treatment of choice. It is no longer an "alternative" form of therapy but rather has challenged traditional therapies to become more goal oriented, clearly focused, and centered on the development of the patient's existing strengths and abilities. All therapy has now become brief therapy!

More than 100 books on brief therapy have been published in the past decade. This statistic, in and of itself, is amazing. The publishing trend, along with the increasing expectation, and even demand, of third-party payers for briefer forms of therapy, has catapulted brief therapy from its former "stepchild" status vis-à-vis long-term psychotherapy to peer status, with both clinical and research respectability, in a relatively short time.

Although the number of publications is remarkable, their clinical utility has generally not been all that remarkable. Ironically, some of the longest books on brief therapy do little more than ponderously review theories of doing therapy briefly, while the very short books say little more than that brief therapy has great promise and applicability. Few books offer much information or guidance about actually doing brief therapy, actually applying its strategies in day-to-day clinical practice with adults. This is *not* to say that no clinically useful articles and book chapters have been written on brief therapy—on the contrary, there are some excellent articles and chapters. But they are scattered across the psychotherapy literature, leaving clinicians and trainees with really no single reference text or sourcebook to consult.

Our purpose in developing this book was perhaps a bit presumptuous: to set a new standard for publishing in the area of brief therapy. Our hope was to provide clinicians-in-training, as well as experienced clinicians, with the most clinical-friendly presentation of these intervention strategies and treatment methods in print. We wanted it to have immediate clinical utility. Hence we have compiled, in a single sourcebook, the best and most effective treatment strategies and interventions targeted to the treatment of individuals and couples. Each strategy is carefully described, and then clearly illustrated with clinical case material, by acknowledged leaders in the field of brief therapy. The chapters follow a common format: First, they describe the origins of a particular treatment orientation. Second, they specify the clinical indications for the treatment strategies unique to that orientation. Third, they describe the strategies in detail. And fourth, they illustrate the strategies with clinical case material from both an individual and a couple treatment context. Each chapter describes at least three representative brief intervention strategies.

We planned for the book to appeal to a broad audience. Typical brief therapy books address only the treatment either of individual clients by individual-oriented therapists or of couples by family-oriented therapists. But this book is meant to be clinically useful to both kinds of therapists, and particularly to the majority of clinicians, who are most comfortable working with individuals and will see couples, but rarely, if ever, work with whole families.

Hence this book brings together brief therapists from a wide variety of theoretical persuasions to present their strategies for working with individuals and couples. Part I contains strategies that are based primarily on cognition and behavior. First, Richard Stuart makes a strong case for the use of brief integrative behavior therapy. This approach is well researched and has clear strategies that are frequently used by clinicians of all theoretical persuasions. Frank Dattilio then highlights why cognitive-behavior therapy has gained a strong following among clinicians. He shows how this approach grew out of behavioral therapy and drew on many behavioral strategies, yet differs with its strong emphasis on changing cognitions. Charles Huber then describes rational-emotive behavioral therapy, emphasizing strategies that have more of a cognitive as well as systems perspective. Here the therapist actively challenges irrational forms of thought. Finally, Arnold Lazarus, frequently cited as the founder of behavioral therapy, presents his multimodal approach. An integrative model, it tailors treatment along seven different modalities—behavior, affect, sensation, imagery, cognition, interpersonal relationships, and biological processes—utilizing strategies that are dependent on the outcome of a very thorough assessment process.

Part II presents a variety of theoretical approaches whose roots lie in traditional psychotherapy. Leigh McCullough's essay on psychodynamic strategies is rooted in her work on characterological problems. Her approach involves an emphasis on emotions and emotional change. Bruce Ecker and Laurel Hulley offer a depth-oriented approach that uses many strategies common to other approaches. Michael Stadter and David Scharff highlight the contributions of object relations theory, one of the four branches of psychoanalytic thought. Some might be surprised to find their approach in a book on brief therapy, but their chapter shows how these strategies may be tailored toward brief efficient interventions. William Nicoll, James Bitter, Oscar Christensen, and Clair Hawes, like Steven Slavik, Len Sperry, and Jon Carlson, highlight the Adlerian approach. Although, this intervention is rooted in analytical thought, it is actually much more integrative, using interventions with thoughts, feelings, and behavior. Robert Wubbolding highlights a reality therapy approach, with strategies that are clear and simple following the WDEP (Wants, Doing, Evaluation, and Planning) system.

Part III offers a variety of newer, more innovative approaches. Michael Hoyt and Scott Miller describe a stage-appropriate approach to brief therapy whose origins lie in solution-focused and constructivist theories. Their model highlights Prochaska's model of stages of change. Jean McLendon then shows how focusing on clear communication and resourcefulness has many strategies that fit a brief therapy model. Wade Luquet presents the imago relationship therapy of Harville Hendricks. His approach has clear stages of intervention with many strategies for work with couples and families. Luciano L'Abate then describes how psychoeducational strategies are the intervention of the future, contending that talk alone cannot bring about successful brief interventions. Gerald Sklare shows how solution-oriented strategies can be used in an educational setting. Andrew Leeds and Francine Shapiro describe EMDR (eye movement desensitization and reprocessing), presenting some well-crafted strategies on working with individuals and couples who have

experienced traumatic stress. Finally, Len Sperry describes the biopsychosocial approach, which has its roots in biological change.

This, then, is an ambitious book that we trust will open up the world
of brief therapy strategies to you and enrich your practice.

Jon Carlson
Len Sperry

Contributors

James R. Bitter, Ed.D., is a professor of counseling at East Tennessee State University and a past president of Virginia Satir's Avanta Network. He has published several articles and book chapters on family therapy and made numerous presentations nationally and internationally. He serves as a trainer with the Adlerian Training Institute in Boca Raton, Florida.

Jon Carlson, Psy.D., Ed.D., is a professor of psychology and counseling at Governors State University in Illinois and a psychologist at the Lake Geneva Wellness Clinic in Wisconsin. He is past president of the International Association of Marriage and Family Counselors and editor of *The Family Journal: Counseling and Therapy for Couples and Families*. He holds a diplomate in family psychology (ABPP) and marital and family therapy (ABFamP). He is the author of 25 books and 120 articles, in addition to being a driving force behind several major video series, including "Brief Therapy Inside Out."

Oscar C. Christensen, Ed.D., is professor emeritus in the counseling and guidance department at the University of Arizona. He is internationally acclaimed as one of the foremost trainers of Adlerian family counselors and a pioneer in open forum family counseling. He has trained family therapists throughout the world, in classrooms, on film, at workshops, and through his books. He also serves as a trainer with the Adlerian Training Institute.

Frank M. Dattilio, Ph.D., ABPP, is a clinical associate in psychiatry at the University of Pennsylvania School of Medicine and a visiting lecturer at the Harvard School of Medicine. He holds a diplomate in both behavioral and clinical psychology and maintains a clinical practice in Allentown, Pennsylvania. He is author/coauthor or editor of 10 books and more than 100 professional articles and book chapters. His works have been translated into more than a dozen languages, and he is internationally acclaimed for his work in the field of cognitive-behavior therapy.

Bruce Ecker, M.A., L.M.F.T., a co-originator of depth-oriented brief therapy (DOBT), teaches this modality widely, at John F. Kennedy University graduate courses, major clinical conferences, agency staff trainings, and continuing education workshops. He is coauthor of *Depth Oriented Brief Therapy*; a volume on the psychology of involvement in spiritual groups and practices, *Spiritual Choices: The Problem of Recognizing Authentic Paths to Inner Transformation*; and various chapters and articles on DOBT. He is in private practice in the San Francisco East Bay area. His previous career in physics research produced many professional publications and presentations both in the United States and abroad.

Clair Hawes, Ph.D., is a psychologist with an extensive private practice in Vancouver, specializing in couple therapy. She has authored books, articles, and chapters on her approach to couple therapy and has provided training workshops throughout North America and Europe. Coauthor of the marital enrichment program *Couples Growing Together*, she also serves as a trainer with the Adlerian Training Institute.

Michael F. Hoyt, Ph.D., is a senior staff psychologist at the Kaiser Permanente Medical Center in Hayward, California, and a member of the clinical faculty of the University of California School of Medicine in San Francisco. He is the author of *Some Stories Are Better Than Others* and *Brief Therapy and Managed Care*; editor of *The Handbook of Constructive Therapies* and the two volumes of *Constructive Therapies*; and coeditor of *The First Session in Brief Therapy*. He is a well-known speaker and workshop presenter.

Charles Huber, Ph.D. is a professor of counseling and educational psychology at New Mexico State University. Also a practicing psychologist, he holds diplomates in both family psychology and behavioral psychology (ABPP). He has authored and edited 10 books and numerous articles, primarily in the areas of cognitive-behavioral and family systems theory and therapy.

Laurel Hulley, M.A., a co-originator of depth-oriented brief therapy, maintains a private practice in the San Francisco East Bay area and develops clinical trainings for Pacific Seminars. She is coauthor of *Depth Oriented Brief Therapy* and of several chapters on clinical methodology and theory, and she is coproducer of a training video series distributed internationally. She is a cofounding board member of the Julia Morgan Middle School for Girls.

Luciano L'Abate, Ph.D., ABPP, was on the faculty of Georgia State University for most of his academic career, where he was director of the Family Psychology Training Program and the Family Study Center. He retired as professor emeritus of psychology in December 1990. He is the author or coauthor of more than 250 papers, chapters, and book reviews in professional journals, and he is the author, coauthor, editor, or coeditor of 30 books and one book in press. His work has been translated into Chinese, Finnish, French, German, Japanese, Italian, Polish, and Spanish. He was awarded the title "Family Psychologist of the Year for 1994" by Division 43 (Family Psychology) of the American Psychological Association. He has lectured and given workshops around the world.

Arnold A. Lazarus, Ph.D., ABPP, is a distinguished professor of psychology emeritus at Rutgers University and is President of the Center for Multimodal Psychological Services in Princeton, New Jersey. The recipient of numerous awards, including the First Annual Cummings Psyche Award, he was honored by the American Psychological Association Division of Clinical Psychology for his distinguished professional contributions. He is the author of 16 books and more than 200 journal articles. A past president of several professional organizations, he currently serves on several professional editorial boards. In 1999, he received Lifetime Achievement Awards from the California Psychological Association and the Association for Advancement of Behavior Therapy.

Andrew M. Leeds, Ph.D., is a California-licensed psychologist with twenty-five years of private practice psychotherapy experience. He practices in Santa Rosa, where he specializes in the assessment and treatment of acute and chronic PTSD, anxiety and dissociative disorders, addictive behaviors, and depression, and provides relationship counseling. A senior trainer with the EMDR Institute, he received his own initial training in EMDR in 1991. As a senior EMDR trainer, he has conducted some 60 training programs in Belgium, Canada, England, France, Japan, and the United States. An invited presenter at four of the first five annual EMDR international conferences, he has also presented papers on EMDR at a number of national and regional professional associations, including the California Psychological Association, the American Psychological Association, the American Psychiatric Association, and the Society for Psychotherapy Integration. He serves on the editorial advisory board for *Traumatology*, an electronic journal. In 1996 he helped establish and now serves as moderator of the EMDR Institute electronic discussion list. He is the author of "Lifting the Burden of

Shame: Using EMDR Resource Installation to Resolve a Therapeutic Impasse," in *Extending EMDR: A Case Book of Innovative Applications* edited by Phil Manfield.

Wade Luquet, M.S.W., Ph.D., is in private practice in North Wales, Pennsylvania, and an associate at the Relationship Center in Spring House, Pennsylvania. He is an instructor and coordinator of the Marriage and Family Therapy track in the Graduate Counseling Program at Eastern College in Saint Davids, Pennsylvania. He is the author of *Short-Term Couples Therapy: The Imago Model in Action* and co-editor and contributor to *Healing in the Relational Paradigm: The Imago Relationship Therapy Casebook*. He is Associate Editor of the *Journal of Imago Relationship Therapy* and the author of several book chapters and journal articles.

Leigh McCullough, Ph.D., is an associate clinical professor and director of the Psychotherapy Research Program at Harvard Medical School. She was the 1996 Voorhees Distinguished Professor at the Menninger Clinic and received the 1996 Michael Franz Basch Award from the Silvan Tomkins Institute for her contributions to the exploration of affect in psychotherapy. She is the author of *Changing Character: Short-Term Anxiety-Regulating Psychotherapy for Restructuring Defenses, Affects and Attachments* and she is on the editorial board of *Psychotherapy Research*. She conducts training seminars in short-term psychotherapy worldwide and maintains an independent clinical practice in Dedham, Massachusetts.

Jean A. McLendon, M.S.W., C.C.S.W., is a private-practice psychotherapist and organizational consultant based in Chapel Hill, North Carolina, where she also staffs and directs Satir system training programs. She is a faculty member of Satir Institute of the Southeast; Avanta: The Virginia Satir Network; and Antioch's whole systems design graduate program in Seattle. She is an approved supervisor of the American Association of Marriage and Family Therapy and a charter member of the American Family Therapy Academy. She has published several articles and book chapters and has presented Satir model workshops to professional groups in Europe, Canada, the Middle East, the South Pacific, and across the United States. She is featured in the award-winning video series "Family Therapy with the Experts."

Scott D. Miller, Ph.D., is a cofounder of the Institute for the Study of Therapeutic Change in Chicago and conducts workshops and trainings worldwide. With his colleagues Barry Duncan and Mark Hubble, he has produced four books: *Handbook of Solution-Focused Brief Therapy, Escape from Babel, Psychotherapy with Impossible Cases,* and *The Heart and Soul of Change.* He is also coauthor (with Insoo Kim Berg) of *Working with the Problem Drinker* and *The Miracle Method.*

William G. Nicoll, Ph.D., is associate professor and chair of the counselor education department at Florida Atlantic University. He served as the national trainer in brief therapy for the American Counseling Association and is the director of the Adlerian Training Institute in Boca Raton. His primary interests are in the areas of brief therapy and family interventions with school-related problems. He has published numerous articles and book chapters and conducted more than three hundred training workshops throughout Europe, North America, and South America.

David E. Scharff, M.D., is codirector of the International Institute of Object Relations Therapy in Chevy Chase, Maryland. A psychoanalyst, psychiatrist, and family therapist, he is a clinical professor of psychiatry at Georgetown University and the Uniformed Services University of the Health Sciences. He is a former president of the American Association of Sex Educators, Counselors and Therapists. Among his twelve books are *The Sexual Relationship* and (with Jill Savage Scharff) *Object Relations Family Therapy, Object Relations Couple Therapy, The Primer of Object Relations Therapy,* and *Object Relations Individual Therapy.*

Francine Shapiro, Ph.D., the originator and developer of EMDR, is a senior research fellow at the Mental Research Institute in Palo Alto, California. She serves as executive director of the EMDR Institute in Pacific Grove, California, and heads the EMDR Humanitarian Assistance Programs, a nonprofit organization that coordinates disaster response. She does pro bono trainings worldwide. She has been designated as one of the "cadre of experts" of the American Psychological Association and the Canadian Psychological Association's Joint Initiative on Ethnopolitical Warfare. She is on the founding editorial advisory board of the journal *Traumatology.* She has written more than 30 articles and chapters and three books: *EMDR: Eye Movement Desensitization and Reprocessing, EMDR,* and *EMDR and the Paradigm Prism.* An invited presenter at most major psychology conferences over the past ten years, she has served as adviser to three trauma journals. She was awarded the 1993 Distinguished Scientific Achievement in Psychology Award, presented by the California Psychological Association.

Gerald Sklare, Ed.D., is a professor in the department of educational and counseling psychology at the University of Louisville. He has authored many articles and the book *Brief Counseling That Works: A Solution Focused Approach for School Counselors*. He has also presented many workshops on solution-focused brief counseling throughout the United States for mental health agencies, school districts, and professional organizations.

Steve D. Slavik, M.A., is in private practice in Victoria, British Columbia, specializing in marital counseling. He also delivers group programs to British Columbia First Nations groups. He has been editor of *The Canadian Journal of Adlerian Pshchology* since 1995 and has published a number of articles in Adlerian journals.

Len Sperry, M.D., Ph.D., is vice-chair and professor in the department of psychiatry and behavioral medicine at the Medical College of Wisconsin. In addition, he holds appointments as professor of family and community medicine and as professor of preventive medicine. He is board certified in clinical psychology, preventive medicine, and psychiatry, and is a fellow of the American Psychological Association and of the American Psychiatric Association. He is a member of the American Family Therapy Academy, the American College of Preventive Medicine, and the American College of Psychiatrists. He has published twenty-eight professional books, including *The Disordered Couple*, and more than 200 chapters and journal articles. He is on the editorial board of 10 professional journals, including the *American Journal of Family Therapy* and *The Family Journal*. He is listed in *Who's Who in America* and *Best Doctors in America*.

Michael Stadter, Ph.D., is a clinical psychologist in private practice in Bethesda, Maryland. He is dean of students at the International Institute of Object Relations Therapy in Chevy Chase, and is on the faculty of the Washington School of Psychiatry in Washington, D.C. He has served as assistant director of the Psychological Center at Georgetown University and as director of the Center for Psychological and Learning Services at American University. His experience with brief therapy includes work in clinics, private practice, and the development and administration of EAP programs. He is the author of *Object Relations Brief Therapy: The Relationship in Short-Term Work*.

Richard B. Stuart, D.S.W., ABPP, is Director of the Clinical Psychology Respecialization Program of the Fielding Institute and Clinical Professor Emeritus in the Department of Psychiatry and Behavioral Sciences at the University of Washington. A past president of the Association for the Advancement of Behavior Therapy, he is the author of more than 100 professional publications and has had 35 years of experience in the delivery and supervision of individual, couple, and family therapy.

Robert Wubbolding, Ed.D. is the director of the Center for Reality Therapy and professor of counseling at Xavier University in Cincinnati, Ohio. He has taught reality therapy in North America, Asia, Europe, and the Middle East. He has authored many publications, including *Using Reality Therapy, Understanding Reality Therapy, Reality Therapy for the 21st Century*, and *Employee Motivation: What to Do When What You Say Isn't Working.*

Part I

1

Brief Integrative Behavior Therapy
with Individuals and Couples

Richard B. Stuart

Behavior therapy arose at a time when psychoanalysis was the overwhelmingly dominant treatment approach. Early behaviorists believed that psychoanalysts relied on untestable assumptions about the etiology and structure of the human psyche, placed far too much emphasis on pathology, and offered a very slow and exorbitantly expensive form of therapy that could not be objectively evaluated (Kazdin, 1978; Stuart, 1971). In contrast, behavior therapy has been synonymous with strength-oriented, relatively brief therapy, essentially all aspects of which are measurable. Although its initial scope was fairly narrow, behavior therapy has not been static in the years since its inception: it has undergone a continuous process of evolution and now encompasses an integrated and verifiable theory of the etiology and change of human behavior.

After discussing the meaning of the word *brief*, this chapter will outline some of the principles of this evolving integrative model of behavior therapy (IBT). It will then suggest some guidelines for, and illustrations of, the clinical application of IBT with individuals and couples.

The Meaning of Brief

To many in the mental health community, the word *brief* implies "suboptimal." When a therapy is described as brief, the connotational subtext is often that the patient will be offered less help than is really needed. But this connotation is in the mind of the beholder. Those committed to an extended process of developmental therapy will view any effort to curtail the duration as contrary to the patient's interest (e.g., Miller, 1996). But others, who view long-term therapy as too costly, too time-consuming, and/or too likely to foster dependency, will place a high premium on approaches that can achieve their goals quickly (e.g. Bagarozzi, 1997).

The duration of therapy is normally defined by the number of sessions, although it is equally influenced by the length and/or spacing of sessions. Because *brief* is a relative term, it can be understood only by reference to some standard of length. Lowry and Ross (1997) asked 234 psychologists to estimate how many 50-minute individual sessions were "necessary to return a person with a particular disorder to a 'normal range of functioning' without the use of medications" (p. 272). Across the list of problems, an average of 30–40 sessions were deemed necessary, ranging from 11–16 for work problems to 79–104 for multiple personality disorders. In addition to the nature of the problem, however, the therapist's orientation also affected the number of sessions considered necessary. Those who identified themselves as working from a psychodynamic orientation believed that an average of 41–52 sessions would be needed, while an average of 23–29 sessions were deemed necessary by those who claimed eclectic, behavioral, or cognitive-behavioral orientations.

When treatment limits are determined by therapists' orientations, they are theoretically meaningful. But in the real world, two other forces contribute powerfully to decisions about the length of therapy. Third-party providers dictate the number of sessions based on considerations of medical economics. Managed-care organizations (Haas & Cummings, 1991) and even state and federal guidelines (Stomberg, Loeb, Thomsen, & Krause, 1996) set limits at 10–20 sessions, regardless of the clinical issue. In addition, clients decide how long they are willing to stay in therapy in keeping with their own beliefs about its cost-effectiveness. Clients have generally been found to terminate therapy at the *lower end* of the range of sessions for which they can be reimbursed (Olfson & Pincus, 1994). Even before the ascendance of managed care, Koss and Butcher (1986) found that the majority of treatment offerings consisted of fewer than 25 sessions. Apart from the cost of therapy in time and money, it is possible that in this era of wonder drugs, the 15-second sound bite, and the "one-minute" manager, philosopher, partner, or parent, clients have only a short attention span. It is also possible that clients may sense that after several sessions their rate of improvement reaches an asymptote, diminishing the treatment's cost-effectiveness after the crisis has passed.

Many years ago, Stuart and Tripodi (1973) found an unexpected explanation for a client's early termination of therapy. Court-referred delinquents and their families were randomly assigned to conditions in which treatment was limited to 15, 45, or 90 days. The results showed that the 15-day treatment did not allow enough time to initiate all the changes that were needed, and that the 45-day treatment produced the best outcome. Of particular interest was the fact that those in the 90-day treatment achieved results comparable to those in the 45–day treatment during the *first half* of their treatment, but systematically *deteriorated* during the second half. Analysis of audiotapes of the sessions revealed that therapists and clients both searched for problems to justify the continuation of therapy, and that this search had an iatrogenic impact.

What, then, is the duration of *brief*? For the purpose of this chapter, brief is defined as one to eight one-hour sessions, distributed over a period of up to 12 weeks. While this is clearly not enough time to help clients build a new personality structure, it is often sufficient to help them meet the challenge of many, if not most, of the issues that motivate them to seek outside assistance.

The Nature of Intervention Theory

Discussion of the nature of any one theory of psychotherapy becomes more meaningful if it is placed within the context of alternative points of view. A few observations about the context in which IBT arose will help to shed light on its similarities and differences with respect to alternative points of view.

Virtually all theories of personality and therapy accept the basic premise that behavior is a function of the interaction between personal characteristics and environmental influences (Equation 1).

$$(1) \ B = f \, PE$$

Theories of personality put their emphasis on the person, with the supposition that much of behavior is trait-driven and is highly consistent across situations (Equation 2).

$$(2) \ B = f \, Pe$$

As early as the 1930s, some theorists and researchers began to feel skeptical about the validity of descriptions of personality characteristics. They instead presented evidence that situational demands often shape behavior, which they therefore began to construe as principally state-driven. Therefore they emphasize the importance of the environment in shaping behavior (Equation 3).

$$(3) \ B = f \, pE$$

And so the theoretical battle lines were drawn between two very disparate camps, one headed by orthodox psychoanalysts and the other by radical behaviorists.

Fortunately, during the past three decades, reason and perspective have returned to both sides through the gradual ascendance of integrative theories (e.g., Reisman, 1971). An increasing number of personality theorists have acknowledged that environmental forces can result in differences in individual behavior in varied situations. And behavior therapists have acknowledged that people's behavior often does show strong cross-situational consistency as they choose and shape the environments in which they live. The result has been a noteworthy consilience (Wilson, 1998) as the various schools of psychotherapy and behavior therapy move toward each other. Despite the wide diversity in both global approaches, with subsystems working from very different assumptions as rationales for a wide variety of techniques, almost everyone accepts the theory represented by a qualified Equation 1. The qualifications include the assumptions that P consists of a broad array of measurable cognitive and affective characteristics, and that E is a system that is in a never-ending coevolutionary interaction with the individual (Maturana & Varela, 1992).

Facilitating this drift toward the integration of theories is the gradual acceptance of a common epistemology by all but the extremists in the personality and behavioral camps. Behaviorists have always eschewed what they regarded as the subjective hypothetical constructs that constituted the core of most theories of personality; for example, Watson (1913) did not consider topics like consciousness to be "proper objects of investigation" (p. 177), a view echoed by Skinner (1953) four decades later. The approach of these behaviorists relied on observable intervening variables (MacCorquodale & Meehl, 1953) in efforts to strengthen and/or predict behavior rather than to explain it. But as the human side of science came to the fore, the grip of rigid objectification loosened and "neobehaviorism" (Smith, 1986) emerged. Fueled by the birth of cognitive science, which applied sound research methodologies (Baars, 1986), behaviorists' rejection of the "black box" of human consciousness was overcome as "cognitivism" (Thagard, 1992) was added to and radically altered the scope and logic of their approach. Meanwhile, personality theorists have increasingly accepted the need to empirically test the descriptive and explanatory language that they employ. This is particularly true of those who offer briefer therapy approaches (e.g., Book, 1998; Messer & Warren, 1995; Ryle, 1992; Strupp & Binder, 1984). The result is a widening common arena in which an integrative theory that draws on knowledge from many discoverable aspects of the human condition may flourish.

Despite the basic assumptions that many therapeutic approaches share, important differences do become obvious in an examination of the points at which they elect to initiate change. Insight-oriented therapies typically begin by promoting cognitive changes through increases in self-understanding and/or insight. Therapies that stress emotion typically make early use of some form of abreactive or cathartic technique, sometimes in association with relabeling to promote new feelings. Skill-building therapies begin by building clients' behavioral repertoires. And environmentally focused interventions begin by modifying situational constraints and opportunities. Regardless of how the therapists initiate or evaluate their intervention, most clients enter therapy because they feel bad and consider therapy a success only when they feel better—ideally through the achievement of some identifiable objectives.

In summary, while in the not-too-distant past fairly sharp differences separated the behavioral and psychodynamic traditions, agreement on the value of empirical findings has recently tended to bring them much closer together. The rift is narrowed even further as brief intervention methods have evolved, given this observation by Koss and Butcher (1986): "While school identification exists in brief psychotherapy, most approaches are considerably more eclectic in their choice of interventions than is true of long-term therapy" (p. 644).

Keys to Effective Brief IBT

IBT is a large cluster of approaches drawn from classical and operant conditioning and research on cognitive and affective processes. Early in the development of behavior therapy, integrative approaches were suggested (e.g., Goldfried & Davison, 1976), and they have continued to proliferate since. Regardless of the blend of techniques, IBT offerings share a number of common denominators (see, for example, Fishman & Franks, 1997; Kazdin, 1978; Spiegler & Guevremont, 1993; Stuart, 1980). For example, all accept social learning theory principles (e.g., Bandura, 1977) as a metric for explaining the biopsychosocial elements of human behavior. All share the optimism that at least some degree of change is always possible, given the assumption that learned behavior can be altered when clients master new, more constructive actions. All view assessment as an ongoing process that rests heavily on an appraisal of clients' strengths and skills (Wallace, 1966). And all use an active approach to therapy (London, 1964) in which clients and therapists collaborate in designing a series of microexperiments to find the most cost-effective (and therefore the least intrusive) means to achieve the clients' goals. Finally, virtually all these offerings objectively assess the outcome of each behavior-change effort and use positive results to justify continuation of the change and negative results to signal the need to develop a different approach.

An interesting way to track the rapid evolution of behavioral theories is to follow the shifts in emphasis of some of its principal exponents. Albert Bandura, whose *Principles of Behavior Modification* (1969) was the most widely cited behavior therapy text for years, gave social cognition a very central place in his approach when he published *The Social*

Foundations of Thought and Action (1986) 17 years later. And Michael Mahoney, who took an essentially operant view of cognition in his *Cognition and Behavior Modification* (1974), moved rapidly toward a constructivist position with the publication, 17 years later, of his *Human Change Processes* (1991). These are but two of the seminal thinkers who have sharply broadened the scope of behavior therapy, making it truly integrative in nature.

Strategies of Effective Brief IBT

Brief therapy must accomplish most of the same goals as long-term therapy, but must do so quickly (Koss & Butcher, 1986; Small, 1971). Three core strategies and a set of special techniques provide the keys to effective IBT.

Strategy 1: Early Determination of Suitable Goals

The sine qua non of IBT is the effective assessment of clients and determination of goals. Most clients' concerns can be defined in ways that make them amenable either to brief or to long-term therapy. For example, a request for help in deciding whether to change jobs can be framed either as a straightforward choice between alternatives or as a reflection of an underlying personality problem that is expressed as indecision at critical choice-points. Brief therapists will frame such a problem in terms of *how it can be solved*. This framing focuses attention on identifying skills that the client is lacking, skills that are in the client's repertoire but need refinement, and/or skills that the client possesses but is not utilizing. This necessarily involves at least a cursory review of the client's learning history with respect to the skills at issue, but it is markedly different from the search that would be conducted by a therapist who focuses on *why the problem occurred*. Answers to "why" questions are always speculative and tend to involve lengthy incursions into the past in search of hypotheses about psychic structure and function.

Brief therapists help maintain their focus on solving problems by translating those problems into goals for change. The first step is to briefly explore the *psycho*logic of each problem—that is, how the client construes challenges and tries to meet those challenges (Mahoney, 1991).

This often involves asking the clients to reflect on the reason for holding certain positions. But rather than exploring the validity of these beliefs, the therapist takes them as indications of the individual's learning history and of the rationales that engender patterns of behavior. In this sense, every expressed concern can be construed as an attempt to solve a problem, and every presenting complaint can be construed as a problem-solving effort gone awry.

In keeping with the increasingly prominent role of cognition in behavioral intervention, IBT therapists usually pay close attention to the content and style of the client's thinking. In order to get the change process started, it is often necessary for the therapist to help the client redefine the problems and think differently about the options. Kelly (1955), the guiding spirit of the cognitive component of cognitive-behavior therapy, recognized that "a person's processes are psychologically channelized by the ways in which he anticipates events" (p. 46). From a different theoretical perspective, Fisch, Weakland, and Segal (1982) reiterated this view: "All purposive human behavior depends greatly on the views or premises people hold, which govern their interpretation of situations, events, and relationships" (p. 5). Accordingly, it is important to understand clients' beliefs about how they arrived at, and how they can change, their current situations. Helping them refine their thinking can greatly enhance their ability to plan and carry out more effective courses of action.

This process almost always involves some interpretation of the impact of their family of origin and other past experiences on their present beliefs, with the goal of promoting better integration of thought, in contrast to the regressive interpretations common to many forms of long-term therapy (Koss & Butcher, 1986). To reach this understanding, there must be some discussion of the client's view of life. As the client's beliefs are discussed, the therapist tries to identify and possibly change those beliefs that are based on past experiences but that do not apply to the present, or at least to introduce metacognitive monitoring that will limit the impact of these intrusions of the past into the present (Nelson, Stuart, Howard, & Crowley, 1999). It is also useful to assess the client's style of thinking—to determine, for example, whether it is flexible enough to allow for change and rich enough to allow for understanding the complexities of new situations. Change in specific beliefs and/or styles of thinking is often the necessary precursor of behavioral change.

While some complex models are available for including cognitive, affective, behavioral, and situational factors in assessment (e.g., Haynes, Leisen, & Blaine, 1997), a simpler approach may also be used. The therapist can begin the first session with a brief self-introduction, followed by an explanation of the purpose of the session. Then, by asking questions, the therapist induces the clinet to describe himself or herself, including a quick summary of his or her developmental histories. During the client's self-disclosure, the therapist has an opportunity to assess his or her mental status, style of self-presentation, and attitudes toward therapy, and to gain an understanding of the "themes" that are associated with happy and sad moments. The information collected in this way is then analyzed through use of a clinical decision tree (such as that presented in Figure 1–1) to select a sequence of goals for brief IBT.

The therapist may then ask the client to describe the reasons for seeking (or having been referred for) therapy, and to list any other concerns. In the interest of therapeutic efficiency, therapists are highly active during this process. Once the client's concerns have been expressed, clarified, and understood, the therpist reframes each "problem" as the client's attempt to solve a certain problem, and explain its *psychologic*. For example, if the client is a boy who acts too aggressively toward other boys, the therapist may reframe this "problem" as an attempt to create a macho image to gain status and friends. Or a man's depression might be understood as a means to delay, if not avoid, looking for a new job. Each concern is then further translated as a *goal for change* The aggressive boy could be helped to seek status by being elected class president, while the depressed man could be helped to define the kind of job and work situation he would like to find. Goal formulation is then completed by *articulation of the specific adaptive skills* that the client can use to attain each objective. The aggressive boy could be taught how to listen to classmates to learn about their interests, rather than try to dominate every encounter by becoming the focus of (even negative) attention. And the depressed man could be helped to develop the skills he would need in a new job, write a better résumé, etc.

Not all attempted solutions are equally effective: some simply don't work, while others may result in more serious impairment of general functioning and even endanger the client or others. These efforts-gone-awry are the essence of psychopathology and must be assessed. Rather than beginning with the goals that the client first expresses, the therapist must first address any that pose **the threat of harm to self or others.**

Figure 1–1: Deciding on the Sequence of Intervention

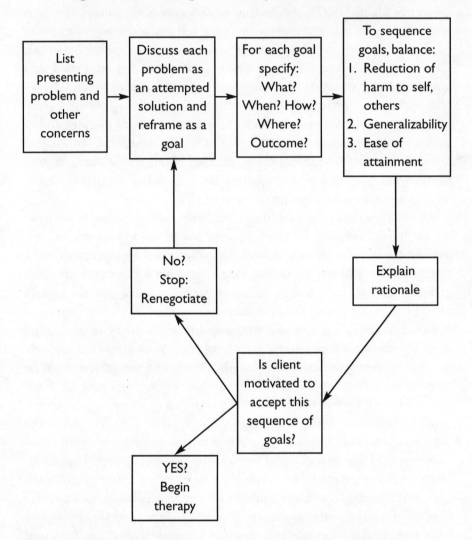

Ethical and professional standards require that these be addressed first. In deciding upon a sequence in which to address the remaining concerns, the therapist faces a series of difficult choices. Two considerations should influence this decision: the changes that will have the greatest impact, but also the steps that the client is able to take. Often, making the changes that would offer the greatest benefit requires the client to make considerable change, and stressing those changes might sap the client's motivation for treatment. Conversely, the less central goals that are readily within the client's reach may seem too trivial and might therefore also undermine motivation. So when choosing goals, the therapist must find the goal with *the most far-reaching impact that is within reasonable reach of the client's current repertoire*. Having decided on a sequence, the therapist discusses its logic with the client and seeks his or her agreement.

At this point the therapist determines the client's suitability for brief therapy. When the safety of the client or others is at issue, it is *never* appropriate to arbitrarily limit the number of sessions. And when a client's goals would be best served by what might be construed as a "corrective developmental experience," IBT is contraindicated. Brief therapy is inappropriate for adolescents and young adults who turn to their therapist as a role model or for perhaps their first opportunity to experience a close relationship with someone who does not attempt to control their behavior. In a similar vein, IBT is inappropriate when attainment of the therapeutic goals requires learning an extended series of new skills; for example, a client who has never had a successful romantic relationship decides that it is time to find a partner and marry. Finally, some goals, such as the wish to clarify personal values and the search for new meaning in life, are best served by therapy offered within a relaxed time frame.

Strategy 2: Empowering the Client

In brief IBT the success of the intervention will be highly dependent upon the therapist's ability to teach clients enough about the logic of behavioral change to be able to plan and carry out goal-attaining changes in their own behavior. In essence, successful clients learn how to be their own therapists, so that they can generalize the therapeutically mediated changes to a variety of new situations.

Ryle (1992) has very eloquently described the importance of explaining treatment rationales as core intervention tools: "We all construct our relation to reality and rely upon abstractions of experience and rules to guide our actions" (p. 196). Many clients who experience recurrent problems, he noted further, approach their lives with a set of assumptions about how to the world works "which they have been unable to revise despite being aware of bad outcomes, and usually despite having received plenty of good advice" (p.196). In his view, therapists face a dual challenge: to understand their clients' perspectives, including the dynamics of their failure to learn; and to offer them an alternative logic that will be more effective than the one with which they entered therapy. In essence, this means accepting that:

1. A person's behavior always makes sense when his or her logic is understood.
2. Repeated unsatisfactory outcomes are probably attributable to flaws in the choice of goals or the means to achieve those goals.
3. People are not likely to make lasting behavioral changes unless they replace habitually unsuccessful ways of reasoning with more adaptive frameworks for construing and planning how to change their lives for the better.

In IBT the therapist can "think aloud' while framing the client's problems in actionable terms and reviewing options for the actions to be taken. The first few times, the therapist may merely ask the client for feedback about the utility of the plan. Later in therapy, the therapist can play a less active role, starting the process but then merely providing feedback while the client takes more responsibility. The therapist can augment this process by suggesting readings that further explicate the principles being presented. Techniques of bibliotherapy (Marrs, 1995; Riagg, 1995) strengthen another core component of IBT, its *psychoeducational* nature, while also possibly shortening its duration.

Strategy 3: The Function of Goal Attainment

The third principal factor that differentiates IBT from long-term therapy relates to the function of goal attainment. The long-term therapist sees each proximate goal as a steppingstone toward achievment of the next goal. In insight-oriented models, this process often means delving more deeply into the past—that is, diverting attention from the present problem to an exploration of its antecedents—before eventually establishing links between past and present and (hopefully) the means to control them. In long-term therapy, each time a goal is reached, the question to be answered is: Where can we go next? In IBT the smallest possible number of goals with the highest potential for generalizable benefits are selected. Each a time the client reaches a goal, the question to be answered is: Will this change enable the client to progress without additional help from the therapist? This difference has a profound impact upon the selection of techniques of intervention.

Techniques of Brief IBT

Effective brief IBT requires a distinctive set of techniques to improve the efficiency and efficacy with which services are delivered.

Facilitating a Quick Start

Collecting information in written form prior to the first session greatly enhances the therapist's ability to complete an accurate assessment in the first session. Materials specifically adapted for this purpose are widely available (e.g., Stuart, in press-a; Wiger, 1997; Zuckerman, 1997). It is also helpful for the therapist to provide the client with a written description of the treatment approach to be used, including any time limits, as well as practice guidelines (such as ethical obligations, fees, and state laws). Providing this information before therapy begins helps to quickly socialize clients into their role, which can greatly expedite the achievement of positive results.

Enhancing Therapist Influence

Establishing and refining the relationship between the therapist and the client is the essence of many forms of long-term therapy. When the expected number of contacts between them is small, however, a client's negative first impression of the therapist may be hard to overcome. Therefore therapists should take great care in how they initially present themselves. One way to help forge a quick bond is to present oneself as a real person through selective self-disclosure. It is also useful to explicitly define the therapeutic relationship as a collaborative one, in which client and therapist will collaborate to create a framework for understanding and overcoming client concerns. In addition, the importance of *realistic* encouragement of the client cannot be overstated (Brown, 1998; Frank & Frank, 1991). As therapy begins, a well-timed and accurate expression of positive expectations can profoundly energize the client. But the therapist's encouragement must be realistic to avoid misleading the client with unrealistic optimism that might encourage the repetition of unproductive or even counterproductive patterns. Once positive results are achieved, satisfaction with the change will replace the positive energy that the therapist must supply at first.

Promoting Quick Change

Effective brief therapy is dependent on the client's following through. Clients are more apt to "do their homework" when they fully understand the time-limited nature of the contact, when they understand exactly what they are being asked to accomplish, and when they believe that the change is a step toward achieving a goal of their own choosing. In addition, since clients who agree to make changes in good faith often forget the details when it is time to act, providing written instructions (e.g., Stuart, in press-a) greatly facilitates adherence.

Maintaining Therapeutic Focus

After the therapist and the client agree on the goals and methods of their collaboration, the therapist should remain focused on this contract. Working from a clear protocol (e.g., Stuart, 1980; in press-b) can help a therapist devote full attention to building the client's skills and overcoming the natural resistance to change. In addition, a therapist who has a plan of action in mind is able to quickly reframe the emerging concerns that the client brings to each session in metaphors of succeeding levels of change.

Case Example:
Brief IBT with an Individual

Presenting Problem

Sandy is a 37-year-old woman who has asked for help in combating a mounting problem of mixed depression and anxiety. She came to the first session wearing a neat but somewhat out-of-fashion business-style suit.

She spoke in faltering tones, often looking away in embarrassment to avoid eye contact. At various points in describing her history, her eyes welled with tears, she sighed, and she fell silent for 30–45 seconds while composing herself enough to continue. She had always hoped to marry and have a family but was now resigned to spending the rest of her life alone with her two dogs and one cat, as a "spinster who is far too old for her age." She had given up on men because most were untrustworthy, and she had no faith in her ability to identify, much less attract, one she could trust.

Developmental History

While she described her childhood as essentially "normal," Sandy admitted that her father, a generally mild-mannered man, was intermittently unemployed due to bouts of alcoholism. She described her mother as a "saint." Her parents divorced when she was 13, her mother remarrying one year later. Shortly after the marriage, her stepfather's long-standing cocaine dependency became evident, and her mother had the marriage annulled. Throughout Sandy's childhood, she was responsible for cleaning the house, cooking, and caring for her two younger sisters while her mother worked. She did reasonably well in school, but she feels that she did not reach her academic potential because she had so little time to study.

After a series of poorly paying jobs, Sandy learned programming at night school and began to write and debug programs on a contract basis in her home. She found the work isolating, since she had contact with other people only when she received orientations to new jobs or handed in the completed product. During her twenties, she dated off and on, having two semi-live-in relationships, each of which lasted about a year. When she was 30, she married a man 10 weeks after she met him at a church singles' function. After marrying him, she learned that he was heavily in debt due to compulsive gambling. She used all of her savings to help him pay off some of his debts, but when his gambling continued, she filed for divorce. The divorce was granted, but she had to assume $30,000 of the community debt incurred though her husband's gambling. She did not date in the four years since her divorce.

Formulation

Sandy's work history made it clear that she was able to succeed in an intellectually challenging task. She appeared very personable, but her aura of vulnerability suggested that she could be exploited. She seemed a good example of the internalized coping style, showing excessive intropunitiveness and overcontrol (Beutler & Clarkin, 1990). She was very lonely because she worked alone, had no close relationships with men, and saw other adults mainly at church on Sundays or while doing routine chores like grocery shopping. Even when she met a potential male or female friend, her self-doubts and bleak expectations inhibited her from making contact. Possibly her depression sapped her energy and caused her social isolation, but her depression may also have been the result of her loneliness. In the first instance, an antidepressant might be the answer, while in the latter case, increased social contact would be the solution. Her anxiety was construed as a form of social phobia; she had learned though bitter experience that she was not a good judge of people. Two therapeutic goals was extablished: relief from the anxious depression that had plagued her for at least the previous four years, and an increase in her sense of self-efficacy. Because of the latter goal, it was decided to begin treatment by attempting to build her social skills, holding drug therapy as a possible later option.

Intervention Plan and Outcome

The treatment plan offered to Sandy is best summarized by its three interim goals.

1. *Goal: to increase Sandy's range of social contacts.* Because she worked in isolation, Sandy was encouraged to find a salaried job as a programmer, even if it meant taking a modest cut in pay. To do so, she needed help in preparing a self-promoting résumé and in rehearsing interview skills. Because she attended a church in which the average age of the congregation was over 60, she was encouraged to sample churches in other parts of town in order to find one with younger members. And because so many of her evenings were spent alone, she was encouraged to start taking night classes in

which she could make new friends and begin to test her academic potential. She settled on a program in computer science. She was also helped to identify other interests (spiritual healing, housing for the homeless, and protection of animals) and to become involved in organizations promoting the causes that she valued. While depression had hindered her mobilizing the energy she needed to get started, she did have the skills needed to make these changes, and doing so gave her a beginning sense of mastery of her life.

2. *Goal: to help Sandy articulate, examine, and reformulate some of her assumptions about men and what intimate relationships could offer.* Sandy's internal working model of relationships was one in which men were self-indulgent and undependable, and women were long-suffering, with little to offer men besides caretaking. She was helped to see the origin of these beliefs in her developmental history. She was also encouraged to look at the lives of others to see if she could find contrary examples—happy, mutually satisfying long-term relationships. That exploration allowed her to see that her beliefs were a choice: she could view all relationships as inevitably dysfunctional; or she could expect—and in fact create—a relationship that would bring true companionship.

3. *Goal: to help Sandy find and develop the kind of relationship she now believed to be possible, at least in principle.* Sandy was helped to articulate a description of the kinds of women and men she wanted as friends, and the kinds of interactions she wanted to have with them. Then she was encouraged to start reaching out, concentrating less on making new friends than on following through on the other steps she planned to take. She soon began to meet men for coffee after church, for hikes and bird-watching, and to study. With help, she defined how she wanted to be treated by men, and the steps she could take to make it more likely that she would receive such treatment. This led to dating and the real potential of a long-term relationship.

It took eight sessions spread over four months for Sandy to make major changes in the social fabric of her life. Her morose fatalism was replaced by the self-empowering, optimistic belief that she could do a great deal to create the kind of relationships she hoped to have. A crisis came when, after dating a really nice man several times, she began to feel uneasy. The therapist interpreted her uneasiness as her not knowing how to interact with a man who wanted, not to be cared for, but to have a mutually respectful relationship. The therapist then helped her use her anxiety as a cue to take steps that would increase the level of her connection with the man, who might become a lifelong partner.

Because Sandy was actively involved in planning her own therapy, she followed through on the steps she agreed to take. The therapist would have examined any failure to follow through by asking three questions: Was she clear about what was expected? Did she have the necessary skills to take the recommended step? Did she see the step as relevant to her goals? For therapists, asking *the client* these questions helps them reformulate instigations so that the client's more likely to follow them. Significantly, in IBT it is instigations that fail, not clients. For example, if Sandy had been unable to find a new job despite her best efforts, her IBT therapist might have suggested that she find other contract workers and try to arrange some shared work space. And if she did not meet reasonable men through the methods she was using, the therapist might have suggested other approaches, such as placing a personal ad.

In summary, at least four factors contributed to the success of Sandy's treatment. Already mentioned are the shift in her core beliefs and her development of a new social repertoire. The third was the help she received in learning when to rely on her feelings and when to rely on her thoughts. Before treatment, her feelings had been the primary cues of her behavior—that is, because she felt depressed and had little energy, she did nothing. During therapy she was encouraged to do what she knew she should do, even if her feelings gave her contradictory messages. As a result, she reached out even though she would have preferred to stay alone. Later, she was helped to decide when her feelings should take precedence over her thoughts, as when she met men whom she thought she should like but really didn't. But when she did meet a man who was right for her, and she felt inclined to end the relationship, she learned to superimpose her knowledge of what she *could* do over the emotions that were telling her what she *should* do. Finally, she was able to borrow some of her therapist's optimism. One cannot overstate the impact of realistic positive expectations upon clients' behavior. This optimism enabled Sandy to envision outcomes that had eluded her throughout her life.

Considerations in Brief IBT with Couples

With brief IBT, individual therapy is easier because the therapist has to overcome the resistance of only one client; at the same time, it is more difficult because the client must be helped to change the behavior of others over whom the therapist has no influence. But conjoint therapy is easier because the therapist can intervene directly with two clients who are each other's significant other—each person in effect becomes a cotherapist for the other. Yet it is also more difficult because the therapist must overcome the resistance of two people by breaking up the "system" that has sustained their familiar albeit problematic interaction. As Haley (1974) noted:

> People in relationships to each other tend to govern each other's behavior so that their relationship remains stable, and it is in the nature of governors that they act so as to diminish change. Implicit in this way of looking at relationships is a premise which might be called the first law of human relations: *when one individual indicates a change in relation to another, the other will respond in such a way as to diminish that change.* (p. 222)

In Haley's view, therapists face the challenge of changing not only the way couples interact from day to day, but also the core processes that sustain their relationship over time. Meeting this challenge involves helping the partners express some of their unspoken expectations and negotiate a shared theory of their relationship. In effect, they are helped to move from an unconscious to a conscious relationship (Hendrix, 1988).

Assessing couples is also more challenging than assessing individuals. For individuals, the *DSM-IV* provides a ready, if not universally valid set of descriptors and categories. But with a couple, two individuals who have different levels of skill and possibly different levels of mental health or psychopathology interact in forming a relationship. The therapist must decide how much of the ensuing problem is attributable to individual pathology, and how much to the interaction between the partners and/or to external circumstances. In brief treatment, the therapist needs an efficient way to structure this assessment. One such way is to focus on the presenting problems rather than on individual diagnoses. Table 1-1 offers one such classification, identifying the presenting problem, assessment issue, and potential intervention implications

Once the assessment has suggested the general goals of the therapy, the therapist should be aware that, while many of the skills developed in individual therapy are useful, conjoint therapy is *not individual therapy for two*. Every comment made by either partner or by the therapist is heard by the other, is taken personally, and can have the impact of stabilizing or destabilizing the relationship. Care must be taken to structure the kinds of interactions that will be constructive for the relationship, and to anticipate the potential impact of every observation and suggestion by the therapist.

Case Example: Brief IBT with a Couple

Presenting Problem

The initial issue that brought Jim and Julie to therapy was a conflict over whether Jim should take a new job. Taking the job would mean more pay, but it would also mean that Jim would have to work more hours, so more of the child-care responsibilities would have to shift to Julie, who already felt overworked. Further discussion revealed their concern about a lack of intimacy in their marriage—the principal sign of which was the fact that they had not made love in over three years. They agreed that they had been "drifting apart" for years and that they each did what was expected of them but felt more annoyed than satisfied by the other's presence. Despite these problems, both said that they would rather have the marriage work than expose their daughters to divorce.

Background

Both Jim and Julie reported that they grew up in stable, loving homes; both prided themselves on the fact that their parents were still married. When they met, at work at ages 21 and 22, respectively, both were still

Table 1-1: Classification of Presenting Problems in Conjoint Therapy

Presenting Problem	Assessment Issue	Intervention
Marital enrichment	The relationship has been generally satisfying, and neither partner presents with individual pathology.	Offer group intervention with carefully screened, high-functioning couples aimed at making good marriages better.
	The relationship has generally failed to offer expected satisfactions and the partners report "growing apart"—i.e., experiencing widening disengagement.	Offer individual therapy, which begins by helping the couple return to courtship mode; explore creating a new relationship contract with greater potential satisfaction; and offer skill training as needed.
An external crisis—e.g., illness of one of the partners, a child, or a parent; loss of job; etc.	The crisis is external, and the partners normally solve problems well together.	Assume the integrity of the relationship and offer specific crisis-management skill training.
	The crisis is one in a series of challenges that the partners find difficult to resolve.	Assume a relationship with dysfunctional aspects, and build problem-solving skills.
A breach of the explicit or secret (Stuart & Jacobson, 1985) contract of the relationship—e.g., an affair, refusal to have a planned child, etc.	One partner has reached the "point of no return."	Help the partners dissolve their relationship as compassionately as possible.
	Neither partner has reached that point, and the relationship appears to have the potential to offer sufficient satisfaction to both.	Help the partners reformulate their contract, develop forgiveness (not forgetfulness), and develop skills (as below).

(Table 1-1: continued on page 24)

Presenting Problem	Assessment Issue	Intervention
A specified functional problem—e.g., dissatisfaction with intimacy, inequity in the balance of home/family responsibilities, etc.	The partners are unskilled in the basics of interaction—i.e., communication, two-winner negotiation.	Offer therapy aimed at helping the partners acquire or enhance the needed skills.
	One partner presents with problems requiring individual attention—e.g., major health or mental health concern.	Consider an appropriate referral.

living at home. They began as friends, finding that they shared basic values, as well as interests in hiking, movies, and sampling microbreweries. They soon began to date and were married after knowing each other for two years—a little over 17 years ago. Both admitted that part of their motivation to marry was their desire to achieve independence from their families of origin. In the first years, they realized that Jim was more concerned about money and was a social isolate, while Julie was more spontaneous and liked to be in groups. Over time, each stopped hoping that the other would change, coming to accept their differences. They tried to have children for a few years, then Julie gave birth to their twin daughters, who are now 8. Julie stayed home with the girls for the first 18 months, but because Jim's job did not pay well, she returned to work. Both of them spend the majority of their time working on the job, taking care of the house, or being responsible parents for the girls. Jim watches sports on TV when he can steal an hour, and Julie occasionally, when she can get away, goes shopping or for a walk with a friend. They have no shared interests now other than the children and their home.

Formulation

A therapist could construe this couple's problem as external, because it involves a job change, or as sexual, attributable to physiological causes and/or the lack of intimacy. Or both problems could be construed as the result of skill deficits in both partners, who really do seem to be well matched. While they married in part to solve personal problems—achieving independence from their parents—their knowledge of and affection for each other seemed to be their strongest motives. Neither violated any terms of their relationship contract by, for example, having an affair. They also appear to have compatible, albeit not identical styles. Both have the skills to do reasonably well in outside employment, and by their own account they function very well as parents. Perhaps because they have learned to accommodate themselves to the idiosyncrasies of each other's style, they do not present with the level of conflict seen in many couples who seek therapy. Instead, their relationship seems best described as "indifferent." Developing skills that would enhance their communication, decision making, and intimacy could have a very positive impact upon their relationship. This appeared to be a relationship that could, and should, be greatly improved.

Intervention Plan and Outcome

Because their health insurance policy did not cover couple therapy, and because money was tight, Julie and Jim agreed that their therapy would be limited to six sessions spread over four months. They also agreed that they would tackle problems one at a time, a process that might be thought of as "partialing the variance" in their presenting complaints.

1. *Goal: to help Jim and Julie regain some intimacy.* Achieving this goal required two important steps. First, they had to agree to spend at least 45 minutes alone together every day, and to have at least one evening or one half-day alone every week. It was explained that unless partners have time to concentrate exclusively on each other, they are unlikely to develop a feeling of closeness. Julie and Jim were helped to complete a Caring Days Inventory (Stuart, 1980; in press-b) in which they identified a number of small, daily acts through which they could convey positive feelings, including affection, concern, and respect.

2. *Goal: to help Jim and Julie resolve the employment issue.* To reach this goal, Jim and Julie were taught the skills inherent in principle-driven negotiation. They learned to determine their own desires, to express these wishes clearly, and to clarify each other's requests to be sure they are understood. Then they learned how to agree on one

or more principles that they could use to frame and evaluate the process of making bids and counteroffers in efforts to reach two-winner agreements. At first Jim clearly wanted the job, and Julie wanted to avoid additional responsibilities. They agreed in principle that child-care hours should be counted as much as work outside the home for pay, and that their workloads should be equal. Then they decided on the amount of money they needed to make ends meet, save for the children's education, and secure their retirement. With the therapist's prompting, they came to the realization that the extra money Jim would earn would more than meet their financial needs. They then agreed that some of the extra cash could be used to pay for extra child care, so that Julie would not have to give up her few precious hours of relaxation.

3. *Goal: to increase their physical intimacy.* It was unreasonable to expect change in this realm until Jim and Julie developed greater affection through caring days and greater trust in their ability to respectfully resolve disagreements. Once they made these changes, they were both ready to discuss lovemaking. Several obstacles were identified. They had a small house, and both were apprehensive that their daughters would hear them having intercourse. Jim had previously been the only one to initiate sex and had stopped when he felt rejected too often—a change that Julie construed as his having lost interest entirely. Finally, Jim liked to make love late at night—when, unfortunately, Julie was often too tired to be interested. Each of these issues was addressed in order. First they agreed to try to make love when the girls were at friends' houses on the weekends, or away from the bedrooms in which the girls slept when they were home. Then they agreed that either one could express interest in sex whenever they felt at all interested, but that Julie would do most of the initiating—at least five times per month—because Jim was more often ready to respond. And with initiation under Julie's control, she could choose the times of day that worked well for her.

It took two sessions to establish and consolidate time together and the caring days behaviors. The job issue was resolved in a single session, as was the problem of lovemaking. The final two sessions were devoted to helping the couple digest what they had learned and to plan ways to use it in the future. In retrospect, the considerable skills and goodwill that each brought to their marriage had been undermined by their common tendency to ignore problems, while their feelings of disengagement had increased. In effect, the frustration associated with each problem was compounded as the next problem arose, until the cumulating negative energy seemed to make the problems unresolvable. This condition can be illustrated as:

Problem → Problem → Problem → Problem

As an alternative, they learned to identify and address each problem as it arose, as respresented by:

Problem → Solution   Problem → Solution   Problem → Solution

Mnemonics like this one, as well as a treatment log and written instigations that clients can keep and use for reference, greatly aid the maintenance of changes made in therapy.

The outcome of this intervention was very satisfying, but it was by no means guaranteed. Jim and Julie did not present with any hidden barriers to change—no undisclosed affairs, no health problems that precluded intercourse, and no personal psychopathology. Had these problems existed, more conjoint and possibly some individual sessions would have been needed to overcome them. Moreover, both partners had positive family-of-origin experiences, which helped them to cultivate positive orientations to relationships. If either or both had suffered from dysfunctional internal working models of relationships, these too would almost surely have required more than brief therapy.

Conclusion

In today's mental health environment, therapists must be prepared to deal with an ever-widening array of diagnostic concerns and to do so within the strictures of an increasingly more draconian managed-care environment. To meet this challenge, every therapist must be skilled in one or more approaches to brief therapy. But when should time-limited intervention be offered? Clearly it is not the universally applicable silver bullet that insurance companies and government regulators purport it to be. Unfortunately, there is no acid test to help therapists differentiate between opportunities to deliver effective brief- and long-term intervention. Sometimes problems that appear to be simple adjustment disorders prove to be only the tip of the iceberg, foreshadowing complex underlying pathology. And at other times, clients who have been accurately diagnosed with major mental disorders derive substantial benefit from help in meeting one or two current challenges. Therapists thus face the prospect of offering either too little or too much help.

As a general rule of thumb, therapists cannot go wrong by beginning all treatment as though it were going to be time-limited. This practice is the surest means of honoring the ethical prescription that clients be offered the least intrusive intervention. At the end of a designated number of sessions, therapist and client can assess their results and determine whether the progress they have achieved warrants terminating their contact or contracting for additional service. Of course, the client has the option of returning for additional sessions if and when the need arises. This approach is one way to replace outmoded models in which a client was expected to have regular contacts with the therapist whether or not they were needed, so that the therapist would be available if and when problems did arise.

The modal treatment offering today is therefore very likely to be time-limited. These services will be most effective when the therapist chooses an appropriate theory to guide the work, frames problems in actionable terms, quickly establishes a collaborative relationship with the client, and develops and follows through on a focal plan for therapeutic change in a series of small steps. Fueled by the therapist's realistic optimism, a surprising amount of sustainable change can be accomplished in only one to six sessions. It is hoped that IBT, as it is described here, using these strategies and techniques, will help to make this potential a reality.

References

Baars, B. (1986). *The cognitive revolution in psychology.* New York: Guilford.

Bagarozzi, D. I. (1997). Marital and family approaches. In S. R. Sauber (Ed.), *Managed mental health care: Major diagnostic and treatment approaches* (pp. 164–186). New York: Brunner/Mazel.

Bandura, A. (1969). *Principles of behavior modification.* New York: Holt, Rinehart, & Winston.

Bandura, A. (1977). *Social learning theory.* Englewood Cliffs, NJ: Prentice-Hall.

Bandura, A. (1986). *The social foundations of thought and action: A social cognitive theory.* Englewood Cliffs, NJ: Prentice-Hall.

Beutler, L. E., & Clarkin, J. F. (1990). *Systematic treatment selection: Toward targeted therapeutic interventions.* New York: Brunner/Mazel.

Book, H. E. (1998). *Brief psychodynamic psychotherapy: The CCRT method.* Washington, DC: American Psychological Association.

Brown, W. A. (1998). The placebo effect. *Scientific American, 178,* 90–95.

Budman, S. H., & Gurman, A. S. (1988). *Theory and practice of brief therapy.* New York: Guilford.

Fisch, R., Weakland, J. H., & Segal, L. (1982). *The tactics of change: Doing therapy briefly.* San Francisco: Jossey-Bass.

Fishman, D. B., & Franks, C. M. (1997). The conceptual evolution of behavior therapy. In P. L. Wachtel & S. B. Messer (Eds.), *Theories of psychotherapy: Origins and evolution* (pp. 131–180). Washington, DC: American Psychological Association.

Frank, J. D., & Frank, J. B. (1991). *Persuasion and healing.* Baltimore: Johns Hopkins University Press.

Goldfried, M. R., & Davison, G. C. (1976). *Clinical behavior therapy.* New York: Holt, Rinehart, & Winston.

Haley, J. (1974). Marriage therapy. In H. Greenwald (Ed.), *Active psychotherapy* (pp. 189–223). New York: Jason Aronson.

Hass, L. J., & Cummings, N. A. (1991). Managed outpatient mental health plans: Clinical, ethical, and practical guidelines for participation. *Professional Psychology: Research and Practice, 22,* 45–51.

Haynes, S. N., Leisen, M. B., & Blaine, D. D. (1997). Design of individualized behavioral treatment programs using functional analytic clinical case models. *Psychological Assessment, 9,* 334–338.

Hendrix, H. (1988). *Getting the love you want.* New York: HarperPerennial.

Kazdin, A. (1978). *History of behavior modification*. Baltimore: University Park Press.

Kelly, G. A. (1955). *The psychology of personal constructs* (Vol. 1). New York: Norton.

Koss, M. P., & Butcher, J. N. (1986). Research on brief psychotherapy. In A. E. Bergin (Ed.), *Handbook of psychotherapy and behavior change* (pp. 627–680). New York: Wiley.

London, P. (1964). *The modes and morals of psychotherapy*. New York: Holt, Rinehart, & Winston.

Lowry, J. L., & Ross, M. J. (1997). Expectations of psychotherapy duration: How long should psychotherapy last? *Psychotherapy, 34,* 272–277.

MacCorquodale, K., & Meehl, P. E. (1953). Hypothetical constructs and intervening variables. In H. Feigl & M. Brodbeck (Eds.), *Readings in the philosophy of science* (pp. 596–611). New York: Appleton-Century-Crofts.

Mahoney, M. J. (1974). *Cognition and behavior modification*. Cambridge, MA: Ballenger.

Mahoney, M. J. (1991). *Hunan change processes: The scientific foundations of psychotherapy*. New York: Basic Books.

Marrs, R. W. (1997). A meta-analysis of bibliotherapy studies. *American Journal of Community Psychology, 23,* 843–870.

Maturana, H. R., & Varela, F. J. (1992). *The tree of knowledge: The biological roots of human understanding*. Boston: Shambhala.

Messer, S. B., & Warren, C. S. (1995). *Models of brief psychodynamic therapy*. New York: Guilford.

Miller, I. J. (1996). Some "short-term therapy values" are a formula for invisible rationing. *Professional Psychology: Research and Practice, 27,* 577–582.

Nelson, T. O., Stuart, R.B., Howard C., & Crawley, M. (1999). Metacognition in clinical psychology. *Clinical Psychology and Psychotherapy, 6,* 73–79.

Olfson, M., & Pincus, H. A. (1994). Outpatient psychotherapy in the United States, II: Patterns of utilization. *American Journal of Psychiatry, 151,* 1289–1294.

Reisman, J. M. (1971). *Toward the integration of psychotherapy*. New York: Wiley.

Riagg, W. N.-B. (1995). Bibliotherapy in unipolar depression: A meta-analysis. *Journal of Behavior Therapy and Experimental Psychiatry, 28,* 139–147.

Ryle, A. (1992). *Cognitive-analytic therapy: Active participation in change. A new integration in brief psychotherapy*. New York: Wiley.

Skinner, B. F. (1953). *Science and human behavior*. New York: Free Press.

Small, L. (1971). *The briefer psychotherapies.* New York: Brunner/Mazel.

Smith, L. D. (1986). *Behaviorism and logical positivism: A reassessment of the alliance.* Stanford, CA: Stanford University Press.

Spiegler, M. D., & Guevremont, D. C. (1993). *Contemporary behavior therapy.* Pacific Grove, CA: Brooks/Cole.

Stomberg, C., Loeb, L., Thomsen, S., & Krause, J. (1996). State initiatives in health care reform. *The Psychologist's Legal Update, 8,* 1–16.

Strupp, H. H., & Binder, J. L. (1984). *Psychotherapy in a new key: A guide to time-limited dynamic psychotherapy.* New York: Basic Books.

Stuart, R. B. 1971). *Trick or treatment: How and when psychotherapy fails.* Champaign, IL: Research Press.

Stuart, R. B. (1980). *Helping couples change.* New York: Guilford.

Stuart, R. B. (in press-a). *Resources for individual, couple, and family therapy.* New York: Guilford.

Stuart, R. B. (1998). Updating behavior therapy with couples. *The Family Journal, 6,* 6–12.

Stuart, R. B., & Jacobson, B. (1985). *Second marriage.* New York: Norton.

Stuart, R. B., & Tripodi, T. (1973). Time-constrained treatment of delinquents: An experimental evaluation. In R. Rubin & J. Hendricks (Eds.), *Advances in behavior therapy* (pp. 121–133). New York: Academic Press.

Thagard, P. (1992). *Conceptual revolutions.* Princeton, NJ: Princeton University Press.

Wallace, J. (1966). An abilities conception of personality: Some implications for personality measurement. *American Psychologist, 21,* 132–138.

Watson, J. (1913). Psychology as the behaviorist views it. *Psychological Review, 20.* 158–177.

Wiger, D. E. (1997). *The clinical documentation sourcebook.* New York: Wiley.

Wilson, E. O. (1998). *Consilience: The unity of knowledge.* New York: Wiley.

Zuckerman, E. L. (1997). *The paper office* (2nd ed.). New York: Guilford.

Annotated Bibliography

Beutler, L. E., & Clarkin, J. F. (1990). *Systematic treatment selection: Toward targeted therapeutic interventions.* New York: Brunner/Mazel. While not specifically addressing brief therapy, these authors offer an invaluable model for relating client concerns to intervention strategies and tactics—the key to offering clinically responsible brief therapy.

Budman, S. H., & Gurman, A. S. (1988). *Theory and practice of brief therapy.* New York: Guilford. These authors present a very thoughtful and detailed model of brief therapy in a range of clinical problems. Their work is noteworthy for its ability to integrate attention to devleopmental issues in clients with techniques for promoting adaptive functioning.

Haynes, S. N., Leisen, M. B., & Blaine, D. D. (1997). Design of individualized behavioral treatment programs using functional analytic clinical case models. *Psychological Assessment, 9,* 334–338. This article offers an invaluable model for linking theory to objectively measurable practice.

Mahoney, M. J. (1991). *Human change processes: The scientific foundations of psychotherapy.* New York: Basic Books. No set of readings on therapy is complete without this monumental work on theory integration, culminating in a profoundly valuable operational approach to constructivist intervention.

Stuart, R. B. (1980). *Helping couples change.* New York: Guilford. This book also offers techiniques for use in brief therapy with couples.

2

---✸✸✸---

Cognitive-Behavioral Strategies

Frank M. Dattilio

Cognitive-behavior therapy (CBT) has now gained recognition among mental health therapists, researchers, and practitioners as a traditional approach to psychotherapy. Currently more than 20 modalities are referred to as cognitive and behavioral, and together they have generated more empirical research and resulted in more clinical outcome studies than any other psychotherapeutic modality in existence (Beck, 1991). CBT—as opposed to cognitive therapy (CT) and behavior therapy (BT)—combines both cognitive and behavioral principles in a short-term treatment approach.

Some in the field believe that practicing either cognitive or behavior therapy alone, without doing both, is very difficult. While purists maintain that the two modalities are distinctly different, in reality they have a great deal of overlap. Many of the distinct differences fall within the realm of the definitions of the terms *cognitive* and *behavioral*. Persons (1995) elaborated extensively on this issue by raising the question of whether all therapies are cognitive, but cognitive and behavioral components appear to be part of the fabric of most therapeutic modalities (Alford & Norcross, 1991).

Behavior Therapy

Behavior therapy (BT) had its origins in the 1950s and early 1960s in the United States as a radical departure from the dominant psychoanalytic perspective. Its main tenet was simply that behavioral conditioning techniques could be effective and a viable alternative to traditional psychotherapy in changing behavior (Bandura, 1961). In contrast to other therapeutic approaches, it applied principles of classical and operant conditioning to the treatment of a variety of problematic behaviors (Wolpe, 1958). Not surprisingly, it encountered harsh criticism and resistance from traditional psychotherapists.

In the early 1960s Albert Bandura developed his social learning model, which combined classical and operant conditioning with observational learning. Bandura focused on cognition, which had been ruled out by the radical behaviorism of B. F. Skinner. During the 1970s BT emerged as a major force in psychology and made a significant impact on the mental health field. Behavioral techniques and strategies were developed and expanded specifically to be applied to the field, and they quickly became viewed as the treatment of choice for certain psychological problems.

In the 1950s Joseph Wolpe and Arnold A. Lazarus had begun to use findings of experimental research with animals to help treat phobias in clinical settings. At the same time, Hans Eysenck, basing his work on Hullian's learning theory and Pavlovian classical conditioning, focused on experimental analysis and the evaluation of therapeutic procedures. Wolpe's development of the technique of systematic desensitization, based on the classical-conditioning model, illustrated how principles of learning theory that were derived from the experimental laboratory could be applied clinically to individuals with anxiety, depression, and a host of other problems (Wolpe, 1973).

A second force in the evolution of behavior therapy involved principles based on operant conditioning. Operant behavior—actions that operate on the environment to produce consequences—became a strong focus in treatment. Operant conditioning rests on the premise that if environmental changes brought about by a specific target behavior are reinforcing, the behavior will likely be strengthened. Likewise, if the environmental changes produce no reinforcement, then behavior is less likely to recur. B. F. Skinner notably based his work on the principles of operant conditioning, particularly with psychotic patients in the United States. For Skinner, actions that were reinforced tended to be repeated, and those that were discouraged tended to be extinguished. *Positive reinforcement* was a procedure in which certain desired behaviors on the part of an individual were followed by the presentation of something such as praise or money as a consequence. *Negative reinforcement*, conversely, involved the removal of unpleasant stimuli from a situation once a certain behavior had occurred. Negative reinforcement usually was unpleasant, and therefore the individual was motivated to exhibit a desired behavior in order to avoid the unpleasant condition.

In the 1970s and 1980s, behaviorists of both the classical-conditioning and operant-conditioning models excluded any reference to mediational concepts, such as cognitive processes, attitudes, and beliefs. Since then, however, the behaviorist movement has conceded a legitimate place to thinking, even to the extent of giving cognitive factors a central role in understanding and treating behavioral problems.

Cognitive Therapy

While cognitive therapy (CT) in theory dates back to the days of Epictetus (A.D. 60–117), it did not come into fruition as a mode of psychotherapy until the early 1950s, with the advent of the work of Albert Ellis. At that time Ellis, who is considered the grandfather of CT, developed his rational-emotive therapy (RET). More recently, as a result of Ellis's reconsideration of the prominent role of behavior therapy in his approach (Ellis, 1995),[1] it has been renamed rational-emotive behavior therapy (REBT). In the early 1960s and 1970s, Aaron T. Beck developed his approach of CT as a result of his research on depression (Beck 1963, 1964, 1967). Beck had observed that depressed patients had a negative bias in their interpretation of certain life events, which contributed to their cognitive distortions.

As a result of his clinical observations and experimental testing, Beck

---

[1]Ellis's work is covered more extensively in Chapter 3.

developed the cognitive theory of emotional disorders and, in particular, the cognitive model of depression (Beck, 1976). He defined cognitive therapy as an active, directive, structured, collaborative, and psychological education model for brief psychotherapy. While he originally developed it for the treatment of depression, over the past thirty years the model has been expanded to effectively treat a host of disorders, including anxiety disorders (Barlow, 1988), panic disorder (Dattilio 1987, 1990), obsessive-compulsive disorder (Salkovskis, 1989), generalized anxiety disorder (Borkovec & Matthews, 1988), and posttraumatic stress disorders (Dancu & Foa, 1992). Although CT has been applied to a broad range of disorders, anxiety and depression are probably the two most widely researched pathologies using cognitive therapy.

According to CT, psychological problems stem from commonplace mistakes and problems, such as faulty learning, incorrect inferences based on inadequate or incorrect information, and a failure to distinguish adequately between imagination and reality (Kovacs & Beck, 1979). Consequently, based on erroneous assumptions, individuals often formulate rules or standards that are excessively rigid and absolute. Such rules and standards are derived from what Beck, Rush, Shaw, and Emery (1979) and Beck, Freeman, et al. (1990) term *schemata*, or complex patterns of thought that determine how experiences will be perceived and conceptualized. These schemata, which develop early as the guiding rules in one's life, shape personality and constitute the basis upon which one codes, categorizes, and evaluates experiences. These schemata or dysfunctional beliefs are often not articulated clearly in an individual's mind but may exist as vague concepts of what should be (Beck, 1988). They can, however, be uncovered by examining the logic and themes of one's automatic thoughts. They are usually employed even in the absence of environmental data and may serve as a type of Procrustean mold, distorting and selecting incoming data so as to fit and reinforce preconceived notions (Beck et al., 1979). This distortion of experience is maintained through the operation of characteristic errors in information processing. Several types of fallacious thinking contribute to the feedback loops that support psychological disorders: for example, systematic errors in reasoning, termed cognitive distortions, are present during psychological distress and result from various distortions (defined later in this chapter).

They develop early in life as a result of personal experiences as well as through parental and societal influences. The cognitive therapist works to learn the specific content of a client's cognitions and/or beliefs and style of thinking and to observe patterns of behavior. Maladaptive behavior patterns that contribute to dysfunctional interaction are also a strong focus of treatment. Clients are taught to identify and report in detail their dysfunctional cognitions as well as behavioral patterns, noting when they occur and their impact on their specific feelings and emotions.

As a reality-based intervention, cognitive therapy accepts the life situations of individuals and focuses on altering only their biased views of themselves, their situations, and the impoverished resources that limit their behavioral and emotional response repertoires and prevent them from generating solutions. CT is therefore an active, structured, and usually time-limited approach to the treatment of emotional and behavioral disorders. It teaches clients to take a number of steps in addressing their problems, including monitoring negative automatic thoughts; recognizing connections between cognition, affect, and behavior; critically examining these underlying thoughts; substituting more objective interpretations for these negative cognitions; and learning to identify and alter distortions or dysfunctional beliefs and maladaptive behavior patterns that predispose individuals to difficulties in functioning.

A collaborative empiricism between client and therapist ties these strategies together in a system that identifies the problem, designs and executes tests of specific hypotheses, and evaluates certain behaviors and beliefs.

The Practice of Cognitive-Behavior Therapy

As with most other therapy modalities, one of CBT's initial goals is for the therapist to develop a rapport with the client. Collaboration between client and therapist is essential in the change process and indeed is probably one of the most important strategies for generating change.

Providing a rational and effective structure is another key issue, both for the entire course of treatment and for individual therapy sessions. Such a structure assures continuity and focus on the issues at hand and makes the best use of time and effort. Once a structure has been established, the therapist and client collaborate in developing a list of specific problems to address in therapy.

Once they have completed the problem list, the therapist may begin to narrow the therapeutic focus and, in collaboration with the client, develop an agenda for the succeeding sessions. The typical session will begin with a review of the previous week's events. Then the client's homework assignments are discussed, along with any difficulty that the client experienced while completing them. Some flexibility is maintained with the session structure, should the client wish to focus on a more immediate or urgent problem. Specific interventions or strategies are contingent on the skill level of the client, as well as the nature of the presenting problem. (This juncture of strategies dictates whether the emphasis is placed on a cognitive or a behavioral approach, or both.)

The last part of each session is devoted to a collaborative assessment and evaluation of the homework from the previous session. The homework assignment for the subsequent session is discussed as well. The therapist may receive feedback from the client in evaluation of the current session. As a result of this format, a gradual yet structured session termination occurs, which also sets the stage for the succeeding session.

Treatment Strategies

A number of strategies[2] within the armamentarium of CBT were designed specifically to aid clients in testing the reality of their cognitions. These strategies can be classified as either cognitive or behavioral in approach, but usually much overlap occurs. The following approaches are adapted in part from Freeman and Dattilio (1992).

Cognitive Strategies

Collaborative Empiricism

Collaborative empiricism is a strategy in which therapist and client work together in partnership to understand and solve the client's problem. Empiricism is the process of collecting data to evaluate the evidence

---

[2] While the terms *strategies* and *techniques* have been distinctly defined in this text, there is considerable overlap in what is constituted by each term. Therefore, the terms are sometimes used almost interchangeably, since strategies comprise a number of therapeutic techniques. Also, due to space limitations, only a few strategies are listed here. Additional strategies are presented within the case material, later in the chapter.

for and against current and alternative beliefs (Dattilio & Padesky, 1990, p. 3). Collaborative empiricism is used with every application of CBT, from depression and anxiety to working with couples, families, and groups. A cornerstone of CBT, it is used throughout the entire course of treatment.

Downward Arrow

The term "downward arrow", first coined by Beck et al. (1979), refers to the actual use of downward pointing arrows to aid clients in understanding the logic and sequencing of their reasoning. A client makes a statement that involves an ingrained belief; the therapist responds by asking, "If so, then what?" This elicits a sequence of thoughts and beliefs that aids in uncovering the client's underlying assumptions. The downward arrow technique can to help uncover the core belief or schema that is fueling an individual's dysfunctional thoughts. It can be used in the treatment of most disorders. For example:

I won't speak in front of a group for fear of making a mistake

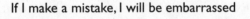

If I make a mistake, I will be embarrassed

If I risk embarrassment, I risk being ridiculed

If I am ridiculed, particularly by my peers,
then I am finished socially

Socratic Questioning

This open form of questioning allows individuals to arrive at their own conclusions through self-knowledge. It is used primarily during the exploration and/or assessment phase.

Cognitive Restructuring

In this strategy, a client changes his or her basic beliefs or schemata, based on the acquisition of new information. It is used primarily with perceptual distortions in all types of disorders.

Labeling of Distortions

By learning to label distortions, clients are able to automatically identify their dysfunctional thoughts and monitor their cognitive patterns. This type of monitoring leads to more accurate routes toward change. For a more detailed description, see Burns (1980). This strategy is used globally for most disorders.

Questioning the Evidence

Once clients learn to question the actual evidence in support of their beliefs, the process of substantiation (verifying) is initiated and becomes automatic following any irrational thought statement. This technique allows clients to assess whether their own statements are based on erroneous information. It is a cornerstone in facilitating change during cognitive restructuring.

Examining Options and Alternatives

This technique is an attempt to avoid the trap of seeing "no way out" of a circumstance or situation. It entails going back over all the possible options and alternatives in a situation. The therapist's specific task is to work until the individual generates new options. This technique is used most commonly during periods of depression or with difficult interpersonal relationships.

Reattribution

Placing all blame on oneself is a distortion commonly seen among clients, particularly in guilt-ridden or depressed cases. In reattribution, the individual appropriately distributes responsibility to the rightful parties and sheds the notion that any single individual is responsible for all problems and difficulties. This strategy is typically used when addressing an individual's self-esteem.

Decatastrophizing

This strategy aids individuals in balancing their focus on a worst anticipated state. They learn to evaluate the situation and ask themselves, "What is the worst thing that might occur?" They can then ask, "If the worst occurred, would it be so horrible or unbearable?" This strategy is particularly useful with anxiety-disordered individuals as well as with distressed relationships.

Listing Advantages and Disadvantages

In attempts to sway clients away from dichotomous thought patterns, instructing them to list the advantages and disadvantages of a situation allows them to change their perspective and balance out the alternatives.

Paradox or Exaggeration

In this strategy—the inverse of decatastrophizing—the therapist takes an issue or idea to the extreme, allowing the client to view the absurdity of an exaggerated viewpoint. Such exaggeration often aids the client in developing a more balanced perspective. It is usually used only when the aforementioned strategies fail or are less effective.

Turning Adversity to Advantage

Recasting an unfortunate situation as a source of advantage can be very helpful. For example, being rejected by the school of one's choice may be an indirect route toward pursuing a more promising alternative. This strategy is used most frequently with depressed individuals and those with low levels of self-worth.

Collaborative Set

This term, coined by Jacobson and Margolin (1979), indicates the need for couples to view their conflicts as mutual and to realize that they are likely to be resolved only by working conjointly. Some authors (e.g., Abrahams, 1982) believe that conflict resolution or communication training is impossible unless both partners are willing to collaborate.

Cognitive Rehearsal

Many target behaviors for change rely on mentally visualizing the desired outcome. The use of cognitive rehearsal may aid individuals in practicing assertiveness, confronting others, and so on. This strategy is particularly vital when working with socially inhibited individuals.

Behavioral Strategies

While cognitive therapy involves the primary use of the preceding strategies, behavioral strategies are also used in conjunction to facilitate change.

These behavioral strategies are more frequently used in CBT, both with individuals and with couples.

Assertiveness Training

Assertiveness training involves both cognitive processes and behavioral rehearsal. The therapist teaches or models the desired behaviors that the client wishes to acquire. The behaviors are acted out in real life (*in vivo*). This strategy is particularly used for clients with the anxiety disorders, such as social phobias or agoraphobia, and in couple therapy. Individuals with almost any type of disorder, however, can benefit from assertiveness training and strategies related to confronting difficult situations.

Behavioral Rehearsal

This strategy is the behavioral counterpart to cognitive rehearsal. Here, instead of visualizing desired behavior, the client rehearses the actual behaviors themselves: asserting oneself in public, getting up and going to work, and so on. The therapist then gives the client feedback as a means of guidance to develop effective responses and styles. This strategy reinforces existing skills and should be employed whenever a behavioral change is needed.

Graded Task Assignments

This strategy establishes priorities for achieving target behaviors, from approaching a parent to overcoming a fear of meeting new people. The client arranges the specific tasks in steps, from the least anxiety-producing or threatening to the most anxiety-producing. This arrangement allows the client to gradually approach facing the threatening object or event, in divided doses, regardless of the disorder.

Bibliotherapy

Prescribing reading assignments has always been a strong characteristic of cognitive-behavior therapy. Many readings can be assigned to clients as homework, including books designed for the general public, such as *Feeling Good* and *The Feeling Good Handbook* (Burns, 1980, 1989) and *Fighting for Your Marriage* (Markman, Stanley, & Blumberg, 1994). Many of these books contain assessment forms, homework forms, exercises, and templates for recording various activities. These readings are not meant to replace therapy but are assigned as adjuncts to serve as supportive educational tools to the actual therapeutic process.

Relaxation and Meditation

Relaxation, meditation, and focused breathing programs have proved to be helpful for clients with anxiety disorders, teaching them to distract themselves and gain control over their anxiety. But this strategy may be used with any client who experiences any degree of anxiety or stress.

Overbreathing

This strategy involves teaching clients how to overbreathe and then encouraging them to hyperventilate in the office. It is effective in showing them that they can attain breathing control and thereby reduce many of their symptoms. This strategy is typically used only for those with heightened levels of anxiety.

Social Skills Training

This strategy involves reviewing and instructing the client in behaviors that are necessary for social interaction: maintaining conversations, good posture, and eye contact; assertiveness skills; and techniques for self-expression and conveying individual thoughts and opinions. Social skills training is used primarily with individuals who have obvious skill deficits.

Shame Attacking

In this strategy (promoted most by REBT therapists), clients engage in activities that emphasize their concern for what others may think of them. A typical example might be to have the client ride a public bus and, while the bus is en route and carrying a full load of passengers, announce each stop out loud. The point is to help the client see that people really react minimally even to such unusual behavior and that their thoughts really do not matter to others. Shame attacking is used primarily with obsessive-compulsive patients who are guilt-ridden; with social phobics; and with those with low levels of self-esteem.

Time-out

This method allows clients to deliberately break away from the situation at hand and redirect their focus, allowing for a period of emotional and behavioral de-escalation. It is used with individuals who experience difficulty with anger management and with couples in conflict.

Homework

One of the most important features of CBT is the use of homework assignments. Because the actual therapy sessions are limited to only one or two hours per week, activities that support the treatment must continue outside the sessions. Self-help assignments can serve as a continuation of what was addressed in a session. Homework is also an integral part of the collaborative process between client and therapist. Assignments typically include the techniques and strategies already listed. They are tailored to the specific problem and result from the collaborative process during treatment.

Clinical Applications with an Individual: Case Example

Rozina, a 48-year-old Romanian-born female, migrated to the United States with her family when she was 10 years old. An only child, she was raised by her parents, who died at an early age due to coronary artery disease. Rozina was always described as a tough, independent individual who was vociferous about her feelings. She was noted for being intimidated by few and for having very few fears. She did extremely well for herself in life, graduating from college with a degree in business administration. She quickly earned herself a position in sales with a high-tech business equipment distributor and worked her way up to regional manager. Since she was always on the "fast track" with her career, she had little time for personal relationships. In many ways, she tended to be a loner, and although she dated occasionally, she never developed any serious intimate relationships. An extremely hard-working individual, Rozina took pride in her work. She lived a comfortable life and was considered worldly, having traveled to may parts of the globe.

One icy winter night in January, as Rozina slept soundly, a fire ravaged a state mental facility several miles across town. The authorities evacuated the facility's mental patients, but in the process a 32-year-old male suffering from severe schizophrenia escaped, wearing just a pair of shoes and his underwear. He traveled across town on foot, darting through alleyways and residents' backyards in a frenzied state of confusion. He developed a severe case of hypothermia and randomly came to a halt on Rozina's back porch. He crouched down in a corner of the porch and he fell to rest. Sometime in the early hours of the morning, he died with his head between his knees.

Shortly after dawn, Rozina came out of her back door on her way to work and discovered the frozen, icy-blue figure huddled against the corner of her porch, almost like an intricately carved ice sculpture. Her scream left her almost breathless in the cold morning air, but she managed to scurry back into the house to catch her breath. A myriad of disbelieving thoughts raced through her mind, until she came to the decision to call the police. She waited in the house until both the police and the local coroner arrived and recovered the body from her porch. Since most of the morning had been consumed with providing the police with a detailed report of her experience, and with dealing with her own anxiety over the shock of the incident, she called in sick to work.

During the next days, Rozina experienced a chronic state of anxiety, experiencing difficulty both in her sleeping patterns and in her concentration. Surprisingly, her symptoms fell short of posttraumatic stress disorder in that she experienced only some autonomic activity and only about one day of flashbacks of the image of the man crouched on her porch. She reported a rather quick recovery, with almost no difficulty sleeping two nights after the incident.

Approximately two years later, during the summer months, Rozina experienced a panic attack, with the classical symptoms: increased heart rate, difficulty breathing, and so on. Her symptoms, she recalled, were similar to the momentary jolt of anxiety that she experienced two years before, when she had found the frozen, dead body on her porch. The episode of panic caused her to anticipate future attacks, and she developed an obsession over anticipating them. The anticipatory anxiety began to generalize to other situations. For example, she had trouble going into certain rooms of her house or opening closets for fear of what she might encounter.

It is somewhat ironic that Rozina's anxiety occurred two years after her traumatic experience rather than within a six-month period. Nonetheless, she experienced panic attacks on a regular basis, at least two to three times per week. He autonomic symptoms consisted of increased heart rate, difficulty breathing, lightheadedness, tingling in the hands and feet, and a feeling of faintness. She reported that these symptoms would occur spontaneously within a 10-minute period, lasting sometimes as long as 90 minutes. The symptoms made her feel out of control of her faculties, and she feared at times that she would lose control and possibly even die.

Rozina's family physician conducted a thorough physical examination, including blood studies and an electrocardiogram. Upon receiving normal results, the physician started her on an initial dose of alprazolam (0.25 mg, one tablet three times per day, p.r.n.). He referred her to a clinical psychologist specializing in cognitive-behavior therapy, in order to treat her panic symptoms.

At the initial visit, the therapist conducted a complete intake and history. Rozina was also administered a psychological test battery, which included the MMPI-2 (Hathaway & McKinley, 1989) and the Body Sensations Questionnaire (BSQ) (Chambless, Caputo, Bright, & Gallagher 1984). She was also administered the Beck Depression Inventory (BDI) (Beck, Ward, Mendelsohn, Mock, & Earlbaugh, 1961) and the Beck Anxiety Inventory (BAI) (Beck & Steer, 1990), in addition to the Modified Post-Traumatic Stress Inventory (Falsetti, Resick, Resnick, & Kilpatrick, 1992).

During the subsequent sessions, Rozina was oriented to the SAEB system, a strategy specifically for panic disorder, designed to track automatic thoughts, emotions, and behaviors and how they relate to panic symptoms. The acronym *SAEB* stands for "Symptoms, Automatic thoughts, Emotion, and Behavior." These words describe the elements that many panic victims report give rise to the alarm that facilitates their panic.

The SAEB system was developed as a result of numerous clinical cases in which panic sufferers were frustrated by their inability to convey to others, including the treating clinician, the exact sequence of events that occur during a panic attack (Dattilio, 1990; Dattilio & Salas-Auvert, 2000).

In this system clients identify the initial symptom or symptoms that precipitate the panic episode (Dattilio, 1994). These symptoms are listed by utilizing such inventories as the BSQ and the BAI, or other empirically derived panic measures, supplemented by specific questioning during the interview phase. If the individual has experienced more than one attack, uncovering the SAEB sequence can help expose their repetitive character. If recalling the symptoms presents a problem, either because the patient is blocking or simply has poor recall, then the use of panic-induction exercises may be helpful, as defined by Clark (1986) and as portrayed in additional case studies (Alford et al., 1990; Dattilio, 1990; Dattilio & Berchick, 1992).

Once the symptoms have been identified and their sequence established, the therapist aligns each symptom with specific automatic thoughts and accompanying emotions and behaviors. These can be obtained firsthand by using either the patient's recollection or a panic-induction exercise. The clinician can also use the patient's own reports in a weekly panic log (Dattilio & Salas-Auvert, 2000).

The assembled sequence of panic attack elements—symptoms, automatic thoughts, emotion, and behavior—can then be represented in a diagram, to show the patient how automatic thoughts and their accompanying emotions work to escalate the attack.

The diagram in Figure 2-1 shows how Rozina's sequence of events unfolded. First an abrupt increase in heart rate led to difficulty in breathing and subsequently lightheadedness, tingling in the hands and feet, and a feeling of faintness. Once the sequence was established, the automatic thoughts accompanying each symptom were listed in a corresponding vertical column. Finally, in a third vertical column, the associated emotion and behavior were listed. Vectors were then drawn, to demonstrate to Rozina how the catastrophic thought content might occur in reaction to autonomic symptoms and how these thoughts contribute to the subsequent behavior and to the subsequent escalation of these symptoms (Dattilio, 1990). This strategy is demonstrated in detail in a videotape presentation (Dattilio, 1996) and is also outlined in detail later in this chapter.

Rozina was then taught a course of progressive muscle relaxation that

Figure 2-1 Rozina's Panic Sequence Using the SAEB System

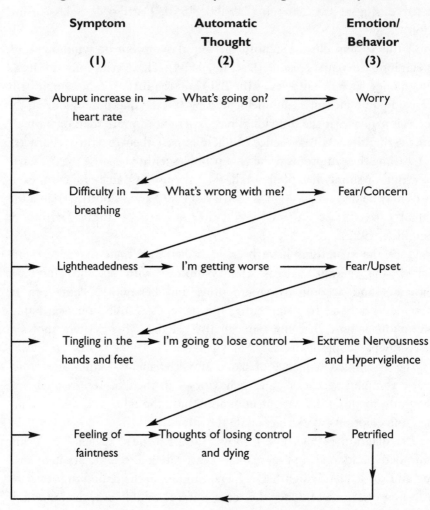

included deep breathing (inhaling through the nose and exhaling slowly and continuously through the mouth). She was taught to regulate her breathing in this manner and was instructed to practice it at least once a day for 20 minutes using an audiocassette tape that she and the therapist made together. This style of relaxation involves the one outlined by Borkovec and Matthews (1988).

The treatment sessions then consisted of helping Rozina reconstruct

Columns 2 and 3 of the SAEB system, replacing them with more balanced responses with a less catastrophic tone.

Once Rozina had acquired some of these coping skills, the next step was *in vivo* exposure to situations that might be fearsome for her. For example, Rozina had had difficulties opening closet doors in her home, anticipating that she might find something that would startle her. When questioned in detail about her thinking regarding the closets, the logic of her reply was: "I know it sounds silly, but finding a frozen dead man on the back of my porch is also something uncommon. Therefore, why would I not expect that something else could happen like that upon opening a concealed area in my home?"

Consequently, a Subjective Units of Discomfort (SUD) scale was collaboratively constructed with Rozina. The scale consisted of a list of possibilities, ordered hierarchically, ranging from 0 (no anxiety-producing situation) to 100 (the most anxious situation imaginable) and filling in the interim gaps in units of 10.

Rozina's hierarchy included items such as opening the back door of her home early in the morning, prior to sunrise; opening storage closets that she had not visited for some time; and going into a dark cellar or attic and turning on the light spontaneously. All of these events involved the potential for being startled by an unexpected incident, which of course, Rozina could state in one sense was "irrational." But the debate always ended with "But then again, you never know." The attempt was to remain sensitive to the emotional component that was present, particularly in light of her previous trauma, yet to keep her focused on her cognitions and behaviors.

The idea here was to expose Rozina to potentially anxiety-producing situations while helping her to control her anxiety, particularly her anticipatory anxiety. This was done by teaching her controlled, deep breathing (inhaling through the nose and exhaling slowly and continuously through the mouth) while she at the same time reassured herself of the unlikelihood of encountering anything traumatic. Once she was confident that her breathing and anxiety were under control, she was imaginally exposed to the lowest level of the hierarchy. Rozina and the therapist walked through the hierarchy, all the way up to the most severe anxiety-producing imagery, until she could imagine being in this situation with little or no anxiety. Much of our work focused on having her control her autonomic activity and regulate her breathing in order to thwart the onset of panic. Once scaling the hierarchy was accomplished successfully on an imaginal level, Rozina was then exposed to it *in vivo*. At this point, the therapist actually came to Rozina's home and walked through the hierarchical events, helping her utilize cognitive-behavioral coping skills at the same time.

Rozina eventually reached the point where she could open up doors and cupboards without anxiety or the anticipation of a panic attack. Part of the treatment included helping her deal with the rare event that she might indeed experience another unusual episode and decide how she would cope with it. Despite Rozina's trauma of discovering the frozen dead man on her back porch, she actually handled the situation quite well. One of the issues that surfaced in the process of treatment was the concept of "being out of control," symbolized by unexpected events. Rozina was the type of individual who always needed to be in "complete" control of her life, but the trauma of discovering the dead man seemed to bring home the reality that there are some things in life that she simply cannot control. This issue hit so close to home, however, that it was difficult for Rozina, and it eventually became a hurdle that she had to overcome.

Treatment lasted approximately three months, at which time Rozina was panic-free. She subsequently attended five additional monthly sessions in order to address the issue of "control in her life" and how to relinquish control of those things that she could not affect. The aforementioned CT and BT strategies appeared to work well with Rozina because they appealed to her practical side and provided her with a structured format for addressing her distressing symptomatology. They also served as a prelude to helping her face her struggle with self-control.

Many of the same strategies that are employed with individuals in therapy can also be applied to couples and families as well (Dattilio, 1998). Some of these strategies are reviewed below and illustrated by the conjoint therapy of a couple in distress.

Cognitive-Behavior Therapy with Couples

Cognitive-behavior therapy has recently received attention in the professional literature as a tool of integration useful with couples and families (Beck, 1988; Dattilio & Padesky, 1990; Dattilio, 1990, 1994, 1998). CBT as applied to couples has evolved out of the behavioral school of thought, when theorists of this school first applied their techniques to couples in the mid- to late 1960s. While cognitive techniques were reportedly being applied to couples as early as the late 1950s (Ellis, Sichel, Yeager, DiMattio, & DiGiuseppe, 1989), the first published studies using behavior therapy with couples did not appear in the professional literature until the late 1960s or early 1970s (Stuart, 1969; Liberman, 1970). The implementation of cognitive techniques in clinically controlled outcome studies actually occurred much later (Margolin & Weiss, 1978), and during the 1980s and early 1990s, increasing attention was given to the effectiveness of the cognitive component of treatment (Baucom & Epstein, 1990; Dattilio, Epstein, & Baucom, 1998).

The primary tenets of CBT as applied to couples involve: (a) the modification of unrealistic expectations in the relationship, (b) the correction of faulty attributions in relationship interactions, and (c) the use of self-instructional procedures to decrease destructive interaction. A primary agenda of CBT is identifying the partners' schemata or beliefs about relationships in general and, more specifically, their thoughts about their own relationship (Beck, 1988; Epstein, 1986) and how these thoughts affect their emotions and behaviors.

As we have seen, basic beliefs about relationships and the nature of couple interaction, or schemata, are often learned early in life from primary sources such as parents, local cultural mores, the media, and early dating experiences. By contrast, automatic thoughts are "surface thoughts"—ideas, beliefs, or images that individuals have from moment to moment that are situation specific (for example, "My wife is late again; she doesn't care about my feelings"). Automatic thoughts usually stem from an individual's schemata, one's underlying core beliefs that are inflexible and unconditional in character.

A therapist working with a couple from a cognitive-behavioral perspective must focus equally on each partner's expectations about the nature of an intimate relationship. Discerning the distortions in evaluations of experience derived from those expectations is critically important. Cognitive distortions may be evident in the automatic thoughts that the couple report, or they may be uncovered by means of systematic or Socratic questioning regarding the meaning that a partner attaches to a specific event. Spouses' automatic thoughts about their interactions with each other commonly include inferences about the causes of pleasant and unpleasant events that occur between them.

Cognitive-behavior therapy with couples focuses on the cognitions and beliefs that are identified as components of relationship discord and as contributing to each partner's subjective dissatisfaction with the relationship. This approach moves to the core of the relationship difficulty by focusing on hidden as well as obvious here-and-now problems, rather than by dwelling on early childhood traumas.

When addressing the issue of change in relationships, several major focal areas in the cognitive-behavioral model are essential. These include: beliefs about the relationship, unrealistic expectations, and causal attributions and misattributions. (For a detailed explanation of these concepts, refer to the case study later in this chapter or to Dattilio, Epstein, & Baucom, 1998.)

Assessment

There are numerous self-report and behavioral methods for assessing couples and families. Unfortunately, space limitations in this book preclude a detailed presentation. For a more comprehensive overview, the reader is referred to Baucom and Epstein (1990) and to Dattilio, Epstein, and Baucom (1998).

Self-Report Questionnaires

Despite the rapid growth of cognitive-behavioral couple and family therapy, relatively few self-report scales are available for assessing the five major types of relationship cognitions. Epstein and Eidelson's (1981) Relationship Belief Inventory (RBI) was developed to tap unrealistic beliefs about close relationships, with subscales assessing the assumptions (a) that the partners cannot change a relationship, (b) that disagreement is always destructive, (c) that heterosexual relationship problems are due to innate differences between men and women, as well as standards, (d) that partners should be able to mind-read each other's thoughts and emotions, and (e) that one should be a perfect sexual partner.

Baucom, Epstein, Rankin, and Burnett's (1996) Inventory of Specific

Relationship Standards (ISRS) assesses an individual's personal standards concerning major relationship themes, including the nature of boundaries between partners (autonomy versus sharing), distribution of control (equal versus skewed), and partners' levels of instrumental and expressive investment in their relationship.

Finally, one of the best methods of assessment is the actual treatment process itself, since clinicians continue to conceptualize the couple's problems even after treatment begins.

Clinical Application with a Couple: Case Example

Roger and Caren were a young couple in their mid-thirties who had been married for five years with no children. This was the first marriage for each. Roger was employed as a shipping clerk with a local publishing warehouse, and Caren was employed part-time as a salesperson in a department store.

As a result of their constant bickering and growing alienation from each other, the couple was referred by a family friend for couple counseling. Both reported the tension as ongoing for the past two years, particularly as a result of Roger's recent infidelity.

Background

Roger and Caren had met at a picnic through mutual friends. They dated only six months prior to marrying. Both said that their marriage progressed extremely well for approximately two years, after which Caren discovered that Roger was having an affair with a female coworker. The affair had surfaced after Caren noticed that increasing sums of money had vanished from the savings account with no explanation. She eventually confronted Roger, after he came in late one evening, and after much prodding by Caren, he confessed to the affair. Roger suspected that his wife knew about his infidelity and felt it better to confess than to get caught. Caren demanded that he discontinue his affair and seek help. He made promises to her on several occasions, only to be caught having contact with this woman over the Internet. Finally, Caren threatened to leave Roger unless he sought professional help immediately and discontinued his contact with this coworker altogether. At that point Roger contacted my office and set up an appointment for himeself and his wife.

First Session: Initial Assessment

During the initial two-hour assessment, I saw Roger and Caren together and obtained a complete history of their relationship, along with details regarding their single lives prior to dating.

Roger and Caren had dated only six months prior to marrying. Neither had dated very much before their introduction, and they claimed that their decision to marry was very spontaneous. Both stated that they were raised in stable environments, with no history of divorce in either family of origin. Both sets of parents urged Roger and Caren to seek couple counseling after their arguing had gone on for more than one year. Roger had made no previous attempts at counseling, but Caren had been in therapy for almost a year upon graduation from high school for self-esteem problems and for problems with interpersonal relationships. She denied any use of drugs or alcohol. Roger admitted to some alcohol use after high school but no other substance.

Aside from obtaining background information, the initial session was devoted to developing a conceptualization of the presenting problem. Roger and Caren agreed that they were bickering and arguing almost constantly, because of tension over Roger's infidelity. Caren described her concern as arising from her lack of trust in Roger and his terrible violation of their marriage vows. She said she constantly questioned his whereabouts and his honesty about contact with any female coworkers. As a result of being so shocked by Roger's clandestine affair, she claimed, she now felt compelled to keep track of his time whenever he left the house. Each time he returned home from being out alone, she gave him the third degree. She was obsessed with balancing the checkbook and telephoned the bank every week for the account balance in order to be sure that he was not withdrawing extra money. She incessantly reviewed his cellular telephone bills, called any phone number that appeared unusual, and checked his e-mail messages on a regular basis.

Roger's major complaint was that despite his attempts to remain faithful, Caren's constant suspiciousness and questioning were actually causing him to be resentful. During these periods of agitation and arguing, he felt the urge to escape and call this other woman. While he understood that this would obviously be destructive to the marriage, he claimed that Caren was driving him back to infidelity or simply to end their marital relationship.

During the initial assessment, Roger and Caren were both presented with the Marital Attitudes Questionnaire (Revised) (MAQR), developed by Pretzer, Epstein, and Fleming (1993). They were instructed to complete the inventory separately and bring it along to the next session. They were also oriented briefly to the cognitive-behavioral model of couple relationships (Dattilio & Padesky, 1990; Epstein, 1986) and were recommended to begin reading the book *After the Affair* by Janis Abrahams and Michael Spring (1996). Individual appointments were then made for both, in order to probe more into their individual schemata about themselves and their relationship.

Second Session

During this individual session with Caren, her responses to the MAQR were reviewed. The majority of her responses that were marked with a 1 ("strongly agree") fell within the area of a general disbelief that the relationship could change. These items were used as a tool to initiate discussion about areas of conflict.

Socratic questioning was employed to ascertain Caren's automatic thoughts about her relationship and the potential for change: "I am so leery of Roger's ability to change"; "He has lied to me too many times already"; "I feel as though I was deceived about our entire relationship"; "I have no idea whether or not he's out there seeing other women and making a fool of me."

As can be seen from Caren's automatic thoughts, she maintained a fairly negative perspective of her marital relationship. Probing uncovered her primary relationship schemata, which consisted of: "I have always been unlucky in relationships, I'll never be happy"; "I set myself up to be used"; "No one wants to love me, my love isn't good enough"; "People don't change, and it is unrealistic for me to think that Roger will."

Many of Caren's beliefs stemmed from her negative experiences with interpersonal relationships in the past, which left her with the general belief that relationships for her rarely last. This schema, was also tied into an emotional component: fear of abandonment.

The essential goal of this session with Caren was to develop a clear and detailed conceptualization of how she viewed herself and her marital situation and, most important, how she viewed her future in the relationship with Roger (Beck Rush, Hollon, & Emery, 1979). It was clear from her statements and beliefs that a negative bias in her thinking directly distorted her view of the relationship. Instead of viewing Roger's infidelities as a result of his own issues and conflicts in their relationship, she viewed

Figure 2-2: Dysfunctional Thought Record

DIRECTIONS: When you notice your mood getting worse, ask yourself, "What's going through my mind right now?" and as soon as possible jot down the thought or mental image in the "automatic thought" column.

DATE TIME	SITUATION	AUTOMATIC THOUGHTS	EMOTION(S)	DISTORTION	ALTERNATIVE RESPONSE	OUTCOME
	DESCRIBE: 1. Actual event leading to unpleasant emotion, or 2. Stream of thought, daydream, or recollection, leading to an unpleasant emotion, or 3. Distressing physical sensations.	1. Write the automatic thought(s) that preceded your emotion(s). 2. Rate your belief in automatic thought(s) (0 to 100%)	DESCRIBE: 1. Specify sad, anxious/angry, etc. 2. Rate degree of emotion (0 to 100%)	1. All-or-nothing thinking 2. Overgeneral-ization 3. Mental filter 4. Disqualifying the positive 5. Jumping to conclusions 6. Magnification or minimization 7. Emotional reasoning 8. "Should" statements 9. Labeling and mislabeling 10. Personalization	1. Write a rational response to the automatic thought(s). 2. Rate your belief in the alternative response (0 to 100%)	1. Rerate your belief in automatic thought(s) (0 to 100%) 2. Specify and rate subsequent emotions (0 to 100%)

Questions to help formulate the ALTERNATIVE RESPONSE: (1) What is the evidence that the automatic thought is true? Not true? (2) Is there an alternative explanation? (3) What's the worst that could happen? Could I live through it? What's the best that could happen? What's the most realistic outcome? (4) What should I do about it? (5) What's the effect of my believing the automatic thought? What could be the effect of changing my thinking? (6) If (person's name) was in this situation and had this thought, what would I tell him/her?

them as being due to her own inadequacy—a not uncommon belief among spouses who have been the recipient of infidelity. For Caren, this clearly tied into her schemata of low self-esteem and fear of abandonment.

As a homework assignment, Caren was requested to begin processing her automatic thoughts through the Dysfunctional Thought Record sheets, which she was fully oriented to use during this session (see Figure 2.2).

Third Session

The third session involved an individual assessment with Roger. Here the same format was used as in the previous appointment with Caren: his responses to the MAQR were reviewed. Socratic questioning about several of his responses to the questionnaire items ascertained his Roger's automatic thoughts about the relationship, along with his beliefs about why he chose to step outside of the relationship with Caren and jeopardize his marriage.

- "I am trying like hell to stay away from other women, and Caren's doing everything to drive me back to infidelity."
- "I am weak and vulnerable to the attention of other women, which sometimes leads to a physical relationship."
- "Caren picks and questions everything that I do and isn't giving me a chance."
- "What's the use of trying if I am being accused of fooling around anyway?"
- I make one mistake, and I am pegged as a cheater for life."

Upon probing more into Roger's automatic thoughts I learned that many of his thoughts stemmed from the underlying belief that he could never meet up to the expectations of others. Hence, when women showed him attention because of his physical attractiveness, he found this very reassuring. He experienced difficulty saying no to certain women's advances. His underlying beliefs carried the theme: "It's very difficult for me to say no to women for fear of rejection"; "I have trouble resisting women's advances since I feel so empowered and confident when they show me acceptance."

As a result of this exercise, Roger was helped to understand how his underlying beliefs predisposed him to automatic thoughts that he would be rejected if he declined women's advances. This undoubtedly affected his interaction with Caren, contributing to much of the tension in their relationship. In both Roger and Caren's upbringing, several childhood incidents had a profound effect on their thinking styles. For Roger, it was his rejection by females during his early adolescence; for Caren, it was trust in interpersonal relationships with her peers. It was pointed out to both that these previous incidents contributed to their schemata in the relationship and to the conflicts with which they struggled. These issues were addressed with a specific focus during the individual sessions and then later on during the conjoint visits.

An essential key to addressing the conflict in this relationship seemed to be to defuse the current tension over issues of trust and honesty. Unless this was accomplished, it seemed, further headway could prove difficult, since all the tension would likely revert to this point of conflict. It was also important to remind Roger and Caren that the issue of infidelity represented deeper issues in their individual lives and in their marriage and that one objective was to avoid getting stuck on focusing exclusively on the affair.

Fourth and Fifth Sessions

In the fourth session, which included both Roger and Caren, the agenda involved explaining in more detail the cognitive-behavioral model and placing specific emphasis on the cognitive distortions that occur in marital interactions. Cognitive distortions were explained as types of fallacious thinking that contribute to the feedback loops supporting marital dysfunction in communication. Below is a list of errors that were discovered in Roger and Caren's reasoning. These were identified during this conjoint visit, using input from both as we went through the basic concept of each term.

- *Arbitrary inferences.* Roger arrives home a half-hour late from work, and Caren concluded, "He was probably out running around on me again."

- *Selective abstraction.* When Caren failed to answer Roger's greeting the first thing in the morning, he concluded, "She's pissed at me again."

- *Overgeneralization.* After having an argument with Roger, Caren stated, "All men are alike."

- *Magnification and minimization.* Roger viewed the trouble with his marriage and stated, "My entire life is a shambles."

- *Personalization.* Roger stated to himself, "Caren has no confidence in me—I guess I am really a louse!"

- *Dichotomous thinking.* Caren stated, "Because Roger has been unfaithful, that makes him untrustworthy in every way."

These errors were highlighted during the session in attempts to have Roger and Caren become more aware of the distortions that occur in their daily thinking.

Subsequent to this review of the cognitive distortions, I explained to Roger and Caren that, as a result of the gradual deterioration in the relationship, they had both come to view each other in a negative frame (Beck, 1988; Dattilio & Padesky, 1990; Dattilio, 1998). In other words, those qualities that they once had admired in each other were now viewed as being undesirable and constituted the negative frame in which they perceived each other. This again was due in part to distortions that developed in the course of their relationship.

I decided to begin the next session by addressing the conflict at hand with both partners:

Therapist: Okay, now I'd like to focus on the conflict that seems to be the foremost issue—your trust, Caren, in Roger's ability to remain faithful, and Roger's fear of giving in as a result of retaliating against what he perceives as Caren's constant nagging.

Caren: That's right. Right now I am extremely skeptical of his word since he has lied to me so much. I really doubt that he'll change, and I emotionally cannot afford to be humiliated and disrespected anymore.

Therapist: So you, Caren, are not very optimistic about this entire counseling process. What about you, Roger?

Roger: Well, I think that she's being unfair. I don't know what the hell she wants. I promised to change, and I'm trying! I've been faithful for almost three months now. She just can't lay off. Since I am being accused all of the time, what's the use?

Caren (*interrupting*): That's right. Not when you say you're coming home at five-thirty and you come strolling in at a quarter to seven with no explanation of where you've been. What am I supposed to think? You must think I'm a real idiot, Roger!

Therapist: Okay, look, we need to hear each other out. But it won't be a very productive session if you fall into a dead-end pattern of arguing again. So let's establish a ground rule that we will not interrupt each other when speaking?

Roger: Yeah, I'll agree to it. But she's the one who can't stop her mouth.

Therapist: I'll get to her in a minute, Roger, but I want an agreement from you.

Roger: Sure, you have my word.

Therapist: Okay. Now, Caren, do you think that you can agree to this?

Caren: I don't know. He lies so damn much. I just have a lot of trouble sitting here listening to some of his bull without jumping into the conversation.

Therapist: Well then, let's do this. Would you, Caren, be willing to write down your thoughts, or what we call your automatic thoughts, when you hear these statements that Roger makes?

Caren: You mean right now?

Therapist: Yes, right now in the session. The same way I had you do when we met individually.

Caren: I guess so.

Therapist: Now, I'd like you to take your pen and note pad and write down the automatic thoughts that you had when Roger made his last statement. I think the statement was, "I promised to change and I'm trying. She just won't stay off my back."[3]

Caren: (She writes them down.) All right, here they are.

Therapist: Caren, will you read them out loud?

Caren: "One: Yes, big deal—a couple of months, and he thinks he's Mr. Fidelity. Two: As soon as I start to let my guard down, he'll be right back to running around on me. Three: 'What do

---

[3] Note: Caren takes a few minutes to write down her automatic thoughts. This strategy is known as the Pad and Pencil Technique, first introduced in Dattilio and Padesky (1990). It is used to help couples refrain from interrupting each other during heated sessions.

I want?' he says. I just want him to stay faithful so I can trust him. Four: Every time he goes out with those damn friends of his, he gets into trouble."

Therapist: Okay, good. Now, Caren, I'd like you to take the evidence for each one of those statements that you made and balance it with a rational thought statement right next to it. I would also like you to label the distortion according to the terms that we discussed earlier. For example, let's take your first thought: "Big deal—a couple of months, and he thinks he's Mr. Fidelity." Now what evidence do you have that supports the notion that he believes he has it made because he's remained faithful for a couple of months?

Caren: Well, none really. Just his cocky attitude and the fact that he's already cheated on me.

Therapist: Is it cocky? Or is he trying to maintain a confident attitude?

Caren: Well, I don't know—you have a point.

Therapist: All right, so just because he's acting confident doesn't mean that he feels that he has it made, does it? Maybe it's a way he's trying to preserve some dignity or reassure you—maybe even reassure himself?

Caren: No, I really have no evidence to back that up.

Therapist: And how would you label this distorted thought according to our model?

Caren: Probably a combination of "selective abstraction" and "mislabeling."

Therapist: That's right! So how might you write up your rational thought statement?

Caren: Well, let's see. (She writes.) "One. Well, I guess a couple of months is pretty good so far. This has been the longest that he's been faithful. I guess the positive attitude is a key force in his staying faithful. Maybe it's a good sign. But . . . it's just tough because it's such an emotional thing for me since his infidelity took me by such surprise—I feel so rejected."

Therapist: I understand this, and you are well within your right to feel this way. We don't want to downplay your emotions—they're important. But at the same time, we don't want them to interfere with your ability to get beyond being stuck. So we need to try to mediate your emotions somehow while remaining sensitive to them so that we can go forward.

Caren: Yeah—I think that's good. It's something I guess I need to deal with. I know he's trying, and I want to trust him. I really do!

I then asked Caren to weigh the evidence for the other three statements and then to rationally restructure her thoughts—and to do it in front of Roger, so that he could witness her efforts to balance her distorted statements and at the same time remain sensitive to her emotional state. The remainder of her thoughts are given below, with the cognitive distortion identified.

Emotion	Automatic Thought	Cognitive Distortion	Rational Restatement
Depressed/ Angry	As soon as I start to let my guard down, he'll be right back to running around.	Overgeneralization	I really have no evidence to support this. Perhaps letting my guard down a bit might just help to give him some reinforcement for staying faithful.

The same procedure was used with Roger in addressing some of his distortions.

| Anger | There she goes. She just can't get it through her head to lay off. | Arbitrary Inference | This is Caren's way of expressing herself. It doesn't mean that she is necessarily condemning me. |
| | Sometimes I believe that she | Personalization | That's ridiculous. If she wanted to |

almost wants me	end the marriage,
to fail.	then she'd do
	that, not set me
	up for failure.
	She's frustrated.

By allowing each partner to witness the other's restructuring of automatic thoughts, they viewed each other in an alternative light as they heard themselves rehearse the positive "flip side" of their thoughts. They were also able to witness each other make a concerted effort to view things in a different light, which often has a positive impact on partners' respective views of each other.

Therapist: As a result of this little exercise, what are you both thinking right now?

Roger: Well, personally, I feel as though maybe she is able to see the optimistic side of my situation, but I am still a little leery about whether or not she'll stick with that. It will probably change back to the negative as soon as we leave here.

Caren: I feel the same way. It was good to hear him say something different for a change, but I still don't trust him.

Therapist: Surely the changes will come in time. It will require some time to get us unstuck. But the point of this session is to help you both to see that by monitoring your thoughts and making some adjustments, you can envision how things could change. As a homework assignment, I would like you to continue with this exercise, particularly each time you begin to become irate with each other. In addition, I would like you to both begin just challenging some of your own thoughts about the situation in order to consider an alternative to what you are telling yourselves. Hopefully, this will begin to have some effect on the emotion that is contributing to your feelings about the situation.

I would also like you to consider doing one nice thing for each other every day. It doesn't have to be anything major, but some small gesture of kindness in order for us to break things up a little. Let's see how this affects you.

I scheduled the appointments for no more than one week apart, to allow enough time for them to complete the assignment but not too much time. I also encouraged Caren and Roger to do some additional reading to supplement the exercises that they learned in therapy. Such books as *Love Is Never Enough* by Beck (1988) or *Fighting for Your Marriage* by Markman, Stanley, and Blumsberg (1994) are commonly recommended.

Sixth Session

The sixth session was a follow-up to the previous session's assignment. Both Roger and Caren claimed that, for the most part, their week had gone a bit smoother except for a minor blow-up over Roger's late arrival home from work one evening. When we reanalyzed their argument in the therapy session, we determined that their conflict had come as a result of deviating from their structured assignment and reverting to their negative frames. Caren accused Roger once again of meeting a female, which caused Roger to throw a tantrum. The couple were encouraged to review their conflict and analyze their automatic thoughts again, applying the techniques of rational restructuring by weighing the evidence and identifying cognitive distortions. Once again, they were encouraged, not to ignore their emotions, but to attempt to mediate them as best that they could through the cognitive-behavioral techniques that they learned. Each had been able to do a few positive things for the other, which helped to enhance a sense of hope in the relationship.

Subsequent Sessions

The subsequent sessions focused on the same pattern: reinforcing the techniques that they had learned through the cognitive-behavioral model and addressing the underlying issues of trust and vulnerability.

As the conflicts began to subside, Roger was able to concentrate on remaining strong and avoiding the temptation to be unfaithful. Several individual sessions were dedicated to addressing his low self-esteem and to applying cognitive techniques in social situations. In addition, it was suggested that he consider some individual therapy for himself. The same was eventually recommended to Caren.

Subsequently, the sessions focused on the couple's emotional dependency needs for each other and their actual fears of failing in their relationship. The duration of treatment was six months, with a total number of sessions of around 20. A one-year follow-up showed both partners were enjoying a more improved relationship, with less anxiety over Roger's infidelity.

Roger and Caren seemed to respond well to a CBT approach because both were both somewhat dependent, concrete individuals who required structure in their life. CBT appeared to offer them this and aided them in pulling out of their crisis so that they could go on to address some of the other interpersonal issues in their relationship.

It is important to note that cognitive-behavior therapy with couples and families is most effective if conducted against the backdrop of a systems framework. Cognitive-behavioral strategies are also very integratable with a number of other couples and family modalities and can be used effectively in combination (Dattilio, 1998).

Summary

This chapter has provided a brief overview of contemporary cognitive-behavioral strategies for the mental health practitioner.

The more popular strategies of both cognitive and behavior therapy have been emphasized here, along with their clinical application with an individual as well as a couple in distress. Many of the strategies listed in this chapter can be used interchangeably, although they may vary slightly depending on the disorder or circumstances involved.

While CBT does have its limitations, it remains one of the most efficacious and well-researched modalities in existence.

References

Abrahams, J. L. (1982, November). *Inducing a collaborative set in distressed couples: Nonspecific therapist issues in cognitive therapy.* Paper presented at the annual meeting of the Association for the Advancement of Behavior Therapy, Los Angeles.

Abrahams, J. L., & Spring, M. *After the affair.* New York: HarperCollins.

Alford, B., & Beck, A. T. (1997). *The integrative power of cognitive therapy.* New York: Guilford.

Alford, B. A., Beck, A. T., Freeman, A. & Wright, F. (1990) Brief focused cognitive therapy of panic disorder. *Psychotherapy, 27* (2), 230–234.

Alford, B., & Norcross, J. C. (1991). Cognitive therapy as integrative therapy. *Journal of Psychotherapy Integration, 1* (1), 175–190.

Bandura, A. (1961). Psychotherapy as a learning process. *Psychological Bulletin, 58,* 143–159.

Barlow, D. H. (1988). *Anxiety and its disorders.* New York: Guilford.

Baucom, D., & Epstein, N. (1990) *Cognitive-behavioral marital therapy.* New York: Brunner/Mazel.

Baucom, D. H., Epstein, N., Daiuto, A. D., Carels, R. A., Rankin, L. A., & Burnett, C. K. (1996). Cognitions in marriage: The relationship between standards and attributions. *Journal of Family Psychology, 10,* 209–222.

Baucom, D. H., Epstein, N., Rankin, L. A. & Burnett, C. K. (1996). Assessing relationship standards: The Inventory of Specific Relationship Standards. *Journal of Family Psychology, 10,* 72–88.

Beck, A. T. (1963). Thinking and depression: 1. Idiosyncratic content and cognitive distortions. *Archives of General Psychiatry, 9,* 324–333.

Beck, A. T. (1964). Thinking and depression: 2. Theory and therapy. *Archives of General Psychiatry, 10,* 561–571.

Beck, A. T. (1967). *Depression: Clinical, experimental and theoretical aspects.* New York: Harper & Row.

Beck, A. T. (1988). *Love is never enough.* New York: Harper & Row.

Beck, A. T. (1976). *Cognitive therapy and the emotional disorders.* New York: International Universities Press.

Beck, A. T. (1993). Cognitive therapy: Past, present and future. *Journal of Consulting and Clinical Psychology, 61*(2), 194–198.

Beck, A. T., Freeman, A., et al. (1990). *Cognitive therapy of personality disorders.* New York: Guilford.

Beck, A. T., Rush, A. J., Shaw, B. F., & Emery, G. (1979). *Cognitive therapy of depression.* New York: Guilford.

Beck, A. T. & Steer, R. A. (1990). *Beck Anxiety Inventory manual.* San Antonio, TX: Psychological Corp.; Harcourt Brace Jovanovich.

Beck, A.T. (1991). Cognitive therapy as the integrative therapy. *Journal of Psychotherapy Integration, 1*(3), 191–198.

Beck, A. T., Ward, C. H., Mendelson, M., Mock, J., & Erbaugh, J. (1961). An inventory for measuring depression. *Archives of General Psychiatry, 9,* 295–302.

Barkovec, T. D., & Matthews, A. M. (1988). Treatment of nonphobic anxiety: A comparison of nondirective, cognitive, and coping desensitization therapy. *Journal of Consulting and Clinical Psychology, 56,* 877–884.

Burns, D. (1980). *Feeling good: The new mood therapy.* New York: Signet Books.

Burns, D. (1989) *The feeling good handbook: Using the new mood therapy in everyday life.* New York: Morrow.

Chambless, D. L., Caputo, G. C., Bright, P., & Gallagher, R. (1984). Assessment of fear of fear in agoraphobics: The body sensations questionnaire and the agoraphobic cognitions questionnaire. *Journal of Consulting and Clinical Psychology, 52*(6), 1090–1097.

Clark, D. M. (1986). A cognitive approach to panic. *Behaviour Research and Therapy, 24,* 461–470.

Dancu, C. V., & Foa, E. R. (1992). Post traumatic stress disorder. In A. Freeman and F. M. Dattilio, (Eds.), *Comprehensive casebook of cognitive therapy* (pp. 79–88). New York: Plenum.

Dattilio, F. M. (1987). The use of paradoxical intention in the treatment of panic attacks. *Journal of Counseling and Development, 66,* 66–67.

Dattilio, F. M. (1990). Symptom induction and de-escalation in the treatment of panic attacks. *Journal of Mental Health Counseling, 12*(4), 515–519.

Dattilio, F. M. (1994). Families in crisis. In F. M. Dattilio and A. Freeman (Eds.), *Cognitive-behavioral strategies in crisis intervention* (pp. 278–301). New York: Guilford.

Dattilio, F. M. (1996). *Cognitive therapy with couples: Initial phase of treatment* (Videotape). Sarasota, FL: Professional Resource Press.

Dattilio, F. M. (Ed.). (1998). *Case studies in couples and family therapy: Systemic and cognitive perspectives.* New York: Guilford.

Dattilio, F. M., & Berchick, R. J. (1992). Panic and agoraphobia. In A. Freeman and F. A. Dattilio (Eds.), *Comprehensive casebook of cognitive therapy.* (pp. 89–98). New York: Plenum.

Dattilio, F. M., Epstein, N. B., & Baucom, D. H. (1998). Introduction to cognitive-behavioral techniques with couples and families. In F. M. Dattilio (Ed.), *Case studies in couple and family therapy: Systemic and cognitive perspectives.* New York: Guilford.

Dattilio, F. M., & Freeman, A. (1994). *Cognitive-behavioral strategies in crisis intervention.* New York: Guilford.

Dattilio, F. M., & Padesky, C. A. (1990). *Cognitive therapy with couples.* Sarasota, FL: Professional Resource Press.

Dattilio, F. M., & Salas-Auvert, J. A. (2000). *Panic disorder: Assessment and treatment through a wide-angle lens.* Phoenix, AZ: Zeig, Tucker.

Ellis, A., & Harper, R. (1976). *New guide to rational living.* New York: Lyle Stuart.

Ellis, A., Sichel, J. L., Yeager, R. J., DiMattia, D. J., & DiGiuseppe, R. (1989). *Rational-emotive couples therapy.* Psychology Practitioners Guidebooks. New York: Pergamon.

Epstein, N. (1986). Cognitive marital therapy: A multilevel assessment and intervention. *Journal of Rational-Emotive Therapy, 9,* 13–22.

Epstein, N. (1992). A case of cognitive therapy with couples. In A. Freeman and F. M. Dattilio (Eds.), *Comprehensive casebook of cognitive therapy.* (pp. 267–275). New York: Plenum.

Epstein, N. & Eidelson, R. J. (1981). Unrealistic beliefs of clinical couples: Their relationship to expectations, goals and satisfaction. *American Journal of Family Therapy, 9,* 13–22.

Eysenck, H. J. (Ed.). (1964). *Behavior therapy and the neurosis.* New York: Pergamon.

Falsetti, S. A., Resnick, P. A., Resnick, H. S., & Kilpatrick, D. (1992). Post traumatic stress disorder: The assessment of frequency and severity of symptoms in clinical and nonclinical samples. Paper presented at the 26th annual convention of the Association for the Advancement of Behavior Therapy, Boston.

Freeman, A., & Dattilio, F. M. (1992). *Comprehensive casebook of cognitive therapy.* New York: Plenum.

Freeman, A., & DeWolf, R. (1990). *Woulda, coulda, shoulda: Overcoming mistakes, regrets and missed opportunities.* New York: HarperCollins.

Freeman, A., & Greenwood, V. (Eds.) (1987). *Cognitive therapy: Applications in psychiatric and medical settings.* New York: Human Sciences Press.

Hathaway, S. R., & McKinley, J. C. (1989). *Minnesota Multiphasic Personality Inventory-2.* Minneapolis: Regents of the University of Minnesota.

Jacobson, N. S. (1991). Behavioral marital therapy. In A. S. Gurman & D. P. Kniskern (Eds.), *Handbook of family therapy* (Vol 1). (pp. 556-591). New York: Brunner/Mazel.

Jacobson, N. S., & Margolin, G. (1979). *Marital therapy: Strategies based on social learning and behavior exchange principles.* New York: Brunner/Mazel.

Kovacs, M., & Beck, A. T. (1979). Cognitive-affective processes in depression. In C. E. Izard (Ed.), *Emotions in personality and psychopathology* (pp. 417–442). New York: Plenum.

Liberman, R. P. (1970). Behavioral approaches to couple and family therapy. *American Journal of Ortho-psychiatry, 40,* 106–118.

Margolin, G., & Weiss. R. L. (1978). Comparative evaluation of therapeutic components associated with behavioral marital treatments. *Journal of Consulting and Clinical Psychology, 46,* 1476–1486.

Markman, H. J., Stanley, S., & Blumberg, S. L. (1994). *Fighting for your marriage*. San Francisco: Jossey-Bass.

Persons, J. (1995). Are all psychotherapies cognitive? *Journal of Cognitive Psychotherapy, 9*(3), 185–194.

Pretzer, J., Epstein, N. B., & Fleming, B. (1983). The marital attitude survey: A measure of dysfunctional attributions and expectancies. *Journal of Cognitive Psychotherapy, 5*, 131–148.

Salkovskis, P. M. (1989). Obsessions and compulsions. In J. Scott, J. M. G. Williams, & A. T. Beck (Eds.), *Cognitive therapy in clinical practice* (pp. 50–77). London: Routledge & Kegan Paul.

Stuart, R. B. (1969). Operant-interpersonal treatment for marital discord. *Journal of Consulting and Clinical Psychology, 33*, 675–682.

Stuart, R. B. (1980). *Helping couples change: A social learning approach to marital therapy*. New York: Guilford.

Wolpe, J. (1958). *Psychotherapy by reciprocal inhibition building*. Stanford, CA: Stanford University Press.

Wolpe, J. (1973). *The practice of behavior therapy* (2nd ed.). New York: Pergamon.

Annotated Bibliography

Baucom, D. H., & Epstein, N. B. (1990). *Cognitive-behavioral marital therapy*. New York: Brunner/Mazel. This book is considered to be one of the bibles of CBT with couples. Its excellent theory, research, and case examples provide readers with everything they need, from assessment to treatment.

Beck, J. S. (1995). *Cognitive therapy: Basics and beyond*. New York: Guilford. This text is the best on the market for those wishing to develop a comprehensive overview of cognitive-behavior therapy. It includes plenty of examples on how to employ the various techniques and strategies discussed in this chapter.

Dattilio, F. M. (1998). *Case studies in couple and family therapy: Systemic and cognitive perspectives*. New York: Guilford. This comprehensive text provides several chapters on the straight use of CBT with both couples and families, along with case examples. It offers an excellent overview of how CBT can be integrated with 16 other modalities of couple and family therapy, with a dialogue between the contributors and the editor.

Dattilio, F. M., & Freeman, A. (1994). *Cognitive-behavioral strategies in crisis intervention*. New York: Guilford. While this book is geared toward crisis situations, it nonetheless provides a nuts-and-bolts application of CBT for a wide variety of clinical disorders, as well as special areas of concern such as ethics, medication, and so on.

Dattilio, F. M. & Salas-Auvert, J. A. (1999). *Panic disorder: Assessment and treatment through a wide-angle lens*. Phoenix, AZ: Zeig, Tucker. This book covers panic disorder from A to Z, from an extensive history of the disorder to assessment, treatment, and follow-up. It addresses the broad spectrum of treatments and provides extensive case studies for each modality along with an exhaustive list of references, resources, and a model treatment plan.

3

Rational-Emotive Family Therapy: ABC, A'B'C', DE

Charles H. Huber

Introduction

My graduate training and supervised clinical experience provided me an introduction to the concepts and practice of rational-emotive behavior therapy (REBT). My early postdoctoral training and supervised experience included two years as a fellow at the Institute for Rational-Emotive Therapy in New York, where I had the opportunity to work with and be supervised by REBT "masters," including Albert Ellis, Richard Wessler, Ray DiGiuseppe, and Dominic DiMattia. Within this context, I realized the critical importance of assessing, intervening, and evaluating outcomes from a specific cognitive-behavioral perspective. The basis for that perspective was REBT's emphasis on *rational and irrational beliefs* as a means of understanding human functioning.

Later, as I developed expertise as a family psychologist, systems theory in concert with REBT came to constitute the guiding core of my research and clinical practice. It is within this guiding core that rational-emotive family therapy (REFT) evolved. Although the term *family* appears in its name primarily as a means of distinguishing REFT from traditional REBT, *family* as a unit of focus in REFT is synonymous with *system*. Thus, the primary unit of focus in REFT is the particular system under consideration, be it an individual, a couple, or a family. Further, whatever the immediate unit of focus, REFT always gives concurrent consideration to the interconnections and simultaneous interactions of multiple systems of influence that contribute to any individual, couple, or family system's overall functioning. The *client-system's beliefs*, however, are the predominant emphasis in REFT assessment, intervention, and evaluation. This applies whether the client is a family, a couple, or an individual and to those significant persons with whom he or she is in interaction, even though these latter persons may never be physically present in the therapy session.

This chapter describes REFT as a brief therapy for individuals and couples and offers case illustrations. It presents REFT's essential clinical strategies by organizing them under the umbrella of the *metastrategy* ABC, A'B'C' (read "A-prime, B-prime, C-prime"), DE. Like communications (like its "surface/report" and "command/meta-" levels), clinical strategies also occur at two levels. The second level, the command or metastrategy, qualifies what takes place at the first level.

Problems arise when a clinical strategy at the first or surface/report level is contradicted by what is "commanded" at the second or meta level (for example, attempting intervention before an adequate assessment is made). Maintaining full and consistent awareness of the metastrategy *contributes to a context wherein the singular clinical strategies will be optimally implemented* (for example, only after an assessment is conducted is an intervention implemented; further, the intervention emanates directly from the assessment).

First I offer a brief overview of REFT's position on rational and irrational beliefs. Then I describe REFT's position on problem formation, so as to facilitate more efficient and thereby briefer therapeutic practice. The essential clinical strategies under the ABC, A'B'C', DE metastrategy are then detailed, and specific indications for their use as a brief therapy strategy are suggested. Finally, two case illustrations show the application of these strategies, first with an individual client-system and then a couple client-system.

Rational and Irrational Beliefs

Individuals and couples are belief-governed systems that behave in an organized, repetitive manner, and from the patterning of their behaviors can be abstracted the governing principles of their daily living (Jackson, 1977). These beliefs represent the norms that contribute to the direction of behavior within the system.

Most system beliefs are unwritten and operate covertly. Initially, they develop as simple *inferences* that all members of the system (or the individual, in a one-person system) make relative to the repetitive patterns of interaction they observe occurring around them. "Partner A does the grocery shopping; Partner B does the cooking." "I am a fine student." "I am a marginal student." I am an athlete." "I am not interested in athletics." "We visit our parents every other Sunday." A common couple-system belief, held at the inference level, unstated but understood by both, is "We make major decisions together."

Such system beliefs at the inference level are *nonevaluative*—that is, they are simple statements of fact or presumed fact. REFT emphasizes the importance of addressing system beliefs as *evaluations*, or the degree to which the member or members of the system evaluate something as desirable or undesirable (Wessler & Wessler, 1980). Consider, for example, a newly married couple who came from families that dealt with conflict quite differently:

> Open discussion of problems and accompanying feelings of anger or frustration were always encouraged in Sarah's family. She, her parents, and her siblings would often get into loud shouting matches. They were able, however, to adequately resolve their differences in this manner and, in the aftermath of such problem-solving sessions, often joked about their seemingly volatile interactions. Ken's family, by contrast, valued calm, deliberate problem solving. When expressions of anger or hurt feelings arose, family members would withdraw into themselves until they were able to come together again in a calmer manner and resolve their differences. Prior to marrying, Sarah and Ken experienced few significant difficulties. Several months into their marriage, however, Ken's withdrawal and Sarah's open expression of anger became a vicious cycle of increasingly greater with-

drawal and more intense angry feelings exhibited by each respectively.

Whenever difficulties arose, Sarah and Ken both maintained their own individual beliefs, which they had learned in their families of origin. At the inference level, their common system belief—which they unconsciously followed and applied to themselves—was "We handle difficulties the way they were handled in our parents' home." Unfortunately at the evaluation level, the rigidity (i.e., "We *must*...") with which they *demanded* adherence to their respective system beliefs contributed to increasing discord between them. The more Sarah expressed her anger, the more Ken withdrew; the more he withdrew, the more she expressed her anger.

REFT stresses the role played by *rational* and *irrational* system beliefs with respect to individuals' and couples' functioning. Rational system beliefs are those that have personal significance for the system member or members and that *evaluate* situations in an adaptive, helpful manner. Here *personal significance* refers to the importance of a belief to members of that individual or couple-system, (e.g., "Loyalty is an important value for us") not just some passing thought ("What a pretty day").

Rational system beliefs are also relative in nature. They contain no set right or wrong but consider every situation as unique and potentially calling for a different response. When individual and couple-systems are able to think about their circumstances in a relative manner, they are more likely to experience pleasure; sometimes they also experience displeasure, such as sadness, annoyance, and concern. Although these latter emotions are not necessarily pleasurable, they are considered appropriate responses to negative circumstances; they do not significantly interfere with the system's pursuit of desired goals or, if these goals are forever blocked, the selection and pursuit of new goals. "Helpful" feelings (relative to the circumstances encountered) accompany rational system beliefs, which are nonabsolute, adaptive statements of personal significance (Dryden, 1984).

Irrational system beliefs are those that have personal significance for the members of an individual or couple-system and are stated in an absolute, unhelpful manner. Feelings accompanying irrational beliefs include depression, anger, and guilt. These "hurtful" emotions go hand in hand with exaggerated *evaluations* of situations and thus are maladaptive even to very negative circumstances because they generally impede the pursuit of the goals that members of the system desire.

A client-system's beliefs and the degree of rationality or irrationality characterizing them are the primary focus of REFT. Until Sarah and Ken are able to move to a more relative and thus rational position with regard to their couple-system rigidly held belief, significant discord will very likely continue in their relationship. For example, from "We must handle difficulties the way they were handled in our parents' home," REFT might facilitate movement toward "We can try to [i.e., "We don't *have to*"] handle difficulties the way they are handled in our parents' home, but we can also look for our own [i.e., "new and/or different"] ways as well."

Rationality characterizes adaptive system beliefs and thus optimal individual and couples' functioning. The more an individual or couple-system interactions are characterized by rationality, the more readily that system is able to be open to and assimilate new information, so as to either maintain or change its beliefs as it evolves in its life-cycle development.

Problem Formation

All individuals and couples encounter expected as well as unexpected life difficulties. REFT views recurring difficulties as a consequence of individual and couple-systems' responding in absolutist and/or exaggerated (i.e., irrational) ways. When the same difficulties continuously recur within an individual or couple-system, a predominance of absolutist and/or exaggerated beliefs accompanies the ineffective solutions that the system employs to defuse the impact of the difficulties. Fisch, Weakland, and Segal (1982) offered insight into the logic of this common occurrence:

> But why would anyone persist in attempting solutions that do not work and, indeed, often make things progressively worse? . . . we explain the persistence of unproductive behavior on the basis of a few simple observations involving a minimum of inference and theoretical constructs: (1) From early in life, we all learn culturally standard solutions for culturally defined problems. These standard solutions often work, but sometimes they do not. Since they have been learned largely at an unconscious or implicit level, to question or alter such solutions is very difficult. (2) When people are in stressful situations, as they are when struggling with problems, their behavior usually becomes *more*

constricted and rigid. (3) Contrary to the widespread view that people are illogical, we propose that people are *too* logical; that is they act logically in terms of basic, unquestioned premises, and when undesired results occur, they employ further logical operations to explain away the discrepancy, rather than revising the premises. (p. 287)

REFT maintains a solution focus relative to the specifics of problem formation. Thus, when expected as well as unexpected life difficulties become problems (a *problem* being defined as "a recurring difficulty that has proved resistant to attempts to resolve it"), the difficulty is made worse by employing poor problem-solving strategies (i.e., unsuccessful solutions). The majority of these solutions are not necessarily unsuccessful in and of themselves but rather represent either an exaggeration or denial of the dynamics of the individual or couple's experience. *REFT posits the single overarching principle that problem formation is the predominance of unsuccessful solutions accompanied by absolutist and/or exaggerated beliefs.* Ellis (1993) referred to this notion as "the primacy of absolutist shoulds and musts" (p. 6). He stated further in this regard:

> RET assumes, in other words, that you are often a profound musturbator and that once you strongly construct absolutist *musts* and *must nots* you will very easily and often, when you, others, and the world contradict them, slide yourself into "logical" but misleading inferences that "confirm" and add to your disturbed reactions. . . . RET's cardinal rulewhen people are thinking, feeling, and acting neurotically is "Cherchez le should! Cherchez le must! Look for the should! Look for the must!" RET assumes that people with disturbance overtly and/or tacitly have one, two, or three underlying musts, that these can usually be quickly found, and then actively and forcefully disputed and changed back to preferences. (Ellis, 1993, p. 8)

The ABC, A'B'C', DE of REFT

REFT as a format for brief therapy with individuals and couples organizes its essential clinical strategies under the umbrella of the metastrategy: ABC, A'B'C' (read "A-prime, B-prime, C-prime"), DE. This ABC, A'B'C' DE metastrategy contributes to the creation of a context wherein each of the individual strategies will be optimally implemented. These individual strategies are detailed in the discussion that follows. Full and consistent awareness of the metastrategy is encouraged throughout, however, so as to promote the most effective and efficient use of these strategies for brief therapy assessment, intervention, and evaluation.

Assessment: ABC, A'B'C'

As an overarching principle for brief therapy, REFT maintains the importance of assessment throughout the course of therapy to maximize therapeutic efforts and minimize therapeutic duration. Assessment begins by determining an individual or couple client-system's ABC, A'B'C': the cognitive, emotive, and behavioral frames of reference that the system is experiencing relative to the concerns being presented for treatment. Assessing these frames of reference is an ongoing process, done continuously during the therapeutic process. Its purpose is to understand what is occurring within the system so as to make suitable interventions, both at the onset of treatment and subsequently.

Recall that REFT formulates *problems* as "unsucessful solutions accompanied by absolutist and/or exaggerated system beliefs." Accompanying these "problems" are typically distressing and unsatisfying emotions and behaviors. Individuals and couples who are involved in an unresolved conflict tend to become stereotyped in the repetitive mishandling of this conflict, with the result that they narrow observations of their circumstances to focus primarily on the conflict. Consequently, they dissociate their more competent ways of functioning from their conflict circumstances. When most individuals and couples present for therapy, they assert the more dysfunctional aspects of their interactions; these they perceive to be the areas most relevant to treatment. These dysfunctional aspects are first assessed according to an ABC assessment: A = activating event; B = client-system's belief; C = emotional and behavioral consequences.

The ABC assessment of dysfunctional interactions represents only one segment of a client-system's present functioning. No matter the intensity or duration of the difficulties that individuals and couples experience, there are always situations or times when, for some reason, they handle the difficulty well (O'Hanlon & Weiner-Davis, 1989). Anxious individuals sometimes feel comfortable trusting their personal resources to handle stressful circumstances; depressed individuals sometimes feel optimism about their future; combative couples sometimes spend an enjoyable evening together; and so on. Most individuals and couples, however, consider these less difficult or difficulty-free times to be unrelated to those times when the difficulty is fully felt in all its pain and discomfort, so they do little to better understand or amplify these better-functioning times.

Most therapists are trained to be enthusiastic psychopathologists. Were they to expand their focus of assessment, they would find that almost all individuals and couples already have the skills and resources to resolve their presenting complaints. As Ellis (1987) posited of all human beings:

> Their very nature is, first, to have probabilities and realistic expectations, and hopes of fulfilling their goals and wishes, and to feel appropriately sad, sorry, displeased, and frustrated when these are not met. But, being somewhat allergic to probability . . . when they have strong and paramount desires they very frequently, and often unconsciously or implicitly, escalate their longings into unconditional and rigid insistences and commands. (p. 373)

Concurrent with any difficult circumstances in the lives of individuals and couples, there are almost always *exception times,* which occur whenever a difficulty is being adequately dealt with. Successful solutions are a part of the repertoire of all individuals and couples—most just don't realize it. They say to themselves, "We must employ solution A or fail." For whatever reason, Solution A seems to them to be the right (logical, best, only) choice. As a result, they lump together and exclude other alternatives. But if individuals and couples experiencing conflict expanded their perspective, they would see that they already possess the skills and resources to resolve their problems (de Shazer et al., 1986). Assessing the dynamics of one or more exception times relating to the presenting concern constitutes the next step of the strategy. A'B'C' represents the activating event (A'), the client-system's belief (B'), and the emotional and behavioral consequences (C') of *competent* ways that the system has functioned but that for reasons unknown are disassociated from the conflict circumstances.

In assessing ABC, A'B'C', REFT recognizes that all individuals and couples will likely at some time have rational as well as irrational beliefs about their circumstances. Assessing ABC and then A'B'C' assists individuals and couples in identifying their rational beliefs (as well as their irrational beliefs) and places them in a position to be able to put the former to greater use. Particularly as a brief therapy strategy, this approach significantly diminishes any need to "reinvent the wheel." Therapists, instead, can put readily available "spare tires" to much greater use.

The steps of the ABC, A'B'C' assessment are thus:

1. *A*: the nature of the individual or couple's complaint (unsuccessful solutions, reframed as desired goals) and how the complaint is generally being unsuccessfully addressed,
2. *B*: the client-system's belief accompanying the unsuccessful solution and the degree of rationality-irrationality characterizing that belief,
3. *C*: the emotional and behavioral consequences accompanying A and B,
4. *A'*: a detailed description of a successful solution that was employed by the individual or couple during a time they were functioning in a more competent manner in similar circumstances (the exception time),
5. *B'*: the typically more rational client-system's belief that accompanied the successful solution of the exception time,
6. *C'*: the emotional and behavioral consequences accompanying A' and B' as the individual or couple functioned more competently during the exception time.

The ABC assessment illustrates the individual or couple's dominant dilemma, while the A'B'C' assessment exemplifies the "spare tire" relative to the individual or couple's overall functioning. This information becomes the focus for therapeutic intervention during the debate (D) and enactment (E) portions of the ABC, A'B'C', DE metastrategy.

Intervention: DE

Following assessment, the therapeutic intervention centers on two essential clinical strategies: debate (D) and enactment (E). Debate (D) asks the individual or couple to compare and contrast the benefits and/or detriments of their system belief (B) that frames their unsuccessful solutions (A) and the accompanying distressful emotional and behavioral consequences (C), with their system belief (B') that frames the more successful solutions (A') of the exception times and the accompanying satisfying emotional and behavioral consequences (C'). Following debate, intervention is then aimed at enactment (E)—rehearsing, reviewing, and confirming the value of the rational B' in those circumstances wherein the irrational B had typically been the norm. This is all done in a manner that encourages an overall philosophy of greater rationality.

Webster's New Collegiate Dictionary defines *debate* as "a process wherein a question is discussed by considering opposing arguments." In REFT, debate (D) challenges the individual or couple to consider the opposing positions represented by their ABC (the unsuccessful solutions, the irrational system belief that frames them, and the distressful feelings and behaviors they experience); and their A'B'C' (more successful solutions, the rational system belief that frames them, and the more satisfying feelings and behaviors). While the ABC and A'B'C' are all considered, the primary emphasis during debate is on B and B'. Debate is accomplished by engaging the individual or couple in three important tasks (Huber & Baruth, 1989).

The first task is to facilitate considerable *cognitive dissonance* for an individual or couple by comparing their irrational system belief with its rational counterpart and then compiling evidence that disconfirms the benefits of the irrational belief. The second task is to have the individual or couple explore the *rational counterpart* of the irrational belief in a way that affirms the greater benefits of the rational belief. The third task is to review and confirm how the irrational belief contributes to *distressful emotional and behavioral consequences* while the rational belief offers enhanced opportunity for greater emotional and behavioral satisfaction (or less dissatisfaction).

Following successful debate, the individual or couple is then engaged in enactment (E). This involves rehearsing, reviewing, and confirming the step-by-step manner in which their rational B' will characterize upcoming circumstances in which their irrational B would have typically been the norm. Initially, the therapist accomplishes enactment by in-session interactions with an individual client "thinking aloud" or by monitoring such interactions between the two partners of a couple. Thereafter the therapist encourages the individual or couple to agree upon outside-of-session homework tasks.

As therapy progresses and the individual or couple clients report their circumstances as improved, the therapist reinforces the idea that they are able to get the rational B' of their "exception time" to recur through their own volition (e.g., "What exactly were you thinking in that more successful and satisfying situation that you were not thinking when you were less satisfied?" "What are you going to think to employ successful solutions more regularly?"). Further, as a part of that process, the therapist helps them tie more satisfying (or less dissatisfying) emotional and behavioral consequences to their efforts to enact their rational B' in more circumstances.

With those individual or couple clients who report their circumstances as unchanged, the therapist still seeks to expand upon and enact employing the rational B' of identified exception times (e.g., "It is my experience that if people don't think rationally, their situation gets worse, not just stays the same. What were you all thinking to keep things from getting worse?"). The emphasis then again moves to the rational B' of the exception times. If the client reports that circumstances are becoming worse, the therapist's emphasis would again be "What have you been thinking to prevent things from becoming *even more* troublesome than they are?" Again, the focus would be on enactment employing the rational B' of these exception times.

The therapist pursues the D and E to the degree that ongoing therapeutic progress is evident. At times, clients may seem "stuck," and minimal or no meaningful progress may be apparent. In such circumstances, the therapist should be willing to engage clients in reassessing their original goals as well as the significance of the ABC and A'B'C' earlier identified. New goals and/or a more personally significant ABC or A'B'C' will typically emerge, allowing successful debate and enactment to take place.

Evaluation

Individuals and couples can live normal, satisfying lives in many possible ways, not just in one static standard way from which any deviation is considered maladaptive or abnormal. Accordingly, individuals' and couples' presenting complaints—their statements of persistent difficulties that hinder their pursuit of life as they wish (reframed as goals)—are the primary foci for evaluating the efficacy of the ABC, A'B'C', DE metastrategy and of the essential clinical strategies that it connects with therapeutic progress.

Given this caveat, the most important indicator of success is an individual or couple's statement of contentment with the therapeutic gains; that is, the agreed-upon goal has been sufficiently achieved and the complaint resolved. The individual or couple that enters therapy as complainants preferably should leave as noncomplainants. Several criteria are used to qualify and quantify clients' reports.

First, as a component of assessment during the course of therapy, the therapist should regularly ask himself or herself, "To what degree and with what frequency is the individual or couple: (a) utilizing the rational B' emanating from the identified exception times; and (b) moving toward an overall position of greater rationality?" Second, as the individual or couple begins to report movement from a complainant to a noncomplainant position, the therapist should inquire, "What has happened to account for the perceived changes?" Again, the main evaluative criteria are reports that indicate a shift to utilizing the rational B' more frequently, as well as an overall position of increased rationality. While rational system beliefs are the obvious emphasis, the individual or couple must be actively behaving and feeling in a manner that they characterize as more consistently satisfying than before.

Clinical Indications

Rational-emotive family therapy was essentially conceived as a "clinical perspective" rather than as an academic or research perspective. As such, REFT represents an evolving set of practical, clinical procedures (Huber & Baruth, 1989). The metastrategy ABC, A'B'C', DE provides a therapeutic context in which REFT's essential clinical strategies can be optimally implemented. Hence this metastrategy—and the essential clinical strategies for which it provides a context—is indicated in addressing virtually any condition that becomes a focus of psychotherapeutic intervention. The ABC, A'B'C', DE metastrategy is most simply a means of making the often very complex interactions of individual and couple-systems more concrete and thus more amenable to therapeutic intervention. From a brief therapy perspective, the opportunity to simplify the process by reducing the number of variables (i.e., beliefs) under consideration is clear (Huber & Backlund, 1991): greater efficiency and effectiveness in the immediacy of the treatment milieu.

Given this wide-range applicability, in some circumstances different foci of attention within the ABC, A'B'C', DE metastrategy (and thus within its essential clinical strategies as well) may predominate, as may the particular manner in which a particular strategy is employed. For example, for clients who have certain presenting conditions (e.g., they are developmentally disabled, psychotic, or paranoid), verbal intervention efforts alone may be insufficient to convey an understanding of the irrationality of their beliefs, despite the therapist's competent efforts to demonstrate the greater benefits of more rational beliefs. In such cases, the inclusion of significant persons in therapeutic efforts would be indicated. The ABC, A'B'C', DE metastrategy would still provide the structure for the therapeutic efforts, however, the client's environmental context would be changed by emphasizing A and A' more than B and B' during ABC, A'B'C' assessment and DE intervention. These cases are rather extreme, however, and very few potential clients for brief therapy are likely to present with such dysfunction that ABC, A'B'C', DE is contraindicated.

As described in the two case examples that follow, a thorough initial clinical interview and formal standardized assessment are recommended. Certain diagnostic findings will be more amenable to brief therapy than others as would be the case with any clinical strategy. For example, Axis I diagnoses that suggest a situational or primarily environmental etiology, relatively higher Axis V GAFs (highest level past year), and assessment profile results finding rigidity and exaggeration in systems' interactions are indicated criteria.

Case Example with an Individual

Background

The client, Kevin, is a recently divorced 35-year-old graduate student who has sole custody of his two daughters, ages 6 and 8. He sought help in order to better deal with the anger he felt toward his former wife and with the frustration he felt in addressing the daily needs of two daughters. His primary presenting concern was his relationship with his daughters: He was feeling overwhelmed by the responsibility of raising them on his own. Exacerbating this feeling was his employer's increasing impatience with his late arrivals at work in the morning.

The therapist conducted an initial clinical interview to gather background information, as well as a formal standardized assessment to gain a direction for the therapy. Instruments utilized included: the Millon

Clinical Multiaxial Inventory, the Irrational Beliefs Test, and the Fisher Divorce Adjustment Scale. The clinical interview and standardized assessments resulted in the following diagnostic profiles:

DSM-IV:

Axis I: 309.24 Adjustment Disorder w/anxiety
Axis II: V71.09 No diagnosis
Axis III: None
Axis IV: Family Disruption
Axis V: GAF = 64 (current)

GAF = 79 (highest past year)

These diagnostic findings supported a shorter-term, brief therapy for Kevin as well as the clinical applicability of ABC, A'B'C', DE. No major personality disturbance was evident. The Axis I diagnosis posited the benefits of a new level of adaptation following a significant stressor. Assessment on Axis V suggested a favorable prognosis given the attainment of that new level of adaptation. Further, Kevin's Irrational Beliefs Test profile, relative to specific scales denoting absolutistic, demanding beliefs, indicated that rigid interactional patterns were a significant contributor to the current distress. The Fisher Divorce Adjustment Scale profile, while identifying continuing grief and feelings of anger, also reported Kevin as having a relatively higher level of adjustment in the area of "rebuilding social relationships," suggesting that some progress relative to his presenting complaints had already occurred prior to the therapeutic intervention.

Session Transcript with Commentary

The transcript with commentary that follows includes excerpts from the third session with this client and explanatory comments highlighting the manner in which ABC, A'B'C', DE was employed. In the preceding session, Kevin's expectations for therapy had been addressed. After reconsidering the presenting complaints, the therapist tied them to potential therapeutic goals, prioritizing one goal that Kevin would see as having the greatest impact on his current circumstances and identifying criteria that would offer evidence of progress toward the attainment of that goal.

The session begins with a summary of the previous session's efforts.

Therapist: Kevin, last time we got together, you offered me an overview of what was going on, and we agreed on what you'd like to gain from therapy. You mentioned that you recently got divorced and that your two girls were living with you. You noted difficulties with that, and today we were going to see together how you might resolve some of your concerns about taking care of the girls and developing a better relationship with them, particularly around your morning schedule. So maybe if you could just summarize a little bit for me where you are with that today.

Kevin: It's pretty much the same as I told you last time. Mornings are really terrible. There are just too many things to do, and the girls aren't cooperative. They end up fighting, and I end up yelling and screaming about things like getting their teeth brushed and getting dressed. Getting myself ready to go to work then becomes a major thing. When this happens, I get frustrated, and I just get so mad at my ex-wife. . . . How could she possibly do this to me, leaving me in this situation while she's off having a good time.

Therapist: It's like "I'm stuck with everything!"

Kevin: That's right. I feel like I am really stuck, and I'm resentful, and I'm having a hard time coping with getting things done on schedule. It seems like every morning when they get up, all the girls do is fool around. It's gotten to where I am late to work half the time, and I'm worried my boss is only going to put up with so much.

As Kevin recaps his feelings of anger and frustration, the therapist is carefully considering how Kevin is thinking about his circumstances rationally and irrationally. In the following interaction, the therapist asks about the children, as a means of focusing the session in order to address specific ABC and A'B'C' interactions. He affirms Kevin's feelings about his former wife and concerns regarding his employer but seeks to maintain him on the agreed-to primary goal: improving the relationship between himself and his two daughters.

Therapist: You mentioned that you feel upset toward your former wife and concerns about your job, and those are things we might want to look at at some point. But right now it might be best to consider just how things are going with the girls, because you mentioned last session that that was your primary goal. That's something you want to see improve.

Kevin: Well, that's causing the most problems right now for me.

The therapist then asks for a description of a specific complaint time in order to identify an ABC interaction where the client-system (Kevin and his two daughters) was unsuccessful in attaining the agreed-upon therapeutic goal. The more concrete the client's blow-by-blow illustration, the easier it will be to clearly delineate the A, the B, and the C.

Therapist: You mentioned that the mornings seem to be a difficult time for you and your daughters, where your relationship sounds to be quite stressed. Could you describe for me what happened during a specific morning recently, one that was really hassled?

Kevin: Yesterday had to be one of the worst days.

Therapist: Could you give me a blow-by-blow description of yesterday morning?

Kevin: The alarm goes off at ten to six, and I make coffee and start having a cup. I decide to get the kids up five minutes earlier to see if we can't eliminate some of the time problems. They don't want to get out of bed. They whine, "Oh, we don't want to go to school today." They want to play around, and so I finally drag them out of bed and into the bathroom to shower, and then they don't want to take a shower. I finally get them both in the shower together.

Therapist: You're pushing them all the time.

Kevin: I'm pushing, I'm just chomping right at their backs, and then they're playing, goofing around, squirming. And my older girl dumps the shampoo, the whole thing, right on the younger one's head and wastes it all. It's a big mess, and she starts crying because the soap is in her eyes, and so they're fighting in the shower, and I go in there and yell at them, "You guys get washed off and get out right now and get dressed!" Sometimes—usually if I get mad enough to yell at them, "This is it,

I've had it!"—they will, but yesterday not only did they not, but they kind of laughed, and I really got mad at that. I understand that they're just young kids, but it makes me mad, frustrated. Then I realized that it was already seven and they weren't dressed and hadn't eaten their breakfast yet, and the bus was leaving in 30 minutes. In the meantime I wasted a lot of time with them, and I still had to finish getting ready for work in order to be there on time.

Therapist: And you mentioned that you were very frustrated about that.

Kevin: Oh, definitely! I don't understand why it has to be such a hassle. I mean, I think it's a reasonable schedule, and why can't they just do it? I don't know.

Therapist: It was probably a lot easier when your former wife was there because you had someone to share it with.

Kevin: Oh, yes.

Therapist: And so it is going to be a lot harder now for you, but it sounds like you're thinking, "It's got to be easier than this!"

Kevin: Yes, I do. I remember when I was married, it wasn't like this. It seems to me that the girls just get more obstinate and stubborn, and I almost start thinking, "They're just doing it to me."

Therapist: So it's almost like it's personal now.

Kevin: Yes. It seems like lately every morning gets worse. The fights get more intense. They start off where they left off, and it's getting to the point where it's just intolerable. I mean, I'm really upset about it.

The A, the B, and the C have been identified:

A = Kevin's determination to "push" the children into cooperation (and the children's apparently expecting and/or waiting to be pushed).

B = Kevin's (and also, although seemingly unspoken, the children's, relative to their position) angry, irrational demands and insistence.

C = Kevin and the children's tension and anxiety and increased pushing and pushing back.

Given the primary importance of the B in the ABC sequence, the therapist follows up briefly to confirm this element.

Therapist: It sounds like both you and the girls were almost demanding, "It's got to be easier! This is too much!"

Kevin: For sure. I was tired, my stomach was just twisting, it was hurting, and I was just going, "I can't believe this. This is unreasonable. This is terrible!"

In this excerpt, while the specific words vary, Kevin has reiterated his absolutistic thinking. The client-system's irrational B seems clearly to be an absolutistic demand. The therapist then shifts the focus from identifying the ABC interaction of the complaint time to identifying an exception time illustrating a specific A'B'C' interaction, in which under similar circumstances Kevin and the girls experienced more successful (or less unsuccessful) solution, as well as a more rational belief and pleasant (or less unpleasant) consequences .

Therapist: Can you think of a day recently, maybe a morning this week, when you and the girls got along better, or at least not as badly as you described yesterday? Maybe it was a better morning, or maybe a not-so-bad morning? You said that this morning wasn't as bad as yesterday.

The therapist here seeks to elicit a specific exception time during which Kevin saw the therapeutic goal attained to some satisfactory degree: when the client-system did not experience the complaint or the complaint was less intense or "not so bad." Again, the therapist makes the inquiry, not just for the sake of seeking an exception per se, but for the express purpose of delineating the A'B'C'.

Kevin: The girls were invited to a birthday party on a Friday after school; and they were excited and had been planning it for a couple of weeks. I told them that unless they cooperated, they weren't going to go to the birthday party, and I really meant it. They laid out the clothes and got all ready to go to school the night before. The next morning things went so smooth. In fact, we had 25 minutes extra, we were ready to go 25 minutes early. At five minutes after seven, I looked at the clock, and they were ready to go to school, and they were happy and I felt good. I even felt like coloring a picture with them before they went to school, and we sat down and did that and watched some TV for a few minutes and kind of did some parent-child stuff, and it felt good. It was just really different.

Therapist: So it sounds like it was a lot more comfortable for you and for the girls in how you were feeling and what you were doing.

Kevin: Yes.

Therapist: You mentioned a couple of things about that Friday morning, but it seems to carry back to Thursday night. You mentioned that you and the girls had set their clothes out and got all ready to go to school on Thursday night. You also mentioned that you identified some consequences for them, and they apparently accepted the potential of your implementing them.

Kevin: Sure. I told them what would happen of they didn't cooperate and what would happen if they did. They were happy and excited, and I think they were just in a more cooperative kind of mood. We didn't have any kind of tension Thursday night.

Clearly, Kevin sees the exception time as different only because of the excitement generated by the birthday party. His perception of it as an isolated incident has thus far prevented him from appreciating the significance of his and the girls' more successful solution (the A'), their thinking in a more rational manner (the B'), and the positive feelings and behaviors (the C') that accompanied the A' and B'. Therefore, he attributes the positive outcome only to the change in the children's mood. The function of the therapist is to emphasize the change in Kevin's and the children's mutual way of thinking and choice of solutions, and connect this to the more positive outcome. The therapist does this without discounting Kevin's position but rather seeks to *add* to the manner in which Kevin perceives the exception time.

Therapist: It sounds like the girls were more cooperative because of the party, Kevin. But it also sounds like when you compare that Friday with yesterday morning, or maybe the night before yesterday morning, you and your daughters did some things differently than you typically do, and you were thinking differently than you probably typically think. That Thursday night you set some guidelines down. The girls seriously accepted those guidelines. Then you all did things to prepare

for Friday morning. It sounds like you all were thinking,
"Tomorrow morning will be a lot easier if we prepare for it
tonight."

Kevin: At the time, I didn't exactly say that, but yeah, that's what I
was probably thinking. In fact, we sat down and had a family
talk in which I communicated pretty much what you just said.

Therapist: What did you talk about?

Kevin: I told them it was important to me for them to get dressed and
be responsible in the morning, and it was really hard for me
when they weren't. I asked for their cooperation and suggested that we begin right then. We put their clothes out and
did some other things to be ready to go as soon as they woke
up. It was a good time between us. We also spent some time
and read a storybook, since they were being so cooperative
and were ready for bed early.

Therapist: So you all were probably thinking something like, "Mornings
can be hectic, but tomorrow will be easier if we prepare
tonight." You weren't demanding that the next morning be
easy.

The A'B'C' of Kevin's report of a more successful time in realizing the
therapeutic goal has been identified:

A = preparing for the next morning the night before
B = "I/we *want* (not demand or absolutistically expect) that the mornings go more smoothly."
C = greater satisfaction and more pleasant interactions between Kevin
and his daughters

The therapist now initiates debate (D) by challenging Kevin to consider the positions he has presented for the ABC and A'B'C' interactions.
The therapist first facilitates doubt about the benefits of the B (i.e., the
absolutistic demand) that accompanies the unsuccessful solution (the A)
and the conflictual emotional and behavioral consequences (the C). Simply introducing an alternative perspective has already raised such doubt,
namely, that there was a time recently when they *wanted* but did not necessarily *demand* that the morning would proceed smoothly and acted

accordingly to attain what they wanted; they were not tension-filled and acting hostilely toward each other, as they likely would have been were they demanding of each other and their circumstances. Debate continues through a more specific comparison of the benefits of the more rational B' that accompanied the exception time's A' and C' with the more irrational B accompanying the complaint time's A and C. The objective is to affirm the greater benefits of the more rational B'.

Therapist: I'm wondering. You mentioned that yesterday morning was a real bad morning. Did you prepare for yesterday morning the night before, as you did for that Friday morning two weeks ago?

Kevin: It was a lot different. We ate dinner late, and the kids wanted to watch some TV, and so we did that. I got a long-distance call and was on the phone for well over an hour with my sister. By the time I got off the phone, it was real late, and they had begun to watch another TV show, which still had a half-hour remaining. I said, "Hey, it's late and you've got to get to bed." They were angry about that and pretty uncooperative. I had to push them to straighten their room, and finally they did it. Then they didn't want to go to sleep and kept getting out of bed and having all these excuses, and I was just so glad to finally have them fall asleep. I was unbelievably frustrated with them.

Therapist: It sounds like you went to bed frustrated and you woke up just as frustrated.

Kevin: If not worse.

Therapist: Let's go back to that Thursday evening before what I'll call the successful Friday morning. It sounds like you were thinking on that Thursday evening, "I want the morning to go easier, and so we need to get prepared for it tonight." You think that's possible?

Kevin: Yes, I think so.

Therapist: It sounds like the night you were rushed, you were thinking, "Well, the morning's got to go easier, because tonight is hard." And it was like, "This is going to *have* to be this way!" There wasn't any preparation, just an expectation, a demand even, for something that used to occur when there were two adults to handle morning responsibilities, not just one.

Kevin: Yes, and that's the way it usually is.

Therapist: You mentioned that you and your daughters usually have difficulties, but you just described a situation where it wasn't so bad. In fact, it was quite good, and you noted feeling very good about it. It went pretty smoothly when *you and the girls* thought something different and did something different, and those different things occurred the night before. But they had a very important impact on the next morning.

Kevin: Yes, I can sure see that. I think probably by the time I picked the kids up from school at two-thirty, we were already preparing for the next day. It was an up kind of experience.

Therapist: It's great that you and the girls want the mornings to go more smoothly, but the fact of the matter is that typically they will be full of hassles, and just demanding that they not be hasn't been working very well.

Kevin: Yes. That sure is the case.

Therapist: Again, though, what happened when your mutual thought was "We want the morning to go easier," and you and the girls spent some time the previous evening preparing for it?

Kevin: I think it will take a little more planning on my part, barring any unforeseen long-distance calls or the like, but yeah, you're right.

Therapist: Sure, those things are going to arise. But even if they do, if you and the girls are thinking that you want the next morning to be better instead of demanding that it automatically be so, you might prepare a bit less, but you could probably still spend a little preparation time with the girls, not just for the sake of spending preparation, but because that significantly contributed to a time you were successful in having the girls respond well to you and they were successful in doing that.

Kevin: Yes. Sort of like expecting the morning to be hard and getting ready for it, instead of just demanding that the morning take care of itself.

Therapist: If you had a choice, would you rather put in a little more effort in the evening and have a more comfortable morning, or have somewhat of an easier evening and then have things go crazy in the morning?

Kevin: Well, definitely I would like to have an easier morning, because it really ruins my day when it starts off so badly.

Following this successful debate, the therapist then moves to enactment (E) to rehearse, review, and confirm the step-by-step manner in which Kevin might apply the more rational B' more frequently. During this final portion of the session, the therapist helps Kevin imagine how he and his daughters might employ this session's understandings in the coming week in a specific situation. This discussion provides further opportunity to confirm Kevin's willingness and ability to employ the greater rationality inherent in B' that he has acknowledged to be more beneficial.

Therapist: Let's anticipate a scenario that will arise during the coming week where you and the girls can experiment with what we talked about today. In the time we have remaining, we can rehearse how to best implement in that upcoming situation.

This has been a fairly typical session where ABC, A'B'C', DE is employed. Kevin has begun to identify the benefits—for himself and his daughters—of changing their way of thinking about their circumstances. The therapist helped him recognize the A'B'C' elements of an exception time and then compared these (during D) with the ABC circumstances of a complaint time. He was then able to consider and then rehearse (during E) a different solution and belief and to reexperience those more positive emotional and behavioral consequences, all of which will increase the probability of future success in his and his daughters' morning routine. Success is defined as movement toward the agreed-upon therapeutic goal: in this case, more cooperative mornings when Kevin and his daughters more cooperatively and pleasantly adhere to their schedule. On such mornings, they all have more positive interactions and therefore a better relationship.

Kevin participated in four more sessions, for a total of seven. His family's morning routine improved almost immediately following this third session, and his lateness to work in the morning was likewise alleviated.

The final sessions addressed his feelings toward his former wife. The ABC, A'B'C', DE metastrategy was again employed, but the client-system under consideration then was Kevin and his former wife. While she was never physically present in the sessions, the irrational and rational beliefs of that client-system were likewise explored and employed to progress toward a second therapeutic goal. (The following case example refers to a different couple.)

ABC, A'B'C', DE:
Case Example with a Couple

Background

The couple, Cindy and James, have been together approximately three years. Cindy is employed as a medical office manager and James is a high school teacher and coach. During the past several months, the couple reported increasing tension and episodes of overt verbal conflict, primarily in regard to the amount of time James spends with his coaching responsibilities. Cindy describes James as a devoted coach and teacher, but when they first met he coached only football. This school year he has agreed to expand his coaching to basketball and baseball as well. James confirms that his coaching time has increased, particularly involving long hours of after-school and weekend practices and significant travel to games. He explains his acceptance of the increased coaching responsibilities as an opportunity to earn extra income to save for the down payment on the home he and Cindy plan to purchase.

James complains of Cindy's constant criticism of his increased coaching, a point he finds particularly irritating, given that its purpose is to finance the home they both desire. Cindy has made many requests of James to spend more time with her, and his numerous promises to do so have been broken, she reports. On several specific and hurtful occasions, she recalls, James was "too busy with his teams" to respond adequately to her requests for his help in handling difficulties she was experiencing at work and with her parents.

The therapist initially undertook a clinical interview to gather background information and conducted a formal standardized assessment to help provide direction to the therapy. The instruments utilized included the Millon Clinical Multiaxial Inventory, the Irrational Beliefs Test, and the Family Environment Scale. The results of the clinical interview and standardized assessment indicated the following diagnostic profiles:

DSM-IV:

JAMES:

Axis I:	309.28 Adjustment Disorder w/Mixed Anxiety and Depressed Mood
Axis II:	V71.09 No diagnosis
Axis III:	None
Axis IV:	Relationship Disturbance
Axis V:	GAF = 61 (current)

GAF = 80 (highest past year)

CINDY:

Axis I:	309.28 Adjustment Disorder w/Mixed Anxiety and Depressed Mood
Axis II:	V71.09 No diagnosis
Axis III:	None
Axis IV:	Relationship Disturbance
Axis V:	GAF = 61 (current)

GAF = 80 (highest past year)

These diagnostic findings supported a brief therapy with this couple as well as the clinical applicability of ABC, A'B'C', DE. No major personality disturbance was evident in either partner. Their Axis I diagnoses posited the sufficient benefits that a new level of adaptation would provide, given that the stressor might persist. Assessment on Axis V suggested a favorable prognosis, given the attainment of that new level of adaptation. Further, both partners' Irrational Beliefs Test results suggested that rigid interactional patterns were a significant contributor to their current distress. Their Family Environment Scale results, particularly their high valuing of family cohesion, likewise suggested rigidity and less openness to alternative experiencing as contributing factors.

Session Transcript with Commentary

The transcript with commentary that follows includes excerpts from the fourth session with this couple and explanatory comments highlighting the manner in which the therapist employed ABC, A'B'C', DE. In the second session, the therapist interpreted the couple profile emanating from the clinical interview and the formal assessment data with regard to the couple's expectations for therapy . After considering their presenting complaints, the therapist helped the couple reframe these complaints to potential therapeutic goals, prioritizing one goal (i.e., "sharing more pleasant couple time together more often") that would, in their view, have the greatest impact on their current circumstances and identifying criteria that would offer evidence of progress toward attainment of this goal. In the third session, the therapist employed ABC, A'B'C', DE to direct efforts in this regard. This fourth session began with a review of the what had occurred since the previous session, emphasizing the couple's use of the B' they had identified. But because of a new situation, the previous session's efforts were apparently given minimal, if any, attention. The session excerpts that follow begin approximately 12 minutes into the session.

> Cindy: James, what about the other night when you were watching TV and I began telling you about my crazy day at work, and you just ignored me and kept watching TV?
>
> James: You know I had to travel to Albuquerque with the team the following day. I didn't just ignore you. I was real tired, just trying to relax, and I asked you if we could let it go until I returned home and we'd have all day Sunday to talk.
>
> Cindy: And come Sunday, you spent the day in front of the TV watching football. Not once did you turn that damned thing off, not even when I reminded you of the promise you made on Friday.
>
> Therapist: James, what was going through your mind at that time?
>
> James: Well, at first I was just thinking how tired I was and how I just wanted to relax and enjoy the game. To be honest, I had forgotten all about what I had said Friday night. When Cindy

reminded me and started to get angry, I guess I got kind of mad that she wouldn't just let me have some time to take it easy. When she pushed it further, I got madder and thought, "That's enough. I'm not going to put up with that!"

Therapist: Cindy, you mentioned a few of your thoughts in that situation already. Was there anything else you were thinking at that time?

Cindy: I just wanted James to listen to me. The whole thing got blown completely out of proportion. All he had to do is spend a little bit of time with me.

Therapist: James, in that situation, what I hear you strongly asserting to yourself as well as to Cindy was "I'm tired, and I must have some time to relax!"

James: I think so. It felt that way; I didn't get home until after 2 A.M, and I was just tired.

Therapist: Cindy, it sounds like your belief there was sort of the same as James's: "He promised, and therefore I must be listened to!"

Cindy: Close enough.

Therapist: That was a time that you both tried something, and it really didn't work for either of you. As I understand it, both of you were really upset, and in fact, the way you both have recounted those circumstances here, it sounds as though you're both still upset when you recall what happened.

James: Definitely.

Cindy: I don't know about being upset, but that's the kind of stuff that pushes my buttons.

Therapist: So it's a very unpleasant remembrance for you.

Cindy: Yeah, it is that.

The partners spontaneously recount a specific situation that illustrates their most recent conflictual interaction. In observing and responding to their mutual interaction, the therapist promotes assessment of the activating events of the unsuccessful solution (A) and explores the couple's emotional and behavioral experiences during this unsuccessful solution, confirming their negative consequences (C). Foremost, the therapist seeks to assess the couple-system's irrational belief (B) that frames the A and C. After identifying the ABC of James and Cindy's unsuccessful solution, the therapist refers back to the A'B'C' interaction that the couple had described in the previous session, when their noted goal was seemingly realized, at least to some minimal degree. The spontaneously recounted complaint time paralleled the complaint time offered in the previous session and thus also paralleled the exception time that had been described as well. Had this not been the case, the therapist would have pursued a different exception time that did parallel the just-described complaint time.

Therapist: That was a time that wasn't real successful for you. I'd like to ask you to return to the time we discussed last session. James, then you saw yourself as being able to postpone responding to a request by Cindy, and Cindy, you saw James as able to follow through in an appropriate manner. Could I ask you to talk to each other again about that Saturday three weeks ago? I think, James, you had to spend all Saturday morning at practice and then repair equipment. You had promised to take Cindy out to lunch when you got home.

James: I remember.

Cindy: I think it was easier for me that time, because you came home and right away suggested we go out for dinner instead of lunch. I was pleasantly surprised because I thought you'd be too tired to do much of anything and would just forget what you'd promised.

James: Thinking back, I remember wanting to ask you to dinner because I thought it would be a lot nicer than just a lunch, and I knew we hadn't spent much time together at all during the week. We had such a nice evening.

Cindy: It just seems like those times that don't happen very often. It was sweet of you to consider my feelings without my having to ask you to.

Therapist: Cindy, you still seem to feel very good about that situation. James spontaneously asked you to dinner, but as I recall, you did something too that helped make it happen.

Cindy: James's response to me there was a fair one. I was thinking that the situation was a fair one. If I didn't think the situation was fair, then I would have had a problem with it, like I did this week.

Therapist: Remember you were thinking, "I want James to follow through on his promise, but it doesn't have to be exactly what was originally promised or right now."

Cindy: Yes. The fact that he remembered and just asked for a postponement rather than ignoring the promise altogether was important to me.

Therapist: You judged the situation and felt it to be a fair one, and that was your input. James, do you recall your thinking there?

James: Yeah. I was thinking that I did want some relaxation time, but also I wanted to give Cindy some time too.

Therapist: So, "I want some downtime, but time with Cindy is important too."

James: Sounds right.

Therapist: That's beautiful the way that worked out. Recall how we talked about you two moving from "have to" to "want to," and how the latter contributed to your feeling a bit more relaxed and open to compromise? It sounds like you both still feel very good about that time. You even moved closer to each other here in the session as you were describing it again.

Cindy: Yeah. It wasn't him in one corner and me in the other. We were like teammates.

James: Yeah. A real neat way to describe it to me, the coach.

Therapist: Both of you seem much more relaxed and peaceful now than when we started the session.

James: I'm a lot more relaxed.

Cindy: Me too.

After this reidentification of the A'B'C' of the exception time of the previous session, the therapist initiates debate (D) by challenging the couple to consider the positions they had presented in describing their ABC and A'B'C'. The therapist aims at facilitating doubt about the helpfulness of B, the irrational belief that frames their unsuccessful solution time and conflictual consequences. Debate continues with another comparison of the benefits of the more rational B' that frames their exception time A' and C'. The objective is to affirm the greater benefits of the more rational B'.

Therapist: You just described a situation where you both were thinking the same unspoken thought: "I *want* to have, but I don't *have* to have . . ." You were both successful and the tension dissipated or never even arose. But in the more problematic situation that you experienced this past week, you were both thinking another unspoken thought: "I *must* have . . ." Then there were a lot of tension and tense negative actions. Consequently, what I would ask you is, if you had a choice, and relating back to your goal for therapy, which is a more beneficial, helpful belief for you two?

James: Well, I'll tell you, every time we get into the "must have" thing, it causes problems.

Cindy: Yeah. As long as both our needs are met to some degree, we both win, like a win-win a bit less, rather than one of us wins and one of us loses.

Therapist: Again, as you both talk about this "win-win a bit less," you both seem visibly more comfortable and loving toward each other.

Following successful debate, the therapist moves to enactment (E) to rehearse, review, and confirm the step-by-step manner in which James and Cindy might apply their rational belief more frequently. They interact in the session so as to employ the session understandings as they might do in the coming week. Given the less-than-successful effort of the past week, the therapist structures the enactment around the complaint time of the previous week. Thus, this enactment offers further opportunity to confirm the couple's willingness and ability to employ the more rational couple belief whose benfits they have just confirmed.

Therapist: Could we reconsider the circumstances of the situation you both described when you first came in today? It was particularly tension-filled situation that's likely to recur. James, you wanted some downtime and promised Cindy some time too. And Cindy, you wanted some time with James.

Cindy: Well, he typically wants to do nothing but lie around all day Sunday, but I need some time from him. James's relaxing some is okay, but if he asked to do something together with me without my having to ask for it, it would be a big plus.

James: The thing with Sunday is that I am really tired and have to have at least one day of downtime.

Therapist: Listen to what you just said now. "I *must* have . . ."

James: Yeah, that is a real strong belief for me, I guess.

Therapist: Let me back you up. How about dinnertime? Could I ask the two of you to put the belief "I *want to* but I don't *have* to." firmly in your mind? James, you could say; "I want to have downtime, but I don't have to," and you might even add to that "total downtime" or "a full day's downtime." Cindy, you could say, "I want to have time together, but I don't have to," and you might similarly add to that "a total day" or "immediately." Would you talk about dinner on Sunday, with the "want to" instead of the "have to" thoughts firmly in mind?

Cindy: I think as long as we get together for at least dinner on the Sunday following a Saturday trip, I would be okay with that.

Therapist: You're right on target. I'm hearing "I want to, and I'm willing to compromise to get what I want." Perfect!

James: I know I have not been sensitive to your feelings, but I think I can be more so. I guess I've been doing way too much "have to" thinking about both my teams and your needs and feeling I had to make a choice of one or the other, and it was frustrating no matter which choice I made. Your saying dinner is okay on Sunday following a Saturday trip . . . I'd be able to have some downtime and yet still give you the attention I really want to . . . what you said earlier about "win-win a bit less."

Therapist: Sounds like you are both willing to compromise a bit more to get what you want. Is what you're saying?

Cindy: Yeah. I still want promises to be followed through on, but I'd be willing to compromise some.

Therapist: And James, that's something you'd be willing to experiment with.

James: Yeah. Sure. I think it will work. I'd like to try it.

Therapist: Starting right away then.

Concluding Summary

Every psychotherapeutic approach either explicitly or implicitly suggests how it thinks it should be viewed in the context of other approaches. Stances range on a continuum from "the ultimate truth as revealed by

God" to "this might help us get through the day." REFT is conceived of and offered in this chapter as a "clinical perspective" rather than as an academic or research, perspective. As such it represents an evolving set of practical, clinical strategies that provide several distinct advantages (Huber & Baruth, 1989). REFT's metastrategy, ABC, A'B'C', DE, and the essential clinical strategies for which that metastrategy offers a context, have been described in this chapter.

Individual and couple-systems behave not only on the basis of observable words, actions, and emotions, but also on the basis of beliefs about one's own and others' behaviors. The ABC, A'B'C', DE metastrategy and its essential clinical strategies are a means of making this interaction very plain. They posit particularly how certain types of beliefs contribute crucially to the existence and persistence of recurring difficulties as well as their alleviation. (*A client-system belief is not necessarily the same as the belief of a singular individual in isolation; it is a "common" belief that describes the manner in which both members of a couple interact or in which an individual client and significant other persons in his or her environment interact.*)

In addition, the client-system beliefs emphasized in the ABC, A'B'C', DE metastrategy and its essential clinical strategies are *evaluations*, reflecting the degree to which the members of the system evaluate something as desirable or undesirable (Wessler & Wessler, 1980). Rational client-system beliefs have personal significance for the system members and *evaluate* situations in an adaptive, helpful manner. Irrational client-system beliefs also have personal significance for system members but are stated in an absolute, unhelpful manner, considering the present circumstances.

These latter points were highlighted in the two case examples. When Kevin and his daughters were experiencing conflict, they were mutually thinking (their system belief), "The mornings *must* go easily." But when mornings went smoothly, they were mutually thinking, "I/We *want* the morning routine to go smoothly," and they prepared the night before to help this happen. Cindy and James, when they were in conflict, were thinking, "I *have* to have . . ." but when they were relating better with each other, they were thinking "I *want to* but I don't *have to* . . ." From a brief therapy perspective, the opportunity to simplify the process by reducing the number of variables (i.e., beliefs) under consideration is clear (Huber & Backlund, 1991): greater efficiency and effectiveness in the immediacy of the treatment milieu.

While REFT presupposes the primacy of the system beliefs in treatment, these beliefs are not the only focus; effective therapy also considers and deals with a number of interrelated factors. REFT's ABC, A'B'C', DE metastrategy alerts the therapist to the importance of essential and specific process elements, thereby escaping the often bewildering array of extraneous content issues that are available for consideration. Not only are the B and B' elements important, but so is assessing the A, C, A', and C' and then actively engaging in D and E. All are critical elements.

The case presentations particularly highlighted the process of identifying the rational B' by investigating the exception time A' and C'. The therapist assumed that both Kevin and his daughters and the couple James and Cindy had areas of competence upon which they could draw in order to surmount their expressed concerns. It was assumed that exception times characterized by a more rational system belief existed. This belief and the successful solution times and the accompanying satisfying emotional and behavioral consequences had simply been discounted, in concert with absolutist irrational system beliefs, recurrent unsuccessful solution times, and accompanying distressful emotional and behavioral consequences. Herein too, from a clinical perspective, the opportunity for simplifying the process by utilizing skills and understandings already in the family's repertoire is clear (Huber & Driskill, 1993). Again, greater efficiency and effectiveness in the immediacy of the treatment milieu make for briefer therapy.

References

de Shazer, S., Berg, J. K., Lipchik, E., Nunnally, E., Molnar, A., Gingerich, W., & Weiner-Davis, M. (1986). Brief therapy: Focused solution development. *Family Process, 25,* 207–221.

Dryden, W. (1984). *Rational-emotive therapy: Fundamentals and innovations.* London: Croom Helm.

Ellis, A. (1985). What is rational-emotive therapy? In A. Ellis & M. Bernard (Eds.), *Clinical applications of rational-emotive therapy* (pp. 1–30). New York: Plenum.

Ellis, A. (1987). The impossibility of achieving consistently good mental health. *American Psychologist, 42,* 364–375.

Ellis, A. (1993). Fundamentals of rational-emotive therapy for the 1990's. In W. Dryden & L. K. Hill (Eds.), *Innovations in rational-emotive therapy* (pp. 1–32). Newbury Park, CA: Sage.

Fisch, R., Weakland, J., & Segal, L. (1982). *The tactics of change: Doing therapy briefly.* San Francisco: Jossey-Bass.

Huber, C. H., & Backlund, B. A. (1991). *The twenty minute counselor: Transforming brief conversations into effective helping experiences.* New York: Continuum.

Huber, C. H., & Baruth, L. G. (1989). *Rational-emotive family therapy: A systems perspective.* New York: Springer.

Huber, C. H., & Driskill, P. G. (1993). *Equilibrium family therapy: A basic guide for the helping professions.* New York: Crossroad.

Jackson, D. (1977). The study of the family. In P. Watzlawick & J. Weakland (Eds.), *The interactional view.* New York: Norton.

O'Hanlon, W. H., & Weiner-Davis, M. (1989). *In search of solutions.* New York: Norton.

Wessler, R. A., & Wessler, R. L. (1980). *The principles and practice of rational-emotive therapy.* San Francisco: Jossey-Bass.

Annotated Bibliography

Ellis, A. (1994). *Reason and emotion in psychotherapy: A comprehensive method of treating human disturbance.* (Rev. ed.) New York: Carol. The first edition of this book, published in 1962, was the seminal work in cognitive-behavior therapy. This revised edition describes the origins of REBT and how it differs from other therapeutic approaches. It is an excellent background resource for developing a foundation in rational-emotive philosophy and practice.

Huber, C. H., & Backlund, B. A. (1991). *The twenty minute counselor: Transforming brief conversations into effective helping experiences.* New York: Continuum. This book condenses and simplifies the major concepts and methods of rational-emotive family therapy for the professional looking to practice from a brief therapy perspective.

Huber, C. H., & Baruth, L. G. (1989). *Rational-emotive family therapy: A systems perspective.* New York: Springer. This seminal work first introduced the position that "family beliefs" are qualitatively different from the beliefs of individual members of a family system. It details the course of rational-emotive treatment from a systems perspective. It includes several case illustration chapters, with session dialogue and commentary to highlight key points.

Walen, S., DiGiuseppe, R., & Dryden, W. (1992). *A practitioner's guide to rational-emotive therapy* (2nd ed.). New York: Oxford University Press. A superb "practitioner's resource," this book offers step-by-step guidelines for diagnosis and treatment from a traditional rational-emotive behavior therapy perspective.

Yankura, J., & Dryden, W. (1997). *Special applications of REBT: A therapist's casebook*. New York: Springer. The chapters constituting this book describe and illustrate (through actual case material) special applications of rational-emotive behavior therapy. Chapter 5, "Rational-Emotive Family Therapy," discusses the use of the ABC, A'B'C', DE metastrategy with families.

4

~∞∞∞~

Multimodal Strategies with Adults

Arnold A. Lazarus

Introduction

Adolf Meyer (1866–1950), considered by many the dean of American psychiatry, coined the term *psychobiology*, and emphasized the need to study the whole person in terms of biological, psychological, and sociological processes. As Muncie (1974) points out, for Meyer, "the fundamental concept of psychobiology was that of integration" (p. 705). Today attempts to integrate somatic therapies and psychosocial therapies have become standard fare. Thus, what Sperry calls "biopsychosocial therapy" and what I term "multimodal therapy" are very much in keeping with Meyer's perspicacious and comprehensive philosophy. Indeed, attempts to provide patients with a seamless biopsychosocial treatment regimen are widespread. Although narrow and rigid school adherents are still extant, as we enter the twenty-first century, most theoreticians and clinicians seem to favor a broad-spectrum approach to patients. There is far-reaching agreement that treatment needs to be holistic and must consider intraindividual, interpersonal and systemic factors at all levels of functioning—physical, psychological, social-environmental, and political. Some also argue for the inclusion of a separate transpersonal or spiritual dimension.

Sperry (this volume) asserts that biopsychosocial therapy is not a new treatment approach but rather endeavors to combine a set of systematic strategies for enhancing treatment outcomes. The same may be said of multimodal therapy. In my view, the multimodal orientation offers particular assessment tactics and strategies that enhance diagnosis and promote a focused range of effective interventions.

The Essence of the Multimodal Orientation

Multimodal therapy (MMT) is a psychotherapeutic approach that places most of its theoretical underpinnings within a broad-based social and cognitive learning theory but draws on effective techniques from many disciplines without necessarily subscribing to their particular suppositions (i.e., it espouses *technical eclecticism*). MMT is predicated on the assumption that most psychological problems are multifaceted, multidetermined, and multilayered, and that comprehensive therapy calls for a careful assessment of seven parameters or "modalities"—behavior, affect, sensation, imagery, cognition, interpersonal relationships, and biological processes. Because the most common biological intervention is the use of psychotropic *drugs*, the first letters from the seven modalities yield the convenient acronym BASIC I.D.—although it must be remembered that the "D." modality represents the entire panoply of medical and biological factors.

The multimodal approach was developed mainly from clinical follow-ups that showed a fairly high relapse rate in patients who received "narrow band" rather than "broad spectrum" treatment (Lazarus, 1989). Addressing the usual A B C variables (affect, behavior, cognition), as many systems do, tends to overlook or omit significant sensory, imagery, interpersonal, and biological issues. Untreated excesses and deficits in these areas of human functioning may leave patients vulnerable to backsliding. It is assumed that the more a patient learns in therapy, the less likely he or she is to relapse. In other words, therapeutic *breadth* is emphasized. Over many years, my follow-ups have revealed more durable treatment outcomes when the entire BASIC I.D. is assessed, and when significant problems in each modality are remedied (Lazarus, 1989, 1997).

MMT (multimodal therapy) is, in a sense, a misnomer because there is no actual treatment method that is totally distinctive to this approach. There are, however, distinct *assessment procedures* that tend to facilitate treatment outcomes by shedding light on interactive processes and by pinpointing the selection of appropriate techniques and their best mode of implementation. In MMT one endeavors to use, whenever possible and applicable, *empirically supported methods* (Chambless et al., 1998). Thus, its practitioners are at the cutting edge of the field, drawing on scientific and clinical findings from all credible sources. This technically eclectic outlook is central and pivotal to MMT. It is important to understand that the MMT approach sees *theoretical* eclecticism, or any attempt to integrate different theories in the hopes of producing a more robust technique, as futile and misguided (see Lazarus, 1992, 1997). On the other hand, a systematic, technical eclecticism opens many avenues that enhance therapeutic understanding and effectiveness (Lazarus, Beutler, & Norcross, 1992).

Particular Assessment Procedures

Let us now consider how the BASIC I.D. format yields several distinctive assessment procedures. Most of these assessment strategies are specific to the multimodal approach. They were developed solely on pragmatic grounds—they tend to enhance treatment understanding and facilitate psychotherapeutic outcomes.

The BASIC I.D.

By thinking in BASIC I.D. terms, a clinician or counselor is apt to leave fewer important avenues unexplored. It is important to grasp the essential components throughout a person's seven modalities: What *behaviors* does he or she want to increase or decrease? What *affective* reactions are proving disturbing? What are the client's precise *sensory* pains and pleasures? What intrusive *images* need to be replaced by positive visualizations? What dysfunctional beliefs and faulty *cognitions* are in need of restructuring? Who are the client's significant others and what essential processes are at play vis-à-vis his or her *interpersonal* network? What are the important facts about the client's *drug* use (recreational or prescribed) and his or her general medical/biological well-being? Besides gaining an understanding of the separate BASIC I.D. components, it is crucial to appreciate the *interactive effects* among and between the modalities. When focusing on any particular modality, the question to ask is: What impact does this have on the other six modalities? One inquires of a client, for instance, "When you have that particular thought, how do you act, what emotions do you experience, what sensations do you feel, what images come to mind, what people are involved, and how does it affect your physical well-being?

The Multimodal Life History Inventory

After the initial interview, most literate clients receive a 15-page Multimodal Life History Inventory (Lazarus & Lazarus, 1991, 1998). The Inventory is not given to clients who are deluded, deeply depressed, or highly agitated. Basically, it provides a therapeutic "road map" that aids in clinical decision making by helping to identify a wide range of potentially salient problems throughout the BASIC I.D. It also generates a valuable perspective regarding a client's style and treatment expectations. The Multimodal Life History Inventory provides detailed background information and is typeset in such a manner that makes it easy to determine specific excesses and deficits across a client's BASIC I.D.

Second-Order BASIC I.D. Assessments

Second-order BASIC I.D. assessments may be conducted when therapy falters. For example, an unassertive person who is not responding to the usual social skills and assertiveness training methods may be asked to spell out the specific consequences that an assertive modus vivendi might have on his or her behaviors, affective reactions, sensory responses, imagery, and cognitive processes. The Interpersonal repercussions would also be examined, and if relevant, Biological factors would be determined (e.g., "If I started expressing my feelings, I may become less anxious and require fewer tranquilizers"). Quite often, this procedure brings to light such factors as noncompliance and poor progress as reasons for the nonresponsiveness. A typical case in point concerns a man who was not responding to role playing and other assertiveness training procedures. Upon traversing a second-order BASIC I.D. assessment, he revealed a central cognitive schema to the effect that he was not entitled to be confident, positive, and in better control of his life, because this would only show up his profoundly reticent and inadequate father. Consequently, the treatment focus shifted to a thorough examination of his entitlements.

The Structural Profile Inventory

A 35-item Structural Profile Inventory (SPI) yields a quantitative BASIC I.D. diagram depicting a person's degree of activity, emotionality, sensory awareness, imagery potential, cognitive propensities, interpersonal leanings, and biological considerations (see Lazarus, 1997). The SPI is particularly useful in couples therapy, where differences in the specific ratings reflect potential areas of friction. Discussion of these disparities with clients can result in constructive steps to understand and remedy them. Herman (1993) and Landes (1988) have established the reliability and validity of the SPI. Herman (1991, 1997) has also shown that client-therapist similarity on the SPI is predictive of psychotherapy outcome.

Multimodal therapists make use of several other assessment instruments (e.g., the Expanded Structural Profile and the Revised Marital Satisfaction Questionnaire), which are printed and discussed in Lazarus (1997). Moreover, when applicable, we administer well-known measures such as the Beck Depression Inventory and the MMPI.

Tracking

A method called *tracking* may be employed when clients are puzzled by affective reactions: "I don't know why I feel this way," "I don't know where these feelings are coming from." The client is asked to recount the latest untoward event or incident. He or she is then asked to consider what behaviors, affective responses, sensations, images, and cognitions come to mind. Thus, our client who reported having panic attacks "for no apparent reason" was able to put together the following string of events.

She had initially become aware that her heart was beating faster than usual. This brought to mind an episode where she had passed out after imbibing too much alcohol at a party. This memory or image still occasioned a strong sense of shame. She started thinking that she was going to pass out again, and as she dwelled on her sensations, this cognition only intensified and culminated in her feelings of panic. Thus, she exhibited an S-I-C-S-C-A pattern (sensation, imagery, cognition, sensation, cognition, affect). Thereafter she was asked to take careful note whether any subsequent anxiety or panic attacks followed a similar "firing order." She subsequently confirmed that her two "trigger points" were usually sensation and imagery. This alerted the therapist to focus on sensory training techniques (e.g., diaphragmatic breathing and deep muscle relaxation), followed immediately by imagery training (e.g., the use of coping imagery and the selection of mental pictures that evoked profound feelings of calm).

The BASIC I.D. lends itself to other assessment and treatment tactics that keep the clinician on track and enable him or her to address issues that might otherwise have been glossed over. Lazarus (1997) presents these methods in some detail.

Clinical Indications

When would one not work multimodally? In other words, what types of issues, problems, or disorders will preempt the use of the Multimodal Life History Inventory and the development of Modality and Structural Profiles, and nullify a detailed BASIC I.D. assessment and its attendant procedures—bridging, tracking, and second-order assessments? The obvious answer is that when a clinician is confronted by a client with serious psychopathology (e.g., active delusions, extreme depression, pervasive anxiety), or when a situation calls for an immediate highly focused crisis-intervention sequence, the emphasis is on methods that are likely to be circumscribed, intense, and clinically robust. Conversely, there is no need to delve into broader or deeper issues with clients whose problems call for immediate and obvious interventions. Thus, a successful female executive who was uncomfortable in airplanes sought treatment because her job called for frequent air travel. (She required no more than three desensitization sessions coupled with mental imagery and autohypnotic skills that she could use as needed.) A high school principal asked for help in dealing with a couple of insubordinate teachers. (In this case, the initial hypothesis of a possible assertiveness deficit turned out to be incorrect.

The client was adequately assertive but mistakenly believed that he would undermine his position if he asked the superintendent to intervene. He subsequently turned to his superior for assistance to good effect.) A 70-year-old widow seemed to need little more than a good listener who could help her learn to integrate into the retirement community where she was residing. Of course, in these instances, administration of the Multi-modal Life History Inventory may be considered in order to determine if there are other separate or related issues that warrant attention.

It is not uncommon to encounter high-functioning individuals whose problems call for a *bimodal* sequence—cognitive restructuring (a focus on misinformation and missing information) and social skills training. Some clients need little more than a good shoulder to cry on (metaphorically speaking), an active listener, or an authority figure who will affirm their own perceptions or judgment, or offer reassurance and good advice. Thus, there is no slavish attention to the multimodal spectrum across the board, but when indicated, the well-trained multimodal clinician has an imposing armamentarium of assessment and treatment strategies at his or her disposal.

Research Findings on Overall Effectiveness

It is, of course, far easier to study the impact of a specific technique than to measure the effectiveness of an entire clinical armamentarium such as MMT. Nevertheless, colleagues in Holland and Great Britain have attempted to do so. Kwee (1984), a Dutch psychologist, obtained encouraging results when conducting a controlled-outcome study using MMT with severe obsessive-compulsive patients, as well as a group of extremely phobic individuals. Williams (1988), a Scottish psychologist, in a carefully controlled outcome study, compared MMT with other treatments in helping children with learning disabilities. He emerged with clear data pointing to the efficacy of MMT in comparison with the other methods.

In essence, it should be understood that MMT is a comprehensive orientation that is extremely flexible and ardently strives to match the best and most effective methods with the appropriate treatment style for each individual. As I have emphasized elsewhere (Lazarus, 1993), relationships of choice are no less important than techniques of choice for effective psychotherapy. A flexible repertoire of relationship styles, plus a wide range of pertinent techniques, seems to enhance treatment outcomes. Decisions regarding different relationship stances include when and how to be directive, supportive, reflective, cold, warm, tepid, formal, or informal. The need to be "an authentic chameleon" was stressed.

Clinical Applications with An Individual:
Case Example

Bob, a 48-year-old advertising copywriter and speechwriter employed by a large corporation, suffered from bouts of depression, had problems maintaining an intimate relationship (he was twice divorced), expressed concerns about his relationship with his son and daughter from his first marriage, and felt unappreciated at work. Previously, he had been in couples therapy and had seen various individual counselors and clinicians from time to time, but he felt that he had derived minimal benefits from counseling and psychotherapy.

During the initial rapport-building session, it became clear that he was starving for affirmation. He latched on to any positive comment: "You are obviously a good wordsmith," "It sounds as if you are a truly concerned and caring father," "Why do you blame yourself for the breakup of your marriages? 'It takes two to tango,' as the old cliché puts it."

At the end of the initial interview, as is customary with literate clients who are not excessively depressed or otherwise too disturbed or distracted to focus on filling out questionnaires, Bob was handed the Multimodal Life History Inventory (Lazarus & Lazarus, 1991). He was requested to complete it in his own time, advised not to attempt to finish it in one sitting, and asked to bring the completed Inventory with him to the next meeting.

The therapist usually studies the LHI after session number two, so by the time the client returns for the third session, the impressions gleaned from the Inventory are discussed and treatment priorities are established. But before perusing the entire document, it is my custom to turn to the bottom of page 4, which inquires about the client's "expectations regarding therapy." Bob had written: "I expect my therapist to be actively involved—he will disclose pertinent things about himself, advise me, direct me, and enter into a two-way process. . . . I do not want a remote or distant father figure. As you will see on page 2, I was raised by one of those." Contrast this with another client's expectancies. She had written: "A good therapist is an active listener who says little but hears all." It would be naïve to assume that clients always know what they want and what is best for them. But without slavishly following their clients' scripts, if therapists had more respect for the notion that their clients often sense how they can best be served, fewer blunders might result.

In Bob's case, the therapeutic trajectory was clearly enhanced by my willingness to self-disclose. (I would talk about strategies that I found helpful in my own marriage and with my own children, and I discussed problems that I had encountered in various work situations and tactics that had proved useful for me.) He took very kindly to the fact that I transcended the usual clinical boundaries by meeting him for lunch on a couple of occasions (see Lazarus, 1998a). He also appreciated the fact that I was quite forthright in offering advice ("I don't see a downside to your asking for a raise. If I were you, I'd go for it").

The LHI brought to light several interconnected problems. His behaviors were characterized by many avoidant tendencies: affectively, he was apt to wallow in self-pity; at the sensory level, generalized muscular tensions seemed widespread; his mental imagery was replete with pictures of failure and derision from peers; his cognitions were fraught with statements of self-denigration, perfectionism, and categorical imperatives; and his interpersonal relationships were characterized by extreme cautiousness and envy of his older brother who, he claimed, his parents had favored. In light of these findings, and because Bob described himself as an avid reader, he was given two books for bibliotherapy, *Don't Believe It for a Minute!* (Lazarus, Lazarus, & Fay, 1993) and *The 60-Second Shrink* (Lazarus & Lazarus, 1997).

Bob scored 32 points on the Beck Depression Inventory, which indicated a significant depression and suggested the advisability of antidepressant medication. He was not averse to seeing one of the psychopharmacologists with whom I have a good working relationship, and he started taking Prozac, which was soon changed to Effexor due to some untoward side effects. He tolerated the Effexor very well and within two to three weeks reported feeling far less enervated and depressed.

Initially, in addition to the antidepressant medication, the treatment procedures employed were standard cognitive-behavior therapy strategies—relaxation training, positive-imagery exercises, cognitive restructuring (especially antiperfectionistic teachings), and assertiveness training. Bob made good progress across several dimensions but there seemed to be three sticking points. (1) Tensions between Bob and his live-in girlfriend were escalating. (2) He was feeling resentful at work because his boss was rarely complimentary. (3) His anger toward his first former wife (the mother of his children) had intensified and was proving disruptive. Above all, my attempts to augment Bob's overall level of assertiveness were falling on deaf ears.

A second-order BASIC I.D. assessment was attempted by asking Bob to picture himself attaining some of his immediate goals—achieving harmony at home with his girlfriend, coming to terms with his boss and his first wife, and behaving more assertively. These situations were addressed one at a time, and Bob was asked to discuss the repercussions in each modality. But he was unable to visualize any of these circumstances. "Something is blocking me," he reported. I said, "Well, let's go back to you and Grace [his girlfriend]. Try to picture a calm, companionable, and congenial scene with her, and tell me what interferes with it." Bob appeared to sidestep my request and waxed eloquent on the theme of the maternal censure and paternal distance he had endured as a child. He thereupon volunteered that his extreme hypersensitivity to any real or implied rebuke from Grace was probably a reaction to his childhood baggage. He grew emotional when recounting that his brother, who was a year and a half older, was allegedly praised for the very things that led his parents to punish and criticize him.

At this juncture, the use of a time-tripping technique held promise. I asked Bob to picture himself as an adult, going back in time to console his alter ego. The 48-year-old Bob stepped into an imaginary time machine and visited himself at various ages, starting at 5 years and ending at 14. This evoked strong feelings that abated upon repeated exposure (a form of desensitization), but these excursions also elicited relevant associations to the effect that he instantly felt like "a little kid" when he perceived himself to be slighted or unappreciated. Hence, in his interactions with Grace and with his boss, he often responded in ways that were age inappropriate. (More information on time tripping appears in Lazarus, 1997, 1998b.)

As a homework assignment, Bob was asked to continue taking these time trips into the past about twice a day for 10-minute intervals. At his next session, he mentioned an important revelation. It became evident to him that he had developed a certain degree of what Seligman and his colleagues (1968) termed "learned helplessness" when it came to asking for affirmation, support, or assistance from significant others. His parents, he said, led him to avoid asking for things because denial of his requests was almost guaranteed. As he now perceived it, he carried these feelings into his adulthood. These factors lay behind the common thread of bottling up his feelings and avoiding confrontations, which extended into all of his relationships.

It seems to be of little importance whether or not insights of this kind are genuine or specious. As is often the case, and as was true with Bob, they tend to provide the fuel that can propel actions that have hitherto been avoided. Thus, Bob was now primed to remedy several problem situations by deliberately cultivating a forthright, assertive, outgoing, and nonavoidant modus vivendi. Consequently, our treatment focus was now centered on various behavior-rehearsal and role-playing procedures to prepare him for heart-to-heart talks with Grace, his first wife, his children, and his employer. We both agreed that any discussion with his parents—both in their eighties—would prove futile. He vetoed my suggestion that a meeting with Bob, Grace, and me might prove productive, stating that he preferred to "go it alone."

Outcome

MMT has no ironclad adherence to weekly sessions—especially when clients need time to practice homework assignments. Thus, Bob had 14 sessions over a period of seven months. His gains were clearly evident. He is no longer depressed (although the psychiatrist he sees for medication wants him to continue with his prescription for several years). The net result of his newfound nonavoidant behaviors is far greater interpersonal satisfaction and closeness, including a substantial increase in salary.

It is noteworthy that although Bob was not a resistant or especially difficult, combative, or seriously disturbed individual, he could easily have continued to suffer needlessly for the rest of his life. Many strategies and tactics were covered in the 14 sessions (e.g., medication, relaxation training, mental imagery methods, cognitive disputation, bibliotherapy, and assertiveness training), but significant psychosocial gains accrued only after the highly focused time-tripping sequences were introduced. Theoretically, these procedures extinguished some of his childhood agonies and freed him to start taking the risk of acting like an adult. Since the therapist-client relationship is the soil that enables the techniques to take root, it must be remembered that the therapeutic alliance was deliberately tailor-made to fit Bob's needs and expectancies. To reiterate: clinical effectiveness is often dependent on a salubrious combination of the correct techniques within the context of an appropriate relationship.

Clinical Applications with a Couple: Case Example

In some cases it is unnecessary to traverse the entire BASIC I.D. because problems loom large and clear in a couple of obvious areas. I will now discuss a couple whose problems were clearly delineated by completing the Structural Profile Inventory (SPI) and the Marital Satisfaction Questionnaire (MSQ).

Ted, aged 24, and Amy, aged 21, had dated for two years before marrying. "We have been married for less than six months, but it was shortly after we got married," said Amy, "that things started going wrong." Both avid skiers, music lovers, hikers, and animal activists, they saw eye to eye politically, enjoyed the same kinds of foods, had the same tastes in movies, and shared a great deal in common. Amy was completing her undergraduate education, and Ted was in his second year of law school. They both agreed to defer any plans to have children until they were both settled occupationally. So wherein lay the problem?

"It's hard to put it in words," Amy stated, "but I'd say, speaking for myself, that I have sensed a growing distance between us, and Ted strikes me as having become irritable, grumpy, and disgruntled." Ted conceded that he had become "difficult to live with," but he attributed his dysphoria to the demands being placed on him at law school, a fact that Amy contended could account for only part of the discord.

The initial session was primarily a rapport-building consultation. We discussed how they met, what attracted them to each other, the compositions of their families of origin, and their joint decision to seek counseling before their marriage landed on the rocks. Neither Ted nor Amy could articulate exactly what was amiss. Amy reiterated her uneasy sense of a growing emotional distance between them and her feeling that Ted was "testy and crabby." Ted volunteered only that he felt under a lot of pressure and that Amy was less understanding than he would wish. At the end of the session, I gave them each a Marital Satisfaction Questionnaire (MSQ) and a Structural Profile Inventory (SPI) and asked them to fill them out separately at home and bring them to our next session. (These measures are published in Lazarus, 1997.)

We had scheduled a second session 10 days later. Two days after our first session, Ted called and asked if he could meet with me alone prior to our next joint meeting. Many therapists refuse to see individual partners but insist on working solely with the couple. I see such refusals as unfortunate because in couples therapy there are three main components to be considered—each individual and the dyad. Nevertheless, as most clinicians can attest, in many instances requests for an individual meeting early in the therapy are usually a sign that an *affaire d'amour* will be revealed. And indeed, after Ted asked and was assured that I would treat as strictly confidential anything he revealed to me, he disclosed that for the past two months he had been having sex with one of his classmates.

Obviously, declarations of this kind raise serious ethical and professional concerns. In my opinion, it would be unacceptable to continue couples therapy while colluding with Ted by hiding the truth from his wife. It certainly was not up to me to divulge Ted's extramarital liaison. Yet in my opinion, any counselor or therapist who would urge Ted to own up, come clean, and confess the truth to Amy ought to be forbidden to treat clients. I have seen many instances of incalculable and completely unnecessary damage from this type of advice.

I explored the reasons that lay behind Ted's decision to have an affair, how committed he really was to Amy and their marriage, whether he viewed his lover as a potentially better life partner, and if divorce counseling rather than marriage therapy might be indicated. Ted was adamant that he loved Amy, wanted to spend the rest of his life with her and raise a family, and stressed that his lady friend was less attractive, less intelligent, and less pleasing than Amy, but that sexually she was exciting and outgoing, whereas Amy was inhibited and often appeared uninterested in sex. I pointed out that this lacuna could be addressed and probably remedied, but that I would not be willing to continue seeing them in couples therapy knowing that he was having extramarital sex. Ted strongly assured me that he would terminate the affair there and then. I stressed that I was not telling him to end the affair but only that I would not continue seeing them as a couple if the affair continued. He assured me that the relationship had "run its course" and that he preferred to have an exclusive relationship with Amy. I emphasized that I had no way of checking up on him, nor would I want to, and that I would simply trust him and assume that he would not deceive me. He asked if it was advisable to discuss the affair with Amy, and I advised against it. In my book *Marital Myths* (Lazarus, 1985), I underscored the inadvisability of making such confessions and discussed a case in which a young man followed his counselor's advice to own up to an affair, whereas "his needs might have been better served had he cut out his tongue" (p. 26).

There are some facts that need to remain strictly personal and private. The notion of sharing everything with one's spouse, going from A to Z, is another unfortunate and damaging myth. I urged Ted to think about what he had learned from his assignations and to decide whether he truly desired to have a monogamous relationship with Amy, and I offered to discuss these components in future individual sessions if necessary. I also said that I would like to meet Amy alone for a few sessions to gain a better appreciation of her basic makeup.

Amy and Ted returned to their second marriage therapy session armed with the MSQ and SPI documents that they had completed. A quick calculation showed that they both expressed a high degree of marital satisfaction. Scores on the MSQ range between 16 and 160 points, with most couples in therapy scoring under 100 points. Amy's score was 132 to Ted's 135. An item analysis showed that both partners expressed dissatisfaction with their sexual relationship.

Similarly, the SPI also revealed only one notable difference between them: The Interpersonal ratings showed Amy to be more gregarious than Ted. Whereas she gravitated to people, enjoyed social gatherings, and cultivated friendships, Ted was more of a loner. Upon hearing this, Ted knowingly muttered, "I guess that's why there's often a tug-of-war between us." He was referring to the fact that Amy frequently made social arrangements despite his protestations.

The foregoing issue was readily resolved: They would meet each other more or less halfway. Amy would willingly attend various functions without Ted (selected cocktail parties, visits to certain family members, some religious services), and she would go out with her friends to plays and movies that Ted was not interested in seeing. Ted, in turn, would willingly attend selected dinner parties that Amy and her friends were fond of having, and he and Amy would visit his parents and her parents every three or four weeks.

The sexual impasse proved trickier. When asked to explain their respective dissatisfactions, both Ted and Amy were vague and offered no specific details. Ted said that Amy was "inhibited," but when asked to explain what this meant, he spoke in generalities. Amy complained that Ted was "inattentive," and she hinted that she had problems asking Ted for certain forms of attention. When Ted added that she often seemed uninterested in sex and he thought her libido was low, Amy retaliated by asserting that her libido was "just fine." I recommended that Amy and I meet to discuss these issues, and we set up an appointment for the following week.

It was not easy for Amy to be outspoken about her sexual feelings and desires, and it took the entire hour to piece together the following information: She incorrectly believed that she suffered from a sexual deficiency because she required direct clitoral stimulation to achieve an orgasm and was unable to climax during penile vaginal stimulation. It was strongly emphasized that her erotic spectrum was entirely "normal." I showed her relevant passages to this effect from the writings of Masters and Johnson, and I read her Zilbergeld's (1992) affirmations: "And Nature gave women a clitoris, an organ that has nothing to do with reproduction and whose only function is sexual pleasure. Interestingly, she put the clitoris in a place that makes it difficult for a penis, thrusting or not, to stimulate it. Maybe she thought that other kinds of sex than intercourse should be part of the plan" (p. 71). "As the penis moves in and out of the vagina, it tugs on the vaginal lips, which are attached to the hood of the clitoris. But this stimulation is insufficient to produce orgasm in most women" (p. 101).

These issues were embroidered a week later during a conjoint session with Amy and Ted. Amy then took the risk of describing her ideal sexual scenario. It involved foreplay (kissing, cuddling, and breast stimulation) followed by sexual intercourse, and it culminated with either oral or manual stimulation to the point of orgasm. She was entirely willing to provide Ted with vaginal, manual, or oral stimulation as per his desire. She also mentioned that on occasion she would like to try using a vibrator while Ted suckled and fondled her breasts. Up to this point, sex had consisted of foreplay, intercourse, and little else, after which Amy usually went to the bathroom, where she masturbated to orgasm feeling "abnormal." I pointed out that we had now written a series of satisfying and exciting sexual scenarios and recommended that the couple try them out. We scheduled an appointment three weeks later.

Amy began the session by stating that the marriage was now "on track." Ted reinforced this perception by adding that it was "better than ever." They reported that their social activities were in harmony and that sexually they had worked out an eminently satisfying trajectory. They had been seen four times in couples therapy and each had had one individual session. Considerable territory had been traversed in a short time, and the use of two multimodal therapy measures had brought to light some focal issues that called for specific remediation.

Summary

After outlining the elements of the multimodal therapy orientation, this chapter has described the assessment and treatment of two relatively straightforward cases, an individual (Bob) and a couple (Amy and Ted). Bob's significant depression called for antidepressant medication in addition to several specific behavioral, cognitive, and interpersonal strategies. The use of precise multimodal methods (a second-order BASIC I.D. assessment, time tripping, and specific homework assignments) led to satisfying results. The couple, Ted and Amy, presented with several dyadic conflicts and posed ethical choice points. The use of two multimodal instruments (the Marital Satisfaction Questionnaire and the Structural Profile Inventory) highlighted their basic differences and pointed the way to effective interventions. Specific sex therapy procedures were also called for.

It is my opinion that the treatments described in this chapter offer some distinctive features, and it is up to the reader to decide if he or she agrees or disagrees. It seems to me that several technical strategic, procedural, ideological, and ethical issues have been raised that should provide food for thought. There will obviously be considerable overlap between what is herein described and what clinicians of other orientations practice and prescribe, but there are also some points of departure that should open avenues for further exploration and enlightenment.

References

Chambless, D. L., Baker, M. J., Baucom, D. H., Beutler, L. E., Calhoun, K. S., Crits-Christoph, P., Daiuto, A., DeRubeis, R., Detweiler, J., Haaga, D. A., Johnson, S. I. B., Mockery, S., Mueser, K. I. T., Pope, K. S., Sanders, W. I. C., Chum, V., Stoical, T., Williams, D. A., & Woody, S.R. (1998). Update on empirically validated therapies II. *The Clinical Psychologist, 51,* 3–16.

Herman, S. M. (1991). Client therapist similarity on the Multimodal Structural Profile as predictive of psychotherapy outcome. *Psychotherapy Bulletin, 26,* 26–27.

Herman, S. M. (1993). A demonstration of the validity of the Multimodal Structural Profile through a correlation with the Vocational Preference Inventory. *Psychotherapy in Private Practice, 11,* 71–80.

Herman, S. M. (1997). Therapist-client similarity on the Multimodal Structural Profile Inventory as a predictor of early session impact. *Journal of Psychotherapy Practice and Research, 6,* 139–144.

Kwee, M. G. T. (1984). *Klinishe multimodale gedragtstherapie.* Lisse, Holland: Swets & Zeitlinger.

Landes, A. A. (1988). *Assessment of the reliability and validity of the Multimodal Structural Profile Inventory.* Unpublished doctoral dissertation, Graduate School of Applied and Professional Psychology, Rutgers University.

Lazarus, A. A. (1985). *Marital myths.* San Luis Obispo, CA: Impact.

Lazarus, A. A. (1989). *The practice of multimodal therapy.* Baltimore: Johns Hopkins University Press.

Lazarus, A. A. (1992). Multimodal therapy: Technical eclecticism with minimal integration. In J. C. Norcross & M. R. Goldfried (Eds.), *Handbook of psychotherapy integration* (pp. 231–263). New York: Basic Books.

Lazarus, A. A. (1993). Tailoring the therapeutic relationship or being an authentic chameleon. *Psychotherapy, 30,* 404–407.

Lazarus, A. A. (1997). *Brief but comprehensive psychotherapy: The multimodal way.* New York: Springer.

Lazarus, A. A. (1998a). How do you like these boundaries? *The Clinical Psychologist, 51,* 22–25.

Lazarus, A. A. (1998b). Time tripping. In H. G. Rosenthal (Ed.), *Favorite counseling and therapy techniques* (pp. 124–126). Bristol, PA: Accelerated Development.

Lazarus, A. A., Beutler, L. E., & Norcross, J. C. (1992). The future of technical eclecticism. *Psychotherapy, 29,* 11–20.

Lazarus, A. A., & Lazarus, C. N. (1991). *Multimodal Life History Inventory.* Champaign, IL: Research Press.

Lazarus, A. A., & Lazarus, C. N. (1997). *The 60-second shrink: 101 strategies for staying sane in a crazy world.* San Luis Obispo, CA: Impact.

Lazarus, A. A., & Lazarus, C. N. (1998). Clinical purposes of the Multimodal Life History Inventory. In G. P. Koocher, J. C. Norcross, & S. S. Hill (Eds.), *Psychologists' desk reference* (pp. 15–22). New York: Oxford University Press.

Lazarus, A. A., Lazarus, C. N., & Fay, A. (1993). *Don't believe it for a minute! Forty toxic ideas that are driving you crazy.* San Luis Obispo, CA: Impact.

Muncie, W. F. (1974). The psychobiological approach. In S. Arieti (Ed.), *American handbook of psychiatry* (vol. 1., pp. 705–721). New York: Basic Books.

Seligman, M. E. P., Maier, S. F., & Geer, J. (1968). The alleviation of learned helplessness in the dog. *Journal of Abnormal Psychology, 73,* 256–262.

Williams, T. (1988). *A multimodal approach to assessment and intervention with children with learning disabilities.* Unpublished doctoral dissertation, University of Glasgow.

Zilbergeld, B. (1992). *The new male sexuality.* New York: Bantam Books.

Annotated Bibliography

Dumont F., & Corsini, R. J. (Eds.). (2000). *Six therapists and one client.* New York: Springer. Six therapists from very different orientations are presented with a hypothetical case history and are asked to describe how they would go about treating the client. Each chapter also provides a commentary written by a colleague, and the editors provide an introduction and overall critique. The step-by-step account of multimodal therapy can be compared with the five other approaches in dealing with the same case.

Dryden, W. (1991). *A dialogue with Arnold Lazarus: "It depends."* Philadelphia: Open Universities Press.

The introduction and eight chapters in this book are the outcome of an intensive series of interviews conducted by Professor Dryden. They provide a clear picture of the origins of the multimodal concept and the factors that led to its refinement. The book covers the range from theoretical to practical applications, training, and supervision, with a particularly interesting chapter on "Dos and don'ts and sacred cows."

Lazarus, A. A. (1997). *Brief but comprehensive psychotherapy: The multimodal way.* New York: Springer. Is it possible to conduct brief, time-limited, and focused psychotherapy and yet not cut corners? How can one be brief and also comprehensive? Is this not a contradiction in terms? As this book clearly demonstrates, the multimodal approach lends itself to broad-based yet short-term therapy. As Cyril Franks points out in the foreword, this book presents "an efficient, effective, teachable, demonstrably valid and comprehensive approach without being rigid."

Part II

5

Short-Term Therapy for Character Change

Leigh McCullough

This form of short-term dynamic psychotherapy was developed from many years of research to try to identify the most effective methods for healing long-standing personality disorders. In the process we found this treatment was also useful in resolving Axis I disorders, such as anxiety and depression, and so our scope has broadened.

The treatment involves three main strategies or objectives: *defense restructuring, affect restructuring, and self/other restructuring.* These objectives (or change processes) were developed because of the main obstacles to change that my colleagues and I were continually facing.

The obstacles were as follows:

1. *Patients were unaware of their maladaptive defensive behavior*
   Patients were often unaware of their maladaptive defensive behavior, so of course they could not change it. If patients do not know that they are intellectualizing, or passive-aggressive, or

masochistic, they are not going to be able to change their behavior or stop doing it. Either you have the behavior or the behavior has you. Therefore we set as a subgoal "the recognition of defenses."

2. *Patients were not motivated to give up their defenses*

Even patients who were aware of their maladaptive responses, would often say, "So what?" or "That's the way I am." And they would remain stuck and unmotivated to change. No matter how bad the defensive behavior, they felt, it must be better than the alternative, or they would not continue it. (Examples: Suicide can be better than continuing a life of unbearable pain. Masochism may be preferable to anger if you hate yourself when you are angry and feel a certain pride in being tough on yourself.) No change is possible if the patient clings to the maladaptive response. Therefore a second subgoal became "relinquishing or giving up the defenses." This obstacle appears to be one of the most resistant to change.

These two goals make up the first main objective, *defense restructuring*, which means altering long-standing maladaptive defensive responses and replacing them with some form of adaptive emotional response.

These objectives, however, are only one aspect of the change process. Even when patients could see what they were doing and wanted to stop doing it, their behavior often still would not change. The next obstacles involved patients' phobias about affect:

3. *Patients were unable to experience certain feelings*

Patients may realize that they need to grieve, or to stand up for themselves, or to be tender with those they love, and they may even strongly want to do so. But many people remain very uncomfortable or completely blocked in the inner experience of these feelings. Therefore the subgoal of "experiencing of affect" was developed to expose the patient to the inner emotional experience until it became tolerable and comfortable.

4. *Patients were reluctant to express feelings interpersonally*

Even when patients are able to feel anger, grief, or tenderness in their therapist's office, the ability to express these feelings often does not generalize to the outside world. Therefore, the subgoal of affect expression was developed to help such patients build skills for interpersonal expressions of feeling.

These two affect subgoals make up the objective *affect restructuring.* Achieving this objective forms the bulk of treatment for many patients, especially those who score above 50 or 60 on the Global Assessment Scale ("moderate to mild impairment in functioning").

For many patients—especially those with a serious impairment in functioning (i.e., below 50 on the Global Assessment Scale)—the restructuring of defenses and affects is often blocked. Many patients have felt criticized or overwhelmed by the process of restructuring defenses or affects. For this reason, we developed the objective of *self/other restructuring* to overcome two further major obstacles to growth and change:

5. *Patients held negative internal images of others*

   Some patients feel so alienated or distrustful of others that they need to spend time building a strong alliance with the therapist and building social supports outside of treatment. The subgoal of "alteration of inner representation of others" was developed.

6. *Patients held negative internal images of the self*

   Patients who cannot face their defenses or affects often feel so much shame and poor self-esteem that specific attention needs to be given to improving their positive feelings about themselves, replacing morbid self-deprecating thoughts and feelings with self-compassion and healthy pride.

Treatment Modality

The treatment is based on the psychotherapy manual *Changing Character: Short-term Anxiety-Regulating Psychotherapy for Restructuring Defenses, Affects, and Attachments* (McCullough-Vaillant, 1997), and its accompanying workbook, *Transforming Affect* (McCullough, Kaplan, Andrews, Kuhn, Wolf & Lanza, 2000, in press.)

This approach is based on the following premises:

1. A person's maladaptive behaviors can be understood as attempts to protect the self (*defenses*).
2. The person attempts to protect the self by avoiding the experience and/or expression of avoided feelings (*adaptive affects*).
3. The feelings are intolerable because of the anxiety or other conflicted feelings that they arouse (e.g., *inhibitory affects* such as shame, guilt, fear of rejection, etc.).

In order to change these maladaptive defensive behavior patterns, the person must first recognize them as defensive, feel motivated to modify them (defense restructuring), identify the avoided feelings, experience them in the therapy sessions, and learn to express them interpersonally in new and adaptive ways (affect restructuring), thus altering the sense of self in relation to others (self/other restructuring).

The core maladaptive conflict can be thought of as an affect phobia (i.e., fear of one's own emotional responses because of conflicted feelings associated with them). The treatment can be conceptualized as an exposure (to conflicted feelings) and response prevention (of defensive avoidance) to achieve desensitization of the feared but adaptive affects.

Therefore, treatment has three main objectives: defense restructuring (recognition and relinquishing of defenses), affect restructuring (experiencing and appropriately expressing conflicted feelings), and self/other restructuring (altering the maladaptive inner representations of self and others). Although the treatment follows the fundamental structure of psychodynamic psychotherapy (i.e., analysis of defenses blocking conflicted feelings), it employs the technology of behavior change to speed up the therapy process. The goal of the therapy is rapid reduction in symptoms as well as adaptive change in long-standing character problems.

Space permits only a brief overview of this treatment model, but it is described in detail in the psychotherapy manual *Changing Character,* mentioned above. The following case example will illustrate the three basic objectives of this model and a number of interventions used to achieve them.

Case Example:
The Betrayed Idealist

The betrayed idealist was a 21-year-old college student who had been depressed and in therapy since he was a young child. At the time he entered therapy, he was on Prozac but was severely depressed nonetheless. His Beck Depression Inventory score was 30. He had a cousin who committed suicide, and he was concerned that he might do the same. Although he was an excellent student, he was having trouble doing his schoolwork. He was well liked by his classmates, but he hated being a male and felt that all aggression was male-derived and bad.

He had come to treatment because his girlfriend had had an affair with his best friend and he felt unbearably betrayed. He simply could not believe that his best friend could have done such a thing. But he was living with this best friend and was trying to be friendly and to "put it past him."

He had a 20-session treatment that cured his lifelong depression, resolved the problem with the betrayal, and resulted in significant character change. At three-year follow-up, his gains were not only maintained but much improved.

Diagnostic Formulation (DSM-III-R):

Axis I:	Major Depressive Disorder
Axis II:	Self-Defeating Personality Disorder (Depressive)
Axis III:	None
Axis IV:	3
Axis V:	GAF = 46 (current)

GAF = 60 (highest past year)

AT TERMINATION:

Axis I and II:	Did not meet diagnostic criteria
Axis III:	None
Axis IV:	1
Axis V:	GAF = 75

Core Dynamic Focus

It was obvious that this young man needed to become comfortable with his feelings of anger at his girlfriend and the best friend who betrayed him. Upon presentation his anger was almost entirely denied and turned toward himself. His sense of self was so extremely negative, however, that treatment quickly switched from focusing on anger to focusing on how he viewed himself and others. In addition, he had no idea how masochistic he was being to himself, and this needed to be made conscious, so he could begin to work on it.

Dynamic Formulation

There were three main dynamic conflicts:

1. *Conflicted feelings (i.e., phobic affect) around anger or assertion.* He was afraid and shamed to experience or express anger, so he used various defenses to block it, such as passivity, depression, masochism, and suicidal ideation. His anger was blocked due to fear of rejection as well as shame about aggression and his masculinity.

2. *Conflicted feelings around care for self.* He had a very poor self-image (i.e., negative feelings about the self) due to the excessive shame that blocked adaptive feelings of confidence and entitlement. To avoid meeting his own needs, he used defenses such as denial (of these needs) and reaction formation and altruism (excessive care of others).

3. *Difficulty with closeness resulting in loneliness and longing.* He felt he did not matter to his parents or to others. He used defenses such as projection (they are not interested in me) and dissociation into work or partying because of the pain of emotional deprivation and longing.

Overview of Treatment

During the first three sessions, we focused largely on anger but also dealt with self-esteem issues when they blocked his ability to be angry. Anger was the main focus because it was extremely difficult for this very hurt young man to be living in close quarters with his best friend, when so much anger was not being addressed. He reported trying to be friendly to Mark and trying to "put it behind him." Later sessions focused on self issues and relationship issues.

Initial Evaluation

Therapist: Can you tell me what problem brought you to treatment? What would you like help with?

Patient: Um . . . like we spoke on the phone. The most immediate problem in my life is basically the aftermath of this, uh, situation with my now ex-girlfriend and best friend.

He tells a long and highly intellectualized account of how he went away for the summer, leaving his girlfriend and his best friend living together. He had made an agreement with his girlfriend that they could date other people. But he did not date other people and in fact made an effort to be faithful to her. He had been attracted to another woman over the summer but worked hard to avoid her. But he did not ask his girlfriend to do the same for him. He reports that it never occurred to him that she and his best friend would become involved.

I repeatedly confront the possibility that he might have set up this situation—but he insists that his friend since age 5 was someone he never would have imagined could do such a thing to him. (This is why I call him the "betrayed idealist." It is entirely possible that his denial was defensive, but the treatment was successful in spite of it.)

Therapist: Okay, let me give you some feedback on what I've heard until this point.

Patient: Okay.

Therapist: You've had an incident where your best friend and your girlfriend slept together, and it's very painful to you. I was planning to look at the painful feelings and see how you managed them in a way that either resolved them or caused your pain. But then you went on to tell a whole other aspect of this issue, which makes it look very different to me.

Patient: Which is?

Therapist: Which is that you've been devastated by this apparent betrayal—and I say "apparent betrayal" because you and your girlfriend had explicitly made an agreement at the beginning of the summer that you two could date other people.

Patient: Yes.

Therapist: Now what I'm hearing is that your words, your explicit agreement with her at the beginning of the summer, was not at all what you were feeling inside.

Patient: Yeah.

Therapist: And as the summer went on, you had certain expectations about her, or hopes that she felt the same. But it sounds as though you felt very strongly inside that you didn't want her to have other relationships, and you yourself in fact behaved very differently from your words. You said, "I really didn't want to have other relationships," and yet you had said that to her and led her to believe that you might.

Patient: No, well . . .

Therapist: That it was likely, you see?

Patient: No, I would not say that I had led her believe that I might. I think it was understood from past conversations over the course of the year . . . that she thought it was likely, but certainly much more likely than her, which I think both of us considered so far out in left field as to virtually not be worth discussing.

Therapist: Hm, that she might have a relationship [was so far out of the question that it was not worth discussing].

Patient: That she might . . . that she might . . . because . . .

Therapist: Why would it be virtually not worth discussing? Why would she be so loyal to a man who very likely might not be loyal to her?

Patient: Um . . .

Therapist: You see, I'm wondering about that.

Patient: No, no, I understand that. I think that . . . you see, I think that, um . . .

My point here is that there are some significant problems with closeness and sense of self. He is unable to tell his girl-friend that he wants her to be faithful, and he possibly feels unentitled to do so. But he makes some assumptions that are not at all in line with reality. These are important topics to focus on, but at this point I persevere in focusing on anger because his living arrangements with the friend who betrayed him make this the highest priority. (Later in the session, he tells how afraid of anger he is, in his very convoluted language.)

Patient: I think it was more the perception that if I get very pissed off with this person [early on in a relationhip] and they decide they never want to be with me again, well, then I haven't destroyed anything.

Therapist: Um-hm.

Patient: Whereas in the middle of the relationship, if I blow up at her and we get into a fight and she walks out the door and never comes back, well, shit . . .

Therapist: So anger's frightening to you, [because] you could actually lose the person altogether? There's not a sense that you can lose your temper and feel safe?

Patient: Anger as a whole is frightening to me. It's sort of like I find anger not a particularly appealing emotion.

Anger has taken on a phobic quality for him. It is not a feel-ing that will give him strength to solve a problem. I need to "desensitize" him to his angry feelings, but each time I try to focus on anger, he moves away from it.

Therapist: So it sounds like you get angry, like the rest of us do, and it sounds like when you get angry, there's a force in you, a very strong force—

Patient: Yes, particularly with my family. *[He had told a story of fight-ing with his sister.]* In my relationship with my girlfriend, I tried to do it in a more logical manner. When I get really, truly angry—like after I found out about this [betrayal]— my first instinct is to look for a bag of golf clubs and wrap them all around a tree. . . . And probably the reason I do that—

Therapist: Do you mean literally [doing this—wrapping golf clubs around a tree]?

Patient: If I could, I probably would.

I am beginning to assess his capacity for impulse control. If he has a history of losing his temper and destroying property, I would not proceed with an intense experience of affect because it could lead to acting out. Instead, I would work very cognitively to notice when the smallest signal of anger was arising and teaching him methods to control it. But his history is one of extreme overcontrol of feeling, so it seems appropriate to try to reduce his inhibition somewhat, so that he can experience the anger in fantasy and direct that energy in an adaptive way.

Therapist: Have you [actually] hit a tree with golf clubs?

Patient: No.

Therapist: Uh-huh, but that's the feeling [the wish].

Patient: That's the feeling. And—and I could see a perception that—from really early on, I used to be told by my mother, "Be careful, you don't know your own strength." I don't perceive myself at all as a large person or a strong person, and yet the one reason why I probably never raised my voice in front of my girlfriend is because even the conception of getting angry enough at someone to hit them frightens me so badly that I would never, ever put myself in a situation where I'd even be tempted to hit someone.

This is a good example of an "affect phobia." He finds it very hard to focus on this topic. During this evaluation—which lasts for three hours—he requests a break. When he returns and I ask him what he would like to be called, he says, the following.

Patient: It doesn't really matter, whatever you'd prefer. Because I've long since learned that people will call me whatever they like, regardless of what I say.

Therapist: Regardless of what you say? So you're powerless? You're a nonactor, huh?

This comment about his needs not mattering is an obvious case of his not voicing his needs— not asking for what he wants. He had not voiced his needs to Rebecca over the summer, so I decide to put aside the focus on anger for a few minutes and explore his ability to care for himself.

Patient: No, it's just that I—I hate that people say . . . I introduce myself as Mike, and if they're friends of mine, they call me Mike. Basically, friends call me Mike, and in more formal situations, they call me Michael.

Therapist: Let me just point this out. You prefer to be called Mike, but there's some way that you don't assert yourself sufficiently to get people trained to do what you please.

Patient: Uh—huh.

Therapist: See, there's a dismissal, but in fact you *do* care, because you do have a preference.

Patient: Yeah, I do have a preference.

Therapist: Right, so you do care. But you let yourself fall through the cracks. Can you see that? And it's a small thing, but [here it is happening] between me and you. We need to watch those kinds of things where you give yourself away, don't you think?

Patient: Yeah. No, it's just funny [laughs] because I somehow end up revealing myself in these ways that I never mean to. [Later] I might have said something to offend you or to waste your time.

I am quite struck by the enormity of his lack of entitlement, and I decide to confront it strongly.

Therapist: Wait a minute. It's amazing how you can really dismiss yourself.

Patient: I have no idea. It just would be . . .

Therapist: It's terribly important to understand. You kind of grinned and shrugged it off, and yet that's a tragic statement you've just made. You come here because you've been depressed since you were a boy and very seriously so. Am I wrong on that?

Patient: At times, yeah.

Therapist: Yeah, right. And if you walked away from here, [you're saying] it's *my* time that would be wasted, not *yours*. So [it's like you're saying] you're not worth anything—you don't matter.

Patient: Well, I mean . . . yeah, I mean, essentially . . . essentially I am much more likely always to consider other people in the situation as being more significant than me. My parents have always said this: You will sacrifice yourself for the sake of a friend, regardless of what's going on in your life. And that is true. If a friend calls me up and says, "I need to talk," I will absolutely put down everything I am doing and talk to them.

Therapist: Were you that giving with Rebecca as well?

Patient: Yes.

[later]

Therapist: It's just a wave of sadness going through my body, to think that a young man with so many gifts carries that feeling [that he doesn't matter]—

Patient: Well, it's not so much that. [*He jumps in and interrupts me, just as I am saying something quite emotional, and on his behalf.*]

Therapist: You know, you talk over me, do you notice? You just talk over me. I went into the sadness [of your situation], and you've pulled away from it. There must be so much pain in there.

He goes into a very highly intellectualized rambling, but he gets choked up.

Patient: If you had a perception that the last two hours were somehow treated by me . . . you say, I mean, maybe do you have doubt and confusion. Having doubt would somehow be, I think . . . It's really that I would perceive your . . . my having doubt, and you or your confusion or having the time wasted or having you be having a wave of sadness would more be a perception of disappointing and letting you down.

Therapist: You're here to make *me* feel good about *you*?

Patient: It's not so much that I'm here to make you feel good as much as I'm *not* here to offend you.

Therapist: Hm, you're *not* here to offend me. You're full of pain right now. Can you just stay with the pain that's coming up rather than [using] that quick mind of yours? What's hurting you right now? Just see if you can stay with those feelings. There's a life of pain that we're seeing.

This is exposure to feelings and an attempt to prevent the defensive response of intellectualization—his "quick mind." He speaks very rapidly, and I am trying to slow him down so that he can feel something.

Patient: I'm really . . . [*he becomes choked up with sadness*]

Therapist: Yeah, take your time. It's okay.

Patient *[sighs]*: It's not like what we discussed in the last two hours.

>*He begins to intellectualize again, but I refocus him on the pain.*

Therapist: You're full of pain right now. Where is [the feeling] in your body? Where's the hurt in your body?

Patient: Literally?

Therapist: Literally.

Patient: My chest.

Therapist: Now [it seems] you're holding back, and there's so much in there. Can you put some words on the worst part of it right now and share it with me?

Patient: Sometimes I think that I just *[very quiet, crying]*

Therapist: Yeah.

Patient: I'm just sick of dealing with my own things. That's why I deal with other people's things, and I don't deal with my own. And it's certainly true after all that happened with Mark.

Therapist: So you're constantly having to live from the outside in. Do you know what I mean? Rather than the inside out. You lose yourself.

>*I use this phrase to differentiate internal locus of control from external locus of control. Mike's actions were largely driven by the needs of others—externally. But although this intervention will increase insight, it is not the best thing to do at this point. I should have stayed focused on the painful feelings and deepened that affective experience rather than move to the intellectual analysis of it.*

Patient: Certainly with respect to my best friend, I was amazed that, as things developed and since this all happened, how much I still wanted to make sure that he wasn't pissed off at me and that he wasn't hurt by this. Because I really didn't want to violate the chance of us remaining friends.

Therapist: You're being so good, huh?

Patient: I try to be very nice to people. *[Laughs.]*

Therapist: Well, you sure do. And we can laugh about it. That's a strength in you—that you can make a joke about it. But you know, that's a tragic burden to bear—[having to be so nice, even to those who have betrayed you].

>*I am validating the defense—it is also a strength—but I am*

> *pointing out the costs, too, and bringing us back to the*
> *painfulness of it.*

Patient: Yeah, basically. That's true throughout all relationships in my life.

Therapist: You know, as you talk, my chest is getting tighter and tighter. It's like you're a human slave to others. I mean, isn't that a reason to get depressed over time? There's some quality about it that's obviously oppressive and creates depressive symptoms.

> *Here I self-disclose my own very pronounced reactions to*
> *his story, to highlight the poignancy of his situation.*

Patient: But there is also some quality about it, something that I get back from these people that I need. [End of Initial Evaluation.]

Second Session

In the second session, he explains that his girlfriend and his best friend were the two people he felt the closest to in his life. This encouraged me to focus on how betrayed, and thus angry, he must have felt.

Patient: I guess that a lot of people were surprised that I was so calm when I found this out. And [my best friend] said, "Well, gee, why didn't you hit me?" But you know, when he told me, my first instinct was to kind of fall into his arms and be hugged by him and to . . . and to hug him back, not to hit him.

Therapist: To fall into his arms?

Patient: Not to fall . . . I mean, to—to, like, be held by him, to be comforted by him. One of the things that was so bizarre about this experience is that I found that the two people who I was hurt by were the two people who, in any other crisis in my life, I would have depended on before anybody else, including my family. And so I really at the time felt like there was no one else to turn to except them. I don't ever remember having the urge to hit him. At the same time, I've made passing jokes with people: "Oh, yeah," I'd say, "we kind of had a bloody breakup, especially after she got the ax in her head."

Therapist: So [you moved the angry feeling] into jokes.

Patient: I know that there's some expression of anger in that. But it doesn't ever translate into my thinking about putting an ax in her head.

Therapist: But you *did* think about putting an ax in her head. You had the thought [in the joke].

Patient: Oh yeah, okay, fair enough. The thought *did* pass through my mind.

Therapist: On an intellectual level.

Repeatedly I emphasize that we are exploring feeling in fantasy. It is important to repeatedly make this distinction during the work on anger.

Patient: On an intellectual level.

Therapist: Right, but you haven't let yourself have the full force of that feeling—and there's some real resistance to doing that. I want to make very clear—we're not talking about behavior. *[I repeat the distinction between thoughts and behavior, yet again.]*

Therapist: We're talking about the restriction you place on your own emotional responses, which is amazing. Because you're a powerhouse of a guy. Look at those words: "that bloody breakup," "an ax in her head." Those are vivid and intense and powerful images.

Patient: I always thought it was kind of a pun. I mean—

Therapist: See, you want to make it intellectual, but [those images] come from somewhere.

Patient: Yeah, I know it does.

Therapist: That doesn't come from a passive, ineffectual person.

Patient: No, that's true. I know I need to be angry at them. I know that I need to be vocally and maybe even emotionally violent with him. I think the reason that I didn't hit him, that it didn't occur to me to hit him, is simply because—I mean, this sounds trite to say—I don't believe in fighting. And I've never gotten into a fight, except for this one when I was attacked by four guys and I was beaten up. [I] could have fought back, but I wouldn't have, you know.

Repeatedly throughout this session I comment that we are not working toward hitting anyone. We are only looking at the feelings. But it is noteworthy that he was severely beaten and made no attempt to fight back.

Therapist: So *[back to your best friend]* you thought you'd really like to crack him—that you really hate him. What are you feeling when you remember that? What's in your body? What's the buildup there, as you think about it right now? He's walking out of the room, and you're having "I really hate you" kinds of feelings. Where do you experience that hate?

Patient: I don't know, it kind of makes me—it kind of makes me feel a little tired, actually.

> *Being tired is a sign of inhibition. When someone is angry, the person is activated, not exhausted.*

Therapist: Uh-huh. Is that hate, or is that [tiredness] something else?

Patient: I don't know. It's probably just being fed up with the whole situation.

Therapist: Hm. And that's not hate, is it? It's important. Do you see?

> *Being "fed up" keeps the turmoil within him, and I am trying to help him see that. But it might have been preferable to explore the tiredness by asking, "What makes you feel so tired?"*

Patient: It's not even so much that. I don't know. Maybe it's not even so much that I hate him as I was just feeling . . . I was about to say that . . . I'm really sick of this shit.

Therapist: You've changed the anger now. You've twisted it around so that you're [the one who is] sick. He gets protected. You get slammed. You've got a lot of power in you, but do you see what you're doing? It's back on you. Why do you have to be the sick one? Where's the fight toward him? Let's go back to that.

Patient: Where's the fight?

Therapist: Yes, where's the fight? Where's that feeling [you mentioned before], "I'd like to crack him"?

Patient: I don't know the answer to that.

Therapist: How did your body feel when you wanted to crack him [the other night]?

Patient: Oh, okay, I see what you're saying. Let me just try to recreate the whole thing in my mind. Kind of just, I guess, in my arms, my chest, and my head.

Therapist: You looked tight.

Patient: I get just this supreme burst of energy for a moment. And then, as it kind of comes and then goes, the whole thought kind of dissipates as the surge of energy goes.

Therapist: Let's go back to the surge of energy. See if you can get into that in your thoughts and fantasies here, where it's not going to hurt anybody, and it's going to help you. Let's see if you can. By the way, murderous feelings aren't the only feelings that we have. You know, [we'll also look at] tender feelings, sad feelings. But you've gone off a lot [from anger]. Let's go back to the angry feelings toward him. Try to see if you can bring [the angriest feelings] up. Is that . . . You look like you just don't want to do this.

Patient: No, no.

Therapist: Is there a reluctance you're feeling?

Patient: No, there's not a reluctance. It's just, I'm trying to figure out . . . the question is how do I feel when I get really angry at him? What would I do if he were right in front of me, and I was really angry at him? Well, I—I don't know. Somehow throwing people against the wall always seemed like the most effective thing to me. *[He makes a fist and raises his arm.]*

Therapist: Actually the muscles in your arms are all tight now. Let's see, how would you do that? Just imagine gripping him, and let yourself feel it. Where would you grab him?

> *It would have been good to remind him, again, that we are not talking about doing this in real life but only acting it out in fantasy. I feel sure he knows this distinction, but it still is a good idea to repeat it several times.*

Patient: By his shirt. By the front of his shirt.

Therapist: Um-hm. By his shirt.

Patient: And . . . I'd run him backward into a wall.

Therapist: You'd throw him backward. That's a powerful image, of throwing him backward.

Patient: I'd run him backward into the wall.

Therapist: And then what? What would he do then?

Patient: I don't know. I've never seen Mark in a fight.

Therapist: But he thought he would have slugged you if you treated him the same way—so? What comes to your mind? Where are you going to go with this?

Patient: *[softly]*: [Grab him] by his chest.

Therapist: Is this hard to look at? You know, you're restraining yourself.

Your voice is quiet. There seems to be some discomfort around the angry feelings—which we might expect.

It is important to point out to the patient when there is a pulling back from the anger. In this case, the sudden quieting of the voice indicates some discomfort with the angry feeling.

Patient: Yeah, I mean . . .

Therapist: Let's look at it. Something's coming up right now.

Patient: You mean, like . . . it has to be a balance between beating him and causing him pain, having him know that it's happening. But not—I have no idea. Not killing him.

Therapist: Hm, it's interesting how you pull back. You've gotten quiet, and this is the longest you've been silent since I've known you. *[both laugh]* We can laugh about it, but do you see that we are—

Patient: I was originally going to say, not put him in the hospital, but then I thought about it and decided there would be a certain pleasure if I put him in the hospital.

Therapist: Right, but there's some shrinking back from your power. You just were getting going, and then you pulled back. I keep asking you about the hesitation or the anxiety about it, and you have a very hard time articulating it. I don't think you're conscious of it.

Patient: I don't know quite . . .

Therapist: But your head is bowing.

Patient *[overlapping]*: I don't know quite what you mean.

Therapist: Your stance is usually moving around, but when I got you talking about beating him, you got constricted. It suggests to me there's some real discomfort [with the angry feelings].

Patient: Yeah, I know that. I mean, there probably is.

Therapist: Can you put any words to it? It may not be on the tip of your tongue, that's okay. But what would be the fear here?

This anxiety-regulating intervention follows the exposure to the angry feelings. Exposure typically elicits some inhibitory affect. Then this inhibitory feeling needs to be focused on until it is not such a block to the feeling.

Patient: The fear is that if I go off and hurt someone, I'm responsible for hurting them.

Therapist: You're mixing up action with feeling. We're just talking about *feelings* right now.

Patient: Right.

Therapist: And you're leveling judgment and blame on yourself for feeling.

Patient: I mean, it just—like, I can't . . . I can't go through the process of beating him to death and going, okay, now I've beaten him, and what happens to him? Do I put him in the hospital? Do I kill him? And then go, you know, how does that make me feel? Well, it makes me feel responsible for the fact I put him in the hospital and killed him. Like I don't . . . I can't imagine an actual physical expression of force that I would find appropriately orgasmic in this situation. But I think that . . . like, by running him backward into a wall, I would just like to run him through a series of walls. It's the steady application of force.

This last statement is a conglomeration of fears about feelings, shame about anger, and wishes to act. In my next intervention, I stay focused on the intensity of the feeling.

Therapist: Exactly. And that feels orgasmic, doesn't it?

I intentionally pick up on his strong emotional language to try to keep him exposed to the strong feeling. The sexual implications are explored later in treatment. The other topic we were just discussing is shelved for the moment but we should return to it: his feeling guilt for his wish to put his best friend in the hospital. I often point out that morality should be tied to behavior but not to our inner feelings, because we all have violent feelings at times. But for now we continue with the exposure to angry feelings.

Patient: I think that the only time it would finally become orgasmic is when I collapsed of fatigue. It's just *[very intensely]* I have all this anger toward him, and I could—I could never run him through enough walls. *[He starts to cry.]* No wall would ever replicate the feeling I had when he told me that he had slept with my girlfriend.

Therapist: Well, let's try.

My goal is to help him put the feelings on the fantasied person and take the torment off of himself.

Patient: That will never make him understand that. *[He says this with great intensity, but it is clear that he is containing the turmoil within himself.]*

Therapist: Well, let's turn the tables right now. 'Cause you're [in turmoil]—it's full in you now. Let's try.

Patient: No, I can never kill him, because if I killed him, then I wouldn't have the satisfaction of him living with that.

Therapist: Um-hm. This is your fantasy, let's go on

At times like this I often say, "It's your fantasy. You can make your fantasy whatever you want it to be."

Patient: The only pain that would be an appropriate pain is one that he had to live with.

Therapist: So [it sounds like you want to] violate him and keep him conscious, just on the edge of death. You want to do [this] just short of killing him. So are there torturous feelings coming up along with the murderous feelings. Hm?

I am intentionally presenting images of his doing something physical to keep the feeling in his body rather than on the level of mental revenge.

Patient: Yeah.

Therapist: Look how tight your body is.

Patient: What it is more than anything else is a desire to give him the pain that he gave me.

Therapist: So let's do that right now.

This is an encouragement to face the warded-off angry feelings—continuing the exposure procedure.

Patient: And I can't give him that pain physically, because this was not a physically painful event in my life. *[He is still in enormous turmoil, and it shows in his tone and body language.]*

Therapist: The tears running down your cheeks tell me differently. It's a tremendously physically painful event, emotionally painful. Let's go with it. Let's not argue that. Let's just put some of that pain on him and see how it feels for you. See, you're staying tight. Let's go to it. You keep fighting me on this, and you're the one who stays hurt.

Here I am both trying to prevent the defensive response, and encouraging exposure to the feared feeling.

Patient: I don't—I mean, I guess I don't understand exactly.

Therapist: You do understand exactly. Actually, you have a fantastic perception, you know, understanding of it. You said, "I couldn't slam him through enough walls to feel the pain that I felt." So I challenge you on that. Let's see what you'd have to do.

As a rule of thumb, I try to encourage patients to turn the tables—of course only in fantasy—to the same degree of intensity as the pain they felt. If someone is hit, they will want to hit back. If someone is sadistically treated, they will want to retaliate sadistically—on a feeling level.

Patient: I think the only thing that could ever give him enough pain . . . is if I did to him what he did to me.

Therapist: See, you're taking it away from your feelings. You're taking it back into the realm of humiliation, thought, emotional pain. Let's just stay with running him through the walls, because that's where your energy is. You've gone back to that again and again.

It is typical for patients to construct "mental revenge" of the sort that was done to them. It is natural and human to do so, but in my experience, it does not lead to change in the problem. I intentionally try to translate his experience into bodily feeling, because this is where I have seen change happen. If he is able to feel an energized and powerful anger rather than a victimized anguish, he is going to be able to act much more masterfully in his interpersonal interactions.

Patient: But, I guess what I'm saying is—and this may mean that I'm more twisted than you even thought—the only way I perceive of myself being able to fuck with him enough is by doing to him what he did to me. Like, I don't think that physical pain, he goes to the hospital, he gets over it, he leaves . . .

Therapist: We can look at that later, that's fine. But right now you're avoiding looking at the angry feeling, and it's going to hurt you if it stays bottled in you. You keep saying your anger isn't strong enough, and I'd like to challenge you on that. How would you make your friend feel it at your own hands? You know, with a mind like yours, you keep saying, "Oh, there's nothing I could do." And I challenge you on that.

I have to be quite forceful because this very intelligent and intellectualizing young man will run away from feelings into thoughts immediately if I don't stay focused on the feelings.

Patient: I don't think that there is physical [act] . . . to replicate, to make him feel what I feel. There has to be, in my mind, an idea of a past, and there has to be an idea of the future, and I don't see that in the physical.

Therapist: Well, we've got just a few more minutes, and you can block me, and I'll be useless to you.

This young man is in visible agony, and I don't want to let him go until he can focus some of the angry feelings away from his image of himself onto the image of someone else. I am concerned that if I don't, he will be depressed and in anguish for another week. This is an example of "wrestling with the defenses" to try to effect change.

Patient: No, I don't . . . understand. I just don't understand . . .

Therapist: What you're saying is, your anger is useless. The truth is, you're pulling back from it. There's a sense of the release [that you would get if you let yourself get mad]. You want to give him the pain you felt. Now stay with that.

Patient: I think that if it has to be physical . . .

Therapist: I'm asking you to explore that.

Patient: I guess, I mean—yeah, like I'd run through wall after wall. I'd feel tired, not feel exhausted, just feel like . . .

Therapist: Relieved?

Patient: Yeah, relieved. And like I had hit him enough. And like, after a while, instead of building after each hit, the energy would just go away. And I kind of think I would be out of breath a little. And I would just get up and leave.

Therapist: Yeah, well, how does it feel having that much of this fantasy? Is there any relief in it? In actuality?

Patient: Um, well, I feel a bit energized.

Therapist: You feel a bit energized?

This is a good sign that he is activated rather than tortured.

Patient: Yeah.

Therapist: What else? How does it feel seeing Mark bloody? Bruised?

Patient: I don't feel bad. *[He says this with quiet certainly—but also surprised relief.]*

Therapist: So you're not punishing yourself for your feelings? You're letting yourself have the feelings.

Patient: Yeah, I mean, if I look at him on the floor, I don't feel bad.

Therapist: What are you feeling? I mean, if you look at him on the floor. You don't feel bad. What would be your words to him? What's your take on it?

Patient: Basically that that's probably inadequate but the best approximation.

Therapist: Yeah, this isn't as bad as you should get.

Patient: Like this is "Now you begin to understand."

Therapist: Uh-huh. Now he begins. All right. Let me just stop you right here.

It is close to the end of the second session, and I sum up what we've done. It is not sufficient merely to elicit feelings. The end goal of therapy is to find the inner strength to make the necessary changes. So after every session of experiencing affect, the therapist needs to put a cognitive cap on the feeling—to help the patient appropriately guide the feeling in interpersonal relationships. I begin by cautioning him not to feel forced to deal with Mark if he doesn't feel ready to do so.

Therapist: Be patient now. Wait until you're really easy with these feelings.

Patient: Right.

Therapist: You know it may happen inadvertently, because you two are living together.

Patient: Right.

Therapist: But optimally you and I would work on this over a period of weeks, and you'd get really easy with those feelings, and you wouldn't . . . because right now it's so new. There's a lot more in you. It hasn't gone away completely yet. You're still feeling pumped up?

Patient: Yeah.

Therapist: [Feeling angry and energized] feels better than feeling helpless and anguished, doesn't it?

Patient: Yeah.

Therapist: Remember how you felt when you said, "I want him to feel the pain that I felt"?

Patient: Um-hm.

Therapist: You know, you had tears running down your cheeks. It was intensely painful for you at that moment. And I was having to really tug at you to get you to put [the anger] out on him in imagery. Compare how that felt with how you feel right now.

Patient: Right now I feel—I feel like I could just . . . I don't know, like he's bound to get what he deserves.

Therapist: Rather than your getting the beating.

Patient: Yeah.

Therapist: You've taken the beating for years. You've had depression for years. You've taken the beating 'cause your anger is so over-controlled. Does that make sense to you?

Patient: Um-hm.

Therapist: And you have a lot of hesitation about it. It wasn't your fault. You learned this from the way you were raised, and people were trying to raise you right. But you overcontrolled it to the point where you put yourself in anguish, and you're the one that gets beat up over and over and over again. So you and I are going to work to shift that. You see how this has just been done—this is what the imagery is used for initially.

I am trying to teach him what we are doing—giving him a "map of the territory."

Patient: Hm.

Therapist: Initially just to stop the pain inside of you and then ultimately to resolve, if possible, and process. [End of 2nd Session]

After this session, he goes back to his apartment and feels freed up enough to have a talk with his best friend. There is minimal relief, as very little is said or resolved, so he remains depressed—though less so. This is a sign that the angry scene must be returned to and worked through until he is much easier with these feelings. This is what we do next in the third session. Notice in this following session that he is much more activated with both grief and anger than he was in the second session. It is common to see a patient become more activated—and comfortable with express-ing feeling—with each successive practice.

Third Session

Therapist: What does it mean about his feeling for you?

Patient: It's not that . . . it's not that what he did is not a violation of love and care. The fact of the matter is that I know he cares about me, and I know that he values my friendship, but I just don't see anymore that because of that he deserves my forgiveness. *[With great emphasis, and waving his arms forcefully]* I don't see that I have to work through this with him. I don't see that I have to get beyond this. And I don't see that we have to remain friends anymore, because the fact of the matter is, maybe there is something that he can do that is just too big.

This is a very different presentation from the previous two sessions. Mike seems much more activated, but he still reports that he was depressed the night before. This is a signal to me that his anger at his best friend may still in part be blocked.

Therapist: You have a lot of force in you about this, and there's a lot of anger in your words. Are you aware of it? But there's also some pain and depression in there too. Am I right on that? You said that last night you got to this point but then you just got depressed. Is that correct?

Patient: Right. Some days I feel like my life is like a movie and everything is just kind of a continuing saga that develops, and life changes, and life becomes this or that. And it just seems kind of a sad and long film. A sad development that we go through all these years of happiness together, we come to college, we get along great with friends, we're all best friends, we all get along *[starting to cry]*, and then he leaves. And everybody knows why. Everybody knows what's going on. It just seems so—so sad. Like life is this uncontrollable process *[a movie]* that you just watch go by. Everything that happened with her, and you don't have much control over it, and then you just—just *[crying hard]* . . . I don't understand what happened. I don't understand what I'm supposed to do now that my best friend isn't someone who I can be friends with. I want to be able to stand up and say, no, it's time for me not to equivocate every relationship I have, to try and preserve every relationship I have. I want to stand up

for myself and say—this is the time when I really need to say—
"You fucked up too big. I don't care to have you in my life anymore." But I don't see how to do that. I don't understand how
to continue after I've done that.

Therapist: What's the worst part of it? If you do risk standing up to him?
*This is an anxiety-regulating intervention to help him bear
losing his lifelong friendship.*

Patient: It's awful [to lose someone so important]. *[crying hard].* It's
all of me.

Therapist *[Quietly]*: It feels huge to you. It's all of you. *[I pause for a
long time while he is sobbing.]* Tell me about that. It's all of
you. How do you mean?

Notice that Mike is not conflicted about grieving (though many people
are). When Mike and I reach the emotional separation that happens
because he is able to let himself feel how angry he is at Mark, the grief
comes naturally and fully.

Later in the session Mike had to begin to see that he had some power
in the choices he made in his life—that he was not just a sitting duck.

Therapist: You were so animated when you first started this session, and
now you look like you're suffering quite a bit. You're tired. Is
this how you were feeling last night? Is your head hurting?

Patient: Something always comes back to keep me. . . .

Therapist: Who's doing it? What's coming back to get you right now?
Who's hurting you right now?

Patient: He is.

Therapist: Who is hurting you? Your friend?

Patient: Yeah.

Therapist: He's not here right now. Who's the only person who can do
this to you emotionally?

Patient: I guess myself.

Therapist: It's really important to be aware of that, because it gives you
the control.

Patient: I see.

Therapist: It's a reflexive habit of a lifetime. So many of us are taught this
way of taking it on ourselves and dragging ourselves down.
True, it doesn't feel like you're making a conscious choice, but

nonetheless, the only person who can make you feel this bad is you. Not anyone else. I mean, your friend can do all kinds of things, but you could be furious with him. You have an alternative. And you have felt more energized and better when you have felt furious. Am I right on that?

Patient *[softly]*: Yeah.

Therapist: You have a terrible pattern of a downward spiral and pulling yourself down. That's been lifelong, hasn't it?

Patient: No, not that I pulled myself down when I was depressed. It just happened.

We have to return to the angry imagery until he is able to leave the session and not get depressed. In some cases, it is necessary to continue to focus on anger for another six or eight sessions, but in this case, one more session is sufficient to make him comfortable enough with the feeling to use it adaptively outside the session. Adaptive and authentic interpersonal expression of feeling is the ultimate goal of this treatment.

Patient: I always think I have him inside of me. I trusted [him] completely. I encouraged him to live with my girlfriend because I believed there was *no way* this would ever happen. I gave him all the trust I had. I called him. I supported him in his work over the summer. I have always tried to be there for him, to lend myself for him. And then he did this, and I don't know that I care to have a friendship anymore. I don't think that he deserves it. I think that loyalty and honesty are the way you come through it. And not only did he . . .

He automaticallly goes into intellectualizing about the anger, and I have to repeatedly focus him on bodily feeling. He is complaining rather than feeling.

Therapist: Yeah. Now what are you feeling right now? Inside?

Patient *[yelling]*: Fucking furious. Not only did he do this to me, not only did he go and sleep with my girlfriend, then he bullshits about what goes on. . . . He tells me one thing, and then I find out another thing is so *[Still yelling].*

Therapist: So if he were right here in front of you right now, what would you be doing with this fury?

Patient: Screaming at him. *[He is writhing around in the chair—but he looks terribly tormented, not freed up.]*

Therapist: Well, take it out on him, not on yourself! How do you put that out on him? You know, you're turning away. How would you grab him? Where's the fight in you right now? Just go for that.

Patient: He . . . [He continues to writhe in the chair, rubbing his head with his hands and looking tortured.]

Therapist: See, you're in turmoil. How do we put that out on him, not you? Let's beat up him, not you. If you poured it out on him—there's so much in you, isn't there?

Patient [heavy breathing]: He comes walking in, and he sees me, and it's like nothing's wrong! [Said with great emphasis.]

Therapist: Yeah.

Patient: Like, okay, we've moved past this. Well, bullshit, we haven't moved past this. [He is yelling these words and moving all over the place in the chair—as though he cannot bear to sit still with the force of feeling that is coming up.]

Therapist: Okay, so if you imagine grabbing him, what would you say to him? How would you grab him?

Patient: I've done this before in here.

This is true, but he hasn't done it as forcefully or passionately.

Therapist: Okay, let's see what you can do if you let out all that energy. It's a huge amount of energy.

Patient: He comes walking in like he can make everything right, like nothing went wrong, like this is somehow forgivable. Well, guess what? It's not!

He yells these words and is enormously activated, but I need to make sure he is consciously feeling the anger, not just venting helpless frustration.

Patient: It is not forgivable. It is not a forgivable action. In living with her, he had my trust, like I never thought that he'd do this. I never thought this was a possibility because I trusted him. Would I encourage him to live with my girlfriend if I thought he was going to go off and sleep with her? It wasn't just my girlfriend, she was like the world. [He is very angry in his tone—but is still visibly tormented. It is as though a lot of feeling is coming up through massive, self-attacking defenses.]

Therapist: What do you do to him when he comes walking in? That really makes you mad. Let's look at what you do to him with those impulses in you right now.

Patient *[yelling]*: He walks in and I just throw him against a wall. I just want to . . . *[Head bent down and in hands—very tortured looking—and writhing in pain.]*

Therapist: Yeah, go ahead.

Patient: I just throw him against the wall because I'm so pissed off. And I'm so sick of his shit. *[Yelling, crying, and holding his head in his hands, as he moves his head back and forth.]*

Note that he is crying defensive tears that are a result of blunted anger. The clue that the tears are defensive—or self-attacking rather than self-soothing—is that he makes statements about his own pain ("I'm so sick of this shit"). These feelings may be in part grief about losing his best friend, but they are so largely a "victim response" that the therapist needs to continue to encourage him to direct the anger away from himself. On the videotape, he looks as though he is tearing his hair out.

Therapist *[very animated]*: Let's not tear *your* hair out. Are you tearing *his* hair out? Let's think, what do you want to do to *him*?

Patient *[sobbing]*: *writhing all over the seat, very dramatically. This is not grief that resolves loss, but a tortured depressive crying.*

Therapist: Uh-huh. So let's . . . yeah. So let's let you have at least that thought. 'Cause you're getting beat up right now. Let's . . . So where do you hit him?

Patient *[sobbing]*: His face. And I throw him against the wall, and I— I want him gone.

Therapist: Yeah, you want him gone. So let's just hit him, and—

Patient: I won't be able to stop until he's gone.

Therapist: So let's let yourself hit him as hard as you can, and let's get it all out.

Patient *[sobs]*: I don't want him around anymore!

Therapist: Uh-huh. Let's just make you easy with these feelings. There are just feelings. You don't have to be so afraid of them. Huh? Do you just see yourself pounding on him?

Patient *[through sobs]*: Yes.

Therapist: What's the worst part of that right now?

Patient: Nothing.

Therapist: Let's let yourself go with it. Let's just imagine you pounding with all the force in you. There's so much force in you. You said you wanted to kill him. You want him out of here. Can you imagine letting yourself do that, because that's the turmoil in you right now? These murderous impulses toward him. And we're just looking at the feelings. That's all they are. What's in your thoughts right now?

I am saying these words as he sits with his head in his hands. But now he appears calmer. He is no longer writhing in his seat

Patient: I don't feel bad.

Therapist: You don't feel bad for having these feelings?

Patient: For killing him.

Therapist: You don't feel bad for having feelings of killing him?

Patient: If I beat him to death, it doesn't matter. I don't feel bad.

Therapist: Well, let's look at that. He's lying there on the ground, you've beaten him to death, and you're just looking at him. What would you say then? Let's just imagine as he's dying, what would you say to him? What would you want to see in his eyes?

This intervention is intended to try to reach the grief of the loss of the relationship. In this case, it works very powerfully.

Patient: *[sobbing hard now, but the tears do not come with negative self-statements. They seem like genuine grief.]*

Therapist: What brings the tears now?

Patient: He's gone.

Therapist: He's gone. What you see is that he's dead? And he's not there anymore? This person was always there. *[The indicator that his tears represent grief rather than defensive self-attack is that his thoughts are predominantly with the loss of Mark— not with what he himself did wrong, or how his life is destroyed.]*

Patient: *[sobs]* [End of 3rd Session]

Notice that he is much less conflicted about grief than about anger. He sobs openly and fully about the loss of Mark. There were some conflicts in the second session about losing part of himself if he gave up Mark. But we worked through that fairly quickly and it does not get in the way now.

In the fourth session we continue the grief about his loss of his friendship—and discover that their boyhood friendship and playfulness had offered him tremendous sanctuary from the tumultuous conflict of his family.

It was after this session that dramatic changes began to take place that are still in effect years later. His anger had been freed up enough for him to comfortably speak with his best friend in a way that felt satisfying to him. A few weeks later he asked his friend to move out. He told him he was still open to talking about this problem between them and wanted to resolve it. But during the coming months, his friend never approached him. This was further cause for mourning—not only the betrayal, but the realization that his lifelong friend could not grow with him. He mourned this greatly.

A few sessions later he reported changes in reaction to the anger:

Patient: I don't have to answer to a whole bunch of people. I don't have to justify where I'm going. I don't have to explain all these things to a bunch of people. I can just go do it. I can feel this, or I can have that. That newer sense of myself as a person—

Therapist: Yeah.

Patient: That has made me feel a lot better about me. It hasn't made me feel like [doing schoolwork] particularly much more, but it has made me feel better about making decisions. I'm kind of feeling like, "This is where I'm off duty, see everybody later."

Therapist: So you took the ball and ran with it, then.

These changes followed what he called "three long sessions," but they served to free him up enough to function at school and do the work of therapy. Therapy continued for a total of 20 sessions, during which we did extensive work on his sense of self as well as on closeness and how he related to people.

The first three sessions focused on anger, as transcribed above. In the fourth session Mike deeply grieved the loss of Mark. The fifth through eighth sessions focused on his sense of self and how he gave himself away to people. He had said to me in the first session, "My life is a movie. Anyone can write it." I dealt with this briefly when I focused on his lack of entitlement around asking people (in this case, me) to call him by the name he wanted. In these later sessions, I readdressed this issue of his feelings not mattering in greater depth. His main pattern was that he lost his own desires to others. In fact, he had a history of giving far too much in relationships. We traced this pattern back to his childhood, where his mother expected him to be excessively sensitive to her and his sisters. Furthermore, his mother had taught him to greatly dislike all things "male" or "aggressive," so that he in fact was "disgusted" by his own needs almost totally. We traced this pattern throughout his relationships, from early life to the present, and we did a lot of cognitive restructuring around his belief that maleness is bad. We redefined aggression versus assertive, authentic responding and looked for effective male models in his life. During this time his sense of entitlement and compassion for himself grew.

In the ninth session he referred to me as his "universal advocate" and said that my support felt like "unconditional love." When I asked him how it felt to have this support in his life, he first said that it felt "unnatural," and then he became sad and tearful, but he had a hard time discussing it. In the next five sessions we focused on his loneliness since childhood and his longing for closeness with others. His view of others began to change, and he began "writing his life."

In the fifteenth session he reported feeling a lot less depressed. Of his interactions with friends, he happily reported, "I made something go my way!" He was seeing very clearly the neglect of his early life—how his parents were never home and how hard this was for him. His compassion for himself increased, and his ability to care for himself, and to ask for reciprocity from others, was much improved.

In the final four sessions (16–19) we focused on his relationship with his parents. He had always felt that he did not matter to them. When I suggested that they come in for a session, it precipitated a crisis. He was certain that they would never take the time from their busy schedules to drive three hours to my office. In fact, they were eager to do so, but he had never asked for this type of attention. This session helped him see that they were far more devoted to him than he had realized, but that he needed to ask loudly and clearly for them to respond to him.

At the termination of treatment in the twentieth session, I asked him what had helped him the most.

Patient: The fact that I could come in here and just get really [angry]. And, in some ways, that's what I did [when I came in here] last fall, when I got really angry with him. I had someone I could scream and yell at, and I could get out the screaming and yelling that I needed to do in a lot of ways—and get me in a position where I could really understand and feel okay with the fact that I was really pissed off.

Therapist: So feeling okay with being pissed off is what [helped alleviate your depression].

Patient: Yeah. I mean, when this first started happening [I was uncomfortable]. I was concerned. You were talking to me a lot about how important it was to allow myself to be angry, and I was kind of concerned that I was being sold a product that I didn't really want to buy.

Therapist: Right.

Patient: And it was especially of concern because it was over someone so important to me. But I don't feel that way anymore.

Therapist: What changed about that? [What made you decide to go along with me?]

Patient: I was desperate. I was feeling so bad that I had nothing to lose. And I had no alternatives. Now I realize that I don't miss my best friend. I miss our friendship, but I don't miss having him around. You know, I haven't seen him yet. I haven't talked to him, thought about him a little. But, you know, I went out last night and saw friends. And what I'm realizing is that [in losing the friendship] what I lose is someone who I really, right now, don't mind losing, and what I gain is strength and a confidence to take more control. I haven't been [depressed]. I walked around Wednesday when I got to campus and did errands all day and just kind of sang all day. I haven't been this energetic since, I don't know, since my first semester in college probably.

The point is that in relatively few sessions, we were able to begin to reverse a lifelong character trait of passivity and severe depression. Not everyone has the strength to work this deeply and quickly, but this young man did.

It bears repeating that anger is not the only focus in this treatment. In fact, we spent only three sessions on anger but six sessions on his sense of self, six sessions on grief and/or longing for closeness, and four sessions on this relationship with his parents and siblings. But I have highlighted the work on anger in this chapter for the following reasons:

- Freeing up conflicted anger often helps alleviate depression. My colleagues and I see this over and over again, and it needs to be documented. This case was a dramatic example of how anger work can rapidly lift a depression.
- Working with vivid angry images is often extremely difficult for patients. We need to help them face and bear these feelings.
- Working with angry imagery is also extremely difficult for therapists, and we need careful study and training in these powerful and effective techniques.

Obviously, the anger work *alone* would not have resulted in the long-term changes that transpired. The subsequent work dealing with his care for self as well as his relationships with others was essential to maintaining his changes. But since anger may be the most difficult of these feelings to work with, I have highlighted it here.

At three-year follow-up, he is in graduate school and working energetically in a field that he loves. He no longer feels depressed and has not needed antidepressant medication. He has built a new set of friendships that are more balanced and has stopped being involved with women for whom he has to do all the giving.

Reference

McCullough-Vaillant, L. (1997). *Changing character: Short-term anxiety-regulating psychotherapy for restructuring defenses, affects, and attachments.* New York: Basic Books.

6

Depth-Oriented Brief Therapy: Accelerated Accessing of the Coherent Unconscious

Bruce Ecker and Laurel Hulley

Introduction: Combining "Brief" and "Deep"

The dexterity of process and the swiftness of change that were made possible by the nonpathologizing brief and systemic therapies emerging since the 1960s come at a great price: avoidance of the unconscious and emotional dimensions of human experience. Revolutionary as these new movements were (see, for example, Watzlawick, Weakland, & Fisch, 1974; Hoffman, 1981; de Shazer, 1985), they still held to a potent fragment of the psychoanalytic legacy—the presupposition that brevity and depth are mutually exclusive. Believing this to be a false dichotomy and working to fully operationalize the clinical application of constructivism, we have developed a therapeutic system—depth-oriented brief therapy or DOBT (Ecker & Hulley, 1996, 2000)—in which going straight into the unconscious roots of symptom production is the very means of making the work so effective that it becomes brief.

The therapeutic strategies of DOBT are based on its core principle of symptom production, *symptom coherence*. That is, a symptom or problem is produced by a person because he or she harbors at least one unconscious construction of reality—one set of reality-defining themes, purposes, meanings, and frames—in which the symptom is compellingly necessary to have, despite the suffering or trouble incurred by having it. Conversely, when there is no longer any construction within which the presenting symptom is necessary, the person ceases producing it.

At the start of therapy, of course, the client views the symptom as having no coherence at all. She or he regards the symptom as senseless and valueless, something involuntary and victimizing, laden with negative meanings about the self or others (bad, sick, stupid, crazy, deficient). In DOBT this set of initial predictable views is referred to as the client's *anti-symptom position*—*anti* meaning simply "against" having the symptom. But clinical experience shows that this is an incomplete account of the client's emotional relationship to the symptom.

DOBT is based on the empirical finding that the coherence of the symptom—how having it is *necessary*—is inevitably present in a very separately held, unconscious position of the client. We refer to this as the client's *pro-symptom position*—*pro* in the sense of being "for" having the symptom. The themes and purposes in this pro-symptom construction of reality constitute the deep sense and strongest emotional significance of the symptom in the client's world of meaning. To find the client's pro-symptom position is to find *the emotional truth of the symptom*.

The principle of symptom coherence should not be narrowly construed as merely a function-of-the-symptom model. It is far more comprehensive than that and applies to the production of functionless as well as functional symptoms (Ecker & Hulley, 2000). Which type the symptom is becomes apparent in DOBT, empirically and nonspeculatively, as the necessitating construction is revealed.

We will first describe DOBT's therapeutic strategy and several techniques that implement it. We will then indicate the symptoms, problems, and clients with whom this approach is applicable. Next we will provide case examples from individual and couples therapy. Our final remarks form the closing section.

Strategies of Depth-Oriented Brief Therapy

A threefold therapeutic strategy defines DOBT: *discovering* the client's unique, unconscious constructions that require the symptom; *integrating* those constructions, making them fully accessible by virtue of being routinely conscious to the client; and *transforming* them, so that the symptom is no longer necessary. The work moves recursively among these three activities, following no rigid sequence, until the client has stopped producing the symptom.

Carrying out this strategy accurately and briefly requires methods that are both *experiential* and *phenomenological*. The reason for this is basic: in order for a person to change a construction of reality, he or she must first access it, and *constructions are actually accessed only by fully entering into them as a subjective experience.* This process requires the therapist to work phenomenologically—that is, to work entirely within the meanings that make up the client's constructions—and refrain from making interpretations or in any way imposing meanings foreign to those constructions (such as "better" narratives, trick reframes, DSM diagnoses, etc.).

The terms *construction* and *construct* as we use them refer to any representation of any aspect of reality. They include emotional, perceptual, and kinesthetic representations as well as verbal-cognitive ones. (On the constructivist concept of representation, see Mahoney, Miller, & Arciero, 1995.)

The therapist begins the work by providing accurate empathy for the client's suffering (his or her anti-symptom position) and clarifying what the client regards as the symptom—the specific thoughts, feelings, behaviors, and/or circumstances the client wants changed but has been unable to change. The discovery work then begins, and it is guided by this central logic: *What construction exists that makes the symptom more necessary to have than not to have?* This search has four variations:

- How, and in what context, does the symptom express an important need or priority in the client's world?
- How is the symptom an actual success for the client, rather than a failure? To what unrecognized problem is the symptom a solution, or an attempt at a solution?

- What unwelcome or dreaded consequences would result from living *without* the symptom? What would happen if the symptom didn't occur?
- How would the client have to change so that the symptom would cease to occur, and how is it important to the client *not* to make that change?

These guiding questions define how the therapist thinks, listens, and navigates within the client's material, but they are *not* used as point-blank questions. The real answers to these questions are truly unconscious, and the therapist's task is to use skills and methods that *elicit* the key material that answers these (unasked) questions experientially and rapidly. The goal of the discovery work is for the *therapist* to understand the emotional truth of the symptom very clearly: the client's specific themes and purposes that necessitate the symptom.

On the basis of that clarity, the therapist then ushers the client into *integrating* this material. Symptoms are generated by living as though their necessitating emotional truth is not the case. Integration reverses this: The client lives in direct awareness of how the symptom's emotional truth *is* the case. Once the client's pro-symptom emotional reality has been discovered, we "pitch a tent" right there. We "set up camp" and go nowhere else, for several sessions if necessary, so that the client comes to experience every occurrence of the problem or symptom *from* and *in* the emotional reality of how and why, in the client's world of meaning, that symptom is necessary. A remarkable experiential shift results: The client discovers that the mysterious power of the symptom to persist is nothing other than his or her own power to persist in carrying out themes and purposes that feel urgent. In a word, the client experiences *agency* in relation to the symptom. It is as though the involuntary muscle whose flexing produces the symptom has become a voluntary muscle. The suffering entailed in having the symptom is real, but is worth enduring because it is far preferable to the much worse suffering expected from living *without* the symptom. None of this is apparent from the client's initial, anti-symptom view of the problem, but when the client integrates his or her pro-symptom position, it becomes not only apparent but vividly real—not as an interpretation or reframe received from the therapist, but as the client's own emotional truth, discovered (not invented) in the sessions.

When the coherence and deep sense of the symptom have become self-evident, former notions of being defective, irrational, and powerless are dispelled. This natural depathologizing is a significant shift in the client's view of self and is one of the more important and broad therapeutic effects of this approach, beyond symptom relief.

Transformation of the client's pro-symptom construction, ending symptom production, frequently occurs spontaneously during sustained integration. This process can be understood intuitively: People are able to change a position that they (experientially) know they have, but they are unable to change a position that they do *not* know they have. Every individual, as the creator/installer/authenticator of his or her own reality-defining constructs, has the capacity to revise or dissolve those constructs but is quite unconscious of wielding that power or of having already used it to set up versions of reality that are now causing problems.

If integration does not spontaneously trigger transformation, the therapist applies the following methodology to do so. First the therapist prompts the client into vividly accessing the already-discovered and integrated target of transformation, the pro-symptom emotional reality. Then, simultaneously and along with it in the *same field of awareness,* the therapist prompts the client to access and vividly experience a different, compelling construction of reality that sharply disconfirms the pro-symptom construction. Faced with incompatible constructions of reality in the same field of awareness, the client will revise or dissolve pro-symptom constructs in order to restore consistency (a process of schema revision described by Piaget, 1971; Kelly, 1955; Festinger, 1957).

Techniques

As a therapeutic system, DOBT is defined by the strategies already described, carried out within the assumption of symptom coherence, not by any particular set of techniques. Of the techniques we regularly use, some have been created for DOBT, but many others are adapted from various experiential modalities, such as Gestalt, focusing, Jungian, Ericksonian, inner child work, mind-body communication, NLP (neurolinguistic programming), EMDR, and so on.

As used in this approach, the term *experiential* means inhabiting the emotional reality of the client's pro-symptom position, truly accessing it subjectively and not merely talking insightfully to the therapist *about* that emotional reality. Such accessing, which may or may not involve intense emotion or catharsis, is brought about through simple tasks designed to cause the client to "bump into" unconscious constructions arising directly in experience. Then, with coaching from the therapist, the client deepens into this material and further "unpacks" it. For example, rather than having a client talk *about* his anger toward his father, the therapist asks him to express the words of anger directly to his image of his father.

Effective use of experiential techniques in DOBT requires skills of cueing and evoking imaginal, subjective process, and of guiding a client's attention to become focused and absorbed into selected features of subjective experience. (For research on the use of concrete, vivid language to foster the accessing of nonverbal, emotional constructions, see Martin, 1991; Watson, 1996.)

Most of the following techniques are illustrated in the case examples later in this chapter and so are described only briefly here.

Engagement is a simple but important precondition for the successful accessing of pro-symptom positions. It consists of having the client *imaginally place him- or herself in a scene or circumstance in which the symptom is or would normally be occurring*. Then the client's pro-symptom position, though still unconscious, is actively *engaged* and is most ready to be brought into conscious experience. Engagement is of course already established whenever the symptom is actually occurring in the session (as when the symptom is presently occurring in relation to the therapist or others).

Symptom deprivation is used to discover the unwelcome or dreaded consequences that would result from living without the symptom. The client is asked to imaginally experience being without the symptom in the very circumstance in which she or he normally produces the symptom. Because the symptom is in some way highly important to have, being without it is likely to give rise to some new dilemma or distress. The nature of this dilemma or distress begins to reveal the specific themes and purposes that make having the symptom necessary. (Symptom deprivation is not to be confused with the "miracle question" central to solution-focused brief therapy. Although both techniques prompt the client to construct and sample a symptom-free state, the strategies and goals they serve are paradigmatically different.)

Cycling builds upon the discovery technique of symptom deprivation to achieve integration. In symptom deprivation the client finds that some unwelcome experience has developed as a result of (imaginally) being symptom-free. For cycling, the client is then asked to imagine having the symptom again, and discovers with surprise that the unwelcome feature disappears. The experience of agency then dawns upon him or her—the experience of having a strong purpose for producing the symptom, namely, to avoid that unwelcome consequence of not producing it. The client can be cycled in and out of having the symptom several times, if necessary.

Imaginal interaction is a large group of techniques in which the client focuses attention on an image formed in imagination—often some significant person or some part or aspect of the client's own psyche or body—and then speaks to and interacts with that image, and regards it as having its own autonomous responses. Disowned pro-symptom material can often be brought into awareness in this way, as in experiential dreamwork, inner child work, two-chair dialogue, or mind-body communication, to name a few examples.

Verbal magnet techniques use a simple but well-designed verbalization to attract unconscious emotional constructions into consciousness. In *sentence completion,* the therapist composes and gives the client the first part of a sentence to say out loud. The client does so without prethinking how the sentence will end; notices whatever completing words spontaneously arise in his or her mind; and says them. It is a remarkable fact of clinical experience that fully unconscious emotional themes and purposes cannot resist the temptation to complete a well-chosen sentence fragment. Certain phrases press forth with a life of their own, sometimes even before the client consciously grasps their significance. As adapted for use in DOBT (which differs from other uses—see Branden, 1971; Gumina, 1980), the wording of the offered sentence fragment needs to be concise, concrete, and evocative of the emotional necessity of having the presenting symptom. The client says the fragment over and over, each time seeing what else arises to complete it.

Another simple verbal magnet is the *overt statement.* The client makes a succinct, highly personal, declarative statement of the material that has emerged so far, directly to the emotionally relevant figures, either visualized or in the flesh, or to the therapist. As a result, the client subjectively deepens into the verbalized theme. Unconscious material closely linked to the verbalized piece then comes into awareness, and the client then forms an overt statement of this new material. The process repeats, in effect reeling into awareness one linked construct after another (a method we term *serial accessing*).

The therapist can also compose and offer the client a complete *trial sentence*. This allows the client to sample subjectively material that the therapist infers or hypothesizes to be present, in order to determine experientially if it *is* accurate, that is, an emotionally true fit to the client's existing constructions. The therapist might say, "There's a sentence I'd like you to try out saying, in order for you to see if it fits and feels true for you, or change it in any way to *make* it true if it's off in some way. The sentence is, . . ." The content of a trial sentence should be closely linked in meaning to already-conscious material. If the sentence does adequately verbalize an emotional truth, the client will immediately feel a resonance in saying it.

Between-session tasks are created at the end of every session for the purpose of maintaining and/or furthering integration of newly conscious material, which otherwise tends to submerge again into unconsciousness. Integration is not complete until the pro-symptom themes and purposes have become routinely conscious parts of the client's daily life, especially whenever the symptom or problem is happening.

Our mainstay between-session task is the twice-daily reading of an *index card* on which is written succinct, candid words of the client's emotional truth. The phrasing is generated collaboratively so as to best capture the client's felt sense of meaning, but it should be the therapist who physically writes the words. At the beginning of the next session, the therapist asks what the client experienced in staying in touch with the emotional truth on the card.

Another between-session task is a nightly five-minute *review of the day* in which the client identifies any situation in which the symptom occurred and what it was in that situation that triggered pro-symptom themes and purposes known from the in-session work—in other words, how having the symptom was necessary in that situation. The client logs this information, using short phrases that will aid memory, and brings this record to the next session to review with the therapist.

In the task of *using the symptom as signal*, the therapist explains that whenever the symptom now begins to occur, it is a *signal* to actually *experience*, right in the moment, the emotional truth of its necessity, despite its very real costs. For success in this task, it is important to include in the session an imaginal rehearsal of the symptom happening and of recognizing it as a signal. Also, the therapist gives the client an index card on which is written (always with first-person immediacy) the theme and purpose necessitating the symptom, to be read upon noticing the signal—the symptom—occurring.

Disconfirmation techniques are used for transformation of pro-symptom constructs when integration alone has not spontaneously brought this about. As already noted, the strategy consists of having the client experience subjectively both the pro-symptom emotional reality and some other, incompatible construction of reality simultaneously, in the same field of awareness. The experiential quality of the disconfirmation is essential and is not achieved merely by attempting to refute, convince, or "correct" the client by contrasting "irrational beliefs" with "rational" ones; or by strategically maneuvering, shaping, or paradoxing a client into new behaviors. The attitude of the therapist in DOBT is one of cooperating with the *client's* enormous power to maintain or dissolve constructions of reality. An experiential disconfirmation cues the client's psyche to use its own native, self-organizing power to revise or dissolve constructs so as to restore a consistent reality.

Disconfirmation techniques differ mainly in terms of whether the source of the incompatible new constructs is external or internal. *External* disconfirming constructs can come from a family member during a session, the therapist, a book, or daily life happenstance. The therapist must guide the client's attention so as to hold the new construct in the same field of awareness with the pro-symptom material it disconfirms, transparently inviting the client if necessary to "let in" the new material in order to feel this juxtaposition. We call this process *construct substitution*.

Internal disconfirming constructs come from one of the client's own other positions—either a construct that the client already possesses but has held apart from the pro-symptom construction, or one that he or she creates with the therapist's coaching. A number of seemingly different techniques can carry out this process of *connecting positions,* such as inner child work; Gestalt two-chair work; experiential dreamwork; cross-linking techniques of NLP; empowered reenactment techniques; and identity-exchange role-play in couple and family therapy.

Trauma-resolution techniques are required if symptoms of PTSD or the emerging content of the material indicates that the pro-symptom emotional reality contains trauma. In such cases, the therapist does *not* "pitch a tent" because sustained, explicit integration is likely to be only retraumatizing. Instead, the therapist applies specialized techniques effective for dissolving traumatic reality-constructions. Three techniques we have found effective are EMDR (eye movement desensitization and reprocessing), TIR (traumatic incident reduction), and empowered reenactment. Safe, successful use of these techniques requires proper training and so we will not attempt to describe them here (see Wylie, 1996a, 1996b, for an accessible account of a comparative study of innovative trauma-dispelling techniques).

Clinical Indications for DOBT

We have had consistent success using depth-oriented brief therapy for time-effectively dispelling anxiety, depression, panic, agoraphobia, attachment problems, attention difficulties, low self-esteem, complicated bereavement, sexual problems, underachievement, procrastination, sequalae of childhood abuse, adult eating disorders, and a wide range of interpersonal, couple, and family problems (Ecker & Hulley, 1996, 1998a, 1998b, 1998c, 1998d, 2000). DOBT is highly suitable as the therapy component of drug and alcohol treatment programs because of its focus and speed in getting to the underlying psychology driving the addictive behavior.

DOBT does not require high-level verbal/conceptual/analytical insight on the part of the client, because the process is experiential and phenomenological. For this reason, it is applicable to diverse socioeconomic, cultural, and age groups, including children. Everyone lives in his or her own constructions of experiential-emotional reality and has the native ability to place attention on these habitually unattended constructions and subjectively experience and know them.

DOBT is also applicable with the majority of clients presenting the global, rigid patterns of "character disorder." With such clients, the work tends to be less brief than usual, though still far briefer than if traditional in-depth modalities were used. In DOBT the aim is for the *therapist's* assumptions and methods not to limit the pace of the work, and to proceed at the pace that the *client* can tolerate. DOBT is unlikely to be effective for clients at the most severe end of the spectrum.

Case Example:
Individual Therapy

Ted, 33, described himself laughingly as "a drifter." He had dropped out of vocational training years ago and had never held a job for more than a few months. He said, "I'm getting nowhere. It's like I just can't keep at it in anything. Kinda like, what's the use, you know? And then I give up and change to something else, and then it goes the same with that." His chronic aimlessness had finally started to alarm him. The therapist set out to discover how and why this symptom of "getting nowhere" was actually necessary for him. The transcript begins ten minutes into the first session. Techniques demonstrated include symptom deprivation, sentence completion, trial sentence, imaginal interaction, overt statement, connecting positions and between-session index card.

First Session

Therapist: I wonder if, for a minute or two, you'd be willing to take a kind of glimpse down the road of achievement, just in imagination. I'd like you to just imagine that you've had a good job for over a year, and you've just been told you've been doing good work and you've gotten a raise. *[Pause.]* Can you sort of try on that reality for a minute, and tell me what you notice it feels like?

Ted: Sounds great. Sure would solve my money problems.

Therapist: Okay, good, keep going. Actually imagine it—doing so well holding that job. What else comes up for you in that reality?

Ted: *[Pause]* Probably get my father off my back.

Therapist: How does it get him off your back?

Ted: *[Short laugh]* Things aren't so great between me and him. I mean, he's always telling me, "You know, there's nothing in life you can't have. If you really want something, you can get it." That's his attitude. And so I've kind of got all this pressure on myself, like I should be able to just head straight for something and reach the goal. So it's like, why am I not getting it, what's happening? What's wrong with me? There must be something really wrong with me, is how I feel. *[Describes a childhood and adolescence full of being criticized, blamed, and shamed by father. There was no physical abuse.]* Even if he, like, broke something of *mine,* if I just mention, "What happened?" he'd just tear me down.

Therapist: Mmm-hm *[pause.]* If you're willing, would you go back into that reality you were trying on? You've held a job for over a year and you've been doing good work and you've gotten a raise. *[Pause.]* And then you tell your dad the good news. Imagine actually telling him—maybe by phone, maybe face to face, whatever feels right—telling him, "Dad, I've done good work this whole year, and I've been given a raise. And I wanted you to know how well I'm doing." See how it feels to tell that to Dad. Right to Dad.

Ted: *[Gazes at floor in silence, then gives a short laugh]* You know, I don't know why, but what you're asking me to say makes me really *edgy.* I can't even remember it.

Therapist: Edgy? You get real edgy when you start to tell Dad you're doing well?

Ted: Yeah, like—I can't even focus on the words.

Therapist: Okay. Sounds like telling Dad some good news about success is *real* uncomfortable in some way. Makes you feel edgy. *[Pause.]* I'm real curious about what comes up if you complete this sentence to Dad. Just picture him—and try out saying, "If you think I'm doing well—." Just say those words, and when you reach the blank at the end, see what comes up to complete the sentence, without prethinking it. "If you think I'm doing well—."

Ted: If you think I'm doing well, then—*[pause]*—you'd stop being on my case all the time.

Therapist: Good, okay, run it through again, and see what comes up next. "If you think I'm doing well—."

Ted: If you think I'm doing well—then when I visit home, I wouldn't have to get torn down at some point.

Therapist: Good. Again.

Ted: If you think I'm doing well—that would prove him right. That would like—something about his ways, how successful he is at everything—oh yeah, I know what it is! It would prove he's been successful as a *parent* too! *[Pause.]* It would say that since I went after what I wanted and got it and became successful, that would prove he's a successful parent, he did okay, and how he treated me is no big deal 'cause I've gone out there and done okay, and so he's blameless. He could say, "Well, look, you turned out okay."

Therapist: What *do* you want him to feel about how he did as your dad?

Ted: *[With angry edge]* I want him to see what a f—king asshole he was and to feel like *shit* about it. He made *me* feel like shit, then he walks away like it's nothing, it's no big deal.

Therapist: I see. He really mistreated you, made you feel horrible, really hurt you, and you want him to *know* it and see that he *failed* as father and feel bad about it.

Ted: Yeah, you bet.

Therapist: And so if he sees you going off and doing things that look so successful—?

Ted: Then forget about it—he'll *never* know what a lousy father he was.

Therapist: So try out completing this sentence: "The way I can make Dad realize what a lousy father he's been is—" Just say it out loud to me, and see what comes up.

Ted: The way I can make Dad realize he's been a lousy father is— *[Falls silent without completing sentence. Gazes at floor.]*

Therapist: What's happening?

Ted: *[Angry edge gone; voice now lower and slower]* Well, when you asked me to say that, the words I heard in my head were, "Me being a mess." *[Pause.]* And it was kind of a shock.

Therapist: *[Pause]* So it's a shock to realize you may be *keeping* your life a mess, making sure success *doesn't* happen, for this crucial purpose—making Dad realize how bad he treated you.

Ted: Yeah.

Therapist: So I wonder if you'd be willing to picture Dad and try out saying it right to him—something like, "To me what's most important is getting you to see that you failed at being a father because you treated me so bad. That's so important to me that I'm willing to keep my life a mess to get you to see that."

Ted: You want me to say that to him?

Therapist: Yes, because that *seems* to be the emotional truth of it. I'm asking you to picture him and say it right to him, and see for yourself if it's true to say that.

Ted: But it's really *screwed up* to deliberately keep myself so messed up.

Therapist: Well, I understand it's not at all that you *like* keeping your life a mess. It's not that you like it. It's that you seem to have this powerful purpose of getting Dad to *get* it and care about how he hurt you. And the mess, the lack of any success, is your way of trying to make that happen.

Ted: Right, right. That helps—putting it that way. Okay, what is it I should say?

Therapist: Whatever words are true about what you suddenly realized, that shocked you. In really personal terms, right to your picture of your father. If it makes it easier, you could start with, "I hate to admit this, but—."

Ted: *[Laughs]* Yeah. *[Pause.]* I hate to admit this, but—*[pause]*—if I do okay and make big bucks—*[pause]*—you'll think you did fine, and you'll never get it how bad you messed me up. And how *you* screwed up as a father.

Therapist: Good. Do you want to add that part about, "I'm hoping that seeing my total *lack* of success is what will make you get it"?

Ted: Yeah, right. What I'm hoping will make you get it is seeing my total *lack* of success.

Therapist: Want to change the wording in any way?

Ted: No, no, it fits. Kind of weird, though. *[Pause]* I mean, it's actually a relief, in a way, 'cause like I said, it's always seemed like something must be really wrong with me that I never get anywhere.

Therapist: Yes, there really seems to be this kind of powerful *purpose* you have, that you're trying to carry out, by getting nowhere. I'm going to write down those words you said to Dad on an index card for you to keep with you and read each day, to help you stay in touch with this. Okay? I mean, you've gotten in touch with how it's really, really *important* to be getting nowhere, so use the card to just *stay* in touch with that as you go through each day, till our next session. Just stay in *touch* with it; don't try to *change* anything, for now.

His card read, "The most important thing to me is to get Dad to see how he failed at being a father to me. I hate to admit it, but that's *so* important to me that I'm willing to keep my own life a mess, and get nowhere, to get him to see how badly he screwed up by tearing me down all the time."

Second Session, Two Weeks Later

Therapist: How'd it go with the card?

Ted: Well, at first I'd look at that card, and like it's so *true,* but it would just make me feel down, y'know? But then, after a few days it changed, and I got more pissed over it—like, how long am I just gonna keep my life on hold, y'know? Waiting for my father to get it?

Therapist: Waiting for him to get it. Sounds like you think he *could* get it. *[Pause.]* Would you try out saying this sentence to me? Just try it out, even if it's mechanical at first, to see how it fits for you: "My father is a man who's *willing* to recognize his own big mistake."

Ted: My father's a man who's willing to admit he made a big mistake. *[Looks down into his lap shaking his head.]* F—k!

Therapist: Or trying out saying, "My father is a man who's *willing* to openly admit his mistake and apologize for causing harm."

Ted: *[Still looking down and shaking his head, low voice]* Oh, man! *[Rueful laugh.]* I mean, what could I be thinking? He never does any of that with *anybody. Never. [Pause. Snorts.]* What a joke.

Therapist: Mm-hm. So would you try out saying to me some words for what it seems you just saw? Maybe, "I see that my father can never give me what I most want from him."

Ted: *[Long pause]* My father can never give me what I most want from him.

Therapist: *[Pause]* How is it to get in touch with that?

Ted: I just want to fight it! It's f—king outrageous!

Therapist: Yes. Outrageous. Tell that directly to Dad. Picture Dad and *tell* him, "I *refuse to accept* that you can't give me the acknowledgment and apology and honesty I want from you, and I'm going to fight to *make* you come up with that for me."

Ted: *[Gazes at his lap in silence, now looking melancholy instead of angry.]*

Therapist: *[Pause]* What's happening now?

Ted: *[Sighs]* When you said "apology and honesty"—like, yeah, that's *exactly* what I want, and that's *exactly* what he'd never do. With me or with anybody.

Therapist: The sound of your voice and how you look—you seem kind of down, right now.

Ted: Well, yeah. *[Big exhale.]*

Therapist: Mm-hm. *[Pause.]* Would you try out saying to me, "If I really get it that my father will *never* have the emotional honesty to see what he did to me—."

Ted: Then, it's like I got no father. I mean, it feels like that—like I got no father. *[Pause.]* Never really did. *[Pause.]* And never *will,* that's the thing. Never will. And I just want to fight that, y'know?

Toward the end of the session, the therapist worked with Ted to find phrases to write on an index card that would capture the most important parts of what he had experienced in the session. The following card resulted, and Ted agreed to read it every day, and especially when around Dad: "Even though keeping my life a mess is starting to really scare me, it would feel even worse to accept that Dad will never change, never face how he treated me, never apologize. I don't accept that! It feels too outrageous and too fatherless. I *will* keep trying to make him come up with the apology and honesty I want from him, in the one way I have: me being a mess." By staying in touch with the emotional truth on this card, Ted would be in the best position to revise it.

The second session had brought Ted to a critical point. He was standing with one foot in his old pro-symptom emotional reality, in which the only way forward was to get Dad to change and give him healing understanding; and he had the other foot in a new emotional reality, in which the way forward is through grieving and accepting Dad as he is. At this point, Ted was not yet at all ready or willing to bring both feet into the new position.

Note that the new possibility of grieving—accepting that Dad will never change—did not come from the therapist as an externally imposed solution. Ted bumped into this possibility himself, as a result of being prompted to make conscious his presupposition that *Dad could become willing* to make the desired change. As soon as this construct was conscious, it came into contact with Ted's own greater knowledge of his father, which was incompatible with it (an example of integration resulting in connecting positions so that pro-symptom constructs are experientially disconfirmed).

In the remaining sessions (10 more, for a total of 12, spanning six months), the work consistently focused on bringing to light Ted's specific themes and purposes that made it necessary to *resist* accepting and grieving Dad's intractability. This included themes and purposes involving separation fears, powerlessness, tragic waste of time and potential, self-responsibility, and risk of failure. By making these various positions of resistance experientially conscious, Ted was able to dissolve some of them and begin to accept others as inherent vicissitudes of life. Some of the index cards given to Ted in the course of these sessions summarize this material:

"Since Dad would think my success proves his *fathering* was a success, I refuse to *have* any success. How he thinks and feels is more important to me than how my own life goes."

"I don't *want* it to be true that Dad can't ever admit he treated me wrong, or feel bad about it, because then I'd know I've been wasting my life for *nothing*. And I'd have to accept being completely powerless to get the acknowledgment I deserve. No way!"

"My only way to feel connected with Dad is by struggling to get him to understand and care about how he hurt me. If I drop that struggle, I feel so disconnected, alone, and on my own that my stomach clenches up."

"Even though being so wired into Dad keeps my life on hold while I wait for him to finally have a change of heart and apologize, it feels even scarier to go forward without him, without a father behind me."

"If I go on without Dad and decide to get somewhere on my own, then I'm responsible for my own life. That feels really scary, so I'm holding back."

At the beginning of the last session Ted mentioned that he had signed up for an electronics training course. This was something he had been considering for several weeks, and the therapist had used his interest in the course as an opportunity to check concretely for any remaining unconscious vestiges of unwillingness to be successful without first getting remorse from Dad. The method of doing this was to invite him to try out saying some of the sentences from his "deck" of index cards from previous sessions, sentences bluntly expressing his various themes of unwillingness. None of these had a compelling, autonomous, unconscious grip on him anymore. Some were still active issues, but Ted could now tolerate grappling with their unresolved, ongoing, essential quality. Ted summed it up with, "Feels like I'm ready to stick with something—ready enough, anyway." As a result of fully feeling and owning his pro-symptom positions, Ted had been able to shift them, though his new level of autonomy and separation was understandably a bittersweet achievement. He said that he had accepted that "my father will go to his grave never *getting* it. He's just living in his own world of 'ain't-I-great.' "

Just over two years later, Ted called for another session—a couple session. He and his girlfriend had decided to get married, and they wanted help with a sexual problem. Ted had completed his electronics certificate program and had landed a job in the quality-control testing department of a manufacturer. He'd had a few bouts of "losing interest" early in the program, "but it didn't really throw me off anymore, because I knew what was going on, you know? Haven't lost steam for quite a while now."

Discussion

When a therapy client such as Ted arrives at knowing and feeling the themes and purposes that compose the symptom's emotional truth, he experiences this as his own view of reality, his own intense purpose within that view, his own powerful way of carrying out that purpose, maintaining a symptom that had seemed to be happening *to* him. The client has discovered a powerful, life-organizing position that he has had all along but did not know he had. Eliminating the symptom means not carrying out the ardent purpose necessitating it, and not carrying out that purpose is unconsciously expected to bring dire consequences and a suffering far worse than the familiar suffering *with* the symptom. The client arrives in therapy having already unconsciously and powerfully made the choice to endure the familiar suffering *with* the symptom rather than the dreaded suffering *without* it. In the current example, Ted's suffering due to underachieving had been far preferable to the suffering of separation, injustice, and grieving that would develop if he moved on in his own life.

Table 6-1 shows Ted's pro-symptom position, indicating how the various constructs constituting it link together to form the whole. The four-level hierarchy of constructs shown is a deep structure that we have found to be a universal pattern of self-organization of emotional realities or positions. The constructs at each level establish a reality that is the basis for the very existence of the constructs at the next-lower-numbered level. At the most governing or superordinate level are unconscious *ontological* constructs defining the essential nature of self, others, or world. From this definition of reality derives a construct of *compelling purpose*, a broad plan or life strategy for how to have safety, well-being, or justice. This unconscious governing purpose in turn dictates how the person unconsciously construes (frames) the *meaning of the immediate, concrete situation*. Finally, the unconscious frame applied to the discrete situation determines the person's conscious, manifested response in the form of *concrete thoughts, feelings, and behaviors,* including the presenting symptoms.

Identifying this hierarchial structure of psychological self-organization has important implications for carrying out highly effective, in-depth psychotherapy. It provides an unambiguous, technical description of the symptom's coherence or emotional truth. It also provides an orienting framework that guides the therapist in the midst of what is sometimes a welter of material generated by the client. Our clinical experience consistently indicates that the minimal level of accessing and integration required for effective in-depth resolution is level 3, the governing *purpose* operating in the client's pro-symptom position. Levels 3 and 4 are the inherent targets of DOBT's strategies and techniques, making this a therapy of third- and fourth-order change—a technical definition of its "depth."

Table 6-1. Ted's pro-symptom position, showing the hierarchical organization of the constructs constituting it and the coherence of his symptoms of under-achieving. Shading indicates unconscious, nonverbal constructs cast here in verbal form.

ORDER OF CONSTRUCT	CONSTRUCT
1st Order *Concrete thoughts, feelings, behaviors (presenting symptoms)*	• Loses interest in vocational pursuits, terminates them • Aimlessness; lacks purpose or direction • Sense of personal failure and defectiveness
2nd Order *Meaning of the concrete situation*	• This job/opportunity is my chance to create more failure that will be further evidence to make Dad finally realize how badly he has hurt me. • To do well at this job/opportunity would be a disaster because that would prove to Dad he did fine as a father and he'd never know how much he hurt me.
3rd Order *Broad purposes and strategies*	• Stay connected with Dad by struggling to make him remorseful for how he treated me.
4th Order *Nature of self/others/world (ontology)*	• I cannot survive on my own, disconnected from Dad. • I am emotionally injured and wronged by Dad and need the healing and the justice his remorse would give me. • It is possible to get Dad to change if I try hard enough.

Case Example:
Couple Therapy

Kim, 34, and Mel, 35, said that their every attempt to talk on their own about their deepening conflict only made it worse. At the point that they came for couple therapy, the fighting had reached a crisis level.

Kim described the problem as Mel "quietly gathering up all the power, financially and otherwise," by not sharing information and decision making, keeping her always "in the dark" and "under his control." She described how "being really in charge of my life" was centrally important to her; how she used to *be* powerfully in charge of her life, successful in a position of managerial responsibility in a male-dominated field. She said, "I picked Mel because he was strong enough to be okay with *my* strength—he wouldn't get blown away by it." Then when she became pregnant with the second of their two girls, now 3 and 5, "somehow nearly every way I'd set up to have control over my life began to crumble," including what she had thought was a relationship based on power sharing. "Now I'm a stay-at-home mom, and Dad's out making the money and the decisions, and I don't want to live like this!" The stress of surviving from paycheck to paycheck would be bearable, she said, "if he didn't cut me out of the loop and leave me living basically alone doing child care."

For Mel, the problem was that "I run my own small business and I work my butt off for our family day and night, and instead of ever hearing any appreciation from Kim, she's always angry at me and picking fights."

With these definitions of the "symptoms," the therapist began searching for pro-symptom themes, meanings, and purposes that would answer these (unasked) questions: How is it *necessary* to be usually angry and fighting, rather than harmonious and close? How is it *important* to have Mel in charge, leaving Kim out of decisions and information on finances and other worrisome matters?

Midway through the first session, after unfruitful initial attempts at discovery, the technique of symptom deprivation yielded important clarity. The therapist asked them both at once to simply imagine sitting down together and having a kind of "business meeting," in which Mel briefs Kim on all the main facts of their current situation, including upcoming financial decisions, uncertainties, and risks. The therapist said, "I'm not saying I think you *should* have such a meeting. I'm only asking if you would *imagine* doing it, because I want to find out a little of what that experience would be like. Just imagine—and if it helps, you can close your eyes to really *picture* the scene—in which Mel is fully spelling out for Kim one major piece of the situation, and then another—*[pause]*—and another—*[pause]*—and just notice how this *feels* to you—*[pause]*—and also how the other seems to be feeling or responding, there in your image."

After a short silence with closed eyes, Mel spoke first. He smiled nervously and said, "It's a real definite image I get of Kim becoming really pale, and she starts talking a mile a minute, and her eyes look kind of panicky over what she's hearing from me. And it's like she wants me to know how to take care of it all, but she can tell from the facts that it's not like that, there are real risks here, and I *don't* know how to make everything okay. And that scares her even more." An unwelcome experience—Kim's intense fear—had arisen for Mel as a result of no longer excluding her from information and decisions.

In order to usher Mel further into experiencing this emerging theme, the therapist asked him if he would look right at Kim and complete this sentence: "I don't tell you things because if I did—." Mel said, "I don't tell you things because if I did—you'd get real scared. *[Pause.]* You know, it's a relief to say that because it's like something I'm always tense about, without even knowing it." Prompted to do the sentence completion again, Mel said, "I don't tell you things because if I did—you'd see how shaky *I* am about some things, and that would *really* scare you." And again: "I don't tell you things because if I did—things would be even harder, with you scared and me then having to calm you by explaining things as they develop day by day. I'm exhausted as it is! I think I'd actually rather have you angry that I'm *not* telling you."

The therapist turned to Kim and asked her, "Does this makes sense to you? Did you *know* that not telling you things is his way of trying to protect you from great fear and insecurity? And himself from exhausting emotional efforts?" She replied, "No, I didn't. And what's surprising to me—and actually kind of embarrassing—while we were imagining our business meeting, and also when Mel was saying that stuff, imagining actually hearing about everything sort of *scared* me! I had a feeling of 'Fine, fine, please *don't* tell me!' " The therapist recognized that Kim had now bumped into one of her own pro-symptom positions, a position of fearfulness in which she *wanted* to be shielded from knowing life's dangers; a position very different from the strong, tough self with which she consciously identified.

The therapist invited Kim more deeply into this material by asking her to make an overt statement to Mel: "Would you stay right where you are, in touch with that, and say it again, directly to him? I know there's an incredibly *strong* side of you, and this fear isn't the whole picture at all, but it's what you're in touch with right now, so just see what it's like to say it right to him." Kim looked at Mel and said, "Those things are scary, and I'm sort of glad you're *not* telling me what they are." The therapist asked how it was to say that to him. "It's weird because it's so not how I think of myself," she said, "but it sure is what I'm feeling." With this confirmation of emotional accuracy, the therapist offered a trial sentence by saying, "I wonder if it would be true for you to tell Mel, 'I *appreciate* how you're shielding and protecting me from these scary things.' See if that fits for you to say, or let us know if it doesn't."

Kim voiced this trial sentence, and her eyes immediately became teary. After a silence she said, "Wow—that brings up a *lot*." The trial sentence had acted as a verbal magnet and pulled into awareness important unresolved material formed in childhood. She told the therapist of a father who "basically abandoned us all" when she was 9, and a mother who was not at all up to the ordeal of surviving as a single parent in poverty. Evictions occurred. Kim and her younger sister always keenly felt their mother's fretful anxiety, insecurity, and indecisiveness, and Kim resolved never to let her own life get so out of control and never to be so "weak" like mother. "*I* had to take care of *her*; *I* had to be the strong one," Kim explained.

The therapist now understood that in the unconscious emotional reality of Kim's pro-symptom position, she was about 9 years old, feeling unprotected and very frightened of the dangers of the big world, and needing a strong, protective adult presence. Bravely making *herself* be that strong protector who was in control of circumstances was her key life-strategy for keeping those unresolved childhood terrors in check.

Working now to foster integration of this position, the therapist guided Kim to feel and know the coherence of all this material explicitly by prompting, "Tell Mel the simple connection between what you went through with Mom, and how you appreciate his shielding and protecting you now." Kim was silent as she felt for and found this connection, and then she verbalized it to Mel, saying "I always felt so *un*protected.

Nobody ever gave *me* protection, and it was so *scary*. I'm always so focused on having to be strong that I don't even notice how scared I really am—how much I want *my* turn being protected. *[Pause.]* I *do* appreciate how you shield and protect the children and me."

As underlying themes emerge during DOBT, the therapist prompts the client to experience how these themes are connected with the concrete presenting symptoms. Seeing such an opportunity here, the therapist continued, "And see if you can also feel the connection to your anger. *[Pause.]* Tell Mel how it *also* makes sense that what's been coming out of you so often is *anger*." Kim looked at Mel again and said, "It's that— when I'm angry, I feel strong, like I have some control. It's what I just said: If I'm angry, I don't feel how scared I really am."

As a between-session task to promote integration of the themes and purposes that had been found so far, the therapist collaborated with Kim and Mel to write index cards for each of them to read daily. Mel's card read, "The side of her that *wants* to feel protected *wants* me to shield her from our troubles, and not tell her things. But then she has no way to feel *she's* being strong—and then old fears flare up. So she gets angry, which makes her feel strong again. When Kim seems angry, it often means she's scared." Kim's card read, "He knows how scared I can be. He shields me from our troubles—keeps me out of the loop—because he'd rather I be angry than feel my fear. And so would I."

The rich crop of symptom-maintaining, unconscious material unearthed using DOBT in this session might give the deceptive impression that these clients must have been highly self-aware and therefore "easy." Actually they were not particularly self-aware or even growth oriented. The flow and effectiveness of the work was due to the therapist's adhering closely and continuously to DOBT's way of thinking (symptom coherence) and way of working (experientially accessing clients' *pro-*symptom positions, without judging, pathologizing, or even trying to change these positions).

In closing, the therapist commented, "It's striking that keeping Kim from feeling fear has been so important to both of you. It's like you've both been on the same team but didn't know it." This was not a facile positive reframe invented by the therapist, but an acknowledgment of an emotional truth that both partners had discovered for themselves in the session.

In the second session, one week later, both partners agreed that the main effect of the cards had been feeling "much friendlier" toward each other than they had for months. They didn't know how "solid" this friendlier feeling was, however, and this in itself was a kind of tenseness, but "overall it felt much better to finally be on the same page about the problem, even though the problem itself isn't actually solved yet," as Mel put it.

The therapist understood that for Mel to fully share information might *frighten* Kim, but it also would *empower* her. In order to probe for how it might be important to Mel to keep the latter from happening, the therapist used sentence completion, saying to him, "What I'd like you to try out now is to say and complete this sentence, without prethinking it, as you look at Kim: 'If you have *all* the information and reach your *own clarity* about what we should do—' " This sentence fragment was designed to act as a verbal magnet for material revealing how, in Mel's world of meaning, it is necessary for him to have far more control over information and money than Kim does.

Mel said, "If you have all the information and reach your own clarity about what we should do—then what do you need *me* for?" Note the difference between the therapist's making an interpretation versus having the client bump into his own emotional truth. Mel was asked to say and complete the sentence again, and then again. Two other endings formed, "—then you'll know when I screw up" and "—then you might *see* me as a screw-up." The therapist then offered the fragment, "If you see me as a big screw-up—" and Mel without delay completed it with, again, "then what do you need *me* for?"

Right here the therapist "pitched a tent." The whole session was spent at this campsite, unhurriedly but very persistently drawing forth, deepening, and integrating Mel's unconscious position of fearfully expecting emotional abandonment unless he supplied vitally needed abilities and resources that the other did not have. *That* construction of reality was the emotional truth of his power gathering in the relationship. In the course of the session, he had a sustained, subjective experience of that construction, feeling and expressing very specifically that his security of connection to Kim required making himself vitally needed by her. Feeling and "owning" this emotional truth was uncomfortable for him, but he proved able to do it. This work was carried out with a few more steps of sentence completion, some focusing (attending to a nonverbal "felt sense" of emotional meaning until it can be verbalized), overt statements to Kim and to images of his parents, and some construct-substitution work with Kim based on what Mel had revealed. Finally the therapist wrote down on index cards the overt statements of the most important themes that had emerged.

One card was written as a statement to Kim and his parents jointly, visualized as standing together in front of him: "I'm sure that you don't want me for myself, but only for what I can do for you. I expect you to cut off from me if I don't come up with something you totally need, and I'm always hiding how afraid of that I am and how urgent it always feels to get you to really, really need me."

A second card combined some of his overt statements to Kim: "I couldn't bear to be without you, so I want you to be unable to be without me, or the insecurity I feel is intolerable. You're so strong, and I'm scared that if you have all the information and reach your own clarity about what we should do, you won't need me. So I have to keep you from knowing what's going on."

Kim too collaborated on the card she received: "I'm enormously important to him, even though his behavior looks like I'm not." This new meaning for his behavior was a pivotal construct substitution for her.

The themes and purposes brought to light in these first two sessions proved to be all that was needed to substantially eliminate the problem patterns they had presented. Over the next seven sessions, Kim and Mel reexperienced these same emotional truths from many different angles and further integrated them as life-circumstances activated them in different ways. Sessions were two weeks apart after the fourth, for a total of nine sessions over three months. It was a case of people being able to change positions they now experienced having. Kim's great wish for being and feeling protected became a very familiar, routinely conscious part of herself, which both amused and confused her for a while, because her strengths and bravery were very real, too. Her confusion ended when she realized that she did not have to have a policy that defined which side was more real or how to know which to go with in any given situation with Mel. *Both* were real, and she would know at the time which to go with. She had been very touched by discovering Mel's awareness of and concern for her fearful, unprotected, young side, and this permanently detoxified his role as information controller. This role itself changed, as he described by saying, "My 'default setting' has changed from making damned sure she's *not* getting the information, to just being the *keeper* of the information and handing it over as she wants." His previously unconscious model of attachment was now something he and Kim frequently joked and teased about. He was hardly free of it yet, but the notion of being loved and wanted for who he was, rather than for what he did, was an intriguing if still hard-to-trust possibility, and he was in an ongoing process of getting used to it. Now that he no longer felt unappreciated by Kim and was experiencing greatly diminished anger and accusations from her, spending time with her and the children became appealing again, and he engaged in more coparenting, alleviating what for her had been one of the worst problems when therapy began.

Conclusion

In depth-oriented brief therapy, deep, swift, lasting change is made possible by the therapist's conviction in: the coherence of symptom production; the immediate accessibility of unconscious constructs; and the use of experiential-phenomenological methods. With these convictions, the therapist can consistently carry out DOBT's methodology: the discovery, integration, and transformation of clients' symptom-maintaining constructions of reality (pro-symptom positions). DOBT challenges the long-dominant view that it requires much time to reach and revise unconscious emotional constructions that were formed in childhood and that have maintained symptoms for decades. It defines clearly which constructs are pivotal (those of purpose and ontology) and how to guide the client to find and change them. It shows that clinicians can work time-effectively and still fully engage the deep-rooted, passionate themes and purposes most important in people's lives.

References

Branden, N. (1971). *The disowned self*. Los Angeles: Nash Publishing.

de Shazer, S. (1985). *Keys to solutions in brief therapy*. New York: Norton.

Ecker, B., & Hulley, L. (1996). *Depth oriented brief therapy*. San Francisco: Jossey-Bass.

Ecker, B., & Hulley, L. (1998a). Briefer and deeper: Addressing the unconscious in short-term treatment. *Family Therapy Networker, 21* (1), 75–83.

Ecker, B., & Hulley, L. (1998b). *Compulsive underachieving* [video and viewer's manual]. Depth Oriented Brief Therapy Video Demonstration and Training Series, 497 E. Oakland, CA: Pacific Seminars.

Ecker, B., & Hulley, L. (1998c). *Down every year* [video and viewer's manual]. Depth Oriented Brief Therapy Video Demonstration and Training Series, 1097SP. Oakland, CA: Pacific Seminars.

Ecker, B., & Hulley, L. (1998d). *Stuck in depression* [video and viewer's manual]. Depth Oriented Brief Therapy Video Demonstration and Training Series, 1096T. Oakland, CA: Pacific Seminars.

Ecker, B., & Hulley, L. (2000). The order in clinical "disorder": Symptom coherence in depth oriented brief therapy. In R. A. Neimeyer & J. D. Raskin (Eds.), *Constructions of disorder*. Washington, DC: American Psychological Association.

Festinger, L. (1957). *A theory of cognitive dissonance*. Evanston, IL: Row, Peterson.

Gumina, J. M. (1980). Sentence completion as an aid to sex therapy. *Journal of Marital and Family Therapy, 62*, 201–206.

Hoffman, L. (1981). *Foundations of family therapy*. New York: Basic Books.

Kelly, G. (1955). *The psychology of personal constructs*. New York: Norton.

Mahoney, M.J., Miller, H. M., & Arciero, G. (1995). Constructive metatheory and the nature of mental representations. In M. J. Mahoney (Ed.), *Cognitive and constructive psychotherapies* (pp. 103–120). New York: Springer.

Martin, J. (1991). The social-cognitive construction of therapeutic change: A dual coding analysis. *Journal of Social and Clinical Psychology, 10* (3), 305–321.

Piaget, J. (1971). *The construction of reality in the child*. New York: Ballantine. (Original work published in 1937.)

Watson, J.C. (1996). The relationship between vivid description, emotional arousal, and in-session resolution of problematic reactions. *Journal of Consulting and Clinical Psychology, 64* (3), 459–464.

Watzlawick, P., Weakland, J., & Fisch, R. (1974). *Change: Principles of problem formation and problem resolution*. New York: Norton.

Wylie, M. S. (1996a). Going for the cure. *Family Therapy Networker, 20* (4), 21–25, 29–37.

Wylie, M. A. (1996b). Under the microscope: Scrutinizing some promising approaches to treating PTSD. *Family Therapy Networker, 20* (4), 22–29.

Annotated Bibliography

Dell, P. (1982). Beyond homeostasis: Toward a concept of coherence. *Family Process, 21,* 21–41. An important recognition and articulation of the concept of coherence within the family systems branch of psychotherapy.

Ecker, B., & Hulley, L. (1996). *Depth oriented brief therapy: How to be brief when you were trained to be deep, and vice versa.* San Francisco: Jossey-Bass. A complete guide to the therapeutic methods and conceptual framework of DOBT, with numerous case examples.

Ecker, B., & Hulley, L. (1998). Briefer and deeper: Addressing the unconscious in short-term treatment. *Family Therapy Networker, 22* (1), 75–83. A close look at a single session of depth-oriented brief therapy with a couple in chronic conflict, illustrating how focusing directly on the unconscious emotional basis of the problem can be the very means of making therapy brief.

Ecker, B., & Hulley, L. (1999). DOBT: Insights in a small space. *Family Therapy News, 29* (7), 27–28. A DOBT case study of couples therapy for loss of sexual desire, weight problems and the struggle of a logic-based man and a feelings-based woman to communicate.

Ecker, B., & Hulley, L. (2000). The order in clinical "disorder": Symptom coherence in depth oriented brief therapy. In R. A. Neimeyer & J. Raskin (Eds.), *Constructions of disorder.* Washington, DC: American Psychological Association. Four case examples of anxiety and panic are used to show that symptoms diagnosed as "disorder" in standard psychiatric taxonomy actually express psychological constructions having a predictable, well-defined order no different from that giving rise to non-symptomatic, non-"disordered" functioning. The rapid accessibility and resolvability of this coherent unconscious structure are demonstrated.

Greenberg, L., & Pascual-Leone, J. (1995). A dialectical constructivist approach to experiential change. In R. A. Neimeyer & M. J. Mahoney (Eds.), *Constructivism in psychotherapy* (pp. 169–191). Washington, DC: American Psychological Association. This technical theoretical model is at the forefront of how cognitive science has come to understand psychological process and change. This model corresponds closely to DOBT, though the two were developed independently.

Guidano, V. F. (1995). A constructivist outline of human knowing processes. In M. J. Mahoney (Ed.), *Cognitive and constructive psychotherapies* (pp. 89–102). New York: Springer. A succinct description of how the mind's dynamic system of self-organization constructs subjective reality.

Mahoney, M. J. (1995). Theoretical developments in the cognitive and constructive psychotherapies. In M. J. Mahoney (Ed.), *Cognitive and constructive psychotherapies* (pp. 3–19). New York: Springer. A review of the successive revolutions in understanding within the cognitive psychology camp, from its early, naïvely rationalist forms in the 1970s, through the computer-metaphor, information-processing, and connectionist models, to the constructivist view of how the mind's multilevel self-organizing activity shapes experiential reality.

Mahoney, J. J., Miller, H. M., & Arciero, G. (1995). Constructive metatheory and the nature of mental representations. In M. J. Mahoney (Ed.), *Cognitive and constructive psychotherapies* (pp. 103–120). New York: Springer. This article lays out the core concepts that define the constructivist view of psychological process and self-organization.

Neimeyer, R. A. (1995). Constructivist psychotherapies: Features, foundations, and future direction. In R. A. Neimeyer & M. J. Mahoney (Eds.), *Constructivism in psychotherapy* (pp. 11–38). Washington, DC: American Psychological Association. A guided tour of constructivist psychotherapy, identifying how constructivist and nonconstructivist approaches differ and how various constructivist therapies differ from each other.

Neimeyer, R. A. (1997). Problems and prospects in constructivist psychotherapy. *Journal of Constructivist Psychology, 10,* 51–74. A further explication of the diverse sensibilities within the constructivist paradigm and a response to criticisms arising from both inside and outside the constructivist movement.

7

⟨⟨⟨⟩⟩⟩

Object Relations Brief Therapy

Michael Stadter and David E. Scharff

Introduction

History

Object relations theory constitutes a particular perspective on personality, development, and the conduct of psychotherapy. It is one of the four major branches of psychoanalytic thought (Pine, 1990). This approach puts the individual's need to relate to others at the center of human development. The infant's efforts to relate to the mother constitute its first and most important tendency. When this experience with the caretaking person is internalized, it results in part of the psyche being structured on the model of that person. It is then called the internal object and becomes a basic building block for continued psychic structuring as aspects of self-organization relate to it internally. No other perspective on the human condition puts as much emphasis on our need to depend upon and relate to others.

Many writers have contributed to the development of core object relations concepts, both from an intensive psychoanalytic perspective (Fairbairn, Klein, Winnicott, Bowlby, Bion, and Guntrip) and from the standpoint of couple and brief interventions (Balint, Malan, Dicks, and Winnicott). These masterfully creative clinicians have greatly aided us in developing our own approach to brief therapy with individuals and couples. In-depth presentations of our brief therapy paradigm can be found in Stadter (1996), D. Scharff and J. Scharff (1991), and J. Scharff and D. Scharff (1998), where the primary references to our sources can be found.

Key Elements of Object Relations Therapy

Object relations brief therapy emphasizes four points:

1. *The uniqueness of each individual client or couple and the particular relationship that develops with a specific therapist at a distinct point in time.* Careful diagnosis is important, but purely descriptive classification systems (e.g., DSM-IV) are not as valuable as *assessment* that emphasizes the *underlying psychodynamics* of the client's suffering and symptoms. Any categorization must acknowledge the uniqueness of each client or couple that is not fully accounted for by diagnostic types. The object relations therapist repeatedly asks, "Who is this person or couple in front of me?" No matter how experienced the therapist, each individual and couple must be approached with an attitude of "not knowing" and of hopeful discovery. Therefore training and experience are crucially important: no "cookbook" approach can really help. Depending on the clients and the situation, five sessions may be too many or two years of three-times-per-week therapy may be too little. Therapy has to be tailored to each situation.

2. *The repetition of past patterns of relating.* Clients are helped to identify and change unconscious patterns of interacting with others and themselves that have been in place for years or even decades. For these people, the past keeps happening over and over again. Object relations brief therapy aims at helping clients to have a present and future that becomes different from that repetitive past.

3. ***The healing power of the therapeutic relationship.*** The object relations approach holds that very little of benefit can occur in therapy
unless the therapist and client develop a positive relationship. The
effectiveness of technical interventions depends upon the relationship and is secondary to it. Guntrip (1969) writes, "The technique
helps us to investigate the problem which the therapeutic relationship, when it is therapeutic, enables the patient to reveal. It is the
relationship with the therapist that creates the situation in which
the problems can be solved." The relationship factor in therapy is
just as important whether it lasts for one session or for one year.

4. ***Understanding relating is the way of relating.*** *Transference* and
countertransference are the technical terms for the patterns of emotion and ways of relating that we study in therapy in order to gain
understanding of clients' inner worlds. Even in brief therapy, the
therapist is aware of the unconscious forces and patterns in the way
clients relate to the therapist (transference) *and* in the way the therapist is feeling and relating in response to clients (countertransference). The therapist looks for ways to interpret and to comment
upon this. Moreover, the therapist tries to connect these reenactments in the session—the transference-countertransference pattern—with clients' past patterns of behavior, feeling and thinking.
This type of interpretive work requires considerable skill and creativity. Often patterns cannot be fully interpreted in brief therapy,
but therapists' awareness and internal processing, even when
unspoken, should further the therapeutic process.

This is part of *containment* (Bion, 1967), a special unconscious
process in which the person (in this case the therapist) is able to
take in and tolerate painful mental states of another person (e.g.,
anxiety, frustration, anger) that that person is unable to tolerate or
understand. The therapist's ability to stay with the difficult affect,
take it in, work toward understanding, and empathically communicate with the client helps to detoxify painful, even overwhelming
emotions. Containment is a process that is essentially unconscious
but that leads toward conscious understanding. The object relations
approach—with its emphases on the uniqueness of each client and
therapist, the therapeutic relationship, and the value of unconscious

reenactments for clarifying internal object relations—can deepen the work of therapists from other theoretical orientations.

Strategies

While it is important for clinicians to think in terms of technique and strategy, many therapists overemphasize technique and strategic interventions without giving adequate attention to the nature and quality of the relationship that has developed between client(s) and therapist. An object relations approach always keeps in mind the context of the relationship. So-called "excellent" or "correct" strategies fail when they are implemented within a poor therapeutic relationship. For heuristic purposes, we will discuss strategies individually. In practice, each strategy has to be considered within the unique environment that has developed between the therapist and client or couple and that psychologically holds the client(s) by providing a sense of safety and trust. Not all strategies are utilized in every case—but nothing can be accomplished without the first one.

Object Relations Strategies

1. Develop a therapeutic alliance: engage the client's curiosity in the inner world.
2. Set a dual focus: symptomatic and dynamic.
3. Get selected historical material to help with focus setting and to understand repetitive patterns.
4. Invite the client to examine the way client and therapist are relating.
5. Interpret dynamics and patterns when possible.
6. Use nonpsychodynamic techniques as appropriate.
7. Consider serial brief therapy.
8. Try to provide a new ending for old experience.

Detailed Description of Each Strategy

Strategy 1: Develop a Therapeutic Alliance

Therapy cannot proceed without the client and therapist making an alliance (conscious and unconscious) in the service of therapeutic progress. The object relations therapist operates from a stance of empathic attunement, sensitively and nonjudgmentally trying to understand the client's concerns and interacting with the client in a manner that conveys respect, competence, and compassion. This stance, in common with that taken by therapists from most orientations, facilitates the development of the therapeutic alliance. Since brief therapy raises the challenge to develop a working alliance quickly, the clinician must first be aware of the common tendency to feel hurried or impatient. Rapid development is different from hasty development. We cannot push the process faster than clients can tolerate. When we try to speed this up without adequate sensitivity to clients' readiness, they will often experience a repetition of earlier unempathic relationships or may defensively idealize the therapist.

Second, when therapists direct attention to describing and understanding clients' pain, it helps them feel understood and more willing to work. Third, the shared process of discovery during history taking increases the alliance. Fourth, collaboratively setting a focus with clients assists alliance building. Finally, using knowledge of clients by attending to transference and countertransference reactions permits therapists to use clients' internal language better and helps to solidify the therapeutic relationship.

Strategy 2: Set a Dual Focus: Symptomatic and Dynamic

Setting a therapeutic focus is the distinguishing difference between brief and long-term dynamic psychotherapy (Stadter, 1996). In object relations brief therapy, we set a focus collaboratively with the client on two levels: symptomatic and dynamic. The symptomatic level typically addresses the psychological pain or the functional impairment that brought the client in—for instance, a sexual problem, or failing grades, or difficulty at work. Sometimes this is all that can be done. But whenever possible, a dynamic focus is also agreed upon that centers on the client's underlying psychodynamic structure. While it is not always obvious, the two foci are usually connected. Work on the dynamic focus assists in the work on the symptomatic focus. We work to understand links between the symptomatic focus and the client's dynamics. If an appropriate dynamic focus cannot be found, the therapy is usually more supportive than interpretive.

Strategy 3: Get Selected Historical Material to Help with Focus Setting and to Understand Repetitive Patterns

Even in very brief object relations therapy, it is essential to develop an understanding of clients' object relations patterns through history taking. Taking a history is frequently therapeutic in itself. The client is able to see—sometimes for the first time—understandable patterns in what previously seemed chaotic. The box highlights some of the most important issues we address in gathering historical data (Stadter, 1996).

Taking an Object Relations History

- Each client or partner's impression of parents, other members of the family of origin, and other important figures who contributed to the client's personality structure
- Recurring patterns of interpersonal interactions (e.g., repeatedly being in an abused position in relationships), including a history of the couple's relationship when there is a long-term partnership or marriage
- Best and worst levels of past functioning
- Family history of psychological disturbance, substance abuse, and loss
- Past suicidal, self-defeating, psychotic, or other regressive behavior
- Significant issues relating to health
- Previous individual and couple therapy

(Adapted from Stadter 1996)

In long-term therapy, a client usually revises his/her history over time. In brief therapy, the original history often has to remain unchallenged.

With couples, however, partners often have different views of individual and shared history, a matter that may become the focus.

Strategy 4: Invite Clients to Examine the Way They and the Therapist Are Relating

It is expected that individuals or couples will reenact some past relational patterns in the sessions. This offers an affectively powerful, here-and-now opportunity for learning. For clients to do this kind of experiential work in sessions can be quite anxiety provoking; not all clients can do it. But when it is tolerable and possible, the therapist directs the client's attention to this arena by saying, for instance, "I noticed something that occurred just now and wondered if you felt I didn't want to listen to you," or, "How did you feel when I made that last comment?"

Strategy 5: Interpret Dynamics and Patterns When Possible

Interpretations are the cornerstone of psychodynamic therapy, as are verbal interventions through which therapists make previously unconscious material conscious, or link events in a causal way new to clients (Scharff & Scharff, 1998). Given the time constraints of brief therapy and/or particular client dynamics, depth interpretation may not be possible. If we push too tenaciously, we can damage the therapeutic alliance and cause the therapy to fail (Piper, Joyce, McCallum, & Azim, 1993). The object relations brief therapist works to understand, interpret, and link the external conflict or situation with the internal situation and its effect on the here-and-now of the therapeutic relationship (Scharff & Scharff 1998). In all object relations work, the therapist uses transference and countertransference to make sense of the client's situation, so the here-and-now of transference-countertransference is used first for facilitating the therapist's understanding and then in formulating interpretations.

Malan (1963, 1976), and later Davanloo (1980), devised a way of thinking about the short-term client, termed the *triangle of conflict* and the *triangle of the person,* two images that they keep in mind to organize their thinking about clients' issues and that guide their interpretive focus. In the triangle of conflict, a concept drawn from Freud's drive theory, they trace the connection between impulse, anxiety, and defense. In the triangle of the person, they trace clients' feelings and actions toward the therapist, feelings toward important figures from the past such as parents, and feelings toward others in the present or recent past. Then the therapist uses these three angles in formulating interpretations (Davanloo from a more forceful and confrontational interpretive stance than Malan). In line with current thinking in object relations and self psychology, Stadter (1996) evaluated how clients treat themselves and added to interpretation the client's attitudes toward self and others, now and in the past. The interpretation of these phenomena adds "self" as a fourth nodal point to the interpretive thrust of the triangle of the person and brings a new dimension of immediacy to the process (Figure 7-1).

A sample interpretation in individual therapy with a man links the past and a current external relationship with the client's self. The therapist might say, "You keep away from your wife sexually now [external relationship] because you are afraid she will take you over [a self experience] as your mother used to do [past relationship]." But to link such an interpretation to the transference, the therapist might draw on a sense of the

Figure 7–1: Interpretive schema including linkage to self

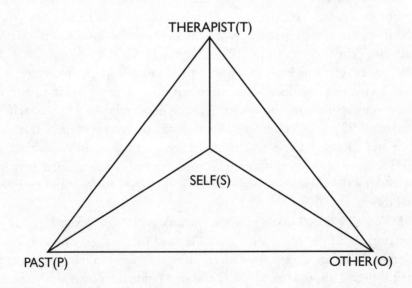

(From Stadter 1996 by permission)

client's reluctance to speak about the transference by adding, "You are also afraid of being here with me [here-and-now transference] in case what I say will somehow put you in danger of being taken over by me [self's fear in here], as you often feel dominated by your husband [external relationship]." In this way, the two interpretations would link all three angles of the triangle with the position of the self in its center.

In couple therapy, interpretation generally moves toward helping to understand the partners' shared construction of dynamics, the underlying reasons for their shared reenactments, and their shared transference to the therapist.

For instance, in couple therapy, a therapist might go on to include the wife of the man in the example above, by saying to her, "In a complementary way, you tolerate his sexual withdrawal [external relationship] because you are afraid of being an overwhelming person [self experience] as you felt your mother was to you and your father [past relationship]." Then the therapist could link both of these individual patterns to the couple's shared transference by saying, "I sense you both are afraid my comments will push you into a destructive pattern and that I will be like the intrusive, know-it-all mothers you both feel you had."

Strategy 6: Use Nonpsychodynamic Techniques as Appropriate

To conduct brief therapy from an object relations perspective, the therapist does not need to restrict technique exclusively to psychodynamic ones (e.g., interpretation, reflective listening, history, confrontation, dreamwork, etc.). In fact, the use of other interventions, such as hypnosis or techniques from cognitive, Gestalt, or behavior or sex therapy, can complement the psychodynamic perspective.

When giving directive instructions to clients, we need to be aware of the effect of the role shift. We ask ourselves, for instance, how teaching a client to reduce anxiety through deep muscle relaxation affects transference. How do clients feel when the therapist recommends cognitive therapy techniques to deal with guilt while at another time remaining more silent in order to permit the client to "stay with" the guilt?

When therapists are ready to explore the integration of different approaches with clients, selective nondynamic interventions often expedite therapy on particular issues. While the nondynamic technique enlarges the client's response repertoire, the dynamic perspective attends to the meaning of the client's suffering and symptoms and provides knowledge about the client's resistance.

This last point can be crucial with any form of therapy. For instance, consider the problem of lack of client compliance with cognitive-behavioral and sex therapy assignments. Understanding and interpreting the unconscious dynamics involved in noncompliance are often necessary for effective progress. With many clients, attention to transference, countertransference, and unconscious processes in general facilitates change, even when using nonpsychodynamic techniques.

Strategy 7: Consider Serial Brief Therapy

Therapists should consider not only the present work with a client but also how the current experience may affect continued growth and development. Attention to the dynamic focus works on themes or issues that operate beyond the current brief encounter. Seen from this perspective, an individual piece of brief therapy becomes part of a larger process of change that may include periodic brief therapy throughout clients' lives, which we call "serial brief therapy" (Stadter, 1996).

The process can be viewed as follows: A client has experienced a process of change—in the context of a unique, consistent relationship at one time of distress—through a relationship with a reliable therapist. At times of future distress or developmental need, he or she returns for further work. In this way, individual episodes of therapy build upon earlier episodes. The whole is greater than the sum of its parts. Serial brief therapy can be viewed as a developmental approach to psychotherapy over a person's life cycle (e.g., Budman & Gurman, 1988).

Strategy 8: Try to Provide a New Ending for Old Experience

Many clients, especially character-disordered ones, live very little in the present. Their lives are strangled by their inability to encounter others directly. Instead, they experience people through the distorted prism of their past experience. Unconsciously, they select friends and partners on the basis of similarity to important past people in ways that limit and trouble their lives. Gaining awareness of this pattern allows them to experiment with new ways of relating.

Repetitive experiences are replayed in the therapy relationship, so the brief therapist attempts to respond in a manner that offers new outcomes to old experiences. Therapists must be more than just a projection of good elements in clients' minds; they must, in their own reality as persons, bring something new, something clients have not experienced before (Guntrip, 1969). Such interactions can be profoundly therapeutic because they disconfirm clients' beliefs (unconscious or conscious) that they will be responded to in a particular way. This may be the most important lesson of therapy.

Clinical Indications for Each Strategy

Object relations brief therapy (like many brief therapy models) is the treatment of choice for highly motivated clients in situations deriving from developmental and externally imposed crises where there is relatively little severe underlying disturbance, or in which the resonance with deeper issues does not principally involve entrenched characterologic patterns (Scharff & Scharff, 1998). But external factors such as limited motivation or financial resources, or moving out of town, may also preclude long-term therapy. In these instances, brief therapy can often provide timely if limited help. In keeping with the emphasis on the unique dynamics, strengths, and weaknesses of the particular client, the model does not a priori exclude a client from this form of brief therapy (Stadter, 1996). The careful choice of the focus for a particular client is crucial if the therapist and client are to work effectively within the constraints of dynamics, pathology, and external limitation.

As we noted above, we do not use all strategies in every case. For example, when a client is highly defensive, is nonpsychologically minded, or has limited motivation, little work may be done in the area of the dynamic focus. The emphasis is on the symptomatic focus (Strategy 2). In such cases, the therapist may not emphasize the examination of the way client and therapist relate (Strategies 4 and 5). Nevertheless, even then, the object relations therapist internally processes such information. Similarly, in many cases there is no need to introduce nonpsychodynamic techniques (Strategy 6). Again, the guiding principle is to customize the therapy to address the uniqueness of the person or couple at a particular point in their lives.

The box lists six selected questions used in object relations brief therapy.

Selected Questions for Brief Interventions

- Can a clear focus be defined?
- Can the client quickly develop a positive, collaborative relationship with the therapist?
- Can the client tolerate the frustration of a brief approach?
- Is this a client for whom brief therapy is better than long-term therapy?
- Has the client responded positively to trial interpretations or interventions in the evaluation session(s)?
- Can the client benefit from brief discontinuous courses of therapy (as opposed to needing a continuous long-term relationship) in order to change in ways that are significant?

(Adapted from Stadter, 1996)

Can a Clear Focus Be Defined?

The single most important difference between brief and long-term dynamic psychotherapy is the setting of a therapeutic focus. If time is limited, then the therapy must be centered in some way. Otherwise, much may be touched on but nothing resolved. With a focus, quite disturbed clients can be helped even in very brief interventions.

For example, Rhonda, a paranoid woman who was at times delusional, came for only two sessions. She thought she should quit her job as a secretary because she was convinced she would be fired. The therapist helped her focus on how to deal practically with the crisis and how to manage her intense anxiety, which grew out of feeling incompetent and undervalued. She worked out a system that enabled her to check out how her performance was viewed externally by her supervisor—who actually saw her as an excellent secretary. When seen several years later, she was still able to handle the job—and she was still quite paranoid.

In another example, Mr. and Mrs. Donald were seen as a couple for Mrs. Donald's increased anxiety after Mr. Donald's recent heart attack. She had begun to badger him about his eating and exercise. One result was that he began to avoid her sexually. In brief therapy, the focus on her anxiety and his sexual avoidance (the symptomatic focus) led rapidly to an understanding that Mrs. Donald had a lifelong fear of loss and abandonment beginning with threats from her parents to send her away, while Mr. Donald feared intrusiveness from his obsessively controlling parents. The health crisis had heightened these vulnerabilities, which was resolved in three sessions so that the couple were able to find each other sexually again.

Sometimes, as with Rhonda, only a symptomatic focus is possible, one that works exclusively with the psychological pain and functional impairment. Whenever possible, however, a dynamic focus is set that centers on the client's or couple's underlying psychodynamic structure, as with the Donalds.

If an appropriate dynamic focus cannot be found, the therapy is usually limited to being supportive rather than interpretive. Malan's (1976) research showed that clients who are curious about their inner world do better in brief therapy than clients who are uninterested in their own dynamics. So an important question for the brief therapist is: How can I creatively engage the client's curiosity about him- or herself? As a general rule, the more disturbed the client or the briefer the therapy, the more specific the focus.

Can the Client Quickly Develop a Positive, Collaborative Relationship with the Therapist?

If not, the therapist and client will need to work together for an extended period of "pretherapy" until trust and collaboration develop. For instance, Sally, a woman in her forties, moved into individual dynamic therapy only after many years of supportive treatment. She had been severely sexually abused as a child and had many dissociative symptoms. It took three years of treatment before she was able to trust the therapist enough to risk talking about matters that were centrally important and meaningful to her.

Abused and hostile clients often require this kind of extended treatment approach. Even then, an agreed-on focus may lead to more rapid progress.

Can the Client Tolerate the Frustration of a Brief Approach?

For some clients, the yearnings and rage at disappointment stimulated by brief work require the therapist to recommend longer-term treatment. This is especially the case for many clients with borderline and dependent personality disorders. For some of these clients, however, attention to the focus and the limits of therapy can often make the rigors of brief treatment manageable.

Is This a Client for Whom Brief Therapy Is Better Than Long-Term Therapy?

We have noted that clients with external or developmental crises may want—and need—only brief therapy. Brief work can also be especially helpful for some clients when it confronts the key issues of loss and dependency by focusing on the limited contact with the therapist. Similarly, time constraints can help confront obsessive or narcissistic clients with the impossibility of "having it all."

Has the Client Responded Positively to Trial Interpretations or Interventions in the Evaluation Session(s)?

One of the best methods to determine whether a client can benefit from brief therapy is to "try out" interpretations or interventions that would be used in a brief, focused approach. If the client does not respond positively, then a long-term or modified approach should be considered.

Can the Client Benefit from Brief Discontinuous Courses of Therapy (as Opposed to Needing a Continuous Long-Term Relationship) in Order to Change in Ways That Are Significant?

As we discussed previously, serial brief therapy is a way many clients use therapy. The following vignettes illustrate when it was useful (Alan, and Sol and Nancy M.) and when it would not have been effective (Sally).

Alan was seen from the age of 18 to 25 for five episodes of brief therapy. The episodes ranged from 3 to 20 sessions in duration, for a total of

50 sessions. When he began treatment, he was a profoundly schizoid, suicidal, asexual young man. When he was last seen in treatment, eight years later, he had an enthusiasm for life, was professionally successful, had a network of personal relationships, and was aware of and dealing with his sexual self. Alan had internalized the therapy process and was continuing to do important work on his own. He found it helpful to return repeatedly for therapy to further his personal journey (Stadter, 1996).

Sol and Nancy M. first came asking for sex therapy when, in their midtwenties, they had been married four years. A course of psychodynamic sex therapy twice a week for about four months gave them sexual functioning that they had not previously had (Scharff, 1982, pp. 131–132). They returned to the therapist many times in subsequent years for marital strain, when they could not process developmental issues: career change and growth for both Sol and Nancy, issues of child development in their daughter, and ways of relating to their own siblings and parents. They came as a couple and individually, and in one series, Sol came with his brother and father for 10 sessions to work on issues of the family business. Over 15 years, they were seen for a total of 70 sessions.

By contrast, however, Sally, whom we described above, could not have benefited significantly from serial brief therapy. She needed the extended presence of a therapist in a consistent, nonabusing relationship in order to be able to modify her old destructive patterns.

Clinical Applications with an Individual: Case Example

This case is presented to convey the use of strategies and the therapist's use of countertransference reactions to understand the client and further therapy. Ronald, a 24-year-old single man, had just begun his second semester in law school and was acutely anxious because of his so-so performance during the first semester. He was having difficulty sleeping and couldn't concentrate on his studies. He felt humiliated and self-critical for feeling out of control. He wanted therapy to be conducted within the 15 sessions his insurance covered, but he expected it would take less time than that "if it helps at all."

First Session

In the first session, I (M.S.) was impressed by Ronald's narcissistic issues and also felt saddened by how hard he was on himself. He talked movingly about almost always being disappointed in himself. Remembering times of my own lack of self-acceptance, I thought, "I'm going to be disappointing to him because I won't meet his standards." But I also felt some irritation with an arrogant, entitled quality that he had. For example, when I explained to him that I expected clients to file their own insurance forms, he replied, "I realize that that's the way you do it for other people, but couldn't you make an exception for me?" My reactions gave me some understanding of his inner world. I thought that in his insecurity, he felt he needed special treatment.

At the end of the first session, we agreed to work on the symptomatic focus of trying to get his anxiety to a more manageable level and to help him be able to concentrate well enough to study. He said, "In law school, you can easily fall hopelessly behind in a few weeks." I also made a tentative suggestion to Ronald that I was impressed by the extremely high standards that he set for himself and thought that they might be connected with the intensity of his anxiety. He seemed to accept that idea, so the issue of his "all or nothing" standards gave a dynamic focus concerning his narcissistic character. So we were able to set the beginnings of a dual focus (Strategy 2). Additionally, the discussion of his high standards evoked his curiosity about his inner world and supported our new alliance building (Strategy 1).

Also, in this session Ronald mentioned that he had been athletic in college but had not engaged in any exercise since coming to law school because he had felt he didn't have the time. I suggested that vigorous exercise is sometimes quite helpful in managing anxiety, and recommended that he try some jogging, which he had previously done in college. (Strategy 6: nonpsychodynamic intervention). He agreed to try it.

I was aware in this session of a countertransference feeling of pressure to help him reduce his anxiety quickly and to "prove" instantly that therapy could be helpful to him. Earlier in the session, he expressed skepticism as to whether therapy would help at all. I thought my plan to direct our attention toward symptomatic relief was sound, but I wondered if I was also responding to his "show me but I don't think this will help" attitude.

Second Session

I came to better understand Ronald's critical attitude during this session (Strategy 3: history taking). He was the oldest of four children and the only son. His parents divorced when he was 10. He admired his mother, who alone raised him and his three sisters. He said, "She was principled and a hard worker," but she was also depressed and a martyr. He worried about her because she was often unhappy.

Ronald had been estranged from his father since the divorce. He was contemptuous of his father for never finishing high school, and he also hated him for physically and emotionally abusing his mother and himself. The father seemed to want to spend time with Ronald, but things usually degenerated when he—the father—yelled or hit him. His father always seemed disappointed with Ronald.

Ronald had a serious romantic girlfriend throughout college, but they "just grew apart." It sounded to me as though he lost interest in her as "not enough for him." Recently he became depressed over breaking up with a woman he had dated for three months.

In the first session, Ronald had said he was always disappointed with his performance. Now he corrected that, saying that during his senior year in college he was "perfect"—he was popular, got good grades, and held high office in student government. He noted that it was always difficult for him to trust people, and he was ashamed about going through this present crisis. He hoped someday to run for political office—U.S. Senate or even higher.

I found, as I often do when I learn more about a client's background, that I felt more empathy with Ronald. I realized that the pressure I felt to prove myself was part of an identification with him. It was the way his father frequently caused him to feel. He was relating to me in unconscious identification with his father, while I identified with his victimized self. I further reflected that academic success was important to his self-image because it differentiated him from his much-less-educated father. I wondered about unconscious identifications with his mother's depressive, martyred stance and also about whether he might expect some similar self-sacrificing devotion from any woman that he would be involved with. I did not share any of these speculations with Ronald at this point. But these insights did help me to maintain my empathy for him in the face of his critical attitude and helped me, later in the therapy, to resist the pull to be like his father: I felt it, but did not act it out.

The preliminary foci that we had set in the previous session still seemed apt. He said his anxiety had diminished some and that jogging had been helpful, but his sleep disturbance and inability to study continued. I proposed that during the next several sessions we work on his anxiety by using some behavioral relaxation training. He readily agreed (Strategy 6: nondynamic interventions). This practical focus on symptom alleviation seemed wise because he was asking directly for it, because the symptoms were quite disruptive, and because he seemed to need "proof" that therapy could help. On the other hand, I wondered if I was acting out a transference-countertransference dynamic, with Ronald being his critical father and me being the Ronald who would inevitably fail in the father's eyes. If that dynamic held sway, therapy would inevitably fail. I felt unsure of my decision but was heartened by the benefits he had reported from jogging and by his eager response to the relaxation suggestion.

Third to Seventh Session

In these sessions we worked on relaxation exercises and readings on self-help cognitive therapy of depression. As he found these helpful, I relaxed and felt his idealization of me grow, and I no longer feared premature termination.

Eighth to Twelfth Session

I did the most interpretive work (Strategy 5) during this phase. By Session 8, his functioning had returned to levels prior to receiving his first semester's grades. I felt, though, that unless he was more aware of his narcissistic issues and better able to cope with them, he would likely have recurring crises of this sort. I noted that we were about halfway through our contract, but he denied having any reaction to that.

As we focused on a few interpretive themes, we continued to look at his narcissistic vulnerability. We discussed how his grandiose standards for success intensified his disappointment and suffering when he didn't meet them. We connected his strife-ridden childhood, especially his father's influence, with his labile self-esteem. He had unconsciously internalized his father's abusive, critical characteristics and frequently treated himself as his father had treated him (self-past link). He also often treated other people as his father had treated him and his mother (past-self-other interpretation). When we talked about his critical dismissive attitude toward me during the first session (therapist-self-past interpretation), I invoked the transference-countertransference. When he defined a situation as a failure, I explained the depression and self-pity he experienced as an unconscious identification with his depressed mother (past-self connection). During this period Ronald said he thought I was disappointed in him. I suggested that he felt I was responding to him as his father had (therapist-self-past interpretation). The interpretations concerning me and our discussions about the way we were relating are examples of directing attention to the way the client and a therapist are relating (Strategy 4).

Ronald was an active collaborator during these sessions and was often enthusiastic about understanding elements in his personality that had previously been mysterious. He had difficulty acknowledging his own critical stance with other people and initially felt criticized when I pointed it out. It was painful for him to consider that not only was he the victim of his father's attacks, but he had also unconsciously attacked others (past-self-other interpretation). He had organized part of his life to demonstrate emphatically that he was not like his father (e.g., by becoming highly educated). At some points, when I pointed something out that he hadn't yet seen, Ronald would feel "put down." We looked at this as a part of the extraordinarily high expectations he would have for himself as well as his difficulty with envy.

Thirteenth and Fourteenth Sessions

Ronald requested that we schedule our last three sessions every other week to permit him an opportunity to deal with his difficulty in getting a summer job. With mixed feelings, I agreed to meet every other week. Diluting the experience of termination concerned me, but spreading out the last sessions could help him deal with the blows to his self-esteem that are part of a job search. Less frequent sessions toward the end of a contract can also be useful in relapse prevention and in reducing the difficulty of termination for the client.

Ronald had a history of denying the importance of relationships in his life and failing to mourn their endings. He said, "When it's over, it's time to move on." By contrast, his preoccupation with other types of losses (e.g., loss of self-esteem, loss of confidence in his academic prowess) was obsessive. Our relationship had been important to him; now, losing a supportive connection with a trusted older man had meaning that he was reluctant to acknowledge. When we discussed ending therapy (Strategy 4), he discounted its significance (see the fifteenth session, below). I did not pursue his reaction to termination very persistently. After therapy had ended, I felt that I had not done enough on that important issue. I had felt that greater exploration of termination would have evoked strong resistance. Nevertheless, in my countertransference I became aware of my own resistance to dealing with the pain and loss of endings. In retrospect, I may have come to feel less significant to him than I was and therefore acted out by failing to confront this minimizing of the importance of our relationship. Later, I realized that my feelings of inadequacy about handling his termination were, in part, an identification with his own feelings of inadequacy.

Fifteenth Session

Ronald landed a good summer job. He came to the last session with both triumph and sadness. He denied his feelings had to do with this being our last session. I felt sad when he then said maybe he hadn't really changed or gotten much from therapy. I asked how he saw himself now compared with when we began five months previously.

Like a lawyer, he cited the evidence: much less anxiety, eating and sleeping well, studying effectively, greater appreciation of his brittle self-esteem, recognition of the tyranny of his all-or-nothing expectations, and awareness of his need to be "special." I thought to myself that this list would be pretty impressive in any therapy, but especially so from someone who was disappointed with therapy. Ronald movingly said that he was amazed to note this array of improvements. He hadn't been in touch with them minutes before. We looked at this lack of awareness as a dramatic example of his predisposition to be self-critical. I acknowledged that his life wasn't perfect and that he was still struggling, but I noted, too, that it was hard to hold on to good experiences.

Our discussion of these issues as he terminated provided him with "a new ending for old experience" (Strategy 8). He was able to end with some understanding of the important dynamics of his vulnerability to disappointment and his difficulty in holding on to "good-but-imperfect" experience. As I connected the pattern back to the relationship with his father, I felt particularly saddened that it was so difficult for him to hold on to good experience unless he was feeling grandiose. This was a manifestation of a periodic inner sense of emptiness, a state that many clients with prominent narcissistic issues frequently feel, which can be thoroughly addressed only in long-term treatment.

Ronald's disappointment in therapy and in me was also a way to diminish his pain over the loss of the relationship by seeing it as less valuable. I acknowledged the gains that Ronald had listed and suggested that further work in open-ended therapy on his self-esteem issues might eventually be useful since he intended to hold positions of influence. He agreed and said that probably the government would be better run if more of our leaders had been in therapy.

Clinical Applications with a Couple: Case Example

For this couple, many years of shared low sexual desire had been complicated by an increasing problem with the husband's impotence. I (D.E.S.) was initially concerned that long-term individual therapy might be needed because the husband's inhibited desire seemed to be part of a pervasive problem with identity and with fear of a dominating exciting object. Nevertheless, brief sex therapy alone proved sufficient.

Dr. and Mrs. T. were both 35 when an adoption agency referred them, just a month after they adopted an infant girl, Tammy. Never sexually assertive at best, Dr. T. had experienced erectile failure occasionally during the infertility evaluation and procedures and in their attempts to conceive. After that time two years ago, he had shown little interest in sex. Mrs. T. had hardly noticed at first, being busy with her own career as a sports executive. But gradually she realized she felt neglected. Eventually the couple admitted to the adoption social worker that their sexual difficulty detracted from their otherwise loving relationship.

During the evaluation, Dr. T. admitted freely that he had become distracted from sex by his interest in professional and community matters. He was also consciously aware that he withdrew from sexual encounters because of his fear of erectile failure, but he underscored his feeling that he had not been motivated about sex since marriage. This was not true during vacations, when the couple relaxed and enjoyed sex easily. Diagnostically, the problem was one partly of erectile instability and performance anxiety, and partly of inhibited sexual desire. In the evaluation, after understanding the presenting problem and establishing a symptomatic focus, I moved toward understanding a dynamic focus (Strategy 2) by getting a brief history from each partner (Strategy 3). This process also helped establish a therapeutic alliance (Strategy 1).

Getting the Husband's History

Dr. T.'s interest in sex had always been rather low. During his years in boarding school, he had several short homosexual encounters, which spoke to his difficulty in establishing an adolescent sexual identity. He had no sexual interest in men, nor any homosexual encounters after high school. He said that his relationship with his parents had been good, as was the parents' relationship itself, until his mother began to look her age while his father's energy continued unabated. Then when Dr. T. was in college, his father ran off with another woman. Dr. T. had felt his mother's hurt although he still got on well with his father.

Getting the Wife's History

Mrs. T. told me she was the baby sister, with an athletic older brother in a loving family. Pushed to be as athletic and competitive as her brother, she never had much confidence as a woman. The difficulty with her sense of feminine sexuality left her on shaky ground in now asking Dr. T. to be more interested in her sexually.

In the evaluation I saw the couple separately and together. When I saw them for an interpretive session, they brought their (month-old) adopted infant, and I was therefore able to see their physical awkwardness with the baby.

I imagined a similar awkward uneasiness with their own and each other's bodies. The whole uncomfortable situation was not, however, the slightest bit unloving.

Setting Symptomatic and Dynamic Foci

I told the couple they shared in the avoidance of sexuality because of a shared shakiness about themselves as sexual people. I had already encouraged Dr. T. to tell his wife of his anxiety and shame about erectile failure. (Strategy 6: nondynamic technique of suggesting disclosure). He had done so, to their shared relief. I said now that underneath the performance anxiety that led to the erectile difficulty, there seemed to be a shared difficulty with desire, which Dr. T. expressed for both of them. I suggested we begin sex therapy, with the option of turning to marital or individual work. We worked to further our alliance as I explained what I understood of the link between symptomatic and dynamic foci. I wondered silently if Dr. T. would eventually need intensive psychotherapy. But as the partners were open, friendly, articulate, and trusting, I felt that my optimistic countertransference should predict a good treatment outcome. That feeling was quickly dashed.

The couple agreed readily to my suggestions for treatment. Before we could even begin treatment, however, Dr. T. said he was scheduled to spend several weeks in an important postgraduate training program during the summer. This required getting them to examine our therapy relationship (Strategy 4). My own schedule dictated that I begin treatment immediately or else refer them to a colleague. When I told them this, Dr. T. became obviously anxious. I spoke about the way this choice required him to face the defensive way he put his marriage second to professional interests. Mrs. T. colluded with his avoidance. I could feel my own anxiety and disappointment when she encouraged him to go to the course. Using my own countertransference feeling as a clue to their fear of closeness, I said I understood their shared fear of risking closeness. With this help, Mrs. T. was able to say that she could hardly bear to ask him to stay in town and put their relationship first. She related this to her guilt about asking for anything for herself, just as she thought her mother would never offend her father by asking for consideration.

This encounter offered our first opportunity to use the nature of our relationship to therapeutic advantage. Their struggle to decide on treatment was a blow to my excessive optimism about them. At least I was now warned about the extent of their resistance, including their own overoptimism that being warm and reasonable—and distant—would be enough for their marriage. Now thinking that it might be difficult to hold them in treatment, I felt on guard. After considerable distress, Dr. T. finally decided to stay for therapy. Within hours of doing so, he felt he had passed a crisis of commitment. He said, "I feel like a new man, almost as if I had just made a decision not to leave my wife. It's like the decision makes me different from my father."

The early sex-therapy exercises of gradually increasing sexual experience went well (Strategy 6: nondynamic elements). The couple relaxed with the protection from anxiety and felt the loving feelings they had been missing. But when I assigned genital stimulation, Dr. T. reported in several sessions that he could feel no arousal. When asked if he had any dreams, he obliged promptly.

"Two nights ago I dreamt that a teacher I hardly knew at medical school came over and sat down to talk to me. He never would have then, all the more so because he was arrogant about students. That was the dream. I had read the day before that he had killed himself because he was depressed. That reminded me of my wife's brother, who had been depressed but did not kill himself. He got through it. We used to worry that her brother had an organic condition, just as I worry that my impotence is organic."

Since we knew from physical evaluation that his sexual difficulty had no organic basis, I said we could look to the dream for help with causes. Mrs. T. joined in, "I worry that he is uninterested because I'm just not sexually attractive." And she continued to elaborate on the feeling that she had a boyish figure. She had not had a menstrual period until the age of 21, presumably because of physiological inhibition from the strenuous exercise of college athletics. "I never feel I can be sexy like a real woman. I never got there: I got stuck at 14."

I said to them, "You both feel your bodies are deficient. This contributes to your sexual fear and disinterest, Dr. T., and to your feeling, Mrs. T., that you cannot expect any better" (past-self dynamic interpretation). They then reassured each other about their mutual attraction to each other's bodies and other attributes.

I also pointed out the anxiety in their relationship to me, "the medical school teacher" of the dream. They shared a fear that I might be disdainful of them and also that their condition would kill me off—making me unavailable to them just when they needed me to work on these issues.

During the next two sessions, the couple reported that Mrs. T. became easily aroused, while Dr. T. enjoyed the massage without arousal or erection.

I now began to feel the anxiety that they shared. Perhaps they were less easily treatable than I had thought. In the countertransference, I began to absorb their doubts, to feel they would "kill off" my efforts to help them. So now, in the countertransference, I was experiencing them as disappointing objects—an identification with the people who had disappointed each of them earlier in life. I had the fantasy that they might leave treatment without improvement, and that if they did, I would be relieved. To use the language of their symptoms, I felt "sick of treating them" and, in a way, lost my "desire" to do so. They had now unconsciously recruited me to join in their shared unconscious view that sexual desire would bring them to a hopeless and potentially lethal impasse. So in this transference-countertransference replay of their internal problem, I now felt seduced by them into an empty hopefulness, and I felt let down by the failure that they also feared.

The signs of impasse persisted until Dr. T. brought in a second dream. He began by assuring me that it was completely unrelated to the therapy, a warning that alerted me to the probability that it was.

"I was standing with 10 or 15 people in a large room with our backs to the wall. It occurred to me that we were going to be executed one by one. My first reaction was to be defeatist. I took off my jacket and rolled up my sleeves, just as I did a few minutes ago in here, and I thought, 'If they are going to do it, I hope they'll hurry. Waiting is agony.' They were demonstrating how people died by carbon monoxide poisoning, the same way that that teacher of mine in medical school died recently. They showed that you went to a bed covered with garbage bags, and you have a gas mask with oxygen until it is changed to carbon monoxide. I realized they hadn't started, and it was a long time. I thought, 'I don't want to die, so why not fight?' I asked to use the telephone. I called my mother, but there was no answer. My fight juices were finally going by now, so I just walked out the front door of the office. I took off my shirt because somehow it was a telltale sign, and I started to run. It felt terribly slow. After two or three minutes, I realized a motorcycle policeman was following me. I kept running for my life. I was running past strip places on a highway, gas stations that were closed because it was 2 A.M. The policeman caught up with me. I thought he was going to catch me, but just at that moment, a bad guy came out of a trailer and took a shot at the cop, who took off after him. So I got away."

This dream allowed for a full dynamic set of interpretations and was a vehicle for linking the sexual symptomatic focus and the dynamic one (Strategy 5). Dr. T.'s associations left all three of us in no doubt that the execution he feared was the sexual exposure of the exercises (Strategy 4). Mrs. T. was the one to notice that the odd method of execution—on a bed that felt threateningly smothering—recalled the assigned sexual exercises on the bed, which she covered to protect it from being stained with oil. In the dream, he had called his mother as he had done in his youth when he felt helpless. He said, "Hers is the one number that hasn't changed all these years. I was counting on her. She should have been home in the middle of the night, but she wasn't there. So I ran for my life." I said that I was the cop he feared. He replied, "No doubt about that!" But Mrs. T. joined in to add that she had also identified with the cop, since he often treated her as being after him to do things. He talked about fearing being controlled by the demand for sex implied by me in giving exercises, by his wife in being attractive to him, and even by himself since he cared for her.

I now asked him about the building in which the dream occurred. It reminded him of his junior high school, the one he had left to attend boarding school to escape his mother. But when he left home, he missed her terribly. When I said he might have felt he had to leave home as a young teenager out of his fearful recognition of his parents' sexual life, he replied, "Well, they did have a last child just after I left. In fact, we named Tammy after that sister."

The fear of the persecuting object was now out in the open in a way that fully connected the sexual symptom, the dynamic focus, and the transference—in the dream, in Dr. T.'s acknowledged fear of sex, in his acknowledged fear of me, and in the person of their infant named for a child born of the parents' intercourse. The couple could also see the way their transference fear echoed the feelings they were trying to keep at bay between themselves (self-past-other-therapist connection).

I summed up my speculations about this dream: Dr. T. had felt threatened with annihilation by me as the representative of parental sexuality. He also felt afraid of being annihilated by sex itself and by the smothering engulfment of his wife, who now stood for the seductive and threatening part of his mother, but who stood at other times for the cop–bad parent. But he was also expressing a fear of sex for both of them, for Mrs. T. identified with the threat of sex that he expressed. He had been on the run, but early in their marriage and early in therapy, they both had. I ended by saying, "You can't get aroused when you're on the run, Dr. T., just as you, Mrs. T., couldn't get pregnant when you ran so much that you had no menses!" Although I was the cop and executioner in the treatment, it was Mrs. T. who had been in that role up to now. She had accepted it because she felt no one would willingly have her.

In the exercise following this session, Dr. T. was easily aroused, and the treatment followed a rapid course to successful completion. Dr. T. became able to relax through any periods of anxiety, and his fear receded. Mrs. T. also found it easier to avoid backing off lest she be seen as the cop. The couple found a new level of integration of their sexual and emotional intimacy.

This couple got what they came for in therapy. Their loving relationship and their motivation allowed them to work through their shared problem and their individual parts of it quickly but thoroughly. We worked on the symptomatic focus of their shared loss of sexual desire through interpretation of dynamic elements of overlapping areas of their internalized worlds, especially that of shaky sexual identification and low self-esteem in regard to sexual functioning. They brought their daughter, Tammy, with them to the last meeting. The exchange between her and her parents had a new, lively rhythm.

Follow-up

I heard from the T.s on two occasions. First, I got an announcement of a natural birth from them eighteen months after termination. There, pictured with his doting parents and 23-month-old sister, was a baby boy.

Three years later Mrs. T. came up to me at a theater. She said that she wanted me to know they had been able to conceive another child, and their marriage had remained solid and loving. Treatment had turned their life around (Strategy 8: a new end for old experience).

Concluding Summary

These two cases illustrate the use of the dual focus—on symptoms and psychodynamics—in the conduct of object relations brief therapy. It is the use of the transference-countertransference pattern to link dynamic elements—the past, the self, internal objects—to the here-and-now of the relationship with the therapist that clearly distinguishes this mode of brief therapy. This is true even when therapy has a supportive quality by focusing mostly on symptom relief, or when it draws technically from the nondynamic therapies, as we illustrated by sex therapy in the case of Dr. and Mrs. T. and in the cognitive-behavioral interventions with Ronald. Derived from theories that have mainly been tested in long-term therapy, object relations brief therapy is a sophisticated way of relating to and treating clients, a powerful tool for change and growth.

References

Bion, W. R. (1967). *Second thoughts*. London: Heinemann.

Budman, S. H., and Gurman, A. S. (1988). *Theory and practice of brief therapy*. New York: Guilford.

Davanloo, H., ed. (1980). *Short-term dynamic psychotherapy*. New York: Jason Aronson.

Guntrip, H. (1969). *Schizoid phenomena, object relations and the self*. New York: International Universities Press.

Malan, D. H. (1963). *A study of brief psychotherapy*. London: Tavistock.

Malan, D. H. (1976). *The frontier of brief psychotherapy*. New York: Plenum.

Pine, F. (1990). *Drive, ego, object, and self: A synthesis for clinical work*. New York: Basic Books.

Piper, W. E., Joyce, A. S., McCallum, M., and Azim, H. F. A. (1993). Concentration and correspondence of transference interpretations in short-term psychotherapy. *Journal of Consulting and Clinical Psychology*, 61(4), 586–595.

Scharff, D. E. (1982) *The sexual relationship: An object relations view of sex and the family*. London: Routledge and Kegan Paul.

Scharff, D. E., and Scharff, J. S. (1991). *Object relations couple therapy*. Northvale, NJ: Jason Aronson.

Scharff, J. S., and Scharff, D. E. (1992). *The primer of object relations therapy*. Northvale, NJ: Jason Aronson.

Scharff, J. S., and Scharff, D. E. (1998). *Object relations individual therapy.* Northvale, NJ: Jason Aronson.

Stadter, M. (1996). *Object relations brief therapy.* Northvale, NJ: Jason Aronson.

Annotated Bibliography

Scharff, D. E., and Scharff, J. S. (1991). *Object relations couple therapy.* Northvale, NJ: Jason Aronson. Explains the object relations rationale for sex and marital therapy, including several cases of brief work, especially when the symptomatic focus is on fear of separation.

Scharff, J. S., and Scharff, D. E. (1992). *The primer of object relations therapy.* Northvale, NJ: Jason Aronson. A brief, easy way to get the fundamentals of object relations theory and practice.

Scharff, J. S., and Scharff, D. E. (1998). *Object relations individual therapy.* Northvale, NJ: Jason Aronson. The comprehensive up-to-date theory for application to brief and long-term treatment. Contains an extensive section on brief therapy.

Stadter, M. (1996). *Object relations brief therapy.* Northvale, NJ: Jason Aronson. The complete text on our way of viewing brief therapy with individuals. Includes a history of the theory and many illustrative cases.

8

※※※

Adlerian Brief Therapy: Strategies and Tactics

William G. Nicoll,
James R. Bitter,
Oscar C. Christensen, and
Clair Hawes

Introduction

Adlerian brief therapy (ABT) is an extension of Alfred Adler's original approach to psychotherapy, which he termed Individual Psychology. Like all dynamic approaches to therapy, Adlerian psychotherapy has evolved substantially over the past sixty years. But the foundational principles and concepts first put forward by Adler in his psychology remain as the cornerstones of Adlerian brief therapy. Indeed, most current models of psychotherapy, and particularly the so-termed brief therapies, are rooted in the principles of individual psychology theory and the approach to psychotherapy first developed by Adler.

It was Adler who first suggested that the emphasis in therapy should focus more upon understanding the social contexts of human behavior, examining the interaction patterns between people, and facilitating cognitive and behavioral change, than upon analyzing intrapsychic processes. Over the course of the twentieth century, alternative therapeutic paradigms focusing more on facilitating cognitive and behavioral change through direct, brief, and resolution-oriented processes have gradually developed to the point where they now predominate the practice of counseling and psychotherapy. This chapter will be devoted to delineating the characteristics, underlying principles, and specific strategies and tactics involved in Adlerian brief therapy. This schema for the brief therapy process provides mental health practitioners with a framework that enables the integration of strategies and tactics from across the spectrum of brief therapy models.

Characteristics of Adlerian Brief Therapy

Adlerian brief therapy, like most brief therapy models, is characterized by five essential characteristics: time limitation, focus, an optimistic and directive counseling style, viewing symptoms as solutions, and the assignment of new behavioral tasks. By time limitation, we refer to the fact that the counselor and client work within an acknowledged time-limited context. Therapist and client essentially establish a contract with one another at the first session regarding the number, frequency, and duration of therapy sessions. This therapeutic contract is understood to be subject to review and modification as therapy progresses. The beginning time limit on treatment serves two essential functions for therapy. First, it conveys an optimistic expectation that change, progress, and growth are possible and within a relatively brief time period. Second, the establishment of a time limitation serves the function of motivating both client and counselor to get to work more quickly and directly than when time is considered to be unlimited.

The issue of time limitations is often misunderstood to mean that the counselor-client relationship ends at the final session. But in Adlerian brief therapy the counselor-client relationship is considered to be ongoing but intermittent, somewhat analogous to the family practitioner–patient relationship in medicine. The counselor and client work intensively for a brief period of time around the client's current presenting issues and symptoms. Once significant progress has been realized, treatment is terminated—or more accurately, interrupted. It is made clear by the therapist that in the future, should the client choose to return to therapy to work on further or new issues in his or her life, the therapist remains available. Treatment is therefore intermittent, with time provided for the client to integrate and consolidate the changes into his or her life before moving on to other areas of concern.

The second primary characteristic of Adlerian brief therapy is focus. Indeed, a more accurate descriptor for the ABT model would be "focused, intermittent, brief therapy." Adlerian brief therapy is more about focus than about time. Counselor and client agree to focus their work for a specific period of time upon a single key area or issue of concern to the client in his or her interpersonal life. Other issues may be addressed at some future point, but for now the client and therapist stay focused on resolving the client's presenting concern(s). The idea of focusing therapy on but one single issue of current concern is perhaps what best defines Adlerian brief therapy. As noted by Wells and Phelps (1990), the key to successful brief therapy is therapeutic "focusing."

A third characteristic of ABT involves the nature of the counselor-client relationship. The counselor takes a direct and active role in therapy. It is the therapist's task to structure the session and work with the client as a partner in understanding the dynamics of the issue and in bringing about both cognitive and behavioral change. The ABT counselor-client relationship is furthermore based upon an optimistic, empowering attitude in regard to the client's capacity to change. Through a focus on the capabilities and strengths of the client—including even the skill and competence the client demonstrates in using his or her symptoms effectively—the counselor empowers the client by aligning with his or her competence rather than aligning against symptoms, viewed as deficits, weakness, or pathology. From the ABT perspective, traditional diagnostic-based labeling and treatment of possessed pathologies, disabilities, or deficiencies serve only to discourage the client and reinforce symptomatic behaviors as defense mechanisms. Being pathology focused may actually prolong treatment by increasing resistance and mistakenly reinforcing the idea that the client is unable to handle life effectively and competently.

The fourth characteristic of Adlerian brief therapy involves the therapist's perspective regarding the client's presenting symptoms and problematic behaviors. The client's presenting behavioral patterns are understood not as the problem(s) per se but rather as limited, mistaken, or counterproductive solutions to some underlying focus issue based in the client's cognitive schema (i.e., lifestyle) and based upon which he or she attaches meaning to, or interprets, life-events and makes behavioral choices. The client's presenting symptomatic behaviors are not the problem! Rather, the problematic behaviors are viewed as counterproductive solutions utilized in an attempt to deal with some issue in the client's life. ABT views the client as being "stuck" in a cycle of using the same behavioral patterns (often with increasing intensity) to resolve a problem without realizing that these patterns may actually maintain the problem, avoid the problem, or in many cases, exacerbate the problem. Much as a driver steps on the gas pedal of an automobile to get it unstuck from a hole of mud or ice, the client intensifies the same solution (first-order change), which unfortunately serves only to dig deeper into trouble.

Viewing presenting behavioral patterns not as problems but rather as the client's solutions to an underlying cognitive issue is similar to the way in which medicine views presenting symptoms. Presenting medical symptoms are often actually the body's solution to infection or disease processes. For example, coughing is merely the body's method of solving the problem of an obstructed trachea. Similarly, a high fever is the solution used by the body to fight an underlying infection. So too, ABT views the client's presenting symptomatic behaviors as the methods the client is currently utilizing to try to deal with some other underlying issue or concern in his or her life.

Finally, the fifth characteristic of ABT is the assignment of behavioral tasks for the client to carry out outside the therapeutic sessions. Actively demonstrating behavioral change, rather than passive suffering and emoting, is clearly established as the expectation for the client. Change is understood as taking place between counseling sessions, not within counseling sessions! The client is expected to actively engage in the alternative behavioral solutions discussed in therapy in his or her daily life between ABT sessions.

Basic Principles

Three basic principles of Adler's psychology are particularly relevant to brief therapies and to ABT: purposiveness, lifestyle, and social embeddedness. Presenting behaviors and symptoms are understood as serving, or intended to serve, a purpose or function for the client. The client most often is not consciously aware of the function that his or her actions actually serve; this purposive aspect of behavior occurs at a level of unaware-ness or preconsciousness. It follows logically from this principle that a client's presenting symptoms, such as anxiety or depression, are best understood not as problems themselves but rather as solutions. The client in ABT is viewed as presenting the therapist with a description of mis-taken, misguided, and/or counterproductive behavioral solutions to some underlying life problem or life task.

Adler's concept of lifestyle forms the basis for the ABT therapist's per-ception of the true problem issue for the client. The concept of lifestyle refers to an individual's unique cognitive schema, or rules for understand-ing self, life, and others; it involves the client's idiosyncratic style of per-ceiving and living. Thus, it follows that problems in living stem less from the objective situations confronting us than from the subjective meanings we each attach to these life situations. Each individual, in essence, writes his or her own set of rules about life, self, and others so as to be able to understand and make meaning out of life events and have a schema for how to effectively cope or deal with them. The key then to ABT is to iden-tify the client's underlying lifestyle rules that led to the presenting symp-tomatic behavior. Change then is a two-step process requiring first a reorientation of the client's lifestyle rules and, second, an exploration of new behavioral solutions.

Finally, Adler's foundational concept of social embeddedness is also central to the perspective and approach taken by the Adlerian brief ther-apist. Individual behavior can be understood only within the larger social context in which it occurs. Most significant among the social contexts in which we all function are the family system, the occupational system (including corporate and educational systems), the couple system, the community, and the culture. Thus, the ABT model assumes a systems per-spective by seeking the purpose or function that the symptom serves in the client's relationships within the social context(s) in which he or she functions and the part those systems, in turn, may also play in maintain-ing these problematic symptomatic behaviors.

Understanding Symptomatic Behavior

Every therapeutic approach has, at its foundation, some implicit or explicit assumptions about behavior that serve to guide the therapist in assessment and intervention processes. Based upon the principles delineated above, Adlerian brief therapy begins by assessing the dynamics of the client's behavior on a three-tiered basis (Figure 8-1). This three-tier model can be applied to understanding behaviors at any systemic level: individual, family, couple, cultural, business, or organization. The brief therapist begins treatment by striving to understand the client's presenting concerns at all three levels.

Figure 8–1: Three levels of behavior

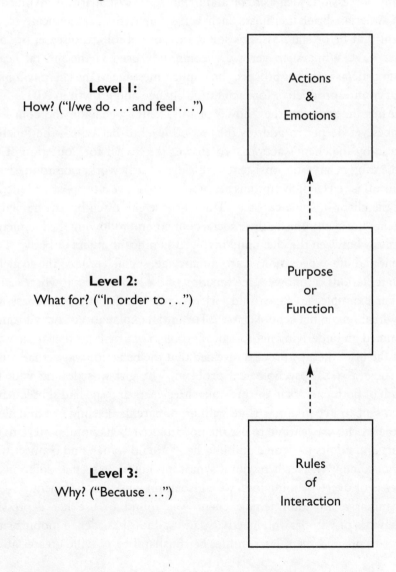

Level 1:
How? ("I/we do ... and feel ...")

Actions
&
Emotions

Level 2:
What for? ("In order to ...")

Purpose
or
Function

Level 3:
Why? ("Because ...")

Rules
of
Interaction

The first level of assessment is to identify the client's precise actions and emotions and the social context in which they occur. This level of behavior assessment focuses upon what the client actually does and how he or she feels while engaging in that behavior. The ABT counselor works with the client to determine exactly in what situations or circumstances the presenting issue occurs (and does not occur) and "how" the client is acting and feeling in relation to the presenting issue. It is important therefore to employ the tactic of altering the language of therapy. Verbs that imply possession, such as *to be* and *to have*, are systematically avoided by the Adlerian brief therapist. Such verbs implicitly communicate to the client that he or she possesses some form of pathology, disease, or character flaw. While such verbs are commonly used in the mental health diagnostic/assessment process, the implicit message to the client is considered counterproductive for facilitating change and growth in ABT.

After determining the "how" of the client's behavior, the counselor probes yet deeper to address the second level of behavior—the function served by the client's actions—to answer the "what for" question of the presenting behavior. Consistent with Adler's early work, causation (determinism) is rejected. Symptoms are assumed to serve a purpose or function for the client in some capacity. This purpose can often be ascertained by placing the symptoms in their social context and following the interaction patterns between the client and involved significant others or between the client and life expectations (career, marriage, social, etc.). As the sequence of interactions is followed, the function of the behavior is slowly revealed.

For example, an 8-year-old girl was referred for inattentiveness and daydreaming in her school classes. The initial explanation from educators assumed an underlying neurological problem of attention-deficit disorder, but the brief therapy process revealed that the behavior was actually used to solve a social-psychological problem. The girl was dealing with the death of both parents in the previous three years and she had subsequently been sent to live in a new state with grandparents. Feeling lost and alone in the world, she learned to use the nonattentive behavioral pattern to get peers and adults to "come and find her," attend to her, and connect with her in some way. Her behavioral symptoms could be seen as solutions to a sense of overwhelming loss, social isolation, and abandonment.

Similarly, an adult female client was found to use her depressing behaviors of withdrawal, inactivity, and sadness in order to mobilize first her parents and then, later in life, her husband to provide greater attention, assistance, and service. In both of these cases, the response patterns of others helped reveal the goal or purpose of the behavior. It is also important to note, however, that neither client was consciously aware of the purpose or function of her symptomatic behavior.

The third and deepest level of understanding behavior involves investigating the client's idiosyncratic rules of interaction. This level answers the third and final question: "why" the client handles life in this manner. "Why" refers here not to causal factors but to the rationale or the idiosyncratic logic system underlying the presenting behavior patterns.

Various theoretical models of counseling and therapy have referred to this idea, using such terms as the client's *basic assumptions, apperception, phenomenological perspective, private logic, belief systems,* and so forth. The essential component driving all behavior is understood to be the client's idiosyncratic cognitive schema, a cognitive framework through which he or she attaches meaning to life experiences and based upon which he or she consciously or unconsciously chooses behaviors. The rules of interaction concept is consistent with the theoretical principles of all cognitive-based therapies, from Adler's individual psychology to constructivism.

The Rules of Interaction concept holds for counseling and therapy at all systemic levels. In couple counseling, we strive to understand a couple's unique, unwritten "contract of expectations" (Hawes, 1989). All couples relate to one another based upon a set of assumptions and expectations regarding their relationship, one another's roles, and the normative expectations for fulfilling those roles. So too in family counseling, most approaches recognize the need to address the "family rule system" (Nichols & Schwartz, 1995), the unique metarule system that organizes family interaction patterns and structures. At the macrosystemic level with organizations, businesses, and cultures, we observe the same dynamic. The focus is always upon understanding the preconscious set of rules by which meaning is attached to events and upon which behaviors are chosen: the organizational culture, the corporate culture, or a shared world view. At the root of all human behavior (individual, familial, organizational, or cultural) lie rules of interaction.

Once these rules are recognized and understood, all behavioral patterns become understandable and, to some extent, predictable. If an individual starts with an assumption (a rule of interaction) that the world is a dangerous and threatening place, then it follows logically that he or she will approach social interactions very cautiously or defensively. The resultant goal (purpose) of avoiding perceived threats can then be realized through a variety of specific behavioral patterns, including withdrawal, the development of phobias and social isolation, or assuming a hostile and aggressive posture (i.e., a "preemptive strike" position), whenever one perceives a potential threat to his or her psychological or physical safety.

ABT's assessment strategy utilizes a variety of tactics or techniques to obtain an understanding of the client's behavior at all three levels. Intervention strategies are then focused first on initiating change in the client's rules of interaction and then on assisting the client to find alternative behavioral strategies for resolving the presenting issue from this new perspective. Unless the client can view or understand life from a different perspective, real and lasting change will not occur! Without a shift in perspective, one may observe short-term changes or first-order behavioral changes (i.e., change without change) that are merely new ways of doing the same old thing.

These three interrelated levels of behavior might be viewed as analogous to a child's bop-bag or punching-bag toy. The first level, behavioral actions and emotions, would be the head of the toy. The second level, purpose or function of behavior, would be the body. The rules of interaction would constitute the weighted bag at the bottom of the bop-bag. Thus, while one might temporarily move the location of the head (symptomatic behaviors) and even the body to some degree (purpose) through forceful intervention aimed at the head (symptom), eventually the bob-bag will return to its original position (i.e., homeostasis). A client, like the bop-bag, will maintain lasting change only if intervention is successfully focused on the third level of behavior, the rules of interaction (i.e., the weighted base). Just as one must move the weighted base of the bop-bag if the head is to remain permanently in a new location, so too in brief therapy one must focus on shifting the client's rules of interaction if lasting behavioral change is to result.

Strategies in the Adlerian Brief Therapy Process

The three levels of behavior can be translated into a four-strategy schema for the brief therapy process. These four strategic steps are identified with the acronym BURP: (B) behavioral description of the presenting issue, (U) underlying rules of interaction identification, (R) reorientation of the client's rules of interaction, and (P) prescribing new behavioral rituals. This four-strategy process is not necessarily followed in a simple, mechanistic manner. Rather, the Adlerian brief therapist follows this general four-strategy process more in terms of a structured flow rather than in a lock-stepped manner. Variations in the process may be necessary, given the particular client and presenting issue. The four-strategy model merely provides the brief therapist with an overall framework from which to work in each session as well as throughout the therapeutic process.

Strategy 1: Behavioral Description of the Presenting Issue

In obtaining a description of the presenting issue, the therapist seeks a detailed behavioral description as to how the problematic situation manifests in the client's daily life. The tactic of changing the client's language from implied possession of pathology to actively attempting to deal with a life situation is crucial at this stage. The therapist must help the client to describe the presenting issue of concern in behavioral (i.e., actions and emotions) terminology. This requires the client to utilize action verbs (ending in *ing*) when discussing the focus issue. The therapist gently directs the client away from the use of verbs implying possession or determinism, such as *to be, to have, to cause,* or *to make.* Such verbs (e.g., "I am . . . ," "I have . . . ," "I suffer from . . . ," "He makes me feel . . ."), while commonly used by clients and mental health professionals in describing a presenting problem or diagnosis, are countraindicated in Adlerian brief therapy. Such terms carry an implicit message that the client is somehow afflicted by or possesses some personality flaw, disorder, dysfunction, or disease that he or she has little or no power to control or change. Another tactic used to this end is to avoid the term *problem* (implying you "have a problem") and rather always asking the client, "What do you want to change or improve in your life?" which more optimistically implies growth and improvement in how one deals with life situations.

Using terminology that implies the possession of pathology places the client in a double-bind situation. The therapist is left asking the client to change that over or for which he or she has no control or responsibility.

For example, rather than allow a statement such as "I am depressed," the counselor might ask the client to describe specific times and situations in which he or she felt sad and depressed. Questioning tactics during the Strategy 1 process focus on such things as "What did you do the last time this occurred?" "Who else was affected?" "What did they do?" and "How did you respond?"

Through such questioning, the therapist not only obtains a more complete understanding of the presenting issue and symptoms but simultaneously facilitates the early stages of the reorientation process (Strategy 4). Changing the language of therapy subtly establishes a new perspective on the presenting symptom(s), involving a focus on one's cognitive processing and behavioral choices rather than upon passive victimization, personal flaws, and involuntary suffering. Utilizing action-oriented terminology to describe the presenting issue(s) produces something akin to hypnotic suggestion, conveying the implicit message that one chooses to use certain behaviors and therefore always has the capacity to choose different behaviors. Without directly stating so, the therapist begins to shift the client's perspective from "What I suffer from . . ." to "How I deal with . . .": in other words, from an external locus of control to an internal locus of control.

Another useful tactic for gently moving the client away from a passive, suffering perspective toward an active, problem-resolution perspective is to ask such questions as "Tell me about the last time this occurred," "What happens when you are anxious (depressed, out of control)?" and "Who is most affected by your symptoms?" By attending to the client's responses, a therapist can begin to identify how the client acts and feels, under what situations the symptoms are most likely to occur, and who (or what areas of life) is involved or affected by the symptomatic behaviors.

In addition, by carefully following the sequential nature and recurring patterns of problem-related interactions, the therapist begins to gain an understanding of the possible purpose or goal of the behavioral symptoms. Much as one observes a sport or game that one does not already know, the therapist observes the patterns of interaction and begins to sense and understand the purpose, or objective, of these actions and some underlying rules that determine how the client "plays the game of life."

Asking questions about the situations in which the symptoms are most likely to occur and who is involved or affected also helps move the therapist's understanding to the second level of behavior: the purpose or function of the symptoms. By identifying who in the client's social environment is affected by or involved in the symptomatic behavior, and the specific social situations in which the problems occur, the ABT counselor can develop hypotheses as to the possible conscious or preconscious purpose served by these symptoms.

Strategy 2: Identifying Underlying Rules of Interaction

The second strategy in the overall ABT process is to ascertain the essential rules of interaction that serve to maintain the presenting symptomatic behavior. Careful attention to the client's description of the presenting issue, the situations in which it occurs, and the behavioral sequences involved will provide the brief therapist with clues as to the possible purpose that the client's problematic behaviors serve (or are intended to serve). It may also assist the brief therapist in forming hypotheses as to possible underlying rules of interaction, based upon which the client perceives, attaches meaning to, and chooses behaviors in his or her life.

Seeing the presenting situation from the client's perspective (i.e., rules of interaction) makes the client's behaviors (or symptoms) completely understandable and indeed logical. This enables the ABT therapist to strategically align with the client rather than against the client's symptoms. The therapist positions himself or herself, not as an adversary, but as an ally. In this manner, resistance to therapy can be avoided, or at least minimized. Resistance is a process involving two opposing forces. In ABT the therapist's strategy is to minimize resistance by withdrawing his or her oppositional "force" and positioning himself or herself in an understanding and supportive role alongside the client. Only when the client feels understood and accepted, rather than criticized and attacked, is he or she likely to be receptive to working with the counselor toward change.

The ABT therapist can use numerous tactics to quickly gain accurate insight into the client's rules of interaction. While it is not within the scope of this chapter to discuss all possible tactics in detail, a few might be mentioned. Early childhood recollections have been found to be useful when they are understood not as historical events but rather as metaphors for the client's current rules of interaction (Mosak, 1972). For example, a woman in her mid-thirties came to therapy due to mild depression and feelings of unhappiness and uncertainty as to what to do about her life (occupational and marital problems, etc.). The woman offered an early memory of being alone on the screened porch of her home watching a party at the house next door and wishing she could join them but unsure if she would be accepted. The memory served as a metaphor for her life, viewing the world "out there" as interesting and exciting but also laden with the potential for rejection or failure, thus leaving her unwilling to let go of the security and safety of the known. Therapy therefore moved to a focus not upon her passive suffering from a mysterious afflic-tion called depression, but upon her choice (costs versus benefits) between remaining safe and seeking to discover her own potential in life.

Family stories and family genograms are tactics that can help reveal rules of interaction derived from the client's family system (Nicoll & Hawes, 1984). For example, an African-American male in his late twen-ties came to counseling because of career decision-making problems. He had begun at least five different master's degree programs, but about mid-way through his course of studies, he always found the field ill suited to him. A powerful family story that he recalled told how each generation had worked hard and suffered since the times of slavery to ensure that the next generation could go one step further in life than they had. The client's parents, aunts, and uncles were all professional people with degrees in medicine, law, and so on. It became clear that the client's prob-lem was to find some way to carry on the family mission of going "one step further." He essentially avoided inevitable failure by moving from field to field "trying" to find one where he could be more successful than the previous generation.

Asking the "magical question" ("How would your life change, be dif-ferent, if you did not suffer from these symptoms?") described by Dreikurs (1954) and later by proponents of solution-focused brief ther-apy, is another tactic that can be useful for ascertaining the underlying rules of interaction. For example, when asked, "How would life be dif-ferent if you didn't suffer from insomnia?" the client replied that she'd be fresh and alert enough to interview for jobs, take a job, and then finally not have to rely upon her parents for everything, including a place to live. The symptom of insomnia could be seen as a solution to this client's fears of dealing with life successfully on her own. Through the use of a sleeping disorder, she took the position of protecting herself from failure by avoid-ance. In ABT the "magical question" is understood as a technique to identify the underlying issue (rule) that is often the source of the client's resistance to change.

A variety of similar tactics or techniques can be utilized by the ABT therapist to better understand the underlying rules of interaction upon which the presenting symptomatic behavior is based. Often these techniques result in useful metaphors for the presenting issue, which can then be used to facilitate cognitive change and suggest behavioral options. In any case, at this point in the ABT process, the therapist should be able to align with the client's symptoms by recognizing that given these rules of interaction and this situation, he or she too would behave in a similar manner (i.e., the symptoms follow logically from the rules of interaction). But the therapist also recognizes that the client could choose to consider alternative perspectives in addition to the one currently held. This sets the stage for intervention strategies that facilitate a cognitive shift in the rules of interaction and seeking behavioral solutions based on the new perspective.

Strategy 3: Reorientation of the Client's Rules of Interaction

Essential to successful intervention and problem resolution is the therapist's ability to facilitate a cognitive shift in the client's understanding of the presenting issue through reorientation. This is the most critical strategy in the ABT process. During the assessment process (Strategies 1 and 2), the therapist will have obtained a fairly clear picture of the dynamics of the client's behavior at all three levels (how, what for, and why). Now the ABT process can be directed to facilitating change. But it cannot be stated too strongly that essential to a successful initiation of change processes is the careful attention paid to the preceding assessment strategies and the accurate identification of the dynamics of the presenting problem at all three levels of the client's presenting symptomatic behavior. The great paradox of brief therapy is that the key to successful brief interventions is to proceed slowly and carefully through the assessment stages.

The dynamics of change begin with reorientation—assisting the client to view his or her behavior from a different perspective. Albert Einstein is said to have stated that one cannot solve a problem by using the same thinking that created it. This insight is very much to the essence of Adlerian brief therapy. The therapist seeks to help the client obtain a new perspective, insight, and understanding or to attach a new meaning to the presenting issue. Once the client can be assisted to understand the issue from a new perspective, he or she will seek new behavioral options that are consistent with this new position.

For example, if the client's rules of interaction consist of themes that he or she is inept, incapable, and likely to fail at anything attempted, then such a client is highly unlikely to engage in any challenging task. Rather, such an individual may develop myriad behaviors (symptoms) that all serve the function of protecting himself or herself from failure. Avoidance, procrastination, displays of incompetence, forgetfulness, excessive anxiety, and so forth may all be used as excuses for poor performance or to solicit others to step in and provide assistance. Without an alteration in this perspective, the client will engage only in first-order change processes; that is, finding new ways of doing the same thing—avoiding personal failure.

Many therapeutic intervention tactics may be employed within the reorientation strategy process. These tactics all serve to reorient the client's current perceptions (rules of interaction) relative to the presenting issue(s). Reframing is perhaps the most central tactic of the ABT process. It is actually begun during the first few minutes of therapy, when the client is asked to describe the presenting issue(s) in behavioral terminology. Presenting issues may be understood through three possible "frames of reference": the medical, the moral, and the relational. Most clients present in therapy with an understanding of their difficulties based on the moral or medical frame of reference. The medical frame of reference sees the symptoms as the result of some medical or neurological flaw or pathologic process, such as depression or phobias, attention-deficit disorder or a personality disorder, or a genetic predisposition such as proneness to uncontrolled angry outbursts "like all men in my family." The medical frame carries the implicit message that responsibility for controlling the symptomatic behaviors remains outside the client's abilities and therefore requires medical intervention of some type (e.g., medication or surgery).

Other clients present in therapy with an understanding based on a moral frame of reference. Such clients will explain that their symptoms are the sign of a moral or character flaw, such as laziness, obstinancy, immaturity, selfishness, defiance, lack of motivation, and so forth. Such moral explanations are most frequently seen in marital and family therapy, where a spouse or child's behavior, viewed as the source of all problems, is said to be based in some moral or character deficiency. Implicit in this frame of reference is the message that sole responsibility for change lies with the spouse or child, and everyone else is a passive, innocent victim. ABT works to move the client(s) away from a moral or medical frame of reference and toward a relational frame; that is, one concerned with how individuals interact with one another or the social environment and the resulting problem-maintaining behavioral cycles.

Additional reorientation tactics may also be utilized in the process of ABT. Relabeling, for example, may be used to place a positive connotation on a behavior seen negatively or a negative connotation on a behavior previously viewed as positive. For example, a mother who did everything for her two daughters and who described herself as a "good, devoted mother" was relabeled a "disabling mother" in therapy, noting that both daughters acted as if they were incapable or disabled in a competition for their mother's attention and service. In another example, a defiant adolescent was relabeled as one who was "determined and a chip off the old block," connecting his behavior to father's perception of himself. Thus, the father-son relationship problems could be viewed as the son's attempt not to rebel or "defy Dad," but to emulate or "be like Dad."

Humor is also frequently used in ABT as a tactic for initiating the reorientation process. Indeed, helping the client see the humor in the presenting behavioral patterns can begin a cognitive shift. The client begins to view the problem situation from a disassociative and analytical rather than an associative and emotional perspective. Further, humor adds positive affect to the presenting issue, with its existing negative affect, thereby attaching a new meaning and perspective to the issue. It is important that in using humor, the therapist be aligned with the client and focus on the behavioral patterns themselves and not be seen as putting the client down or laughing at him or her.

Additional tactics that can assist in reorientation have been identified and described by many models of counseling and therapy. For example, the tactic of externalizing the symptom—talking about the symptomatic behavior as an external threat to the client rather than an internal flaw—has been described and utilized in narrative therapy (White & Epston, 1990). Utilizing metaphors can be a highly effective tactic for clients in viewing themselves and their situation differently (Kopp, 1995). Useful metaphors often arise during the process of uncovering the client's rules of interaction (Strategy 2). For example, a 15-year-old girl was brought to therapy because of her sullen, passive defiance of parental demands. Both her parents and her younger brother were quick to identify and criticize all her misdeeds. Given the girl's identified interest in art, she was invited to draw a picture or mural that would portray her view of the family relationships. This tactic is often referred to as relationship imagery, in which the client creates a picture that represents his or her view of the relationship using only animate or inanimate objects but not people. In this case, the girl drew a picture of three circling hawks and a field mouse hiding under a rock. The picture created a very powerful metaphor that moved the family to understand that what they had perceived as merely passive defiance was actually based in fear and self-protectiveness. The reorientation process therefore consisted of discussing how hawks would create an environment safe for a field mouse, thereby helping the family begin the process of resolving their issues and building a new relationship pattern.

It is usually most effective for the therapist, in the reorientation process, to assume a nonthreatening, one-down position vis-à-vis the client. This approach is sometimes referred to as "Columbo tactics," based on the 1970s television detective show. Such a therapeutic position helps to minimize resistance and empower the client to seek and discover alternative aspects of the presenting issue. In the one-down "creative misunderstanding" tactic, the therapist expresses his or her confusion about a contradiction between the stated intent of the client and the behavioral strategies employed: for example, "I hear you telling me that you want your husband to spend more time with you, yet you also tell me that you attempt to convey this message by meeting him with criticism and complaints when he comes home. Help me understand this now—how will your behavior facilitate a desire on his part to spend more time with you?" "Active wondering" is another useful one-down tactic, in which the therapist offers the client alternative perspectives or hypotheses to consider regarding the dynamics of the presenting problem: for example, "I'm not sure here, but I can't help but wonder if perhaps sometimes your depressive episodes don't also work for you a little by helping you avoid difficult situations and mobilizing others to take care of you."

In the process of facilitating a cognitive reorientation in the client's understanding of the presenting issue, the therapist might utilize any number of tactics, of which just a few have been noted here. The choice of which to use must be based on the nature of the presenting issue and the characteristics of the client. In all cases, however, the therapist must maintain a position of acceptance and alignment with the client rather than mistakenly assuming an oppositional stance aligned against the client's symptoms. Such a position is likely to result in overt or covert resistance and thereby undermine the therapeutic process. Indeed, some clients may even attempt to lure the therapist into a position of criticism of the client's views and behaviors. The function of such attempts may be to defeat therapy by engaging the therapist in a subtle power struggle, in which, of course, the client need only continue the symptomatic behaviors to win, while responsibility for therapeutic failure can be placed entirely upon the therapist. This pattern is frequently observed with clients who have been sent to therapy by some authority figure or who are so fearful of change that they seek to avoid it and place blame on the therapist for their nonimprovement.

Strategy 4: Prescribing New Behavioral Rituals

The final strategic step in the ABT process involves prescribing new behavioral rituals. Such rituals consist of new behavioral tasks for the client to perform outside of therapy. Brief therapy, as stated previously, is based upon the assumption that change occurs not within the therapy session but rather between therapy sessions. The client is not allowed to assume the role of passive sufferer but instead is expected to actively engage in the change process outside of therapy.

Rituals can be defined as regular, repeated actions that serve to reaffirm or maintain underlying rules of interaction for a system. Religious rituals, for example, are used to reaffirm church members' belief system. Ritual activities (e.g., salesperson of the month) in the workplace can be seen as reinforcing the corporate culture, thereby defining and reaffirming what is important or valued in the organization.

Similarly, a client's symptoms might be viewed as ritualistic behaviors that serve the function of reaffirming for the client his or her underlying rules of interaction. As such, they often develop into self-fulfilling prophecies. Experiencing a panic attack, for example, might serve to help a client avoid a feared situation while simultaneously reaffirming the underlying rule of interaction that he or she is somehow flawed and incapable of coping with certain life situations effectively. Consequently, when the client is assisted to view his or her symptoms and situation differently (i.e., reorientation), he or she will need to learn new behavioral options (rituals) that will help him or her deal with the presenting situation more effectively and that will simultaneously reaffirm the new, healthier perspective regarding self, others, and life.

Performing a ritual involves taking action. This last step in the ABT process involves prescribing new behaviors for the client to utilize when dealing with the presenting concern from a new perspective. At this point in treatment, the therapist can use either of two types of therapeutic tactics, based upon what he or she has learned about the client during the therapy process. The first type is "compliance-based tactics," which assume that the client is motivated to work with the therapist and implement change in his or her life situation. The second group of tactics are "noncompliance-based," in which the client is thought likely to try to sabotage his or her own progress in order to remain in the safe, or advantageous, position of bearing symptoms. As a rule, it is best to begin with compliance-based tactics and move to noncompliance-based tactics only if deemed necessary by the client's sabotaging responses or resistance to change. One can always move from compliance to noncompliance tactics, but once a therapist assumes a noncompliance-based position, it is difficult to move back to compliance-based approaches.

Many types of compliance-based rituals can be used, depending upon the needs of the client. For example, the therapist might introduce new interaction steps into a repetitive sequence between a husband and wife for handling conflict (i.e., changing-the-choreography rituals). Or an individual might be taken out of, or placed into, an ongoing problem interaction to change the sequence (i.e., changing-the-actors rituals). Other commonly prescribed rituals include restoring positive rituals, connecting rituals, desensitization rituals, and boundary-making rituals (Nicoll, 1997). All involve prescribing specific new behavioral interactions that are to be performed on a regular, repeated basis and that reaffirm the new meaning or understanding associated with the presenting issue through the reorientation process.

In noncompliance-based tactics, the therapist takes the paradoxical position that change should not occur or, at least, not too quickly. For example, a noncompliant client may expect the therapist to engage in a power struggle with him or her over the presenting symptomatic behaviors. But when the therapist cautions against change, the client is placed in a double bind. Refusing to change will align the client with the therapist, whom he or she is however consciously or unconsciously attempting to defeat. But defeating the therapist (or those who sent him or her to therapy) requires the client to initiate growth and change—despite the therapist's cautions. Either outcome is acceptable to the therapist.

Therapists use three basic tactics within the noncompliance-based approach. The first tactic is to prescribe the symptom. When the client maintains that he or she is unable to control the symptomatic behavior, the therapist suggests that the client actively engage in the problematic behavior but at an increased rate or intensity or at a different time or location. Regardless of whether the client is successful, simply making the attempt confirms that the client does indeed have some control over the behavior. This information is used to return to the previous stage of reorientation for further exploration in therapy.

A second noncompliance tactic is paradoxical positioning. Here the therapist unexpectedly aligns with the symptom and suggests to the client that it may be adaptive and functional at the present time. The client is instructed not to change at the present time, as to do so would be risky. For example, an adolescent client had developed a debilitating fear or phobia that he would contract the HIV virus. Accordingly, he had withdrawn from all extracurricular and social activities and spent most of his time at home expressing his worries and concerns to his parents, who in turn attempted to reassure and console him. Three therapists had unsuccessfully used compliance-based tactics; the present therapist obtained additional information during Strategy 2 and chose to take the paradoxical position of suggesting that the client was punishing or "grounding" himself for not living up to his own high standards. Therefore, he suggested, perhaps parents should stop reassuring and catering to him and instead let him "ground himself" until he felt it no longer necessary. The outcome was that the adolescent was outraged at the therapist's suggestion that he continue to worry and isolate himself, and chose to "defeat" treatment by resuming his normal life activities and refusing to worry obsessively about HIV/AIDS.

The third noncompliance tactic is to restrain change. In this situation, the therapist instructs the client to move toward change very slowly and gradually. This approach is particularly useful with clients who are likely to self-sabotage or defeat themselves through overambitious goals and expectations. The client who sets unrealistic standards for his or her success is likely to then take any setback or slight relapse as proof of treatment failure and return to the status quo. By cautioning against rapid change, the therapist can congratulate the client for occasional setbacks as signs that he or she is growing and implementing changes at a realistic, gradual pace.

Regardless of which tactics are used, the strategy of prescribing new behavioral rituals involves the client in actively making behavioral changes in his or her life outside of the therapy session. It cannot be emphasized enough, however, that the success of these prescriptions is based entirely upon the therapist's ability to successfully bring about a shift, change, or reorientation in the client's original rules of interaction. The reorientation strategy is the key to change. It is the shifting of the "bop-bag's" base. Only when the client can view his or her symptoms from a new perspective will he or she be prepared to seek and then employ alternative behavioral strategies. The new behavioral rituals that the therapist gives the client are directives for handling the presenting situation differently that simultaneously reaffirm this new perspective. Two case examples may illustrate the change process delineated by the ABT framework.

Clinical Indications

The four-strategy process of Adlerian brief therapy is generally applicable to all presenting issues in counseling and psychotherapy, although some modifications may be necessary in particular instances. Presenting concerns related to interpersonal problems, psychosomatic complaints, and psychological adjustment difficulties not based in any identifiable medical etiology lend themselves particularly well suited to Adlerian brief therapy. In addition, the four-strategy process, and the tactics related to each, can be useful in helping clients with somatic-based complaints (such as with chronic illness, disability and biologically based disorders), as well as the entourage of significant others involved with the client, cope more effectively with the problem.

There are several instances, however, in which the ABT approach must be modified and/or combined with other treatment modalities to provide optimal treatment to clients. For example, when biological factors are implicated, the ABT model should be used only in conjunction with a holistic approach incorporating medical interventions and case management assistance. Also, when issues such as childhood abuse, alcohol and drug abuse, or grief and loss are identified in the course of the first two assessment-related strategies, the therapeutic contract is best modified to incorporate long-term, supportive treatment modalities, such as support group counseling. In all situations, the issue of time must not be misunderstood as restricting treatment to a specific number of sessions. Rather, ABT is to be viewed as a focused, short-term, intermittent treatment process. Time, in relation to number of sessions, time per session, and the spacing of time between sessions must be used flexibly based upon the presenting issue(s) and needs of the particular client.

Clinical Applications with an Individual

A 21-year-old male, Derek, came to counseling due to recent problems with panic attacks. These attacks suddenly began shortly after he returned to his university campus for a third year of study. The problem had escalated to the point that he was initially hospitalized and then sent home for treatment, as the attacks prevented him from living on campus and continuing his studies. Since returning home, the attacks had significantly decreased, but he was concerned about possible recurrences.

When the therapist asked Derek to describe one of his most recent panic attacks, the young man stated that they typically occurred in the evenings at his dormitory. He would awaken feeling very agitated and frightened and sweating profusely, to the point that he had difficulty breathing. On several occasions, his roommates had to call for emergency assistance from the campus medical center. Such attacks had never occurred in his first two years of study. Questioning related to the social context of his life revealed that during those years his older brother was a graduate student at the same school but had graduated the previous spring semester. This was the client's first semester "out in the world" alone.

The therapist used the tactic of early childhood recollections, which revealed Derek's memory of being alone in the kitchen with his alcoholic father. "My father and I were laughing and joking about something, when suddenly he turned around and hit me in the mouth with his fist as hard as he could. I bounced off the wall and fell to the floor. I never could figure out what I had said or what happened to cause him to hurt me like that." This memory served as a metaphor for Derek's underlying rules of interaction, revealing his idiosyncratic view of the world as fraught with potential dangers and quite unpredictable and of himself as relatively naive and vulnerable. Further, as the youngest of three boys with an explosive, alcoholic father, he had learned to cope or survive by aligning closely with older, protective family members, such as his eldest brother and his mother: "I was the type of kid always clinging to Mom's apron strings or tagging along with my older brother."

In this case, the three levels of behavior can be quickly observed during the first two stages of brief therapy. Rather than viewing Derek as "suffering from" mysterious panic attacks, a position of powerlessness and victimization that would only reaffirm his existing perceptions of self, the therapist reframed his presenting issue in relational terms, viewing him as someone who, based upon early life experiences, had come to perceive the world as being very dangerous and unpredictable, a place where one can be easily hurt (rule of interaction). Consequently, Derek's approach to life was to seek safety and security by aligning with individuals he viewed as stronger and more capable than himself and protective of him (purpose). When placed in a situation without such supports, he responded by unconsciously reminding himself of how dangerous his situation could be, and he employed panic attack symptoms (behaviors). Interestingly, the result of these symptoms was to obtain protection and support, first through hospitalization and then through returning to living at home under the safety and protection of his mother. Thus, he found safety and protection once again, only this time through the anxiety disorder symptoms. His presenting symptom, anxiety, served as his "solution" to an underlying issue of avoiding an unpredictable and dangerous world, by remaining in the protection of a safe environment.

Treatment then focused on identifying Derek's strengths and capabilities and finding ways to gradually use these methods to handle life situations even when they were unpredictable. Tasks were assigned to gradually engage him in more activities (education and part-time employment) where he would have to function on his own. His anxiety level was monitored as a gauge of how potentially dangerous each situation was to him, and he was assisted in developing alternative strategies for dealing with life events or requesting assistance without reverting to full-blown panic attacks. But the therapist always maintained the alignment with the symptom by noting that Derek always had this very effective strategy to fall back upon when things seemed too overwhelming. Over the course of the next several sessions (scheduled semiweekly), progress was observed, until Derek decided that he no longer needed to check in regularly with the therapist but could always return if he felt a need for a "booster" session if things seemed to be getting too stressful for him to handle alone or with support from his mother, friends, or siblings.

Clinical Applications with a Couple

A young couple, Bob and Mary, came to therapy due to their uncertainty as to where to go with their relationship. They had met during medical school and had now been dating for over seven years. On at least four separate occasions over the course of the relationship, they had announced a formal engagement, only to break it off, split up, and then reunite. Both were now physicians with their own practices well established. When asked to give some examples of times they decided to cancel marriage plans and end the engagement, a pattern emerged. In each instance, as the wedding date neared, Mary felt increasingly anxious about the potential success of their marriage. Eventually she would announce the engagement ended and express fears that the marriage would not work.

Each time this occurred, Bob would feel devastated and then set out to demonstrate to her that her fears were ill founded. Mary, in turn, would then feel bad about all he was going through just for her and agree to return to the relationship, which would then quickly proceed through the stages of dating, engagement, wedding plans, Mary's increasing anxiety, breaking the engagement, and finally Bob's attempts to win her back.

On one occasion, Mary noted her desire to have children and expressed strong doubts that, given the demands of his practice, Bob would have time to be a devoted, involved father. After she broke off the engagement, Bob set out to prove just how much he was willing to go through to be both a successful physician and a devoted, involved father. That spring he volunteered to coach two local Little League teams, attending every game and practice faithfully. Mary noted, "How could I not go back to him after he was willing to go through that much work and stress just to demonstrate to me how good a father he would be?!"

Since the couple had expressed the importance of church and their religious beliefs even in their initial telephone call for an appointment, the therapist decided to use a tactic for identifying the couple-system's underlying rules of interaction (sometimes referred to as the couple's contract of expectations) that were respectful of the role religious beliefs played in their lives. Bob and Mary were each asked to share their favorite religious story or parable from memory (i.e., without biblical consultation). This tactic is based on the idea that favorite childhood stories are most easily recalled, because they represent in some way how we see ourselves and our own lives metaphorically through the story.

In this case, Mary spoke of the story of the Good Samaritan who, upon coming upon a poor, suffering man at the side of the road, took pity on him and picked him up and gave him water, food, and clothing. This story fit very well with Mary's approach to life, having dedicated herself to working in a community clinic for low-income patients. Bob, on the other hand, always liked the story of the Prodigal Son, which he recalled was about a father who had two sons, one of whom went off into the world behaving irresponsibly and the other of whom stayed home and toiled on the farm with his father year after year. Years later the irresponsible son returned, and the father celebrated by ordering the slaying of a fatted calf and a feast. Bob noted that he always identified with the older brother who stayed home and did all the right things, and yet nobody had ever slain a fatted calf for him—though he deserved it even more than his brother!

These stories were used in ABT to help the couple understand how they each approached life and their relationship. Bob came to see how he used "good, responsible" behavior as a means of justifying his demands for getting what he wanted over the objections of others. Mary, in turn, quickly recognized her pattern of dismissing or sacrificing her own needs in order to take care of others first. Thus, their relationship contract appeared to be based upon a rule system whereby Bob got what he wanted by "toiling away in the fields," proving his worthiness, while Mary felt sorry for his noble suffering and continuously put his needs, or wants, above hers.

During the reorientation process, the therapist used the tactic of active wondering. He couldn't help but wonder, he said, if part of Mary's reason for coming to counseling was to have the therapist take responsibility for Bob's emotional well-being, so that she could leave and move on with her life without feeling guilty. This observation resulted in an immediate recognition response from Mary. Bob too noted the patterns of his behavior, not only in his relationship with Mary but with family members and professional colleagues as well. Discussion between the couple moved quickly at this point to Mary's expressing her true desire to leave the relationship but had feelings of guilt in doing so since Bob was such a "good person who really needs me." The result of this single session of brief couple counseling was that Mary felt empowered to decisively state her intention of ending the relationship permanently, while Bob asked to return for additional individual sessions to work on developing better relationships with his family and colleagues that did not result in overt appreciation but covert resentment.

Summary

These case studies illustrate the application of the Adlerian brief therapy process in individual and couple counseling. Different clients and different presenting issues will require the use of alternative tactics, but the overall process and strategies for effecting growth and change remain the same. ABT interventions follow a pattern of first identifying specific behaviors and emotions utilized by the client(s) in relation to the presenting problematic life situation. Then the therapist utilizes appropriate tactics to obtain a clearer understanding of the client's underlying rules of interaction that maintain the problematic cycle of behavior (i.e., the idiosyncratic cognitive schema that is used to assign meaning to life situations). Based upon this understanding, the therapist guides the client toward considering the presenting symptoms or issue from a new, alternative perspective (reorientation), then assists the client in identifying new behavioral strategies (i.e., behavioral rituals) for resolving the presenting concern.

References

Christensen, O., Bitter, J., Hawes, C., & Nicoll, W.G. (1997). *Strategies and techniques in brief therapy: Individuals, couples and families.* (Training manual available from the Adlerian Training Institute, P.O. Box 276358, Boca Raton, FL 33427.)

Dreikurs, R. (1954). The psychological interview in medicine. *American Journal of Individual Psychology, 10,* 98–122.

Hawes, E. C. (1989). Therapeutic interventions in the marital relationship. In R. M. Kern, E. C. Hawes, & O. C. Christensen (Eds.), *Couples therapy: An Adlerian perspective* (pp. 77–114). Minneapolis, MN: Educational Media Corporation.

Kopp, R. R. (1995). *Metaphor therapy.* New York: Brunner/Mazel.

Mosak, H. H. (1972). *Early recollections as a projective technique.* Chicago: Alfred Adler Institute.

Nichols, M. P., & Schwartz, R. C. (1995). *Family therapy: Concepts and methods* (3rd ed.). Boston: Allyn & Bacon.

Nicoll, W. (1997). Brief therapy: Strategies and techniques. (American Counseling Association National Workshop materials, Alexandria, VA.)

Nicoll, W. G., & Hawes, E. C. (1984). Family lifestyle assessment: The role of family myths and values in the client's presenting issues. *Individual Psychology, 41*(2), 147–160.

Wells, R. A., & Phelps, P. A. (1990). The brief psychotherapies: A selective overview. In R. A. Wells and V. J. Giannetti (Eds.), *Handbook of the brief psychotherapies.* New York: Plenum Press.

Annotated Bibliography

The following texts are suggested for individuals seeking further information regarding Adler's individual psychology theory as a basis for Adlerian brief therapy:

Adler, A. (1979). *Superiority and social interest: A collection of later writings* (by H. L Ansbacher & R. R. Ansbacher, Eds.). New York: W.W. Norton.

Dreikurs, R. (1973). *Psychodynamics, psychotherapy and counseling.* Chicago: Alfred Adler Institute.

Mosak, H. H. (1977). *On purpose.* Chicago: Alfred Adler Institute.

Shulman, B. H. (1973). *Contributions to individual psychology.* Chicago: Alfred Adler Institute.

The following readings are suggested for information regarding specific therapeutic strategies and techniques consistent with Adlerian brief therapy:

Carlson, J., & Manaster, G. J. (Eds.). (1989). Varieties of brief therapy [Special issue]. *Individual Psychology: The Journal of Adlerian Theory, Research, and Practice, 45*(1 & 2).

Fisch, R., Weakland, J.H., & Segal, L. (1982). *The tactics of change: Doing therapy briefly.* San Francisco: Jossey-Bass. This text on brief strategic therapy from the Mental Research Institute in Palo Alto is very consistent with and complements the principles, strategies, and tactics of Adlerian brief therapy.

Kern, R., Hawes, E. C., & Christensen, O.C. (1989). *Couples therapy: An Adlerian approach.* Minneapolis, MN: Educational Media.

9

Efficient Adlerian Therapy with Individuals and Couples

Steven Slavik,
Len Sperry,
and
Jon Carlson

It is well established that brief therapy is both cost-effective and thera-peutically effective. Various theories have been proposed to account for its effectiveness and to justify its use (Sperry, 1989). But little litera-ture describes the actual strategy of brief therapy, as distinct from the spe-cific tactics and techniques used in its implementation.

The purpose of this chapter is to focus on the strategy of brief or, as we prefer, efficient Adlerian therapy. Unlike other approaches described in this book, which elaborate four or more strategies, we will describe only one strategy. But this single strategy is supported by several tactics. It defines at least one perspective and plan of action without detailing actual techniques used. Efficient Adlerian therapy joins problem-focused and solution-focused therapies in that it is not a curtailed version of a therapy initially seen as long term; it was originally designed to be as efficient as possible (Ansbacher, 1989).

Efficient Adlerian Therapy:
Historical Background and Basic Concepts

Alfred Adler received his medical training at the University of Vienna in 1895 and practiced general medicine before focusing on psychiatric issues. In 1902 Freud invited him to join his discussion group, later the Vienna Psychoanalytic Society, of which Adler became president in 1910. Soon thereafter, Adler resigned from the society, largely because of Freud's pressure for uniformity and strict allegiance to his theory. Contrary to popular belief, Adler was never a disciple of Freud but rather a colleague whose viewpoint increasingly diverged from Freud's. As Adler's view developed into a system, he established the Society for Individual Psychology in 1912. Before he died in 1937, Adler had published more than 300 books and articles articulating an approach to psychotherapy that today would be described as essentially constructivist and systemic, emphasizing briefer treatment and solution-focused interventions (Carlson & Sperry, 1998a).

A number of concepts inform Adlerian psychotherapy (Adler, 1956). *Holism* is the suggestion that the individual is a unified whole; individual motivation unites perceptual, affective, cognitive, and conative processes into a coherent unity. One's *goal* is an image of what one will be when perfect or complete, serving as a model of the unity of the individual. Instead of accepting oneself as a human being among others, one strives for the *superiority* felt in the goal, thereby avoiding a felt sense of inferiority. *Apperception* is the perception of one's capacities and environment "as if" they were resources and opportunities to achieve one's goal. *Community feeling* is the apperception that one is a welcome part of the cosmic and social world and is capable of dealing with the tasks of life as they present themselves. Presence of community feeling differentiates a horizontal striving for communal welfare from a vertical striving for self-aggrandizement. Lack of community feeling is shown in *pessimism,* the conviction that anything one does will turn out badly; and in *self-discouragement,* the reluctance to try to solve problems and to better oneself, avoiding challenges that may increase one's community feeling.

Thus Adler described only one motivating force: a striving for perfection or completion in order to overcome life's challenges. This striving itself creates a sense of inferiority, aiding in the creation of the direction for the striving in the form of a final, fictive goal. Behavior is then directed by this image of the goal. Motivation "pulls" the individual: behavior is motivated by the final goal and the individual's concern for the future. Action is oriented in and toward a social context in which others could be apperceived as equal; but—given pessimism and discouragement and the sense that one does not belong—one may not understand that one is, or act as if one were, equal to others. Many personal and interpersonal problems become issues of status.

Efficient Adlerian therapy, derived from Adler's approach to psychotherapy, was developed over the past 10 years by us in response to the demand for briefer, outcomes-based psychotherapy. While consistent without the basic theoretical premises articulated by Adler, this approach has been tailored and adapted to the unique needs of North America. In other words, efficient Adlerian therapy is an inculcated therapy approach.

Efficient Adlerian therapy is based primarily on the unique theoretical assumption that all people are equal. This belief can be summarized simply as: The therapist has no privileged knowledge or position in regard to the client. The therapist is a consultant in human affairs who, in cooperation with a client, helps to solve certain problems or difficulties the client currently or habitually experiences in living. A therapist acts as a consultant in this process, rather than as an expert on another's life, and relies on client cooperation in matching solutions to situations. Since the client may be unacquainted with equality, the burden of cooperation lies primarily on the therapist rather than on the client (LeShan, 1996). In efficient Adlerian therapy, the premise of equality explicitly structures all therapist-client meetings from beginning to end.

Basic Strategy

Generally speaking, Adlerian therapy tends to be reasonably efficient. Nothing special needs to be said about motivating or justifying efficiency as such. It seems to be built into the purposes of Adlerian therapy and the typical training of Adlerian therapists. Other than the standard techniques of Adlerian therapy (Carlson & Slavik, 1997), in combination with the quick wits of therapist and client, no methods get to the heart of a problem more quickly than the client can understand and do something about it and the therapist can focus on, suggest, and motivate a solution. Whether 1 or 100 sessions are sufficient, efficiency is a universal strategy in Adlerian therapy. The basic strategy is to *make a difference* to a client as effectively as possible (Bitter, Christensen, Hawes, & Nicoll, 1997), while never doing for clients what they can do or can learn to do for themselves. Alternatively, the therapist should never be more ambitious for success than the client.

Tactics

Engage the Client

It is vital for the therapist, at the beginning of therapy, to engage the client in cooperation and collaboration. This cannot be overemphasized. Premature termination and failure of therapy are often the result of poor engagement (Sperry, 1999). Engagement is made positively where possible, through clarification of what the therapist can and will do (and often through clarification of what is not possible, such as ensure what a third party will do) and what is expected of the client. Without cooperation, the possibilities of tailored treatment (Carlson & Sperry, 1998b) are limited. If engagement fails—that is, if the client does not make and/or keep a contract—cooperation can be elicited negatively, for a short term, by either the refusal to participate, or the explicit and temporary agreement to participate, in covert attempts to make the therapist responsible for the client, and by clarification of those efforts. The therapist can explain the adage to "do nothing for another that one can do for oneself."

Focus Treatment

In therapy, the *client's* problem is addressed, not the therapist's take on life, or his or her need for high numbers of appointments, prestige, affiliation, or income. The client, with the therapist's help, states, clarifies, and defines the problem, what may constitute a solution, the action necessary, and when it is solved. This does not preclude the therapist's joining, empathizing, clarifying, reframing, using technique, offering suggestions, persuading, arguing, or talking about oneself. But the client is the arbiter of satisfaction regarding results.

Emphasize Client Strengths and Competence

The client is assumed and shown to be competent in many ways. Any individual has strengths, competencies, talents, and skills to address life. Perhaps they are underdeveloped or underrated, discounted, or disregarded. In the mistaken attempt to prove that one is a "person" or better than oneself, a client's ambition may lead to a devaluation of his or her "commonplace" abilities. It is the therapist's work to locate and perhaps to train, encourage, and make use of the competence a client has, to build on strengths. In this work, the therapist neither pampers nor abuses the client but cultivates a position of mutual respect. The therapist does not do anything for the client that is within his or her own capabilities; nor does the therapist expect the client to do anything that he or she is clearly untrained to do.

The *attitude* that, of course, the client can handle and solve the presented problem must predominate sessions. The attitude that "God does not present us with problems we cannot handle, particularly with help," must prevail. Without encouraging any specific solutions, optimism that the client has acted and will continue to act in ways beneficial to self and others—and that others have good will—must pervade sessions. This attitude is particularly important for the client with a "yes, but" attitude, denying the effectiveness of any specific suggestion. This occurs frequently if working with laid-off, middle to late-aged workers who have no plans and who consider themselves trapped by circumstance.

The therapist does not fall into a client's trap of seeing the client (or a partner) as incompetent, malicious, or stupid. Efforts to do so are always reframed positively. One option is to say, "Well, miserliness is a virtue these days, isn't it?" Another is to try, "Gosh, it would be nice if we could get rid of the problem so easily, but we usually criticize in others what we don't let ourselves do." As a last resort, for the recalcitrant critic, one can simply agree with a criticism and work with it as a restriction of options in the client's life, reminding the client any time he or she tries to venture away from it.

Think "Short Term"

The therapist thinks "short term" continually and so thoroughly that he or she never invites the client to do anything in the office except solve the problem. The therapist is so "short term" that he or she makes problems into practical issues whenever possible, resorting to "psychological" solutions only when necessary. For example, guilt can be interpreted as regret, and then something can done about it (Mosak, 1987). Issues can be broken down into small steps to create manageable short-term goals for immediate or more immediate experience of success.

From the moment of saying "I'm glad to meet you" to "It's been a pleasure to work with you," the therapist is assessing the attitude of the client that may have led to the experienced difficulty and seeking the most expedient way of relieving it. This process is based on the Adlerian assumption that individuals create their own difficulties through being unwilling to act differently. Formal diagnosis is not always important; informal assessment of interpersonal style and dominant attitude (which *can* lead to a DSM-IV diagnosis) is vital (Carlson & Sperry, 1998).

The therapist also keeps sessions focused, on time, and of a set length. These are components of standard practice, but they also keep clients focused and encourage the idea that it is they who can, indeed must, make use of the time they have. This sense of responsibility reinforces the idea that clients are consulting, not depending on, a therapist. In times of financial restraint, a standard practice emphasizes efficiency.

Reframe Issues in a Positive Light

All problems and all solutions are social and relational in nature. Adlerians seek, where possible, to reframe issues in social terms. Casting others' and clients' behavior and intentions in a positive social light reframes issues as relational; such reframing often allows clients to think better of themselves and others (Eckstein, 1997) and to feel less distress regarding themselves. Adlerians may also seek to modify convictions, but this is usually done through the medium of behavior. Successful behavior—that is, behavior that alleviates the problem—changes the way one looks at life and at one's feelings and in fact changes one's feelings. Success may prove that it is unnecessary to think in a certain way. For example, success after treating people more openly may show that it is unnecessary to assume all are "out to get you" and may reduce obsessions (Slavik, 1998a).

Problems are, more specifically, problems of equality, that is, of pessimism or discouragement. Solutions are the client's learning that he or she is in fact equal and belongs. Solutions typically have the nature of saying, "I can speak up and take my place," or, "I can live without insisting on having my way here." These solutions change the arrangements of life that lack of community feeling engenders (Slavik, 1998a) and ultimately reduce pessimism and discouragement.

Emphasize Mutual Respect and Equality

The consulting model of efficient Adlerian therapy assumes that mutual respect between client and therapist helps to pinpoint and evaluate issues of status that a client may habitually generate. The therapist attempts to change status issues into issues of task resolution and into questions of how all parties involved in difficulties may participate in a solution. The client does not have to demand to be a "person" but merely notice that he or she already is. The consulting model requires a therapist who is keenly aware of (but is not obsessed with) perceived issues of dominance and submission. Nonetheless, many clients do not want to enter into a problem-solving process and prefer to remain compliant with therapist suggestions (Garner, 1972).

The Treatment Process

Efficient Adlerian therapy is a process, not a procedure. The description offered here is not a statement of "do this first, then do that." It initially describes a flow of information between client and therapist regarding how a client thinks and the expectations of the therapist. Some therapists tend to be formally and others informally oriented. A formal therapist might insert assessment procedures into this process at appropriate times and have a plan. An informal therapist might seldom have a plan, except for a few set questions, and prefer to follow cues offered by the client.

1. The therapist invites a statement of the problem. "What brings you to see me today?" or "How can I help today?" suffices to start the discussion. There are no particularly right or desperately wrong ways to start a process of focusing on behavior and thinking. If working with a couple, the therapist invites a statement from each of them; as much as possible, one does not allow either of them to say, "I'm here for the same reason he/she is." Their individual statements and the problems with which each partner comes forward tell the therapist much about why the "problem" is not solved. In instances where parents—or others—insist on agreeing on the recalcitrance of a third party, this solidarity itself might exacerbate the problem. This can be addressed, or the therapist might initially accept the problem at face value.

2. The therapist helps to clarify the presented issue, simplify it, or cast it in concrete, transactional terms. He or she seeks to simplify the problem, or at least its statement. Whether the client lets it be simplified or wants to keep it complicated predicts the success of the therapy. Sometimes at this point a therapist can discuss why and for whom the problem is a problem. It happens that clients bring in others' problems as if they were their own.

3. The therapist asks for the best solution, if any, that is under the control of the person experiencing the distress: "If you could have it any way you wanted, how would you solve this problem?" On hearing a solution, the therapist can often enough just recommend, "That sounds sensible. Why don't you go ahead and do it that way?" Then the client may state his or her hesitations, reasons that may or may not appear to be in alignment with common sense. One well-known pitfall is to endorse a solution that depends on a third party's benevolence or cooperation. The therapist may ask The Question (Carlson & Slavik, 1997). Using The Question helps focus on the interpersonal aspects of a difficulty, even though it may not direct one to an immediate solution.

   At this point the therapist begins to assess the compliance of the client. The therapist must be alert to compliant attitudes that interfere with problem solving (Garner, 1972). If a client appears to be looking for a "packaged" solution, the therapist must decide how to deal with this. Our usual methods at this point have been to encourage a client to work for himself or herself to find a best solution. But this sometimes does not work, and clients refuse engagement and defer to one's "expertise," usually without utilizing whatever "expertise" one is seduced into offering. With some pessimistic clients this is an ongoing problem of which the therapist must be continually aware.

4. If the client offers no best solution, the therapist may suggest one that might easily work (in his or her mind). It can be offered tentatively: "Here's a suggestion. I don't know if it would work for you. You might try . . . What do you think?" Another, more directive way to suggest a solution is: "Have you tried . . . ?" or "Why wouldn't you do . . . ?"

   It often works that clients adopt and adapt such solutions, perhaps because of the therapist's supposed expertise in these matters or simply because of the permission implicit in the suggestion. Many clients have merely said, "I never thought of that." The next session is telling. In any event, the therapist's suggestions are just "priming the pump" and perhaps dispensing with dead wood on the therapist's mind. Suggestions can be accepted, rejected, or modified, or they may lead to greater knowledge of the person. In particular, the response to a suggestion may lead to a better idea of why common sense is not used. This procedure also aids in the differentiation of the discouraged client from the pessimistic client. The discouraged will move forward, however slowly, but the pessimistic will not. For example, if the therapist suggests to a man who has had an affair that he "forget it, make amends, repair and improve the relationship with your wife," and the client decides to keep his guilt, then the therapist can ascertain what attitudes prevent forward movement.

5. On the other hand, if the client offers a best solution, the therapist encourages it: "What could you do to help this happen?" While it may need some shaping in order to be concrete and under the control of the client, it is probably a direct way to solve the problem, in line with the client's thinking and plausible in the client's mind. With a couple, the therapist may have to help negotiate a way for both to see a win-win solution.

6. The therapist looks for and encourages strengths. He or she looks for prosocial, cooperative behavior that the client already knows how to do and encourages it, both in line with the solution to the presented problem and otherwise as a means of morale raising and support for the client. The therapist always looks for strengths and solutions that answer the question, "What did you do/what can you do to improve things?" As well, in each session the therapist looks for ways to promote the client's morale.

7. If a solution is not found in such practical ways, the therapist may ask for early memories and interpret them (Carlson & Slavik, 1997; Slavik, 1991). The therapist may do this many times: he or she does not write down an early memory and refer back to it in later sessions. It appears effective for the therapist to forget it and ask for it again, interpret it again, to suit the session. Given early recollections, one can use the information to inform, guide, or modify the client's direction of movement in cooperative directions that make sense to the client (Slavik, 1995). One can use early memories to adduce couple complementary and seek a solution at that point (Slavik, 1998b).

8. The therapist discriminates between the discouraged and the pessimistic client. The discouraged need encouragement and the experience of success. The pessimistic need well-structured, collaborative, long-term therapy and self-education (Maniacci, 1996). One may choose to refer a pessimistic client or begin to shift to a longer-term approach. A DSM-IV diagnosis will likely have been formulated by now, which aids in further treatment formulation (Carlson & Sperry, 1998b).

9. As a last resort, particularly for the pessimistic client, the therapist may suggest an *assessment* and describe the procedure and its purpose. The point of assessment is to prolong (short-term!) therapy, to encourage the client, to know him or her better, to educate the client, and to slow matters down. Some assessments, such as the Life Style Assessment (Shulman & Mosak, 1988), allow great precision in focus on strengths and convictions. Doing a phenomenological assessment allows a stronger relationship to develop, in

which the client is frequently willing to reveal more about himself or herself. Many other efficient, though less brief, treatment modalities are available (Mays & Croake, 1997).

10. Other techniques can be called upon (Carlson & Slavik, 1997), with the agreement and cooperation of the client, to aid in self-knowledge and to develop alternative methods of dealing with challenges. Some prefer a conversational method, in which individuals can openly, without guilt, discuss how and perhaps why they do things, and the effectiveness of their methods. The openness and self-acceptance required can often be established in a few sessions; with the therapist's help in clarifying goals and methods, it is an efficient, effective means of therapy for some. Nonetheless, effectiveness in this method definitely depends on the client, on what he or she is willing or interested in hearing and discussing.

Case Study: An Analysis of Individuals Within a Couple Therapy Context

Discouragement and pessimism are perhaps the vital concepts in efficient Adlerian therapy (Myers & Croake, 1996) and worth further comment. Discouragement and pessimism do not describe feelings, any more than encouragement means "helping one to feel good." Discouraged individuals do not necessarily feel discouraged; pessimism is not necessarily the "sourness" of Scrooge. Both the discouraged and the pessimistic can feel happy, particularly when life happens to present the results demanded to satisfy their goals. Rather, they both have constricted views of the world—and of themselves in the world—that limit their willingness to consider the point of view of others and that enable them to justify, for example, "getting it for themselves" or letting others make their decisions. Discouragement and pessimism are restrictions of life enforced by restricting or restraining beliefs about life (Kamsler, 1990). Individuals justify their constrictions in living as "reality" or part of human nature.

The discouraged are reluctant to try anything new. They perhaps perceive but avoid facing challenges that might, if faced successfully, cast themselves in a more positive light. But with the discouraged, the emphasis is on their *reluctance*. They are willing to discover or to be shown a better way—just. Their reluctance may be situational rather than chronic. It may be that they, even often, see their circumstances as those where it is best to go slow and drag their heels. Of course, it may as well be chronic, characterologic reluctance, as with an individual who utilizes passive-aggressive methods. The many versions of "I am ineffective [here and now], but I try" represent discouragement. For the discouraged, the world is difficult but not impossible.

The pessimistic, however, are *convinced* that whatever they attempt will fail. The world is clearly a place where one will be defeated unless one acts in a certain fashion. Often pessimism will appear in lifestyle convictions: "The world is a hard, steely environment where I have few means to assert myself." They see no possibility that the world will change to suit or aid them, and this view frequently justifies specific behavior that is difficult for others.

The distinction between discouragement and pessimism seems to lie in the focus of the limiting convictions. The discouraged feel a lack of self-efficacy; they might more often blame themselves than the world. The pessimistic know they are living in a ruthless and rigid world where they must squirm to find a place or any satisfaction. As a diagnostic tool, the distinction is unimportant; as a way to evaluate methods of work, it is vital in determining strategy (Carlson & Sperry, 1998).

A case exemplifying discouragement and pessimism might clarify the distinction. Herb and Olivia, both in their fifties, present themselves for couple therapy. They both have been married twice before. Their presenting problem is an impending divorce that both claim they do not want yet seem powerless to call off. They both say they want to reconcile or at least to "try" one last time before a divorce. The therapist, perhaps foolishly, took the case. When pursued, it appears that Herb is afraid of being "taken" financially in either divorce or marriage, yet he is paying Olivia $1,500 a month as part of a separation agreement until the divorce. Olivia doesn't "trust" Herb; he doesn't intervene for her when his mother and adult son "slight" her, and he "refuses" to let her have friends. She is very sensitive to his frequent, silent irritation and anger.

His earliest memory: "One day I was walking home from school with my sister. Bees attacked us, and my sister told me to hide in a hole under a tree. When I jumped in, I discovered the bees were coming from there, and

I got stung." His conviction: "When I do what women tell me to do, I get stung." With this conviction, Herb will not be very cooperative with women.

Her earliest memory: "I remember my dad carrying me around on his back one day at the farm. It made me feel real special." The conviction: "Men should elevate me and make me special." Likewise, with this demand Olivia does not put herself into Herb's shoes to understand his financial problems.

The complementarity of these attitudes is apparent: When Olivia expects Herb to make her special (financially), he is afraid of being stung, and he balks, or else resents that he does so much for her. She then becomes very indignant at not being taken seriously and increases her demands to be made special.

On the face of it, when presented carefully with the interpretation of her early recollection and confronted with the unreality of expecting to be carried through life, Olivia seemed to be able to recognize her demands for being special and modulate them slightly. Herb never did acknowledge his expectation of being "stung" in his relationship with Olivia. He appeared to be extremely pessimistic in regard to being treated fairly by women. He made some concessions in order to please her, with a careful eye to her appreciation of his efforts. As therapy ensued, however, Olivia returned to her complaints of being treated poorly, and perhaps it was more "reality based" at this time. They divorced. Herb was definitely pessimistic in his expectation of the world. Nor was he interested in modifying this apperception.

Working with pessimism tends to be problematic in time-limited, brief therapy (Maniacci, 1996). The therapist must be careful to maintain the consultant relationship instead of becoming an expert on how the client should live. The relationship can be deepened within the guideline that the client is an equal: no condemnation occurs and no guilt is incurred, so that the client has at least one instance where society is not his or her enemy. Adlerians place a greater focus on the importance of the relationship and its initiation into community feeling than do some other short-term therapies.

Motivation will be the first issue. Where there is felt discomfort, one can work. Focus on limited issues for specific gains is recommended. A longer-term focus on self-education is also suggested by some, where the client faces and tests his or her self-imposed restrictions (Maniacci,

1996), but this may exceed motivation. Manaster (1989) asks the same question we have: "What does one do with a client with whom one has rapport and a cooperative understanding of the nature and specifics of the client's problems when no, little, or insufficient change has occurred at the end of time-limited therapy?" He concludes, "I can only suggest continuing, albeit with rethinking, study, and consultation" (p. 247)— and we would add, with careful consideration about whether the client or the therapist has the problem.

Summary

Efficient Adlerian therapy is based on the cooperation of the therapist and the client and relies on this cooperation to make a difference to the client. The basic strategy of an efficient Adlerian therapist is to focus on the presenting problem of the client as a task in which the therapist acts as a consultant. The therapist clarifies and simplifies the problem and encourages and suggests solutions. Efficient Adlerian therapy focuses on formulating positive and reasonable goals that pull clients from their current states of "tunnel vision" or narrow interpretations of their situations. The therapist is also aware of the range of interventions available and can discern, through the metaphors of discouragement and pessimism, how to tailor treatment effectively.

References

Adler, A. (1956). *The individual psychology of Alfred Adler: A systematic presentation in selections from his writings* (H. L. Ansbacher & R. R. Ansbacher, Eds.). New York: Basic Books.

Ansbacher, H. L. (1989). Adlerian psychology: The tradition of brief psychotherapy. *Individual Psychology, 45*(1 and 2), 26–35.

Bitter, J. R., Christensen, O. C., Hawes, C., & Nicoll, W. G. (1997). *Adlerian brief therapy with individuals, couples, and families.* Unpublished manuscript.

Carlson, J., & Slavik, S. (Eds.). (1997). *Techniques in Adlerian psychology.* Washington, DC: Accelerated Development.

Carlson, J., & Sperry, L. (1998a). Adlerian psychotherapy as constructivist psychotherapy. In M. Hoyt (Ed.), *The handbook of constructivist therapies; Innovative approaches from leading practitioners* (pp. 68–82). San Francisco: Jossey-Bass.

Carlson, J., & Sperry, L. (1998b). Assessment, diagnosis, and tailored treatment. In J. Carlson & L. Sperry (Eds.), *The disordered couple* (pp. 1–12). Bristol, PA: Brunner/Mazel.

Eckstein, D. (1997). Reframing as a specific interpretive counseling technique. *Individual Psychology, 53*(4), 418–428.

Garner, H. H. (1972). The confrontation problem-solving technique: Applicability to Adlerian psychotherapy. *Journal of Individual Psychology, 28*(2), 248–259.

Kamsler, A. (1990). Her-story in the making: Therapy with women who were sexually abused in childhood. In M. Durrant & C. White (Eds.), *Ideas for therapy with sexual abuse* (pp. 9–36). Adelaide, South Australia: Dulwich Centre.

LeShan, L. (1996). *Beyond technique: Psychotherapy for the 21st century.* Northvale, NJ: Jason Aronson.

Manaster, G. J. (1989). Clinical issues in brief psychotherapy: A summary and conclusion. *Individual Psychology, 45*(1&2), 243–247.

Maniacci, M. P. (1996). An introduction to brief therapy of the personality disorders. *Individual Psychology, 52*(2), 158–168.

Mays, M., & Croake, J. W. (1997). *Treatment of depression in managed care.* New York: Brunner/Mazel.

Mosak, H. H. (1987). Guilt, guilt feelings, regret, and repentance. *Individual Psychology, 43*(3), 288–295.

Myers, K. M., & Croake, J. W. (1996). Major depressive disorder during childhood. In L. Sperry & J. Carlson (Eds.), *Psychopathology and psychotherapy: From DSM-IV diagnosis to treatment* (pp. 417–461). Washington, DC: Taylor & Francis.

Shulman, B. H., & Mosak, H. H. (1988). *Manual for life style assessment.* Muncie, IN: Accelerated Development.

Slavik, S. (1998a). Cultivating confidence. *The Canadian Journal of Adlerian Psychology, 28*(2), 1–10.

Slavik, S. (1998b). Using early memories to elicit complementarity in couples counseling. In H. G. Rosenthal (Ed.), *Favorite counseling and therapy techniques* (pp. 158–163). Washington, DC: Accelerated Development.

Slavik, S. (1991). Early memories as a guide to client movement through life. *Canadian Journal of Counselling, 25*(3), 331–337.

Slavik, S. (1995). Presenting social interest to different life styles. *Individual Psychology, 51*(2) 166–177.

Sperry, L. (1989). Contemporary approaches to brief psychotherapy: A comparative analysis. *Individual Psychology, 45*(1 and 2), 4–25.

Sperry, L. (1999). Biopsychosocial therapy: Essential strategies and tactics. In J. Carlson & L. Sperry (Eds.), *Brief therapy strategies with individuals and couples*. New York: Brunner/Mazel.

10

<hr>

Brief Reality Therapy

Robert E. Wubbolding

Introduction

Reality therapy began in opposition to psychological theories that emphasized the endless discussion of how problems originally started, the reasons for mental disturbance, clients' fixations, and the need to gain insight. By contrast, it emphasizes that the most efficient and effective therapy is centered on current issues that, while they are the results of personal history, are best addressed as *current* problems requiring *current* decisions and solutions.

History

William Glasser developed reality therapy in a mental hospital with the help of Dr. G. L. Harrington. They insisted that patients work at productive projects, such as building sidewalks and gardening. The main requirement was that these jobs be different from the work and the lifestyles that preceded the onset of the patients' mental problems (Glasser, 1965).

In the past 30 years, the principles of reality therapy have been refined and applied to education (Glasser, 1990, 1991, 1998; Glasser & Wubbolding, 1997; Wubbolding, 1997) and relationships (Glasser, 1995). Moreover, they have also been applied in seminal fashion to short-term therapy (Glasser & Wubbolding, 1995; Wubbolding, 1988).

Choice Theory

Choice theory, the basis of reality therapy, as a short-term therapy was formerly called *control theory* or *control system therapy*. While this theory has a long history, Glasser (1980, 1985) further developed it is a basis for counseling and educational practice.

In the years 1980–1996, many alterations in the theory were made: needs were inserted, as well as the concept of the quality world, which is seen as the core of human existence. Four components of behavior were suggested, and the levels of perception were amplified. Most of all, choice was given a central place. Consequently, it became evident that *choice theory* was a more appropriate name than *control theory*. In order to understand the strategies used in brief reality therapy, it is crucial to understand choice theory.

Components of Choice Theory

Motivation

The motivations for all behavior originate from within. Contrary to the precepts of the popular "external control psychology" (Glasser, 1998), people are not motivated by external rewards or punishments. Nor can they be controlled through external coercion. Rather, they are driven to satisfy five motivations or needs that are innate genetic instructions and that all people possess. First is the need for *survival or self-preservation*. Second is the urge to *belong or be involved* with other people. Third is the urge to *attain power or to achieve*, which includes the urge to gain recognition, to maintain self-esteem, and to feel self-worth. Fourth is the urge *to attain freedom, independence, or autonomy*. People are born with the inclination to make choices and to stand on their own two feet. Finally, the urge for *fun or enjoyment* is the fifth drive in human behavior. In fact, it is the payoff for learning. Children learn by having fun, by playing.

These five needs are universal. Everyone has them. They are also general, not specific. But they are not fulfilled directly. They are satisfied, instead, through the *quality world,* which is every person's ideal world, containing their intense desires, images of their treasured possessions, and their valued personal beliefs.

Most proximately, people's behavior is generated when their needs and wants are not fulfilled in the quality world. The discrepancy between what a person wants and what he or she is getting at a given moment ignites the behavioral system to make some impact on the external world.

The implication for brief therapy is that all problems are here-and-now problems. They are rooted in unfulfilled wants and needs. While personal history is important, it is of little value in reality therapy to repeatedly discuss past pain and trauma. In effect, the reality therapist says to clients, "Look but don't stare at the past. You have no control over it, and it need not overwhelm you now. It is more helpful to desist from revisiting it, and instead to assess the path that your life is currently taking." Knowing *how* does not register knowing *why.* It is a waste of time to identify the pothole that damaged a car before you have the front end aligned. The reason is that all problems are current.

Focus on Behavior

The client's current behavior, the result of unmet needs and wants, constitutes the presenting problem that is the focus of brief reality therapy. This behavior is the contact point for the effective use of reality therapy strategies. It is usually seen in the context of relationships that are often dysfunctional or less than desirable. Even if the problem is not exclusively a disturbed or inadequate relationship, the therapist helps the client examine and improve the relationships as a way to lessen his or her pain. For example, a client's decision to place a senile parent in a nursing home can be accompanied by emotional pain, stress, guilt, loss, and the like. But enhancing relationships can bring the family together and thus make the process bearable.

Components of Behavior

Behavior is made up of four components: actions, cognitions, emotions, and physiology. All four are seen as dynamic and generative. Arguing and fighting are most obviously *actions;* and the inner discourse of "I can't" or "I can" is *cognition.* Shame, resentment, and other *emotions* are seen neither as static conditions nor as causes of actions but as being generated accompanying acting and thinking, and the result of unmet wants and needs. Thus a person is said to be *"depress-*ing," *"guilt-*ing," or *"anxiety-*ing."

Even *physiology* can be described as an active behavior. For instance, anyone who has had chronic headaches and backaches knows that these conditions are not static. They are active ongoing behaviors generated to achieve a purpose.

The strategies used in reality therapy are based on the preeminent principle that all behavior is a choice. Central to choice theory is the principle that behavior is neither random nor thrust upon people from the external world. It is chosen. Still, some behaviors are more easily controlled than others. Actions can be influenced by emotions. And feelings are not explicitly selected. No one says, "I'm going to feel depressed today." But if behavior is treated "as if" it were a choice, clients can gain new understandings and perceive that they have more control over their lives than they previously thought.

All behaviors are also purposeful. We choose them in order to impact the external world for the immediate purpose of fulfilling our wants and for the ultimate purpose of satisfying our needs. When clients realize this, the strategies make more sense to them. Still, purposes often are unknown to others and can be unclear even to the person behaving. Thus, some behaviors appear to be aimless and senseless. But to the agent, they have significance even though he or she may be reluctant or unwilling to disclose the purpose.

Perception

If behavior is a generated purposeful output, perception is the input received and that results from our purposefully maneuvering the external world. We may perceive that our wants are fulfilled or unfulfilled and our needs met or unmet. The brain processes incoming information, which is seen as satisfying or unsatisfying, useful or useless, helpful or harmful, pleasant or painful, or simply neutral. From this storehouse, it makes a comparison between a want that is connected to a need and a perception that the want or need is unfulfilled. From this discrepancy comes behavior.

The process of brain functioning is analogous to a control system such as a thermostat. The mechanism "wants" the room temperature to be 72 degrees, so when it perceives it is 68 degrees, it signals to its behavioral system that a discrepancy exists and that it should generate heat. That is, the thermostat wants the "perception" that the room is 72 degrees.

The implication is that the brain can be fooled. We can take drugs or engage in addictive behaviors to gain a perception that all five of our needs are satisfied. Our need to belong is satisfied. We feel a sense of power. We experience a sense of freedom from stresses and pressures, as well as much fun and enjoyment. But these experiences are momentary, illusory, and destructive in the long run.

By helping clients establish, maintain, and intensify their relationships, reality therapists help them to find positive alternatives to acting out destructive thoughts and harmful feelings, and the unhealthy physiology that may accompany the other behavioral components. Reality therapy's strategies are thus designed to enhance clients' relationships.

Reality Therapy Strategies

Brief reality therapy focuses on dysfunctional relationships as the immediate source of a client's pain and misery. Glasser (1998) states that all problems are rooted in flawed relationships. Moreover, these wounded relationships are *current*. Thus the therapist explores how clients can become more effectively allied with the people around them and thereby fulfill their five psychological needs.

The delivery system for brief reality therapy is summarized in four letters: WDEP, for Wants, Doing, Evaluation, Planning (Wubbolding, 1991) The therapist helps clients explore what they *want,* especially regarding their interpersonal relationships. They discuss what they are currently *doing,* especially their activities, their self-talk, and their feelings. They are also helped to *evaluate* their own lives, whether they are effectively connecting with the people around them. They may formulate *plans* (treatment plans) related to the five psychological needs, with emphasis on relationship improvement.

W (Wants)

The quality world is the bank of specific wants or desires connected to the need system. Thus, it is crucial that the client perceive the therapist as a warm, caring, accepting helper.

Then as quickly as possible, the reality therapist helps the client define wants and goals for the counseling session. These wants or goals can be general. Useful questions include: "What do you want from today's session?" "What do you want to take away with you when you leave today?" "What do you want to do differently as a result of our conversation?" They can also be connected with each need: belonging ("Who is the most important person in your life?" "To whom do you want to be close?"), power or achievement ("What would you be doing if you were to feel a sense of pride in your work, in school, in your relationships, etc.?"), freedom ("What choices are you hesitant about making?"), and fun ("What kind of fun do you want to have that you are not having?" "If you were to be enjoying life, what would you want to have that you are not having?" "If you were to be enjoying life, what would be different for you?" "Who would you be having fun with?")

D (Doing)

The therapist and client discuss all the components of behavior, including actions, feelings, cognition, and physiology. But clients often begin by telling the therapist how they feel or what is happening in their lives at present. Usually the discussion centers on a problem: what is wrong, or why they are unhappy. The reality therapist asks detailed questions about current actions: how has the client been spending time, what happened yesterday or in the *recent* past, what did he or she say? Current feelings also receive special attention, but they are always connected with the client's actions. Questions center on what the client *did* when depressed, angry, or guilty, and especially on actions that accompanied positive feelings, such as contentment, acceptance, hope, trust, and accomplishment.

Most practitioners of reality therapy are counselors, therapists (psychologists and social workers), child-care workers, or case managers. Few are medical personnel. Consequently they do not generally prescribe medication. They do, however, discuss how the client is functioning from a biological or physiological point of view. Their questions explore how the client expresses stress in "body behaviors" (i.e., backaches, headaches, high blood pressure, insomnia, overeating, excessive sleeping, and many others). Appropriate referrals are made for physical complaints.

This approach recognizes that all behaviors are composed of the four components—action, cognition, feeling, and physiology—which cannot be separated one from another. Thus, a depressed person has a different physiology from a positive, upbeat, hopeful person. A runner has a different physiology from a "couch potato." A person who is depressing has an appropriate physiology. The physiological behavior is congruent with the other components, and vice versa.

The reality therapist then identifies ineffective self-talk related to choice theory. This inner discourse differs from the self-verbalizations of rational-emotive behavioral therapy (Ellis, 1975). Ineffective self-talk related to choice theory includes implicit statements, such as:

1. "I have no choices. I am powerless." Such statements often accompany feelings of powerlessness, hopelessness, and lack of inner control.
2. "Nobody is going to tell me what to do." This statement is an internal utterance of an individual who is filled with anger, resentment, rage, and hatred.
3. "Even though my current actions are not getting me what I want, or are not helpful to others, I will choose to continue to repeat them."

This is the inner language of many people who have minor problems, as well as individuals and families who are more seriously disturbed or dysfunctional.

Feelings are discussed but not belabored. Negative emotions are seen not as causes but as symptoms of frustration or unmet wants. When people are depressing, their behavioral system is signaling them that their choices are very ineffective. The therapist asks, "What do you think these bad feelings (of depression, sadness, worry, fear, anxiety, anger, shame, or resentment) are telling you about your relationships?"

Discussion centers on action, because that component of the behavioral system is the most easily changed. When it changes, the other components of thinking and feeling follow, because all components are inextricably linked. There is a saying, "*You can act your way to a new way of thinking more easily then you can* think your way to a new way of acting."

E (Evaluation)

The heart of the therapy delivery system is the client's self-evaluation of his or her behavior, wants, and perceptions. Because this is a strategy, it is described later in this chapter.

P (Planning)

Treatment plans do not focus on "curing," "resolving," "remediating," "settling," or "untangling" past problems. Rather, because all problems are seen to be current, their solution is appropriate for brief therapy (and managed care). Plans are built around "enhancing," "increasing," "lessening," "alleviating," "improving," "boosting," "progressing," and so on. Moreover, plans focus on building more need-satisfying relationships *no matter what the presenting problem is!*

Detailed Description of Reality Therapy Strategies

Strategy 1: Helping the Client Self-Evaluate

If the strategies are analogous to the stones of an arch, client self-evaluation is the keystone. Without it, the system crumbles, and the other strategies are useless. It is essential that clients continually monitor their own actions, thoughts, feelings, and wants. No one makes changes without previous self-evaluation. It can be said that people have an undying belief in things that do not work; clients who seek help often repeat the same behaviors, hoping that this time the outcome will be different. Accompanying such actions is the underlying self-talk that "I can control other people." Feelings of frustration, anger, and rage as well as physiological symptoms such as insomnia are often linked to these actions.

Thus the task of the reality therapist is to help clients to evaluate the effectiveness of their actions in achieving the fulfillment of their wants and to evaluate the impact of their actions on others. Questions include: "Is what you are doing getting you what you want?" "Are your current choices helping or hurting your family or your friends?"

Many people are incapable of making judgments on the basis of inner norms or even of perceiving the impact of their behavior on others. Such individuals are asked to decide if their actions are against the law, the rules of the institution, or the unspoken expectations of their employer, family, or society in general.

None of us changes our behavioral direction or specific behaviors unless we make a judgment that such change is necessary. Clients' behaviors will not change until they realize, "My current direction or my specific actions are not effective, not getting me what I want, not satisfying my wants and needs in either the short run or the long run."

More specifically, the reality therapist asks clients if their specific actions today, yesterday, or recently were helpful in getting what they want. They are also asked to evaluate the appropriateness of their wants. They are asked to conduct a courageous assessment of the realistic attainability of their wants and goals. And they are encouraged to see the therapy not as a cure but as a way to learn tools useful for life. Self-evaluation of their degree of willingness to work at the therapy is part of the first session. Some clients want an outcome without making the effort. They want others to change but fail to see their own part in causing or maintaining the problem. Clients are thus asked to determine the amount of energy they wish to expend in addressing the possibility of change.

The effectiveness of self-evaluation depends on the creativity of the therapist in asking questions as well as the willingness of the client to genuinely commit to it. Later in therapy, if clients have not made changes in their personal or interpersonal lives, the therapist will return to this strategy. The condition of being "stuck" is due to ineffective self-evaluation.

Strategy 2: Teaching the Client Directly or Indirectly

The effective use of reality therapy in brief therapy includes the direct teaching of the concepts. The therapist teaches clients in clear understandable language about helps and hindrances to the betterment of their mental health.

- *Don'ts*. The therapist teaches the client the ABCs of what *not* to do: Don't Argue, Blame, Criticize, Demean, make Excuses, Find fault, Give up when mistakes are made, or Hold grudges. The therapist elaborates on these *don'ts* and teaches the harmful effects of each one.
- *Do's*. Communication is enhanced by language that is nonargumentative and nonblameful. I-messages, self-affirmations, and effective self-talk can be learned. "I have choices," "I am more effective when I live within reasonable boundaries and respect others," and "If my current actions are not taking me in an appropriate direction, I'll change them" constitute inner discourse that is life enhancing.

Similarly, the therapist teaches clients the WDEP system. They learn to talk to their families using the language of inner control rather than external control. They learn to continually ask themselves such questions as, "Is your current behavior bringing you closer together or further apart?" (Glasser, 1998).

Such self-evaluation is not as easy as it appears. Clients who have developed unexamined habits of behavior find it difficult to self-evaluate. A major part of recovery from addictions is the art of learning: "If something is not helping me, I need to change." "If my relationships have deteriorated, I need to look at what I'm doing and change it, rather than project the blame on everyone else." For some individuals and couples, such fearless self-inventory is difficult to operationalize. Thus the therapist becomes a teacher. Successful teaching depends on therapists' knowledge, their ability to use the language of their clients, and timing (or presenting) the ideas when the clients are ready to hear them.

Strategy 3: Planning for Quality Time

Clients can be taught to set aside specific time frames for high-quality, mutually need-satisfying activities. For people in wounded relationships, this quality time should be brief, repetitious, noncombative, and enjoyable to both parties. The parties talk about topics that are enjoyable to both, and they refrain from arguing and preaching.

The purpose of quality time is to build a storehouse of pleasant memories and perceptions in order to counterbalance the painful ones. Excruciating and painful perceptions cannot be remediated; they can only be replaced by pleasant and recently embedded experiences. From these perceptions and skills, the following tool is built.

This strategy applies to individuals or couples who are experiencing stress, grief, or alienation. These behaviors are often demonstrated by feelings of depression, loneliness, and anger, as well as actions such as withdrawing, arguing, and criticizing self or others.

Spending quality time is usually a doable strategy, because clients generally want at least a "vacation" from the problem, a time when they can set it aside, with the idea that they can dredge up the pain later.

The value of this strategy is connected with that of teaching. Clients learn indirectly that they have more choices than they first considered. They learn that they can do something to address their frustration and pain. The good feelings are a payoff for changing their actions. They learn that by changing their actions, they can change their feelings, attitudes, and perceptions.

Strategy 4: Utilizing the Solving Circle

In this strategy, clients are to imagine that they have a piece of magic chalk and are asked to draw a chalk mark around themselves. Glasser (1998) suggests that relationships can be enhanced when individuals and couples imagine themselves enclosed in a circle. From within this circle they can utilize the procedures summarized by the WDEP formula in examining a relationship. The partners define what they want from each other, examine what they are doing, describe in detail each other's strengths, and most emphatically, state their own specific plans for improving their relationship. None of the ABCs are allowed to encroach into the circle. This strategy is most effective when clients have already learned to avoid destructive methods of communication and to look to a future mutually satisfying solution.

This strategy is also most useful after clients first have been taught that their own behavior originates from within. Nothing "makes" them angry. There is no such thing as an "attack" of anxiety. Feelings that our behavior has external causes are generated when we don't have what we want. If the solving-circle strategy is used too soon, before the client has gained a foundation of commitment and knowledge, it can backfire and become an "exacerbating circle." The skillful therapist can diagnose when clients are prepared to talk to each other in a helpful and civilized, not argumentative, manner.

Clinical Indications for the Strategies

Reality therapy does not define specific strategies for specific presenting problems or diagnoses. The axiom "sometimes solutions have nothing to do with the problem" applies here. Because problematic behaviors spring from unmet needs and wants, reality therapists help clients fulfill their wants and needs—that is, choose more effective behaviors. Thus the therapist need not confront a client's depression directly. "Depress-ing" is a systematic, ineffective action, as well as a cognitive behavior and a feeling behavior. Consequently, the therapist can help the client make better choices that are inwardly more productive and helpful than "depressing."

Reality therapy sees most psychological problems as connected with damaged relationships. Even if clients do not admit to an impaired relationship, improving their already-satisfactory alliances can help address the negative presenting problem.

Clinical Applications with an Individual: Case Example

Frank is a 62-year-old man whose wife died of cancer 11 years ago. Their three children are grown and have their own families. Two of them live far away and one lives about 100 miles from Frank. After Frank's wife died, he had the support of family and friends, went to therapy, and seemed to grieve in a slow but normal manner. He has now been retired from a successful business for four years and is in good physical health, but he has withdrawn from civic, social, and family involvements that had been rewarding but that gradually lost their attractiveness. Frank seeks therapy because it was suggested that he has been alone too much, watches television excessively, cries for no specific reason, eats intermittently, and withdraws from friends and activities. He states that he has trouble sleeping at night but dozes during the day as he watches soap operas. A religious man, he says he would never commit suicide because it is morally unacceptable. He was interested in several women who were also attracted to him, but he has not seen any of them for many months. He admits to being depressed, lonely, and alienated from people who, he said, "might be inclined to reach out to me."

Helping the Client Self-Evaluate

After listening empathically to Frank's *current* situation, the therapist asks many questions designed to help him make explicit his inner self-evaluations.

- "How realistic is it for you to feel a little better in the next week?"
- "Who is a very important person in your life, and how does it help you if you don't reach out to him or her?"
- "If you make no changes in how you spend your time, will you change how you feel?"
- "If you did change your routine even slightly, what would be the impact on how you are feeling?"
- "What is the worst thing that could happen if you had a failure in a relationship?"
- "What qualities do you have that people would find attractive?"
- "During the times you feel slightly better, what are you doing that is different from your actions when you feel down in the dumps?"

Frank would never have made even a tiny change if he hadn't self-evaluated first. His "depress-ing" was his way of coping with his loss and fear. When he decided that his life direction was not adequate for him, he decided to change. He then became willing to make plans related to involvement with other people, to gain power and to have fun no matter what effort was entailed.

Teaching the Client Directly and Indirectly

Reality therapy involves direct instruction: the therapist directly taught Frank the basics of choice theory. But indirect teaching was also emphasized. In asking questions based on the WDEP formula, Frank learned to define what he wanted and to evaluate his actions by asking himself appropriate questions. The most significant learning for him (as for many clients) was that he had far more control and many more choices than he dreamed possible. Because therapists see "depress-ing" clients as having countless opportunities to feel better, clients learn almost as a side effect of therapy that there is hope for a better future and that they can realize that hope by making small but significant choices.

Planning for Quality Time

Because Frank lived alone and had few friends or acquaintances, the therapist helped him initiate an exercise program, which consisted of casual walking at first and then brisk walking. He was to do this exercise several times a day and to monitor how he felt, both while doing it and after he stopped. Immediately after his walks, he made special note of his actions and recorded how they were different from his feelings in previous weeks.

The purpose of this strategy was to help Frank make some relatively small changes, with a view to gaining an in-control, positive feeling and thereby relinquishing *some* of the out-of-control feelings of self-pity and depression. He was then ready for further action.

Utilizing the Solving Circle

The solving circle was used only as part of the therapy sessions. Frank, along with the therapist, brainstormed questions about his "lonely-ing" and "depress-ing" choices, as well as solutions to them.

- "What would you be doing if you felt better?"
- "What do other people do who feel positive and hopeful?"
- "Would you do some of these things even though you don't feel great?"

- "What will you do today that is better than what you would have done if we had not talked?"
- "Whom would you call today?"
- "What is the name of a woman whom you formerly knew? Would you call her today to say hello?"

The therapist asked many other questions, and Frank answered them. By using the solving circle, Frank developed target behaviors and specific plans related to the four needs. In his brief reality therapy, Frank did not solve all problems, but he learned a process and addressed the genuinely ineffective choices that he had been making for several years. Such is the goal of brief reality therapy: to learn a process, to gather a set of tools, and to take very large steps described as "improvements," "enhancement," "lessening," "improving," and so on.

Clinical Applications with a Couple:
Case Example

John, 38, and Lenore, 36, have been married for eight years. It is the second marriage for both. John had no children from his first marriage, and Lenore had two who are now with them: James, 14, and Heather, 10. John works for a large company, travels to plants around the country, and is sometimes away for five to seven days at a time. Lenore is the owner of her own business, which requires her full commitment each day, many evenings, and on several weekends per month. For about one year, they have seen very little of each other. Their few times together each week, usually late in the evening, are characterized by bickering, blaming, and an unwillingness to compromise. The children are being raised, for the most part, by sitters and grandparents, who supervise them, entertain them, and take care of their needs as best they can. Recently Lenore, John, James, and Heather spent a day at an amusement park. During that time Heather chose to become lost for three hours, and James was caught stealing prizes from one of the booths. James is in danger of flunking and repeating his grade, and Heather is acting out in minor ways in school. There is no suspicion of child abuse or substance use among the family members.

No detailed history is taken in reality therapy, except to determine if there is a history of violence or other abuse. While all human beings are products of their histories, nothing can be done to alter the past. Moreover, clients who indulge in an extensive discussion of the past often come to believe that it is more important than it need be in therapy. Reality therapists see such protracted conversations as superfluous.

John and Lenore approached a reality therapist in a state of mild desperation. They hoped that therapy would help them. But they were unclear about the possible benefits.

The therapist first helped them reach the conclusion that they wanted to stay together. They also agreed that they were willing to work at improving the relationship. They were mildly committed, in that they wanted results, but they had not reached the conclusion that it was *they* who would need to make some changes.

Helping the Client Self-Evaluate

The therapist allowed the clients to describe their situation. They expressed their intense dissatisfaction by arguing, blaming, complaining, and criticizing each other.

John: We came because we're fed up with this marriage. She works night and day and on weekends. When the kids see her, the first thing they say is " 'Bye, Mom" and I hardly see her because of her schedule.

Lenore: Wait a minute—you work just as much. Don't blame me. The kids don't even see you enough to say "Bye." Your job takes you away from this so-called family at least as much as mine.

John: But you don't have to work that much. It's because you want to work.

Lenore: Of course I want to work. What is there for me at home when you're gone so much? I supported myself when I was yonger and had a career. Why should I give it up now?

John: Nobody said to give it up, but you don't have to work 80 hours a week.

Lenore: It's not 80 hours a week. See, this is how he exaggerates.

John: I'm surprised you listened. You usually don't pay any attention to me.

Lenore: You're the one who works day and night. You're gone all the time. I couldn't possibly pay attention to you even if I wanted to.

John: So you admit that you don't want to have any conversations with me.

Lenore: I didn't say that.

John: Well, what did you say? Just what do you mean when you make such remarks?

The dialogue between them proceeded in the above manner for about five minutes. The therapist then interrupted:

Therapist: I have a question. You said you wanted to work on the marriage and try to make it better, or at least tolerable. Is this conversation that you are having right here and now fairly typical? Is this the way you usually talk to each other?

They agreed that while they saw each other only sporadically or sometimes were too tired to engage in conversation, they often used the "silent treatment," and even assailed each other with this kind of language on a regular basis.

During this first session, the therapist then asked them a multitude of self-evaluation questions. These were, of course, interspersed throughout a longer discussion.

- "If you continue to talk this way, are you going to improve or undermine your marriage?"
- "What impact does this type of communication have on each other, on the relationship, and on your children?"
- "Do blaming and criticizing and unceasing arguing accomplish anything that you can be proud of?"
- "If you spend time together only when you are tired, what does that say to you and to your children about the importance and the priorities of the various family relationships?"
- "If both of you continue to work as much as you do, what will happen to your marriage? Can it realistically survive?"
- "If neither of you is willing to change, will your children be helped or hurt?"

- "How realistic is it for you to push the other person to make changes?"
- "When you try to verbally outmuscle each other, does the other person weaken and give in or become more resistant and hardened?"
- "If someone else heard this conversation, what would he or she say about this marriage?"

Interventions focusing on client self-evaluation were especially useful and even necessary to facilitate change. After hearing the many self-evaluation questions, John and Lenore came to the realization that if the marriage were to last and if the family were to remain intact, both of them would need to make changes. They concluded that both needed to make rapid and radical changes.

Teaching the Client Directly

John and Lenore were at first restrained from making rapid and radical alterations in their patterns of behavior. The therapist, however, directly taught the WDEP system, emphasizing that a complaint such as "You always work too late" is actually a less effective way to express a want than "I would like to be with you more." They were taught to ask themselves the self-evaluation question, "Is what I am about to say going to bring us closer and help the relationship, or is it going to impact it negatively?" At this stage of the therapy, they were encouraged not to make grandiose plans.

They were also taught the need system and how attempts to externally control the other person threaten the satisfaction of needs. They were taught that if the relationship was to endure and prosper, there would have to be at least *some* overlap or congruence between the quality world and the behaviors of each person. They made a plan to practice these skills in a specific part of their home each day for five minutes.

Planning for Quality Time

John and Lenore learned to improve their style of communication especially during the times when they were not exhausted from work. The therapist then helped them make plans to set aside the problems for a while and to lessen their work overload so that these areas of their marriage and family were functioning smoothly. They would not discuss the children's or their own problems. They would not even discuss mutually agreed-on solutions to problems. These experiences, the therapist explained, are designed to build a reservoir of positive experiences and pleasant memories, and to provide a firm basis for compromise and problem solving.

Utilizing the Solving Circle

Focusing the solving circle, John and Lenore were encouraged to use the same place in the house where they practiced the communication skills. They would draw an imaginary circle around themselves. While they were in this circle, their conversation would be limited to the following:

- How to solve their problems and settle their differences
- What each one brought and would bring to the relationship
- What each person was willing to change in the future in order to bring them closer

If this strategy is built on the previous ones, it can be effective. Problem confrontation is built not on personal combativeness, but on commonality.

The four strategies described in this chapter are best used as a unit and as a system, since they are interdependent and developmental. Their use in this case enabled John and Lenore to make significant strides by lessening their work, communicating more satisfactorily, spending time together, engaging the children in conversation and activities, and learning the fine art of self-evaluation.

The value of these strategies lies not in achieving finality or total solutions, in curing, or in accomplishing irrevocable closure. Their merit lies rather in making initial and even major changes, and in learning life skills that are applicable to virtually any problem.

Concluding Summary:
Reality Therapy as a Brief Therapy

Hoyt (1995) has identified eight characteristics of brief therapy and managed care that provide a backdrop to reality therapy.

1. Specific targets. Reality therapy centers on helping clients formulate plans to enhance their lives in the areas of self-preservation, belonging, power or achievement, freedom, and fun or enjoyment. The reality therapist knows that any problem can be lessened when these needs are met and has a theoretical and practical scheme for approaching the presenting problem.

2. Early intervention. All human beings have general needs and specific wants. When they evaluate their behavior early in the therapeutic process, they can make changes. The therapist builds a relationship quickly with clients, helps them evaluate their behavior, teaches them choice theory and reality therapy, and helps them follow through on treatment plans.

3. Clear definition of patient-therapist responsibility. Often reality therapists begin by asking clients what they want from this first session as well as from the entire therapeutic process. Therapists describe what they want from clients and what they have to offer them. For instance, therapists want clients to come on time, to be willing to talk, to be open to suggestions, and to implement plans.

4. Flexible use of time. Phone calls, letters, and brief or extended visits are used as deemed appropriate.

5. Interdisciplinary cooperation. Reality therapists work within the boundaries of their limitations. Referrals to medical professionals, recovery groups, and the like are made as needed.

6. Multiple formats and modalities. Reality therapy is used individually, in family counseling (Wubbolding, 1993), or in groups (Wubbolding 1991, 1997). It has many applications to schools and classrooms (Glasser, 1990, 1991; Wubbolding, 1993) and to management/supervision (Wubbolding, 1996).

7. Intermittent treatment. In a short time—1 to 10 sessions—clients can learn the principles and gain some tools for life enhancement.

Still, some clients return on an episodic basis to deal with other issues or to develop new ways to cope with diverse relationships.

8. Results orientation and accountability. Clients evaluate their own behavior and their own progress. A favorite inquiry by reality therapists is: "What would others see you doing if you were to have a better relationship (if you were to be feeling better, if you were to be a more productive and cooperative employee, etc.)?"

Reality therapy has always been a brief therapy. In fact, in earlier years it was occasionally and mistakenly criticized as a "quick fix" because it was not a psychoanalytic approach. While it can be used on a long-term basis with individuals or groups for personal growth, it is quite useful in the age of short-term, solution-focused, outcome-based brief therapy.

References

Ellis, A. (1975). *New guide to rational living*. New York: HarperCollins.

Glasser, W. (1965). *Reality therapy*. New York: HarperCollins.

Glasser, W. (1980). *Stations of the mind*. New York: HarperCollins.

Glasser, W. (1985). *Control theory*. New York: HarperCollins.

Glasser, W. (1995). *Staying together*. New York: HarperCollins.

Glasser, W. (1990). *The quality school*. New York: HarperCollins.

Glasser, W. (1991). *The quality schoolteacher*. New York: HarperCollins.

Glasser, W. (1998). *Choice theory*. New York: HarperCollins.

Glasser, W., and Wubbolding, R. (1995). Reality therapy. In R. Corsini (Ed.), *Current psychotherapies*. Itasca, IL: Peacock Publishers.

Glasser, W., and Wubbolding, R. (1997). Beyond blame. *Reaching Today's Youth, 1* (4), 40–42.

Hoyt, M. (1995). *Brief therapy and managed care*. San Francisco: Jossey-Bass.

Wubbolding, R. (1988). *Using reality therapy*. New York: HarperCollins.

Wubbolding, R. (1991). *Understanding reality therapy*. New York: Harper-Collins.

Wubbolding, R. (1991). *Using reality therapy in group counseling* [Video]. Cincinnati, OH: Center for Reality Therapy.

Wubbolding, R. (1993). Reality therapy. In A. Horne & J. L. Passmore (Eds.), *Family counseling and therapy*. Itasca, IL: Peacock Publishers.

Wubbolding, R. (1993). *Managing the disruptive classroom* [Video]. Blooming-
ton, IN: Agency for Instructional Television.

Wubbolding, R. (1996) *Employee motivation*. Knoxville, TN: SPC Press.

Wubbolding, R. (1997). School as a system. *Journal for Reality Therapy, 16* (2),
76–79.

Wubbolding, R. (1997). *Using reality therapy in group counseling*. Cincinnati,
OH: Center for Reality Therapy.

Annotated Bibliography

Glasser, W. (1998). *Choice theory*. New York: HarperCollins. This book contains
an overview of the theory that underlies the practice of reality therapy: a summary of needs and the quality world as sources of motivation. It includes
applications to interpersonal relationships and community education.

Glasser, W. (2000). *Reality therapy in action*. New York: HarperCollins. Specific
cases of Dr. Glasser's own style of therapy are presented, including specific dialogues and explanations of how his comments are grounded in choice theory.

Wubbolding, R. (1988). *Using reality therapy*. New York: HarperCollins. This
brief summary of choice theory gives practical ideas on how to use the environmental and procedural components of reality therapy. Applications are
made to adolescence, marriage, and management of employees.

Wubbolding, R. (2000). *Reality therapy for the 21st century*. New York: Harper-
Collins. The procedures are significantly expanded, with multicultural applications and adaptations presented based on the author's international
experience. In addition, research findings validating the use of reality therapy
are summarized. The emphasis here is on how readers can use reality therapy.

Part III

11

∞

Stage-Appropriate Change-Oriented Brief Therapy Strategies

Michael F. Hoyt
and
Scott D. Miller

> *A journey of a thousand miles*
> *must begin with a single step.*
> —Lao-tzu (c. 604–531 B.C.E.)

We find it useful in brief therapy to think about what would be best in a given moment to identify, encourage, promote, amplify, and help maintain clients' desired changes. We seek collaboration and expect forward movement, a significant shift from earlier orientations. In 1904, Sigmund Freud placed the concept of *resistance* to change at the center of his evolving theory of therapy. Based on his observation that clients would frequently and often vigorously reject the interpretations he offered, he concluded that "patient[s] cling to [their] disease and . . . even fight against [their] own recovery." Overcoming these resistances by provoking and then "working-through" them was, he came to believe, "the essential function of [treatment] . . . the only part of our work which gives us an assurance that we have achieved something with the patient" (Freud, 1915–1917).

While the concept of resistance has seen many modifications over time, the belief that people sabotage or otherwise subvert the change process survives (Anderson & Stewart, 1983; Singer, 1994). "Resistance," pio-

289

neering family therapist Lyman Wynne (1983, p. vi) once observed, "is a thorn that by any other name pricks as deep." *Secondary gain* (Freud, 1909; Weiner, 1975), *habit strength* (Dollard & Miller, 1950), *homeostasis* (Jackson & Weakland, 1961; Hoffman, 1981), *self-protection* (Mahoney, 1991), *lack of motivation* (Malan, 1976; Sifneos, 1992), and the recent and popular characterization of people as *being in denial* are just a few of the terms used nowadays that reflect Freud's original concept. This belief, as Mahoney (1991, p. 18) has noted in his massive and systematic review of psychotherapy process research, has led to "one of the most important points of convergence across contemporary schools of thought in psychotherapy: Significant psychological change is rarely rapid or easy."

Shifting Toward Working *With*

It's easier to ride a horse
in the direction it's going.
—Cowboy adage

In 1970, Speer pointed out the irony of basing therapeutic approaches to change on theories of how people do *not* change. Some 14 years later, brief therapist de Shazer (1984) developed this insight in his now-classic paper, "The Death of Resistance," in which he argued that traditional theories of resistance were tantamount to pitting the therapist against the client in a fight that the therapist had to win in order for the client to be successful. In contradistinction, de Shazer suggested shifting the focus of therapeutic activity to the study of how people *do* change. From this perspective, clients could be seen as having unique ways of *cooperating with* rather than resisting the therapist in their mutual efforts to bring about desired changes.

Borrowing concepts from an earlier resistance-based framework, de Shazer and his colleagues (e.g., Fisch, Weakland, & Segal, 1982; Segal & Watzlawick, 1985) developed a rudimentary system for classifying different types of client-therapist cooperation. They described the therapeutic interaction as an active, doing type (referred to as the *customer-seller* relationship), a passive-reflective type (referred to as the *browser-listener* relationship), or an uncommitted, waiting type (referred to as the *visitor-*

host relationship). The purpose of the classification system was to provide therapists with a "thumbnail" for cooperating with their client in the development of interventions that were tailored to each client (de Shazer, 1988). This system has evolved into the well-known solution-focused therapy taxonomy of *customer/complainant/visitor* (see Berg, 1989; Berg & Miller, 1992; de Shazer, 1988; Miller & Berg, 1991). As Shoham, Rohrbaugh, and Patterson (1995, p. 153, emphasis added) explain:

> Here the distinction between customer, complainant, and visitor-type relationships offers guidelines for therapeutic cooperation or "fit" (de Shazer, 1988; Berg & Miller, 1992). If the relationship involves a *visitor* with whom the therapist cannot define a clear complaint or goal, cooperation involves nothing more than sympathy, politeness, and compliments for whatever the clients are successfully doing (with no tasks or requests for change). In a *complainant* relationship, where clients present a complaint but appear unwilling to take action or want someone else to change, the therapist cooperates by accepting their views, giving compliments, and sometimes prescribing observational tasks (e.g., to notice exceptions to the complaint pattern). Finally, with *customers* who want to do something about a complaint, the principle of fit allows the therapist to be more direct in guiding them toward solutions.

Recognizing that "imposition generates opposition" (Hoyt, 1999), the basic idea is that working *with* the client's stage of motivation, language, goals, and theories of change (Duncan, Hubble, Miller, & Coleman, 1998) often obviates or simply dissolves "resistance." We may know that we're helpers (or at least think that we are), but the client may not—or may not be ready or looking for what we think would be helpful. With this understanding, "resistance" can be seen quite differently from the conventional psychiatric pejorative. Not identifying and honoring the client's treatment goals may make it necessary for the client to "resist." Clients who are described as "noncompliant" or "resistant" may be in a power-politics struggle (Tomm, 1993), engaged in counteroppressive practices to refuse being psychologically colonized or bent in directions they don't want to go (Hoyt, 1998). In such cases, *vive la résistance!* The client's response signals an opportunity to repair a mismatch.

Stages of Change

What is the hardest of all? That which you hold
the most simple; seeing with your own eyes what
is spread out before you.
—Johann Wolfgang von Goethe

Around the same time that de Shazer and his associates were developing their ideas, another group of clinicians in a very different setting were coming to a similar conclusion, namely, that traditional schools of therapy were "more about why people do not change than how people can change" (Prochaska, 1999, p. 228). Based on the realization that *most* people change *without* the benefit of formal therapy, Prochaska and his colleagues extended their analysis beyond the therapeutic setting that had been the focus of the de Shazer group and began studying how people change naturally, spontaneously, and on an everyday basis (Prochaska, 1999, 1995; Prochaska & DiClemente, 1982, 1983, 1984; DiClemente & Prochaska, 1982). In the nearly two decades of research that followed, they discovered:

> a phenomenon that was not contained within any of the leading theories of therapy. Ordinary people taught us that change involves progress through a series of stages. At different stages people apply particular processes to progress to the next stage. (Prochaska, 1999, p. 228)

As Norcross and Beutler (1997, pp. 48–49) have summarized, in this *transtheoretical model* change unfolds over a series of five (or six) stages of motivational readiness:

> *Precontemplation* is the stage at which there is no intention to change behavior in the foreseeable future. . . .
> *Contemplation* is the stage in which people are aware that a problem exists and are seriously thinking about overcoming it but have not yet made a commitment to take action. . . .
> *Preparation* is a stage that combines intention and behavioral criteria. Individuals in this stage are intending to take action immediately and report some small behavioral changes. . . .

Action is the stage in which individuals modify their behavior, experiences, and/or environment in order to overcome their problems. . . .

Maintenance is the final stage in which people work to prevent relapse and consolidate the gains attained during action. . . . [M]aintenance is a continuation, not an absence, of change. . . . Stabilizing behavior change and avoiding relapse are the hallmarks.

Prochaska (1993, p. 253) adds a final stage, perhaps more ideal than realistic:

Termination, in which "there is zero temptation to engage in the problem behavior, and there is a 100 percent confidence (self-efficacy) that one will not engage in the old behavior regardless of the situation."

In their aptly named article, "In Search of How People Change," Prochaska, DiClemente, and Norcross (1992, p. 1107) focus on "*when* particular shifts in attitudes, intentions, and behaviors occur." Movement through these stages generally happens in two ways. First, change may advance linearly, proceeding gradually and stepwise through the stages from start to finish. The second, and by far the most common form of progression, is characterized by advance, relapse, and recycling through the stages. This is the process intimated in the popular saying, "Three steps forward and two steps back." Sudden transformations in behavior are possible, too, such as Jean Valjean's change from sinner to saint in Victor Hugo's *Les Misérables* (Alexander & French, 1946; Hoyt, Rosenbaum, & Talmon, 1992) and the celebrated overnight conversion of Ebenezer Scrooge in Charles Dickens's *A Christmas Carol* (W.R. Miller, 1986).

Both Prochaska's and de Shazer's theories of the change process have the advantage of shifting the guiding metaphor for clinical practice from one that emphasizes therapist power to one that stresses collaboration and facilitation. Within both systems, therapy is not a matter of using "techniques, strategies, and other clever maneuvers . . . for the good of the clients" (de Shazer, 1986, p. 73). Rather, therapists are thought of as "joining with," "working together," or "cooperating with" clients in an attempt to facilitate their unique process of change. Prochaska's work is supported by a wealth of empirical data, a critical feature in today's health care environment that requires both individualized treatment and accountability from third-party payers (Hoyt, 1995; Hubble, Duncan, & Miller, 1999; Johnson, 1995; Miller, Duncan, Hubble, & Johnson, 1999).

For the majority of people, reaching lasting change takes time and sustained effort. This does not mean, however, that treatment *must* necessarily be a long-term and intensive process in order to be successful. In their research, for example, Prochaska et al. (1992) found that people who moved from one stage to the next during the first few sessions of treatment doubled their chances of taking effective action to solve their problem in the next six months. A movement of two stages as much as quadrupled the chances of success (Prochaska, Velicer, Fava, Ruggiero, Laforge, & Rossi, 1997).

From this vantage point, the traditional distinction between long and brief forms of therapy can be seen as a muddle. Indeed, the length of treatment is largely irrelevant to successful outcome. Rather, *effective* therapy is a result of working cooperatively with people to facilitate their movement to the next stage of change. Research shows that such movement generally occurs early in the treatment process or *not at all*. Nearly all large-scale, meta-analytic studies, for example, show that people's response in the first few sessions is highly predictive of eventual outcome (Hubble, Duncan, & Miller, 1999). In one representative study, Brown, Dreis, and Nace (1999) found that people *not* reporting movement by the third visit on average showed no improvement over the entire course of treatment regardless of the model of treatment their therapist employed (e.g., brief versus long-term, psychological versus medical, etc.).

Prochaska et al. (1992) demonstrated that stage of change is a better predictor of treatment outcome than the client's age, socioeconomic status, problem severity, goals, self-efficacy/esteem, and existing social support network—variables that continue to be used despite their low predictive power. As one example of the predictive power of the stage-of-change model, consider the results of a study on the moderating effects of stages of change in drug treatment for anxiety and panic disorder (Prochaska, 1995). Following treatment, stage-of-change measures predicted more of participants' progress than assignment to either active drug or placebo conditions. In other words, the persons's stage of change had more predictive power than the psychoactivity of anxiolytic medication (Beitman, Beck, Deuser, Carter, Davidson, & Maddock, 1994)!

Research to date further shows that therapists improve the chances of success when treatment is tailored to the client's stage of change. For example, several studies have found that stage-appropriate treatment interventions result in greater recruitment and retention of people in the treatment process (see Brogan, Prochaska, & Prochaska, 1999; Reis & Brown, 1999)—two serious problems in outpatient practice (Prochaska, 1999). Other studies have shown that stage-appropriate treatments produce degrees of success equal to those observed in intensive programs but at much lower cost—outcomes of considerable importance for those interested in meeting current demands for efficiency and accountability (Miller et al., 1999; Prochaska et al., 1997).

Illustrating Stage-Appropriate Practice

The readiness is all.
—William Shakespeare
(*Hamlet*, act V, scene ii)

Combining Prochaska's transtheoretical model of stages of change with strategic and solution-focused therapy (de Shazer, 1985, 1988; Miller, Hubble, & Duncan, 1996) suggests some differential intervention strategies, as discussed at length by Miller, Duncan, and Hubble (1997, pp. 88–104):

> *Precontemplation* : Suggest that the client "think about it" and provide information and education;
>
> *Contemplation* : Encourage thinking, recommend an observation task in which the client is asked to notice something (such as what happens to make things better or worse), and join with the client's lack of commitment to action with a "Go slow!" directive;
>
> *Preparation* : Offer treatment options, invite the client to choose from viable alternatives;
>
> *Action* : Amplify what works—get details of success and reinforce;
>
> *Maintenance* : Support success, predict setbacks, make contingency plans;
>
> *Termination* : Wish well, say goodbye, leave an open door for possible return if needed.

Let's take a closer look at some of these transtheoretical ideas and how they can help provide a framework for integrating techniques and practices developed by various schools of brief therapy.

Precontemplation

Prochaska (1999, p. 228) indicates that people in this first stage "are not intending to change or take action in the near future, usually measured in terms of 'the next six months.' " These are the people typically labeled "resistant," "in denial," or "character disordered" in traditional treatment approaches. In reality, however, these people may "not have a clue" that a problem exists. Alternatively, they may feel there is a problem, but they, as of yet, may not have made a connection between this problem and their contribution to its formation or continuation. Quite often, people in this stage have actually tried to change. Their lack of success, however, may have caused them to become demoralized. As a result, they avoid thinking, talking, or reading about ways to solve the problem. As might be expected, people in this stage are often not interested in participating in treatment (Prochaska, 1995). Most often, they come at the behest or mandate of someone else (e.g., parent, partner, probation officer, court). As such, they may portray themselves as under duress or the victim of "bad luck."

Ruth, a 52-year-old woman who was ordered into treatment after receiving a citation for driving under the influence of alcohol (Miller et al., 1997), is an example of someone in the *precontemplation* stage. Despite previous arrests on similar charges, Ruth indicated that she did not have a problem with alcohol.

Therapist: Ruth, tell me just a little bit about what brings you in today?
    Ruth: I got a, uh, ticket for driving under the influence.
Therapist: (*nodding*)
    Ruth: Actually, I only had one or two drinks, but I hadn't eaten much, and probably some of the medication I had taken contributed to that.
Therapist: (*sympathetically*) Yeah, and, so, you got a ticket?
    Ruth: Yeah, I got my license suspended and I have to come here or someplace for counseling. I've been evaluated, very unfairly I might add, as having a *big* problem.

Therapist: A *big* problem.

Ruth: Yeah, according to these tests, which I don't think are very reliable, uh, that's what they say, and there is no recourse. I have already tried to do something about it, but the state says that if I want my license back, I gotta come here.

Contemplation

The process of change continues in the second stage. According to Prochaska (1999, p. 229), people in the *contemplation* stage "intend to change in the next six months." In traditional treatment approaches, these people are frequently referred to as the "yes, but" clients—those who earnestly seek the therapist's help and advice, only to reject it once it is offered. In reality, however, people in this stage recognize that a change is needed but are unsure whether it is worth the cost in time, effort, and energy. In addition, they are concerned about the losses attendant to any change they might make.

Consider the following dialogue from a first session with a woman who is experiencing difficulty making a decision about whether to marry (Miller et al., 1997). On the one hand, Meg knows that, in order to make this important decision, problems in the relationship must be discussed with her potential mate. At the same time, however, she worries about the consequences that might ensue from such a discussion:

Meg: I don't like the way things are right now, but I don't want to, we have a very nonconflictual relationship, so I don't want to fight with him. We always have a good time. I just want to figure out, you know, should we marry or, uh, *(laughing)* just be merry.

Therapist: Do you think that if people are assertive and let other people know what they want, do you think that makes conflict?

Meg: *(shifting in chair)* No, I don't, but it's difficult to do.

Therapist: Well, perhaps.

Meg: I have tried to talk with Michael about this and tell him, you know, but . . .

Therapist: Sometimes people mistake aggressiveness for assertiveness, and they say things that thwart the other person, the conversation, and you don't want that to happen?

Meg: No, but I have tried to talk with him and tell him what I want. Like last week, we were coming home from this party we'd been to, and I told him how I was feeling, how I wanted to talk about our, you know, relationship, where we were going.

Therapist: Did he hear you?

Meg: Yeah, well, at least to start, but then the same old thing, the subject got changed.

Therapist: What did you do then?

Meg: I just laughed to myself.

Preparation

The third stage is *preparation*. According to Prochaska (1999, p. 230), people in this stage "intend to take action in the immediate future, usually measured in terms of 'the next month.' " Their main focus is on identifying the criteria and strategies for success as well as finalizing the development of their plan for change. *Preparation* is also characterized by the client's experimenting with the desired change—trying it on for size, noticing how it feels, and then experiencing the effects. For example, a person experiencing problems with drugs or alcohol may delay using temporarily or even modify the conditions under which they typically use (Prochaska & DiClemente, 1982). In contrast to the two previous stages—wherein the client's relationship with change is more tenuous and delicate—clients in the *preparation* stage are rarely given negative psychological labels. Indeed, these clients are often considered the ideal—their customership is on a surer footing, and their intention to take action fits with traditional ideas about the change process (Prochaska et al., 1992).

The following dialogue from the fifth visit with a man struggling to overcome obsessive and compulsive thoughts and behaviors can be used to illustrate this stage:

Peter: Well, you know, working on my symptoms is where my head is at. I've really been working on setting up this behavior program.

Therapist: Uh-huh.

Peter: In many ways, though, the bottom line is that it is like a diet. You know?

Therapist: Uh-huh.

Peter: You can do it this way or that way. But any way you do it, *if you do it*, you're gonna lose some weight.

Therapist: Right.

Peter: But you still gotta do it.

Therapist: Right.

Peter: Right now, I am thinking about doing it, but I'm not doing it.

Therapist: Uh-huh.

Peter: It's like, I'm having a hard time moving from thinking about doing it to actually doing it.

Action

Following *preparation*, the *action* stage commences. According to Prochaska (1999, p. 230), this is "the stage in which people have made specific, overt modifications in their life-styles within the past six months." Because of a tendency to equate the *action* stage with change in psychotherapy, many traditional treatment models erroneously identify this stage as the one in which *the* treatment takes place (Johnson, 1973, 1986; W. R. Miller, 1986; Prochaska et al., 1992). Research shows, however, that in spite of the field's historical bias toward action, people are *least* likely to be in this stage at the onset of treatment. This mismatch goes a long way toward explaining the persistence of the concept of *resistance* in mental health discourse.

The following excerpt from the fourth session with a woman who sought therapy in order to regain contact with alter personalities that had been lost following a head injury is typical of dialogue in the *action* stage.

Therapist: Have you had an opportunity to try any of the things that we've talked about?

Pamela: Yeah *(slight laugh)*. It was quite fun.

Therapist: Good. I was hoping it would be.

Pamela: Actually, we did not have to do many at all. Nat [*an alter*] left a note for everybody [*the other alters*]. I would say a lot of things changed after that talk with you. That evening and that next day, some different things were tried, and then that next evening Joe [*her partner with whom she had previously been unable to speak regarding her difficulties*] said, "Obviously something is wrong, so what gives?" Chris [*another alter*] was out and she told him. I think it's made a big difference because I'm out and Linda was out earlier in the week, also [*two alters that she had been out of contact with since the head injury*].

(See Schwarz [1998] for discussion of the collaborative treatment of dissociative disorders.)

Maintenance

In this stage, change continues and emphasis is placed on what needs to be done in order to maintain or consolidate gains. In contrast to those in the previous stage, people in the *maintenance* stage "are less tempted to relapse and are increasingly more confident that they can continue their changes" (Prochaska, 1999, p. 231). This is because they have learned from difficulties and temptations that they encountered while passing throught the other stages.

A recent session with a man who had been treated for problems with alcohol and depression illustrates dialogue typical of someone in the *maintenance* stage:

George: I've been thinking that, well, I've really got a lot out of coming here.
Therapist: It shows.
George: Yeah, and I thought about what we talked about last time . . .
Therapist: Uh-huh.
George: About spacing out our sessions . . .
Therapist: Uh-huh.
George: And, well, I think I'm ready.
Therapist: What gives you that confidence, that you're ready?

In the ensuing discussion, the therapist and George explored the reasons for George's confidence, as well as any circumstances he might encounter that would challenge it. This helped to reinforce and solidify George's gains, as well as prepare (inoculate) him for subsequent difficulties.

Termination

According to Prochaska (1993, p. 253), in this final stage there is zero temptation to engage in the problem behavior regardless of the situation.

So defined, this stage may actually be more of an ideal than a realistic or achievable stage of change, although over time some people move past "recovery" to a life and self-image that no longer contain the old problem (see Hoyt, 1994a; Dolan, 1998). More than likely, however, most people stay in the *maintenance* phase. That is, they continue to be mindful of possible threats to their desired change and monitor what they need to do to keep the change in place.

The Temporal Structure of (Brief) Therapy

There is a season for everything, a time
for every occupation under heaven.
—Ecclesiastes 3:1

Time is nature's way of not having everything happen at once. In the course of an event or process, some activities precede others; sequencing gives order and can provide direction. Recognizing that different issues and activities may be appropriate in the early, middle, and finishing phases of therapy may also help to organize and potentiate change interventions.

Therapy can be thought to have five interrelated phases or stages (see Hoyt, 1990, 2000). In actual practice, the phases blend into one another rather than being discretely organized. The structure tends to be epigenetic or pyramidal, each phase building on the prior so that successful work in one preconditions the next. Each phase sets the stage for the following phase: for example, the client typically needs to elect therapy and be selected for treatment before an alliance and goals can be formed; goals need to be established before working through and refocusing can meaningfully occur; a sense of movement needs to precede discussions of homework, relapse prevention, and leave-taking; and all of these anticipate change processes continuing past the formal ending point of treatment and the possibility of a return to therapy as needed.

Schematically, the five phases look like this:

Figure 11-1: The Temporal Structure of Brief Therapy

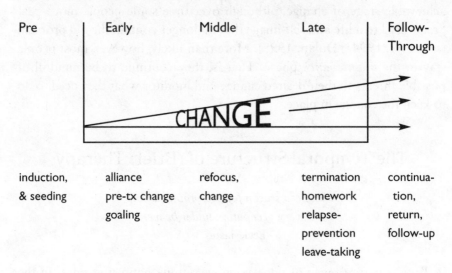

Pre	Early	Middle	Late	Follow-Through
induction, & seeding	alliance pre-tx change goaling	refocus, change	termination homework relapse-prevention leave-taking	continuation, return, follow-up

There is often an interesting parallel between the structure of the overall course of treatment and the structure of each individual session. As seen in Figure 11.2, there is a microcosm-macrocosm resemblance ("Ontogeny recapitulates phylogeny," say the biologists), the activities of each treatment phase mirroring the activities of each session: for example, the client elects (to return to) therapy; the first portion of each session (and treatment) emphasizes alliance building; the middle portion of each session (and treatment) focuses on accelerating change; the latter portion

Figure 11-2: The Temporal Structure of Each Session

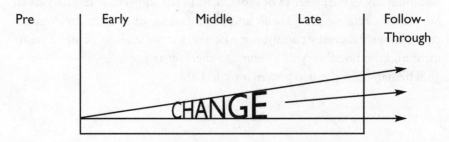

Pre	Early	Middle	Late	Follow-Through

of each session (and treatment) emphasizes how to keep it going; and the follow-through after each session (and treatment) is a time of continuation and possible return.

Each course of therapy can thus be schematically represented as comprising a chain or sequence of sessions, as seen in Figure 11-3.

Figure 11-3: Therapy as a Temporally Structured Sequence of Sessions, Each with a Temporally Structured Sequence

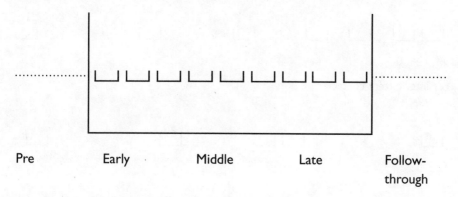

Pre   Early   Middle   Late   Follow-
through

(It can be noted that when a single session composes the entire course of therapy [as happens in approximately 20–50 percent of cases—see Hoyt, 1994b, 1995; Hoyt et al., 1992; Rosenbaum et al., 1990; Talmon, 1990], Figures 11-1 and 11-2 collapse on to one another, the structure of the individual session and the overall treatment, by definition, being self-same [isomorphic].)

One can also schematically depict, as in Figure 11-4, various arrangements in which sessions occur at variable intervals, such as (see Figure 11-4a) having sessions on a regular (e.g., weekly) periodic basis; or (see Figure 11-4b) initially having sessions weekly and then biweekly and then monthly; or (see Figure 11-4c) having sessions episodically or intermittently on an as-needed basis.

Figure 11-4: Some Ways Sessions Can Be Temporally Arrayed

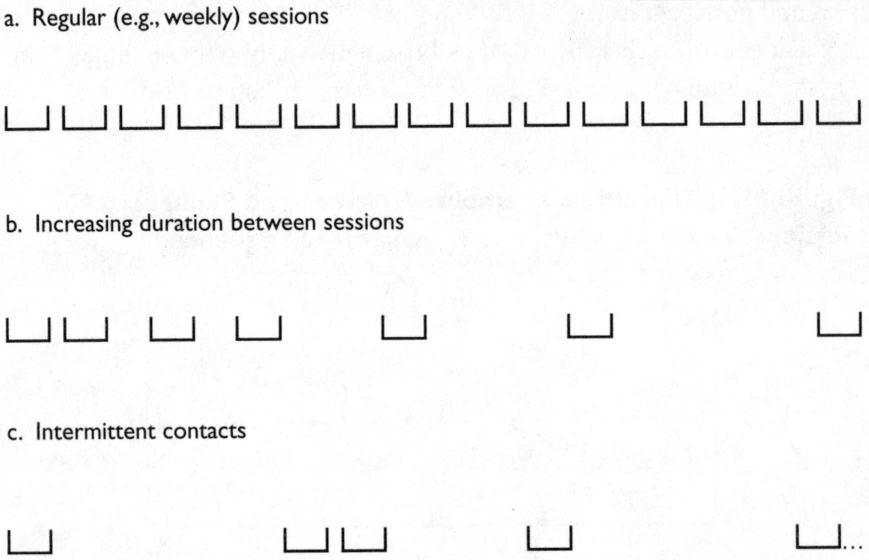

a. Regular (e.g., weekly) sessions

b. Increasing duration between sessions

c. Intermittent contacts

Strategies by Temporal Stage

Organizing is what you do before you do
something, so that when you do it, it's
not all mixed up.
—Christopher Robin
(A. A. Milne, *Winnie-the-Pooh*, 1926)

There are various tasks to be accomplished at each stage or phase of a session (and treatment). While flexibility, innovation, and honoring the client's theories, motivations, goals, and energies ("leading by following") are paramount (Miller, Duncan, & Hubble, 1997; Duncan et al., 1998), we find it helpful to have these ideas available to strategically organize our therapeutic activity across the course of working with clients. In should be noted that as we use the term, *strategies* refers to purposeful, respectful activity; we accept our responsibility as therapists to help make something useful happen *with* the client (see Haley, 1977; Held, 1992; Solovey & Duncan, 1992; Weakland, 1993).

In what follows, we present a sampler of typical questions that might be useful at different phases of therapy. It should be noted that these are "questions (not answers)" (Miller, 1994); that we are looking for "symptoms of solutions" (Miller, 1992) that are often best accessed if we "step off the throne" (Duncan, Hubble, & Miller, 1997a), "recast the client as the star of the drama called therapy" (Duncan, Hubble, & Miller, 1998), and listen carefully to our clients' constructions of what would be helpful (Duncan, Hubble, Miller, & Coleman, 1998).

Pretreatment

Change begins even before we have contact with the client. She/he/they have decided that there is a "problem" and that she/he/they would like assistance to resolve the difficulty. While making an initial appointment, we inquire (a receptionist or even a questionnaire can do this):

- "What's the problem? Why have you called now?"
- "How do you see/understand the situation?"
- "Who's involved?"
- "What do you think will help?"
- "How have you attempted to solve the problem thus far?"
- "When the problem isn't so bothersome, what is going on differently?"

During this initial contact, before the first session, we also recruit the client's cooperation and seed change by asking:

- "Please notice between now and when we meet, so that you can describe it to me, when the problem you called about isn't so bad [when you're less or not depressed, when you're not having panic attacks, when you and your partner are getting along okay, etc.], what you're doing differently then. This may give us some clues regarding what you may need to do more of." [This is a variant of the "First Session Formula Task" described by de Shazer, 1985, p. 137; Weiner-Davis, de Shazer, & Gingerich, 1987]

We may also remark to the client:

- Therapy involves making some changes, not just talking about what's been wrong, so identifying exceptions to the problem that led you to call will help us focus on solutions that may be useful for you."

Early in Treatment and Early in Each Session

As we begin a session and a therapy, we attend carefully to developing a good alliance, inquiring about possible changes since our last contact, and establishing goals for the session and the therapy. Some useful questions include:

- Since we last spoke, what have you noticed that may be a bit different or better? How did that happen? What did you do?" [This question regarding presession change follows up on the earlier request for the client to notice possible exceptions—it may provide information to build upon and also conveys a metamessage of accountability, that the therapist will recall and inquire about agreed-upon tasks and homework.]
- "When is the problem not a problem? When is the presenting complaint not present?"
- "What do you call the problem? What name do you have for it?" [This personification is part of the "externalization" process described by White, 1989a; Roth & Epston, 1996.]
- "When (and how) does [the problem] influence you; and when (and how) do you influence it?" ["Relative influence questioning," following White, 1986.]
- "What's your idea or theory about what will help?"
- "How can I be most useful to you? What kind of therapist would you like me to be?" [See Norcross & Beutler, 1997.]
- "What's on your agenda? What needs to happen here today so that when you leave you can feel this visit was worthwhile?"
- "What are you willing to change today?" [See Goulding & Goulding, 1979.]
- "Given all that you've been through, how have you managed to cope as well as you have?" [This question acknowledges the seriousness of client's complaints and situation while still looking for strengths, resources, and competencies.]

- "If we work hard together, what will be the first small indications that we're going in the right direction?"
- "Suppose tonight, while you're sleeping, a miracle happens, and the problem that led you here is resolved. When you awaken tomorrow, how will you first notice the miracle has happened? What will be the first sign that things are better? And the next?" And the next? [This is the "Miracle Question," following de Shazer, 1988, p. 5.]

In the Middle of Treatment and the Middle of Each Session

Like a pilot checking the flight plan (the intended destination, the present location, the remaining fuel), we keep track of clients' goals and whether we're going in the right direction or if some "course corrections" need to be made. Possible refocusing is directed by the client's response to the following questions:

- "How did that work?" [If an attempted solution perpetuates the problem, something different, that still honors the client's belief structures and view of reality, is needed—see Fisch et al., 1982; McCloskey & Fraser, 1997.]
- "Is this being helpful to you? What might make it more so?"
- "Do you have any questions you'd like to ask me?"

If the client is making progress that is adequate and satisfying to her, him, or them, we attempt to keep in mind the solution-focused principle, "If it works, don't fix it" (de Shazer, in Hoyt, 1996b). We offer encouragement and support and try not to push. If the client is moving forward, we cheerlead rather than mislead, so to speak. We attend assiduously to empowering the so-called "common factors" (alliance and client contributions) that voluminous research (see Lambert, 1992; Lambert & Bergin, 1994; Miller et al., 1997) has shown accounts for most of the variance in psychotherapeutic outcomes. Remembering that the client-clinician alliance is the vehicle and not the destination, however, we don't necessarily focus explicit discussion on the therapeutic relationship unless something seems amiss. *If* we do not experience the client as experiencing us as helpful and supportive or if there isn't movement in the direction of the client's goals, we may inquire:

- "Are we working on what you want to work on?"
- "I seem to have missed something you said. What can I do to be more helpful to you now?"

Late in Treatment and Late in Each Session

Nearing the end of a course of therapy and nearing the end of each session, issues of *termination* become central. This phase can be thought of as subtracting the therapist from the successful equation (Gustafson, 1986; Hoyt, 1990, 2000), a basic heuristic being "You've been doing well with me; how can you continue to do well without me?" There are a number of issues to be addressed, as the following guideline questions suggest:

Goal Attainment/Homework/Postsession Tasks

- "Has this been helpful to you? How so?"
- "Which of the helpful things you've been doing do you think you should continue to do? How can you do this?"
- "Between now and the next time we meet [or, to keep things going in the right direction], would you be willing to do———?"
- "Who can be helpful to you in doing ———? What might interfere, and how can you prepare to deal with those challenges?" [See Levy & Shelton, 1990; Mahrer, Nordin, & Miller, 1995; Meichenbaum & Turk, 1987; Mohr, 1995.]

Goal Maintenance/Relapse Prevention

- "What would be a signal that the problems you were having might be returning? How can you respond if you see that developing?"
- "Suppose you wanted to go back to all of the problems you were having when you first came in—what would you need to do to make this happen, if you wanted to sabotage yourself?" [While independently developed (see Hoyt, 1995), this can be seen as a variant of Norm Reuss's "Nightmare Question"—see Berg & Reuss, 1998, pp. 36–37.]
- "How might [the problem] try to trick you into letting it

take over again?" [For some narrative therapy examples, see Nylund & Corsiglia, 1996; Madigan & Goldner, 1998.]

- "What will you need to do to increase the odds that things will work out okay even if you weren't to come in for a while?"
- "Who will be glad to hear about your progress? How can we circulate the good news? Who in your present or past would support your efforts? Which friends/family make up your community of positive concern?" [See Madigan, 1997; Madigan & Epston, 1995; White, 1993, 1997.]

Leave-taking

- "Would you like to make another appointment now, or wait and see how things go and call me as needed?" [See Hoyt, 2000, for a number of variants.]
- "What is the longest period you can imagine handling things on your own at this time?"
- "If you got stuck and wanted some help, but decided to try something other than therapy, what would you do? Who could you turn to, if not to therapy, if things get difficult again?" [These questions come from Kreider, 1998, pp. 352–353.]
- "How can you recall some of the helpful things we have discussed when you need them?"

Case Illustrations

Stage-Appropriate Brief Therapy with an Individual

Call me another thrower.
—Loren Eiseley
(*The Star Thrower*, 1978)

Doug was a 23-year-old in great distress. His relationship with his girl-friend, Jennifer, had continued to spiral downward. Despite many promises, she had been increasingly nasty and rejecting toward Doug. She had lost another job and was on the verge of being evicted from her apartment. Doug suspected that she had begun drinking and using drugs again, especially speed, despite her angry protestations to the contrary. Finally, during a late-night phone call, she admitted that she had been going to bed with Jeff, whom Doug had thought of as one of his best friends. She dumped Doug. Never before much of a drinker (nor into drugs), over the next several days Doug drank heavily, missed work, and felt miserable.

Doug's parents called and scheduled an emergency appointment. As I (M.F.H.) found out, Doug worked in a law office. He lived with his parents. He described himself as a Christian, dressed with style, and followed pro basketball closely. He had gone out with Jennifer for almost three years. He said that he loved her and that he had been aware of her "vices" but had hoped to reform her. She had not returned any of his recent calls. When Doug had begun talking about Satan and suicide, his parents had become understandably alarmed and had called the HMO psychiatry department.

I took their call and agreed to see Doug and them that day, then asked if I might speak with him on the phone. I introduced myself, saying I'd heard he was having a rough time, and asked if he wanted some help. He said he didn't know, that the call had been his folks' idea. When I asked why they were so concerned, he said he really needed to calm down and have someone to talk with. I told him that I felt I could be helpful with that, and added that we might also talk about "making some changes." I confirmed our appointment time later that day and asked him to think about what else I could do to be helpful, and then hung up.

When he and his parents arrived in the late afternoon, I brought them all into my office. Wearing jeans, running shoes, and a rumpled T-shirt, Doug looked like someone who hadn't showered or slept much in several days—which he hadn't. His parents were almost frantic. They hadn't liked Jennifer but said they appreciated his concern about her and how hard breaking up was—but this wasn't the son they knew. "Should he be hospitalized?" they wanted to know.

I asked Doug if he felt he needed hospitalization to ensure his safety. He didn't think so. "What would be most helpful right now?" I asked, adding that I couldn't influence Jennifer. "Something to help me get some rest and sleep," he responded. "If I get a doctor to come in and give you a prescription, will you promise not to drink and not to harm yourself, and will you come to see me again on Friday?" (It was Wednesday.) He said yes, we reviewed our no-suicide and no-drinking agreement in front of his parents, and I summoned the on-call psychiatrist, who after a brief evaluation gave Doug a prescription for a couple of antianxiety pills. I didn't want to go down the slippery slope of medicating life problems, but he was quite agitated and seemed sincere in his promise not to drink, and I hoped some immediate response to his request would provide some relief and help strengthen our alliance and perhaps build some hope.

I also asked Doug what he did when he wasn't upset and found out some of his interests, including his avid attention to pro basketball. His affect brightened, and he revealed a keen knowledge as we talked about some recent trades the local team had made. We also discussed Jennifer—he nodded and cried when I asked if he thought "it was over." When I asked about ways he had been able to cope successfully with stress in the past that he could use now, he mentioned several (prayer, exercise, talking with friends, reminding himself of what was best in the long run) and agreed to use these over the next few days. I also suggested that he think about the good times and the bad times with Jennifer to see what conclusions he might draw.

We met that Friday, and the next, and the next. He reevaluated his relationship with Jennifer, realizing more of the problems. He still felt very sad but said he no longer felt that he had "failed." We discussed what he thought had gone wrong and what he might want to do differently in the future, once he was ready to move on and someday meet another woman. (He laughed when, utilizing sports jargon, I referred to his next girlfriend as "a player to be named later.") He decided that he had been too much of a "rescuer," that the relationship had been "too one way—I gave and she took."

At our next meeting, Doug reported that Jennifer had called him, long-distance collect. He said he had been sympathetic, but that he didn't get sucked back in. He promised to call her a couple of days later, but she wasn't there when he called at the appointed time. He had then heard through a friend that Jennifer had lost yet another job because of continued lateness and absenteeism, and that she was living with another guy. This fortuitous ("extratherapeutic") sequence of events brought up more disappointment, but Doug said it also helped confirm his decision to let go and move on.

After a fourth weekly meeting, Doug said he felt he was doing better and that he didn't need to come in so often—but that he still wanted to keep meeting for a while. I asked what he thought would be a good schedule, and he suggested three weeks hence. Jennifer was still a topic, but Doug also brought up the situation with his folks. He felt "jammed" (cramped) by them. He said he was a good son but that he needed to live his own way. He had been contemplating moving out but feared his parents would be worried or hurt, especially after the way they had been there for him during his crisis. We discussed times when his parents had been proud of his independence—this "reframe," which allowed him to maintain a "preferred view" of himself (see Watzlawick, Weakland, & Fisch, 1974; Coyne, 1985; Eron & Lund, 1989, 1996), relieved his guilt. It also prefigured his growing readiness to discontinue therapy. We considered several possible courses of action (e.g., living on his own versus roommates), which Doug said he would give more thought to and soon make a decision.

We met two more times, a month apart. He was maintaining his gains ("I'm sorry it had to end that way with Jennifer, but it did"). He was working, socializing, not drinking, and had moved in with roommates. I congratulated him on his good work. We discussed some possible temptations and "pitfalls" and how to avoid them. In leave-taking, he expressed his appreciation and said that he had liked the feeling that he had been given emotional support but allowed to work things out in his own way and at his own pace. We discussed what might be some possible indications to return to therapy. He agreed to recontact me if he felt the need. We wished each other well and said good-bye.

Stage-Appropriate Brief Therapy with a Couple: From Changing Individuals to Changing Relationships

> *Know what you see; don't see what you know.*
> —Addie Fuhriman (1984, personal communication)

While the stages-of-change model was originally developed to describe the individual's progression through the change process, it is also possible to apply the ideas to clincal work with couples and families. In such cases, the stages are applied to the relationship between the individuals in treatment rather than to the individuals themselves.

The following excerpts (from a case supervised by S.D.M.) are taken from the fourth session of therapy with Marcus and Felicia, a married couple who sought treatment for "long-standing communication problems." In their intake information, the couple reported having been in treatment on two prior occasions for the same problem without success. In the first three sessions of the present therapy, the couple were treated as if they were in the preparation or action stage of change. As such, treatment sessons were active in nature (e.g., teaching and practicing communication skills) and action-oriented homework assignments (e.g., "try out the skills you learned in the sessions") were given between visits. While the couple willingly engaged in the skill-building exercises during the sessions, they did not complete the homework assignments.

The fourth session began with the following exchange:

Therapist: Well, welcome. I'm glad you both could get here. The first thing I'd like to know is, is there anything different that's been happening between you since the last time I saw you?

Felicia: I think, I think there is. I think there's *less* communication.

Therapist: Okay.

Felicia: Because we haven't really spoken. Yesterday we got into an argument before we left for work. So we didn't speak all evening.

Therapist: Uh-huh.

Felicia: But I think there's been less communication. So . . .

Therapist: There's been less communication.

Felicia: Uh-huh. I mean, there hasn't been any communication about what we discussed at our last session.

Therapist: Okay.

Felicia: We've been avoiding it.

Therapist: How about you, Marcus? Anything different that you've noticed?

Marcus: Mmm-huh, nothing, other than what Felicia has noticed.

Therapist: You've noticed less communication also?

Marcus: Uh-huh, less communication.

Therapist: What do you think that means?

Marcus: That we have a problem.

Therapist: And what's the problem?

Marcus: Uh, that we're not communicating and we don't have mutual objectives, I don't think.

Both Felicia and Marcus recognize that a problem exists. At the same time, however, neither member of the dyad has *acted* to solve the problem in the time between the present and previous session. Rather, in Felicia's word, the couple has been "avoiding it" [the communication problem].

Such *in*action on the part of this couple might easily be viewed as "resistance" or, minimally, a "lack of motivation." This mindset might, in turn, lead the therapist to engage in activities aimed at "breaking through" the resistance (e.g., confrontation) or getting the clients to *do* something (e.g., encouraging activity or the taking of responsibility, homework tasks, etc.) to solve their problem.

When viewed through the lens of the stages-of-change model, however, the couple is considered neither resistant nor in need of a therapist-provided motivational "pick-me-up." Rather, emphasis is placed on identifying and cooperating with the clients' stage of chage. In this case, the interaction between Felicia and Marcus is typical for people in the *contemplation* stage. As such, therapeutic activities that encourage new thinking, feelings, or observations are likely to be the most congruent with the activity level of the couple's current change process.

In the next excerpt, the therapist follows up on Marcus's comment about "not having mutual objectives" and attempts to help each member of the couple generate new thinking about his or her understanding of the problem as well as goals for treatment. This represents a shift in approach from the previous visits, during which the partners were treated as if they were in the *preparation* or *action* stages.

Felicia: He's the only one who can answer that. I don't know what he wants. He doesn't ever communicate what he wants. So, I don't know what he expects or what he wants.

Therapist: What do you think, Marcus, is that a possibility?

Marcus: Uh, it's a great possibility. I think that when communication is taking place, one has to, I think, understand that you can't verbally abuse someone and expect them to have perfect communication. As a matter of fact, that type of behavior produces just the converse. That person doesn't want to communicate with someone that is verbally abusive.

Therapist: Mmm-huh.

Marcus: And I think that behavior not only causes me to react individually, but I think that's probably a natural reaction for anyone. I don't know anyone that is positive to verbal abuse.

Therapist: Okay. But is it possible that you could incorporate . . . some of, maybe, do you gesture, how does it happen?

Marcus: *[nodding]*

Therapist: When you perceive that she is being verbally abusive, she does what? She raises her voice?

Marcus: Well, she could raise her voice. Not necessarily raise her voice. She uses profanity. She uses it very inappropriately and sometimes very consistently.

Therapist: Mmm-huh.

Marcus: One thing that really gets me is the fact of how she displays this verbal abuse, and it's not setting a good example for our daughter. And I guess that's what makes me so angry at the situation, because of the fact that it's not just impacting me individually any longer—it's impacting our child with this behavior. And, as I said, it was something that I saw early in our relationship. I felt that it would get better. Of course, as you know, this is not our first attempt at counseling. And I'm not beyond the fact that we, as a couple, may have problems. But I know fundamentally that we can't get to our joint problems unless I can get Felicia to look at the behavior that she is displaying because it's not only, you know, tearing me down but it affects me when I see the impact on my daughter. And I think that's more the impact on me, because I'm an adult and can deal with it. But at the same time, I react to her verbal abuse. But it really gets me when I have a daughter and now, you know, she's part of that whole behavior pattern that Felicia has, and I don't like it.

Felicia: Yeah, but you're part of the problem in this relationship too, Marcus. It's not only my doing. It takes two people to work on a relationship. And it's not only about me. It's just like we discussed the last time we were at the therapist's office. You always want to blame me for every damn thing. You never want to take responsibility for your actions. You don't want to be blamed for anything because you think that you can't do any wrong. My sisters see that about you, our friends see that about you, that you never want to be blamed for anything. And you're always trying to impress everybody. You want to impress everybody else, except me. Your family should come before other people come into play about trying to impress people, Marcus.

At this point in the session, the interaction between Marcus and Felicia turns into a heated argument. Each member of the dyad presents his or her view of the problem and each attributes the cause to the other. Specifically, Marcus blames the couple's difficulties on Felicia's "verbal abuse," while Felicia, in turn, credits Marcus's "lack of responsibility" for their problems. Such behavior is not atypical for people in the *contemplation* stage of change. Indeed, a hallmark of this stage, as Berg and Miller (1992, p. 23) point out, is the belief that "the only solution is for someone other than themselves to change" *first*. At the same time, however, the key to maximizing the success of therapeutic intervention from the stages-of-change perspective is accommodating rather than changing this belief.

One brief therapy strategy that has proved particularly useful in such circumstances is relationship-oriented or circular-style questions (Tomm, 1988). Briefly, such questions "attempt to bring forth" patterns that connect "persons, objects, actions, perceptions, ideas, feelings, events, beliefs, contexts" (Dozier, Hicks, Cornille, & Peterson, 1998, p. 192). As such, these questions contrast sharply with the more common lineal-style questions that seek to uncover beliefs about the origin of the problem or goals for treatment.

In the excerpt that follows, the therapist switches from individually oriented to circular questions. The impact on the couple's interaction is immediate. Specifically, they stop presenting their individual positions and opinions and begin to develop a vision of working together as a couple.

Therapist: There's a question that's in my mind, and I've sort of been trying to twist my tongue and figure out exactly how to ask it of the two of you. I'm wondering, what would be signs to the two of you that you were *working together* at resolving these things that happen in your relationship? What would be signs to each of you that you were working together rather than at cross-purposes? Does that question make sense?

Felicia: I'm not . . .

Therapist: Okay. When you actually have one of these episodes where you're obviously at a different place, my sense is that when you're trying to communicate, each of you sort of talks, and it's like, "What the hell?"

Felicia: Yeah, each of us doesn't listen to what the other says.

Therapist: Right, that's the point I'm getting at. So, what I'm looking for is what would be signs—when one of those episodes actually happens—what would be signs to each of you that you were working constructively around that difference rather than at cross-purposes?

Felicia: Sitting down and talking about it, and each of us listening to each other, instead of trying to outdo the other.

Therapist: Okay. And let me ask you this, and *[pointing at Marcus]* you can't give any hints here, okay? What would Marcus say he would notice about you that would give him the idea that you were listening?

Felicia: My not interrupting, because he complains that I always interrupt when he tries to speak to me.

Therapist: Okay. Instead of interrupting, you would . . . ?

Felicia: *[thinking]* Hmmm.

Therapist: Paint a picture for me.

Felicia: I would probably just sit there and listen.

Therapist: Yeah? And how would he know? What would make him say, "She's listening to me!"?

Felicia: Probably just being relaxed and not making any gestures or facial expressions.

Therapist: Okay.

Felicia: 'Cause he says I roll my eyes or I sigh or I look away when he's talking.

Therapist: Okay. How about for you, Marcus? What would Felicia say or, in fact, what would be signs to you that you were working together at resolving these things when they came up rather than being at cross-purposes? What would be signs that your couplehood is working?

Marcus: I don't know. . . .

Therapist: Okay.

Marcus: Because we have this way of communication that is different.

Therapist: Okay. Well, that's obvious to all of us. . . .

Marcus: Yes.

Therapist: That your styles are different.

Felicia: Mmm-huh.

Therapist: What I'm trying to figure out is what it might look like when the two of you are working together at resolving the difference.

Marcus: I think she would say that I would look at her. *[Looks at Felicia.]* I guess that would be what she would say.

Therapist: Anything else that you can think of? Sort of looking at her, maintaining eye contact. Any other ideas?

Marcus: Uh. Probably tell her, "I'm listening."

Therapist: *[looking at Felicia]* Okay.

Marcus: Tell her, "I'm here, I'm with you."

Therapist: So it's not going to be enough just to look. You have to keep going, "I'm with you, I'm with you." Is that right?

Marcus: Yes. She says that—it's really frustrating—she says that I'm not listening when I am!

Therapist: Okay, so to give *her* the idea that you're listening, you *[pointing to Marcus]*, you have to say, "I'm with you, I'm trying, I'm listening, I'm trying."

Marcus: *[nodding]*

Therapist: Anything else that would tell the two of you that?

In the discussion that followed, circular-style questions helped the couple continue to add details to their vision of working together to resolve their difficulties.

As the session neared the end of the hour, the therapist used another strategy from brief therapy—*scaling questions*—as a way to assess the couple's stage of change. Such questions, which can be used at any temporal phase, are based *not* on normative standards but rather on the clients' perception of self and others as well as their impressions of how others view them. As Berg and de Shazer (1993, p. 10; also see Hoyt & Berg, 1998; Miller, 1994) point out, the questions serve to "motivate and encourage, and to elucidate the goals and anything else that is important."

Therapist: So, Felicia, let me ask you: On a scale from 1 to 10, where 10 is the highest and 1 is the lowest, where would Marcus say you are in terms of your interest in having a different kind of conversation? In being interested in working at resolving these differences? Where would he say you are, on a scale of 1 to 10?

Felicia: Probably a 2 or 3.

Therapist: And where would Felicia say you are on a scale of 1 to 10, Marcus? Interested in having these kind of conversations we've been talking about?

Marcus: Probably a 1 or 2.

Therapist: And Marcus, where are you? Where would you say you are in terms of your interest in having a different kind of conversation?

Marcus: My interest is probably about a 9 or a 10.

Therapist: And you, Felicia?

Felicia: I would probably say mine is probably a 5.

Therapist: Okay, a 5. So, Marcus thought you'd be a 2 or a 3; you're saying a 5?

Felicia: Mmm-huh.

Therapist: What is it that Marcus will be noticing more of once he gets the idea that you are actually more interested in having a different kind of conversation? What would he notice different about you that would tell him you are much more interested in having a different kind of conversation?

Felicia: Probably trying to sit down and talk to him when I'm not angry.

Therapist: Okay, trying to talk when not angry.

Felicia: Mmm-huh.

Therapist: Okay, that would be a big one.

Felicia: Mmm-huh.

Therapist: You mean, as opposed to trying to make the conversation work once things have already sort of plummeted?

Felicia: Yeah. Mmm-huh.

Therapist: All right. [To Marcus.] You're saying you're a 9 or 10?

Marcus: Mmm-huh. Felicia probably doesn't think so.

Therapist: You think she'd say you were a 1 or 2?

Marcus: Yeah.

Therapist: Okay. What is it that Felicia would be noticing more about you, once she gets the idea about how much more interested, how much more willing you are? What would she notice different about you?

Marcus: Probably, basically, to know that I am *really* listening.

Therapist: Really.

Marcus: If I look at her, hold her hand, while she is talking.

Therapist: Okay. You're [pointing at Marcus] saying you're a 9 or a 10. You're [pointing at Felicia] saying you're a 5. If the team behind the one-way mirror has some ideas—and I have some ideas—how interested or willing would you be to try them out? A 10 being that, "Damn it, I'll do anything, once." A 1 is, "I'm outta here—straight to the divorce lawyer." I want you to be honest with me here. If the team has some ideas . . .

Marcus: A 9 or a 10.

Felicia: I would be 9 or a 10. I'd be interested, very interested.

Therapist: Okay. I'd like to take a break and go back and chat with them. I really appreciate your helping me fill in the blanks from here.

Marcus: This was really interesting.

Felicia: And helpful. I mean, you know, I mean it's like you said—we do, it's a struggle for us to work at it, but we both *[tearful]* really want it to work, but you know, I'm at the point where I'm not willing to work at it anymore.

Therapist: Right. And I don't sense that that's what either of you want, actually.

Felicia: No, I don't. But it becomes a job on a daily basis, and I'm not willing to work at it anymore.

Therapist: Right. Give me 5 or 6 minutes, okay?

At this point in the interview, the therapist took a break to consult with a team of therapists who had been observing from behind a one-way mirror. (The couple had briefly met this team at the beginning of the session.) Discussion centered on creating a between-session homework task that was congruent with the couple's stage of change. Whereas in previous sessions the therapist and team had conducted treatment as if the couple were in the *preparation* or *action* stage, the therapist and team now decided to treat the couple as if they were in the *contemplation* stage. Consistent with this stage, the couple was encouraged to "go slow"—even stop their problem-solving efforts altogether—and given an observation assignment to help them shift their viewing from conflict to cooperation.

Therapist: We've had a chat behind the mirror with everybody that you saw. Sort of sharing ideas. At least my experience of it is that the consensus is how very hurt each of you has been. That there is a tremendous amount of pain, emotional pain. It shows in your faces. We thought about when you first started talking about how you got together, there was all this brightness; and now there seems to be a distance and hurt and pain. At the same time, a desire to reconnect that hasn't seemed to work. But not for lack of trying. You've both come to individual counseling. You've both come here and tried things out. You both, in a painful way, I think, have tried to get your point across. The result is mostly, at best, frustration and, at worst, exhaustion.

Felicia: *[nodding]* Mmm-huh.

Marcus: *[nodding]* Mmm-huh.

Therapist: And so, it's not surprising to us to hear things like, "Oh, if this doesn't change quick, I want the hell out of this." I would say that makes you normal, that feeling. At the same time, I don't think that's what you want. At least, I don't get that experience yet. I get a thread of hope: around your children, how much you both mutually care about your family. Does this fit for you both?

Felicia: *[nodding affirmatively]*

Marcus: Yeah.

Therapist: When I was thinking about what we could offer, in terms of useful things, I did have some ideas, and the team and I talked about them. But after reflecting with each other about it, our sense is that the amount of the pain, the depth of the pain, and the amount of exhaustion that's apparent, makes me think at least, and I think the team understands, what is required first is a vacation from the constant drive to solve this. Not a vacation where you move out. But a vacation so that each of you can replenish individually and then come back and work together. Because right now both of you are sort of like, "Oh, please don't give anything too much right now." And I think that's wise. What I think, my impression—and I'm willing to hear your feedback—maybe a few weeks' vacation, where you stop trying to figure out and solve this. And you give the other person a vacation from that also. And you simply work quietly, observing the other person for signs that they are being replenished so that you can come back rested and work together, work at figuring out a way to resolve this, like I know both of you want to. Is that helpful?

Marcus: Makes sense.

Felicia: Yeah, it makes a lot of sense.

Therapist: I'm not talking about a laissez-faire . . .

Marcus: Uh-huh.

Therapist: Not just not doing anything. Now, that's not a vacation. A vacation is, you go to Rome. And you know the old saying, "When in Rome . . ." Look for signs that the other is being replenished.

A return appointment was scheduled for a month later. At that visit they both reported that they felt rested and replenished. They also both reported noticing things their partner had done to facilitate their being rested and replenished. Coincidentally, both felt that they had been communicating better as a couple during the vacation period. Time was spent exploring and reinforcing this change in this and two subsequent sessions. By the last visit, the therapist and team were treating the couple as if they were in the *active* or *maintenance* stage.

Summary: Doing What Works

> *Every art and every investigation, and*
> *similarly every action and pursuit, is*
> *considered to aim at some good.*
> —Aristotle (c. 384–322 B.C.E.)
> (*Nichomachean Ethics*, book 1, chapter 1)

Rather than following traditional psychiatric discourse—which tends to discount and exclude clients and places control within the therapist—we are interested in respectful collaboration that more fully appreciates and utilizes clients' strengths, resources, and competencies. Recognizing different stages of change, levels of motivation, and phases of treatment can help clinicians join with clients to empower and promote their active and efficacious participation in therapy.

References

Alexander, F., & French, T. M. (1946). *Psychoanalytic therapy: Theory and applications*. New York: Ronald Press.

Anderson, C. M., & Stewart, S. (1983). *Mastering resistance: A practical guide to family therapy*. New York: Guilford.

Beitman, B. D., Beck, N. C., Deuser, W., Carter, C., Davidson, J., & Maddock, R. (1994). Patient stages of change predicts outcome in a panic disorder medication trial. *Anxiety*, *1*, 64–69.

Berg, I. K. (1989). Of visitors, complainants and customers: Is there really any such thing as resistance? *Family Therapy Networker*, *13* (1), 21.

Berg, I. K., & de Shazer, S. (1993). Making numbers talk: Language in therapy. In S. Friedman (Ed.), *The new language of change: Constructive collaboration in psychotherapy* (pp. 5–24). New York: Guilford.

Berg, I. K., & Miller, S. D. (1992). *Working with the problem drinker: A solution-focused approach*. New York: Norton.

Berg, I. K., & Reuss, N. H. (1998). *Solutions step by step: A substance abuse treatment manual*. New York: Norton.

Brogan, M. M., Prochaska, J. O., & Prochaska, J. M. (1999). Predicting termination and continuation status in psychotherapy using the transtheoretical model. *Psychotherapy*, *36*(2), 105-113.

Brown, J., Dreis, S., & Nace, D. (1999). What makes a difference in psychotherapy outcome? And why does managed care want to know? In M. A. Hubble, B. L. Duncan, & S. D. Miller (Eds.), *The heart and soul of change*. Washington, DC: APA Press.

Coyne, J. C. (1985). Toward a theory of frames and reframing: The social nature of frames. *Journal of Marital and Family Therapy*, *11*, 337–344.

de Shazer, S. (1984). The death of resistance. *Family Process*, *23*, 79–93.

de Shazer, S. (1985). *Keys to solution in brief therapy*. New York: Norton.

de Shazer, S. (1986). A requiem for power. *Contemporary Family Therapy*, *10*(2), 69–76.

de Shazer, S. (1988). *Clues: Investigating solutions in brief therapy*. New York: Norton.

DiClemente, C. C., & Prochaska, J. O. (1982) Self-change and therapy change of smoking: A comparison of processes of change in cessation and maintenance. *Addictive Behaviors*, *7*, 133–142.

Dolan, Y. D. (1998). *One small step*. Watsonville, CA: Papier Mache Press.

Dollard, J., & Miller, N. E. (1950). *Personality and psychotherapy: An analysis in terms of learning, thinking, and culture*. New York: McGraw-Hill.

Dozier, R., Hicks, M., Cornille, T. A., & Peterson, G. W. (1998). The effect of Tomm's therapeutic questioning styles on therapeutic alliance. A clinical analogue study. *Family Process*, *37*, 189–200.

Duncan, B. L., Hubble, M. A., & Miller, S. D. (1997a). Stepping off the throne. *Family Therapy Networker*, *21* (4), 22–31, 33.

Duncan, B. L., Hubble, M. A., & Miller, S. D. (1997b). *Psychotherapy with "impossible" cases: The efficient treatment of therapy veterans*. New York: Norton.

Duncan, B. L., Hubble, M. A., & Miller, S. D. (1998, May 16). *Recasting the client as the star of the drama called therapy*. Keynote presentation at the Therapeutic Conversations 4 Conference, Toronto.

Duncan, B. L., Hubble, M. A., Miller, S. D., & Coleman, S. T. (1998). Escaping the lost world of impossibility: Honoring clients' language, motivation, and theories of change. In M. F. Hoyt (Ed.), *The handbook of constructive therapies* (pp. 293–313). San Francisco: Jossey-Bass.

Eiseley, L. (1978). *The star thrower*. New York: Harcourt Brace.

Eron, J. B., & Lund, T. W. (1989). From magic to method. *Family Therapy Networker, 13*(1), 64–68, 81–83.

Eron, J. B., & Lund, T. W. (1996). *Narrative solutions in brief therapy*. New York: Guilford.

Fisch, R., Weakland, J. H., & Segal, L. (1982). *The tactics of change: Doing therapy briefly*. San Francisco: Jossey-Bass.

Freud, S. (1904). On psychotherapy. In *The standard edition of the complete psychological works of Sigmund Freud* (Vol. 7, pp. 257–268). London: Hogarth Press, 1953.

Freud, S. (1909). Some general remarks on the nature of hysterical attacks. In *The standard edition of the complete psychological works of Sigmund Freud* (Vol. 9, pp. 229–234). London: Hogarth Press, 1959.

Freud, S. (1915–1917). The complete introductory lectures on psychoanalysis. In *The standard edition of the complete psychological works of Sigmund Freud* (Vol. 15–16, pp. 13–463). London: Hogarth Press, 1963.

Goulding, M. M., & Goulding, R. L. (1979). *Changing lives through redecision therapy*. New York: Brunner/Mazel.

Gustafson, J. P. (1986). *The complex secret of brief psychotherapy*. New York: Norton.

Haley, J. (1977). *Problem-solving therapy: New strategies for effective family therapy*. San Francisco: Jossey-Bass.

Held, B. S. (1992). The problem of strategy within the systemic therapies. *Journal of Marital and Family Therapy, 18*(1), 25–34.

Hoffman, L. (1981). *Foundations of family therapy*. New York: Basic Books.

Hoyt, M. F. (1990). On time in brief therapy. In R. A. Wells & V. J. Giannetti (Eds.), *Handbook of the brief psychotherapies* (pp. 115–143). New York: Plenum. Reprinted in M. F. Hoyt, *Brief therapy and managed care* (pp. 69–104). San Francisco: Jossey-Bass, 1995.

Hoyt, M. F. (1994a). Is being "in recovery" self-limiting? *Transactional Analysis Journal*, 24(3), 222–223. Reprinted in M. F. Hoyt, *Brief therapy and managed care* (pp. 213–215). San Francisco: Jossey-Bass.

Hoyt, M. F. (1994b). Single session solutions. In M. F. Hoyt (Ed.), *Constructive therapies* (pp. 140–159). New York: Guilford. Reprinted in M. F. Hoyt, *Brief therapy and managed care* (pp. 141–162). San Francisco: Jossey-Bass, 1995.

Hoyt, M. F. (1995). *Brief therapy and managed care: readings for contemporary practice*. San Francisco: Jossey-Bass.

Hoyt, M. F. (1996a). Introduction: Some stories are better than others. In M. F. Hoyt (Ed.), *Constructive therapies* (Vol. 2, pp. 1–32). New York: Guilford.

Hoyt, M. F. (1996b). Solution building and language games: A conversation with Steve de Shazer. In M. F. Hoyt (Ed.), *Constructive therapies* (Vol. 2, pp. 60–86). New York: Guilford.

Hoyt, M. F. (1998). Introduction. In M. F. Hoyt (Ed.), *The handbook of constructive therapies* (pp. 1–27). San Francisco: Jossey-Bass.

Hoyt, M. F. (2000). The last session in brief therapy: How and why to say when. In *Some stories are better than others* (pages 237–261. Philadelphia: Brunner/Mazel.

Hoyt, M. F. (1999). It's not my therapy—it's the client's therapy. *The Psychotherapy Bulletin*, 34(1), 31-33. Reprinted in M.F. Hoyt, *Some stories are better than others*. Philadelphia: Brunner/Mazel, 2000.

Hoyt, M. F., & Berg, I. K. (1998). Solution-focused couple therapy: Helping clients construct self-fulfilling realities. In M. F. Hoyt (Ed.), *The handbook of constructive therapies* (pp. 314–340). San Francisco: Jossey-Bass.

Hoyt, M. F., Rosenbaum, R., & Talmon, M. (1992). Planned single-session psychotherapy. In S. H. Budman, M. F. Hoyt, & S. Friedman (Eds.), *The first session in brief therapy* (pp. 59–86). New York: Guilford.

Hubble, M. A., Duncan, B. L., & Miller, S. D. (Eds.). (1999). *The heart and soul of change; What works in therapy*. Washington, DC: APA Books.

Jackson, D., & Weakland, J. H. (1961). Conjoint family therapy: Some considerations on theory, technique, and results. *Psychiatry*, 24(2), 30–45.

Johnson, L. D. (1995). *Psychotherapy in the age of accountability*. New York: Norton.

Johnson, V. E. (1973). *I'll quit tomorrow*. New York: Harper & Row.

Johnson, V. E. (1986). *Intervention: How to help someone who doesn't want help*. Minneapolis, MN: Johnson Institute Books.

Kreider, J. W. (1998). Solution-focused ideas for briefer therapy with longer-term clients. In M. F. Hoyt (Ed.), *The handbook of constructive therapies* (pp. 341–357). San Francisco: Jossey-Bass.

Lambert, M. J. (1992). Implications of outcome research for psychotherapy integration. In J. C. Norcross & M. R. Goldfried (Eds.), *Handbook of psychotherapy integration*. New York: Basic Books.

Lambert, M. J., & Bergin, A. E. (1994). The effectiveness of psychotherapy. In A. E. Bergin & S. L. Garfield (Eds.), *Handbook of psychotherapy and behavior change* (4th ed.). New York: Wiley.

Levy, R. L., & Shelton, J. L. (1990). Tasks in brief therapy. In R. A. Wells & V. J. Giannetti (Eds.), *Handbook of the brief psychotherapies* (pp. 145–163). New York: Plenum.

Madigan, S. P. (1997). Re-considering memory: Re-remembering lost identities back toward re-membered selves. In C. Smith & D. Nylund (Eds.), *Narrative therapies with children and adolescents* (pp. 127–142). New York: Guilford.

Madigan, S. P., & Epston, D. (1995). From "spy-chiatric gaze" to communities of concern: From professional monologue to dialogue. In S. Friedman (Ed.), *The reflecting team in action: Collaborative practice in family therapy* (pp. 257–276). New York: Guilford.

Madigan, S. P., & Goldner, E. M. (1998). A narrative approach to anorexia: Discourse, reflexivity, and questions. In M. F. Hoyt (Ed.), *The handbook of constructive therapies* (pp. 380–400). San Francisco: Jossey-Bass.

Mahoney, M. J. (1991). *Human change processes: The scientific foundations of psychotherapy*. New York: Basic Books.

Mahrer, A. R., Nordin, S., & Miller, L. S. (1995). If a client has this kind of problem, prescribe that kind of post-session behavior. *Psychotherapy, 32*(2), 194–203.

Malan, D. H. (1976). *The frontier of brief psychotherapy*. New York: Plenum.

McClosky, K. A., & Fraser, J. S. (1997). Using feminist MRI brief therapy during initial contact with victims of domestic violence. *Psychotherapy, 34*(4), 433–446.

Meichenbaum, D., & Turk, D. (1987). *Facilitating treatment adherence: A practitioner's guidebook*. New York: Plenum.

Miller, S. D. (1992). The symptoms of solution. *Journal of Strategic and Systemic Therapies, 11*(1), 1–11.

Miller, S. D. (1994). Some questions (not answers) for the brief treatment of people with drug and alcohol problems. In M. F. Hoyt (Ed.), *Constructive therapies* (pp. 92–110). New York: Guilford.

Miller, S. D., & Berg, I. K. (1991). Working with the problem drinker: A solution-focused approach. *Arizona Counseling Journal, 16*(1), 3–12.

Miller, S. D., Duncan, B. L., & Hubble, M. A. (1997). *Escape from Babel: Toward a unifying language for psychotherapy practice.* New York: Norton.

Miller, S. D., Duncan, B. L., Hubble, M. A., & Johnson, L. D. (1999). Jurassic practice: Why the field is on the verge of extinction and what we can do to save it. In M. A. Hubble, B. L. Duncan, & S. D. Miller (Eds.), *The heart and soul of change.* Washington, DC: APA Books.

Miller, S. D., Hubble, M. A., & Duncan, B. L. (Eds.). (1996). *Handbook of solution-focused brief therapy.* San Francisco: Jossey-Bass.

Miller, W. R. (1986). Increasing motivation for change. In W. R. Miller & N. H. Heather (Eds.), *Addictive behaviors: Processes of change.* New York: Plenum.

Milne, A. A. (1926). *Winnie-the-pooh.* New York: Dutton.

Mohr, D. C. (1995). The role of proscription in psychotherapy. *Psychotherapy,* 32(2), 187–193.

Norcross, J. C., & Beutler, L. E. (1997). Determining the therapeutic relationship of choice in brief therapy. In J. N. Butcher (Ed.), *Personality assessment in managed health care: A practitioner's guide* (pp. 42–60). New York: Oxford University Press.

Nylund, D., & Corsiglia, V. (1996). From deficits to special abilities: Working narratively with children labeled "ADHD." In M. F. Hoyt (Ed.), *Constructive Therapies* (Vol. 2, pp. 163–183). New York: Guilford.

Prochaska, J. O. (1991). Prescribing to the stage and level of phobia patients. *Psychotherapy,* 28, 463–468.

Prochaska, J. O. (1993). Working in harmony with how people change naturally. *The Weight Control Digest,* 3, 249, 252–255.

Prochaska, J. O. (1995). Common problems: Common solutions. *Clinical Psychology: Science and Practice,* 2, 101–105.

Prochaska, J. O. (1999). How do people change and how can we change to help many more people? In M. A. Hubble, B. L. Duncan & S. D. Miller (Eds.), *The heart and soul of change.* Washington, DC: APA Books.

Prochaska, J. O., & DiClemente, C. C. (1982). Transtheoretical therapy: Toward a more integrative model of change. *Psychotherapy,* 19, 276–288.

Prochaska, J. O., & DiClemente, C. C. (1983). Stages and processes of self-change in smoking: Toward an integrative model of change. *Journal of Consulting and Clinical Psychology,* 5, 390–395.

Prochaska, J. O., & DiClemente, C. C. (1984). *The transtheoretical approach: Crossing traditional boundaries of therapy.* Homewood, IL: Dow Jones-Irwin.

Prochaska, J. O., DiClemente, C. C., & Norcross, J. C. (1992). In search of how people change. *American Psychologist,* 47, 1102–1114.

Prochaska, J. O., Velicer, W. F., Fava, J., Ruggiero, L., Laforge, R. & Rossi, J. (1997). *Counselor and stimulus control enhancements of a stage-matched expert system for smokers in a managed-care setting.* Unpublished manuscript.

Reis, B. F., & Brown, L. G. (1999). Reducing psychotherapy dropouts: Maximizing perspective convergence in the psychotherapy dyad. *Psycotherapy, 36*(2), 123–136.

Rosenbaum, R., Hoyt, M. F., & Talmon, M. (1990). The challenge of single-session therapies: Creating pivotal moments. In R. A. Wells & V. J. Giannetti (Eds.), *Handbook of the brief psychotherapies* (pp. 165–189). New York: Plenum. Reprinted in M. F. Hoyt, *Brief therapy and managed care* (pp. 105–139). San Francisco: Jossey-Bass, 1995.

Roth, S., & Epston, D. (1996). Consulting the problem about the problematic relationship: An exercise for experiencing a relationship with an externalized problem. In M. F. Hoyt (Ed.), *Constructive therapies* (Vol. 2, pp. 148–162). New York: Guilford.

Schwarz, R. A. (1998). From "either-or" to "both-and": Treating dissociative disorders collaboratively. In M. F. Hoyt (Ed.), *The handbook of constructive therapies* (pp. 428–448). San Francisco: Jossey-Bass.

Segal, L., & Watzlawick, P. (1985). On window-shopping or being a non-customer. In S. B. Coleman (Ed.), *Failures in family therapy* (pp. 73–90). New York: Guilford.

Shoham, V., Rohrbaugh, M., & Patterson, J. (1995). Problem and solution-focused couple therapies: The MRI and Milwaukee models. In N. S. Jacobson & A. S. Gurman (Eds.), *Clinical handbook of couple therapy* (pp. 142–163). New York: Guilford.

Sifneos, P. E. (1992). *Short-term anxiety-provoking therapy: A treatment manual.* New York: Basic Books.

Singer, E. (1994). *Key concepts in psychotherapy* (2nd ed.). New York: Aronson.

Solovey, A. D., & Duncan, B. L. (1992). Ethics and strategic therapy: A proposed ethical direction. *Journal of Marital and Family Therapy, 18*(1), 53–61.

Speer, D. C. (1970). Family systems: Morphostasis and morphogenesis. Or "Is homeostasis enough?" *Family Process, 9,* 259–278.

Talmon, M. (1990). *Single session therapy.* San Francisco: Jossey-Bass.

Tomm, K. (1988). Interventive interviewing: Part III. Intending to ask lineal, circular, strategic, and reflective questions. *Family Process, 27,* 1–15

Tomm, K. (1993). The courage to protest: A commentary on Michael White's "Deconstruction and Therapy." In S. Gilligan & R. Price (Eds.), *Therapeutic conversations* (pp. 62–80). New York: Norton.

Watzlawick, P., Weakland, J. H., & Fisch, R. (1974). *Change: Principles of problem formation and problem resolution.* New York: Norton.

Weakland, J.H. (1993). Conversation—but what kind? In S. G. Gilligan & R. Price (Eds.), *Therapeutic conversations* (pp. 136–145). New York: Norton.

Weiner, I. J. (1975). *Principles of psychotherapy.* New York: Wiley.

Weiner-Davis, M., de Shazer, S., & Gingerich, W. J. (1987). Building on pretreatment change to construct the therapeutic solution: An exploratory study. *Journal of Marital and Family Therapy, 13*, 359–363.

White, M. (1986). Negative explanation, restraint, and double description: A template for family therapy. *Family Process,* 25(2). Reprinted in M. White, *Selected papers* (pp. 85–99). Adelaide, Australia: Dulwich Centre Publications.

White, M. (1989a). The externalizing of the problem and the re-authoring of lives and relationships. In *Selected papers* (pp. 5–28). Adelaide, Australia: Dulwich Centre Publications.

White, M. (1989b). Negative explanation, restraint, and double description: A template for family therapy. In *Selected papers* (pp. 85–99). Adelaide, Australia: Dulwich Centre Publications.

White, M. (1993). Commentary: Histories of the present. In S. G. Gilligan & R. Price (Eds.), *Therapeutic conversations* (pp. 121–135). New York: Norton.

White, M. (1997). *Narratives of therapists' lives.* Adelaide, Australia: Dulwich Centre Publications.

Wynne, L. (1983). Foreword. In C. M. Anderson & S. Stewart, *Mastering resistance.* New York: Guilford.

Annotated Bibliography

Duncan, B. L., Hubble, M. A., & Miller, S. O. (1997). *Psychotherapy with "impossible" cases: The efficient treatment of therapy veterans.* New York: Norton. Applies what is know about curative factors—particularly the importance of accommodating the client's frame of reference and theory of change— to getting results with especially "difficult" cases.

Hoyt, M. F. (1995). *Brief therapy and managed care: Reading for contemporary practice.* San Francisco: Jossey-Bass. A practical overview of the current field of brief psychotherapies and some of the dilemmas of today's health care environment, with an emphasis on ways various issues can advance or impede treatment.

Hoyt, M. F. (Ed.)(1998). *The handbook of constructive therapies.* San Francisco: Jossey-Bass. A compendium of leading theoreticians and clinicians—including solution-focused, narrative, strategic interactional, and neo-Ericksonian—describing innovative ways to help clients construct and live within more therapeutic psychological realities.

Hoyt, M. F. (Ed.) (2000). *Some stories are better than others: Doing what works in brief therapy and managed care.* Philadelphia: Brunner/Mazel. A new collection of papers highlighting brief therapy and managed care issues within a narrative constructivist framework.

Hubble, M. A., Duncan, B. L., & Miller, S. D. (Eds.). (1999). *The heart and soul of change: What works in therapy.* Washington, DC: APA Books. Leading researchers and practitioners integrate findings on common factors from various perspectives and offer numerous practical suggestions on how these can be applied in daily clinical work.

Miller, S. D., Duncan, B. L., & Hubble, M. A. (1997). *Escape from Babel: Toward a unifying language for psychotherapy practice.* New York: Norton. Cutting across schools, models, and techniques, the authors identify and clinically demonstrate the factors that really make a difference.

Miller, S. D., Hubble, M. A., & Duncan, B. L. (Eds.). (1996). *Handbook of solution-focused brief therapy.* San Francisco: Jossey-Bass. Brings together practical tools, illustrative case examples, and research findings for delivering effective solution-focused therapy in a variety of treatment settings.

12

⚭

The Satir System: Brief Therapy Strategies

Jean A. McLendon

Introduction

Virginia Satir (1916–1988), renowned educator, author, and systems therapist, is known the world over as the people's family therapist and, across most mental health disciplines, as the Columbus of family therapy. She was a pioneer in her field as she helped lead psychotherapists out of the Freudian world and into the world of empathy and connection. Her power for creating change with her clients came not only from her clarity and understanding about what it means to be human, but equally from her willingness and skill at bringing her essence to the therapeutic relationship. To separate the strategies of the Satir system from Virginia Satir, the person, would purge the system of its creativity, strength, and integrity. For these reasons, this chapter spends considerable effort connecting the reader to the source of the system—Virginia Satir.

Mental health managed-care descriptors of today have only marginal capacity to describe Satir's system of therapy or to convey its power for creating change in clients. For the thousands of therapists who observed her work, she was brief, strategic, solution-seeking, problem-solving, family-of-origin, and communications focused. Her interventions were structural, experiential, and outcome guided. She was unabashedly process driven and "touchy-feely." Her goal was always to raise the self- and system-esteem of her clients. Satir observed time and time again that self-esteem catalyzes creative resourcefulness.

The Satir system is based on several fundamental beliefs that Virginia Satir vocally and faithfully adhered to throughout her career: All people have the capacity to change. Therapy should focus on strengths. Empowerment is gained through experiencing choice. Spirituality is a vital ingredient for health. Her methods also reflected her personal commitment to congruence. She knew how to engage clients quickly, directly, and deeply in their inner world of feelings, thoughts, meanings, perceptions, expectations, and longings. Equally so, she scoped out the external behavioral nuances of the client's personal and interpersonal contexts.

The Satir system teaches, also, that behaviors are simply an attempt to communicate. She strove to help her clients repattern their behavior and build on their strengths so that they would be able to meet the kinds of real-world situations they would encounter outside therapy. And therefore Virginia Satir never hid her disdain for therapies that failed to focus on strengths, sharing with her many students her philosophy that she did what works.

Satir's approach is equally valid for long-term work. The basic and underlying beliefs, goals, and strategies remain the same. Treatment decisions about pace, focus, and depth are made at a moment in time, given the information at hand. When new information is available or when circumstances change, the therapy plan also changes. Constant in her plan, however, is the reality that, for all people, the work of growth, change, learning, and healing is lifelong and life-giving.

Importance of Self-Esteem and Spirituality

Her theories, practices, strategies, and explanations never failed to express a deep knowing that she could always rely on the spiritual essence of her clients as a basis to help guide them throughout their therapy. Although she was ahead of her time with a dynamic, systems-oriented, holistic, multisensory, spirit-filled approach to change, her knowledge was embedded in the old ways of the wise people who came before her. Satir offers to the world, therefore, a superb, strategic, and experiential translation of the teachings of Lao-tsu, the ancient sage and alleged author of the *Tao Te Ching*. Like Lao-tsu, Virginia Satir understood the basis and nature of process. Like Lao-tsu, she knew the power of living in the present while respecting the past.

Strategy: Recipe

Satir was not one to provide recipes for such a creative process as transformation, although she was not reluctant to tell people what ingredients were necessary for positive change. This chapter attempts to reflect on the holographic and dynamic system of this master therapist and to construct a basic recipe for her strategies. In the same way that Virginia Satir cooked up a bit of magic, so the therapist and client must follow the recipe, testing for taste, texture, temperature, and nutrients. Therapy at this level is like a potluck dinner: everybody contributing. Omitting the uniqueness of the therapist or client leaves the dinner tasteless, if not inedible. One tip: Satir said she always started from scratch (McLendon, 1981).

For purposes of metaphor and recall, Satir's six primary strategies are provided in "recipe" form, beginning with the following basic ingredients: *resourcefulness, empowerment, congruence, inner system, patterns,* and *externalization*. Satir's therapeutic tools (the mandala, meditations, sculpting, communication stances, family mapping, inner child work, and the self-esteem maintenance kit) are added to each of the basic ingredients, providing the reader with a template to understand more fully the two case presentations that follow. They demonstrate the blending of Satir's primary strategies and most commonly used tools. Each tool offers a way to express internal cognitive and emotional experiences—experiences that may be tainted and tarnished by rules, expectations, and incongruent communication patterns that were designed at an earlier time for one's self-preservation. Past experiences create programs and patterns for the present and future that may be either limiting or enhancing. Satir strategies and tools help clients assess their need for new programs and access their resources for the desired changes.

The use of Satir system strategies is limited only by the ability of the client and the therapist to communicate openly. What makes sense and what feels helpful at a moment in time is essential feedback. The feeling of safety that is derived from openness and trust in the therapeutic relationship allows the client to enter deep personal spaces where awareness and self-acceptance have been blocked. Like a newly planted flower, safety in the therapeutic relationship must be tended constantly: too much water and it will drown, too little and it will wilt; too much fertilizer and it will be burned, too few nutrients and it will not grow. Resistance to growth choices within the Satir system, therefore, is a comment only about the present, not the future. Safety, support, and stimulation must be added all along the way. Any fracturing or misunderstanding between the therapist and client must be addressed and resolved before proceeding.

Resourcefulness: Self-Esteem Maintenance Tool Kit

Satir's belief that all people have the internal resources to change underscores the strategy of Resourcefulness—the creative utilization of the birth tools of one's self-esteem maintenance kit (Weiner, 1998). These tools are essential for charting new territory and creating new choices. The therapist's job is to help teach and validate the existence of these human tools and then to support their appropriate use. Included in the tool kit are a golden key to open the door to the unknown and to new possibilities; a wishing wand to help surface hope and desire; a courage stick to provide the strength to change; a yes-no medallion to support healthy boundaries and self-care; a detective hat to analyze and sort out input and options; and the wisdom box, referred to earlier, which represents the inner, grounding guidance available to all humans. (Satir, Banmen, Gerber, & Gomori, 1991) Virginia Satir failed to note that the kit lacked a heart. No doubt, with her big heart, she did not think that her students would need such a reminder. But adding the heart to the kit has been immeasurably facilitative in coaching clients toward congruence—which, of course, requires compassion for both one's self and the other(s).[1] The tools of the kit are universal and cross cultures, age, gender,

---

[1] For additional details on clinical uses of the self-esteem kit, refer to McLendon, 1998.

and ethnic groups; however, the specific icons symbolizing the embedded resource may be culture, age, and gender biased. For example, some cultures may not recognize a Sherlock Holmes hat as a symbol for thinking and analysis. Do not limit yourself to a specific expression of a universal.

In her meditations, Satir often presented these tools conceptually, using imagery (Banmen & Banmen, 1991, pp. 76–81). Listening to or reading her meditations reminds the reader of Satir's deep appreciation of the power of the right brain and of the unconscious to feed the soul, inform the mind, and instruct the body. She spoke with a clear, strong, and soft voice when she carried her students and clients into meditative states. Her words were filled with invitations to see, hear, feel, touch, and smell all the affirming concepts she spoke about. When presenting the self-esteem tools in this way, she made one aware of all the glory, goodness, and color of each one (Banmen & Banmen, 1991, pp. 76–81).[2]

Many clients appreciate having their therapist guide them with meditations. Likely, an equal number prefer their therapist to listen and respond to their words rather than overtly lead the conversation. Some see guided imagery as nurturing and a gift from their therapist. Some feel controlled by it. Some believe it is against their religion. Some like the experience but need help in translating their experience into proactive behavioral choices. Clients with high levels of anxiety, depression, distortion, and distractibility will need clear explanations and assistance in making decisions about their readiness and the appropriateness of this particular technique. Openness between the two—the client and the therapist—is therefore critical for this level of joint decision making. Consider each intervention as an experiment, asking "What could have made this better for you?"

The therapist must also assess his or her competence in guiding meditations. There is likely no greater need for trust between therapist and client than when an invitation from the therapist begins with ". . . permission to close your beautiful eyes," as Satir so often did when she began a session. An aura of trust literally flowed from her during her meditations. Her words were always uplifting; her improvisational scripts were steeped in her belief in the positive value and uniqueness of each person. It seemed as if she put her belief system to music: full of

---

[2]Audiotapes are available from Avanta, The Virginia Satir Network, P.O. Box 66958, Burien, WA 98166.

melody and harmony, without the minor discordant chords that signal conflict or disturbance. She did not move into the sorrowful, sad, and frightening sounds and sights of her clients during meditations. When she was confronting the dark scenes, she knew that, at least, the therapist's eyes needed to be open, hands available to touch for support, and ears attuned like antennae to hear and welcome each word that was uttered.

Rather than presenting the self-esteem tools to clients in meditation format, many therapists create concrete versions of each tool. These symbolic icons are kept at hand in the therapy office, available to be picked up, discussed, and used at the appropriate moment. The wishing wand is useful as a metaphor for use during initial sessions, particularly when someone has had little experience in responding to Satir's number-one question: "What would you like to have happen for you?" Placing a beautiful wishing wand lovingly in someone's hands will elicit a response: often a smile, evidence of an acknowledgment of the inner child's historical experiences with the magic of wishing. Enjoying the warmth and levity of these moments is vintage Satir. She loved to laugh with her clients. She spoke often of life being a cosmic joke.

Some clients may appear sad when handed the wand. Perhaps for them, there is pain associated with unfulfilled dreams, or perhaps they feel shame in speaking of their longings. The wand acts like a cotherapist, inviting the dreams, desires, hopes, and yearnings to surface. As with any cotherapist, one observes and follows the client's response to the cotherapist's invitation. Do the hands reach actively toward the wand, or do they pull back? Does the face change color? Is vocalization different in volume, speed, content, or tone? Stay with the energy, whatever its form— pain or pleasure. Welcome its meaning warmly. Knowing the client's inner feelings about these longings identifies the contexts in which the client currently experiences being resource challenged. These hopes and wishes map the way for the client's transformation journey and give hints about what the territory and landscape are likely to be.

Having a set of tools available for both partners in couple therapy sessions is useful. When a couple, trying to resolve a conflict, is surrounded by the full repertoire of self-esteem tools, they become aware of the inherent resources each brings to the relationship. Sharing the similarities and differences in the valuing and usage patterns that each makes with the tools provides rich material for dialogue. Selecting from the tool kit the overlooked or overutilized tool can create a dramatic opening for awareness about one's personal resource patterns. It is not uncommon in many marriages to find that one partner has the detective hat and the other partner, the golden key. Their arguments are about what one thinks is possible and what the other believes is practical. Having each partner reclaim his or her own full set of self-esteem tools can be very useful in helping the couple get unstuck from familiar patterns of dependency and codependency.

Awareness and acceptance of one's unique gifts are critical to operating resourcefully. The therapist who works from the strengths of his or her client searches with the client into the past, discovering ample evidence of the client's inner resources. From this place, growth, change, learning, and healing are based in choice and resource utilization.

Empowerment: The Five Freedoms

Empowerment is the act of authoring choices on behalf of one's health, be it about one's mind, body, or spirit. Authorship of new behaviors is facilitated when awareness of needs is met with acceptance. Application of the client's new learning to behavioral change is an empowering act, requiring courage and encouragement (McLendon, 1997). Empowering acts take place on the inside as well as on the outside of an individual. An example of internal empowerment is the individual, diagnosed with a chronic disease, who becomes a first-rate, conscientious student and loving servant to her self. External empowerment for that person might be sharing her knowledge and instructing and supporting others in healthier living patterns. Whether internal or external, empowerment is fortified by a prerequisite of full, albeit temporary, acceptance of the status quo. Starting with this acceptance reduces resistance, thereby saving time, money, and energy for both the client and the therapist. Satir defined empowerment most succinctly in her poem, "The Five Freedoms":

> *The freedom to see and hear what is here,*
> *Instead of what should be, was, or will be*
> *The freedom to say what you feel and think,*
> *Instead of what you should*
> *The freedom to feel what you feel, instead of what you ought*

The freedom to take risks on your own behalf,
Instead of choosing to be only "secure" and not rocking the boat.[3]

Critical to self-esteem, and the cornerstone of Satir's work, is the ability to claim one's own experience. Thinking, speaking, feeling, or acting in ways that belong to someone else, or to another time and place, infringe on a person's ability to be fully present. Early attempts to assess the level of the client's freedoms must be made while recognizing that, although behavior is communication, unveiling the intended message may take patient and methodical exploration or, if you will, a good detective hat and a compassionate heart. After the first Satir-session question is asked—"What would you like to have happen for you?"—be watchful. The inability to respond to questions about hopes reflects oppression of the five freedoms. Trauma is not a requirement for oppression. A steady, innocuous, and subtle interjection by an important person, over time, that rejects a person's inner claims will dampen the spirit, voice, and activities of almost anyone. Imagine for just a second the impact of hearing the following: "I'm sure you don't really think that." "There's really no reason for you to feel that way." "I don't think you will be happy." "That's not right for you." Not wanting to stay in that negative trance state, take a deep breath and imagine the reverse.

Satir's strategy to help people recreate their birthrights, as stated in the five freedoms, begins by offering the individual an opportunity to tune in to the inherent infringements that come with being socialized. No matter the level of imperfection of the parental figures, whether minor or major, all adults and young adults must evaluate the cost of their own patterns and choices that reflect what others have decided for them. By using such props as ropes, scarves, or belts to dramatize the power of being constrained and denied access to these freedoms, Virginia Satir demonstrated the client's internal imprisonment about common constraints to personal freedom. When using this particular multimodal technique, those observing the work and the client (usually referred to as the star) should be informed that the ropes are symbolic representations of messages. The process of being socialized, civilized, and reared in all cultures leaves the prints of teachers—the big people who take care of children. The way

---

[3] V. Satir, Five Freedoms poster, available from Celestial Arts, P.O. Box 7123, Berkeley, CA 94707.

that a child encodes these messages requires adults to review, and usually rewrite, the messages for more self-responsibility and empowerment. Writing new codes and authoring new texts happens most expeditiously when the client can feel genuine compassion and grief for losses. The pain of recognition opens the system to the universal human need for care and support. This awareness—if it is accepted, and if the anger connected with the awareness is not denied—is freeing for the client, who may then learn about the value of support.

It is ill advised to use this type of psychodramatic intervention without the support of a cotherapist. This technique is not designed for revisiting physical and emotional abuse or neglect. The visuals, however, have been known, in one instance, to trigger flashbacks of abuse for a group member who was observing a star's work with the five freedoms.[4] These responses, when observing group members or family members, must be managed without abandoning the star. It is equally important to express the belief, up front, that the messages sent to the child by the teaching-parental figures were from people doing the best they knew how at the time, no matter how painful or debilitating the results. If this belief is not a part of the therapist's own belief system, this exercise should not be attempted. Using a part of this dramatic intervention is quite feasible and instructive in therapy sessions with individuals and couples. Much like the self-esteem kit tools, ropes are useful metaphors and can be kept available until the appropriate time arises for their use. They will undoubtedly be used for more than showing constraints to freedoms.

To reiterate, empowerment is the act of taking responsibility for authoring one's conscious response to life. It begins with awareness. If acceptance of one's self, others, and one's context can be facilitated, then compassion can grow and a robust articulation of one's unique essence can be achieved.

Congruence: Self, Other, and Context

Congruence is the strategy that most emphatically highlights the significance that the Satir system gives to communication. The value of con-

---

[4] Participant experience in Avanta Process Community workshop, 1989, Crested Butte, CO.

gruence cannot be overstated. It both reflects and requires self-esteem. There is no more powerful strategy for improving one's health, relationships, and performance than congruence. Communication between people is the primary medium for experiencing and assessing the system's coping patterns. And for Virginia Satir, communication was the ultimate connector linking the mind, body, and spirit. How people interact within, between, and among themselves is critical to the kind of interpersonal contexts that can be created. Collaboration, creativity, compassion, connection, and conflict—to name a few—are directly tied to the ways in which people communicate. Simply stated, communication is the act of sending and/or receiving information. It can be conscious or unconscious, verbal or tacit, internal or external. Communication within the Satir model is the most important indicator of how well a system is functioning. One's level of self- and system-esteem drives one's internal experience and therefore in large part determines what and how one communicates.

Focusing on the content of the communication is not as important as listening and noting how the seeds of the problem are reflected in the dynamics of the communication. Following the process of how an individual talks about his or her life, and how members of a client-system address each other, is the gateway to understanding the systemic nature of human intra- and interpersonal problems.

Congruence is the most difficult strategy to grasp and implement. Consistency between the inner and outer world of the communicator is often considered to be the primary requirement for congruence. For example, do the words and actions match the feelings? Consciousness and compassion are, in fact, more critical in determining one's congruence. Were it not so, Hitler could be considered congruent. He was certainly consistent, but he lacked consideration for others and his context. One could also argue as to whether he truly honored his self. But were one to assume that Hitler operated for himself according to the five freedoms, he surely did not grant these freedoms to others. Congruence is inherent in the five freedoms and in the feeling of empowerment when one claims these freedoms for one's self and promotes them for others.

With the proliferation of communication classes, reading and assessing communication for its level of congruence have become increasingly difficult. All too often, the lessons taught are about correct lines and the right words, not about how to manage the feelings that interfere with real understanding and connection: the kind of communication that builds self-esteem. Generally, words are not as important as the more subtle cues of tone, breathing, and demeanor. Sensing incongruence and engaging in a power struggle with clients about one's perception of the discrepancy between the inner experience, or intentionality, and the outer expression are not helpful practices. Humans move toward alignment when they feel safe. They are considerate of others and their world when they have sufficient self-esteem to claim their internal experience and to trust their own value and resourcefulness.

Satir believed that appreciating the implicit intents of incongruent communication is a prerequisite to understanding congruent communication. Further, since all people are sometimes incongruent, she thought it wise for therapists to practice and to take note of their own incongruent communication. The more the therapist owned and understood his or her incongruence and its roots, the more likely that the therapist would understand the intricacies of transforming incongruence into congruence. For Satir, each observed incongruent exchange in therapy was an opportunity for learning and building a more positive connection. Incongruence offers a shield of protection and defense against exposing one's vulnerabilities and accepting one's limitations. In so doing, it blocks intimacy and spontaneity. In essence, incongruence separates one's essence from one's sense of self and from the world around. It is, at its core, a way to cope with fear; it has little value for individuals who have sufficient self-esteem to deal openly and resourcefully with their feelings. Incongruent communication stances are created during childhood when choices are limited. In some obvious or not-so-obvious way, the stances were designed to serve their owners. In fact, all incongruent coping stances are individually crafted, with no two precisely alike. Satir taught, however, that all humans learn four universal and primary incongruent communication stances: placating, blaming, superreasonable, and irrelevant. In each, an essential element is omitted, or not valued, regarding the feelings, thoughts, and needs of the self, the other(s), and/or the requirements of the context.[5] Each of these four major forms of incongruence will be

---

[5] For more in-depth explanation of incongruent communication, see V. Satir, *The New Peoplemaking*, (Mountain View, CA: Science and Behavior, 1988), pp. 80–101; and Satir et al., 1991, pp. 31–61.

presented in the following sections, including descriptions and ideas for transformation. In all cases, the strategic question is: What is missing and needed for wholeness?

Placating

Placating communication is a denial of the five freedoms for one's self. Placating hides one's profound fear of being rejected. The physical posture, or sculpt, used to demonstrate this stance has the individual on one knee depicting a "pushover" quality. The neck and head are tilted up to the other person, showing deference, ingratiation, and submission. The torso is twisted to show the dire condition, with the back side a bit exposed from the stooped, bent-over posture. The eyes and one hand are raised in begging fashion. The other hand and arm are used to cover the heart area. In Satir's words, "To perfect the universal experience of placation, be the most syrupy, martyrish, boot-licking person you can be" (Satir, 1988, p. 85). Trying on this position for longer than a few minutes is not recommended. It is known to cause a feeling of nausea. Though placating is a sign of distrust of one's self, it also shows a lack of trust in the person being placated. Since few placaters can long survive in this condition without becoming resentful and passive-aggressive, distrust is a natural by-product. (In the sculpt, the hand covering the heart slides around to the back, hidden to the other person, and forms a fist.) Expressing the anger associated with placating is an important phase of therapy. To allow and to reinforce placation towards one's self and others breeds suspicion, seduction, and sleaze in a relationship. No one with high self-esteem chooses placation over authentic valuing.

Within placation, however, as with all incongruent stances, is a powerful resource, or seed, waiting to be nurtured and transformed. Placaters orient toward the other and have a natural capacity for caring, compassion, and empathy. These attributes are particularly useful in situations where walking in another's shoes is important. People who tend toward placation as their preferred incongruent stance are naturals for jobs as negotiators, salespeople, and therapists. Families and organizations that have a larger percentage of placaters tend to be more relationship based. In Myers-Briggs terms, they are apt to prefer feeling over thinking as a basis for decision making (Kirsey & Bates, 1978). For a placating client, care, compassion, and empathy for one's self is missing. Having a therapist acknowledge the painful cost of this superficially safe stance can be an eye-opening and heartfelt experience for the client. Congruent articulation must be preceded by awareness, acceptance of the needs underlying placating, and commitment to becoming the author of one's life.

Blaming

Blaming communication claims the five freedoms for one's self and denies them to others. The sculpt that depicts blaming is known throughout the world. The body is tense and tight, leaning—and almost thrust—toward the other person. The index finger of the dominant hand is pointed at the other person. The other arm is appendaged to a slightly raised shoulder, while the hand sits squarely on a slung-out hip. The picture of cocky arrogance is obvious. The message is unmistakable: "You are nothing. I am everything!" Blaming, taken literally and to its limits, can be imagined as the precursor to murder. The posture, if held for a minute or two, reveals the physical cost to the blamer: The body aches. Blaming creates havoc by perpetuating a false sense of grandiosity by hiding one's limitations from one's self and from others.

During the therapy session, it is important to acknowledge the pain of the blamer and the blamed. In MBTI (Myers-Briggs Type Indicator) terms, the SJ (sensing-judging) traditionalist, when under stress and suffering from low self-esteem, is apt to respond with blaming. The transformed blamer brings skill in advocacy and debate. Blamers tend to be high-energy people and do well in entrepreneurial situations. The primary challenge for blamers is to confront their fears and the pain associated with failure. Most likely, there has been shame surrounding mistakes and accidents. Learning that the value of one's essence supersedes one's accomplishments is profoundly liberating to these people. Understanding that failure is an expression of human limitation and not worthlessness is central to transformation for blamers. Although blamers seem to demand perfection from their partners, colleagues, and family members, they are equally demanding on themselves. When they become aware of the wounds that fester beneath their blaming behavior, they can begin to develop empathy with those they blame and those who have blamed them. Often blamers have no idea how painful their blaming is to others or to themselves. When the blamer can release his or her fixation on the other as the cause for vulnerability, then self-assertion, not aggression, is possible. In hierarchical situations and relationships, blaming is usually done by the person with power. Placating is implicitly invited as a response, since it feels like a way to avoid the pain of blame. Since placation over time leads to resentment and anger, blaming may become an unexpected by-product. The placating-blaming dance is one of the most familiar ways human intimates encounter each other when they are feeling vulnerable and lack the self-esteem to deal congruently with stress.

Superreasonable

The superreasonable, or the computing, stance is characterized by the individual's responding to life and his or her world as though feelings do not exist. The sculpt is one in which the body is rigid, upright, chin up and out, shoulders lifted, arms to the side, face muscles still, eyes vacant, chest out, and breathing shallow. In effect, the pose should evidence no sign of life except a monotone voice delivering factual, theoretical explanations. The intent is not dialogue, but rather avoiding the feared feelings of losing control. This stance has received great reward in the Western world of science, business, and academia. Men of this era who were taught as little boys not to show pain or fear, or even not to have these feelings, will have great resonance with the computer stance. There is no juiciness in superreasonableness since intimacy and creativity are blocked. If, however, the value of feelings can be understood and support given while the client undergoes the chaos of feeling, then what were rigid judgments can be replaced with a larger view about life and being human. The added value for transformed superreasonable communicators is sound reasoning that includes facts, feelings, facts about the feelings, and feelings about the facts. As such, they become excellent leaders, parents, and partners. Without feelings, they are unable to be fully present.

Therapeutic work for a superreasonable person must be presented in such a way that it makes sense. The possibility of change must begin with the head. Once the head is engaged, go directly to the heart. Unlike the placating or blaming stance, the computing stance is likely to be devoid of awareness of what the body is feeling unless specifically assisted. Crying and deep laughter—two powerful physical detoxifiers for humans—are luxuries that the computing communicator has not been able to afford.

Emotions are a form of energy that is dangerous; feelings are locked up inside a tightly closed and closely held system. It is not uncommon for middle-aged, superreasonable men and women in their second and third marriages to realize the loss of family and friends, and to take seriously the study of the "universality of emotionality." Many come ready to learn and are quick studies. The corresponding MBTI type is the NT (intuitive thinking). The NT, of course, need not be superreasonable; but if he or she has low self-esteem, under stress, that person will tend to rely on theory and analysis, avoiding and bypassing feelings.

Irrelevant

Irrelevant communication, in its physical and sculpted posture, reflects distractibility and disconnection. To experience the position, or to have a client experience it, turn the feet inward, bend the knees, droop the shoulders down and in, let the arms dangle loosely from the shoulders, and gently move about with a slight bounce. Twirl a bit, as if your attention is flitting like a butterfly. The initial feeling is fun; continue longer, and one feels dizzy. Although this stance is often taught as one that omits all three components of congruence—self, other, and context—the one required omission for this stance is the context.[6] Arguably, when severed from self, other(s), and context, the individual is dead or near death.

Irrelevant communication deflects and creates distance between the person and the stress of the situation. Irrelevant communication is often accomplished with humor and untimely absences; it is usually disruptive and averts attention from that which is too painful to consider. This combination of high stress and low self-esteem tends to short-circuit the individual's connections. In MBTI format, this type of communicator is likely to show a preference for SP (sensing and perceiving). Sometimes referred to as troubleshooters, they often have permeable boundaries and are great scanners of their environment. Too much stimulation, or stimulation under stress, becomes synonymous with distress, and the defense strategy surfaces. The irrelevant communicator's hidden resource is creativity.

---

[6] Confirmed in conversations with Satir, during process community training, summer 1987.

There is value in the perspective of someone who has escaped for a period of time from the grind of the familiar. Helping an irrelevantly oriented client access enough safety and validation to experience the warmth of connection and relationship is a strong motivator for the client's welcoming new ways to cope with stress and esteem problems.

In summary, the strategy of developing congruence in individuals and their relationships is comparable to overhauling a car. As miles and rough handling are to a car, so incongruence is to the person and his or her relationships. The cumulative cost of incongruence is high for all aspects of the system: the mind, the body, and the spirit. Transforming incongruence into congruence is not a cosmetic or superficial modification, nor is it necessarily inexpensive. Unlike repairing an automobile, the "guts" of the individual or human system cannot be removed and replaced. But automobile repairs are rarely so simple as merely adding an ingredient. In the Satir transformation process, the work is always to find what is missing and to add it. Relationships where incongruence is the major mode of communication reduce the possibility for expressions of one's true feelings, sensations, and thoughts and produce the likelihood of shame and low self-esteem. When individuals interact in this incongruent medium, the body-mind-spirit connection atrophies and the whole system suffers. On the other hand, when relationships in which communication is open and essence-based support growth and generativity, then the system hums.

Inner System: Make Contact

Meeting the inner system of an individual or couple is the strategy that connects the therapist to the client-system's essence and universal desire to connect and contribute. Satir had many techniques for entering the inner domain, perhaps none more important than her full expression of genuine interest. For Satir, therefore, change does not happen unless contact is made. Satir died before touching became unacceptable in the classroom, the business place, the doctor's office and the therapist's office. Her teaching about the power of safe, nonsexual touch as a means to connect deeply to the inner longings of an individual was well known. Her videotape *Of Rocks and Flowers,* produced by Golden Triad, is a masterful example of the therapeutic value of touch. She knew to intervene beyond the cognitive and often did so with the use of touch. Equally important, she knew how to touch with her eyes, her posture, and her listening. Touching was never a means in and of itself.

Clients who are unhappy with their therapists often complain about gross examples of disinterest: answering telephone calls during sessions, being late, not keeping appointments, falling asleep, interrupting, and talking over the client. These criticisms may seem pale against grievances of sexual misconduct or unchecked "dual-plus" leveled relationships, but those behaviors carry a message of disinterest. Therapists who want to enter the inner world of their clients and of their relationships will do well to search out genuine and comfortable ways to express their interest overtly. If they find themselves without interest, it is time for some combination of a referral, vacation, consultation, supervision, and/or career shift.

When there is a shared and confirmed sense of comfort between the client and therapist, the connection to the client's inner system can be deepened by using the metaphor of the inner child. The therapist's understanding and concern for the wounds and aspirations of the child-within-the-client stimulate the client's compassion for the childhood experience. Satir proclaimed, in the last sentence of her book, *Making Contact* (Satir, 1976), "I wish you Godspeed and, above all, be loving to yourself." Loving the child that the client was and in truth remains is a deeply humanizing experience for the client. This love of self frees one to care for one's body, mind, and spirit. The client becomes the primary guardian for a healthy future. The path of change is fraught with chaos and pain, but that pain pushes one into action, bringing the great rewards and the great love that proclaim, "I'm really worth my life's being better."

There are numerous ways to introduce the concept of the inner child. Having a client hold a specifically chosen stuffed animal or doll has great potential for most people. (Not so, however, if the therapist is uncomfortable with this technique.) If one uses stuffed dolls or animals as props, it is important to have an ample supply so that a fitting representation of the child can be selected. Having the client share childhood pictures also helps introduce the inner child to the client and the therapist. To know the scars and the dreams of the client is to be able to know the

essence of the client and to care deeply. Making contact at that level is
rejuvenating.

Patterns: The Family of Origin: Six P's

Patterns tell the story of history and project one's narrative into the
future, unless interrupted by change. Virginia Satir operated early on
from the perspective that the most entrenched rules that script the stories
of clients are rooted in their family-of-origin experience, the experience
provided initially by the child's caregivers. The repetitive, early interjec-
tions of learning from these big people form patterns filled with intricate
nuances and subtleties that shape the feelings about one's self, others, and
the world around. Satir gravitated to the exploration of interpersonal
patterns having to do with six areas of living (the six P's): pain, pleasure,
performance, power, plans, and problems. How an individual or couple
relates and responds to these areas of life is most revealing. Consider
these possibilities: When pain cannot be expressed, it goes underground
and surfaces from another angle. When pleasure is prohibited, anger and
acting out emerge. When performance is met with criticism rather than
accountability, learning is stifled. When power is not shared, responsibility is not taught. When plans are held too rigidly or too loosely, empowerment is diminished. When problems are not viewed as opportunities for
learning, they become internalized and unattended. In this way, little
problems become large problems.

The way the story is told, the questions, elaborations, and affect flavor
the therapy material and enliven the transformation process. Satir's strategy to ferret out the process puzzles latticed in the presenting symptomatology usually meant using the following tools in some kind of
combination: family map, family life chronology, and wheel of influence
(Satir et. al., 1991, pp. 369–375; or Nerin, 1993, pp. 93–114). Family
mapping, a term used by many Satir practitioners, provides an opportunity to incorporate all three tools, to make a palette for the colorful stories of the client's growing-up years. Placing a flip chart pad and Magic
Markers in the therapy office is almost as good as having a cotherapist.
The process of outlining and coloring in the client's significant content
can begin immediately or after the therapeutic alliance is formed. I prefer
to use mapping at multiple levels: for assessment, making contact, and

facilitating transformation. When important information is shared. I make certain a way is found to indicate its significance on the print paper. The visual picture tells the story of the people, places, pets, proverbs, events, and important dates that make up the client's story. [7] In my head, I will explore and learn what I can about the interpersonal process patterns associated with each of the six P's. Every member of a couple, family, or larger system has his or her unique experience, no matter how much they have in common. I share my puzzles and stay vigilant to be sure that the story being told is about the person with whom I am present. It is important that the client, or star, differentiate his or her story from the story of siblings, partners, and parents. I pause when space is needed for tears and laughter, for I know that I am in sacred territory.

Adding details, additions, and modifications keeps the family-of-origin experience in close proximity to the therapy dialogue. The map is an ever-unfolding account of what was, is, and can be. It is truly a picture worth more than a thousand words. The more creative the therapist and the client are at finding ways to symbolize the story, the richer the experience. It is not uncommon to have the client or couple remark that their predicament, "stuck place," or symptom makes more sense when placed in the context of their pictured histories. It is also not uncommon for clients to begin dialogues with family members about their history, opening up the possibility for reshaping relationships toward more support. When therapy is terminated, clients often appreciate leaving with their map(s). Rolled up with a ribbon, the maps can represent a graduation diploma. I had one client who refused to work in therapy with me if she had to see her map. The losses represented on the map were massive, and she did not want to experience the pain of those losses. In her alcoholic family, pain was hushed and hidden. The responses to mapping will be varied, and if the mapping interferes with connecting and making contact, it should be discontinued. Its value lies in facilitating contact sufficiently to understand the significant and relevant family-of-origin patterns that are embedded in the interpersonal-process patterns of the client.

---

[7] To see the value of this technique for moving quickly into the relevant process patterns affecting the behavior of a young African-American boy, see the videotape, *Satir Therapy with Jean McLendon*. In *Family Therapy with the Experts*, December 1997, Allyn & Bacon, 160 Gould Street, Needham Heights, MA 02194; order no. T83448.

Externalization: Ownership

Externalization of internal processes is the strategy used most often by Satir system practitioners to drive home and anchor the link between self ownership and choice. Externalizing the various aspects of one's self promotes the concept that we are a complex organic system with many internal layers, levels, and parts. A client can imagine, or have role-played, the voice inside of a loving, deceased grandparent. The love itself can be externalized and viewed and held in the hands of an individual. In working with a gay couple recently, I placed a rather large soft pillow, shaped like a heart and made of purple silk, into their four hands and suggested that their heart connection needed the support and attention of both partners. That heart continues to be a useful symbol for this couple, externalizing their longings. I offered another couple two items on display in my office: a small crystal turtle and a similarly sized, mostly black stuffed loon. The turtle represented the clarity she has about her feelings; the loon symbolized the mystery he has about his feelings. They took hold of the metaphors literally and figuratively. After keeping them at home for two months, they brought them back to therapy. They had wonderful stories to tell about what the turtle and loon had shared with each other.

In another case, I externalized a couple's internal boundaries by placing hula hoops around them and the chair in which they were sitting. Ropes also serve this purpose well. Although I did not have them actually interact with the hoops, they were called to attention whenever one of us noticed codependency. I participated by having my own hoop. Likewise, in using stuffed animals and dolls to externalize the inner child, I often hold a representation of my inner child. My message is that I too have an inner child for whom I must take responsibility. When another client began talking with me and her husband about how vulnerable and sensitive she felt, I walked over to my corner of stuffed items and pulled out the little red-headed doll with a stitched scar on her tummy. Presenting the doll to my client, I said, "I think you are talking about old wounds from your childhood that still need loving care." She reached for the little doll, held it to her breast, and wept. With only my slightest prompting, her husband moved to her side and held her while she cried. Both spouses were victims of incest. They needed validation for their wounds and comforting in a safe environment. Seeing the stitched scar on the doll's tummy made evident the reality of the client's wound. Holding the doll enabled the client to open herself up to the compassion she so much needed. Having her partner be attentive while she held the doll and cried for the scarred doll inside herself deepened the healing.

Another couple, whose long marital history was fraught with years of unresolved conflicts, benefited greatly when I dumped a wadded and knotted assortment of ropes over their laps. I said, "These are like your tangles and knots. Decide which one you think is the most critical one to focus on at this time." The dialogue was rich. They chose a rope that had two colors, that was the thickest of all, and that they felt most strangled their intimacy. During the next several sessions, they told their stories about what the rope represented. Both the husband and wife detailed ways in which their partner had inflicted pain into their being. In both cases, they were able to trace the source of the pain to family-of-origin experiences, and in both cases, their responses to pain in their marriage was the same defense that they had constructed as children. This insight allowed for ownership of choice about a new way to deal with pain. Viewing pain as signaling the need for connection, not isolation, created a path for practicing the skills of intimacy.

When a concrete symbolic form is available to see and touch that can also be spoken to and listened to, the channels for relationship open. When one relates openly to the symbolic object, the embedded experiences represented by that object can be revisited, reevaluated. The here-and-now realness of the experience enhances the depth of feeling and the growth of awareness. Having parts or patterns of one's self explored experientially makes one's experiences easier to understand, own, and modify.

Application of Satir Strategies with a Couple

I have chosen to present the strategic interventions I made with a heterosexual couple whom I have seen eight times over a three-and-a-half-month period. Considering their progress, I expect to terminate treatment very soon. I will refer to them as Sam and Nancy. He is 49 and she, 44. He has a high school diploma and has had a great deal of on-the-job training at the company where he has worked for 25 years. His work is electrical in nature. She has a high school education and training as a dental assistant. She has a part-time job that she has had for more than two years. Sam and Nancy have been married for six years. He was married twice before, for 11 and 12 years, respectively. He has a 25-year-old daughter by his first marriage. Nancy was married once before. Her two sons, John, 17, and Bob, 15, are from her first marriage. Although she was legally married to her first husband for nine years, she had left him after no more than two years. She feared for her life and for her children's lives because of his alcoholism and associated violence. He died when the boys were 12 and 10, shortly before she and Sam were married. After she left the relationship, Nancy never saw her former husband again, nor did the boys see their father, as Nancy and her parents moved with the two babies to another state in order to hide from him. At the time of my first session with the couple, they were living with the two teenage boys in the basement of Nancy's parents' home. This is the home in which Nancy has lived for more than 10 years.

Once in my large office, Sam and Nancy were invited to sit wherever they chose. They chose to sit in the chairs clustered in the middle of the room. All three chairs were able to swivel. I pulled up my chair and a small easel with an 18- by 24-inch print pad and a large basket of Magic Markers. I explained that sometimes it was helpful for me to make notes and diagrams on paper. In that way, I could better remember the discussions and also obtain a better perspective on issues. The couple seemed to agree with this procedure.

Before I could ask the number-one Satir question—"What would you like to have happen for you?"—Nancy immediately told me she was on Zoloft and had been in therapy with a woman whose family was known by her father. She believed that she had made significant progress in her therapy and said that "I am ready now to deal with my marriage." She added, however, that there were "things" that I needed to know about her. I began taking the important history. I put as much of it on the pad as I could, trying to keep up with her story and stay in touch with her. In less than 10 minutes, I had almost filled the page with a vertical, colorful family map showing Nancy's history on the right side of the page. Her marriage to Sam was shown with a lateral solid line between the two of them. Nancy's family was on the right, with her family of origin above. Her first marriage was shown with another lateral line that had short vertical lines crossing the marriage line, showing their divorce. Nancy was able simultaneously to talk and to watch me scribe, sometimes scribble, the people, dates, places, and events of the past that she wanted me to know.

Sam became involved in the conversation, too, making certain that I was coding information accurately. I changed the colors of the markers often, explaining that certain information should "really stand out." Both clients were willing to offer their ideas about the colors that should be used.

Nancy's first marriage had been an abusive one. She had married at that time to escape from her parents' home, where she believed that she had been the "whipping child." When she was a small child, she explained, she was "smothered." Her father died when she was six years old, her mother remarried a "know-it-all" who expected her to be "his servant," and her situation became worse. Because of the abuse at home and with her first husband, Nancy decided that she would never again trust a man. Sam chimed in that Nancy had really been afraid of him at first, always thinking he was going to hit her. He declared, "I've never hit a woman and don't ever intend to." Nancy answered that she was "grateful to God for finding Sam," whom she described as a "good and honest man," but she added, "I don't know why he's married to me. He doesn't seem to care anything about me." She explained that Sam "works long hours and many weekends. When he's not at work, he is always watching sports on television." She wept as she talked about all the ways in which he was not loving or attentive to her. To help their relationship, she had even befriended his daughter, "who doesn't give him the time of day, even though he paid for her college education." I interrupted to see if I had understood the bottom line of her soliloquy: "Seems as if you feel cheated. You waited a long time to find an honest man, but you really feel unloved. You don't know if he wants to be with you. You want to feel connected to him." She acknowledged that I did understand what she was saying. Quickly, she then told me all the ways in which she had tried to be a good wife, and all the reasons that he should be nicer to her.

We were now almost 20 minutes into the session. I interrupted her again, noting that she seemed very hurt and disappointed. But, in the brief time that we had left in the session, I added, I should also hear from Sam. She stopped talking and looked at Sam. His breathing seemed fast, and his face was red. I turned to him, saying, "I know this must have been hard to hear—all the ways that your wife is unhappy with you. But," I continued, "I am very interested in hearing what you want to have happen for you." With an almost explosive burst of stammering and flood of words, Sam told me that he had been taught to be honest, to do what he said he would do, and to work hard. Neither at home nor at his job of 25 years did he feel he was given credit or respect. He lamented:

> Nancy doesn't know what it's like to work all day, never being appreciated, things always changing, and people never satisfied. She doesn't know how I don't want to have to talk or think when I get home. And her boys—they don't know the value of work, and they don't know how to entertain themselves as we did as kids in my family.

I allowed Sam to vent his feelings. Nancy was absolutely still and looked frightened. I moved my chair closer to Sam and put my hand on the arm of his chair, nearly touching his arm. I said in a soft voice, "I think you are really angry." Our eyes had not really met until this moment. He seemed speechless at first, shaking his head to show his exasperation. I moved my hand gently to his lower arm, which was wrapped rather tightly around the chair's wooden arm. I could feel the tightness in his arm. Again our eyes met, and I said, "I can tell you don't know what to do at this point. It seems to me that what you most want is to be understood." He quieted, his breathing became more relaxed, and he nodded slightly, affirming that I understood. I looked at Nancy, who was almost motionless. I asked her if she, too, felt as if she did not know what to do. She motioned "yes" with her head, and her eyes looked soft as she moved them from me to Sam.

We had about 15 minutes left in the session. I said, in an almost Columbo[8] style, "I want to see if I have the right picture. Will you help me?" They looked puzzled. I stood up, backing out of the way, and extended my arms and hands to them, asking them to stand up. They did. I began: "This is my picture of the pain in your relationship at this time." In my mind, I thought, "These are the patterns that perpetuate your problems." I then moved them about a bit, trying to get just the right sculpt. I turned Sam so that his back was to Nancy. I suggested that he pretend to be watching Michael Jordan play ball. He might droop his shoulders a bit to symbolize the burdens and despair he felt, and tighten

---

[8] Television detective from the 1970s who presented himself as not so bright but who always stumbled into the one fact that would unlock the mystery.

the muscles across his back and in his upper arms, to reflect the kind of tension with which he was living. My sculpt was of a blamer trying hard to be superreasonable, although I did not use or need to give him those labels. I could see that he was trying to do as I requested. He was told to relax while I positioned Nancy. I thought for a minute, then said, "Let's try you down on the floor on one knee, a bit wobbly." I asked her to pull on Sam's pants legs, trying to get his attention, and to add whimpering sounds. Sam was to add angry breathing sounds.

It seemed as if this was the picture of their relationship. They agreed. "Good," I affirmed. "We all agree about what is happening." I told them that I believed that their marriage was very important to both of them, and then I asked them to take their postures one more time, explaining, "We have to figure out what can happen for you, Sam, so that you won't have to feel tense and unfulfilled, so that your body can relax more." As I said that, I lightly touched his upper back and shoulder and one of his upper arms. As had happened before, I could actually feel him relax. I went onto one knee to speak to Nancy. I told her that she needed to learn how to stand up and realize what a loving and special woman she was. She seemed to take these words as an instruction and stood up, reaching for Sam. Responding, he opened his arms and hugged her. I said, "I think we can make this a very good marriage." They smiled. "This can be the picture we work toward," I said. Though not necessary in this case, it is often diagnostic and therapeutic after sculpting the problem patterns to request the couple to give their picture of the sculpt they want for a model of their future.

I sat down in my chair, and they followed suit. I wanted to schedule another appointment for the next week, but my travel plans were such that it would be more than two weeks before we could meet again. Although they understood this when we scheduled the initial appointment, I felt regret that we had to wait so long to meet again. Thankfully, the first session ended in a very hopeful place. We had three pictures to work with when we would next meet: (1) the family map that looked like a modern abstract, depicting many of the important people in their lives, with different colors showing the "hot spots" (Nancy's abusive husband and Sam's distant and rejecting daughter were in red; a blue line encircled the family that Sam and Nancy had been trying to blend, including the boys; and a dotted line showed interest in including Sam's daughter); (2)

the sculpt of marital disappointment and pain; and (3) their embrace, representing their marital longings and hopes.

Unfortunately, due to a death in the family, I had to leave town two days before our planned second session. I was nonetheless on the phone with Nancy, dealing with the crises that had happened the night before I was to return home (Sunday): Sam and John, her 17-year-old son, had become physical that Saturday night. John had run away from home, and then Sam had also left, angrily saying that he was tired of her lack of support. He didn't know if he would return. During our telephone call, I gave Nancy appointments for Monday and Tuesday, allowing her to decide how she wanted to use the time—either to come alone or to bring whomever she chose. I remembered the vivid picture of her kneeling on the floor in the sculpt, and I believed that leaving the decision to her indicated my trust in her ability to know what really made sense in this situation. Nancy chose to bring her boys to Monday's session, and Sam on Tuesday.

On Monday, I asked the boys how they were coping, living in small quarters with Sam and Nancy so distant and unhappy with each other. Although the boys mostly grunted, they were able to acknowledge that it was difficult. Nancy explained that John had broken up with his girlfriend and was not having an easy time. She said she was unhappy for John but was really happy that they were breaking up. Bob, her 15-year-old, when asked for his thoughts about John's breakup, said that the girlfriend was "no good for John." I then turned to John, noting that his mother and brother both believed that "you deserve someone better." Do you agree? I asked. He did not answer. Perhaps, I suggested, "your heart, your body, and your head are not yet quite all together on this decision." He looked up as if to agree.

I recalled from my session with Sam and Nancy that Nancy had left her first husband because he was not good for her and her baby boys. Before Nancy and her boys had arrived at my office that Monday, I had opened their flip chart, which now stood in my office, to the family mapping that we had begun several weeks before. Pointing to the page (my "cotherapist" with the good memory), I suggested that, years ago when they were little boys, Nancy had some of the same feelings that John was having. All three looked puzzled. I continued, "You, Nancy, had to leave your husband because he was not good for you and the boys when he drank and got violent. I know it must have hurt you very badly to give up your dreams." She offered, "It was hard, but I knew it was the right decision."

I went over to my self-esteem tool kit box and pulled out the courage stick and the golden key. I held the courage stick for a minute, explaining that it represented courage—the ability to go forward even when you are afraid and don't know what the consequences will be. I presented the stick to John, saying, "I think you have a lot of courage." I then pulled out the golden key and talked about how it opens new doors and new possibilities. I thought out loud, "You are not alone in needing to use your golden key. The whole family needs to find some new ways to be."

I ended the session by spending a few minutes with John. He said he was sad but was all right. I believed him. I reached out to shake his hand good-bye, not knowing if the teenager would be able to respond to this gesture. He did. I felt as though he had shown me briefly, by his handshake and the look in his eyes, that he is not just a boy but a young man. I wished him well and asked if he would be willing to come back at another time. He said that he would.

The following day, Tuesday, I met with Nancy and Sam. They had begun to talk to each other. I went to my self-esteem tool kit and brought out two small stuffed red hearts. I gave one to each, saying, "I think it is very hard to build trust when your hearts have been so wounded." Sam began to cry, telling Nancy that he really loved her and wanted their life together to be different. His tears seemed to melt her heart. In this moment, he broke through the barriers of his blaming and superreasonableness. I felt as if we were back on the path toward problem resolution: He could share himself with her, and therefore she could empathize with him; she felt valued by his sharing and responded from her own strengths. Sam's becoming physical with John, I suggested, was evidence of the difficulty he had in handling his own feelings and stresses. I wondered if he didn't sometimes feel "like a bomb about to explode." He said he did. We talked about the benefit he might derive from a few sessions of counseling for himself. I recalled that he believed the counseling sessions had been helpful for Nancy. He said that he would do whatever he needed to do.

Sam did follow up and met with a male therapist five times. He reported that it was helpful to talk to someone about his life. I said that I thought his being able to talk with a man about his challenges must have been especially helpful. I commented that 49 was a significant age and that he was very wise to be taking the time to really think about his health, his relationships, and his work life.

Sam and Nancy have made excellent progress in using their resources and consciously relating to each other in more positive ways. Whenever during a session I thought that they were successful in using one tool from their self-esteem kit, I would retrieve that tool from my box to show how it was at work in their lives. Sam, becoming more involved with the family, has taken John fishing and supported him at school, trying to obtain special services for his learning disability. Nancy and Sam report that Bob is relaxing more as the home environment becomes less tense. The most dramatic step, however, is that Nancy and Sam have decided to leave the basement of her parents' house and buy their own home. Although Nancy and Sam are thrilled to be making this change, they said that the boys were apprehensive about the effect this move would have on their grandparents.

I suggested that it might now be time to consider a family session to discuss everyone's feelings associated with this big change. Nancy and Sam agreed wholeheartedly. While looking with them at pictures of the new home that would be theirs in another few weeks, we remarked about how much their lives had changed in such a short time. I was so impressed with all that they had accomplished. I told them that it would be a treat for me to meet with them and the boys about such a positive step in their lives.

This couple has weathered a crisis and recovered their love and sense of safety with each other. They must, however, continue to grow together and to develop their self-esteem and compassion for each other in order to sustain their gains. I believe they will.

Application of Satir Strategies with an Individual

Therapy with this individual demonstrates primarily the strategy of externalization of a client's parts of self for increased awareness and authorship. Ann is 45 years old, has a college degree, and works with computers. She is a single mother of a teenage son, Arnold, who has just graduated from high school. She was pregnant when she got married. After a long separation, she divorced her husband when her son was nine years old. The father has offered little in the way of financial or emotional support to his son. He has remarried and has young children. Ann is bright, obese, and depressed, but she finds considerable symptom relief from Prozac, which she has taken for a year.

Ann entered therapy upon the referral of her son's therapist. Because

Arnold had seemed depressed and because he was not working to his potential in school, Ann had sought the help of a child psychologist. Arnold did not take to therapy, but the therapist, noting his mother's anxiety and depression, suggested that Ann could benefit from therapy. She entered the session in my office saying that she had no personal life to speak of, except as Arnold's mother. She thought that she had done a good job as a mother and was proud that her son had graduated from high school, considering how difficult school had been for him. She hopes that, after a few years of being on his own, he would attempt college.

Ann's family map, done on a flip chart pad and visible at most sessions, showed a red line from Ann to her maternal grandmother and the word "resembles" written by this line. This grandmother committed suicide when Ann's mother was four years old. Although Ann never met this woman, various relatives in this large Irish family have told her over the years that she "takes after her." Ann believes it is because of her weight and her appearance and the fact that her grandmother was supposedly very intelligent. Ann was skipped from first grade to third grade because of her intelligence, and she appreciates that she is able to grasp many technical concepts quickly.

Ann's passivity is evident in the way she lives her life. She reads self-help books and talks about how helpful they are, but she has difficulty motivating herself to take action. She wonders if she is lazy but dismisses that idea when she is reminded of the effort she has put forth in rearing Arnold, as well as how hard she works on her job. Although she seems to have benefited from inner child work, when she holds a stuffed doll that has many of her features and recognizes her losses and longings, action is slow and often unsustained. Needless to say, her depression plays a part in her slow progress, but Ann seems to know when she is fighting depression and when she is sliding into the patterns of her childhood and the patterns of her passive-submissive mother.

For Ann, it is important that things make sense to her. I began to wonder which of her parts were fighting the parts that wanted to change. Ann was intrigued with the exploration. I suggested that we lay the parts of the self, as defined by my mentor, Virginia Satir, on the floor and see if we could figure out what was standing in the way of her progress. She seemed pleased. I suspected that she could get more access to energy and awareness if we did our work standing and walking. This idea proved to be true.

I brought out nine pieces of paper, each about a foot and a half long and about six inches wide. Each piece of paper had the label of one part of the self mandala (spiritual, intellectual, interactional, physical, sensual, contextual, emotional, and nutritional). One had the words "Self—I Am" written on it (Satir et al., 1991, pp. 274–282). I spread out the papers on the floor and suggested that we talk about each part briefly. She was then to arrange the pieces in a fashion that would reflect how she was living her life.

Ann was as animated as I ever remember. She said that it was exciting to be looking at her life in such a holistic way. I suggested that she find a place in the room to place the paper "Self—I Am," and to stand on that paper. Once she did that, I suggested that she close her eyes and decide what she wanted to place first on the floor collage of her life, and where she would place that piece of paper. She asked for the "nutritional" part and laid it touching the "self" part to the left. I suggested that she take a deep breath and see what she was feeling. She answered, "This is true. I'm always thinking about what I am going to eat." She noted that she eats uncontrollably after work, in a very unconscious way. She could eat a bag of potato chips without even noticing that she was eating. She explained that she had attempted many different diets, but with little or no success.

I suggested that she continue with her "big picture." She closed her eyes to recenter herself. She opted to place the "emotional" part next, touching the upper left corner of "nutritional." With that, she sighed and commented again, "This is true. I always connect my feelings about myself and others and my life to what and how much I have been eating." Next, she added the "physical." It lay touching "nutritional" on the top right side. She laughed, adding, "Is everything connected to what I eat?" I didn't answer but encouraged her to continue with the other parts of her mandala. When she had finished, I suggested that she center herself on the "Self—I Am" home base and tell me three action items that she believed her picture suggested. She centered herself and again began laughing. "It's too simple. Take carrots and sunflower seeds to work, and drink lots of water." She seemed genuinely pleased with her analysis. When I asked if she meant that she was going on a diet, she was quick to answer, "No! I'm tired of all these years coming with big plans about what I need to do and not being able to carry them out." I supported the wisdom she had gained from experience.

When Ann returned in two weeks, she was excited about having ordered a comfortable chair for her house. She remarked that she had wanted to make some changes in her house for a long time. She reported that she had spent the previous weekend rearranging her house so that she would enjoy it more. In passing, she said that she was eating her carrots and sunflower seeds and drinking water. I wondered what she had done before. "Candy and cookies," she responded.

Two weeks later, she reported that she had invited a friend to her house for dinner. She acknowledged that it had been more than a year since she had had a guest in her home. I was very impressed that she seemed to be in an action mode in a very positive way. She reminded me that, when she had done the mandala, everything in her picture was connected to "nutritional." She acknowledged having known this predilection but had not understood it so clearly. I wondered if we should lay out the picture again. She had drawn the picture for herself the month before but had left it at home. She recreated it on the floor, which again had her standing, stooping, and walking. She was astonished that taking such a few small steps in one aspect of her life seemed to have made such a positive ripple in her life in general. I used a Polaroid camera to capture the configuration, gave her a picture for her refrigerator, and kept one for my records. I commented that, in time, she would have a different relationship with her parts. She noted that her spiritual life was really distant from her "Self—I Am" part. She wondered what would have to happen for that part to be enlivened. She humorously questioned what food she should eat. We both laughed and reminded ourselves about the value of small steps.

The work that Ann is doing is timely. Her life has been devoted to the mandala of her son. She fears that she could become like her mother and her grandmother: depressed, apathetic, and morbidly obese. Externalizing and manipulating her mandala on the floor was an act of increasing her awareness of these fears and of helping her to accept where she is. Authorship seemed to have happened in a natural way, given the urgency of creating a life beyond motherhood. Several weeks later, she came to my office reporting an interaction with her supervisor. For the first time, she had clearly explained what she wanted her role to be at work, and what activities were of low interest to her. Ann was pleased that her boss was already reacting favorably to Ann's suggestions. Ann also was really pleased with herself. She laughed again about the power of carrots, sunflower seeds, and water. She was more loving to her self nutritionally, and she was almost effortlessly directly impacting her contextual and her interactional parts. In fact, she had begun walking for 30 minutes every other day, which made her physical part happy, and in fact she believed it was also providing some satisfaction to her sensual part.

Ann's progress, after many years of struggling with empowerment, seemed to take a leap forward when she took ownership of her mandala. Ownership of her parts has been esteem-building and thought-provoking. The detective hat and golden key have been particularly useful in her work with the mandala. She reported several times that "I do better when things make sense to me." She still must bring her heart on board with her detective hat and golden key. When her son moves away in another month, however, she will have a unique opportunity to experience her inner child's need for nurturance. I hope to help her grieve not only for her son but also for the little girl who, she recalls, was always standing back behind her sister and being overlooked.

Summary

In presenting the Satir system's strategies applicable to brief therapy, this chapter has shown the significance of the relationship of the self of the therapist to the therapist's ability to do effective work. The therapist's inner assumptions about what it means to be human shape the therapist's clinical thought and behaviors. As Virginia Satir said, "There is a close relationship between what I believe and how I act. The more in touch I am with my own beliefs and acknowledge them, the more I give myself freedom to choose how to use those beliefs" (Baldwin & Satir, 1987, p. 35). Satir thought that positive change was possible for everyone. Her recipe for deep and sustaining change included six primary strategies. The first three are resourcefulness, empowerment, and congruence. The second three give form to the former: working with the inner system to make deep contact, assessing the process patterns, and externalizing the client's inner workings for increased ownership and choice. The Satir tools referred to in this chapter, specifically in the two case presentations, are designed to help the therapist connect to the client's essence and underlying needs. They concretize his or her basic concepts about becoming more fully human and actively invite clients into the adventure and spiritual exploration of change, learning, growth, and healing.

Clinical Indications

To be effective, the use of Satir methods must be grounded in a genuine adherence to the basic beliefs undergirding the system. These beliefs about the universal longings and possibilities of humans serve to guide therapists in respecting boundaries, appreciating uniqueness, and creating active methods for engaging the client's strengths. Operationally, these values call forth the therapist's empathy and compassion and willingness to risk congruence.

Although Satir was famous for making contact with the most resistant of clients, generally the prerequisite for successful treatment with this modality is the clients' awareness of pain and desire for more positive connections in their lives. Clients who are depressed may open to awareness but have little energy to follow through with action. Similarly, clients who are overwhelmed or flooded with anxiety and trauma memories may be too distracted to operate in the here and now of the therapy relationship. In these cases, psychotherapeutic drugs are often helpful in assisting clients to gain greater access to the mind-body-spirit connection. The ability of clients to be in awareness of their thoughts, feelings, body sensations, and spirit—or essence—determines the depth and speed with which transformation can happen.

References

Baldwin, M., & Satir, V. (1987). The use of self in therapy. *Journal of Psychotherapy, 3*(1), 17–25.

Banmen, A., & Banmen, J. (1991). *Meditations of Virginia Satir*. Palo Alto, CA: Science and Behavior Books.

Kirsey, D., & Bates, M. (1978). *Please understand me*. Del Mar, CA: Prometheus Nemesis Books.

McLendon, J. (1981). Unpublished notes as member of Satir research team, Richmond, VA.

McLendon, J. (1997). The tao of communication and the constancy of change. *Journal of Couples Therapy, 6* (3 and 4), 35–49.

McLendon, J. (1998). Satir system in psychotherapy. In J.D. Weiner (Ed.), *Action methods in psychotherapy*. Washington, DC: American Psychology Books.

Nerin, W. (1993). *You can't grow up till you go back home.* Gig Harbor, WA: Magic Mountain.

Satir, V. (1976). *Making contact.* Celestial Arts, CA: Ten Speed Press.

Satir, V. (1988). *The new peoplemaking.* Mountain View, CA: Science and Behavior Books.

Satir, V., Banmen, J., Gerber, J., & Gomori, M. (1991). *The Satir model: Family therapy and beyond.* Palo Alto, CA: Science and Behavior Books.

Weiner, J. D. (Ed.). (1998). *Action methods in psychotherapy: A practical guide.* Washington, DC: American Psychology Books.

Annotated Bibliography

Banmen, A., & Banmen, J. (1991). *Meditations of Virginia Satir.* Palo Alto, CA: Science and Behavior Books. Reading this book is a great way to learn the underlying assumptions and beliefs of the Satir system and to develop an appreciation for language as a base for affirming resourcefulness.

Brothers, B. J. (Ed.). *Journal of Couples Therapy.* New York: Haworth Press. This very readable journal focuses on the process issues of therapeutic work with couples. The work of Virginia Satir is frequently featured.

Loeschen, S. (1998). *Systematic training in the skills of Virginia Satir.* Pacific Grove, CA: Brooks/Cole. This author lays out simple and relevant exercises for students who want to develop the basic skills of the Satir model.

Satir, V. (1988). *The new peoplemaking.* Mountain View, CA: Science and Behavior Books. A comprehensive explication by Satir of her values and views about people and how they communicate. The most important of all Satir books, whether written by her or others.

Satir, V., Banmen, J., Gerber, J., & Gomori, M. (1991). *The Satir model: Family therapy and beyond.* Palo Alto, CA: Science and Behavior Books. An encyclopedia of Satir beliefs, tools, and methods.

Satir, V., Stachowiak, J., & Taschman, H. (1975). *Helping families to change.* New York: Jason Aronson. This book presents Satir's early conceptions of congruence. She discusses her beliefs about the use of self in therapy.

Schwab, J., Baldwin, M., Gerber, J., Gomori, M., & Satir, V. (1989). *The Satir approach to communication: A workshop manual.* Palo Alto, CA: Science and Behavior Books. A useful guide for professionals who want to teach the Satir system. It provides exercises for learning basic concepts.

13

---∞∞∞---

Imago Strategies

Wade Luquet

Introduction

Imago relationship therapy (IRT) has its roots in the work of Harville Hendrix, who writes that it evolved out of his relationship with his wife, Helen (Hendrix, 1996). In the 1970s, their common psychology backgrounds led them to begin thinking about the nature of relationships and whether therapeutic healing could take place only in therapy, or if it could occur within a committed relationship itself. They concluded that "since the *wounding* occurred in relationship with one's parents, logic required that the *healing* could occur only in a context which reactivated the wounds. The idea was born, though not then named, that marriage, conducted with the aim of mutual healing, is the most effective form of therapy; thus evolved the phrase 'marriage as therapy' " (p. 3).

Since its early beginnings, IRT has developed its own theory that healing is inherent in committed relationships, as well as a set of skills, a strategy for utilizing the skills, and an international following that includes thousands of therapists certified in the model. In a strategic series of sessions, a couple is taught communication skills and a new way of thinking about relationships by a therapist who acts as a facilitator or coach of the couple's experience. At the conclusion of the course of therapy, the couple possesses the skills necessary to maintain the relationship, as well as a new view of the meaning of their lives together.

This chapter presents the strategic plan that therapists use to teach the Imago skills, and it provides the information necessary to create a paradigm shift for couples. This shift in thinking helps the partners to move into a relational mindset—one that allows them to see the relationship as a healing journey rather than as a painful, hopeless endeavor. IRT sees the pain in relationships as being caused by a rupture in the connection between partners, which causes individual self-absorption rather than an empathic connection. Its main goal is to repair this rupture, which occurs as a result of a power struggle between the partners. Once reconnected, the relationship can become an essential place to foster emotional healing, spontaneous fun, and spiritual awareness.

The relationship can also offer an opportunity for the couple to experience *connected differentiation,* that is, "I can be different but still in relationship with you." This concept allows for each person to become distinct and to develop fully while still being in relationship—a task that is difficult in most relationship models because of the exclusive emphasis either on the individual or on the relationship. In Imago the focus is on collaborative self-development (Luquet, 1996)—committed partners helping each other give birth to their selves.

Imago strategies can be envisioned as a tree. At the base of the tree are the main tenets of the work—the establishment of emotional safety and the use of the couples dialogue. The remaining strategies are the tree's five branches: reimaging the partner, restructuring frustrations, resolving rage, reromanticizing the relationship, and revisioning the relationship. To fully embrace the Imago model, couples need to participate in 10 to 12 sessions of therapy, although couples with extensive problems or intense frustrations may need additional time. Many couples choose to stay in therapy longer because of the possibilities for personal growth that IRT opens up.

In this chapter, I will introduce four strategies that are essential in a brief Imago model, along with the techniques to facilitate these strategies. First I will list the four strategies here, then follow up with a more in-depth description, and finally provide case studies designed to illustrate their use in brief imago therapy.

- *Couples Dialogue and the Creation of Emotional Safety.* Unlike individual therapy, where the couple come in and tell the therapist about the fight they had, in IRT the couple show up in the midst of the fight. The object of their disaffection walks through the door with them. So the first strategy is to teach them how to defuse the frustration, to self-soothe to create an emotionally safe environment to deal with the frustration, and to communicate in a way that allows them to make contact.
- *Imago Psychoeducation.* Once the couple have created some sense of safety, it is important that they learn what lies behind their frustrations; they should also identify the purpose of their relationship. IRT teaches couples that marriage serves the goals of self-development and partner development. This aspect of psychoeducation attempts to offer the couple a new view of marriage, one of hope and meaning.
- *Restructuring Frustrations.* Expressing a frustration in a relationship often does nothing more than increase the existing level of frustration. Anger is often met with anger, so that escalation occurs (Gottman, 1998). This strategy teaches couples how to word complaints in such a way that they are more likely to be heard and reacted to positively.
- *Reromanticizing the Relationship.* Gottman (1993) has shown that couples in long-term stable marriages flood each other with five positive behaviors to every one negative. In other words, they know how to be friends. This fourth strategy teaches couples the importance of caring behaviors as a way of promoting a sense of well-being in each partner, which in turn will increase the emotional safety of the marriage.

Four Strategies of Imago Relationship Therapy

Strategy 1: Couples Dialogue and the Creation of Emotional Safety

Most couples come to therapy as a last resort. By the time they make it to the sessions, they may already have experienced years of frustration, criticism, misunderstanding, and contemptuous and invalidating expression, as well as long periods of silence. One of the fears of the couple, and the therapist, is that they will demonstrate this behavior in the office. Tensions should not be avoided in the therapy sessions, as there is a lot to be learned from these moments, but the couple need a way to calm their flooded neurosystem, reconnect to each other, and feel heard. The skills that are taught also need to be practical enough for the couple to use outside of the therapy room.

The therapist spends the first two sessions teaching the couple to calm and center themselves and to listen to each other fully, using a process called the *couples dialogue*.[1] The therapist begins by educating the couple about how the brain works to protect them from danger through its defense mechanisms of fight, flight, playing dead or freezing, hiding, or submitting. For couples, these mechanisms may take the form of arguing, leaving the room, staring through the partner while he or she talks, or giving in in order to end an argument. Most couples are quick to recognize that they have been utilizing these natural methods of protection, in various forms, in their own fights. This revelation alone helps them to understand a basic problem inherent in most couples' communication: You can't fully hear your partner when your defenses are up.

The therapist then trains the couple in *creating a sense of safety,* or self-soothing, that is immediately accessible. The methods used may include centering, visualization, or meditative techniques. For many couples, this may be their first experience with quieting their minds in this way. Some may have difficulty, whereas others enjoy the approaches.

---

[1] A regular assessment of substance and physical abuse should also be done. Because of the impact of substances on the relationship and the very real possibility that someone *is* getting hurt, it would be impossible and unethical to teach a couple to experience safety when these events are occurring.

There are several forms of effective calming techniques, and it is recommended that the couple be given the opportunity to try several over the course of treatment.

- *Visualization:* Have the couple mentally visualize a safe place. Whether it is a mountain trail or a warm beach, someone's house or riding in their car, whatever place they choose is fine, as long as they can visualize themselves feeling peaceful and safe there. Take a few minutes to have the couple close their eyes and put themselves in their safe place. Let them know that this is the place they will need to visualize later, during the dialogue process you will teach them. If they feel themselves getting anxious or wanting to fight with their partner, they are to take a moment, breathe, and return to their safe place.
- *The Protective Barrier*: Have each partner visualize a protective barrier around himself or herself that protects the partner from the other's words. The partners should allow the barrier to let the words in so they can hear them, but the barrier will protect them from any harm the words can inflict. This exercise is surprisingly powerful in serving as an anchor for the couple to stay calm during the dialogue process. Should the therapist notice that the listening partner wants to respond, a simple reminder about the protective barrier should help that partner lower his or her level of arousal.
- *Breathing and Centering*: Many couples object to being taught a formal meditation practice. They will, however, participate in the meditation technique of breathing and centering themselves. Teach the couple how to take slow, deep, breaths and allow their bodies to sink into their chairs. Help them to clear their minds of thoughts, especially fearful ones, about each other. Help them learn that they can lower their heart rate by clearing their minds of the thoughts aroused by each other's words. Remind them that this process will give them the opportunity to respond, but that they need to listen fully to each other so that they know to what to respond. The therapist may have to whisper "Breathe" several times during the dialogue process so that the listening partner can learn to center during the hard parts of a dialogue.

Teaching couples these calming techniques is an integral part of the success of this work. Some couples, especially those who have been severely wounded by the relationship, may have a difficult time letting down their guard. They may need many experiences of safe communication to "rewire" their brains before they can believe that their partner can make the relationship safe. The couple should spend at least half of their session time practicing these safety techniques in the dialogue process so they can have a regular and sustained experience of a safe and effective communication process.

The couple will learn and experience the couples dialogue at the same time as they are learning and practicing the safety techniques. The dialogue is a three-part process in which the listening (receiving) partner mirrors the speaking (sending) partner's words, validates that the sending partner makes sense from the sending partner's point of view, and offers an empathic connection by taking a guess at how the sending partner may be feeling.

A typical interaction from a couple that has not learned the dialogue process might sound like this:

Diane: I get really upset that you have to work so much. You are spending 11 hours a day at the office, and by the time you get home, I'm too tired from my job and getting dinner ready to have any energy to spend with you. I miss our time together.

Tony: Well, you know I have to work. This is a particularly busy time, and I have to be there.

Diane: But not every day. You're missing so much around here. It's like you're married to the job.

Tony: Well, it's you who has to live so extravagantly. If you did not need the living-room furniture, I would not have to work so hard. And I think you are so tired because you are not getting any exercise.

Diane: When would I have time for that! I don't have the luxury of time like you do.

Tony and Diane show little connection, and they are more concerned with defending their stances than with hearing each other. Their brain defenses are in full swing and the power struggle erupts, yet they have no capacity to hear each other.

That same couple, when taught the couples dialogue process, might sound something like this:

Diane: Tony, I really need to talk to you. Is now a good time?

Tony: Yeah, I can do that. Give me a minute to calm myself. . . . Okay, I'm ready.

Diane: I get really upset that you have to work so much. You are spending 11 hours a day at the office, and by the time you get home, I'm too tired from my job and getting dinner ready to have any energy to spend with you. I miss our time together.

Tony: If I'm getting this, you are saying that you are upset that I am spending so much time at the office. After my 11-hour days and your workday and taking care of home things, you are too tired to spend quality time with me. You say you miss our time together. Did I get that? Is there more?

Diane: Yes. I married you because you were such a good friend, but I don't feel that anymore. I feel distant from you, and I want that to change. I want to feel like we are friends again.

Tony: So you are saying that you married me because we were such good friends and now you don't feel like we are such good friends. You feel distant and you want that to change so that we can be friends again. I can understand that. What makes sense about that to me is that we were such good friends, and now it seems we have so little time to spend together. I imagine you feel distant, disappointed, and lonely. Did I get that?

Diane: Yes, you did. Thank you.

Of course, Tony has some things he will want to say, and he will need to do it within the structure of the dialogue too. And although this dialogue may sound rote and rehearsed, the process provides couples with a safe way to communicate. Clearly, not every power struggle begins with an invitation to talk. Most frustrations erupt spontaneously, and the couple can expect to have a painful, unproductive interaction. But the partners should be taught to return to the conversation after they calm down, using the dialogue process. After a period of practice, the use of couples dialogue will become more spontaneous, requiring less of the imposed format than in the early stages. Eventually, the dialogue may sound more like this:

Diane: I want to talk to you about something. You have been a great friend to me, especially when the kids were very small. You are a good father. So I want you to hear that I get really upset that you have to work so much. You are spending 11 hours a day at the office, and by the time you get home, I'm too tired from my job and getting dinner ready to have any energy to spend with you. I miss our time together.

Tony: So you are getting upset that I spend so much time at work and we have so little time together. I imagine that would upset you. I have been working a lot lately, and I know you have been working, and it puts a lot of burden on you.

Diane: It does put a lot of burden on me. Picking up the kids, getting dinner ready, and doing it all after a full day of work. It's really getting to be too much.

Tony: Well, that makes sense to me. After your day of work and the things you have to do when you get home, I imagine you are tired and lonely and are wondering why you have to do it all yourself. It's a huge job, and I know that my crazy work schedule is really messing things up. If I can respond.

Diane: Sure, I can hear you now.

Tony: I want you to know that I am feeling upset that I might have to change my schedule to help you out with this. I know it's is important, and I'm feeling anxiety at the thought of making a change.

Diane: I bet you are upset, and I can see it will be a stretch to meet my request, and I thank you.

This evolved couples dialogue has the components of communication that Gottman (1998) found in happy and stable marriages: "a softened start-up by the wife, [and] that the husband accepted influence from her" (p. 17). The couples dialogue should eventually evolve into this natural process that gives partners the feeling of being heard and validated but not necessarily agreed with. When two people live together, separate realities are expected. Dialogue is a way of saying. "I can see your reality. Can you also see mine?" Dialogue is not a problem-solving mechanism. Although a solution may make itself apparent, the dialogue's main purpose is to achieve connection and validation. It allows a couple to become authentic with each other—promoting differentiation, but in the context of connection. The problem-solving component will come later, with behavior change request.

To utilize the couples dialogue with a couple, the therapist should have some experience with it personally. Certified Imago therapists must participate in a two-day couples workshop with their partners or a significant friend in order to enter the training program. While this formal training is not necessary, it does make the therapist more comfortable with the process, and couples feel more comfortable knowing that the therapist practices what is preached. (More information on dialogue and safety can be found in Hendrix, 1988, 1992, and 1997; Luquet, 1996; and Luquet & Hannah, 1998.

Strategy 2: Imago Psychoeducation

Once the couple have made a connection through the couples dialogue and creating safety, they need a new way to think about the purpose of their relationship. IRT has a large psychoeducational aspect. Over the next four sessions, the couple will spend half of their time in the dialogue process discussing issues important to them and learning part of the theory behind IRT. The strategy is to teach five ideas that will give hope and purpose to the relationship.

1. *Relationships have an unconscious purpose.* Couples are drawn to each other in romantic love for reasons that are beyond their conscious sight. While they may think they were drawn together, for instance, by good looks or similar interests, actually they were both wounded in the same place developmentally in their childhood. The relationship unconsciously brings them together for the purpose of healing those wounds. IRT posits that we are born in relationship, we are wounded in relationship, and we are healed in relationship. To be healed, we choose partners who possess both the positive and the negative aspects of our early childhood caretaker, as well as someone who mirrors the lost, disowned, and denied parts of ourselves. It is what evolutionary anthropologists call love maps (Money, 1986) and what is referred to in IRT as the imago.

   These words will have little meaning to most couples, so to make it clear to them, the therapist will ask them to do an exercise called the *Imago workup* (Hendrix, 1988; Luquet, 1996). On a sheet of

paper they are asked to write the following about their early childhood caretakers—male and female—as far back as they can remember. (Examples are italicized and noted parenthetically.)

A. Caretaker's positive traits: (*always there, warm, smart, listened to me*)
B. Caretaker's negative traits: (*never there, mean, cold, distant, scary*)
C. What I always wanted and needed as a child was: (*to be noticed and have my ideas respected*)
D1. My recurring frustrations in childhood were: (*I did not get to play with my friends; I was always told what to do; no one listened to my ideas*)
D2. What I did when I was frustrated: (*I brooded, got quiet, withdrew, kept my thoughts to myself*)
E1. My positive memories of my childhood are: (*going to my grandmother's; playing baseball with my dad*)
E2. I felt: (*happy, connected, loved*)

This information is then transferred to a formula of five sentence
stems about the partners' present struggles with each other. The
purpose of this process is to enlighten the couple about how their
past wounds are played out in their present relationship. The formula typically describes the couple's struggle. In the list of stems
below, the letter at the end of each stem corresponds to the information on the already-completed caretaker sheet. (In this example,
the sample answers have been transferred from the caretaker sheet
and appear in italics.)

1. I am trying to get a person who is (B): *(never there, mean, cold, distant, scary)*.
2. To instead always be (A): *(always there, warm, smart, listened to me)*.
3. So that I can get (C): *(noticed and have my ideas respected)*.
4. And feel (E2): *(happy, connected, loved)*.
5. I stop myself from getting this sometimes by (D2): *(brooding, getting quiet, withdrawing, keeping my thoughts to myself)*.

Completing the imago workup allows the couple to understand that committed relationships are a search for the imago. The imago is described as the positive and negative traits of our early childhood caretakers that we carry in our unconscious mind and that we use in the partner-selection process.

2. *Where one partner is most frustrated is where the other partner needs the most personal growth.* Although it is difficult to see it in the midst of a conflict, relationship frustrations serve a purpose. Frustrations are markers for the areas of growth necessary for each individual in the couple, and nobody sees where one partner needs to grow more clearly than the other partner.

Most people are able to fool the world by greeting it with the "presentational self," but intimate partners know each other too well. An artistic, emotional partner knows that an logical, analytic one lacks an ability to empathize and thus screams for it: "You unfeeling bastard! Listen to how I feel for a change." Conversely, the logical partner knows that the feeling partner needs to slow down and think things through: "Calm down and think clearly about this. You are being irrational!" The problem here is not the observations but the way they are expressed. Such disrespectful expressions of frustration immediately trigger the reptilian brain, so that the accused partners become defensive and unable to hear what is really being said. During the course of Imago work, the couple will learn how to talk to each other intentionally and with respect.

3. *Growth comes when we expand our behaviors and thus ourselves. Healing occurs when we get our emotional needs met. Both can occur simultaneously.* We develop in relationship. As children, we experienced growth when our behaviors expanded: learning to walk, learning to read, learning to write, learning to think logically, learning how to choose friends and to participate in productive activities on our own. When the circumstances are right and caretakers parent consciously, children receive praise for their newfound skills and pass through developmental stages with intact self-esteem, a newfound skill, and a continued relationship with the

caretaker. And yet due to circumstances that may have been beyond our parents' control—poor parenting skills, unconscious material finding its way into their parenting, a temperament that does not take in the praise, or a poor fit between the parent and child relationship styles—we may become restricted in an area of our self-development. For example, a child who was educated in a strict school setting may have a difficult time letting loose and having fun as an adult. Parents who do not listen to a child's feelings may produce a child who, as an adult, has difficulty expressing emotions. Like a muscle that goes unused, that part of the person atrophies and becomes difficult to access, becoming what imago considers the "missing self."

Partners seek the wholeness of expression of the other, which is nowhere more evident than in couples' frustrations. The frustrations of one partner are always focused on the missing self of the other. But when a frustration is expressed in its usual attacking form, the other partner cannot hear it. When one partner learns to state frustration as a desire—"I want you to learn to have fun," or "My wish is for you to learn how to appreciate my feelings"—and the other responds with the desired behavior, two things occur simultaneously. The responding partner achieves growth by expanding his or her behavioral parameters, and the partner who is frustrated gets a need met and thus finds healing.

4. *Frustrations in marriage are inevitable and important.* We live in a culture in which the prevailing marriage myth is that we should live happily ever after. Perhaps one of the greatest gifts couples can receive in therapy is learning that "happily ever after" is an empty promise—and that that's okay. Our partners' frustrations hold a key to our personal growth; they focus our attention on the areas where we are weakest. Couples participating in IRT are often told that they should concentrate on areas where they need growth rather than on their strongest points.

Is such a stance contrary to a strengths model of therapy? Actually, it is complementary. Couples know where they are strong. Growth occurs as a result of exercising the weaker muscles. If couples make the stretch to reach out to their missing selves, even though it is difficult, they will become stronger people. Once the partners are in the relationship as conscious, intentional collaborators, frustrations, while still present, will prove less intense and will likely resolve themselves more quickly. The partners know that their frustrations have a purpose and are not grounds for immediate termination of the relationship. All relationships are conflictual, but if during conflict the couple can communicate, new growth can emerge and connection can be maintained.

5. *Conscious relationships can be spiritual vehicles.* Not every couple will want to explore the notion that their relationship can have a strong spiritual component. For those who are open to this idea, though, it may be a pleasant surprise to learn that spirituality can be fostered in a conscious relationship. The Jewish philosopher Martin Buber stated in *Eclipse of God,* "In the act of true dialogic (I-Thou) relation, man becomes a self. And the fuller its sharing in the reality of the dialogue, the more real the self becomes"(1952, p. 125). The prolific Jesuit priest Pierre Teilhard de Chardin wrote in his essay "The Eternal Feminine," "Everything in the universe is made by union and generation—by the coming together of the elements that seek out one another, melt together two by two, and are born again in a third."

Spirituality should not be confused with religiosity. Spirituality preceded religion and is basically a feeling of awe before creation. When two people meet in dialogue, a third entity—the relationship—is created. It is not a constant experience, nor should it be. Spirituality in relationships is fleeting but powerful, and it is created by a deep experience of each other through dialogue. The best way to teach this to a couple is to point it out when it occurs. Deep dialogue can reveal profoundly touching moments, and if at one of these moments you point out that they are experiencing the spirit of relationship, they will know exactly what you mean.

Strategy 3: Restructuring Frustrations

IRT seeks to discover understanding before encouraging behavior change. Encouraging behavior change before understanding is achieved often leads to misunderstanding and more hurt feelings. The receiving partner must fully understand the purpose of the change, as well as its healing potential for their partner, if the change is to be successful in meeting the partner's needs. Simultaneously, the receiving partner will stretch into their own new behavior as they meet the partner's request. Understanding comes through couples dialogue; change comes through behavior change request.

IRT views a couple's frustrations as desires that are stated negatively. When one partner expresses a frustration, the other usually reacts with some form of fight, flight, playing dead, hiding, or submitting. The direct expression of a frustration elicits an equal and negative response from the partner. Therefore, for frustrations to be expressed and acted upon, they need to be restructured into a less threatening format: a desire. "I hate when you are late" becomes " My desire is that you arrive on time." "I hate the way you treat Sarah!" becomes "My desire is for you to treat Sarah respectfully and listen to her feelings."

Expressing a frustration as a desire must be done consciously rather than reactively. This is not an easy task, and it typically occurs in the second round of the interaction—the first round being a fight about the frustration. Recasting the frustration as a desire allows for the softened start-up (Gottman, 1998) so important and prevalent in happy and stable marriages. But expressing a desire does not automatically mean that the desired behavior will be the result. The couple must then be taught how to convert this first step into a specific behavior change request.

The *behavior change request* begins with the stated desire and then develops one or more positive, doable, measurable, and time-limited tasks. "My desire is for you to treat Sarah respectfully and listen to her feelings" becomes "Three times a week, I would like for you to go to Sarah's room, ask her about her day, and listen to her, using the dialogue, for 15 minutes" or "Twice a week, I would like for you to tell Sarah what a beautiful, smart, and strong child she is." These behavior changes will meet a need of the sender—having the partner behave compassionately and respectfully toward the children. Making the changes will likely be the task of the partner who needs to work on positive expression of feeling—the logical person cut off from any ability to emotionally connect with others.

In brief therapy, behavior change requests are introduced after the couple has had an experience of couples dialogue and they are informed about IRT's view of the purpose of marriage. The couple can typically be guided through the process in the sixth session. They are first asked to list their frustrations on a piece of paper, knowing that the other will not see this list. The therapist then helps the couple through the process of translating the list of frustrations into a list of desires. Special attention needs to be paid to how the desire is presented; it should be written in a positive way, without such words as *not, don't,* or *stop.*

Next, the couple is guided through the process of converting desires into specific requests. Each desire is broken into two or three specific requests, in an effort to give the receiving partner a choice of behaviors to which to respond. The couple present the behavior change requests to each other in the dialogue process, as a way of keeping the conversation safe and focused. When completed, the receiver may have a list of 20 or 30 behaviors to choose from to meet the needs of the sender. The other partner will then receive the same. The requests are seen not as "have-to's" but rather as gifts of behavior change that one person can give to another. To give a gift meets the needs of one partner and promotes personal growth in the other. This strategy takes coercion out of behavior change.

Strategy 4: Reromanticizing the Relationship

One of the most overlooked aspects of a couple intervention is the enhancement of positive, caring behaviors. While couples understandably have a difficult time enjoying positive behaviors in the midst of a conflict, positive interaction may be the most important aspect of any couple's therapy. As we have seen, Gottman (1993) reported that long-term stable marriages have a constant ratio of five positive behaviors to every one negative behavior. The use of positive affect—humor, affection, interest, and support in problem-solving discussions—may be the main determinant of a couple's happiness. Gottman (1997) reported that only 30 seconds of positive affect separate marriages that are considered unhappy yet stable from those considered happy and stable.

People often feel that their partners should know what makes them happy. Our sense of entitlement says that our partner should be able to read our mind and know what we need at any given moment. Bitterness often results from these unmet expectations, which may set into motion feelings of futility and resignation, wherein the couple become depleted, discouraged, and contemptuous of each other.

The fourth strategy of IRT is for couples to decide what makes them feel cared for and to educate each other about these needs. They make an exhaustive list of caring behaviors. The therapist reviews with the couple activities—such as belly laughs and surprises—that add to the couple's sense of well-being. With this sense of care and friendship, they can navigate through the frustrations and remain a couple.

The enhancement of positive behaviors can begin informally in the first session, by assigning the couple the homework task of paying at least one compliment to each other each day. The therapist should check this homework each week and add a new task at the end of each session: Take at least one walk together, go out to dinner without the children, give each other a massage. After the couple has gained a communication skill, a new way of thinking about the marriage, and a way of dealing with frustrations, caring behaviors can be addressed formally, usually in about the tenth session. The first task will be for each partner to come up with a caring behavior list.

Not to be confused with the behavior change request list, a *caring behavior list* notes the past and present behaviors that create a pleasurable experience for the partner. The couple are asked to finish the following two sentence stems:

1. The things you do that make me feel loved and cared about are:
2. The things you have done in the past that made me feel loved and cared about are:

The responses should be extensive and may include such items as making a cup of tea for the partner, telling her she looks nice, asking him to go for a walk, rubbing her feet, opening the car door for him, and so on. They should share this list with each other in a dialogue process. This becomes a great opportunity to teach them how to use the couples dialogue in positive conversations: "You like when I bring you a cup of tea. That makes sense because you like it when I think positively of you. I imagine you feel loved and special when I do that for you." The couple are given the task of doing at least one caring behavior for each other each day. This begins the process of flooding each other positively and changing the temperature of the marriage, so that it becomes a warm rather than a cold environment.

Caring behaviors may also take the form of surprises. But what may be pleasurable for one partner may not be pleasurable for the other, and so the gift or surprise should be something that the other wants; otherwise, the gesture will fall flat, and both partners will feel unfulfilled. Partners are encouraged to listen to each other about what pleases them. For example, they may be walking through the mall, and the wife may say, "I really like those earrings," but like most people, she passes them by without a second thought. For her partner to later purchase those earrings for her would be a pleasant surprise. Many such "random droppings" occur in the course of everyday relating that would serve as a guide for surprises; like "I'd like to order that magazine one day," or "It would be nice to have just a few hours away from the baby one day to go to the park," or "We'll have to go into the city one day to shop." The Imago therapist will highlight them and encourage the partners to listen for what the other wants and to offer one surprise a month.

Finally, a powerful behavior to promote is belly laughs. Sustained belly laughs release endorphins that lead to an increased sense of well-being. Many couples at some point quit laughing together and begin to take everything very seriously. Of course laughter at its best is spontaneous, but there are ways to encourage couples to be silly, and the therapist can initiate and support the idea in the sessions. The game "I Can Do That" is a good place to start. In this game, one partner does a motion—for instance, tugging an ear—and then says, "I can do that. Can you do that?" The other mirrors the behavior and adds another one—maybe jumping on one foot—and says, "Yeah, I can do that. Can you do this?" The couple continues the game until they are doing five or six motions and, if all goes well, laughing at the silliness of it. Couples need to laugh together; this kind of activity gives them an excuse to do so.

The best means of knowing whether the caring behavior strategy is working is to listen to the quality of the couple's conversations. If the conversations seem more hopeful and positive and have more shared humor, the couple is adequately utilizing the behaviors. If they continue to be dominated by negativity, and the partners still try to avoid each other outside the session, caring behaviors need to be increased. Often you will hear couples say, "We don't have time to do things for each other." They need to learn the concept of "paying yourself first." Like saving money in the bank, if you give yourself what is left after paying for everything else, you will never have enough. Couples need to pay the relationship first through positive behaviors and dialogue so they will have the energy to deal with the frustrations that inevitably occur. Often this is opposite to the way the couple is thinking, so it may be one of the most important things they learn.

Clinical Indications for IRT Strategies

Imago strategies would seem to be appropriate for all couples under all circumstances. After all, a good marriage should have clear and safe communication, future goals, a means of expressing and acting upon frustrations, and lots of caring behaviors. For most couples, and especially those wounded at later developmental stages, IRT basically involves learning good relationship skills and developing a philosophy and plan for personal growth and the growth of the relationship. But by the time some couples come into therapy, so much negativity has built up that the strategies may have to be altered for a brief model.

For couples in difficult or conflictual marriages, the therapist may have to spend more time on helping them calm themselves enough to at least hear each other. It can be a tough time for both partners, each struggling to get his or her point across, and equally tough for the therapist, who tries to convince them that winning this argument is not as important as hearing that each has a point to make. Although these couples are entitled to learn the strategies used in IRT—good communication, safely expressing frustrations, caring behaviors—it is difficult to get these ideas across fully when both partners are on guard against insults. For couples at this stage of resistance, longer-term therapy may be necessary. Although the Imago therapist is always rooting for the marriage, divorce cannot be ruled out as an option.

Clinical Applications with an Individual:
Case Example

IRT is basically a couple therapy, but it can also be beneficial to individuals who are between relationships. Many people recently out of a relationship will seek therapy to grieve the ending of that relationship and, equally important, to learn how to make better choices in their next one.

Jean, a 42-year-old woman, recently ended her 20-year marriage to Dick, her college sweetheart. Jean has three children by this marriage, one in college and two soon to finish high school. About two years earlier, Jean and Dick recognized that they had little in common anymore and had grown distant. Couple therapy proved unsuccessful except to show them that they might be better off apart. They have been separated for one year and yet remain friends. As Jean says, "We are better friends than lovers."

Jean is still very sad about the ending of her marriage ("I always thought we would grow old together"), but she knows that it was for the best. She thinks about Dick often and questions what she could have done differently. She wants to know how she can do things differently next time: "I don't want to feel that pain again." Before Jean can move forward, she seemed to need to grieve her relationship with Dick, so she was asked to participate in what is called the Good-bye Exercise.

Because Dick was not available, the exercise was done in a Gestalt-type manner, in which Jean visualized Dick in a chair. The therapist then led her through a grieving process in which she would say good-bye to the relationship. First, she was asked to say good-bye to the good things about the relationship. What follows is an abbreviated version of her work.

Jean: I want to say good-bye to the way you touched me. I always loved the way you would run your hand across my back. I always felt supported by that. Good-bye. I want to say good-bye to the way you supported my ideas. You always believed in me. I will miss that. Good-bye.

Next, Jean said good-bye to the bad things about the relationship.

Jean: I want to say good-bye to the way you would come home late and not even apologize. I hated that you took me for granted. Good-bye to that. I want to say good-bye to your self-righteous attitude. You were so smug, and I hated that. Good-bye.

Finally, Jean was asked to say good-bye to her dreams for the relationship. She did so tearfully.

Jean: I want to say good-bye to the idea of growing old with you. We will not get gray together, and that feels sad to me. Good-bye. I want to say good-bye to being together as a couple when our children get married. That dream will not come to pass. Good-bye.

While this one session did not end Jean's grief, it did remind her that she was carrying this emotion with her. Occasionally, although regretfully, she would have to express it so that she could move beyond the incapacitating grip of grief and begin living her new life. To experience the grief now will let her fully commit herself to the next relationship she enters—her stated goal for entering therapy.

Learning Imago Processes as a Single Person

Because Jean attended therapy by herself, she was not able to have a dialogue with her partner. Single clients entering Imago therapy are often referred to Imago singles groups or weekend workshops so they can experience Imago processes with others. In Jean's case, since she wanted to do the work in individual sessions, the therapist explained dialogue, safety, and the behavior change request, and she practiced them. The Imago workup helped her understand that she is likely to unconsciously find someone who looks good at first but also has some negative traits necessary for her personal growth. For a single person looking for a long-term relationship, the real trick is to find someone who is willing to do the psychological work necessary to maintain an intimate relationship.

From the information gathered in the workup, Jean was able to do some "shadow" (Jung) work on herself. Dick had often complained about Jean's "clinging" behavior—she always seemed to be under him when she was home and to ask questions to which he felt she already knew the answers. She was aware of this tendency but felt that Dick's reaction was exaggerated. From the workup, she was able to see that her parents had been critical of her work around the house and at school but were too preoccupied to show her how to do it right. She sought answers from them, but they were short with her, which registered as an abandonment. As she got older, she began to lack confidence and looked to others to show her the way. She did this in her marriage as well and did not want to do it again in a new relationship.

Being able to see this pattern clearly, Jean worked for a few weeks at making decisions at home and believing that they were good decisions. She reported, "I decided to take that business class at the community college, and I did not look back once!" It would take many more decisions like this to make a full change, but she was off to a good start. She also recognized that she might again become involved with someone who would be short with her, and that they would have to work on it when the conflict arose. At this point, Jean's future relationships were becoming conscious to her, and she felt she could enter into them with open eyes.

Relationships are work. Romantic love blinds couples to that fact and gives the sense that relationships are easy and self-sustaining. Single clients need to learn the wisdom of long-term stable and happy marriages: romantic love ends and must give way to mature love. This love causes the partners to stay in the game, through dialogue, even when quitting seems easier. Couples in mature love maintain caring behaviors, even when they do not care very much at a given moment. Feelings of resentment and despair come and go. The real trick is to get through those times without deep regrets by taking the high road: minimal criticism, contempt, and passive-aggressive behavior, and as many caring behaviors as one can muster considering the circumstances.

The best time to learn IRT skills is as a preventive, before or early in a relationship. The purpose of IRT with single clients is to educate them about the nature of relationships, heal wounds from past relationships, look at blocks that prevent them from experiencing good relationships, and help them to become conscious of the purpose of the relationship and its patterns.

Clinical Applications with a Couple: Case Example

Rich and Susan are both 35 years old and met seven years earlier while working together at a computer company. She currently works part-time as a computer consultant, and he is a programmer on the night shift at a software company. They chose this work arrangement so that they could both participate in the care of their 6-year-old son. They decided to seek therapy in anticipation of the birth of their second child in approximately five months.

For the last two years, things did not go well for Rich and Susan, and they figured that the added stress of the baby would only make things worse. Both the level and number of their arguments increased, and their sex life significantly worsened. They were fully aware that their work and sleep schedule, as well as hormonal changes from the pregnancy, made things, especially sex, more difficult. But Rich and Susan felt that there was more to it, since they had made every attempt to spend time together and were committed to the relationship. They felt at a loss about what to do about their present situation. They stated that while they were friends, they were questioning their love for each other, which felt scary to them. Both were on the verge of tears in the first session and seemed to lack hope for the relationship.

Creating Safety and the Couples Dialogue

The therapist spent the first session connecting with the couple and introducing couples dialogue to them. While Imago work is more centered on the couple's learning the work and utilizing it at home, it was important for Rich and Susan to leave with a sense of hope and faith in the therapist (Lambert, 1992; Sperry et al., 1997). The therapist took a brief history and assured the couple that the problems they were experiencing were not unusual and usually responded well to the course of treatment. Its success depended on their regular use of the skills and ideas learned in the session. The therapist explained that they would get new information and skills to work on each week, and that their regular attendance was important to their learning the Imago processes.

After a brief introduction to IRT, the partners were asked to turn toward each other and for three minutes display a typical frustration. That interaction went as follows:

Rich: The other night, we were having such a good time. It felt good to be with you. We were laughing and talking so nicely. Then out of the blue, you asked me what I liked and did not like about the relationship. I was dumbfounded! How could you do that in the middle of this nice moment? It just changed everything!

Susan: I just wanted to know. We were having a nice time, and I thought it was a good time to ask.

Rich: How can you do that? Can't we just have a nice time without your analyzing it?

Susan: It seemed like the right time to me. Why not talk about it then when we're feeling good? When we're fighting is not a good time. What would be a good time to ask about our relationship?

Rich: Maybe never. Can't the moment tell you that I feel good about
    things? You know I don't talk much about how I feel. That's what
    you are good at.

Susan: But I need to know. It's like food to me. I need to know where I
    stand. You don't talk to me. You don't tell me anything about us.
    You're good with sports scores or what appliance we should buy
    according to the consumer magazines, but damn it, I need more
    than that.

Rich: Just hold on to this thought, Susan. When you are like this, I
    don't like the relationship. When you are nice, I like it. Now let's
    drop it.

Susan and Rich were on two different playing fields. Susan wanted to
know where she stood; Rich wanted to leave well enough alone. Their
communication style is best described as a diatribe—one says what is on
his or her mind while the other thinks up a defense, and then the pattern
repeats itself. The argument becomes highly charged, and the reptilian
brain takes over with its fight-flight responses. Susan and Rich were
introduced to the first Imago strategy of creating safety and the couples
dialogue. They were asked to relax and close their eyes. They were
guided to a beach scene, an image they had indicated would relax them.
They spent five minutes in this visualization and were instructed to
return to this place if they felt like responding out of turn during their
upcoming dialogue. The beach scene would become their "safe place"
in which to listen to their partner. They were then instructed in the
three-part couples dialogue process. Although the first few sessions
were awkward, Rich and Susan were eventually able to produce a dialogue like this

Susan: I get really scared when you don't talk to me. You are withdrawn
    sometimes, and it leaves me without any information on how we
    are doing.

Rich: So you are saying that you get scared when I get quiet and with-
    drawn. You don't get the information you need on how we are
    doing. Did I get that? Is there more?

Susan: Yes, I need contact. I know that you do fine with a computer and
    a newspaper and don't need as much contact as I do, but I need
    conversation. I need you as a friend.

Rich: So you feel as if you need more contact than I do. You need for me to talk to you, and you need me to be a friend. Did I get that? Is there more?

Susan: Yes, I think that is why I don't feel sexual around you like I used to. I know that you can just have sex, but I can't do that. I need conversation. I need to be listened to so that I can feel close to you.

Rich: So you think that our lack of conversation and contact is why we don't have sex like we used to. You need to feel close to the person you make love with, and for you that occurs when you are listened to. I can see that. What makes sense to me is that you are a people person and need contact with someone. I imagine that would make you feel ignored, lonely, and invisible.

Susan: Yes. Thank you for listening.

Susan was then able to reciprocate, doing a good job of listening to Rich talk about how he needed time alone; time to think and be by himself. He complained that his life had become work, sleep, and taking care of their child, with very little time for himself. Rich and Susan were able to learn the dialogue in five sessions. They used it three times a week, and during tense moments they were able to establish contact and lessen their frustration with each other. On the occasions when frustration got the best of them, they later returned to the dialogue when they felt safe. They were taught that anger is inevitable and is not necessarily destructive to a marriage unless it is accompanied by defensiveness, criticism, contempt, belligerence, or stonewalling (Gottman, 1994). A crucial part of the process is to return to the issue after calming down and to do so within the structure of dialogue. While issues continued to emerge, Rich and Susan reported that the intensity of their interactions was lessened and that their conversations felt more productive.

Relationship Reeducation

Rich and Susan were interested in Imago theory and its relevance to their marriage. During the course of their work, they were presented with information on safety in communication; child development and its influence on mate selection; the development and restriction of the social self; and IRT's view of the purpose of marriage as a healing vehicle.

Rich and Susan completed the Imago workup and discovered that Susan seemed to be dealing with her parents' having ignored her as a child. The parents were passionate, religious people who paid more attention to their community activities than to her. She longed for their attention but seemed to get it only when she participated in church activities, where the community viewed them as a model family. Susan resented that view because in reality she felt very lonely in her family. Her parents told her where to go, what to do, and how to think, and so Susan learned to look to them for guidance on "what to do next." She became rigid and structured in her personality, yet unsure of herself. She was hesitant with her ideas and sought the closeness in her adult relationships that she had not had as a child. Her social self depended on her feeling and sensing ability.

Rich, on the other hand, came from a very quiet family that did not speak of feelings. But although quiet, the family was structured and had clear, rigid expectations. Those expectations included taking care of your own problems and dealing with them logically rather than emotionally. Rich became a clear, logical thinker, a loner who was good at fixing things but believed that others should fix their own problems. His ability to empathize with others was minimal, and his social self depended on his being able to think logically and accomplish things.

That Rich and Susan were frustrated with each other came as no surprise. What Susan most wanted—empathy and help making decisions—was what Rich had difficulty giving. What Rich most wanted for Susan—to figure things out logically and to do things without his help—was particularly tough for her, because of her early wounding. And yet each was right about the other. Rich needed to learn empathy and to develop his sensing and feeling parts. Susan needed to gain some independence and to develop her confidence and her logical side. Once some understanding of these issues was in place, the couple was able to move on to making behavior change requests.

Behavior Change Request

As stated above, Rich and Susan's main frustrations, or core scenes, were clear: she wanted empathy and help from him, while he wanted her to think logically and do things on her own. These seemingly opposite goals resonate with most couples in therapy: what one wants, the other lacks.

Susan turned one of her frustrations into a desire: "I would like you to listen to me talk about my day." From this starting point, she developed three behavior change requests for Rich.

1. Twice a week, within an hour of your getting home, I would like you to come to me and ask me how my day was and to listen to me for 15 minutes, using the couples dialogue.
2. Once a week after we dialogue, I would like for you to say something like "Boy, it sounds like you had a rough day" or "You had a productive day. You must be proud," so I know you are connecting with what I said.
3. One time a week, I would like you to offer to help me with a situation I am struggling with at home or at my job.

Susan's behavior change requests would challenge Rich to stretch his typical range of behavior. By dealing with Susan on a feeling or intuitive level, as most of her list requested, Rich would have to stretch into behaviors that had lain dormant for most of his life. This corresponds to the Imago principles that frustrations are desires stated negatively, and that desires changed into specific requests exercise the missing self and call each partner into wholeness of expression. Conversely, Rich's requests centered on expanding Susan's thinking and acting parts.

1. Twice a week, I would like you to take a household project that you would normally bring to me and outline a plan of action on paper that you think would solve the problem. Prior to undertaking it, we'll discuss it, and I will listen to you using the couples dialogue.
2. Twice a week, when you get home, I would like an hour to do some things for myself, like exercising, reading, taking a walk, or doing nothing. I would like you to be totally responsible for any household activity during that time.
3. Once a week, I would like you to show me, with enthusiasm, a project that you completed on your own.

Over a three-week period, Susan and Rich each transformed six frustrations into desires and behavior change requests. This gave each of them 18 behaviors from which to choose in attempting to work on meeting his or her partner's needs. They could address the requests at their own pace and were encouraged to move slowly through them so as not to become overwhelmed by the work. Growth is slow and steady. To become enduring habits, the changes need to be consistent and practiced regularly. Rich and Susan had educated each other on the things each needed to do to accomplish personal growth goals. They had received their blueprints for their growth.

Caring Behaviors

Of course, Rich and Susan's life could not be all work and no play. Two sessions were spent working on caring behaviors and creating a vision for the marriage. The therapist gave them statistics about stable marriages and positive behaviors, and they understood that they needed to do more to show that they cared for each other. In one session, they developed a caring behavior list. Each listed activities and behaviors that would make him or her feel loved and cared about. Unlike the behavior change request, the caring behaviors consisted of activities in which the partners were already engaged. This time Susan and Rich looked for an increase in these activities. Some of the items on Susan's list:

I like when you bring me a cup of coffee in the morning.
I love when you get show tickets and surprise me with a night out.
I feel cared about when you rub my back while we watch TV.
I feel cared about when you help me clean up so we can snuggle on the
   couch.

Among Rich's items:

I like when I am doing work at home and you bring me some tea.
I like when you make me stop working and snuggle with you.
I feel cared about when you make my lunch.
I really like when you call me Sweetheart.

The therapist asked them to make an extensive list to give to each other so they would have many behaviors from which to choose to express caring. They were encouraged to do at least one caring behavior a day, and to hug and snuggle more. Such affection does not necessarily mean that sex will follow, which is an especially common thought among men. Many women have reported that hugs begin to feel unsafe because of this expectation. Caring behaviors, surprises, and belly laughs were recommended as daily activities in an effort to promote their feeling of well-being and to increase their "money in the bank" for when the difficult times arise. It is difficult to express caring behaviors when resentments and past wrongs crop up, but it is essential to the survival of any marriage.

In another session, the therapist asked Rich and Susan to develop their relationship vision. They were now about ten sessions into the process and were feeling hopeful about their future together. This session had them map that future by writing down their dream relationship. They acknowledged that they were not in this dream relationship yet. The vision was to serve as a guide and point them in the right direction. Their vision included:

We are friends to each other.
We handle disagreement through dialogue.
We are financially secure.
We take care of our bodies.
We parent our children in partnership.
We take walks together.
We take regular vacations together.
We listen to each other's feelings in dialogue.
We are proud of each other's accomplishments.
We have traditional family rituals.

Creating a vision offers hope to a troubled couple. Newlyweds rarely consider creating such a vision because they are still in the thralls of romantic love. When romantic love ends, however, a relationship vision can act as a guide for the couple. The vision points them in the direction of fulfillment rather than regret and resentment. Rich and Susan established a vision that held the promise of carrying them through the rough early-childhood years, through the various stages of family life, and into a future when they would be alone again. The vision could be changed at any time, and they would have to review it regularly for it to remain meaningful in the marriage, but it served as a starting point for partners who just several months earlier wondered if they would make it through another year.

At the end of their 12-session treatment, Rich and Susan had new skills and a plan for their marriage. The road would not be easy, but now they had a map to guide them. They had learned an essential communication skill and come to recognize the importance of emotional safety. They had forged a new understanding of why they had chosen each other and of the unconscious purpose of their relationship.

Concluding Summary

Imago relationship therapy is an integrative approach to couple therapy that operates in what is referred to as the relational paradigm (Luquet & Hannah, 1998). It sees growth and healing as occurring within the context of committed, intimate relationships. IRT therapists view empowering the couple with skills and ideas as primordial to the therapy. The therapist becomes a coach, or facilitator, to the partners, who, after acquiring some basic skills, do the therapy themselves.

The basic strategies of IRT are to create emotional safety, teach a communication skill, and help couples understand the reason for their relationship, express frustrations in healthy ways, and treat each other with the love and respect with which they entered the relationship. When couples are able to achieve these things, the relationship blooms. When the relationship blooms, the partners can bloom as individuals, stronger and better able to fill in life's basic sentence stem, "I am a person who . . ." Individuals in conscious relationships become conscious individuals.

References

Buber, M. (1952). *Eclipse of God*. New York: Harper.

Gottman, J. M. (1993). The goal of conflict engagement, escalation, and avoidance in marital interaction: A longitudinal view of five types of couples. *Journal of Clinical and Consulting Psychology, 61* (1), 6–15.

Gottman, J. M. (1994). *Why marriages succeed or fail*. New York: Simon and Schuster.

Gottman, J. M. (1997). Why marriages succeed or fail: Report from the love lab. Paper presented at the conference of the Coalition for Marriage, Family, and Couples Education, Washington, D.C. [Audiotape available.]

Gottman, J. M. (1998). Predicting marital happiness and stability from newly-wed interactions. *Journal of Marriage and the Family, 60,* 5–22.

Hendrix, H. (1996). The evolution of imago relationship therapy: A personal and theoretical journey. *Journal of Imago Relationship Therapy, 1*(1), 1–18.

Hendrix, H. (1988). *Getting the love you want: A guide for couples.* New York: Henry Holt.

Hendrix, H. (1992). *Keeping the love you find: A guide for singles.* New York: Pocket Books.

Hendrix, H., & Hunt, H. (1997). *Giving the love that heals: A guide for parents.* New York: Pocket Books.

Lambert, M. J. (1992). Implications of outcome research for psychotherapy integration. In J. C. Norcross & M. R. Goldfreid (Eds.), *Handbook of psychotherapy integration.* New York: Basic Books.

Luquet, W. (1996). *Short-term couples therapy: The imago model in action.* New York: Brunner/Mazel.

Luquet, W., & Hannah, M. T. (Eds). (1998). *Healing in the relational paradigm: The imago relationship therapy casebook.* Philadelphia: Brunner/Mazel.

Luquet, W. J., & Hendrix, H. (1998). Imago relationship therapy. In F. Datillio (Ed.), *Integrative cases in couples and family therapy: A cognitive behavioral approach.* New York: Guilford.

Money, J. (1986). *Lovemaps: Clinical concepts of sexual/erotic health and pathology, paraphilia, and gender transposition in childhood, adolescence, and maturity.* New York: Irvington.

Sperry, L., Brill, P. L., Howard, K. I. & Grissom, G.R. (1996) *Treatment outcomes in psychotherapy and psychiatric interventions.* New York: Brunner/Mazel.

Teilhard de Chardin, P. (1968). *Writings in time of war.* London: Collins.

Annotated Bibliography

The following books contain more information on Imago Relationship Therapy. *The Journal of Imago Relationship Therapy* is available from Psychosocial Press, an imprint of International Universities Press. P.O. Box 1524, Madison, CT 06443–1524.

Hendrix, H. (1988). *Getting the love you want: A guide for couples.* New York: Henry Holt. The best-selling book that began the international interest in Imago Relationship Therapy. Although written for the lay reader, it has much to offer the professional and is recommended reading for clients and those interested in the basics of IRT.

Hendrix, H. (1992). *Keeping the love you find: A guide for singles.* New York: Pocket Books. Hendrix's second book is designed for the single person who is hoping to enter a healthier relationship. This book contains more Imago theory and is also recommended to the professional seeking further information on IRT.

Hendrix, H., & Hunt, H. (1997). *Giving the love that heals: A guide for parents.* New York: Pocket Books. Hendrix and Hunt make IRT principles available to parents. This book is not a book of parenting tips; rather, its premise is that parents have to heal from their own childhood so that they do not pass the wounds on to their children. Parents will also learn how to give children what they need at their various developmental levels.

Luquet, W. (1996). *Short-term couples therapy: The imago model in action.* New York: Brunner/Mazel. The first IRT book written for the professional, it takes the therapist through a step-by-step course of Imago couple treatment. Clear and very practical, many therapists report it is the most dog-eared book in their collection. Contains 36 pages of forms ready for photocopying.

Luquet, W., & Hannah, M.T. (Eds.). (1998). *Healing in the relational paradigm: The imago relationship therapy casebook.* Philadelphia: Brunner/Mazel. Fifteen diverse case studies by various Imago therapy contributors clearly illustrate how to use IRT in the office setting. Beautifully written, this book contains cases that illustrate the concept of developmental wounding, and how to use IRT with various populations and situations. Chapters include working with African-American couples, Hispanic couples, and gay and lesbian couples; and with issues of HIV, ADD, affairs, substance abuse, sexual dysfunction, and spirituality.

14

───∞───

Psychoeducational Strategies

Luciano L'Abate

The purpose of this chapter is to review two psychoeducational strategies for brief therapy with individuals and couples: (1) psychoeducational social skills training (PE-SST) programs, and (2) programmed distance writing (PDW), used in conjunction with computer-assisted interventions (CAI). Usually, both PE-SST and PDW/CAI focus on a specific topic, ranging anywhere from assertiveness for individuals to negotiation, problem solving, or intimacy for couples; are composed of a finite (anywhere from 3 to 10 or more) number of sessions (PE-SST) or assignments (PDW/CAI) respectively; follow prearranged scripts that may vary in structure but are systematically sequential, following a preordained arrangement of plans; and have costs that are known before the intervention.

Carlson and Sperry (1990) are responsible for promoting "psychoeducational strategies in marital therapy" a decade ago. In this model, the professional helper's role is to teach, coach, and impart new skills rather than listen, empathize, and passively be available with a minimum of action, direction, and planning. While traditional talk therapies may tend to gravitate toward the more passive polarity of "relationship skills," PE-SST and PDW/CAI strategies tend to gravitate toward the active, "structuring skills" aspects of help giving. Although these two polarities seem nonoverlapping as presented here, many professional helpers do indeed overlap both strategies in their everyday practice. There are, however, differences between the two roles—"teacher" versus "therapist"—that need highlighting along a continuum of preventive strategies rather than a dichotomous and unrealistic split between relationship and structuring skills.

Preferably, the first strategy, PE-SST, could be considered a *universal primary prevention* to apply to many *at-risk* individuals and couples, to prevent individual distress and couple/marital conflict or neglect/abuse from developing in the first place. PE-SST programs can be used with almost any individual or couple working face-to-face with a professional helper or quasi-professional trainer (L'Abate, 1999-b). Because of their predetermined, already-structured format, PE-SST programs may be administered by para-and semiprofessionals who specialize in one specific PE-SST and nothing else. PDW/CAI, on the other hand, is conceived as *targeted secondary prevention*, seeking to lower rates of established, *in-need* cases of distress and abuse/conflict/divorce for *selected* individuals and couples. This strategy in this case implies working at a distance from a professional helper through correspondence, fax, or Internet, with limited or even no face-to-face contact between patient and professional. *Indicated tertiary prevention* seeks to decrease the amount of disability associated with an already-existing *in-crisis*, clinical, chronic, or critical condition in a distressed individual or couple who definitely needs professional intervention, medication, psychotherapy, and even hospitalization (L'Abate, 1990; Mrazek & Haggerty, 1994, pp. 19–20).

Both PE-SST and PDW/CAI strategies can stand alone or can join synergistically with each other as well as with many other types of intervention. For instance, they can be used in conjunction with traditional verbal psychotherapy and with new nontraditional treatment approaches, like virtual reality therapy, neurobiofeedback, manualized therapies, and eye movement desensitization and reprogramming (L'Abate, 1999c).

The Laboratory Method in Clinical Practice

Over the last third of a century, starting in 1963, my students and I have been involved in an enterprise called "the laboratory method in clinical psychology" (L'Abate, 1973), which served as the basis for subsequent, preventive work with individuals, couples, and families. This method was set up as an attempt to lower the costs of mental health practices; find more cost-effective ways of service delivery; link clinical practice with research; and develop theory on the basis of practice. Part of the motivation for the creation of this method was strictly practical. How can a professional help as many people as possible per unit of her or his time at the lowest possible cost, without sacrificing standards and criteria of responsible practice? I became convinced, and I still am, that the best way to help people who are at risk for personal, marital, or family breakdown and who are in need of some form of help (not necessarility crisis intervention or psychotherapy) is to work at a distance from them through intermediaries in face-to-face situations or, more recently, through the written medium, as in PDW/CAI (L'Abate, in press-a).

The hierarchical approach that would come about through the use of intermediaries (a professional-in-charge, semiprofessional, or paraprofessional) is no different from other existing structures in human enterprises, be they business, medicine, construction, or even the military. The reason for these structures is efficiency. Architects and engineers cannot build skyscrapers with their bare hands. After designing the blueprint of a skyscraper, a host of specialized personnel with different skills are necessary to carry out the actual work. In psychotherapy, there is no way that individual professionals are going to help all the individuals and couples at risk, in need, or in crisis through face-to-face contact (L'Abate, 1990). We have barely sufficient personnel to take care of couples in crisis, let alone couples at risk or in need. There are too many couples at risk and in need to think that the goal of caring for them can be achieved only by qualified professionals.

Consequently, we need to rely either on subprofessional and paraprofessional personnel or on ways, like PDW/CAI, to reach individuals and couples that are even more efficient and cost-effective than the personal contact of one-couple/one-therapist based mostly on talk. Elsewhere, I argue that in psychological interventions talk is both cheap and expensive and, in comparison with other media (nonverbal and written), both inefficient and uncontrollable (L'Abate, 1999c). Personal contact may be necessary with people in crisis, but for every individal or couple in crisis, there are at least four or five other individuals or couples at risk or in need of some kind of preventive intervention. There are not enough professionals trained or interested in preventive work to deal with so many people. Hence, different and cost-effective approaches are needed to reach and help them. In addition to intermediaries, PDW and CAI, among other approaches (L'Abate, 1990, 1992; L'Abate & Odell, 1995), may perhaps allow us to get the job done.

Evaluation as the Cornerstone of the Laboratory Method

Pre-post-intervention evaluation of individual children, couples, and families (L'Abate & Wagner, 1985; L'Abate, Wildman, O'Callaghan, Simon, Allison, Kahn, & Rainwater, 1975) became the cornerstone of the laboratory method. But evaluation without reevaluation may become futile, unless one is responsible for the whole process of evaluation-intervention-reevaluation and follow-up. Evaluation for evaluation's sake may be needed when responsibility for intervention is in the hands of another professional who might not be interested in the final outcome of the intervention. It mattered to me to learn the final outcome of any intervention for which I was responsible, even and especially at a distance from the respondents.

Differentiating Between Technical and Professional Skills

In evaluation, *technical* skills consist of the administration and scoring of test instruments, while *professional* skills consist of interpreting test battery results, reporting psychodiagnostic results, making recommendations to clients, and referring professionals. This distinction is based on two axes of time and knowledge. Technical skills, like the administration of an intelligence test, take more time to apply but require less knowledge than the professional skills necessary to interpret that test. Professional skills, like the ability to interpret the results of an intelligence test, take less time to apply but require much more knowledge: of the empirical background of the test, its statistical properties, its research results, and so on. Paraprofessional skills may be limited to advanced graduate students supervising beginning graduate students with the support and supervision of the professional (Jessee & L' Abate, 1981).

Applying this distinction to preventive interventions, technical skills consist of administering the structured interventions found in enrichment programs and programmed materials, which involves keeping in touch with respondents and reporting to a supervising professional. These technicians need to have people skills in order to establish and maintain rapport, as well as the ability to administer the materials responsibly, with complete notes for the supervisor's consumption. Professional skills consist of abilities in crisis intervention and symptom reduction; decision making about different interventional approaches; and training, support, and supervision of technical personnel.

Changing Behavior at a Distance Through Intermediaries

A variety of considerations prompted the creation of structured interventions for couples and families: the advent of family therapy and the need to develop structured methods of training for couples and families; the relative ineffectiveness of play therapy with children without the involvement of parents and siblings, who saw the "identified patient" (IP) as being the one in need of help, exempting themselves from responsibility for making changes in the family; and therefore the need to avoid accepting the family's definition and making the referred child the IP by evaluating the child alone and "treating" him or her without intervening in the family as a unit.

These considerations prompted me to establish new ways of intervening with couples, using graduate students as intermediaries. Many graduate students had never interviewed a couple or family, or if they had received any psychotherapy experience, it was strictly of an individual rather than a multirelational nature. With the help of these students, I started to create structured enrichment programs for couples and families that involved evaluating them before and after intervention.

Social Skills Training (SST) Programs for Individuals and Couples

The last half-century has seen the development of a plethora of PE-SST programs for individuals, couples, and families (L'Abate & McHenry, 1983). More recently, Berger and Hannah (1999) have edited a handbook that contains most, if not all, of the PE-SST programs for couples available on the market: relationship enhancement; Minnesota couples communication; American association couples enrichment; conjugal relationship enhancement; marriage encounter; practical applications of intimate relationship; prevention and relationship enchancement; Imago relationship therapy; Adlerian enrichment program; MARDILAB; and Enrich-Prepare. Each program's background lies in theoretical (mostly humanistic) and empirical underpinnings. A wide range of research supports some of them, while others are based mostly on impressionistic evidence. The interested reader should consult Berger and Hannah (1999) for an appraisal of these programs.

Structured Enrichment Programs for Couples

Most of the programs listed above have one characteristic in common: they all follow a funnel approach. That is, the same program is applied to a variety of conditions for couples—one size fits all. By contrast, my students and I have followed a more structured approach consisting of a variety of programs that we can match with marital and family problems with greater specificity. Since we were dealing with functional and semifunctional couples who wanted to make things better for themselves, these programs were intended to develop and enrich rather than to change (Kochalka, Buzas, L'Abate, McHenry, & Gibson, 1987; Kochalka & L'Abate, 1997; L'Abate, 1974, 1977, 1981a, 1981b, 1982, 1985, 1986a, in press-b; L'Abate, Kearns, Richardson, & Dow, 1985; L'Abate & O'Callaghan, 1977; L'Abate, O'Callaghan, Piat, Dunn, Margolis, Prigge, & Soper, 1976; L'Abate, Wagner, & Weeks, 1980).

These programs were developed as a didactic way of teaching graduate students to work with couples and families under structured conditions, to minimize anxiety; and they could start working with functional and semifunctional couples before working with dysfunctional ones. Instructions were followed verbatim, from written programs. This practicum experience brought about the creation of a graduate course in preventive approaches with couples, where students would enrich couples and also produce an enrichment program of their choice. These programs produced a library of 50 programs (L'Abate & Weinstein, 1987) and accompanying case studies (L'Abate & Stevens, 1986; L'Abate & Young, 1987).

No theoretical assumptions were made at the time (L'Abate, 1985). The most immediate goal was simply to give a structure for training students to work with couples under controlled conditions that would minimize anxiety and maximize learning (Jessee & L'Abate, 1981). Programs were developed eclectically from different theoretical and atheoretical sources. As this approach grew, programs were developed from a variety of theory-related and theory-independent sources. Three doctoral dissertations (Ganahl, 1981; Sloan, 1983; Wildman, 1976) and a consumer satisfaction survey (L'Abate & Rupp, 1981) evaluated the short-term outcome of these programs, with positive outcomes in comparison with contrast groups. Another doctoral dissertation (Yarbrough, 1983) was completed outside the GSU Family Study Center. In another follow-up study, only a handful out of more than 300 couples and families dropped out. A 15–20 year follow-up received responses from 16 of these couples or families, who by then had changed addresses and, in some cases, had even forgotten what had happened that many years earlier (Cusinato, 1988, unpublished research).

In addition to the primary goal of training students, a second goal enriched (i.e., made things better with) already-functioning couples and families. We found that clinical families could not be enriched at the outset (L'Abate & Weeks, 1976), but they could be enriched *after* the initial crisis that brought them into therapy was resolved—that is, after they had been "normalized" through therapy (Kochalka et al., 1987). By providing a structure by which couple and family members may come together and answer questions that they had never been asked before, they could learn to love and negotiate better than if they had never had this experience.

The 50 programs are divided into lessons (3 or more), with 5 or more exercises per lesson, for a total of more than 1,000 exercises, coded for 9 dimensions of family interaction (Kochalka & L'Abate, 1997). The section of these programs relevant to prevention with couples deals with developmental stages in the family life cycle, starting with premarital issues, marital issues, and sexuality (6 programs), man-woman relationships (7 programs), parenting (6 programs), and late stages of the family life cycle (4 programs). A second section deals with couples/families structurally, according to their level of emotional/educational/intellectual development, from introductory (3 programs), to intermediate (4 programs), to affective (4 programs), cognitive (4 programs), and relational skill building (4 programs). A third section contains programs for non-traditional couples/families (divorce, single-parent, adoption, blended, and dual-employment). A fourth section contains programs for dysfunctional couples/families (general, physically handicapped, mentally handicapped, alcoholics, drugs, and depression).

Each couple (usually obtained from our student body as an experiment for which they received class credit) was interviewed and evaluated on a before-after enrichment basis with a battery of paper-and-pencil marital self-report tests. On the basis of the enricher(s)' impressions, the couple's stated needs and wants, and objective test results, the couple was offered a choice among three enrichment programs that seemed to approximate their needs, as perceived by them, as well as by the enrichers and supervisor. After they chose a program, each couple was usually seen for 6 sessions, after which they were reevaluated with the same test battery and received a feedback, debriefing session (L'Abate & Young, 1987). Each couple was enriched alone with one or two enrichers. Couples were enriched sometimes in their homes and sometimes in the GSU Family Study Center, according to their schedules, the schedules of the enrichers, and the logistics of being seen in either place.

Within each topic (i.e., program) there would be lessons relating to that topic. For instance, if the marital relationship was relevant, then programs related to marital issues were presented for consideration (negotiation, assertiveness, intimacy, etc.). If the major issue requested by a couple was parenting, this program started with a lesson on deciding to have a baby, expecting a baby, parental assertiveness, parental effectiveness, parents and teenagers, and separating teenagers from their parents. Each of these programs would break down into lessons (3 to 6) about processes of decision making, problem solving, and the like.

Because programs are written down verbatim, they can be administered with a minimum of training. Practice took place through role playing, in which "mock" families made up of trainees themselves took turns at being "enrichers" and family members. After becoming acquainted with evaluation and the process of structured enrichment, trainees started to work with a volunteer functional or semifunctional couple, being supervised in group about the process from their notes and/or videotapes. They learned by doing. This approach led to the conclusion that given a specific and clear structure, paraprofessionals with personal but no professional qualifications can successfully be taught to enrich couples. Even though graduate students may not be thought of as paraprofessionals, many of them, especially those with a baccalaureate degree and no clinical experience, had as yet received no substantive training to qualify as professionals.

Case Study in Structured Enrichment with a Couple

Mr. and Mrs. Jones, a middle-aged couple of average educational and economic background, were referred by a local mental health clinic for help in dealing with their children. Mr. Jones had an advanced degree in education. Mrs. Jones had one year of secretarial school. In addition, Mr. Jones, a high school teacher, felt that he had problems controlling his students in class. He had been put on probation after a heart attack and was considering retiring from teaching altogether. Their children, a teenage girl, a teenage boy who dropped out of high school, and a preteen boy in middle school, came in reluctantly. After the initial interview, even though the family had received 10 sessions of family therapy elsewhere, it appeared that their situation was at best chaotic, like a ship without a rudder. Both parents were unable to give any direction to their lives, let alone to the lives of their children. Nonetheless, they spoke quite freely about themselves and each other, holding back very little. The children felt that the parents needed help, and they refused to come in for any other sessions. They had had enough of the therapy and were "sick and tired of that stuff." Hence, the parents were accepted for structured enrichment, even though they were still "clinical" and "in crisis." They were administered the standard GSU test battery consisting of pictures rather than words: Feelings in the Family and the Animal Concepts Picture Series (L'Abate & Wagner, 1985). These tests supported the conclusion that there was still a great deal of confusion and chaos in the way both parents defined themselves as individuals, partners, and parents.

After the test results were discussed, the parents were presented with three possible enrichment programs: Transactional, Death and Dying, and Separating Parents from Teenagers (L'Abate & Weinstein, 1987). The parents chose the Transactional program, which starts with the question:

"What does it mean to be a man or a woman in your family?" Their responses essentially conformed to the traditional stereotyped distinction between the man as provider and the woman as homemaker. The second question was: "What does it mean to be old or young in your family-of-origin?" The differentiating issue was responsibility—the older one is, the more responsibility one has to undertake. The third question was: "What happens to one of you if something happens to the other?" Their responses indicated their awareness of the transactional nature of their relationship.

The two graduate students administering this program felt that the couple should give greater stress to feelings and emotions. The couple cared for each other, but did not know how to express their care. Consequently, the Helpfulness program (L'Abate & Weinstein, 1987) was administered with the couple's permission. In the first lesson, "seeing the good," both partners shared what good they saw in themselves and each other. Mr. Jones had a great deal of difficulty in answering this exercise, especially in seeing the good in himself and in expressing positive feelings toward his wife. The second lesson of this program deals with how caring is expressed in the marriage. When their answers at the presentational level (instrumental role for husband, and expressive role for the wife) were challenged, they were able to dig a little deeper in their relationship and express how lonely they were in their marriage because there was little sharing. They were locked into their fixed, traditional roles and had as yet not found a way to share their inner selves and to become more flexible in their roles, so that the husband would be more expressive and the wife more instrumental. At the end of the session, Mr. Jones indicated his desire to share in the cleaning of the house and in doing the laundry. Mrs. Jones countered by showing more interest in her husband's work difficulties.

The third lesson, "sharing of hurts," dealt with a topic that was crucial in their becoming intimate. Up to the present, they either did not share hurts or dealt with them with pat and superficial solutions. Their inability to share hurts produced distance and inadequate affection and very little sex. Mr. Jones was especially threatened by the whole topic, trying desperately to rely on his role as provider and avoiding the more subtle feelings of affection and trust. Mrs. Jones also indicated conflicts in this area. She wanted closeness and affection but at the same time was afraid of them, since she, like her husband, had never experienced these feelings in her family of origin.

The next lesson, "forgiveness," was interpreted by the couple as consisting of "overlooking." Elaborating on this topic as giving up demands for perfection and accepting our humanness as imperfection seemed to bring up a spark in both of them. They had never given any thought to this topic, even though it was so crucial to their relationship. Mrs. Jones acknowledged her difficulty in forgiving because she collected all her hurts and put them into a gunnysack, to be opened during arguments and fights.

The last lesson of this program, "enjoyment," dealt with what they did as individuals, partners, and parents to enjoy life. Their discussion revealed the paucity of things that they did to enjoy life, since life for them, as well as for their families of origin (during the Great Depression), was oriented strictly to survival and nothing else. When asked to plan something enjoyable for themselves as individuals, as partners, and as parents, they formulated plans for the coming week to be carried out at the three levels, individual, marital, and parental.

Both spouses were then reevaluated with the same tests given at the beginning. This time the results clearly indicated Mr. Jones's serious depression and Mrs. Jones's anger and frustration in dealing with him as a "failure." Mr. Jones's absolutistic thinking made it difficult for him to accept and deal with different shades of gray: "You are either perfect or you are not." "If you are imperfect you are bad; if you are perfect you are good." In the post-test debriefing session, where various individual and marital assets were affirmed ("You both care deeply about each other." "You are very honest and committed to the marriage and to your children," etc.), they indicated that the process had brought to the fore their need for additional therapy. They had brought the children to therapy to avoid looking at themselves as individuals and as a couple. Consequently, they asked for less structured marital therapy. They received it from a more advanced team of graduate students under my supervision. A once-a-month series of three sessions was contracted.

The first therapy session was dedicated to their sharing hurts by performing the Hurt Sharing exercise related to this intervention (L'Abate, 1986, 1997b, 1999). In performing this exercise, they both started to cry uncontrollably and ended up hugging each other tightly. As a homework assignment, they were given Pennebaker's task (1997), to write about their past hurts for 20 minutes a day for four consecutive days (Esterling, L'Abate, Murray, & Pennebaker, 1999). In the next session, they brought their lists and were able to share with each other and with the two therapists their emotionally deprived family backgrounds. Also during the second session they were asked to perform the "drawing of the lines" exercise (L'Abate, 1998; L'Abate & Harrison, 1992) that is now part of a codependency workbook (Table 14-1). This exercise revealed their need to develop and refine more specific priorities in their lives. Consequently, they were given the weekly homework of doing four assignments from the *Negotiation* workbook (L'Abate, 1986b) dealing with: responding to each other, separating being from doing and having; establishing priorities; and holding a marital conference to discuss how each had completed these assignments. They came back for the third and, by contract, final session, quite ecstatic and enthusiastic about the movement that had taken place during the previous four weeks. ("These assignments changed our lives.") They parted from us with our comment that our doors would be open for them and their children.

DW and CAI with Individuals and Couples

Distance writing (DW) has a distinguished history that goes back to the end of the last century with the autobiographical movement (L'Abate, in press). (Brief histories of distance writing can be found in L'Abate, 1991, 1992; L'Abate, 1997a; L'Abate & Platzman, 1991.) The importance of writing in cognitive and personality development has repeatedly been recognized. Most of the research on expressive DW has been reviewed by Esterling et al., in press; L'Abate, 1997a, 1997b; and Smyth, 1998. Clinical applications have been reviewed by Riordan, 1996. The purpose of this approach is to facilitate communication with individuals, couples, and families in addition or as an alternative to traditional face-to-face, verbal contacts between patients and therapists.

DW can be classified according to structure, content, goal, specificity, and level of abstraction. Structure can variously be *open-ended* (OPW) as in "Write about anything that happens every day" in a diary or jounal; *focused* (FDW) an in "Write about all your past hurts for 20 minutes a day for four consecutive days (Esterling et al., in press; Smyth, 1998); *guided* (GWD) as in "I have read what you wrote in your journal and I would like for you to answer in writing the following questions that have arisen from what you wrote"; or *programmed* (PDW) consisting of workbooks oriented toward a particular topic, as discussed below. Goals can be prescriptive or cathartic. The level of abstraction varies from abstract ("Write about the meaning of life") to concrete ("Write in detail about the contents of your closet, including types of clothes and shoes"). The level of abstraction, as one can readily see, overlaps with the specificity (i. e., general-specific), while the content can vary from the traumatic to the trivial (L'Abate, 1990, 1992, 1997a, 1997b, 1997c, in press-a). The rest of this section therefore will deal with programmed distance writing (PDW) as examplified by workbooks for individuals and couples (Table 14-1).

A workbook consists of a definite number of assignments related to a specific topic, usually administered as homework between therapy sessions or independently of them. A homework assignment consists of a series of questions or prescribed tasks to be administered for educational, parapreventive, or paratherapeutic purposes. Assignments can be given in addition to face-to-face treatment, as well as at a distance via mail, fax, or computer. Workbooks therefore represent (PDW) and are the software for CAI. Over the last decade a plethora of workbooks about all possible human conditions have been commercially available.[1]

Workbooks can be used parapreventively, that is, in addition to an ongoing preventive program, like PE-SST programs; as an alternative to such a program; or paratherapeutically, in addition or as an alternative to psychotherapy. L'Abate (1986b) suggested that workbooks can be administered after an individual or couple has successfully surmounted the initial crisis stage of the relationship and is ready to learn new skills along a more structured appraoch. Workbooks can be administered before, during, or after such interventions, provided that feedback, either verbal or in writing, is given after the completion of each assignment.

A preferred way to administer PDW, either with or separate from face-to-face psychotherapy, consists of two phases. In the first phase, at the beginning of therapy, it is better to require *focused* DW (L'Abate, 1997b) by following Pennebaker's (1997) preferred format, which is: "Write for 20 minutes a day for four consecutive days about all the hurts that you have experienced in your life, some of which you not have not disclosed or shared with anyone else." Following this disclosure—and with additional information from history taking, the patient's report of hurts, and possibly test battery results—it is possible to administer a workbook that may fit isomorphically either with deviant scores on an objective

---

[1] For more information about these workbooks, please access:
<http:www.mentalhealthhelp.com>

test (Table 14-1), or with the referral complaint (discussed below).

This strategy requires a certain modicum of clinical experience. Workbooks for Better Living (LLC) (WFBL) does not provide the workbooks described below unless it receives written proof of professional license or certification. But any qualified, credentialed professional willing to try this strategy should be able to administer those workbooks described here almost immediately, since many can be used as structured interviews before assigning them at a distance. Evaluation should take place as a matter of course, on a before-after administration of any workbook. To evaluate workbook use on a before-after basis, the WFBL produces two easy-to-administer-and-score outcome measures: the Self-Other Profile Chart (SOPC) (L'Abate, 1982, 1997b), and the What Kind of Depression? (WKOD?) rating sheet (available from the (WFBL) www.mentalhealthhelp.com).

Table 14-1. Workbooks and Materials Available from the Institute for Life Empowerment (ILE)*

I. Workbooks for Individuals
  A. Youth: Children and Adolescents (ages 8 to 17)
    1. Based on Psychological Test Profiles (General)
      a. Externalizations (Anger, Acting Out, Hostility, and Aggression)

- *Juvenile Psychopathy* can be used either in conjuction with a self-report, paper and pencil test, or simply on the basis of persistent acting-out behavior (3 assignments+).
- *School Conduct* is drawn from different sources to cover socially maladjusted and conduct-disordered youngsters (3 assignments+).
- *School Social Skills (S³)* developed from the test by the same name of Brown, Black, and Downs (1984) contains four different workbooks about Adult and Peer Relations, School Rules, and Classroom Behavior (7 assignments+).
- *Social Training* consists of 20 terms that control behavior and teaches respondents to think before they act (20 assignments).

---

*For more information about these workbooks, please access:
<http:www.mentalhealthhelp.com>

- *Unusual and Troublesome Behavior* is drawn from the Checklist by the same name developed by M. G. Aman and Nirbhay N. Singh for youth in residential and community settings (3 assignments+).

b. Internalizations (Anxiety, Depression, Fears)

- *Anxiety in Youth* drawn from the scale by the same name developed by P. L. Newcomer, E. Barenbaum, and B. R. Bryant (3 assignments +).
- *Emotional Problems* is drawn from a Differential Test by the same name by E. J. Kelly and edited by G. J. Vitali to cover emotionally disturbed youngsters (3 assignments+).
- *Depression Anxiety in Youth* drawn from the scale by the same name developed by P. L. Newcomer, E. Barenbaum, and B. R. Bryant (3 assignments +).

2. Based on Referral Question (Specific)
   a. Externalizations

- *Addendum to Social Training* is written from the viewpoint of how many acting-out individuals think (10 assignments).
- *Anger in Children and Adolescents* is based on the meta-analysis of destructive behaviors by B. Lahey and collaborators (3 assigments+).
- *Juvenile Psychopathy* can be used either in conjuction with a self-report, paper and pencil test, or simply on the basis of persistent acting-out behavior (3 assignments+).
- *Posttraumatic Stress Disorder Symptoms* in children exposed to disaster based on the extensive confirmatory factor analyses by J. L. Anthony, C. J. Lonigan, and S. A. Hecht (3 assignments+).
- *Social Training* consists of 20 terms that control behavior and force respondents to think before they act (20 assignments).

b. Internalizations
See workbooks for adults that can be also applied with few changes in wording to children and adolescents.
c. Both Internalization and Externalizations

1. By Test Profile

- *Self-Others Profile Charts* are two theory-derived workbooks that allow a quick and focused determination of disturbances in Self, in intimate Others, and in both Self and Others (Elementary, Middle School, and High School versions of the Chart available) (6 assignments+).

2. By Referral Question
See workbooks for adults that could be also applied with few changes in wording to children and adolescents.

B. Adults
Evaluation
Social Information Form is an 85-item quantified, either self-report or structured interview about developmental history. 13 pages.

1. Based on Psychological Test Profiles (General)

- *Big Five Markers* consists of L. Goldberg's factor analysis of the Five Factors Model (FFM) of personality (12 assignments+).
- *Butcher Treatment Planning Inventory* was written in conjunction with the first instrument to specifically assess treatment resistance (3 assignments+).
- *Five-Factors Model of Personality* (NEO) is one of the most popular, research-based, trait-oriented personality inventories (12 assignments+).
- *Minnesota Multiphasic Personality Inventory-2* consists of 15 separate workbooks maching the 15 Content Scales (15 assignments+).
- *Personality Assessment Inventory* (PAI) covers most common psychiatric conditions or syndromes, including phobias, anxiety, and traumas, among others (23 assignments+).
- *Self-Others Profile Charts* are two theory-derived workbooks that allow a quick and focused determination of disturbances in the self, in intimate others, and in both self and others (6 assignments+).
- *Meyers-Briggs Type Indicator* is based on the theories of Jung concerning personality types (10 assignments+).

2. Based on Referral Question (Specific)
   a. For Externalization and Acting-Out Disorders

- *AA12 Steps in 4* is a condensation of the well-known approach for alcoholics or addicts who want to work on forgiving themselves (4 assignments).
- *Adult Psychopathy* can be used in conjunction with a short self-report test for incarcerated felons who want rehabilitation (3 assignments+).
- *Addendum to Anger* teaches that there are a variety of angry feelings that can be expressed and controlled in more constructive ways than in the past (7 assignments).
- *Addendum to Social Training* is written from the viewpoint of how many acting-out individuals think (10 assignments).
- *Anger Expression* is based on the research by Forgays, Forgays, and Spielberger (1997) about the factor-structure of the STAXI-2 (5 assignments+).
- *Anger Hostility and Aggression* derived from the work of Eckhardt, Deffenbacher, Spielberger, and associates (the AHA syndrome) (5 assignments+).
- *Gambling* covers how individuals with this addiction think about it (3 assignments+).
- *Social Training* consists of 20 terms that control behavior and force respondents to think before they act (20 assignments).
- *Temper* is based on the original (1982) questionnaire with the same name developed by C. Spielberger and P. London (7 assignments+).

b. For Internalization Disorders

- *Addendum to Phobias* teaches people to learn to express and control their fear (5 assignments).
- *Anxiety* follows the DSM-IV definition of this condition (6 assignments).
- *Anxiety, Depression Fears* are the major emotions that are difficult to control and use positively. This workbook teaches how to control these fears (3 assignments+).
- *Beck Anxiety and Physiological Hyperarousal* based on the tripartite model of depression and anxiety (3 assignments+).
- *Beck Depression Inventory-II* is based on the latest revision of this much-used inventory (3 assignments+).
- *Codependency* helps partners of addicted individuals to set limits on their partners (13 assignments).

- *Dependent Personality* deals with items that describe characteristics that put dependent personalities at risk for depression (3 assignments+).
- *Dissociative Experiences: Form BA* developed from research by L. R. Goldberg (1999) targeted specifically for individuals with dissociative experiences (3 assignments+).
- *Dissociative Experiences: Form TDE* developed from research by L. R. Goldberg (1999) targeted specifically for individuals with dissociative experiences (3 assignments+).
- *Emotional Competence* is based on the work by C. Saarni (1999) on how to become a more competent individual emotionally (10 assignments).
- *Emotional Expression* teaches individuals, who find it hard, to express feelings in a more appropriate and helpful fashion than in the past (3 assignments+).
- *Hamilton's Anxiety Scale* can be used to develop assignments relevant to learning to cope with anxiety (3 assignments+).
- *Hamilton's Depression Scale* uses the items from this scale to develop assignments to learn how to cope with depression (3 assignments +).
- *Loneliness* helps individuals to deal with feelings that make them unable to develop meaningful relationships on their own (6 assignments).
- *Moodiness* is an all-purpose workbook that teaches individuals to express a great many memories that affect their moods (12 assignments).
- *Personality Disorders* are extremely resistant to talk-based interventions. Perhaps through the writing medium and computer-assisted interventions like this workbook these disorders may become more amenable to change (3 assignments+).
- *Procrastination* helps individuals become more aware of and learn to deal with and control their procrastination (6 assignments).
- *Sexual Abuse* is for victims of sexual abuse who should complete it in conjunction with a support or therapy group (9 assignments).
- *What Kind of Depression?* based on the differentiation between depression derived from overdependency and depression derived from self-criticism (5 assignments+).

c. For Both Internalization and Externalization Disorders

- *Brief Psychiatric Rating Scale* permits a very quick confrontation of most symptoms of psychiatric disturbance (3 assignments+).
- *Posttraumatic Stress Disorder* is based on the latest factor analytic study of the scale by the same name (3 assignments+)
- *Posttraumatic Stress Symptoms* helps people who still suffer from painful experiences from their pasts (3 assignments+).
- *Social Growth* can be used as an all-purpose approach to a variety of clinical and borderline conditions (14 assignments).
- *Symptom Scale 77 (SS-77)* covers most severe psychiatric conditions, many already covered by the PAI (2 assignments +).

d. For Normative Experiences

- *Multiple Abilities* is based on the theories of H. Gardner, R. J. Sternberg, and P. Salovey about multiple intelligences (15 assignments).
- *Normative Experiences: Form PSC* developed from research by L. R. Goldberg (1999) is generic and neutral enough to be administered to relatively well-functioning individuals, perhaps on a post-psychotherapy basis (3 assignments+).
- *Normative Experiences: Form IPIP* developed from research by L. R. Goldberg (1999) is generic and neutral enough to be administered to relatively well-functioning individuals, perhaps on a post-psychotherapy basis (3 assignments+).
- *Normative Experiences: Form ABSC* developed from research by L. R. Goldberg (1999) is generic and neutral enough to be administered to relatively well-functioning individuals, perhaps on a post-psychotherapy basis (3 assignments+).
- *Social Skills* based on the Inventory by the same name developed by M. Lorr, R. P. Youniss, and E. C. Stefic (3 assignments+).

II. Workbooks for Couples
   A. Based on Psychological Test Profiles

- *Improving Relationships* deals with the most frequent issues in committed, prolonged, and close relationships (6 assignments).

- *Marital Satisfaction* is based on one of the most frequently administered inventories available commercially (13 assignments).
- *Problems in Relationships* program includes a workbook and a 240-item computer-scored scale to pinpoint major discrepancies among 20 scales of potentially conflictful areas with matching assignments for each of the 20 areas (22 assignments + scale).
- *Relationship Conflict* covers the most stressful areas of conflict, including abuse and fighting (14 assignments).

B. Based on Referral Question

- *Arguing and Fighting* consists of description, positive reframing, and prescription of 7 different aspects of abusive behavior (10 assignments+).
- *Depression in Couples* teaches partners to become aware of how depression develops from past family patterns that produce deadly triangles (8 assignmentss).
- *Intimacy* teaches couples to care, to see the good, to forgive, and to share joys, hurts, and fears of being hurt, qualities that are the essence of love (6 assignments).
- *Marital Violence* teaches partners to control their violence through cognitive processing of their actions. It can be used complementarily with the Partner Violence workbook. (3 assignments+).
- *Negotiation* teaches couples negotiation step-by-step because few learned it from their families of origin (9 assignments).
- *Partner Violence* teaches partners to control their violence and learn to express their feelings in more helpful ways (3 assignments+).
- *Premarital Preparation* helps partners clarify their reasons for wanting to get married (3 assignments+).
- *Stand Up for Yourself!* teaches partners to express themselves in a more constructive fashion (5 assignments).

III. Workbooks for Families
A. Based on Psychological Test Profiles

- *Arguing between Parent and Child* allows the pinpointing of specific patterns of arguing that lead to stress and breakdown in family relationships (3 assignments+).

- *Arguing between Parent and Parent* allows the pinpointing of sources of disagreement between parents and how to solve these disagreements (3 assignments+).
- *Family Environment Scale* links assignments with areas of family functioning that are low in their test profile (3 assignments+).
- *Family Profile Form* contains nine dimensions of family living that correlate highly with other measures of marital and family functioning (3 assignments+).

B. Based on Referral Question

- *Binge Eating* consists of three assignments focused on description, positive reframing, and prescription of this symptom in children and teenagers (3 assignments).
- *Divorce Adjustment for Chidren*, developed by Karin B. Jordan, Ph.D., for elementary school aged children whose parents are divorcing (7 assignments).
- *Domestic Violence and Child Abuse* consist of three assignments focused on description, positive reframing, and prescription of this symptom (3 assignments).
- *Foster or Adoptive Families* helps families who need training, instructions, and suggestions in how to cope with their often novel and difficult responsibilitie (8 assignments).
- *Initial Family Interviews and Feelings* helps families confront feelings and emotions that many families do not know how to express (5 assignments).
- *Lying* consists of three assignments focused on description, positive reframing, and prescription of this symptom in children (3 assignments).
- *Negativity* in families consists of three assignments focused on description, positive reframing, and prescription of this behavior (3 assignments).
- *Relationship Styles* based on the Elementary Pragmatic model developed by Piero De Giacomo, M.D. (3 assignments+).
- *Revised Temper Tantrums* helps parents of children from preschool to adulthood (4 assignments).
- *Shyness in Children* consists of three assignments focused on descrip-

tion, positive refraining, and prescription of this symptom (3 assignments).

- *Sibling Rivalry* consists of three assignments focused on description, positive reframing, and prescription of this symptom (3 assignments).
- *Stealing* consists of three assignments focused on description, positive reframing, and prescription of this symptom (3 assignments).
- *Time-Out Procedures* helps parent(s) of preschool and elementary-school children (4 assignments).
- *Verbal Abuse* consists of three assignments focused on description, positive reframing, and prescription of this symptom (3 assignments).

IV. Appendices
   A. Annotated Bibliography of Selected Self-Help Workbooks
   B. Example of Informed Consent Form
   C. Feedback Sentences for Letters to Respondents
   D. Self-Other Profile Charts (SOPC): Revised Forms for elementary, middle school, high school, college, and adulthood.

Advantages of Workbooks

Workbooks produced by the WFBL for individuals and couples, as listed in Table 14-1 (L'Abate, 1997a), provide many advantages to mental health professionals, students, and researchers, such as saving time in clinical practice without decreasing effectiveness, and consequently saving expenses for practitioners and their patients; conserving energy and effort to deal with specific clinical problems that are outside the range of the practitioner's expertise; maximizing patients' involvement in the treatment process; continuing the delivery of mental health services while the practitioner is sick or on vacation; perhaps decreasing the number of therapy sessions; conforming (reluctantly?) to managed care restrictions; performing research inexpensively under controlled conditions; making treatment available to patients who cannot afford face-to-face counseling or psychotherapy on a weekly basis; reaching populations heretofore thought to be unreachable (shut-ins, handicapped people, the military, missionaries, Peace Corps personnel, incarcerated felons, hospitalized patients, etc.); matching a specific workbook with a specific individual or couple condition, according to a test profile (Table 14-1) or according to the referral question; and with the software of CAI, having the potential to reach much more people that can be reached through talk.

Disadvantages of Workbooks

The most dangerous disadvantage of workbooks lies in faulty matching between the referral problem and the administered workbook. Faulty matching, more often than not, results from incomplete or inadequate evaluation of the individual or couple. As found in research with undergraduates (L'Abate, 1997a) and with seminary couples (McMahan, 1997), initial reactions to homework assignments may result in heightened anxiety and a reduction in performance. Consequently, it is extremely important that an Informed Consent Form (available from WFBL) be administered before any workbook administration, warning respondents about the potential dangers of written confrontation. This formal practice is not too different from the warning that many therapists give individuals and couples from the outset of therapy, that "things may get worst before they get better." Without this warning, both verbal and in writing, however, practitioners may find themselves in questionably defensible positions, ethically and professionally. Furthermore, the practice of written homework assignments needs to be brought out during the very first hour of professional contact. In my experience, giving homework assignments later in the course of therapy without a clear understanding from the very outset that they will be given, will produce unnecessary and often deleterious reactions from individuals and couples, including dropping out of treatment.

Functions of Workbooks

In addition to their advantages, workbooks can serve as: written homework assignments and feedback for treatment coordinated by a professional, especially if each hour of face-to-face counseling or therapy is matched with one hour of written programmed lessons; structured, standardized treatment plans for diagnosis-specific patient needs; guidance for the development of diagnosis-specific treatment plans coordinated with leading mental health assessment tools; and initial patient (individuals, couples, and families) assessment to develop appropriate treatment plans. They can also reduce guesswork in treatment planning for specific mental health conditions and diagnoses; be reproduced without limit, allowing them to be used as often as necessary without additional expense to the professional; furnish the software for CAI, mental health training, prevention, and psychotherapy; provide uniform treatment for convenient outcome analysis administered to a variety of patient populations through verbal (tape-recorded), written, and electronic media, such as video, fax, and PC; permit research to be conducted inexpensively and under controlled conditions that cannot be matched by the spoken medium, minimizing the need for elaborate controls, record keeping, coding, and classification.

Furthermore, workbooks are designed to train beginning graduate students in dealing with a variety of mental health issues in individuals, couples, and families, initially using them as written, structured interviews and guidelines and later as homework assignments; serve as guidelines for mental health professionals in need of specific treatment plans in face-to-face situations or at a distance from patients; offer written homework assignments as alternatives or in addition to ongoing face-to-face professional interventions, provided that verbal or written feedback after completion of such homework is given by professionals; and facilitate research because of their time-saving qualities that allow them to reach as many respondents as possible per unit of a researcher's time.

As explained at greater length in L'Abate (1992) and L'Abate (1997a), administration of workbooks can take place alongside with, in preparation for, or after termination from any face-to-face intervention, allowing for a more precise tailor-making than many verbally oriented interventions.

Ethical and Professional Requirements

Ethical and professional requirements are set in order to avoid the inappropriate and irresponsible use of workbooks by unscrupulous or unethical mental health providers. To protect the rights of clients/patients, as well as the needs of professionals, workbooks and materials produced by the WFBL are protected by worldwide copyright laws and can be used only by qualified professionals and no one else. *Qualified* means professionals who can demonstrate proof of being licensed or certified in the state in which they are practicing.

These workbooks *must* be administered along with an admittedly long and complex Informed Consent Form (ICF), which is available to all purchasers of programmed workbooks from the WFBL. This form can be adapted and shortened to suit the specific needs of clients. It also sets the limits for clinical indications and counterindications for workbook administration. Some parts of the ICF can be administered verbally in a face-to-face professional relationship, provided the patient signs an appropriate waiver. The length and complexity of the ICF are due to legal, ethical, and professional issues that need to be covered in order to protect patients and professionals alike.

Administration of Workbooks

A workbook should be administered only after the patient has understood the nature of PDW or CAI (Computer Assisted Intervention) and has signed the ICF. Before beginning and after completion of each workbook, objective assessment is highly recommended to evaluate its effectiveness. Some evaluation materials are provided by the WFBL free of charge to purchasers.

These workbooks can be administered according to at least two criteria: a result from a test/profile, or a referral reason. For instance, a high depression score on a personality test would require a matching workbook on depression. A self-report inventory "What Kind of Depression?" (WKOD?) to evaluate the type and extent of depression is found in the *Personality Assessment Inventory* workbook. Other workbooks match profiles of a specific test, such as the Brief Psychiatric Rating Scale, or a general-purpose inventory, such as the NEO (Neuroticism Extraversion Openness), to evaluate the Five Factor Model of Personality. If an individual complains of loneliness, procrastination, or past sexual abuse, or a condition for which no objective assessment tool is available, a workbook matches each specific condition (Table 14-1). Workbooks for couples can be administered on the basis of both couple test profiles or for a referral reason Both the *Relationship Conflict* and the *Marital Satisfaction* inventories allow such a specific matching. When a couple complains of arguing or fighting too much, for instance, a specific workbook can be administered for that condition.

Workbooks for Individuals by Test Profile

Individual homework assignments recognize the importance of particular characteristics in the overall functioning of a couple, family, or group. With individuals, these assignments can be administered in cases of comorbidity, where one clinical condition is treated through the verbal, face-to-face approach, while the other is treated through DW or CAI. Workbooks in this section are to be administered by test profile. In this fashion, each assignment or series of lessons matches the same isomorphic dimension on a test profile. If a test profile shows a high score on anxiety, for instance, then the anxiety assignments would be assigned.

Workbooks for Individuals by Referral Question

In contrast to administering workbooks on the basis of a test profile, workbooks can also be administered according to the reason for referral (Table 14-1). This reason may be a diagnosed clinical symptom, or it may be a behavior that is troublesome to the individual or to those who care for him or her. In some cases, the reason for referral may also coincide with the results from a test profile, a welcome coincidence.

Individual homework assignments recognize the importance of individual characteristics in the overall functioning of a couple, family, or group. With individuals, these assignments can be administered in cases of comorbidity, where one clinical condition is treated through the verbal, face-to-face approach, while the other is treated through DW or CAI.

Workbooks for Couples by Test Profile

Some workbooks are devoted to improving semifunctional and dysfunctional relationships in couples involved in long-term and intimate commitments (Table 14-1). It is assumed that the professional administering these workbooks is experienced in working with couples, and they should not be administered by professionals who lack such experience. Except for the *Relationship Conflict* and the *Marital Satisfaction* workbooks, the other five workbooks can be admistered on the basis of the professional's judgment. Of course, administration of each workbook should be coupled with the administration of an Informed Consent Form (furnished with all workbooks provided by the WFBL).

Workbooks for Couples by Referral Question

Assignments from the *Relationship Conflict* or *Marital Satisfaction* workbook need to be assigned after administration of the self-report, paper-and-pencil inventory that is the basis for each workbook. The profile obtained from each inventory indicates which area or dimension of the couple's relationship should be administered first. The administration of each homework assignment from one session to another should follow sequentially from the most deviant to the least deviant area or dimension indicated by the test profile. The more deviant an area or dimension is in comparison with all the other areas or dimensions in the profile, the greater the need to administer its matched lesson. Even though there may be just one assignment for each area or dimension, this lesson could be used for further discussion in the professional's office.

Administration of any self-report inventory should be performed on a before-after intervention basis. To make sure that this test-retest takes place routinely with every couple, it may be necessary, in addition to their signing the Informed Consent Form, to charge the couple for the two pre-post administrations of the inventory from the very beginning of the preventive, training, or therapeutic contract. A discussion of the test results should precede, of course, the administration of matching lessons.

Clinical Application with an Individual: Case Example

This section describes the rationale for a depression workbook used as written homework assignments for depressed individuals, couples, and families as a standard operating procedure in my clinical practice and research (L'Abate, 1986b, 1997a; L'Abate, Boyce, Fraizer, & Russ, 1992; L'Abate, Johnston, & Levis, 1987). The development of this workbook will serve as an example for the creation of other workboks dealing with a wide range of clinical conditions. Depression is one of the major debilitating conditions in human existence. It is present in various forms and differs in degrees of intensity, but in many cases, it remains masked, undetected, and unexpressed, making it difficult to treat. Psychotherapy and medication, although necessary, will not be sufficient to deal with the many people affected directly by this condition. Furthermore, the therapist needs to pay attention to relatives and family members who are directly and indirectly affected by it. Sometimes they are responsible (without meaning to be) for generating and maintaining depression. Depression, no matter how many professionals insist on its physiological genesis, does not grow up in a vacuum. It is the outcome of definite and often deliberate family interactions (L'Abate, 1997b). There will never be a sufficient number of therapists to deal directly with those afflicted by this condition, let alone with those who are indirectly responsible for it and affected by it. If, as some conservative estimates tell us, at least 15 to 25 percent of the population suffers from depression at one time or another, it becomes imperative to develop alternative ways—inexpensive and mass-produced—to help people suffering from this condition, as well as those who are indirectly affected by it.

What was originally a general "focused" assignment ("Write about your depression for one hour every other day, once a week, at predetermined times") became a more specific and systematic workbook ("This is the first homework assignment of an eight-assignment workbook"). It paralleled a theoretical model developed over the years (L'Abate, 1986b). Since the creation of these workbooks, seven depression workbooks have been developed: an empirical one, based on the Minnesota Multiphasic Personality Inventory-2 (MMPI-2) (L'Abate, 1992); a depression program developed on the basis of Beck's cognitive model of depression (Beck & Young, 1985); two depression programs developed on the basis of a two-factor model of depression as self-criticism and overdependency (L'Abate, 1997a); two depression programs based on Hamilton's Depression Scale; and one program based on the Depressive Personality (Table 14-1).

Case examples of using PDW with symbiotically attached individuals have already been published (Jordan & L'Abate, 1995). In my private practice, the depression workbook (L'Abate, 1986b; Table 14-1) has been used the most for the last 15 years. It can be used with depressed individuals (L'Abate, 1997a) as well as with couples. It consists of nine assignments, starting with an assignment on the "drama triangle," where the patient can choose from variations on the three themes of victim, perse-cutor, and rescuer. Assignment 2 deals with the "distance triangle," made up of three roles: distancer, regulator, and pursuer. Assignment 3 asks the patient to define depression and then asks him/her to rank-order 10 "explanations" (all positively reframed) according to how they apply to self. If none applies, there is room for the patient's own explanation. Assignment 4 deals with the "positive element" in depression. If depres-sion is "good" for the patient, then he or she should learn to approach it rather than to avoid it (Weeks & L'Abate, 1982). Consequently, the patient is asked to be depressed at least three times during the coming week and to write about what he or she feels or thinks during those times. Assignment 5 deals with "achieving control" over the depression rather than being controlled by it ("Start it if you want to stop it!"). During the coming week, the patient is to stay depressed from 15 to 20 minutes on at least two occasions and to write about them. Assignment 6 deals with achieving "flexible" control over the depression by continuing to approach it rather than to avoid it. Assignment 7 asks the patient to "let others help." Assignment 8 teaches the patient to "use" depression rather than to be "used" by it. Assignment 9 consists of a feedback form, for the patient's direct feedback about the workbook.

Clinical Applications with an Individual:
Case Example

Background

Walter, a 28-year-old married man, came for therapy with his wife, Victoria, complaining of depressive and suicidal feelings. He had been married once before and had one child from his previous marriage, who was living with his biological mother. Both Walter and Victoria were col-lege graduates, working in middle-level positions in large corporations. While Victoria denied any personal and marital problems, Walter was quick to make himself the patient, exonerating her of any responsibility for his depression. He attributed his condition to: being a child of an alcoholic father and a very passive, codependent mother; having to pay alimony to his ex-wife and child support for his child; considerable debts incurred from his divorce; and pressures at work, where employees were held strictly accountable for both performance and production quidelines.

Both partners were administered the MMPI-2; the Self-Other Profile Chart (SOPC), a very short, easy-to-administer rating of self-attributes and of intimate others who are responsible for the patient's sense of importance (L'Abate, 1997b); and the What Kind of Depression? rating sheet (WKOD?), which is part of the *Personality Assessment Inventory* workbook (Table 14-1). The WKOD? provides two scores for depression, one related to self-criticism/achievement and the other to overdependence on others. Predictably, Walter's MMPI-2 profile showed a very high score (80 percentile) on depression, with average scores, around the 50th percentile, on the other clinical scales. His SOPC showed the expected pattern of a depressed individual, rating self-importance low and significant others high. On the WKOD?, he showed high scores on both self-criticism/achievement and overdependency. Victoria's MMPI-2 profile was unremarkable, failing to show any relevant deviance. By the same token, her SOPC was even and average for both self and other ratings. On the WKOD? she scored low for both self-criticism/achievement and overdependency.

Rationale for Specific Strategy and Choice of Workbook

On the basis of the referral question, the test results, and limited financial resources, it was agreed to meet face to face on a once-a-month basis, with Walter working first on an individual depression workbook based on the content scale of the MMPI-2 (L'Abate, 1992), and then, once this workbook was completed, together with Victoria, on the depression workbook described earlier (L'Abate, 1986). After signing an Informed Consent Form, Walter agreed that he would mail back each completed assignment once a week and receive written feedback in return, together with the next assignment in the workbook.

During the once-a-month sessions with both spouses, historical/developmental background factors dealing with his low self-ratings and high ratings of intimate others were discussed, including the consequences of such a pattern on himself and his relationships with women, including his ex-wife and his present wife. After completing four assignments in the individual MMPI-2 depression workbook, both partners were ready to start the *Depression in Couples* (L'Abate, 1986b) workbook. It was explained to Victoria that her help was needed because, even though she might have denied or not shown any personal issues, in the long run her husband's depression eventually might adversely affect the marital relationship. She agreed to cooperate and completed with Walter all of the depression assignments on a once-a-week basis with once-a-month face-to-face sessions.

Outcome

The total number of face-to-face sessions for this couple, including the feedback session after posttesting, was five. After completing both the individual and couple depression workbooks, both spouses were retested with the same instruments used at the outset. On the MMPI-2, Walter's depression scale was still somewhat high but within normal limits (59th percentile), and the rest of the profile was unchanged. On the SOPC, his self ratings were much higher than his preintervention self-ratings, while his ratings of intimate others remained unchanged, since they were high to begin with. For Walter, the two depression scales on the WKOD? were much lower than the scores obtained at the outset, but they were not yet within normal limits. Victoria's MMPI-2 profile, SOPC, and WKOD? ratings were the same as those obtained at the beginning.

Clinical Application with a Couple:
Case Example

Background

Debbie and Eli, a middle-aged couple, came in for help because of their continuous arguing, bickering, and fighting. They wanted to find out *why* they were arguing and fighting so much. They had been married 18 years and had two children, in middle and high school respectively. Eli, an engineer with an advanced degree, worked for an international company, while the wife stayed home. Their request was answered this way: "If you want to find out *why* you are fighting, it will take at least one year of therapy. Even then there would not be any guarantee that you would really find out the reason or that your arguing/fighting would decrease. But if you want to lower the level of arguing/fighting, it might take half as much time and certainly would cost less money." After some discussion about pros and cons of this proposition, the couple chose to lower the level of arguing/fighting by agreeing to complete written homework assignments related to that topic. Since they traveled some distance, requiring practically a whole day to come and return home, it was agreed that they would be seen initially on an every-other-week basis, provided they would work on the assignments about arguing/fighting. If they did well in completing the homework assignments, then there might be a switch to a once-a-month face-to-face basis.

They were administered the same battery of tests mentioned in the previous case in the first two evaluation sessions. They were also given an Informed Consent Form to bring back to the third session, before deciding whether we (couple and therapist) would want to work together long distance or not. The test battery was scored from the second to the third evaluation session, and the results were discussed in regard to their relevance to the treatment plan. On the MMPI-2, Eli showed a profile of the driven individual, scoring high (around 70th percentile) on the mania and introversion scales. On the SOPC, he scored high on both the self and other ratings, while on the WKOD? his scores were were low. On the MMPI-2, Debbie showed high (around 75th percentile) scores on the hypochondriasis and psychosthenia scales, while on the SOPC her self-ratings were low and her others rating were high. On the WKOD?, she scored high for overdependency and medium for self-criticism/achievement. Between the second and third evaluation sessions, they were asked to write for 20 minutes a day for four consecutive days about all the hurts they had experienced in the past, both before and during their marriage (Pennebaker, 1997).

Rationale for Specific Strategy and Choice of Workbook

At the end of the third evaluation session, Eli and Debbie brought back their writing about past and present hurts. Debbie listed 48 hurts from her family of origin, including losses of loved ones and fears of losing parents and siblings. Eli reported 15 hurts, focusing on his father's rigid discipline and critical comments (which were, however, countered by his mother's unconditional love); a poor if nonexistent athletic record in high school and college (which was, however, countered by high academic achievements); and a couple of love affairs that ended in painful rejections. In sharing their lists of hurts, Debbie and Eli discovered that they had not shared many of them with each other. They were able to cry about their past hurts and hugged each other while they were crying. The therapist praised this experience as an outstanding achievement in their progress toward a closer and more intimate relationship. After some discussion, both spouses agreed to work along two tracks, one face-to-face with the therapist, and the second using homework assignments related to their fighting. Every week they would meet at home at a prescheduled time to share (compare, contrast, and discuss) their respective assignments, whether they came for therapy or not (L'Abate, 1986).

The first assignment of the arguing/fighting workbook (L'Abate, 1992) given to them (each received a copy, to be discussed together after individual completion) consists of ratings about the frequency, duration, rate, intensity, and content of the arguing/fighting. On this assignment, both partners disagreed on practically all the characteristics—duration, frequency, rate, and intensity—of their arguments/fights. Eli downplayed the seriousness of these arguments, complaining that Debbie was "exaggerating" them. They did agree, however, on the content of their fights: money, sex, and the children's discipline. These were unresolved issues for them. During the first three sessions ("You evaluate us, whether you are comfortable with us and want to work together with us"), it was found that Eli controlled the finances while Debbie controlled access to sex. He was "harsh" on the children, while she was "soft" on them.

The second assignment in the arguing/fighting workbook consists of 10 positive "explanations" of the arguments (e.g., "You only fight with those you love"), which they had to rank individually on the basis of validity. If these positive "explanations" were not acceptable, each spouse could come up with his or her explanation. Meanwhile face-to-face, they tackled the issue of money by asking Eli to relinquish the checkbook to Debbie. After protesting that Debbie did not know how to keep it correctly, Eli agreed begrudgingly to give it to her. By the same token, it was found that their sex life was strictly focused on performance, an aspect of their sexuality that Debbie abhorred. Yet she could not come up with any suggestions on what she liked and what she wanted to do in this area. There was very little emphasis, in their sexuality, on sharing pleasure, sensuality instead of only sexuality; there was almost no foreplay; and Eli showed little if any concern about his wife's pleasure. They were given specific written instructions to practice "sensate focus," by alternating in massaging each other's bodies for 20 minutes twice a week without intercourse.

After they brought back the second "explanations" assignment, with a discussion of the assignment and other relevent matters, they were given the third assignment. It consisted of detailed instructions on how to argue/fight really "dirty" by using the seven deadly errors in how to argue (L'Abate, 1992; L'Abate & Harrison, 1992). These errors are deadly because they "kill" both self and partner and consist of abusive patterns, such as blaming the partner and not taking responsibility for self ("you-ing"); bringing up the painful past; mind-reading; making excuses for self but not for other; issuing threats and ultimatums; using bribery and black-mail; and distracting. The detailed instructions told them to set an alarm clock for one hour and then engage in an argument that followed the seven deadly patterns, and that had to be recorded. They brought the tape back with a discussion of how the argument/fight went, then started to relax and reported some of the humorous aspects of the argument. At the end of the session, they were handed scoring sheets. Each spouse had to listen, separately from the other, to what he or she had said on the tape recording, scoring how often each used the seven deadly patterns. They had to score themselves and not the partner. Afterwards they could come together to a "marital meeting" to discuss the results. Essentially, in these assignments, they were put in a metaposition to argue about their arguments.

In the meantime, they reported that they had enjoyed massaging each other but found it difficult to abstain from intercourse. They were told how to increase foreplay, and the husband was given specific suggestions on how he could pleasure his wife in ways that were acceptable if not welcome to her. The therapist explained, at this point, their overreliance on doing and having and unconcern for being (L'Abate, 1996, 1997b). In order to stress and magnify being, they were told to sit on a sofa, after the children were in bed, and hug each other, with no talk, doing nothing but just listening to each other's presence for at least 15 minutes, without words or distractions from the TV, telephone, or radio. They were also told that this was the most difficult nonverbal and nonwriting assignment of all for both to complete (L'Abate, 1998).

After they brought back the scoring sheets for the tape-recorded argu-ment/fight, their scores indicated that Debbie was still involved a great deal with past hurts and a great deal of mind-reading of her husband. Eli, on the other hand, relied a great deal on making excuses for himself (i.e., stressing the importance of work to justify his emotional distance at home) and making none for his wife. He also tended to distract by changing topics abruptly and bringing irrelevant elements into the discussion. On the basis of these scores, Debbie was handed an assignment about bringing up the past, while Eli was handed an assignment on making excuses for self and no one else.

During this session, the couple brought up their concern for their two children's sibling rivalry. They felt that this rivalry had increased since they started treatment. On the basis of this discussion, they were asked whether they could handle a sibling rivalry workbook together, in addition to their individual and couple assignments. They felt they could, and therefore they were handed the first assignment of the sibling rivalry workbook (L'Abate, 1992).

For the next session, they brought back their completed individual assignments and the first assignment of the sibling rivalry workbook. By now their pattern of disagreements over duration, frequency, rate, and intensity did not appear. Moreover, they both agreed on four characteristics of the sibling rivalry. After a discussion about issues deriving from their individual assignments and their joint reports about the sibling rivalry, the husband was handed an individual assignment about "distracting" while the wife was handed an assignment on "mind-reading." Both were given copies of the second assignment for sibling rivalry that, true to standard format, consisted of positive "explanations" for this pattern (L'Abate, 1992).

By the next session, they brought back their completed individual assignments as well as the second assignment of sibling rivalry (which mirrored, as they became more aware, their own bickering and arguing). At this time, they were arguing less than in the past and were becoming more concerned about their children's sibling rivalry.

A common pattern in many couples is to initially come for therapy for themselves but eventually extend their concerns to their children. This couple felt that they had achieved a good handle on their arguments but needed to continue working together on the sibling rivalry. They were given the third and final copy of the workbook, which essentially prescribes the symptom, telling the parents how to start ("Start it if you want to stop it?") the pattern of sibling rivalry by setting an appointment with the children to bicker at each other at a prearranged time and for a specified limit of time ("Go ahead and bicker with each other all you want for no longer than 15 minutes"), on preordained days (Mondays, Wednesdays, and Fridays, or Tuesdays, Thursdays, and Saturdays), and at prescribed times (i.e., after Dad comes home from work; after supper; before going to bed). They were also required to keep notes about what they said to the children and what the children said during the required 15 minutes of bickering with each other.

Within two weeks, the couple reported that the sibling rivalry had ceased to be problematic. But such a sudden and quick improvement was unheard of in the professional literature, they were told. Therefore they should continue to require the bickering to continue at least for another week. Both Debbie and Eli reported no more arguing or fighting with each other and a noticeable improvement in their sex lives.

On the basis of these results, it was agreed to discontinue treatment after 11 therapy sessions, but to evaluate whether any improvement had "really" taken place or whether this was a "temporary flight into health." They were readministered the same battery of tests given at the outset, and a final feedback session was scheduled to discuss the test-battery results and prospects for the future.

Outcome

On the MMPI-2, Eli showed lower scores (one standard deviation) on the mania scale and an increase in extraversion. The wife showed a lowered (65th percentile) hypochondriasis score and a marked decrease in psychosthenia (58th percentile). On the SOPC, both spouses scored high on both the self and other ratings, while the WKOD? showed significantly lower scores on both the self-criticism/achievement and the overdependency scales.

It was clear from the beginning that this couple was not seriously distressed. They cared for each other deeply and were willing to travel great distances to achieve their goal of becoming closer. Both individual and couple strengths determined their greater reliance on the written than on the spoken word.

Clinical Indications

Written homework assignments are relatively new and experimental and are not yet in the mainstream of psychological practice. They differ from traditional practices of most mental health professionals to the extent that they are to be completed regularly in the couple's home or office. These assignments should be prescribed on the basis of: a couple's specific needs or requests; the mental health professional's opinion; and/or a battery of short screening tests, preferably both individual and couple. So many very short rating scales are available that would easily fulfill this purpose that responsible professionals really have no excuse not to use them (with an Informed Consent Form, as indicated earlier).

These workbooks should not be administered to floridly psychotic, fully addicted, or extremely distressed individuls or couples, including: retarded or extremely distressed individuals or couples in need of psychiatric attention; abusive or violent members of a couple in need of incarceration or restraint; distressed couples with a history of abuse and neglect; and chaotic families in chronic and extreme distress. If there is any doubt about whether these workbooks should be administered, a complete individual and couple history and a battery of objective tests should be administered beforehand. Completion of a standard test battery, in addition to its results, may be just one indication of how functional a couple may be.

Concluding Summary

Neither the individual nor the couple cases presented in this chapter demonstrated blatant or serious psychopathology. One could argue therefore that both PE-SST and DW, in its different structures, can be used only with functional and semifunctional individuals and couples. This conclusion may be valid, except that if one were to divide treatment into phases (L'Abate, 1986), the initial distress of the referral symptom or the referral question can be lowered with face-to-face crisis intervention. But after the referral symptom is taken care of, individuals and couples need to learn skills through enrichment and PDW/CAI that will help them over the long haul, in case there are relapses and regressions.

References

Beck, A. T., & Young, J. E. (1985). Depression. In D. H. Barlow (Ed.), *Clinical handbook of psychological disorders* (pp. 206-244), New York: Guilford.

Berger, R. & Hannah, M. T. (Eds.). (1999). *Preventative approaches in couples therapy*. Bristol, PA: Taylor & Francis.

Carlson, J., & Sperry, L. (1990). Psychoeducational strategies in marital therapy. In P. A. Keller & S. R. Heyman (Eds.), *Innovations in clinical practice: A sourcebook* (pp. 389–404). Sarasota, FL: Professional Resource Exchange.

Cusinato, M. (1988). A 20-year follow up of structured enrichment programs with couples and families. Unpublished research, Psychology Department, University of Padua, Italy.

Esterling, B. A., L'Abate, L., Murray, E. J., & Pennebaker, J. W. (in press). Empirical foundations for writing in prevention and psychotherapy: Mental and physical health outcomes. *Clinical Psychology Review, 19,* 79–96.

Ganahl, G. F. (1981). *Effects of client, treatment, and therapist variables on the outcome of structured marital enrichment*. Unpublished Ph.D. dissertation, Georgia State University, Atlanta, GA.

Jessee, E., & L'Abate, L. (1981). Enrichment role-playing as a step in training of family therapists. *Journal of Marriage and Family Therapy, 7,* 507–514.

Jordan, K., & L'Abate, L. (1995). Programmed writing and psychotherapy with symbiotically enmeshed patients. *American Journal of Psychotherapy, 49,* 225–236.

Kochalka, J., Buzas, H., L'Abate, L., McHenry, S., & Gibson, E. (1987). Structured enrichment training and implementation with paraprofessionals. In L. L'Abate (Ed.), *Family psychology II: Theory, therapy, enrichment, and training* (pp. 278–287). Latham, MD: University Press of America.

Kochalka, J., & L'Abate, L. (1997). Linking evaluation with structured enrichment: The Family Profile Form. *American Journal of Family Therapy, 25,* 361–374.

L'Abate, L. (1973). The laboratory method in clinical child psychology: Three applications. *Journal of Clinical Child Psychology, 2,* 8–10.

L'Abate, L. (1974). Family enrichment programs. *Journal of Family Counseling, 2,* 32–38.

L'Abate, L. (1977). *Enrichment: Structured interventions with couples, families, and groups*. Washington, DC: University Press of America.

L'Abate, L. (1981a). Screening couples for marital enrichment programs. In A. S. Gurman (Ed.), *Questions and answers in the practice of family therapy* (pp. 102–104). New York: Brunner/Mazel.

L'Abate, L. (1981b). Skill training programs for couples and families. In A. S. Gurman & D. P. Kniskern (Eds.), *Handbook of family therapy* (pp. 631–661). New York: Brunner/Mazel.

L'Abate, L. (1982). Skill training and structured enrichment for marriage and family life. In P. A. Keller & L. G. Ritt (Eds.), *Innovations in clinical practice: A sourcebook* (pp. 299–308). Sarasota, FL: Professional Resource Exchange.

L'Abate, L. (1985). Structured enrichment (SE) with couples and families. *Family Relations, 34,* 169–175.

L'Abate, L. (1986a). Prevention of marital and family problems. In B. A. Edelstein & L. Michelson (Eds.). *Handbook of prevention* (pp. 177–193). New York: Plenum.

L'Abate, L. (1986b). *Systematic family therapy.* New York: Brunner/Mazel.

L'Abate, L. (1990). *Building family competence: Primary and secondary prevention strategies.* Newbury Park, CA: Sage.

L'Abate, L. (1991). The use of writing in psychotherapy. *American Journal of Psychotherapy, 45,* 87–98.

L'Abate, L. (1992). *Programmed writing: A self-administered approach for interventions with individuals, couples and families.* Pacific Grove, CA: Brooks/Cole.

L'Abate, L. (1997a). Distance writing and computer-assisted training. In S. R. Sauber (Ed.), *Managed mental health care: Major diagnostic and treatment approaches* (pp. 133–163). Bristol, PA: Brunner/Mazel.

L'Abate, L. (1997b). Beyond talk in psychotherapy: Programmed writing and structured computer-assisted interventions. Atlanta, GA: Workbooks for Better Living.

L'Abate, L. (1997c). *The self in the family: A classification of personality, criminality, and psychopathology.* New York: John Wiley.

L'Abate, L. (1998). Discovery of the family: From the inside to the outside. *American Journal of Family Therapy, 26,* 265–280.

L'Abate, L. (1999a). Distance writing and face-to-face approaches to increase couple intimacy. In J. Carlson & L. Sperry (Eds.), *The intimate couple* (pp. 328–340). Bristol, PA: Brunner/Mazel.

L'Abate, L. (1999b). Structured enrichment and distance writing programs for couples. In R. Berger & M. T. Hannah (Eds.), *Preventative approaches in couples therapy.* (pp. 106–124). Bristol, PA: Brunner/Mazel.

L'Abate, L. (1999c). Taking the bull by the horns: Beyond talk in psychological interventions. *The Family Journal: Counseling and Therapy with Couples and Families, 7,* 6-20.

L'Abate, L. (Ed.). (in press). *Distance writing and computer assisted interventions in psychiatry and mental health*. Stamford, CT: Ablex Corporation.

L'Abate, L., Boyce, J., Fraizer, L. M., & Russ, D. (1992). Programmed writing: Research in progress. *Comprehensive Mental Health Care, 2,* 45–62.

L'Abate, L., & Harrison, M. G. (1992). Treating codependency. In L. L'Abate, J. E. Farrar, & D. A. Serritella (Eds.), *Handbook of differential treatments for addictions* (pp. 286–306). Boston: Allyn & Bacon.

L'Abate, L., Johnston, T. B., & Levis, M. (1987). Treatment of depression in a couple with systematic homework assignments. *Journal of Psychotherapy and the Family, 2,* 117–128.

L'Abate, L., Kearns, D., Richardson, W., & Dow, W. (1985). Enrichment, structured enrichment, social skills training, and psychotherapy: Comparisons and contrasts. In L. L'Abate & M. Milan (Eds.), *Handbook of social skills training and reserach* (pp. 581–603). New York: John Wiley.

L'Abate, L., & McHenry, S. (1983). *Handbook of marital interventions*. New York: Grune & Stratton.

L'Abate, L., & O'Callaghan, J. B. (1977). Implications of the enrichment model for research and training. *The Family Coordinator, 26,* 61–64.

L'Abate, L., O'Callaghan, J. B., Piat, J. D., Dunn, E. E., Margolis, R., Prigge, B., & Soper, P. (1976). Enlarging the scope of intervention with couples and families: Combination of therapy and enrichment. In L. Wolberg & M. L. Aronson (Eds.), *Group therapy 1976: An overview* (pp. 62–73). New York: Stratton Intercontinental Medical Books.

L'Abate, L., & Odell, M. (1995). Expanding practices and roles of family clinicians. In M. Harway (Ed.), *Treating the changing family: Handling normative and unusual events* (pp. 321–339). New York: John Wiley.

L'Abate, L., & Platzman, K. (1991). Programmed writing (PW) in therapy and prevention with families. *American Journal of Family Therapy, 19,* 1–10.

L'Abate, L., & Rupp, G. (1981). *Enrichment: Skill training for family life*. Washington, DC: University Press of America.

L'Abate, L., & Stevens, F. E. (1986). Structured enrichment (SE) of a couple. *Journal of Psychotherapy and the Family, 2.* 59–67.

L'Abate, L., & Wagner, V. (1985). Theory-derived, family-oriented test batteries. In L. L'Abate (Ed.), *Handbook of family psychology and therapy* (pp. 1006–1032). Pacific Grove, CA: Brooks/Cole.

L'Abate, L., Wagner, V., & Weeks, G. (1980). Enrichment and written messages with couples. *American Journal of Family Therapy, 8,* 36–44.

L'Abate, L., & Weeks, G. (1976). Testing the limits of enrichment: When enrichment is not enough. *Journal of Family Counseling, 2,* 70–76.

L'Abate, L., & Weinstein, S. E. (1987). *Structured enrichment programs for couples and families.* New York: Brunner/Mazel.

L'Abate, L., Wildman, R. W., O'Callaghan, J. B., Simon, S. J., Allison, M., Kahn, G., & Rainwater, N. (1975). The laboratory evaluation and enrichment of couples: Applications and some preliminary results. *Journal of Marriage and Family Counseling, 1,* 351–358.

L'Abate, L., & Young, L. (1987). *Casebook of structured enrichment programs for couples and families.* New York: Brunner/Mazel.

McMahan, O. (1997). *Programmed writing, personality variables, and couple adjustment.* Unpublished Ph.D. dissertation, Georgia State University, Atlanta, GA.

Mrazek, P. J., & Haggerty, R. J. (1994). *Reducing risks for mental disorders: Frontiers for prevention intervention research.* Washington, DC: National Academy Press.

Pennebaker, J. W. (1997). *Opening up: The healing power of expressing emotions.* New York: Guilford.

Riordan, R. J. (1996). Scriptotherapy: Therapeutic writing as a counseling adjunct. *Journal of Counseling and Development. 74,* 263–269.

Sloan, S. Z, (1983). *Assessing the differential effectiveness of two enrichment formats in facilitating marital intimacy and interaction.* Unpublished Ph.D. dissertation, Georgia State University, Atlanta. GA.

Smyth, J. M. (1998). Written emotional expression: Effect sizes, outcome types, and moderating variables. *Journal of Consulting and Clinical Psychology, 66,* 174–184

Weeks, G., & L'Abate, L. (1982). *Paradoxical psychotherapy: Theory and practice with individuals, couples, and families.* New York: Brunner/Mazel.

Wildman, R. W. (1976). *Structured versus unstructured marital interventions.* Unpublished Ph.D. dissertation, Georgia State University, Atlanta, GA,

Yarbrough, D. M. (1983). *Effects of structured negotiation training on dyadic adjustment, satisfaction, and intimacy.* Unpublished Ph.D. dissertation, University of Georgia. Athens, GA.

15

Solution-Focused Brief Counseling
Strategies

Gerald Sklare

Introduction

Much has been written about this recent approach in brief
therapy/counseling (de Shazer, 1985, 1987; O'Hanlon & Weiner-Davis,
1989; Walter & Peller, 1992; Weiner-Davis, 1992; Sklare, 1997; and
DeJong & Berg, 1998). These and other publications present the theoretical underpinnings and related rationale for the use of solution-focused
brief therapy in different settings and with various issues. Therefore,
many aspects of this theory will not be discussed here; the thrust of this
chapter is, rather, a brief descriptive narration of how to apply solution-
focused strategies. A general review for implementing this approach will
be presented, although the description will be limited due to the brevity
of this chapter. Readers interested in pursuing this approach further are
referred to Walter and Peller (1992), Sklare (1997), and DeJong and Berg
(1998) for more in-depth application procedures.

Solution-focused brief therapy evolved from the ideas of Milton Erickson through the work of Steve de Shazer and his colleagues. In his work with brief therapy, de Shazer began asking clients to take note of the things between sessions that were better (de Shazer & Molnar, 1964). Two thirds of his clients reported positive changes, and 50 percent of the third that initially reported things weren't any better discovered improvements during the session that had at first gone unnoticed. Weiner-Davis, de Shazer, and Gingerich (1987) further developed this concept by requesting new clients to notice what was better in their lives between the phone call they made for their first appointment and their first meeting. They obtained the same results as de Shazer and Molnar. These findings reinforced the notion that clients' problems were not always present. Depressed clients were not always depressed, anxious clients were not always anxious, and so on, even when events that usually trigger these conditions were present. Clients often unknowingly do something different to remedy their difficulties. This led de Shazer and his disciples to shift their counseling thrust from problems to solutions exclusively. This is one of the differences between this approach and traditional counseling methodologies: Therapists recognize that their clients do not always suffer from the difficulties they come to counseling to resolve. Typical mental health providers, by contrast, tend to steer counseling sessions toward maladies and tend to dismiss exceptions. But the existence of these exceptions suggests that solutions have occurred. With the solution-focused approach, as clients identify even slight hints of nonproblem times in the midst of their difficulties, instances of success are exposed. These instances or exceptions are explored in detail. Solution-focused therapists have found that in counseling, you get more of what you talk about. Problem talk begets more problems and a sense of hopelessness, while solution talk begets solutions and a sense of hopefulness. Sklare (1997) claims that one of the major reasons problems exist is that solutions are being ignored. Etiology and diagnosis are deemphasized in favor of the position of philosopher Ludwig Wittgenstein, who stated, "It's a mistake to look for an explanation when all you need is a description of how things work" (source unknown). The strategies discussed when the emphasis is shifted exclusively to solutions may sound somewhat simplistic; but counseling doesn't necessarily have to be complicated to be successful. The fourteenth-century philosopher William of Ockham, who became known as a minimalist, stated, "What can be done with fewer means is done in vain with many" (cited in de Shazer, 1985). When the focus of counseling shifts to solutions, the need for in-depth exploration of the client's history becomes unnecessary.

Another aspect of the solution-focused method that differentiates it from other models of counseling is that the client rather than the therapist determines the goal of the counseling. An underlying belief of solution-focused counselors is that clients are the best experts about themselves and therefore know what they need to accomplish. This concept enables solution-focused therapists to address a wide variety of client concerns. Regardless of the presenting problem condition, the counselor's task is to assist the client in identifying when the condition is absent or less intense and what the client has done to facilitate this difference. The counselor leads a depressed client, for example, whose goal is to reduce his or her depression, through a series of interventions to discover when, at times when the depression is most likely to occur, it has been milder or nonexistent, and how the client has brought about this change.

The solution-focused brief counseling process is a step-by-step sequence of interventions designed to empower clients to recognize their own resources that resolve their issues. In the five-step initial session, the client (1) determines a goal for counseling; (2) presents a hypothetical picture of what life would be like without the problem, (3) explores when the problem has been diminished or absent, and how the client caused that to occur, (4) rates his or her present progress toward the goal and assesses additional actions needed for improvement, and (5) receives a message from the counselor that both complements the client's successes and provides a task to complete prior to the second session.

Second and subsequent meetings consist of having clients (1) identify improvements since the first meeting, (2) explore the ripple effect associated with the changes, (3) acknowledge the counselor's reinforcement of the progress, (4) repeats steps 1–3 several times, (5) rate their progress toward reaching their goal, (6) assess their satisfaction with their progress and determine their needs for future counseling meetings, and (7) receive a message from the counselor that complements the client's successes and provides a task to complete prior to the next session.

The purpose of this chapter is to provide the essential solution-focused ingredients for effective therapeutic change. The major emphases will be to describe when this strategy is appropriate and how to implement the solution-focused process, and to provide several case examples. As this approach is conducted somewhat differently from traditional methods of counseling, the first example will be a word-for-word transcript of an actual case. Although this method has been found successful with many populations and with varied problems, the examples presented will be from my caseload with a preadolescent boy and his mother.

Strategies in the Initial Session

The first session begins with welcoming comments to make the client more comfortable, informed consent information, and a brief description of how the session will be conducted. Since the solution-focused process is somewhat different from what the client may anticipate, the counselor needs to provide a general explanation of how the session will proceed. An example: "Let me tell you how this is going to work. I'm going to ask you a lot of questions. Many of these questions are going to sound kind of strange and therefore will be difficult to answer. I will record some of your answers on my notepad so that I can recall what you have said so I can construct a message for you. Near the end of our meeting, I am going to excuse myself for a few minutes to put my thoughts together so I will be able write you a note that will give you some feedback and suggestions. When I return, I will read you the note make a copy for my records and give you the original to take with you. Do you have any questions about all that?"

Strategy 1: Establishing the Client's Goal in Positive Concrete Terms

Identifying concrete and behaviorally specific goals in the first meeting is a good predictor of productive counseling outcomes and generally results in more rapid client progress (Sklare, 1997). The purpose of identifying a goal in positive concrete terms is to help the client recognize those observable behaviors they would see themselves doing while on their paths to accomplishing their goals. Often, inquiries about a client's goals elicit nonspecific behavioral responses like "I want to feel better about myself" or "I want to be more accepting of others." The therapist needs to help specify the observable behaviors that the client will demonstrate. The therapist's comments to accomplish this include: "What would you notice that you would be *doing* that would tell you that you are feeling better about yourself?" or "So what would others report they would see you *doing* that would tell them that you are being more accepting of them?"

Clients frequently indicate their goals in negative terms: something they don't want to do or that they want to stop doing. Examples include, "I don't want to get so depressed when I'm alone" or "I want to stop being so lazy." What clients don't recognize is that when they no longer want to do something or want to stop something, another behavior must be started that will take the place of the behavior that is being eliminated. Therefore, helping clients to rephrase negative goals into behaviorally observable positive ones gives them concrete objectives to work toward. Counselor interventions that address this are: "If you weren't getting so depressed when you were alone, what would you be doing *instead*?" or "As you begin to see your lazy behavior stop, what would you and others see you start to do?"

Many clients express goals in terms of wanting others to change, thereby defining someone else as the problem, such as "I want my spouse to stop nagging me about everything." Counselor interventions should help clients focus on themselves and what they can do in their situations. Examples include: "What will this change in your spouse do for you?" or "What will you do if your spouse doesn't change?" or "Sounds like you have been trying to change her for a while, which hasn't been too successful. I would like to really help you with this, but I cannot change your spouse. I wonder, is there something else about this I can help you with?"

To implement this aspect of the process the counselor needs to demonstrate empathy to convey an understanding of the client's concerns. The therapist also needs to be able to clearly distinguish among the client's expressions of negative and positive goals. Then an effective solution-focused counselor must redefine the client's goals to starting instead of stopping something. Finally, the counselor must be able to initiate interventions that help the client identify goals in terms of observable concrete behaviors.

The counselor will be able to evaluate the effectiveness of the implementation of this strategy when the client is successful in describing positive goals that consist of observable details that both the client and the counselor can unilaterally visualize. The second strategy (the "miracle question"), described below, provides an additional means for clients to establish and clarify goals.

Strategy 2: The Miracle Question

In the introductory stage of the meeting, the client was forewarned that some strange and difficult questions will be presented. The "miracle question" strategy is one of those questions; therefore, informing the client that the first of the strange questions is about to be asked will ease the transition into this phase of the process.

The miracle question is a hypothetical question that allows the client to imagine what life would be like without the problem. The purpose of this strategy is to have the client create a portrait of success through fantasizing solutions that possibly exist that may have gone unrecognized. The development of these hypothetical solutions—the more the better—enhances the chances that the client will be able to identify instances of success or exceptions to the problem in the third phase of the process. The miracle question is phrased something like this: "Suppose tonight when you go to sleep, a miracle happens that solves the problem that brought you here today. This miracle happens when you are sleeping, so you don't know it happened until you wake up in the morning. When you wake up tomorrow morning, what are some of the things you will notice that will tell you that this miracle has occurred?"

The counselor must be skillful in helping the client describe the new behavior in detail. The client may describe it in general terms, such as "I would be less pressured" or "I would be happy." The client is helped to identify the specific behavior that reduces pressure or causes happiness. To facilitate this understanding, the counselor might say, "So when you are acting less pressured, what would you see yourself doing that would show you this?" or "Who would be the first to notice you were happy, and what would they see you doing that would convey this to them?" This intervention encourages the client to visualize the details of what success looks like.

Reciprocal relationship questions (ripple effect) are also integrated into this segment of the strategy. The purpose of these is to enable the client to recognize how changes in behavior beget changes in the reactions of others. The therapist exposes the client to the ripple effect of the miracle by asking reciprocal relationship questions like "Who will be the first to notice this change in you, and how will they react when they notice this about you? And then how would you react to their reply?" This sequence gives the client a larger picture. This sequence is repeated several times, with the counselor asking, "What else would you notice after this miracle?"

The requisite skills needed to effectively apply this strategy are the same as those required in the goal-establishment phase of the process. The counselor must also be relentless in supporting the client's efforts to identify examples of miracles, even very small ones. This is a difficult task for clients, who mostly focus their energies on what's not working rather than on what is. The therapist's effectiveness in implementing this strategy can be measured by the success of the client's work in identifying miracle-related observable behaviors. The ability of the client to visualize and discuss the realistic reciprocal effects of actions indicates the counselor's success in practicing this aspect of the strategy.

Strategy 3: Identifying Instances of Success and Problem Exceptions

The purpose of this strategy is twofold: to direct the client's attention to occasions when some aspects of the miracle have already occurred, and to help the client recognize his or her resources that contributed to making this miracle happen. Persistent solution-focused therapists are able to ascertain this information through questions that cause clients to explore and assume responsibility for their unrecognized successes. The therapist redirects the hypothetical solutions discussed in the miracle scenarios to reality by introducing this strategy with a question that assumes that exceptions or instances of success have occurred. The client is asked to tell the counselor about these incidents. Examples are: "*Tell* me about some time, either recently or in the past, when some of this miracle you have just described has happened, even if it was just slightly" or "*Tell* me about some moments when that bad situation wasn't quite so awful for you, perhaps when you were just a little less anxious than at other times." It is important that the therapist phrase this question with the expectation that exceptions have occurred. The message conveyed to the client is the belief that success has occurred in the past and that he or she has what it takes to be successful again. Counselors should avoid closed inquiries like "Are there some times when parts of this miracle have already happened?" Such a question implies the miracle may not have happened, which may stifle the process. Clients who have a difficult time noting exceptions or instances of success are encouraged magnify recent events to find successes. A comment like "How about this week or even just today" often helps clients identify a minor incident. Those who still have difficulty can be asked questions that challenge their absolutistic exploration: for example, "Do you mean to tell me that you are always severely depressed a hundred percent of the time, every waking moment of every day of your life?" The client invariably will respond, "Well, not every day." This answer implies that solutions have existed.

After identifying exceptions or instances of success, clients are encouraged to note the details of how these times were different from others. Furthermore, the counselor asks the client what different actions led to the improvement. Helping clients recognize their efforts that facilitate these differences provides them with a mindmap (Sklare, 1997) to use in the future. A typical intervention that yields productive exception exploration is: "What was different about that time when things turned out better for you, and what did you do to help that happen that was different?"

Some clients may give the credit for their success to others: "I didn't go drinking after work this time because my wife told me she would leave me the next time that happened." When this occurs, the counselor helps the client take ownership for the successes with an intervention like "My guess is that you have been warned like that before and you still went drinking after work. So what was it this time that made it different for you?"

When implementing this part of the exceptions strategy, cheerleading or complimenting clients on their accomplishments reinforces their efforts. The effectiveness of cheerleading can be enhanced when the counselor also gives the client the rationale for the compliment. Stating how impressed the counselor is with the client's accomplishments may not be viewed as genuine when unaccompanied by the reason for the compliment. Effective cheerleading consists of a compliment that includes a *because* conclusion that gives the reason the compliment was offered. For example, "I'm really impressed with your effort to go home after work rather than to the bar with your buddies, especially with all the pressure you were under to go with them. That's fantastic *because* it shows how strong you can be when you want to be. It also indicates how important your relationship with your wife is to you." Repeating this entire strategy several times, finding exceptions and instances of success, helps the client recognize resources that may have previously gone unnoticed, thus providing hope and a sense of empowerment.

To effectively apply this strategy, the counselor must have the listening skills to identify and immediately focus on moments of success rather than failure. The ability to recognize the presence of failure talk, as well as the existence of the cracks within it that imply slivers of success, and the skill to refocus the session to success talk are requisite. This is difficult for many therapists, for traditionally they have been trained to focus on what's wrong rather than on what's right. When sessions continually remain problem focused, this is a warning sign that a reversal of emphasis is needed.

The ability to use open-ended questions that help clients rediscover the specific details of their successes is also essential in this step in the sequence. A counselor's effectiveness in implementing this strategy is indicated when the client is able to describe when success occurred, what it looked like, and how he or she made it happen in observable behavioral terms.

Strategy 4: Scaling Present and Future Success

The purpose of scaling is to provide a means for clients to subjectively quantify their progress toward attaining their goals and to identify additional actions that would indicate further progress. Scaling enables clients to recognize the progress they have already made, thereby providing hope and encouragement for further efforts.

Therapists initiate the implementation of this strategy by asking clients to estimate where, on a 10-point scale, they think they presently are in relation to reaching their ideal goal. The intervention is introduced: "If we had a 10-point scale, with 10 being the day after your miracle and 1 being when things were at the worst they could ever be, where do you think you are on that scale right now?" Any score above 1 indicates some form of progress. The client is then asked to provide detailed information that supports the assessment: "So you're at a 3. What is it that you have done to get to a 3?" Assuming and encouraging further progress, the therapist requests the client to envision what a 10 percent improvement would look like: "When you are at a 4, what will you be doing differently that will show you and others that you have moved up your scale?" Again the client is encouraged to be behaviorally specific in replying.

The skills used in this strategy are the same as those used in the earlier strategies. The client's ability to provide scaled ratings with behavioral evidence supporting his or her assessments demonstrates that the counselor has been successful in utilizing this strategy.

Strategy 5: Concluding the Session with a Message

Throughout the entire session, the counselor has been taking notes on goals, miracles, instances of success, exceptions, scaling scores, and any other material that can be used to construct a message for the client. Messages consist of compliments and are bridges that connect compliments to the tasks that are to be completed between meetings. The purpose of this strategy is again to reinforce the client's effective actions and thoughts, support his or her efforts and ideas, and convey that the counselor has carefully listened and is helping identify the path to further success.

The therapist initiates the message strategy, after completing the scaling strategy, by excusing himself or herself to write a note: "Well, I have run out of questions for you, and unless you have some for me, I will need to excuse myself for a few minutes, as I mentioned earlier, to review my notes and put my thoughts together so I can write you a message. While I'm gone, you might want to jot down on a piece of paper the things that happened in this meeting that were the most helpful to you."

The first part of the message that the therapist writes contains at least three compliments generated from the session that reflect the client's resources and efforts. Compliments can be for a client's actions, attitudes, commitments, thoughts, desires, decisions, attributes, or any other strengths noted by the therapist. They are citations of specific behaviors exhibited by the client. They are like seeds planted for future successes, and they also serve as a reminder of past accomplishments. An example would be: "I am very impressed with your persistence to go directly home after work rather than make a stop at the bar with your buddies as in the past, for it shows your commitment to your family."

The bridge is the second part of the message. It is a mechanism that links the compliments to the homework tasks that will follow. Bridging statements are short phrases that recognize or encourage the client's efforts and a suggestion that introduces the task, such as: "Because of your desire to improve your relationship with your family at home, it would seem to be in your best interest to . . ."

The final section of the message is a homework assignment or a specific behavioral task. The seeds for such a task have been suggested in the compliment portion of the message; therefore, the assigned tasks are stated in general terms to encourage the client to create his or her own implementation strategies. Task development is determined by what was accomplished in the session. Most often clients are able to identify instances of success during the session; therefore, tasks usually request the clients to do more of what has already worked for them. An example would be: "Continue doing what you have been doing that has been successful." When clients seem unclear about their goals or are reluctant to take action or stay focused on the problem, the assigned task is to notice when things are somewhat better or when their problem is somewhat diminished. An example of this would be: " Notice between now and the next time we meet when this problem is slightly less of a problem and what you may be doing to bring that about." After completing the message a copy is made for the counselor's records. To conclude the session, the note is read and given to the client.

Effective message writing requires that the counselor have note-taking and writing skills. Note taking should not interfere with the progress of the session, so the therapist must develop methods that facilitate a smooth transition into the next intervention. I have found that restating the comment while writing it down seems to be less disruptive. The ability to record specific successes is important in constructing messages. Sklare (1997) has provided a prompt sheet to assist counselors with their message writing. DeJong and Berg (1998) also furnish tips on constructing messages.

Smiles, head nods, and acknowledgments from the client indicating the accuracy of the points being made in the message rather than confusion serve as an evaluation of this application of this strategy. The client is asked if he or she thinks further sessions are needed, and if so when that should be. Occasionally, only one session is all that is needed to get a client on the right track. Most clients choose to come back for a second session one week later.

Strategies in the Second and Subsequent Sessions

Many of the strategies in follow-up sessions are similar to those in the initial session; therefore they will be noted but not discussed further here. The first session centered on goals and solutions, thereby creating a climate that focused on what was working for clients. The second and subsequent meetings continue this process, as the counselor's interventions convey the assumption that positive changes have continued to occur. In the cases where positive change is difficult to identify, clients are helped to recognize the coping techniques they have implemented to minimize their difficulties.

The second meeting begins with the counselor asking the client, "What's better since the last time we met?" Three client responses are possible: things are worse, everything is the same, or things are better. The first two reflect a lack of improvement, so they will be addressed together here. As the client discusses the situation, the counselor carefully listens for even slight signs of things being better or not quite as bad. Interventions are used to find exceptions, like: "Do you mean to say that a hundred percent of your every waking hour of every day since we last met was worse or the same?" Usually the client will respond to this type of intervention with a comment such as, "Well, not every waking minute." This response indicates an exception to explore, in order to discover what the client was doing to make things better or not allow them to get any worse. De Shazer found that most clients report an improvement.

Once the client reveals a success or even some form of successful coping, the counselor initiates the EARS process. The EARS process is similar to the procedures implemented in the first session.

Strategy 1: Eliciting, Amplifying, Reinforcing, Starting the Sequence Again (EARS)

The acronym EARS identifies the four steps in this strategy. According to DeJong and Berg (1998), the *E* refers to *eliciting* instances of success or exceptions. The *A* refers to *amplifying* successes or exceptions by discussing their differences from problem times and then investigating how they occurred and what the client did to contribute this difference. The *R* refers to *reinforcing* successes through cheerleading and exploring the positive reciprocal relationship outcomes that result from the client's efforts. The *S* refers to *starting the sequence again* by asking the client to identify additional things that are better. The EARS sequence is repeated three or four times. The techniques within each part have already been discussed in the initial interview section and therefore will not be reviewed again.

Strategy 2: Scaling

After the counselor and client have completed the EARS sequence, the counselor implements the scaling strategy, as practiced in the initial session. The scores that the client reports are used to assess progress from the prior meeting and how it was accomplished. If the client reports either a lack of progress or lower scores, the counselor helps the client explore the successful coping skills used to prevent matters from deteriorating further: "So you were at a 4 last time we met, and now you're at a 3. Most people in your situation would have been at a 2 or a 1. How come that didn't happen to you?" The same scaling process in the initial meeting is followed and therefore will not be described again here.

Prior to concluding the session with a message, the counselor asks, "When you are at what number on your scale will counseling be finished for you?" A confidence scale intervention can also be used at this point. This scaling adaptation enables clients to rate their confidence in reaching their goals, where 1 is having absolutely no confidence and 10 having absolute confidence. The implementation of this technique is similar to that for the scaling previously described. If counseling is progressing well, there is generally a two-week interval between the second and the third meeting and a four-week interval between the third and fourth sessions. The intervals are doubled thereafter, until counseling is concluded.

Strategy 3: Concluding the Session with a Message

All solution-focused sessions conclude with the therapist constructing a message for the client, as described previously.

Clinical Indications for Each Strategy

Solution-focused counseling addresses clinical indications differently from other therapeutic approaches. Traditional therapeutic approaches tend to emphasize the etiology of problems, what keeps problems going, what maintains them, and other problem-related issues. Solution-focused therapy, by contrast, focuses on clients' strengths, resources, solutions, successes, and exceptions. Furthermore, traditional theoretical methods usually diagnose from the DSM-IV and treat clients according to the clinical indications prescribed for that diagnosis. The treatment goals are generally determined for the client by the therapist. But solution-focused practitioners contend that clients know themselves better than anyone else does, and therefore clients are considered the most knowledgeable experts about themselves and are responsible for determining their own goals for counseling.

After determining what a client wants to accomplish in concrete behavioral terms, the solution-focused therapist helps the client discover when and how he or she was somewhat successful or was better able to cope with this situation in the past. Therefore, symptom reduction or improvement within the context of a client's self-determined goals minimizes the need for counselors to identify clinical indications for using this approach.

These assumptions and procedures enable solution-focused counselors to apply this method with almost any client, regardless of his or her condition, as they decide the agenda for counseling. A paranoid schizophrenic client may want to cut down on the number of times a day she listens to the voices in her head; therefore, the thrust of counseling becomes discovering when the voices are less frequent and what the client is doing to make that happen.

Since solution-focused therapists apply this process under all sets of circumstances, it may be helpful to discuss several situations that may at first appear to be incompatible with this approach. For one, some clients may be interested in knowing why they are the way they are. The counselor can reframe the direction of counseling by asking, "Suppose you find out why. What would you do differently then?" After the client describes what he or she would be doing differently, the counselor can inquire, "What would it look like if you were doing that?" which returns the session to a solution-focused format.

Some clients may complain they are always depressed. The counselor may ask, "How would you know you're always depressed?" This inquiry implies that sometimes the clients are less of what they claim to always be, which helps them to cite exceptions.

Some clients may state they want to stop doing something, but they make excuses for continuing to do the thing they want to stop. The counselor may play the devil's advocate in this situation, with a comment like, "You must be getting something out of not stopping. So why do you want to quit?" The rationale provided by the client is then used to develop a goal. This procedure is similar to the one used with clients who respond with "yes, but" replies. Counselors can agree with them by stating, "I don't see how you could ever possibly get through this." Clients most likely will "yes, but" this response, thus providing a goal for counseling.

Loss situations require time for mourning and grieving, so solution-focused counseling may be limited in helping clients attain goals connected to the lost relationship. Goals for counseling can be established by asking, "What is it about that relationship that you want to continue?" or "How do you think ——— would want you to go on with your life?" or "What was good about your life with ——— that you want to carry on?" These interventions redirect the session toward solution talk.

Clinical Applications with an Individual

As already indicated, goals for counseling are determined by clients, who therefore decide the agendas for the sessions. Exploring only those issues that clients want to change and discovering when and how change happens is the only case background needed with this approach. This information is explored as the session progresses.

The case presented here is that of a 10-year-old African-American male who resides in a housing project in a midsize city. The boy, Kasey, is in a behavior disorders class. His teacher referred him to a mental health counselor working in the school. The strategies utilized in the meeting follow the solution-focused format and are typical of most solution-focused sessions.

First Session

The session began when the counselor made some introductory comments to help the client become more comfortable with counseling, described the procedures that were going to be followed, and gave an informed consent explanation. Then the counselor tried to determine the student's goal for counseling.

Counselor: What's the reason that you are here?

Kasey: I have problems.

Counselor: What do you mean, you have problems?

Kasey: I like messing with people, and I like fighting.

Counselor: Is that something that you want to stop doing?

Kasey: Sometimes I want to stop. Sometimes I get messed with, and I start to get mean.

Counselor: So if you were to stop messing sometimes, what would you be doing instead?

Kasey: I'd watch TV, play Nintendo, and do my homework.

Counselor: So those are the things you would do instead of messing and fighting and stuff like that?

Kasey: Or if I were in school, I'd do my work and play.

Counselor: I think I have a picture of what you want to do. You're saying that there are times when you don't want to fight, you don't want to mess. And in those times you want to play instead, in a friendly way.

Kasey: Yeah.

Counselor: Here is the first crazy question: Suppose tonight when you go to sleep, a miracle happens. Because you were sleeping, you didn't know this miracle happened, and when you woke up in the morning, the problem that brought you here was gone. No longer were you fighting or messing with people at all. What would be some of the things you would notice the next day that would tell you that there has been a miracle?

Kasey: I won't be doing anything mean to them, to hurt them.

Counselor: So instead of doing mean things, what would you be doing?

Kasey: Go over my friends' house to see what they are doing.

Counselor: So you'd go over to your friends' house to see what they are doing, and not being mean. What would they notice that you were doing that would say to them "Hey, Kasey, . . ."

Kasey: "You've changed."

Counselor: What would they say that you've changed to? What would they see you doing?

Kasey: I wouldn't be pushing them around like I used to sometimes.

Counselor: So instead of pushing them around, what would you be doing?

Kasey: I'd just be talking to them nicely.

Counselor: When they saw you talking to them nicely instead of pushing them around, how would they react to you? What would they do? How would they respond to you?

Kasey: Nice.

Counselor: What would they be doing that would be different that would show they were being nice to you?

Kasey: Like, when they throw the ball and I miss it, they would give me a look and say "That's okay, try to catch it next time."

Counselor: When this happens, how would you be different?

Kasey: Try to help them get the ball.

Counselor: I guess that whole thing would happen different, if you started to make that little change, and that would cause them to change, and then that would cause you to change.

Kasey: Yeah.

Counselor: Tell me, what else would be different if this miracle happened?

Kasey: I wouldn't be calling them names. We'd be joking around, but we wouldn't be calling names.

Counselor: Instead of calling names, what would you be doing?

Kasey: I would call them by their real names, instead of saying "What's up, punk?"

Counselor: When they heard that, what would they do?

Kasey: *(motion jaw dropping)*

Counselor: *(laughing)* Their jaw would drop. They would say, "This is a new Kasey." They would be amazed.

Kasey: They would.

Counselor: You'd just blow their socks off if you did something like that? And after you did that, what would they say to you? How would they act when you talked to them that way?

Kasey: "You've changed!" Sometimes they'd say, "You've changed a lot!"

Counselor: They'd say that. How would they behave toward you?

Kasey: They'd be nice to me.

Counselor: How would they act nice to you? What would tell you they were being nice to you?

Kasey: Like I said—if I miss a ball or something, they would pat me on my back and say, "Try harder next time." Like when we play kickball, and I roll it wrong, and somebody still kicks it far and straight up to me so I can catch it and I miss it, they just pat me on my back.

Counselor: Instead of using different kinds of language and stuff, you'd call them by their names. Who would you be calling by their names?

Kasey: Dominique, Darrell.

Counselor: So you'd be saying "What's up, Darrell?"

Kasey: Yeah. That's one thing I won't change—saying, "What's up."

Counselor: So if all of a sudden you started calling them by their names, saying "What's up, Dominique?" and they are patting you on your back, what would you be doing in return?

Kasey: Patting them back on their back, or hitting them on their shoulder.

Counselor: In other words, you would have a different kind of relationship with them. What else would happen with this miracle?

Kasey: I'd be different, everything would be different.

Counselor: What would you notice that would be different?

Kasey: I'd get up and say "Hello, Mom!" or "Hey y'all, wake up, everybody!"

Counselor: So in other words, the way that you know this miracle happened is that you'd be saying "Hello, Mom! Hello, everybody!" and you'd be up. Who would notice that this change was happening to you?

Kasey: My whole family.

Counselor: They would all notice? What would they say?

Kasey: "Dang, you've changed!"

Counselor: How would they know that Kasey had changed?

Kasey: I'd be helping my mom cook. I'd start cooking before she gets home. Sometimes I would take care of everything. Or I do half of it, and when she gets home, she takes a little break and then she does the other half. Like, tacos—I do the hamburger and the lettuce and heat up the taco shells.

Counselor: Before she gets home? Boy, I bet she would appreciate that, wouldn't she? Helping out like that.

Kasey: Yeah. She appreciates that. I did that yesterday. We had tacos. I heated up the taco shells and cut up some lettuce and tomatoes. She made the hamburger and everything else.

Counselor: Wow, you've already done some of this stuff.

Kasey: Yeah.

Counselor: So your mom would notice that you are helping out. Who else in your family would notice this miracle?

Kasey: My brother and sisters, that I would be playing with them more often sometimes. And I would treat them nice, just like my friends.

Counselor: What would they see you doing that would tell them, "Hey, he's treating me different, like he treats his friends?"

Kasey: Helping them with their homework. Usually when they ask me, I say no. Sometimes I help them, sometimes I don't. That's when I feel like being nice and I be nice.

Counselor: So you'd help them with their homework. That would sure tell them. When they see you doing that, how would they be with you?

Kasey: They stop treating me mean 'cause they know I'm being nice. I'm usually mean to them first.

Counselor: So instead of being mean, they are nice to you.

Kasey: Yeah, 'cause if I'm mean to them, they are mean to me.

Counselor: So whatever you do to them, you get that back?

Kasey: Yeah. Like sometimes I need help with my homework. They'd be helping me do my homework.

Counselor: Let me ask you another question. Tell me about some times when some of this miracle is already happening.

Kasey: Miracle hasn't really happened.

Counselor: Let me run some of this down for you to help remind you.

Kasey: Okay.

Counselor: You talked about talking instead of pushing your friends around. You talked about calling them by their names instead of putting them down, calling them by their real names. And you told me about helping your mom with the cooking yesterday. That's already happened, when you helped with the tacos.

Kasey: Yeah.

Counselor: How did you decide to do that?

Kasey: I just tried to be nice for a change. I just did it.

Counselor: Yeah, but I think there are times when you decide not to do that, but yesterday you decided to do it. How did you decide that? How did that happen for you?

Kasey: Most of the times when I do it, I'm bored. There's nothing good on TV, or I want to eat 'cause I'm hungry. Or I just want to be nice.

Counselor: You know, my guess is that you wanted to be nice. So you have that in you.

Kasey: Yeah.

Counselor: Being nice is inside your soul. And you just decide sometimes that you want to be that way.

Kasey: Yeah. It's where I live at, it gets me all confused, and I just want to be mean.

Counselor: My guess is that you'd be nice if you wanted to, even during those times when you're confused.

Kasey: Yeah.

Counselor: You have that kind of control. How do you do that? How do you make yourself be nice?

Kasey: I just say in my head about 50 times, "Be nice, be nice, be nice."

Counselor: Oh, so you tell yourself, "Be nice." Just like that? That works for you?

Kasey: Yeah. Fifty times. Say it 50 times, and I'm nice. Sometimes it takes me only 25 times to be nice.

Counselor: How did you figure that out?

Kasey: I don't know. I just started saying it one day, and it helped me.

Counselor: Yeah, that's pretty miraculous. Think about that. You were able to figure that out?

Kasey: I figured that out myself.

Counselor: Just by yourself! You weren't watching Oprah on TV?

Kasey: No. Just myself.

Counselor: You figured that out on your own. You must be really smart.

Kasey: I remember when I started saying it. It was, I think, last year, and it just happened. I was bored and didn't have nothing to do. No cartoons or nothing on, and I just started saying, "Be nice, be nice. Don't go in the kitchen and burn up something. Just be nice."

Counselor: Fantastic! So you have a tool. You can make yourself be nice by just saying that. By reminding yourself, "Be nice, be nice."

Kasey: Yeah, 25 or 50 times.

Counselor: That's amazing! Tell me about some other times when you have been able to have this miracle happen for yourself.

Kasey: I've said, "Don't do nothing wrong 'cause you know you might get a treat." And I like treats. I like going out to eat. I just say that so many times, too.

Counselor: So you say, "Don't be mean, be nice."

Kasey: Yeah, "Don't be mean, be nice."

Counselor: And that works, too, 'cause then you get treats.

Kasey: Yeah. Most of the time I just say, "Be nice, don't hurt nobody."

Counselor: "Be nice, don't hurt nobody." Wow, I'm impressed. So that works for you when you are able to do that. Does that help you to say hello, to call your friends by their names, and stop yourself pushing them? Does that work there, too?

Kasey: Yeah, sometimes I get nice to this one guy in my class who gets real mean.

Counselor: So if you are nice to him, what happens?

Kasey: He's nice to me.

Counselor: So you can start it off?

Kasey: Yeah.

Counselor: Another question for you: We have a scale from 0 to 10, with 0 being that this miracle never happens. You are fighting and messing with people all the time, all the time. You have no control over it, is a 0. With 10, you are able to be nice all the time. Where do you think you are?

Kasey: I think I'm a 5.

Counselor: That's impressive. How have you gotten yourself to 5?

Kasey: I used to be mean all the time, until just this last year I started saying those words in my head.

Counselor: So you say, "Be nice, don't hurt anybody."

Kasey: Yeah.

Kasey: And sometimes I lose control. Sometimes I don't.

Counselor: Sometimes you lose control. Tell me about some times when you were going to lose control and you didn't.

Kasey: One time I wanted to do something, and my mom said no, and I was about to sneak, but I didn't.

Counselor: Wait a minute—you didn't sneak?

Kasey: Yeah. I went outside and I was about to go through the alley and through the back door, and I just turned around and took off my jacket and went back in the house.

Counselor: You didn't sneak?

Kasey: Yeah, I was ready to, but I didn't.

Counselor: So normally, you would have sneaked out of the house?

Kasey: Yeah. 'Cause when she has to go to the store and she says she'll be gone two hours, I will sneak. It takes me like 5 minutes to get up to the pay phone and I make calls. Then it takes me about 30 minutes to get back home, and I've wasted my time.

Counselor: How did you do it that time? How did you decide not to sneak?

Kasey: Just turned around, took off my jacket, went back in the house, and calmed down.

Counselor: I know that's what you did, but you had to make a decision about that to be able to do that, didn't you?

Kasey: Oh, yeah. I just thought I'd get in trouble 'cause sometimes she says she'll be back in two hours, but that's when she wants me to sneak. She'll tell me a story 'cause she doesn't want me to go anywhere. She gets back home early, and she says, "Where's Kasey? He's not supposed to go outside when I'm gone!"

Counselor: Oh, I see. So in other words, you decided you didn't want to get in trouble. That's different for you, isn't it?

Kasey: Yeah. I only did it five times.

Counselor: Oh. That's a lot! A lot. 'Cause you didn't want to get in trouble.

Kasey: Right.

Counselor: You know, Kasey, that says something to me about you. That says that you respect your mom and yourself..

Kasey: Yeah. Sometimes I have sneaked out when she told me not to.

Counselor: But those five times were different, for you were able to decide that you were going to listen, and going to show respect, that you were going to show that you care enough about yourself to not get yourself in trouble. That says you can do it when you want to. How did you do that, make it happen this time?

Kasey: I don't know. For some reason, I just did. Like a miracle. Usually when I sneak out when she tells me not to and then comes back early because she forgot her card or something. When I get back home, and she's home—yipes! I'm in trouble.

Counselor: Yeah, but you've thought that before, haven't you? And you still went out, didn't you?

Kasey: Yeah.

Counselor: So it had to be different.

Kasey: I just got tired of getting in trouble.

Counselor: So when you think it through . . .

Kasey: Yeah, when I think it long enough before she leaves, I'll be sitting on the front porch thinking before she goes, "Do I want to get in trouble or do I not want trouble?" And I decide I don't want to get in trouble, take off my stuff, stand up, go back in, and hang my jacket up.

Counselor: You were thinking about the consequences. Thinking about "If I do this, I know what the consequences are—I'll get myself in trouble, and it's not worth it."

Kasey: Yeah.

Counselor: How do you make yourself think about the consequences?

Kasey: I just do it.

Counselor: Yeah, but you know, something tells me that there are some times that you don't do it and some times that you do it. So there's a difference. And what's real important is that if you know what that difference is, you can do it again.

Kasey: And again, and again, and again!

Counselor: See how important that would be? So how do you do it? How do you make yourself think about it before you do it?

Kasey: I just start thinking about it, about when I get in trouble. And if I do it, I'll get a punishment. Sometimes when I'm bored, I don't want to get myself in trouble. Then the next day things get messed up, my friends come back early. Oh no, and I'm stuck in the house!

Counselor: So you don't want to disappoint your friends, either?

Kasey: Yeah.

Counselor: And yourself?

Kasey: Yeah, and my mom.

Counselor: So you don't want to disappoint yourself, your friends, or your mom.

Kasey: Yeah. I don't want to disappoint my father either. I feel great when I do those things.

Counselor: Excellent. What are you going to have to do to get to a 6? You're at a 5 right now.

Kasey: Work hard. Work hard at being nice.

Counselor: So how would you make yourself be nicer? What are you going to have to do?

Kasey: Keep saying, "Don't do it, you'll get in trouble if you do it."

Counselor: Think of the consequences?

Kasey: Yeah.

Counselor: What would happen if you were thinking those thoughts and being nice, and one of your buddies, one of your friends, starts being mean? How are you going to keep yourself nice?

Kasey: Don't hang around them.

Counselor: Don't hang around them?

Kasey: Just don't hang around them until they change.

Counselor: That would work?

Kasey: Yeah.

Counselor: You know, Kasey, I'm real impressed with all that you have been telling me here. You really know what works for you. You have some really good control when you want to be in charge of yourself. You are really good at that. Is there anything else that I need to ask you?

Kasey: Not that I know of.

Counselor: I'll take a couple of minutes to put my thoughts together so I can write you a note.

Message for Kasey

Compliment

I am amazed with your understanding of what you have to do to avoid messing around and fighting. Calling your buddies by their names, talking to them instead of pushing them around, and playing with them help to keep things peaceful.

You also realize that you would be happier if you were to get up on your own in the morning, say hello to everyone in your family after waking up, help your mom cook dinner, and treat the members of your family like you treat your friends. If you were to do these things, you think they would be nicer to you in return.

I am really impressed with your ability to tell yourself to "Be nice and don't hurt anybody" 25 to 50 times in your mind to avoid trouble. Your ability to think about the consequences of doing things that will get you in trouble like sneaking out of the house shows that you respect yourself, your mother, your father, and your friends and also says you don't want to disappoint them.

Bridge

Because of your desire to improve your relationships with your friends and your family

Task

I would like you to notice when you are doing the things to be nice to your family and friends that moves you toward a 6.

Second Session

The second session with Kasey was conducted one week later.

Counselor: What's better or different since last week?
    Kasey: Everything is better.
Counselor: Tell me about it.
    Kasey: I did all my work for school this week, I helped Brad without being asked with his work, and I didn't even complain about it.
Counselor: Is that different for you?

Kasey: It sure is. And you know what, I worked harder than usual in math, and I even did my own reading this week.

Counselor: Wow! Kasey, that's really fantastic.

Kasey: The best thing though was that I stopped myself from fighting with this other kid when I wanted to get into it with him.

Counselor: You did what?

Kasey: I didn't fight, and all these guys were throwing money around trying to get me to punch this kid out, and I didn't get into it with him.

Counselor: That's amazing, Kasey, because that's what you said you wanted to do—stop the fighting and do other things instead like playing football, watching TV and playing Nintendo, and doing homework with your friends.

Kasey: Yes, that's right. And I did it. I even got a club together with five other guys.

Counselor: What kind of club is it?

Kasey: We're called the Club Church 'cause when we meet we talk about God, play games, act out plays, and help each other with our schoolwork.

Counselor: And all this took place since last week.

Kasey: Yes, and I'm the one who got it all going, and I'm the leader of the club.

Counselor: I'm really impressed with all these great things that you have made happen.

Kasey: Yeah. The fight was the hardest thing for me, because you know I really like to fight. It was real hard to walk away from it, especially when these guys started calling me a sissy.

Counselor: I bet that was tough. How did you do it?

Kasey: I thought to myself, "He ain't worth it."

Counselor: With all that pressure on you to fight, you still walked away. Most kids wouldn't have been strong enough to do that, but you did. You must be real proud of yourself.

Kasey: I am 'cause I never did anything like that before.

Counselor: What kinds of reactions did you get from others as a result of your not fighting?

Kasey: Well you know, the kid I didn't fight, we have become friends.

Counselor: Really! And since becoming friends with that kid, what have he and others done?

Kasey: That's when the club started coming together. I guess these guys that I always get into fights with saw me acting different, so they decided we could be real friends now, and they have been nicer to me

Counselor: Kasey, that's what you said you wanted to happen. Now that it's happening, what are you doing with them?

Kasey: Instead of fighting, we talk about stuff that's bothering us.

Counselor: That's real impressive, Kasey. You know, that took a lot of hard work on your part, and I'm curious how you were able to start off this series of things and stop yourself from fighting.

Kasey: I thought to myself, "He ain't worth it."

Counselor: As you said before, that's different for you, and I'm wondering how you made yourself think that way.

Kasey: Well, I had been thinking about what we talked about last week, and in my mind I told myself, "It takes more of a man to walk away than fight," and that's what I did.

Counselor: You're a really a strong person, for it took courage not only to do that but not to act without thinking first.

Kasey: That's what I did—rather than just start swinging away I made myself think about it first, and it worked.

Counselor: Hearing all these things you've been doing leads me to want to ask you where you are on a scale between 0 and 10 toward reaching your goal for counseling, with 0 being at the absolute bottom and 10 meaning you have reached it.

Kasey: I'm at a 9½.

Counselor: That's fantastic! What have you done to make that possible?

Kasey: Not fighting, organizing a club with my friends, helping Brad, praising God, being nicer to my friends, and thinking before I act.

Counselor: What if someone still tries to get in a fight with you and keeps pushing. What will you do then?

Kasey: I can talk about what's bothering him so we can try to straighten things out.

Counselor: And if that doesn't work, what will you do then?

Kasey: Think to myself, "It takes a man to walk away," and I'll walk away.

Counselor: What would you do if he follows you and starts swinging?

Kasey: Just block everything he throws at me.

Counselor: Sounds like you have a plan and are prepared just in case.

Kasey: Yes, I am.

Counselor: What are you going to have to do to move up to a 10?

Kasey: Keep on being nice to others so there won't be any reasons for fights.

Counselor: And when you're being nice, what will others see you doing that would tell them that?

Kasey: I will be talking rather than fighting.

Three more sessions similar to the second one were conducted with Kasey. Both Kasey and his teacher reported marked improvement in his behavior in school as he became less aggressive and more cooperative, and he improved academically throughout the remainder of the year. Solution-focused counseling worked well in this case. Kasey's strengths were enhanced, and he became a believer in his abilities to be successful, as demonstrated in his own words: "I like coming to see you because this is the first time anyone talked to me about the things I do good."

Clinical Applications with a Mother and Her Son

My own experience has been limited to working with individuals and families. The case reported here is with two members of a family, a mother and her 10-year-old son. The solution-focused procedures used were similar to those of couple work. The features that differ will be described. Most pairs of clients or couples who willingly come into counseling together desire to resolve some form of conflict. Therefore, establishing a goal that is compatible with both parties is the first step in the process. The Miracle Question responses provide a picture to both members of the couple of what success would look like. It also provides an opportunity for reciprocal relationship interventions to be directed to both parties rather than soliciting predictions from just one client. With both parties present, an additional witness can be asked to recall exceptions and instances of success that the client does not remembered. Scaling also takes on a wider perspective as both parties can assess each other's perceptions of what would constitute progress on their scales. Basically, in couple work both parties envision a clear picture of what they both have done that has worked in their relationship, what they need to do to repeat past successes, and the additional steps they could take to make things even better.

The case of Kasey has already demonstrated the details of conducting a solution-focused session. Therefore, only the highlights of applying this approach with two clients working on their shared concerns will be presented here.

The mother, Dawn, called for an appointment for herself and her son, Nate, a 10-year-old fourth-grade student. Dawn indicated that Nate's teacher suggested he receive counseling, for he was having academic difficulty. Dawn agreed, for in addition to his school problems, Nate was becoming increasingly uncooperative at home. She stated that she was at the end of her rope with Nate and needed help as well.

In the first meeting, Dawn stated that she spent most evenings trying to read to Nate and help him with his schoolwork. According to Dawn, Nate resisted her attempts to help him. She reported that when he was to do his chores or when she made requests of him he was belligerent and hostile. Dawn wanted Nate to mind her. She also wanted to learn how to be more effective in motivating Nate at home and in school. Nate indicated that his goal was to be nicer to his mother by cooperating with her. Together they established a mutual goal of improving their relationship.

Once a positive goal was established, the therapist posed the Miracle Question and several others several times to Nate and his mother. The key to the success of the session came with one of Nate's replies. He described scenes in which his mother, rather than ordering him around, was being polite to him by saying "please." He indicated that when that happened, he would reciprocate by cooperating with her requests and would tell her "thank you." It was revealed that Dawn and her husband had always placed a heavy emphasis on displaying proper manners, and in Nate's view she was not fulfilling her obligation. Throughout this segment, Dawn learned of Nate's perceptions of her behavior. She had been unaware of the effect it had upon him. Dawn was asked how she would react to Nate's cooperative behavior in response to her politeness. She replied that she would reward Nate by letting him go out of the house and have friends over more often. This sequence continued as the ripple effect of their cooperation led from one positive reaction to another.

After several additional "what else" questions were processed, the therapist implemented the exception/instances of success phase. Dawn recalled several instances when Nate's father had helped him with his homework without any argument. Nate explained that his father was polite by saying "please" and "thank you," and that was the difference. Nate also brought up an exception that had occurred the night before. He had allowed his mother to read to him and gone to bed when asked. His mother was polite that evening, which was different, and that encouraged him to cooperate with her, he said. Several other exceptions were noted, most of them related to politeness.

Upon concluding the exceptions phase, scaling questions were used to assess Nate and Dawn's standing in reaching their goals. By exploring and discovering their resources and unrecognized successes, both realized they already had taken steps to improve their relationship. A 1 (low) to 10 (high) scale was used to rate where each of them stood. Dawn scored herself at a 7 and skeptically questioned whether being polite would make a difference. But she cautiously indicated she would be at a 9 when she saw herself politely urging Nate to cooperate rather than being so demanding. Nate was more conservative as he rated himself to be at a 5. He indicated that his mother would notice he was at a 6 when he would let her read to him for five out of seven requests. The session ended with the counselor constructing the following message.

> I am impressed with how much you want to improve your relationship and do what's best for your family. Dawn, you and your husband are doing a wonderful job instilling proper manners in Nate. You are deeply committed to his success in school, as demonstrated by your attempts to read with him and by trying to help him with his schoolwork everyday.
>
> Nate, you recognize that by doing your chores and homework, you will get along better and get some rewards as well. You also know that when your mom makes requests by saying "please" and by being polite in a calm manner you are more likely to do what she asks.
>
> Because you both want to get along with each other, I would urge both of you to do the things that will help you each to move up 1 number on your scales.

The second and last session commenced two weeks later. Things had improved dramatically both at home and in school. Nate reported that his mother's use of "please" worked. Dawn noted that Nate was cooperating as he was reading and doing his spelling words with her. She also pointed out that on the few occasions when Nate did resist working with her, she calmly and successfully backed off and let her husband work with him. She was amazed that such a simple thing would discharge the negative energy causing so much conflict. Dawn scaled herself as a 9 due to her improved relationship with her son and her ability to motivate him more effectively. Nate was so happy with the progress that he rated himself at a 10. They both realized they had the skills to be successful, and a little push was all that was needed to get them going. Therefore counseling was concluded with a message and a reminder that further nudges were available if needed.

Concluding Summary

With solution-focused brief counseling, clients determine what they want to accomplish. Therefore this model has been found to be versatile and successfull with a wide range of issues and clients. This nontraditional approach favors addressing the successes rather than the failures in clients' lives. Implementing it requires a paradigm shift in counselors' thinking. Underlying this theory is the basic principle, "You get more of whatever you focus upon" (Sklare, 1997). The five-step process of goal setting, creating hypothetical miracle solutions, identifying problem exceptions or instances of success, scaling, and constructing reinforcing positive messages enables clients to recognize their resources and leaves them feeling empowered to change. This approach is not a magic bullet that will work with everyone, but the chances are favorable that it will.

References

de Shazer, S. (1985). *Keys to solution in brief therapy.* New York: Norton.

de Shazer, S. (1987). Minimal elegance. *The Family Therapy Networker,* September-October, 59.

de Shazer, S., & Molnar, A. (1964). Four useful interventions in brief family therapy. *Journal of Marital and Family Therapy, 10*(3), 297–304.

DeJong, P., & Berg, I. K. (1998). *Interviewing for solutions.* Pacific Grove, CA: Brooks Cole.

O'Hanlon, W. H., & Weiner-Davis, M. (1989). *In search of solutions: A new direction in psychotherapy.* New York: Guilford.

Sklare, G. B. (1997). *Brief counseling that works: A solution-focused approach for school counselors.* Thousand Oaks, CA: Corwin Press.

Walter, J. L., & Peller, J. E. (1992). *Becoming solution-focused in brief therapy.* New York: Brunner/Mazel.

Weiner-Davis, M. (1992). *Divorce busting.* New York: Fireside.

Weiner-Davis, M., de Shazer, S., & Gingerich, W. J. (1987). Using pretreatment change to construct a therapeutic solution: A clinical note. *Journal of Marital and Family Therapy, 13*(4), 359–363.

Annotated Bibliography

DeJong, P., & Berg, I. K. (1998). *Interviewing for solutions.* Pacific Grove, CA: Brooks Cole. This book describes the basic steps that a counselor must follow to conduct solution-focused interviews. The authors include many case examples that demonstrate how to implement the solution-focused process. Several chapters are devoted to reporting outcome research on this approach. The appendix provides examples of solution-building tools and forms that help facilitate the process.

Sklare, G. B. (1997). *Brief counseling that works: A solution-focused approach for school counselors.* Thousand Oaks, CA: Corwin Press. This book presents an easy-to-read step-by-step description of how to implement the five sequenced stages of solution-focused brief counseling with children and adolescents. The applications can be generalized to an adult population as well. Several chapters include exercises that enable readers to practice the concepts. Complete case examples are included, as well as ways to overcome typical stumbling blocks. Road maps are also provided, serving as guides to be used in sessions to prompt those new to this approach.

Walter, J. L., & Peller, J. E. (1992). *Becoming solution-focused in brief therapy.* New York: Brunner/Mazel. This text provides extensive background that supports the rationale for solution-focused brief therapy. Its 18 skill-building chapters will equip readers with background to find solutions with clients. Chapters are sequenced to demonstrate the entire solution-focused process from beginning to end. Scenarios from cases, exercises, flow charts, and worksheets are included to help the reader learn solution-focused clinical skills.

16

—⊶⊷—

EMDR and Resource Installation: Principles and Procedures for Enhancing Current Functioning and Resolving Traumatic Experiences

Andrew M. Leeds and Francine Shapiro

Introduction

This chapter presents an overview of eye movement desensitization and reprocessing (EMDR), a research-validated treatment for posttraumatic stress disorder (PTSD), and a related set of procedures known as resource development and installation (RDI), which have been reported to be useful in ego strengthening and stabilization. First, the extant research on EMDR, its theoretical model, and the eight phases of its treatment will be sumarized. The principles and theoretical foundations of RDI will then be discussed. Two cases will be presented. The first case illustrates a simple application of resource development and installation to supplement the standard EMDR PTSD protocol in the brief treatment of a marital crisis. The second case summarizes the brief, strategic use of RDI to stabilize a patient with complex PTSD who was referred for collaborative treatment and to build a foundation for comprehensive EMDR treatment.

History and Development of EMDR

EMDR was initially developed empirically (Shapiro 1995, 1999) by exploring the observed effects of eye movements on consciousness and memory. It was introduced to the field of psychology through a controlled-outcome study (Shapiro, 1989) that showed significant decreases of disturbance in posttraumatic-stress-related memories and improvements in associated symptoms following a single session of an "eye movement desensitization" procedure then termed EMD. Since posttraumatic-stress-related symptoms had generally been found to be stable and resistant to treatment (Breuer & Freud, 1955; Kardiner, 1941; Rothbaum & Foa, 1996; Solomon, Gernity, & Muff, 1992), these findings triggered an initial rush of attention and appropriate skepticism. Over the next few years, Shapiro modified the early EMD procedure, which evolved into EMDR, adding new procedural elements and clarifying and standardizing the sequence of the elements to address observations of rapid treatment responses, blocked responses, and patient feedback. In 1995 a standardized set of basic protocols was published in a reference text (Shapiro, 1995).

While a great deal of attention has focused on the role of eye movements and other forms of alternating, bilateral stimulation used in EMDR, the novelty and skepticism associated with the introduction of eye movements to psychotherapy should not overshadow the other fundamental ways in which EMDR differs from previous methods. While EMDR incorporates a number of familiar procedural elements, it does so in an intrinsically new way and with new criteria for their use. Because EMDR is a complex, patient-centered set of principles, protocols, and procedures and is neither a simple matter of eye movements nor a rote set of unvarying steps, the need for specific training has been repeatedly emphasized (Shapiro, 1991, 1995) to ensure efficacy and patient safety.

Theory of EMDR

The theoretical model evolved to explain the observed treatment effects of the EMDR procedure has been informed by the terminology and early concepts of information processing, associative networks, and state-specific memory originally presented by Lang (1977) and Bower (1981), as well as considerations of research on the neurobiology of learning, trauma, and memory (Shapiro, 1995, 1999). While differing in some of its elements and in its application, the EMDR theoretical model is also compatible with other information-processing models (Chemtob, Roitblatt, Hamada, Carlson, & Twentyman, 1988; Foa & Kozak, 1986; Horowitz, 1979).

Central to Shapiro's original formulation is the premise, not previously specified in other theories, that a capacity for adaptive information processing is a universal and intrinsic feature of the human nervous system and that this system is oriented to physiologically alter stressful and traumatic life experiences toward an adaptive resolution. *Adaptive resolution* is defined to mean that the associated negative affects are neutralized, vivid and intrusive sensory memory elements are shifted to a less vivid, narrative form, and the information related to the experience is integrated into an overall functional self-concept so that it is available in a useful form to guide future behavior.

It is also hypothesized that the functional capacity of the information-processing system can be blocked by experiences that overwhelm the person's available resources. Such experiences include specific traumas and stresses during critical developmental periods. Within the accelerated information-processing model, desensitization effects and cognitive restructuring are viewed as evidence and consequences of "adaptive information processing taking place on a neurophysiological level" (Shapiro, 1995, p. 13). Shapiro (1995, pp. 13–27, 309–341) and Leeds (1998b) provide a more detailed overview of the model and explore possible underlying physiological processes. What needs to be emphasized here is that EMDR is implemented not merely for symptomatic relief but primarily as a way to catalyze learning (information processing) at the most fundamental levels of affect, belief, and behavior. Its observed effects cannot be adequately explained merely as the result of exposure or desensitization, as explored elsewhere (Shapiro, 1998c, 1999). Not only are negative affects, beliefs, and behavioral response sets neutralized and desensitized during the EMDR treatment process, but positive affects, beliefs, and more functional behavioral response sets are enhanced, increasing resiliency and forging an enlarged and strengthened sense of self and identify.

The term *desensitization* and the early emphasis on eye movements in the name for the EMDR procedure have perhaps made it more difficult for clinicians and researchers to conceptualize the roles of EMDR's overall procedures and principles. Emerging theories for explaining its observed effectiveness suggest that the integration of bilateral stimulation with structured treatment produces significant decreases in negative affect and increases in positive affect through a combination of pathways. These include dual hemispheric processing (Nicosia, 1994; Stickgold, 1998), investigatory or orienting response (Dyck, 1993; Macculloch & Feldman, 1996), cognitive loading (de Jongh, 1998; Wells & Papgeorgiou, 1998), and intrinsic positive-affect interest-excitement (Demos, 1988; Leeds, 1998c: Nathanson, 1998; Schore, 1996). Simple conditioning and exposure models such as extinction and desensitization may fail to model the observed treatment effects of EMDR (Van Etten & Taylor, 1998) and related procedures as well as emerging information-processing models. This seems to be particularly the case with the observed effects of the installation phase of the standard PTSD protocol and RDI procedures in enhancing positive affect.

Memory Networks

The concept of *memory networks* is central to the EMDR model. Memory networks are hypothesized to include related memories, affects, images, sensations, and thoughts that may be stored with various degrees of association. Reiser (1990) and Tomkins (1991) have both proposed affect as the central organizing principle in the formation of memory networks and related response sets. The role of affect is given greater emphasis in EMDR's procedures and theoretical model than in other information-processing models.

The five main elements of memory networks in EMDR are:

- *Image.* Images are the sensory elements of a memory network that are most commonly described by patients as visual but that may also include other sensory memories, such as smells and tastes.
- *Thoughts and Sounds.* These are the memories of the initial thoughts experienced and sounds heard at the time of the target memory.

- *Affect.* Affects include the presently perceived and unperceived emotional responses to the traumatic memory, together with their felt locations in the body.
- *Sensation.* Present physical sensations reported by the patient may represent memories of sensations from touch or injury as well as the bodily locations of primarily affective responses.
- *Self-appraisal.* Cognition in EMDR is a current self-appraisal or self-referencing thought or belief by which the patient interprets the affects and other memory elements associated with the traumatic memory. In the standard EMDR PTSD protocol (as described below, in Phase 3), the initial self-appraisal associated with the traumatic memory is generally a negative one. The patient is also asked to select a more adaptive self-appraisal, which the patient would prefer to believe with felt confidence after treatment.

In the standard PTSD protocol (Shapiro, 1995), each EMDR treatment session focuses on a selected target or node of the hypothesized memory network that represents a specific experience with its image, affect, thoughts, sensations, and self-appraisal. Functional and dysfunctional behavioral and emotional responses are hypothesized to reflect aggregations of specific learning experiences as represented by aggregations of nodes in the memory networks, which may be available to varying degrees depending on various state-specific effects and current stimuli.

For example, it is hypothesized that for an adult patient with a single-incident, adult-onset trauma with good premorbid functioning, the unresolved dysfunctional-memory network would consist of relatively few nodes and the functional-memory networks would consist of many nodes. Functional nodes of the patient's memory networks would be readily available during active treatment and would contain information incompatible with the distressing affect and irrational beliefs of the discrete trauma-memory network. Therefore during reprocessing it would be generally expected that treatment responses would be rapid and spontaneous. The patient's adaptive information-processing system would be able to resolve the trauma-memory network quickly, without additional information and without external cueing of functional memory nodes.

On the other hand, for an adult patient with multiple-incident adult trauma and poor premorbid functioning related to unpredictable fear- or shame-inducing experiences in early life—for example, with an alcohol-abusing primary caretaker—the unresolved dysfunctional-memory network will consist of many interconnected nodes, while the functional-memory networks will consist of relatively fewer nodes. If such a patient meets overall readiness criteria (see Phase 1, below) for the standard PTSD protocol, new information might well need to be introduced before or during reprocessing or to be externally cued by the clinician (known in EMDR as the *cognitive interweave*) in order to support the incorporation of a specific traumatic incident into a new more functional memory network. It would also be predicted that such a patient would tend to associate any one specific adult traumatic incident with multiple childhood antecedents (known as *feeder memories*). Therefore while adaptive information processing would be accelerated during EMDR treatment, a more active involvement by the clinician would be needed, and treatment would generally take more sessions to address the many, earlier associated nodes of the dysfunctional-memory network.

A Unique Multimodal Integration

EMDR provides a unique integrative model and a multimodal approach that is compatible with most psychotherapeutic methods. Combined with the growing research data (see below), this has led to EMDR's being incorporated into the work of experienced clinicians of quite diverse previous orientations (Shapiro, in press). EMDR's focus on the relevance of early childhood experiences and the need to permit free association within the treatment process fits well with psychodynamic models and a patient-centered approach (Rogers, 1951). At the same time, EMDR gives importance to current dysfunctional responses and behaviors congruent with classical conditioning and generalization principles from behaviorism (Salter, 1961; Wolpe, 1991). It emphasizes the role of positive and negative self-assessments, which have been central in the development of cognitive approaches (Beck, 1967; Ellis, 1962; Meichenbaum, 1977; Young, 1994). It recognizes the need to address ego state conflicts (Assagioli, 1965; Fraser, 1991; Watkins & Watkins, 1977).

Finally, it places central importance on the role of affect (Demos, 1988; Nathanson, 1992; Tomkins, 1991) in enhancing or inhibiting information processing, together with innate and learned physical responses (Lang, 1979).

Research Base

While few studies of EMDR were published from 1989 to 1993, the experimental literature on it has grown rapidly since 1994. A recent meta-analysis of all (59) psychological and drug-treatment-outcome trials for posttraumatic stress disorder (Van Etten & Taylor, 1998) concluded that "behaviour therapy and EMDR were the most effective psychological therapies for PTSD" (p. 130) and also stated, "The results of the present study suggest that EMDR is effective for PTSD, and that it is more efficient than other treatments" (p. 140).

A recent review of the EMDR research by Shapiro (1998b) notes that since the first study appeared in 1989, additional controlled studies have been completed (Boudewyns et al., 1993; Boudewyns & Hyer, 1996; Pitman et al., 1996; Jensen, 1994; Carlson et al., 1998; Renfrey & Spates, 1994; Wilson, Silver, Covi, & Foster, 1996; Rothbaum, 1997; Wilson, Becker, & Tinker, 1995, 1997; Scheck, Schaefffer, & Gillette, 1998; Vaughan, Armstrong, & Tarrier, 1994; Marcus, Marquis, & Sakai, 1997). Five examined the efficacy of EMDR with combat veterans (Boudewyns et al., 1993; Boudewyns & Hyer, 1996; Pitman et al., 1996; Jensen, 1994; Carlson et al., 1998), a multiple trauma population that would be predicted to require multiple sessions to achieve significant treatment effects on general measures. Of these studies, only Carlson et al. provided a sufficient number of sessions with sufficient fidelity to obtain optimal results. Unfortunately the other studies did not provide sufficient sessions, specific enough measures, or adequate treatment fidelity to fully evaluate treatment effectiveness. Nevertheless these studies generally showed significant improvements with the use of EMDR for combat trauma and compare favorably with all other studies of psychological treatments for combat trauma. Seven studies (Renfrey & Spates, 1994; Wilson, Silver, Covi, & Foster, 1996; Rothbaum, 1997; Wilson, Becker, & Tinker, 1995, 1997; Scheck, Schaeffer, & Gillette, 1998;

Vaughan, Armstrong, & Tarrier, 1994; Marcus, Marquis, & Sakai, 1997) have examined primarily single-episode trauma victims and found generally large treatment effects as assessed with standard psychometrics and independent assessors. While 8 of these 12 studies used wait-list controls or attempted component analyses, 4 studies included active control treatments, 1 with combat trauma and 3 with single-incident civilian trauma. The 4 most recent civilian PTSD studies (Rothbaum, 1997; Wilson, Becker, & Tinker, 1995, 1997; Scheck, Schaeffer, & Gillette, 1998; Marcus, Marquis, & Sakai, 1997) found that 84–90 percent of subjects treated with three sessions of EMDR no longer met criteria for PTSD.

Use of Safe Place in the Stabilization Phase: Extending EMDR via Resource Installation

Current approaches to the treatment of posttraumatic stress disorder generally call for a phased treatment plan that paces the therapy to meet the nature of the patient's symptoms (Courtois, 1988; Herman, 1992; McCann & Pearlman, 1990; van der Kolk, McFarlane, & van der Hart, 1996). Early portions of treatment focus on stabilization, which generally includes patient education, building self-control strategies, and assuring adequate social support ("stage one"). Work on resolving traumatic memories ("stage two") is generally not to be started until patients have been sufficiently stabilized. For patients with intensely intrusive memories, a dissociative disorder, or major deficits related to early childhood neglect and failures of early attachment, these first portions of the treatment plan can require months or years of reparative work and can prove more challenging than the eventual work on trauma memories themselves. When the trauma-focused work has been largely addressed, the therapy eventually moves toward reestablishing deeper interpersonal connections and integrating new skills, goals, and a new identity ("stage three"). In EMDR such a phased approach is encompassed within the eight phases of the treatment plan described below.

With the understanding that EMDR is not merely a simple technique of desensitization but is a comprehensive treatment approach that moves targeted material rapidly and profoundly as it enhances emotional learning, the need for stability and patient readiness before addressing traumatic material is even greater. A number of standardized approaches to modulating affective distress—such as structured muscle relaxation, breathing techniques, autogenic training, hypnosis, and guided imagery—can be useful for some trauma survivors. But early in the application of EMDR to combat trauma and adult survivors of childhood abuse, it was found that many chronic trauma survivors had a paradoxical response to relaxation approaches to modulating anxiety, based on a perceived need to remain hypervigilant.

In the accelerated-information processing model, EMDR is viewed not merely as a technique for desensitizing distressing associations but also as a way to strengthen positive associations. While no published controlled clinical studies have as yet focused on the use of alternating eye movements to enhance positive affect and self-appraisals before addressing traumatic memories, this approach has been incorporated in the clinical application of EMDR since shortly after its introduction. This took the form of the three-pronged protocol, which calls for reprocessing earlier memories and present triggers, and processing positive templates for appropriate future action. The installation phase and the future templates specifically made use of EMDR's ability to enhance positive images, affects, and beliefs (Shapiro, 1991a, 1995). Subsequently Neal Daniels (Shapiro, 1988a) suggested using this effect of EMDR in the preparation phase of treatment, to combine an image of a safe place with alternating eye movement to enhance the ability of combat veterans to experience feelings of calm and peacefulness. Clinical feedback indicated that this procedure was of widespread value, and it was soon introduced as a recommended part of the stabilization phase of EMDR.

Subsequent to Daniels's suggestion, a number of EMDR innovators have reported clinical benefits from incorporating bilateral, alternating stimulation for enhancing positive-memory networks (Greenwald, 1993a, 1993b; Wildwind, 1992). But the use of these procedures for stabilization purposes has not been the specific subject of controlled-outcome studies.

In an effort to bring more attention to the potential for these ego-strengthening and positive-memory-enhancing procedures, Leeds (1995) introduced the term *resource development and installation* (RDI) along with proposed principles for alternating stimulation with positive images, memories, and symbols within the larger framework of the eight-phase EMDR approach. In addition to the early reports cited above, numerous individual case reports of a range of applications to patients with diverse diagnoses have been described in personal communications to us and via postings to the EMDR Institute Discussion listserv on the Internet. An informal survey (Leeds, 1998a) of EMDR Institute–trained clinicians who subscribed to this listserv reported these procedures to be nearly universally safe and effective at enhancing patient stability. An experimental study with an analogue population by Ichii (1998) found that positive attributes of positive memories were enhanced and negative attributes of negative memories were reduced when subjects focused on these memories and engaged in alternating eye movements. Preliminary evidence has been reported that RDI can be effective in the stabilization phase of treatment of complex PTSD (Korn & Leeds, in press). Controlled research will be needed with various clinical populations to explore specific risks and benefits of this procedure. Until such a body of research is amassed, principles established from case reports together with considerations informed by neurobiologial research and theoretical formulations can guide the application of these additional procedures.

Definitions of Terms

The term *resource* is used to refer to both "ego resources" and "self-capacities" as defined by McCann and Pearlman (1990). Resources are normally developed through appropriate modeling by caregivers and authority figures, sharing of stories and metaphors, and instruction in practical and moral precepts. These normal experiences aid development of emotional regulation, adaptive skills (mature defenses), and healthy self-object relations.

Resource development refers to deliberate strategic interventions implemented over a series of sessions that support patients' development of missing or inadequately developed resources.

Resource development strategies focus on the use of images, stories, metaphors, humor, play, and other methods to introduce self-object representations that aid the patient in constructing more adaptive models, defenses, and response sets.

Resource development strategies may be quite focused and prescriptive, such as instruction in principles of assertiveness. They can also be quite general and permissive, such as wondering out loud with the patient about the thoughts, feelings, and behavior of a more positive role model, or presenting a metaphor or brief story without specifying any particular patient responses.

Resource development and installation refers to a set of EMDR-related protocols that focus exclusively on strengthening resources in positive-memory networks while deliberately not stimulating dysfunctional-memory networks.

Resource development and installation protocols are informed by earlier strategies, such as Ericksonian and permissive hypnosis and guided imagery methods for ego strengthening. For patients presenting with limited resources and questionable stability, stabilization and resource development often must become the primary focus. For many of these patients, stabilization methods described by others (van der Kolk, McFarlane, & Van der Hart, 1996; Linehan, 1993a, 1993b) can often be easily integrated into RDI procedures.

RDI is hypothesized to differ from these earlier methods in at least four ways:

- Bilateral stimulation is incorporated into a structured protocol.
- Rapid shifts in affect and physiological state (a "compelled relaxation response" [Wilson, 1996]) regularly occur when bilateral stimulation is added to an activated memory network.
- Spontaneous associations to personally meaningful memories are commonly observed in EMDR and RDI sessions (Leeds, 1998a) in ways that enrich the patient's functioning.
- There appears to be an increased integration of left-and-right-hemisphere-mediated functional capacities (Nicosia, 1994; Stickgold, 1998; Wilson, 1999). This leads both to in-session observed shifts in associated material, and to a generalization of treatment effects as shown in spontaneous new functional capacities. Patients do not need to make a conscious connection between the work done in an RDI session and subsequent more functional emotional,

cognitive, and behavioral responses. That is, a conscious elicitation of the resource is not necessary to ensure optimal functioning.

RDI procedures help patients build new frames of reference. They increase patients' abilities to tolerate present and future stresses by: promoting their ability to accept existing social supports or risk reaching out for new, appropriate social supports; building new self-capacities to resume reworking developmental delays and fill in lacuna; forming new memory networks; and building and strengthening resources needed to address traumatic memories and core dysfunctional schemata. Through RDI, patients' core needs for meaning and a sense of spiritual redemption can also be addressed.

Additional Theory for Resource Development and Installation

Both human and animal neurophysiological and neuroimaging studies indicate that trauma and neglect are capable of producing significant neurological abnormalities that appear to underlie many of the clinical symptoms in patients with such histories (Schore, 1994, 1996; Teicher et al., 1997; van der Kolk, McFarlane, & Weisaeth, 1996). Teicher et al. found that survivors of physical or sexual abuse or pervasive neglect show hemispheric suppression. Patients with such history are severely limited in their ability to make functional use of left-hemisphere-mediated, positive linguistic and cognitive capacities when memories of distressing images, emotions, or sensations are activated in their right hemisphere. Since chronic trauma survivors are flooded with such memories, often on a daily basis, stabilization methods should initially incorporate right-hemisphere-mediated capacities that will remain functionally available at times of left-hemisphere suppression.

Additionally, Schore (1994, 1996, 1997) has emphasized the central role of positive affect in the normal developmental sequence leading to emotional regulation. Patients with certain insecure attachment status show positive-affect intolerance. Chronic, early-trauma, and neglect survivors benefit greatly from developing a greater functional capacity for tolerating stronger affect, rapid affect state changes, and affect modulation before they can tolerate addressing the intense negative affects of traumatic memories (Brierre, 1996; Courtois, 1988; Herman, 1992; Linehan, 1993a; McCann & Pearlman, 1990; van der Kolk, McFarlane, & van der Hart, 1996). These emotional-processing capacities are all mediated via a right-hemisphere—right prefrontal orbital cortex—amygdala circuit that is inadequately developed in survivors of early neglect (Schore, 1994, 1996, 1997). Patients who practice left-hemisphere-mediated-linguistic-based cognitive-behavioral interventions when they are in a calm state (left hemisphere active, right hemisphere suppressed) may find these methods of limited functional value for affect modulation or self-control during somatic, affective, or sensory flashbacks (van der Kolk, McFarlane, & van der Hart, 1996).

RDI procedures emphasize the use of right-hemisphere-mediated memories to develop functional capacities for affect modulation via specific images, body sensations, and memories of positive affect, to access and strengthen functional-memory networks. When clinically indicated and possible, left-hemisphere-mediated cognitive schemata and positive linguistic self-referencing beliefs are deliberately linked with these right-hemisphere-mediated positive-memory networks, together with alternating bilateral stimulation that is posited to enhance bi-hemisphere activation and integration.

Neurocognitive research shows that prefrontal inhibition (Schore, 1994, 1996; van der Kolk, McFarlane, & Weisaeth, 1996) occurs in survivors of trauma and neglect, resulting in the subjective experience of loss of self. RDI procedures are hypothesized to help build a capacity for prefrontal activation via consistent rehearsal of right-hemisphere-mediated functional-memory networks of positive images, affects, and sensations. The literature on the role of positive affect and specific imagery suggests that they help patients recovering from the effects of cumulative and early trauma and neglect develop the ability to activate, tolerate, and integrate right-hemisphere-mediated positive images, affects, and sensations (Baker, 1981, 1983). Clinical exploration of RDI principles and protocols has led to their increasing use by EMDR-trained clinicians across a range of clinical presentations (Leeds, 1998a).

Overview of Eight Phases of EMDR

EMDR treatment consists of eight phases, which are here identified and described separately for purposes of discussion and clarification of treatment strategies. On a practical level, experienced EMDR-trained clinicians find that the tasks and sequencing of these phases necessarily overlap in many cases.

Phase 1: Patient History and Treatment Planning

In Phase 1, the clinician conducts a thorough screening and history taking. The extent of this screening and history will depend on a number of factors, including premorbid adjustment, complexity of clinical presentations, histories involving childhood abuse or neglect, number and kinds of trauma history, and stability of current environment.

It is essential that clinicians take an adequate history, as rushing to begin the reprocessing phases of the standard EMDR PTSD protocol could lead to overlooking such potential contraindications as the need to do more extensive patient stabilization, refer for medication, or build a therapeutic alliance adequate to the specific needs of a more vulnerable or unstable patient. Sufficient history must be obtained to assure that an appropriate, overall treatment plan has been developed.

In EMDR a multimodal-modal assessment is encouraged, such as is described by Lazarus and Lazarus (1991). For a detailed description of history-taking, patient-screening, and selection issues, see Shapiro (1995). A few of the specific cautions to be considered will be mentioned here.

Dissociative disorders

Before offering EMDR reprocessing on either traumatic targets or resource installation, screening for a possible dissociative disorder is essential. EMDR catalyzes a more rapid associative processing that has frequently been reported to overcome amnestic barriers in dissociative patients, flooding them with emotions, traumatic images, and body sensations that can overwhelm their defenses. This can be not only retraumatizing to the patient but can lead to potentially dangerous loss of impulse control, acting out, and parasuicidal and suicidal behaviors. EMDR can be successfully incorporated into the treatment of patients with dissociative disorders, but it should only be done by those with appropriate specialty training and supervised experience in both the use of EMDR and the treatment of dissociative disorders (Fine et al., 1995; Lazrove & Fine, 1996; Paulsen, 1995).

Depression

Depressed mood by itself is not a contraindication for use of the standard EMDR protocol, as patients with PTSD are generally subject to cycling between episodes of hyperarousal and avoidance, with symptoms of both anxiety and depression (van der Kolk, McFarlane, & Weisaeth, 1996). There is substantial evidence from controlled studies that EMDR alleviates symptoms of depression that are associated with PTSD. (See for example Wilson, Becker, & Tinker, 1995, 1997.)

Not all depressive symptoms are associated with posttraumatic syndromes. Patients with apparently endogenous and/or "biologically" based depressions may benefit from and need antidepressant medication, both for stabilization and to be able to participate fully in psychotherapy. Adult survivors of childhood neglect by chronically depressed parents may exhibit early-onset or lifelong dysthymia, not only as a result of genetic factors but due to the impact of inadequate attachment experiences.

Such individuals may never have experienced an adequate "premorbid" period and may therefore lack the adaptive resources needed to respond positively to the standard EMDR PTSD protocol. Specialized RDI approaches have been reported (Korn & Leeds, in press; Leeds, 1997; Wildwind, 1994) to be helpful with these patients, but controlled research is needed to assess their efficacy, risks, and range of applications. Patients where suicide is a risk, including those with a history of hospitalizations to prevent or following suicide attempts, need to be managed conservatively. EMDR should be offered to these patients only by clinicians with appropriate training and experience. Hospitalization to permit more intensive work in a safe environment can be a viable option in certain cases.

Adult Attachment Status, Affect Change and Intensity Tolerance

The capacity to tolerate changes in affect state and affect intensity is often subsumed under ego strength, but it needs to be a central aspect of assessing readiness before commencing EMDR standard protocols. Adult attachment status (Main, 1996) tends to vary, along with the capacity to tolerate affective intensity and change. Case formulation will often depend in large measure on adult attachment status. This should not be confused with adult relationship status, as some patients in stable family or marital relationships may have rather unstable, insecure attachment status (Stein, Jacobs, Ferguson, Allen, & Fonagy, 1998).

Maladaptive Schemas

When patients have impairments in several core schemata, their treatment will be more complex and lengthy. Treatment planning will need to carefully consider sequencing of targets in terms of the need structures, self-capacities, and schemata that the patient most needs and can best tolerate addressing.

Treatment Planning

During the treatment-planning phase, the clinician identifies suitable foci for treatment, which are called *targets*. Formative past events that the clinician and patient view as the foundation for the patient's symptomatology are identified and prioritized to be processed. Current stimuli that trigger pathological responses are identified and will be checked and processed after the targets from the past if they remain sources of dysfunction. In addition, new skills and identity structures that the patient may need in the future will be processed as future templates to ensure that they will be fully integrated into the patient's coping capacity and self-concept.

Not every identified past traumatic event and present trigger will necessarily need to be processed individually. Clinical experience has repeatedly shown that generalization of treatment effects often permits related traumatic events and stimuli to be grouped in clusters and that representative targets may be processed to achieve functional resolution of related targets and broad symptomatic relief.

Phase 2: Preparation

In the second phase of treatment, the clinician prepares the patient in several ways.

- Most important is establishing a supportive therapeutic alliance and a collaborative relationship that will permit honest communication by the patient. The time needed to establish an adequate level of trust varies with the extent to which trust schemata have been violated in the patient's past and the nature of the issues to be resolved.
- The patient is given adequate information to provide informed consent to treatment, including explanations of procedures and a rationale for treatment.
- Helpful metaphors and models of the treatment process are provided to orient the patient and reduce anxiety about a new experience. The patient is instructed in a variety of self-control procedures to increase (or establish) stability in current functioning. These may include training in structured relaxation exercises; self-observation skills; and guided imagery, which can be enhanced with sets of eye movements or other alternating rhythmic stimulation (see Phase 4).
- The patient is taught a stop (hand) signal to enhance the sense of control during processing of traumatic memories.

The extent of work needed in Phase 2 to prepare a given patient for the standard EMDR PTSD protocol will vary greatly depending on an array of patient characteristics. For patients with a single-episode adult-onset trauma with a good premorbid adjustment, only one or a few sessions may be needed to assure stability and readiness. Survivors of prolonged trauma, such as imprisonment and torture, who are suffering from complex posttraumatic stress disorder (Herman, 1992) will need more work in the preparation phase to provide sufficient stability and adequate access to self-control and affect-modulation skills. On the other hand, for survivors of early childhood neglect, suffering from complex posttraumatic stress disorder and adult-attachment-related syndromes (Barach, 1991; Liotti, 1992; Main, 1996), the preparation phase will become the central focus of treatment for an extended period of time to support the patient in developing basic self-capacities for self-care, in tolerating changes and more intensity in negative and positive affects, and in containing impulses for self-injurious and suicidal behaviors.

Phase 3: Assessment

During the assessment phase, the therapist and patient jointly select the target (i.e., traumatic memory, current stimuli, or future template) to be processed. The principal elements of the target's memory network are delineated as the most salient or representative images, beliefs, emotions, and sensations. Baseline ratings of the target are also taken. The components of these procedural steps, the eliciting phrases for each step, and their sequence have been optimized based on years of clinician feedback from a wide range of clinical experience. Each of the procedural steps in Phase 3 leading up to processing with eye movements (or other alternating, bilateral stimulation) should themselves be considered an integral part of the therapeutic process and contribute to the overall treatment effects in a variety of ways (which will be seen in the description of each step).

Delineation and assessment of the selected treatment target begin with identifying a visual image (or an alternative sensory memory, such as a sound or smell) of the most emotionally painful part of the experience. The sensory aspect of an unresolved traumatic memory is believed to be predominantly stored in the right hemisphere, together with associated distressing emotions such as fear and anger generated via the amygdala, which is closely linked to the right hemisphere (van der Kolk, Burbridge, & Suzuki, 1997).

Next the clinician assists the patient in identifying the central, personal negative attribution(s) with which the patient is identified as a result of that experience. This is referred to as the *negative cognition* or NC. In EMDR the negative cognition is a preeminently negative self-appraisal, such as:

- "I am bad."
- "I am worthless."
- "I am unlovable."
- "I am vulnerable."

Psychologically, this step helps the patient to recognize the irrationality of the cognitive interpretation of this experience. Neurologically, it requires the patient to activate Broca's area in the left hemisphere, which has been shown to be functionally inhibited when the traumatic memory is activated (Rauch et al., 1996). Clinically, the negative cognition provides an additional means to activate the dysfunctional memory network or fear structures referred to by Foa and Kozak (1986).

The next step is to help the patient develop a more adaptive self-attribution in relationship to that painful experience, known as the *positive cognition* or PC. This positive cognition is a statement such as:

- "I did the best I could."
- "I am a worthy person."
- "I am lovable enough."

Psychologically, the positive cognition introduces corrective information that is incompatible with the original assessment. It also represents an expression of the treatment goal for the session and can encourage the patient to continue through the processing of the emotionally charged material that lies ahead. Neurologically, eliciting the positive cognition requires the patient to activate left-hemisphere- and prefrontal-mediated areas, which provide analytical skills that are less linked to sensory-based experience and that provide a more symbolic and categorical mode of information processing (van der Kolk, Burbridge, & Suzuki, 1997). Clinically, eliciting the positive cognition helps the clinician assess how "far" the patient "can see down the road" toward adaptation and recovery. In patients with chronic or complex PTSD, the severity of hemispheric suppression (Teicher et al., 1997) can make the identification of an appropriate and ecologically relevant positive cognition a challenging and crucial part of the treatment. A positive cognition that is too far removed from the patient's present perspective or one that is presently unrealistic can inhibit rather than contribute to treatment effects.

The therapist next asks the patient to rate how true the more adaptive statement feels on a scale from 1 (feels totally false) to 7 (feels totally true). During the rating of the *validity of cognition* (VoC), the patient is asked to hold the disturbing image (right-hemisphere) in awareness at the same time as the positive cognition (left hemisphere) and give an affective rating (bilateral activation). This baseline rating of the VoC provides an additional reference point for assessing treatment effects later in the session. This baseline reference can be especially useful when the processing of traumatic material must be extended over more than one treatment session, as even partial increases toward a 7 VoC can provide validating evidence of the patient's gradual progress through challenging material.

Note that sequence of these initial procedural steps facilitates the patient's ability to connect the selected visual image with both the negative and the positive cognitions *before* the associated affects of the traumatic material are fully or explicitly stimulated, to reduce potential interference from intense affective arousal.

Next, the therapist asks the patient to focus on the selected image and the negative cognition and to name the emotions presently felt. Explicitly naming the present emotion establishes further baseline information that can aid in evaluating progress since during the processing of a traumatic memory, the emotional response to the traumatic memory commonly changes several times. If the level of emotional disturbance (see SUD level, below) remains unchanged at the end of the session, knowing the baseline emotional response for the session can clarify for the patient and the clinician whether progress was made. For example, the emotional response may have shifted from intense fear and helplessness to anger. Knowing the present emotion in addition to the negative belief assists the clinician in being able to give needed support and to identify potential beliefs that could block processing.

After identifying the present emotion, the patient is asked to rate how disturbing the specific memory or situation feels in the present, on a Subjective Units of Disturbance (SUD) scale from 0 (calm, no disturbance) to 10 (the most disturbance the patient could imagine).

Finally, the therapist asks the patient to report where the present disturbing emotion is felt in the body. Identifying the location of the physical sensations before and during processing helps further activate the unresolved aspects of the traumatic memory. Asking for the body location helps assure that the patient is feeling something and provides a check against the patient's arbitrarily naming a likely emotion merely to satisfy the clinician's inquiry. Naming the location also provides another way for the patient to observe without judging or having to describe in detail what is being experienced during processing. This shift to an observing stance, which only requires the patient to note where something is felt, furthers treatment goals, as many patients tend to become caught up in self-judging or in overly verbalizing as a way to avoid reexperiencing distressing aspects of traumatic memories.

The physical sensations may represent an aspect of the associated emotions, or they may be linked to the memory of sensations produced during the traumatic event. It is not necessary to determine which of these the sensations may actually represent.

Phase 4: Desensitization

The next three phases (desensitization, installation, body scan) involve alternating bilateral stimulation, together with other procedural elements intended to enhance information processing (Shapiro, 1995). They are collectively referred to as *reprocessing* or *processing*. Forms of alternating bilateral stimulation include:

- back-and-forth eye movements
- alternating auditory tones
- alternating hand taps

Throughout these three phases, any or all aspects of the traumatic-memory network may be simultaneously changing as reported or observed: changes in the vividness or content of sensory memory; changes in affect quality or intensity; changes in self-assessment and thoughts about the memory; changes in the characteristics and location of physical sensations.

When the target to be treated has been delineated and assessed, the therapist first makes sure the elements of the target are active in the patient's awareness and then asks the patient to adopt a nonjudgmental attitude, to just notice whatever takes place while beginning alternating, bilateral rhythmic stimulation. The procedures employed throughout the three reprocessing phases of EMDR were initially developed and later modified based on extensive clinical observations (Shapiro, 1995). They are intended to enhance the rapidity of treatment effects while maintaining the patient's stability and the sense of safety and control over the treatment process and outcome. For example, the instruction to "let whatever happens, happen" before commencing alternating stimulation is intended to reduce demand characteristics and the patient's fear of "failure" while enhancing spontaneous association to relevant aspects of traumatic memories. Indeed, based on extensive clinical observation, it appears that EMDR can enhance the formation of new associations and memory networks that are adaptive for the patient.

At the end of each set of alternating stimulations, the patient is instructed to "rest, take a deeper breath," and is asked, "What do you notice now?" These instructions and the pause engendered by the "deeper breath" appear to further the nondemand, exploratory stance established at the outset, helping the patient to dose the exposure and then to reaccess the most relevant emerging aspects of the target material while permitting the overall continuation of the level and type of affective arousal. Any state-dependent information processing (Bower, 1981; Demos, 1988) associated with a type or degree of affective arousal is thereby permitted to continue and, after the patient provides a verbal report sufficient to determine that emerging material is in fact processing rather than "looping" or remaining stuck at the same informational plateau, to resume. Verbal and nonverbal patient responses during and after each set of alternating stimulations help inform clinical decisions regarding potential changes in length, speed, type, and other characteristics of the bilateral stimulation. The clinician may also remind the patient of relevant information incompatible with the emerging material, when it appears that patient is not attaining or maintaining information processing with changes in the type of stimulation alone. In EMDR treatment this is called the *cognitive interweave* (Shapiro, 1995).

Phase 4 is called desensitization because typical treatment effects lead to decreases in anxiety and distress and in the vividness of sensory recall, along with increasingly adaptive self-attributions. But the desensitization effects are considered to be a consequence of information processing and include an array of rapid changes in eliciting insights, organization of memory, associated affect, and self-concept not observed during classical desensitization procedures. The desensitization phase is said to be complete when the patient can focus on the target memory or situation and rate the level of emotional disturbance at a 0 or 1.

Phase 5: Installation

In the installation phase, the focus is on associating a more adaptive self-assessment with the target memory. Installation involves bringing the target event into awareness at the same time as a more adaptive self-appraisal, and adding alternating stimulation. A more appropriate adaptive belief may have emerged during Phase 4 than the PC initially selcted in the assessment of the target. The VoC of the selected self-appraisal is identified, and then sets of alternating stimulation are offered until the rating of the emotional validity of the more adaptive belief rises to a 6 or 7 or to a level that is ecologically valid for the patient's situation.

Phase 6: Body Scan

Only after completing Phases 4 and 5 is the patient asked to:

- Visualize the formerly painful memory or event, and
- Hold that memory together with the more adaptive statement, and
- Scan from head to toe for any sensations.

If tension or discomfort is found, the alternating stimulation is continued until the patient reports no unpleasant bodily sensations when pairing the target memory and the positive belief. During the body scan multiply traumatized patients commonly report associations to other traumatic memories, which must be processed in subsequent sessions. Treatment is not considered complete until the patient reports no further sensations that may be associated with other significant areas of disturbance. The tension or other disturbing sensation is evaluated and addressed by offering further alternating stimulation in that or a later session, since some uncomfortable sensations, such as from a recent injury or an uncomfortable chair, may not be linked to other significant material. If positive sensations are found during the body scan, the alternating stimulation is continued until the patient reports that the pleasant sensations are not getting any more pleasant.

Phase 7: Closure

At the end of each session, the clinician checks to see that the patient's distress or pain has been reduced. The patient is brought back to a state of equilibrium, either via completed processing or through the use of affect-regulation and self-control methods developed during Phase 2. After the clinician is assured that the patient is feeling comfortable and is well-oriented, the patient is asked to be alert, until the next session, for indications of further changes, positive or negative, related to the presenting symptoms and targeted memories, emotions, and beliefs and to make a record of these in a written log. Other homework assignments are given, and plans are made for the next appointment. These closure procedures are intended to enhance patient stability between sessions.

Phase 8: Reevaluation

At the beginning of each subsequent session, the clinician reevaluates the patient's current level of functioning along with feedback from the patient's log. Targets addressed during prior sessions are reevaluated to verify the stability of treatment effects. Checks are made to determine if any new issues or problems have arisen or if the patient needs to develop additional self-care or interpersonal skills. The treatment plan is adjusted based on the observed responses to treatment. Successful treatment can be determined only with sufficient reevaluation. Within-session treatment effects are not considered a sufficient basis for verifying successful treatment.

The overall goal of EMDR treatment is "to produce the most comprehensive and profound treatment effects in the shortest period of time, while simultaneously maintaining a stable patient within a stable system" (Shapiro, 1998b, 1999). Achieving this goal requires pacing the work according to the patient's observed capacity to tolerate changes in affect state, behavior, and self-concept and as well integrating the responses of the patient's primary social systems to the effects of treatment.

Treatment is considered complete when the patient has reached the treatment goals. These would normally include: significantly disturbing memories are resolved; current stimuli are no longer able to evoke symptomatic responses; and the patient is prepared for likely future situations with an increased sense of resilience and confidence.

Purposes of Resource Development and Resource Installation

Resource development strategies in general and specific RDI protocols are intended to enhance patient stability through a series of ego-strengthening experiences and through the development of discrete impaired self-capacities. RDI is intended to enhance patients' capacities to access adaptive resources in times of stress and, by enhancing their capacity for affect containment, self-soothing, and coping, to promote stability in current functioning. A central aspect of RDI is a focus on generating the positive affects of interest-excitment and enjoyment-joy (Tomkins, 1991; Nathanson, 1992) by combining bilateral stimulation with uniquely positive images, memories, body sensations, and self-appraisals. In successful RDI sessions, patients show rapid shifts to these positive-affect states. For some patients, their positive-associational-memory networks are fairly well developed, and they can easily tolerate the rapid increases in positive affects. For other patients with more chronic problems or early developmental deficits, these positive-associational-memory networks may be nearly nonexistent, and the patient may be almost "allergic" to the positive affects. The need for differential case formulaton, treatment planning, and treatment strategies in such complex cases will be touched on more fully later. Next, the basic RDI protocol will be presented and then illustrated with the first of two case examples.

The Basic EMDR Resource Installation Protocol

Resource installation is a creative and flexible procedure that must be adapted to the unique needs of each patient. The following is a general model.

1. Ask the patient to focus on a challenging current life situation, blocking belief, or maladaptive schema.
2. Ask the patient to identify what quality (or qualities) he or she needs in order to better manage this situation or belief.

- Use your knowledge of the patient's history and current social and personal resources to help the patient identify an experience of this quality associated with positive affect, for which he or she has an image or sensory memory.
- If the patient cannot remember an experience, ask the patient to remember someone else dealing effectively with this type of situation. Consider what qualities the person embodies in that situation.
- Also consider a symbolic representation of this resource that may or may not be obviously linked to a specific memory.

3. Ask the patient to focus on the quality (resource) he or she wishes to strengthen; ask the patient to allow an image (of a person, real or fictional, or any object or animal or a symbol) to arise that represents that quality.
4. Ask the patient to describe the image or memory. Write down verbatim key descriptive words. Prompt the patient, if appropriate, for more detail on the resource for each relevant sensory modality.
5. Ask the patient to notice any positive emotions or sensations he or she feels when focusing on this image or quality. Find out where the patient notices these feelings in the body.
6. Enhance the patient's resource experience by repeating descriptions of the memory or image. Include the sensory and affective qualities and the location of feelings associated with the resource.

Verify the patient's resource experience was enhanced and that there were no negative associations or emotions.

Use clinical judgment to decide whether to do either of the next two steps at this point or after adding alternating, bilateral stimulation to the resource experience.

7. Ask the patient to say a cue word or phrase that goes with the resource he or she wants to enhance.
8. Ask the patient to imagine physically connecting with the resource. He or she can imagine stepping into the body image of the person or animal, or can hold it and feel it dissolve into his or her body.
9. Ask the patient to focus on the image and feelings (and a cue word or phrase, if selected). Add eye movements. Do a brief set of 6 to

14 back-and-forth movements. Then ask what the patient is aware of now.

10. If the patient reports that the resource experience was enhanced, continue with 2 to 3 more sets of alternating, bilateral stimulation, as long as the positive feelings and associations get stronger. Discontinue the alternating stimulation when the resource has been strengthened. Stop if the patient associates to negative material, and consider selecting a different resource or resource experience.

11. Repeat this process for each of the qualities the patient wants to strengthen.

12. Consider the use of a future template to have the patient imaginally practice using the resource(s) between sessions to enhance current coping skills.

13. Keep in mind that reevaluation is an essential element in treatment plans using these methods. In future sessions, check resources that have previously been installed as well as the patient's written log for any feedback. When the patient is ready for stage two, trauma-focused work, consider beginning the session by bringing in—and strengthening with alternating stimulation—the resources needed to address the traumatic material.

14. During trauma-focused reprocessing, consider using previously installed resources as cognitive interweaves.

Clinical Application with a Couple

In this case example, both individuals have a secure attachment status, and RDI protocols were used for stabilization and symptom management in the first stage of treatment. Due to their overall stability and degree of functioning, RDI was rapidly followed by the standard EMDR protocol, leading to a comprehensive and stable resolution of the presenting complaints in both individuals and the relationship in eight sessions.

Background

Stephen and Maryann had been married for 12 years. Stephen was a 14-year firefighter with cumulative work trauma from a number of horrific experiences, including witnessing badly burned bodies and children overcome by smoke who could not be resuscitated.

After nine years of a happy and fulfilling marriage, Stephen became increasingly withdrawn and emotionally distant. Several times he was verbally abusive to his wife and more recently to his 11-year-old son. There was no evidence of work impairment. Yet his CISD (Critical Incident Stress Debriefing) team leader felt inclined to encourage him to consider some individual therapy. Stephen denied needing therapy and said he was doing fine.

Maryann had gone back to school five years before to complete the last two years of nursing training. She had worked as a nurse for the last three years and blamed herself for her husband's change in temperament. Having always taken good care of herself and her family, she felt helpless to bring back the happy family life she had previously known with Stephen.

Six months ago, she turned down a job promotion to become shift supervisor to spend more time with her family. But Stephen had begun spending more of his time away from home and rejected her assistance on home projects. She became quite discouraged and somewhat depressed. After previously regaining and maintaining her premarital weight through careful diet and exercise, she neglected her exercise program, began overeating, and gained 30 pounds.

Seeking Treatment

Maryann decided that she and Stephen needed marriage counseling. She asked him to accompany her to see a psychologist trained in EMDR who was recommended by the CISD team leader and the team's mental health adviser. Stephen initially refused to accompany his wife for counseling, so Maryann went for an individual intake session, where she said she wanted to focus on how she could take better care of herself and perhaps influence her husband to enter marriage counseling.

Second Session

In Maryann's second session, her therapist decided to focus on RDI as a way to help her strengthen her current functioning. The therapist guided Maryann to identify key resources that could strengthen her self-

care program. Her initial goal was to stop overeating and resume her former exercise regime. Maryann easily remembered how, within a few
months of the delivery of each child, she had been able to return to her
prepregnancy weight and measurements. These memories were used as a
resource, which was strengthened via the Resource Installation protocol.

First the therapist asked Maryann to identify the memory that most
represented her capacity for self-care. She identified the time after her second child's birth. The therapist then asked her to select a specific image,
and she selected the memory of the day, 14 days after the birth, when she
first went out for a 40-minute walk/jog. She recalled the still morning air,
the bright sun on the lawns she passed, the feeling of her legs working
hard, her breath vigorous in her chest, and her heart beating strongly. The
positive words associated with this memory were: "I'm strong. I can take
care of myself." Holding this image, the body sensations, and the positive
words in her awareness, Maryann was asked to follow the movements of
the therapist's hand with her eyes. With each of 4 short sets of eye movements, the feelings became stronger and more pleasant.

Next Maryann identified a positive memory of choosing to eat more
selectively and consciously. The memory again came from the time after
her daughter's birth, when she had stopped eating impulsively and gone
shopping for more fresh foods. She remembered passing by the frozen
food section in the store without buying another half-gallon of ice cream,
as she had been doing, and instead buying an assortment of fresh fruit
and vegetables. She said that was really the turning point of her making
better choices about what to eat. She identified the positive words "I
know what I really need" and a feeling in her head, shoulders, and neck
of "certainty." These elements were strengthened with short sets of eye
movements. After the third set, Maryann laughed and said, "You know,
it's funny—I can actually taste how good those peaches were that year."

A future template was employed to help Maryann access these
resources when food urges might arise and when she might consider
avoiding her exercise schedule. For each of these stimuli, Maryann was
asked to notice the negative thoughts and sensations and then to hold in
mind the selected resource while doing a set of eye movements. After
Maryann reported being able to neutralize each of these stimuli, the therapist acknowledged Maryann's work and accomplishments in the session.
She then gave Maryann a list of books on communication skills and
assertiveness and suggested that Maryann select one to read for possible

ideas about how to approach her husband. She stated that they could discuss this together in later sessions.

Third Session

At the third session, Maryann reported that during the week she had been to the gym for the first time in a long time, had stopped overeating, and had returned to her former, balanced eating habits. She said she wanted to focus on gaining the courage and skills to effectively confront her husband with a demand to enter marital counseling. When she imagined doing this, she saw him becoming angry and herself withdrawing in silence. Since this was what had happened recently, she was asked to focus on that recent memory.

She was easily able to see Stephen's angry face and feel the urge to withdraw. Her negative cognition was "I'm worthless." Her positive cognition was "I deserve to be loved." Her VoC was 1. The emotion was shame and fear, with the urge to withdraw. The SUD was 8.

Due to the high SUD and low VoC, her therapist hypothesized that an earlier unresolved and more disturbing memory, known in EMDR as a *feeder memory*, existed that was associated with the high SUD and low VoC. This memory was quickly identified using affect and self-appraisal bridging: a childhood memory from age 9, when she wanted to go to summer camp with her three best friends.

Her mother had taken seven months off work earlier that year, when her youngest brother was born. Her father was worried about spending more of the family's partially depleted savings on the athletics summer camp. When Maryann asked her father if she could go with her friends, he responded uncharacteristically by yelling at her. She ran from the room, feeling humiliated and frightened. Her mother was nursing her baby brother in another part of the house. Not wanting to take attention away from her baby brother, who tended to cry loudly if nursing was interrupted, she went to her room and never spoke to her mother of her desire to go to summer camp. Her father never brought the matter up again either, and she did not go.

The negative and positive cognitions and emotions in this childhood memory were the same as in the recent experience of asking Stephen to join her for marriage counseling. The VoC was a 2. The SUD was an 8. Instead of proceeding directly to process this traumatic memory,

Maryann was first asked to identify any resources that would help her know that she was lovable and worthy. She immediately identified two: her grandmother, with whom she had frequently spent extra time during summer vacations as a child, and the director of nursing at the hospital, who had encouraged her to accept the promotion six months before.

Maryann was asked to identify a specific memory with her grand-mother that was connected with feeling lovable and worthy. She remembered one specific afternoon spent doing a watercolor on Grandmother's screened back porch, and how happy she felt with Grandmother's encouragement about her painting. She felt a sense of pride in her spine and a feeling of being loved in her heart. She identified the words "I'm worthy and lovable." She held the image of her grandmother's face, the positive words, and the feelings in her body with several sets of eye movements. The feelings got stronger. With the second set of eye movements, she cried briefly as she felt a rising sense of appreciation for her grand-mother's love and how much she missed her. With the third set of eye movements, the tears passed, and she reported feeling more strength in her arms and legs and an open feeling in her chest and throat. With the fourth set of eye movements, there were no more changes.

Maryann was then asked to bring up a positive memory of her director of nursing. She remembered an unplanned lunch meeting in the hospital cafeteria, where the director of nursing had praised her work on the unit and encouraged her to consider accepting the supervisor position. Focusing on this memory, she again felt a sense of pride in her spine but now with an open feeling in her face and eyes. The positive words linked with this memory were "I'm capable, and I deserve recognition and support." This resource was strengthened over three sets of eye movements with only positive affects, sensations, and associations.

Maryann then asked to continue to work on the memory of Stephen's recent angry refusal to enter counseling with her by targeting the memory of her father's angry response to her request to go to summer camp. Although less than half the session remained, the therapist agreed to proceed, since Maryann had several resources that could be used to help contain a possible incomplete session. Before proceeding, on rechecking the memory of her father yelling at her, they noted that the SUD had dropped to 6 and the VoC had risen to 4. In addition to humiliation and shame, she now felt some anger.

After the first set of eye movements, Maryann reported that her father's face was becoming clearer in her memory, and she noticed the distress and worry around his eyes. His loud voice expressed his anger and irritation. She said she felt less humiliation and fear and was thinking about how she didn't deserve to be the target of his anger. With the second set of eye movements, she said she was feeling calmer and recognized that her father's outburst at her was due to the financial strain he felt. With the fourth set of eye movements, she said she felt much calmer. Asked to focus again on her father's face in the memory, she reported that she noticed she felt "larger," not like a little kid but like his grown-up daughter. She felt an urge not to run away as before but to reassure him that it was okay, that she would still be proud of him and love him even if the family couldn't afford it. After another set of eye movements, Maryann said she felt relieved, calm, and no longer afraid of her father. Checking the SUD, they found it was down to 0. They went on to an installation of her preferred positive cognition, "I deserve to be loved." The VoC had already risen to a 6, and within two sets of eye movements it had risen "above a 7."

Holding the memory in mind and the positive words, Maryann was asked to close her eyes and scan her body for any feelings. She reported feelings of openness in her chest and strength in her legs and arms. These feelings were strengthened with a further set of eye movements. She was given a standard briefing on possible aftereffects of the session and reminded to keep a log of significant occurrences.

Intersession phone call

Three days after the third session, Maryann called into the therapist's answering service and requested a call back. When Maryann answered the phone, she asked her therapist if it would be "all right" if she didn't wait until after the next session to ask Stephen to come in. Instead of giving a definite answer, the therapist asked why she needed to know. Maryann confessed that ever since the last session, she had been thinking about asking him to come to the next session using some of the assertive methods she'd read about a couple of weeks before. The evening before, after the kids were in bed, she had done just that, and he'd agreed, reluctantly, to come with her the next week if it was "okay" with the therapist.

The therapist was somewhat surprised at the rapid turn of events.

Maryann gave a brief and rather matter-of-fact explanation of how the conversation had gone. Apparently Stephen had gotten angry initially, just as Maryann had predicted, but she had stayed calm and repeated her request without walking away. She then went on to use what seemed to the therapist like some fairly advanced assertive strategies with her husband. For example, she had reminded him of some of the special vows they'd written together into their marriage ceremony 12 years before. Maryann also mentioned that near the end of the conversation he had remarked that she had changed so much in the last three weeks that he was concerned that he better come in to "catch up" with her. The therapist readily agreed with the plan to have Stephen join them for the fourth session.

Once the feeder memory of father's anger had been resolved, apparently Maryann was much less troubled by her husband's angry outburst. While this is a fairly common response, it will sometimes be necessary to reprocess the recent event and then to process a future template before the patient feels ready to adopt new behaviors. The patient's need to address all three aspects, past, present and future, will depend on individual factors from their family-of-origin, extent of their unresolved traumas, and their ability to tolerate change. On the other hand, the spontaneous emergence, in formerly fearful or avoidant patients, of more appropriate behaviors with a matter-of-fact attitude is typical of many patients' responses to EMDR.

Fourth Session

At the fourth session, the therapist and Stephen got briefly acquainted. Things got off to a positive start when Stephen expressed appreciation for his wife's improved self-care, through regular exercise and a better diet, since she started treatment. He said he'd always been suspicious of therapy and the stories he'd heard of people being in lengthy treatment with little change. He said he'd heard good things about the therapist from their CISD team leader and their mental health adviser and decided that maybe this therapist could help him and his wife get back some of the good feelings they used to share. He didn't say anything about his work-related trauma, and rather than press for discussion of his individual issues, the therapist asked instead about what needed to happen to bring back some of the good feelings. Both Maryann and Stephen talked about the need for the two of them to spend more time together. Stephen admitted he'd been avoiding doing that recently because he had been feeling upset a lot and he didn't want to dump on her. He said she deserved better treatment than he'd been giving her and that he didn't understand why he was so jumpy and angry much of the time.

Before the therapist could begin, Maryann jumped in to explain about cumulative trauma and how that affected a lot of career firefighters. "We both know other firefighters who started to get that way after 10 years on the job," she said. "Stephen, you've been doing this for 14 years. What makes you think you're immune to the stress?" With tears in her eyes, she said, "You know how proud I am of what you do. You've saved so many people over the years, but you can't save them all. I know you've seen some horrible things, but you're a good man. You'd have to be a machine not to feel some distress after all these years and all those—well, you know."

Stephen just looked at her for a long time in silence, then turned to the therapist and said, "I've never felt like I could talk about this before without being called a mental case, but after reading your intake forms, I know you can't tell anyone about what I tell you. I guess after what you've done for Maryann, I feel like I can trust you. I've been having nightmares about some of the things I've seen for a while now, and I always figured that meant something was really going wrong. Then a couple of nights ago, Maryann sat me down at our home computer, and we looked at some of those Web sites[1] about trauma and EMDR. I've been reading over the stuff we printed out that night, and I've been thinking that maybe I could use some help getting rid of some of that garbage. I don't really know if it will work. I mean, it seems pretty weird moving your eyes around like that, like when you're dreaming, but it seemed to help you, Maryann, so I'm willing to give it a try."

The therapist agreed to offer some individual EMDR sessions to Stephen and asked if he wanted to set up appointments to come in by himself. They discussed his need to have privacy. Maryann said, "You know, I can't be there to help you when you're at a fire scene, but I wish I could be here to support you and to understand what you've been

---

[1] David Baldwin's Trauma Info Pages: <http://www.trauma pages.com>; EMDR International Association <http://www.emdria.org>; EMDR Institute: <http://www. emdr.com/index/html>

through." After some discussion, he agreed that it would be okay if Maryann sat in on those sessions.

Fifth Session

The next week, the therapist helped Stephen develop a safe place, which turned out to be a quiet spot under a shade tree in their backyard. This was installed and strengthened with a few sets of eye movements. They then identified four key disturbing memories of fire scene deaths and one suicide call. Stephen's negative self-appraisal for each of these scenes was "I am a failure." His initial, preferred self-statement was "I did the best I could."

The first selected memory was of a scene where he and his crew found a family overcome by smoke and fumes in a second-story building. After carrying out two children, the mother, the father, and the dog in the space of a few minutes, he discovered that the paramedic team had been unable to revive one of the children, and he had screamed at them to keep trying. The emotion was anger with a SUD of 9. The VoC was a 2.

Once the reprocessing started, Stephen processed rapidly through a lot of anger, which shifted after several sets of eye movements to self-recrimination, and then sobbing grief for the death of the child and finally some fear about the possibility of losing his own children.

As he returned to the memory of the fire scene, Stephen's SUD had dropped to a 4. He now remembered the grief-stricken faces of the mother and father, and the man saying with tears in his eyes, "Thank you for getting us out. Thank you for saving our little girl. We all would have died without you." With the next few sets of eye movements, the remaining disturbance decreased to a SUD of 0. The preferred cognition "I did the best I could" was installed, and it strengthened to a 6. In discussing what kept it from becoming any stronger, Stephen said, "I'll always remember how that child died. We should be able to do better than that. Maybe what I really need to know is that even when someone dies, I'm a good person." This new self-appraisal was installed with the memory of the fire scene, and it strengthened up to a 7 with just two additional sets of eye movements. The body scan revealed no tension, just a feeling of a weight being lifted off his chest.

Sixth to Eighth Session

The next week, Maryann reported that they had had the best week that she could remember in years. They had worked together on a home improvement project and gone out on a date for dinner and a movie. Stephen said that while he was helping his son with his homework that week, he had spoken more frankly to his son. Stephen reported he had apologized to his son for being so hard on him recently, and they had made plans to go to a college basketball game together. Stephen asked to do more EMDR and worked through two more memories of fire scene deaths, including one that had become a recurring nightmare. At the end of the sixth session, Stephen thanked the therapist and asked Maryann if it would be okay to have the next session to himself. She readily agreed.

At the seventh session, Stephen came in alone and worked on the memory of a suicide call where a man had put a gun in his mouth and shot out the back of his head. The man had called 911 before shooting himself so that his family, who were away for the day, would not be the ones to discover his body. The emergency crew had arrived on the scene a few minutes later, but there was nothing to be done. Stephen was deeply troubled by the man's decision to kill himself. He processed his anger at the man for his self-pity and for abandoning his family. After resolving the memory and completing the installation of his preferred belief, "I'm a good person," Stephen remarked, "You know, I realize part of what was so upsetting to me was that I was starting to think like that man. I was starting to think my family would be better off without me. I realize now, I would never do that. I would never leave them, no matter how bad I was feeling. I know now that even those crazy feelings of failure can pass. I would never do that to Maryann or the kids. I realize now that it's not a sign of failure, it's okay to ask for help when I need it."

At the eighth session, Maryann rejoined Stephen. After checking the remaining memories, it turned out they had apparently been resolved on their own, through generalization of the treatment effects. The session was spent discussing the changes in the family and the marriage over the last two months. Saying that all their initial concerns seemed to have been resolved, Maryann and Stephen asked if it would be okay if they took a break for a couple of weeks and checked in after their family vacation. Three weeks later, Maryann called to say things were going well and that she and Stephen would be in touch if there were any more problems. A month later, Maryann sent a note saying that she had accepted the supervisory position at the hospital. Stephen had also enclosed a "thank you" in which he remarked that he was trying to get one of the other firefighters to come in for a few sessions.

Why This Strategy Worked in This Case

When both husband and wife are having individual problems, marriage counseling that focuses on increasing communication may not address the source of the problems. In this case, individual problems rather than relational difficulties were considered to be the core issues. Both Stephen and Maryann had good premorbid functioning, with stable childhoods, good interpersonal skills, and no significant prior psychological problems. Had there been a history of traumas in their individual pasts or more damaging interactions in their marriage, the treatment would have been more complex and lengthy. The treating clinician made a strategic clinical choice to strengthen Maryann's individual functioning initially rather than to address areas of marital conflict.

These issues underscore the importance of incorporating EMDR into a good overall treatment plan and the need to select treatment protocols based on a solid case formulation. A decision to address the apparent areas of marital conflict as the initial focus might have led to an exacerbation of the marital problems rather than their solution. An initial EMDR focus on Maryann's disturbing memories of her father, before working on better self-care and assertiveness skills, might also have led to an eventual resolution of her problems, but it could have temporarily increased her current distress and prolonged her impulse-control problems with food and exercise. Incorporating EMDR into a good treatment plan involves a number of clinician competencies (touched on below).

The dual potential of EMDR—both to strengthen patient capacities and to address the specific disturbing or traumatic memories associated with current affect dysregulation—was highlighted in this couple's treatment. Their individual responses to EMDR treatment were excellent. Not every couple will respond so rapidly, but their case is typical of those who respond well to these interventions.

Issues in RDI Use

Clinical Indications for RDI

Based on extensive clinical anecdotal feedback, it appears that RDI generally provides positive outcomes for patients with secure attachment status (Main, 1996; Stein et al., 1998), for patients with anxious-ambivalent insecure attachment status, and (with some caveats) for patients with disorganized insecure attachment status or dissociative disorders. Patients with dismissing-avoidant or withdrawn, insecure attachment status generally are much less tolerant of the changes in affect state produced by RDI and need a significantly modified approach that proceeds at a much slower pace (Leeds, 1998c).

Clinical Indications of Missing Resources and/or Inadequate Stabilization

Early use of specialized RDI procedures was often made when selected patients failed to meet selection criteria or to respond positively to standardized EMDR PTSD protocols. While RDI procedures may be chosen to strengthen functioning with many patients, there are clearly many other patients for whom RDI is essential for stabilization because they do not meet the readiness criteria for the standard EMDR PTSD protocol. The following is a list (derived from clinical observation) of indications of missing resources or inadequate stabilization suggestive of the need to provide resource development or installation.

1. The patient is easily flooded with overwhelming feelings of shame, fear, anxiety, or distress, with limited capacity to identify the triggers. At these times, the patient may be unable to speak or may barely be able to articulate coherent thoughts.
2. The patient is not able to identify and describe feelings and, when asked about emotional state, becomes silent, confused, or withdrawn (alexithymic).
3. The patient is unable to make use of standard self-soothing or stabilization strategies (i.e., safe place imagery, relaxation, or coping self-talk), leaving the patient vulnerable to emotional flooding during and between treatment sessions.

4. The patient is avoidant in many areas of life: for example, does not complete projects, withdraws from social connections, minimizes concerns, fails to report significant symptoms.

5. The patient shows persistent depressed mood (dysthymia), low self-esteem, and cognitive distortions, but may not complain of depression, considering these symptoms normal.

6. The patient is unable to tolerate any acknowledgment of success and maintains a consistent self-critical stance.

7. The patient shows active suicidality/homicidality.

8. The patient exhibits poor impulse control: angry outbursts; self-injury; spending money; substance abuse.

9. The patient shows significant dissociative symptoms: time loss; fugue episodes; fragmentary recall of the previous week's events or interactions in session; uncontrolled rapid switching between ego states or alters; uncontrolled flashbacks.

10. The patient shows poor cooperation and communication between ego states (complex PTSD or DDNOS) or alter systems (DID) and engages in threatening, sabotaging, or suicidal/self-injurious behaviors.

11. The patient maintains strong denial over the diagnosis (i.e., DID, eating disorder, substance abuse).

12. The patient shows extreme fear in discussions about trauma processing or EMDR work.

13. The patient is unable to leave an abusive situation or set appropriate limits or boundaries.

14. The patient has an unstable therapeutic alliance.

15. The patient is in a current life crisis or transition requiring psychological focus.

When self-resources are limited and stabilization is questionable, attempts to proceed with the standard EMDR PTSD protocol are likely to produce a number of adverse consequences. Briere (1996) has referred to this problem as overshooting the "therapeutic window." These consequences may include:

1. Increased looping. (The patient activates distressing material during bilateral stimulation, but shows no indications of a shift toward a more adaptive resolution in spite of the use of standard EMDR strategies [Shapiro, 1995] for addressing block responses.)

2. Increased dysphoria and suicidality
3. Increased trauma-related symptoms
4. Increased sense of failure and hopelessness (i.e., "I'll never get well. This won't work for me")
5. Increased dissociation and avoidance behaviors (i.e., canceling sessions, decreased compliance)

Limitations and Cautions for Use of RDI

In patients meeting criteria for DID (Dissociative Identity Disorder) and DDNOS (Dissociative Disorder not otherwise specified), the use of RDI with unprepared alters (ego states) or conflicts between alters (ego states) can lead to inappropriate resource selection or attempts to make changes that pose a threat to other parts of the patient's self system.

In the stabilization phase of RDI treatment, if negative material is associated in a patient with an insecure ambivalent (resistant) attachment disorder, the clinician should seek an alternative resource or shift to a different resource-development strategy. Since the patient is not yet stable, proceeding to process dysphoric material with bilateral stimulation is likely to destabilize the patient further.

A paradoxical response is often observed in patients with insecure avoidant (withdrawn) attachment disorders. These patients may show no change or negative responses such as confusion or increasing anxiety to resource installation due to affect intolerance for moderate to high arousal levels and the rapid affect state changes commonly produced in Resource Installation. Space limitations make an adequate description of specific alternative treatment strategies beyond the scope of this chapter. In general, the emphasis may need to shift to slower strategies that help the patient tolerate the development of a therapeutic alliance. In general, these procedures should be considered by the trained EMDR clinician only after establishing an adequate clinical assessment of the patient's adult attachment status (Stein et al., 1998) and affect and ego-state-change tolerance, and after screening for a dissociative disorder.

Addressing Traumatic Material

Through the judicious, repeated use of RDI, many patients can be assisted to achieve significant decreases in a wide range of presenting symptoms and achieve greater stability. But addressing traumatic material with standard EMDR trauma-focused protocols to process foundational memories, current stimuli, and blocking beliefs remains essential to overall therapeutic progress and to the stability of treatment effects. For patients who meet criteria for stress or a mood or dissociative disorder, as most survivors of significant trauma or neglect do, the use of RDI protocols alone is not considered a sufficient therapeutic intervention, but it can play an important role throughout all three phases of a more comprehensive treatment plan.

Potential Sources and Types of Resources

Many types of resources can be considered for RDI, depending on the patient's need and the clinical presentation. What all these resources have in common is their association with positive affect. There is a preferential hierarchy among them. First are the patients' interpersonal experiences that are capable of generating positive affect, and second is internal locus of control. Thus, memories of patients' own previous or current positive experiences and adaptive coping efforts (ego strengthening) are often the best resources to be developed and installed. But it will not always be possible or effective to use them. Next to be considered might be memories of receiving support, nuturance, or guidance from caregivers, relatives, teachers, positive authority figures, and/or peers. Patients who come from backgrounds where such experiences were rare or nonexistent may not be able to identify such resources or may respond negatively to attempts to use them. Instead they may respond favorably to more abstract or distant resources, such as: memories or images from religious or spiritual sources; figures or symbols from dreams or daydreams that express the patient's capacity for adaptive functioning or coping; or figures from books, stories, movies, TV, or cartoons. Some patients may need active assistance to slowly build up symbolic or imaginal resources through guided imagery or hypnosis. Examples of this would include the image of an integrated, whole person, influenced and guided by "helping selves" (i.e., warrior woman, wise woman, soothing woman) or an image of a positive goal state (Popky, 1996) or future self. Other patients may be able to generate or identify resources through images from art therapy or art homework or other creative endeavors. For patients whose interpersonal experiences have been consistently inadequate or damaging, abstract symbols from nature (such as the sun, the earth, the ocean, or trees) may be the only images that can be associated with soothing or positive affect.

Some clinicians may find they can help patients generate or identify resources through the use of metaphors or stories that illustrate new ideas or perspectives for accessing and utilizing positive resources. Right-hemisphere-mediated activities, such as music or movement, may help patients to have a foundational experience of a positive affective state that can be incorporated into an RDI procedure.

Means of Evaluating EMDR RDI

Within-session indicators of treatment response include stable incremental decreases in anxiety and observable increases in positive affect, such as smiling, laughing, release of worry lines, better coloration, more upright posture, and easier breathing. In addition, patients will often report more positive physical sensations, such as a feeling of openness in the chest, pleasant tingling sensations in the arms or legs, or a feeling of strength. Patients with chronic pain may report decreases or complete alleviation of their pain. Patients will generally report more positive self-statements and greater confidence about facing their life situation.

Follow-up indicators of successful resource installation include patients reporting: that they have used the resource on their own between sessions to better cope with current stresses or flashbacks; and that they have engaged in new, more assertive, limit-setting, or appropriate-risk-taking behaviors (Korn & Leeds, in press). Patients may also report consolidation dreams that contain more positive elements or a change in a recurrent nightmare to a more positive outcome. Subscales of standardized assessment tools such as the SCL-90R (Derogatis, 1991) and the Trauma Symptom Inventory (Briere, 1995) and appropriately selected specialized behavioral self-report measures (Fisher & Corcoran, 1994) may also be appropriate for evaluating the stabilizing effects of RDI procedures on patient mood, cognition, and behavior.

Clinical Application with an Individual

Background

Beth was referred for treatment by Dr. Sheppard, a psychologist who had been providing her with regular twice-weekly psychotherapy for the previous eight years. Dr. Sheppard explained that Beth had been raised in a home filled with danger, neglect, insanity, and religiosity. Beth was the second oldest of four children. The household was in complete disarray throughout her childhood, with bags of garbage in the kitchen, bathrooms filthy beyond imagination, rats and mice running through the house, and frequent periods when there was simply no food to eat.

In spite of being a credentialed mental health professional, Beth's mother was bizarre and possibly psychotic. She presented herself as the perfect homemaker and would comment on how well she was taking care of the house, even while there was nothing to eat and there was filth everywhere. Her mother's bizarre misperceptions of reality were made even more painful by their church community's acceptance of her. Beth's family was deeply involved with the church community, which had been founded by her great-uncle. Over the years, he interceded to keep the police and the church elders from interfering in the family situation. The constant disparity between the family's reality and the mother's descriptions of it led Beth to deeply mistrust her perceptions and her feelings about the deprivation and danger she faced.

Beth was concerned that her EMDR clinician be able to understand the truth of her experience. Soon after being referred, she told of one especially painful memory. One day when she was perhaps 6 or 7 years old, her mother called her over to the living-room window with a large smile on her face. She pointed to the backyard, where Beth's beloved dog lay chained and dying from starvation. Not only was Beth agitated by her helplessness to protect her pet, but she could not grasp why her mother seemed to be so delighted.

Beth's father was a heroin addict and an alcoholic with frequent rages. He kept his drug "kit" by the easy chair in the living room. The wall and ceiling were blood spattered from some of his botched attempts to "shoot up." He kept a loaded gun near him at all times and fired it inside the house for target practice at the roaming rats and mice. His drug habit and his inability to keep a job were the main reasons for the family's poverty.

He sexually abused his oldest daughter, who was his primary sexual partner and who had been assigned the role of "evil one" in the family system.

Beth described being assigned the role of the "good" one, the "cold angel." The mother would send Beth's older sister to take physical and sexual abuse from the father, in order to insulate the mother from his sexual rages. When the older sister couldn't take this anymore, she would turn on the mother. Beth's job was to protect her mother from her older sister and to go to her father when neither her older sister nor her mother could manage his smoldering rage and depression. Beth managed not to be sexually or physically abused by her father.

From the time she was 3 or 4 years old, Beth would run out of the house seeking safety and food. She found refuge at a neighbor's down the street. Don and his wife, Sue, would give her a place to stay for a few hours and some food to eat. Much later, Don unfortunately turned out to be a nonsadistic pedophile. He cultivated Beth for nearly three years, then began to sexually abuse her without his wife's knowledge. When she was too young to baby-sit or work for food money, Beth often had no way to obtain food other than to go to Don and Sue's house. Beth tried to find times to get food only when Sue was there, but her husband became increasingly bold and eventually would molest Beth if his wife left the room for even a few minutes.

To help make ends meet, Beth's mother brought in a steady stream of foster children, for each of whom the state paid her a monthly allowance. From the time she was about 10 years old, Beth was repeatedly raped and molested by many of the foster brothers who were brought into the house.

Beth would have run away from home, but for the fact that she had made it her mission in life to keep her youngest brother, Timothy, alive by finding or buying him food, protecting him from her father's rage, and nurturing him in the face of their mother's neglect. It is certain that Timothy would have starved to death without her protection.

Beth eventually married a member of the congregation, who turned out to be a kind man and a good provider. Together they had several children. The details of Beth's dark past were a secret she did not share for many years. She had been referred to Dr. Sheppard by Pastor Fred, who had provided spiritual guidance and prayer with Beth on a regular basis for years. Without Pastor Fred's unfailing loving kindness and constant encouragement, Beth's life would have been an open wound. Dr. Sheppard asked that Beth begin EMDR therapy once a week and continue their treatment once a week.

At intake, Beth's principal identified symptoms included: intermittent depression; extreme hypervigilance and panic attacks; flights to safety in the mountains; sexual dysfunction and fear of intimacy; inability to trust others or her own perceptions; nightmares; insomnia; visual and auditory flashbacks; and depersonalization experiences when stressed. Her strengths included some college course work and excellent skills in music and education. Her involvement with her children was important to her, but like her other accomplishments, it had not been incorporated into her sense of self-worth. In addition to Pastor Fred, she had one other close friend, Ann, from the church, as well as an extensive but somewhat emotionally distant social network. Beth was clinically assessed as having an anxious ambivalent insecure attachment status.

One of the initial presenting issues was Beth's pattern of fleeing into the mountains a half-day's drive away, to an isolated lake. When she became overwhelmed with fear, she would arrange for someone from the church to care for her children, and she would jump in the car for the long drive to the mountain lake. While Beth was not acutely suicidal at that point in her treatment, she believed her life to be empty and said that she had never truly "stepped into life."

It was clear that after eight years of competent psychotherapy, Beth's situation was still not sufficiently stable for EMDR to be used to address her many past traumatic life experiences. But she had a number of self-capacities, ego strengths, and important interpersonal relationships that could potentially be enhanced and incorporated into her self-concept and sense of self worth.

First RDI Session

After a few initial sessions to build a therapeutic alliance, establish a treatment contract, and obtain more history, Beth was given an overview of how EMDR could be used to address her present symptoms. Her two most obvious symptoms were (a) a compulsive need to drive to the mountain lake in an attempt to escape from recurrent feelings of panic, and (b) an inability to trust that her relationships with Pastor Fred and Ann were "real" and meaningful. To help Beth strengthen her sense of present safety, the clinician suggested that the positive resource of the isolated mountain lake be installed. Beth was asked to imagine being at her special place at the lake. She described the sensory elements of her safe place: the stable, exposed, rocky cliff wall at the far side of the lake, with its small hidden cave and spring; its unobstructed view of the only road in to the undeveloped lake; the soft sound of the late afternoon wind in the trees; the light glinting off the lake surface; an occasional call of a bird. After hearing these sensory descriptions repeated back to her to strengthen the experience, Beth was asked to notice where she felt the sense of safety in her body. She reported feelings of calm in her belly, legs, neck, and back. When asked to identify a positive phrase about herself that went with the image, she said: "I am safe here." Beth was asked to hold the image, the physical sensations, and the positive phrase and to follow the clinician's hand movements with her eyes. With each of three short sets of eye movements, Beth reported that the feelings had strengthened noticeably and she stated that she felt "more present."

The clinician then asked Beth to imagine being able to use this image on her own to rehearse making contact with these feelings. She stated she could easily imagine doing so. She was then asked to think of a stressful situation that she might face in the next few days and to imagine getting the urge to drive to the lake. When she had identified such a stressor, she was asked to again use the image of her safe place to neutralize the anxiety and the urge to flee. When she reported that she could imagine doing so, she was asked to notice the place in her body where she felt the relief. She described a letting-go in her belly and chest. After three more short sets of eye movements focused on the image of the lake and the positive words "I am safe here," she again reported that the positive sensations were strengthened.

Follow-up to the First RDI Session

The next week Beth reported that when the urge to flee had arisen, she had been able to use the image of the lake and the positive words as a way to calm herself. She also reported that the urge had perhaps not been quite as strong, which had made it easy to manage. Attention was then turned to Beth's difficulty in trusting that Pastor Fred and Ann really cared about her after she was out of their presence. This symptom seemed to reflect multiple issues, including mistrusting her perceptions, lack of object constancy, and tendencies to feel abandoned and to depersonalize when alone.

Beth was asked to identify one memory where she could tell that Pastor Fred was truly her friend. She was asked to notice the details of the room, the time of day, and the look on his face. She was asked to locate this sense of trust and connectedness in her body. She reported feeling it in her chest and arms. She said she would like to believe "I can trust my perceptions" when she held this memory in mind. But she stated that this was not something she thought she would ever be able to believe. She was then asked to hold the image of Pastor Fred's face, the room, and the places in her body with the feelings of trust and the positive words, and to follow the hand movements with her eyes. With each set of eye movements, the feelings strengthened in her body, and her face softened in a way that showed a more innocent and more open aspect of Beth. A similar resource was then developed and installed using a specific memory of being with her friend Ann. Beth was asked to rehearse using these specific images of Ann and Pastor Fred, along with the image of her safe place at the mountain lake during the week.

Follow-up to the Second RDI Session

When Beth returned, she reported it had been a difficult week. Her urge to drive to the mountains had been stronger, and she was feeling troubled about the EMDR sessions. She had begun to wonder if she were somehow being tricked into false feelings of security. The clinician reassured her that these responses were normal and asked her to give herself time to judge the stability and dependability of the treatment effects for herself. The clinician reassured her that it was important for her to give accurate reports about how she was feeling and that no judgments would be made of her. Her current mistrust of the "good feelings" was hypothesized to reflect anxiety about the relatively rapid increase in positive affect related to strengthening her sense of connectedness. So the clinician decided not to attempt to install any new resources but to enhance and reinforce the previously installed resources.

Beth was asked to once again imagine she was at her safe place. This image and the sensations of safety and calm were enhanced by repeating verbatim to her the descriptions she had given two weeks before, together with the positive words "I am safe here." Then she was then asked to bring up the specific image of Pastor Fred that had been strengthened before, and to imagine it before her right visual field, together with the bodily feelings associated with that memory. Then she was asked to bring up her image of Ann in front of her left visual field and to hold that and the body sensations that went with that memory, together with the phrase "I can trust my perceptions." She then followed the hand movements between the image of Pastor Fred before her right visual field and the image of Ann before her left, through three short sets of eye movements. During the third set, something both dramatic and subtle happened in Beth's facial expression and breathing. She asked, "Did you feel that?" Not knowing what she meant, the clinician asked her to explain. She reported, "I thought it was an earthquake at first. It's like my whole brain just shifted. Everything feels different." No comment was made except to say, "Just notice that and follow again." At the end of the fourth set of eye movements, there were no further changes. The session was then concluded.

Follow-up to the Third RDI Session

The next week Beth returned looking brighter. She reported that a difficulty had occurred during the week. The clinician noted again, without comment, the discrepancy between her facial expression and her disappointed tone of voice. A pastor who was known to have a drinking problem, Beth said, had angrily accosted some of the members of her youth group. He was clearly under the influence. Rather than tolerate his abusive manner, as she had in the past, Beth decided to confront him directly. She stepped up to him and in a firm, calm voice told him that his behavior was inappropriate, that the young people had done nothing to merit his angry and abusive tone, and that he should go to his offices until he had become more self-collected (meaning sober). He turned even more red in the face but stomped off without further incident. Beth's firm handling of the inebriated pastor left the young people in the room with their mouths hanging open in amazement. Dr. Sheppard confirmed that this behavior was completely unexpected from Beth, who had always avoiding confronting Pastor Smith's drinking problems in the past. This spontaneous emergence of more assertive and protective behavior was taken as evidence that the RDI work done in the previous three sessions was providing Beth with a more stable sense of safety and trust in her own perceptions. This interpretation was further supported by Beth's report that she had been better able to manage her few impulses to flee that week. The remainder of that session and the next were spent in verbally consolidating these gains, taking further history, and doing more treatment planning.

Finding Purity and Soothing the Emptiness

The next week, Beth revealed another symptom that she now wanted to address. She hoped that EMDR could help lessen it. The symptom was a form of pica, in which Beth felt a compulsion to eat chalk. She would go to the store and buy blackboard chalk and eat several pieces until the urge abated. She revealed that this compulsion had begun when she was 3 or 4. She remembered being terrified of her father's rages and of his gun and the rats. She remembered being so hungry when there was nothing to eat. To alleviate the empty feelings in her belly, she would grab some pieces of broken plaster from the bullet holes in the wall and take them to a hideaway under the house. As an adult, she would frequently get the same empty feelings in her belly. She would then go buy chalk to eat. The stimuli for these feelings and urges might be any external stressor, but more commonly they were the auditory and visual flashbacks and nightmares that she still was not willing or able to describe.

Because Beth still did not show adequate ego strength to tolerate trauma-focused EMDR reprocessing, the clinician decided to postpone working with her memories of the onset of the pica symptom. Instead, it was proposed to do further RDI work to address Beth's need to find another coping strategy to use with the urges and to see if a metaphorical solution might provide a temporary solution until Beth could tolerate reprocessing childhood memories.

Beth was asked to recall her safe place along with the words "I am safe here" and the sensations of calm. These were strengthened with a set of eye movements. Then she was asked to bring up the images of Pastor Fred and Ann, the body sensations, and the words "I can trust my perceptions." These additional elements were integrated with a set of eye movements. After Beth reported that these elements were strengthened, she was asked to imagine getting up and walking over to the entrance to the cave with its hidden spring. She was asked to go inside, let her eyes adjust to the dimmer light, and then to go to the spring. Standing by the pure spring, Beth was asked to notice where in her body she felt the urge to eat chalk. To help her identify it the clinician asked her to remember the last time she had felt that urge. When she indicated that the urge was present at a significant level of distress, she was asked to imagine cupping her hands, scooping up the pure water to her lips, and taking it into her mouth. She was asked to feel the cool, pure water in her mouth and then just to notice what happened as she swallowed and allowed it to go down to where she felt the urge to eat the chalk. These instructions were repeated. Then Beth was asked to follow the movements of the hand with her eyes as she "just noticed" what happened. With the first set of eye movements, her face began to soften. Over the next three short sets of eye movements, she reported that the urge to eat the chalk had been replaced with a strange new sense of calm and inner peace. She stated that she had never felt this way before.

As in earlier sessions, Beth was asked to address this urge, the next time it might happen, by using the resource image, the sensations, and a positive phrase which she identified as, "I am fine now." This imaginal rehearsal was then strengthened with additional eye movements. A short time later the session came to a close.

Follow-up to the Fourth RDI Session

The next week, Beth entered with new concerns about some important changes that might be happening with her church. Not until nearly halfway through the session were follow-up data obtained on the resource work done to address the pica. It seemed almost an afterthought to Beth, who explained that she had used the resource image a couple of times and that she had not eaten any chalk. She then went on to talk about other concerns. At each of the next few sessions, follow-up data were obtained regarding urges to flee to the mountain lake or to eat chalk. Beth consistently reported that these urges generally seemed to be less intense and that she easily managed them using these resources.

Follow-up Data and Trauma Work

Nine months after this initial phase of her treatment, Beth reported she was still able to manage these persistent urges. The increased stability produced by this initial phase of RDI helped Beth cope with an external crisis situation that lasted for several months. After this crisis passed, this continued stability permitted EMDR trauma-focused work to begin on the intrusive flashbacks, nightmares, and other symptoms that Beth wanted to alleviate. EMDR memory-reprocessing work was introduced at a slow pace, in consideration of the Beth's slowly developing defenses and self-capacities.

Why These Strategies Were Chosen

Survivors of early childhood abuse and neglect often have difficulty utilizing left-hemisphere-mediated language-based skills to regulate emotional distress when their impaired schemata for safety or defectiveness are triggered (Teicher et al., 1997). After years of pastoral counseling and psychotherapy, Beth continued to experience a profound sense of loss of self and relatedness and was frequently flooded with distressing images, emotions, and urges. To help her develop increased capacities for self-soothing, object constancy, impulse control, and affect modulation that would remain accessible to her at these times, imagery processes were combined with EMDR bilateral stimulation.

Safe place and other resource installation procedures were used to first identify a series of uniquely positive images for safety, trust, and self-soothing, together with their associated sensations and emotions. Mental rehearsal was then used to help Beth practice making use of her imaginal resources when she would feel distressed, frightened, or mistrustful.

Following each RDI session, Beth showed clear behavioral, cognitive, and affective changes with increased stability in functioning. She developed mastery over long-standing impulse control. She also developed parallel changes that had not been addressed specifically, such as greater assertiveness and limit setting.

Several factors contributed to the positive outcomes in the application of RDI procedures in this case. At intake, Beth was deeply impaired in emotional regulation and was prone to loss of adult-ego-state control. But through her long-standing relationships with Pastor Fred and Dr.

Sheppard, she had developed models for new behaviors, thought patterns, and emotional responses. Like many patients with anxious ambivalent attachment problems, Beth was able to tolerate a range and degree of emotional response that permitted the use of these procedures, which tend to produce rapid affect and ego-state changes.

Concluding Summary

EMDR is a comprehensive treatment approach that is informed by an integrative, information-processing model that consists of principles, procedures, and protocols. A substantial body of controlled research supports the application of the standard (PTSD) protocol to posttraumatic and related syndromes. Clinical anecdotal and case reports suggest that a modified EMDR protocol known as RDI, which focuses exclusively on positive-associational-memory networks, can be of significant benefit for enhancing stability in the initial stages of treatment of patients who present with inadequate affect containment, or impulse control and/or affect-modulation problems. There is a need for controlled research to assess the potential for RDI to assist highly unstable patients with insecure attachment status and to explore its efficacy, risks, and range of applications for various diagnostic groups and clinical presentations.

To implement these methods in the treatment of individuals and couples, clinicians need skills in case formulation and supervised training in EMDR. The controlled research on the standard (PTSD) EMDR protocol suggests that rapid and stable alleviation of serious PTSD symptoms can be obtained in as few as three treatment sessions. Clinicians interested in incorporating these methods into the treatment of individuals and couples due to their potential for alleviating patient suffering are encouraged to become familiar with the EMDR literature and to obtain supervised training before attempting to use these methods with patients. Although better results may be obtained by clinicians with more supervised experience, there is strong evidence that clinicians can begin to use EMDR and RDI methods with robust results immediately following initial supervised training.

References

Andrade, J., Kavanagh, D., & Baddeley, A. (1997). Eye-movements and visual imagery: A working memory approach to the treatment of post-traumatic stress disorder. *British Journal of Clinical Psychology, 36,* 209–223.

Assagioli, R. (1965). *Psychosynthesis: A manual of principles and techniques.* New York: Penguin.

Baker, E. (1981). An hypnotherapeutic approach to enhance object relatedness to psychotic patients. *International Journal of Clinical and Experimental Hypnosis, 29*(2), 136–147.

Baker, E. (1983). The use of hypnotic dreaming in the treatment of the borderline patient: Some thoughts on resistance and transitional phenomena. *International Journal of Clinical and Experimental Hypnosis, 31*(1), 19–27.

Barach, P. M. (1991). Multiple personality disorder as an attachment disorder. *Dissociation, 4,* 117–123.

Beck, A. T. (1967). *Depression.* New York: Hoeber-Harper.

Boudewyns, P.A., & Hyer, L. A. (1996). Eye movement desensitization and reprocessing (EMDR) as treatment for post-traumatic stress disorder (PTSD). *Clinical Psychology and Psychotherapy, 3,* 185–195.

Boudewyns, P. A., Stwertka, S. A., Hyer, L. A., Albrecht, J. W., & Sperr, E. V. (1993). Eye movement desensitization and reprocessing: A pilot study. *Behavior Therapist, 16,* 30–33.

Bower, G. (1981). Mood and memory. *American Psychologist, 36* (2), 129–148.

Breuer, J., & Freud, S. (Eds.). (1955). *Studies on hysteria* (Vol. 2). London: Hogarth Press, (Original work published 1893–1895).

Briere, J. (1995). *Trauma symptom inventory professional manual.* Odessa, FL: Psychological Assessment Resources.

Briere, J. (1996). *Therapy for adults molested as children: Beyond survival.* New York: Springer.

Carlson, J. G., Chemtob, C. M., Rusnak, K., Hudlund, N. L., & Muraoka, M. Y. (1998). Eye movement desensitization and reprocessing treatment for combat related posttraumatic stress disorder. *Journal of Traumatic Stress, 11*(1), 3–24.

Chemtob, C., Roitblatt, H., Hamada, J., Carlson, J., & Twentyman, C. (1988). A cognitive action theory of posttraumatic stress disorder. *Journal of Anxiety Disorder, 2,* 253–275.

Courtois, C. (1988). *Healing the incest wound: Adult survivors in therapy.* New York: Norton.

de Jongh, A. (1998). Distraction as an explanation. Internet: EMDR Institute discussion list. November 16.

Demos, E. V. (1988) Affect and development of the self: A new frontier. In A. Goldberg (Ed.), *Frontiers in self psychology* (Vol. 3, pp. 27–53). Hillsdale, NJ: Analytic Press.

Derogatis, L. R. (199). *Scoring and interpretation manual, symptom checklist revised*. Minneapolis: NCS Professional Assessment Services.

Dyck, M. J. (1993). A proposal for a conditioning model of eye movement desensitization treatment for posttraumatic stress disorder. *Journal of Behavior Therapy and Experimental Psychiatry, 24,* 201–210.

Ellis, A. (1962). *Reason and emotion in psychotherapy*. Secaucus, NJ: Citadel.

Fine, C. G., Paulsen, S., Rouanzoin, C., Luber, M., Puk, G., & Young, W. (1995). EMDR dissociative disorder task force recommended guidelines: A general guide to EMDR's use in the dissociative disorders. In F. Shapiro (Ed.), *Eye movement desensitization and reprocessing, basic principles, protocols, and procedures* (pp. 365–369). New York: Guilford.

Fisher, J., & Corcoran, K. (1994). Measures for clinical practice: A source book, Adults (2nd ed., vol. 2). New York: Free Press.

Foa, E. B., & Kozak, M. J. (1986). Emotional processing of fear: Exposure to corrective information. *Psychological Bulletin, 99*(1), 20–35.

Fraser, G. A. (1991). The dissociative table technique: A strategy for working with ego states in dissociative disorders and ego-state therapy. *Dissociation,* 4(4), 205–213.

Freud, S. (1955). Introduction to psychoanalysis and the war neuroses. In J. E. T. Strachey (Ed.), *The standard edition of the complete psychological works of Sigmund Freud* (Vol. 17). London: Hogarth Press. (Original work published 1900)

Greenwald, R. (1993a). Treating children's nightmares with EMDR. *EMDR Network Newsletter, 3*(1), 7–9.

Greenwald, R. (1993b). Magical installations can empower clients to slay their dragons. *EMDR Network Newsletter, 3*(2), 16–17.

Herman, J. L. (1993). *Trauma and recovery*. New York: Basic Books.

Horowitz, M. J. (1979). Psychological response to serious life events. In V. Hamilton & D. M. Warburton (Eds.), *Human stress and cognition*. New York: John Wiley.

Ichii, M. (1998). Effects of eye movements on negative and positive imagery. Personal communication.

Jensen, J. A. (1994). An investigation of eye movement desensitization and reprocessing (EMD/R) as a treatment for posttraumatic stress disorder (PTSD) symptoms of Vietnam combat veterans. *Behavior Therapy, 25,* 311–326.

Jung, C. G. (1916). *Analytic psychology.* New York: Moffat.

Kardiner, A. (1941). *Traumatic neuroses of war.* New York: Hoeber.

Kohut, H. (1971). *The analysis of the self.* New York: International Universities Press.

Korn, D. L., & Leeds, A. M. (in press). Preliminary evidence of efficacy for EMDR resource development and installation in the stabilization phase of treatment of complex posttraumatic stress disorder. *Journal of Clinical Psychology.*

Lang, P. J. (1977). Imagery in therapy: An information processing analysis of fear. *Behavior Therapist, 10,* 224–242.

Lang, P. J. (1979). A bioinformational theory of emotional imagery. *Psychophysiology, 16,* 495–512.

Lazarus, A., & Lazarus, C. (1991). *Multimodal life history inventory.* Champaign, IL: Research Press.

Lazrove, S., & Fine, C. G. (1996). The use of EMDR in patients with dissociative identity disorder. *Dissociation, 9*(4), 289–299.

Leeds, A. M. (1959, June). *EMDR Case Formulation Symposium.* Paper presented at the international EMDR conference, Santa Monica, CA.

Leeds, A. M. (1997) *In the eye of the beholder: Reflections on shame, dissociation, and transference in complex posttraumatic stress and attachment related disorders. Principles of case formulation for EMDR treatment planning and the use of resource installation.* Paper presented at EMDR International Association conference, San Francisco.

Leeds, A. M. (1998a). *EMDR Safe Place survey.* EMDR Institute Discussion listserve. Available E-mail: EMDR@MAELSTROM.STJOHNS.EDU.

Leeds, A. M. (1998b). *How does EMDR work? An exploration of possible neurobiological mechanisms.* Paper presented at the EMDR International Association conference, Baltimore, MD.

Leeds, A. M. (1998c). *Neuroaffective therapy for adult attachment related syndromes.* Paper presented at the EMDR Association of Canada mini-conference, Vancouver, B.C.

Linehan, M. M. (1993a). *Cognitive-behavioral treatment of borderline personal disorder.* New York: Guilford.

Linehan, M. M. (1993b). *Skills training manual for treating borderline personality disorder.* New York: Guilford.

Liotti, G. (1992). Disorganized/disoriented attachment in the etiology of the dissociative disorders. *Dissociation, 5*(4), 196–204.

Macculloch, M. J., & Feldman, P. (1996). Eye movement desensitisation treatment utilises the positive visceral element of the investigatory reflex to inhibit the memories of post-traumatic stress disorder: A theoretical analysis. *British Journal of Psychiatry, 169,* 571–579.

Main, M. (1996). Introduction to the special section on attachment and psychopathology: 2. Overview of the field of attachment. *Journal of Consulting and Clinical Psychology, 64*(2), 237–243.

Marcus, S., Marquis, P., & Sakai, C. (1997). Controlled study of treatment of PTSD using EMDR in an HMO setting. *Psychotherapy, 34,* 307–315.

Martinez, R. (1991). EMDR: Innovative uses. *EMDR Network Newsletter, 1*(2), 7.

McCann, I. L., & Pearlman, L. A. (1990. *Psychological trauma and the adult survivor: Theory, therapy and transformation.* New York: Brunner/Mazel.

Meichenbaum, D. (1977). *Cognitive-behavior modification.* New York: Plenum.

Nathanson, D. (1998). *Locating MEDR: Affect, scene and script.* Paper presented at the EMDR International Association conference, Baltimore, MD.

Nathanson, D. L. (1992). *Shame and pride: Affect sex and the birth of the self.* New York: Norton.

Nicosia, G. (1994). *A mechanism for dissociation suggested by the quantative analysis of electroencephalography.* Paper presented at the international EMDR conference, Sunnyvale, CA.

Paulsen, S. (1995). Eye movement desensitization and reprocessing: Its cautious use in the dissociative disorders. *Dissociation, 8*(1), 32–44.

Pitman, R. K., Orr, S. P., Altman, B., Longpre, R. E., Poire, R. E., & Macklin, J. L. (1996). Emotional processing during eye-movement desensitization and reprocessing therapy of Vietnam veterans with chronic post-traumatic stress disorder. *Comprehensive Psychiatry, 37,* 419–429.

Popky, A. J. (1996, December 6). *Integrative addiction treatment model.* Paper presented at the EMDR Level Two Training, San Francisco.

Rauch, S. L., van der Kolk, B. A., Fisler, R. E., Alpert, N. M., Orr, S. P., Savage, C. R., Fischman, A. J., Jenike, M. A., & Pitman, R. K. (1996). A symptom provocation study of posttraumatic stress disorder using positron emission tomography and script-driven imagery. *Archives of General Psychiatry, 53,* 380–387.

Reiser, M. F. (1990). *Memory in mind and brain: What dreams imagery reveals.* New York: Basic Books.

Renfrey, G., & Spates, C. R. (1994). Eye movement desensitization and reprocessing: A partial dismantling procedure. *Journal of Behavior Therapy and Experimental Psychiatry, 25,* 231–239.

Rogers, C. R. (1951). *Client-centered therapy.* Boston: Houghton Mifflin.

Rothbaum, B. O. (1997). A controlled study of eye movement desensitization and reprocessing for posttraumatic stress disordered sexual assault victims. *Bulletin of the Menninger Clinic, 61,* 317–334.

Rothbaum, B. O., & Foa, E. B. (1996). Cognitive-behavioral therapy for posttraumatic stress disorder. In B. A. van der Kolk, A. C. McFarlane, & L. Weisaeth (Eds.), *Traumatic stress: The effects of overwhelming experience on mind, body, and society* (pp. 491–509). New York: Guilford.

Salter, A. (1961). *Conditioned reflex therapy.* New York: Capricorn.

Scheck, M. M., J. A., & Gillette, C. S. (1998). Brief psychological intervention with traumatized young women: The efficacy of eye movement desensitization and reprocessing. *Journal of Traumatic Stress, 11,* 25–44.

Schore, A. N. (1949). *Affect regulation and the origin of the self: The neurobiology of emotional development.* Hillsdale, NJ: Lawrence Erlbaum.

Schore, A. N. (1996). The experience-dependent maturation of a regulatory system in the orbital prefrontal cortex and the origin of developmental psychopathology. *Development and Psychopathology, 8,* 59–87.

Schore, A. N. (1997). Early organization of the nonlinear right brain and the development of a predisposition to psychiatric disorders. *Development and Psychopathology, 9,* 595–631.

Shapiro, F. (1989). Efficacy of the eye movement desensitization procedure in the treatment of traumatic memories. *Journal of Traumatic Stress Studies, 2,* 199–223.

Shapiro, F. (1991a). Eye movement desensitization and reprocessing: from EMD to EMD/R—a new treatment model for anxiety and related traumata. *Behavior Therapist, 14,* 133–135.

Shapiro, F. (1991b). Eye movement desensitization and reprocessing: A cautionary note. *Behavior Therapist, 14,* 188.

Shapiro, F. (1995). *Eye movement desensitization and reprocessing, basic principles, protocols and procedures.* New York: Guilford.

Shapiro, F. (1988a). Personal communication.

Shapiro, F. (1998b). Eye movement desensitization and reprocessing (EMDR): Historical context, recent research and future directions. In L. Vandecreek, S. Knapp, & T. L. Jackson (Eds.), *Innovations in clinical practice: A source book* (Vol. 16, pp. 143–161). Sarasota, FL: Professional Resource Press.

Shapiro, F. (1999). EMDR and the anxiety disorders: Clinical and research implications of an integrated psychotherapy treatment. *Journal of Anxiety Disorders, 13*, 35–67.

Shapiro, F. (in press). *EMDR and the paradigm prism.* Washington DC: American Psychological Association Press.

Shapiro, F., Vogelmann-Sine, S., & Sine, L. (1994). Eye movement desensitization and reprocessing: Treating trauma and substance abuse. *Journal of Psychoactive Drugs, 26*, 379–391.

Stein, H., Jacobs, N. J., Ferguson, K. S., Allen, J. G., & Fonagy, P. (1998). What do adult attachment scales measure? *Bulletin of the Menninger Clinic, 62* (1) 33–82.

Stickgold, R. (1998). *Current understanding of the psychobiology of trauma.* Paper presented (with B. A. van der Kolk) at the EMDR International Association conference, Baltimore, MD.

Solomon, S. D., Gerrity, E. T., & Muff, A. M. (1992). Efficacy of treatments for posttraumatic stress disorder: An empirical review. *JAMA, 268* (5), 633–638.

Teicher, M. H., Ito, Y., Glod, C. A., Andersen, S. L. Dumont, N., & Ackerman, E. (1997). Preliminary evidence for abnormal cortical development in physically and sexually abused children using EEG coherence and MRI. In R. Yehuda & A. C. McFarlane (Eds.), *Psychobioloy of posttraumatic stress disorder* (Vol. 821, pp. 161–175). New York: New York Academy of Sciences.

Tomkins, S. S. (1991). *Affect imagery consciousness. The negative affects: anger and fear* (Vol. 3). New York: Springer.

van der Kolk, B. A., Burbridge, J. A., & Suzuki, J. (1997). The psychobiology of traumatic memory: Clinical implications of neuroimaging studies. In R. Yehuda & A. C. McFarlane (Eds.), *Psychobiology of posttraumatic stress disorder* (Vol. 821, pp. 99–113). New York: New York Academy of Sciences.

van der Kolk, B. A., McFarlane, A. C., & van der Hart, O. (1996). A general approach to treatment of posttraumatic stress disorder. In B. A. van der Kolk, A. C. McFarlane, & L. Weisaeth (Eds.), *Traumatic stress: The effects of overwhelming experience on mind, body, and society* (pp. 417–440). New York: Guilford.

van der Kolk, B. A., McFarlane, A. C., & Weisaeth, L. (Eds.). (1996). *Traumatic stress: The effects of overwhelming experience on mind, body, and society.* New York: Guilford.

Van Etten, M. L., & Taylor, S. (1998). Comparative efficacy of treatments for post-traumatic stress disorder: A meta-analysis. *Clinical Psychology and Psychotherapy, 5*, 126–144.

Vaughan, K., Armstrong, M. F., & Tarrier, N. (1994). Eye-movement desensitization: Symptom change in post-traumatic stress disorder. *British Journal of Psychiatry, 164,* 533–541.

Watkins, J. G., & Watkins, H. H. (1997). *Ego states: Theory and therapy.* New York: Norton.

Wells, A., & Papageorgiou, C. (1998). Social phobia: Effects of external attention on anxiety, negative beliefs, and perspective taking. *Behavior Therapy, 29,* 357–370.

Wildwind, L. (1949, March). *Chronic depression.* Paper presented at the international EMDR conference, Sunnyvale, Ca.

Wilson, D. L. (1999, June). *An orienting response model of EMDR: Research, clinical applications, and new instrumentation.* Paper presented at the 1999 EMDR International Association conference, Los Vegas.

Wilson, D. L., Silver, S. M., Covi, W., & Foster, S. (1996). Eye movement desensitization and reprocessing: Effectiveness and autonomic correlates. *Journal of Behavior Therapy and Experimental Psychiatry, 27,* 219–229.

Wilson, S., Becker, L. A., & Tinker, R. H. (1995). Eye movement desensitization and reprocessing (EMDR) treatment for psychologically traumatized individuals. *Journal of Consulting and Clinical Psychology, 63*(6), 928–937.

Wilson, S. A., Becker, L. A., & Tinker, R. H. (1997). Fifteen-month follow-up of eye movement desensitization and reprocessing (EMDR) treatment for post-traumatic stress disorder and psychological trauma. *Journal of Consulting and Clinical Psychology, 65*(6), 1047–1056.

Wolpe, J. (1991). *The practice of behavior therapy* (4th ed.). New York: Pergamon Press.

Young, J. E. (1994). *Cognitive therapy for personality disorders: A schema-focused approach.* Sarasota, FL: Professional Resource.

Annotated Bibliography

Overview of EMDR Treatment

Manfield, P. (1998). *Extending EMDR, A case book of innovative applications.* New York: Norton. Exploration of the integrative nature of EMDR, with contributions ranging from behavioral through analytic in the application of EMDR to diverse difficult cases, including a variety of personality disorders.

Shapiro, F. (1995). *Eye movement desensitization and reprocessing, basic principles, protocols and procedures.* New York: Guilford. The primary EMDR textbook, essential for mental health professionals and university courses.

Shapiro, F., & Forrest, M. S. (1997). *EMDR: The breakthrough therapy for overcoming anxiety, stress and trauma.* New York: Basic Books. An authoritative introduction for professionals and laypeople and a casebook for trained EMDR clinicians. Chapters cover various types of traumas, phobias, children, addictions, grief, disease, and future directions.

The following controlled EMDR studies of PTSD have been completed.

Civilian Studies

1. Chemtob, Nakashima, Hamada, & Carlson (in press). Brief psychosocial intervention for elementary school children with disaster-related posttraumatic stress disorder: A field study. *Journal of Clinical Psychology.* This study evaluated the effects of three sessions of EMDR using a lagged-group design with children suffering the aftereffects of Hurricane Iniki. Thirty-two children who had not responded to previous treatments and met the criteria for the classification of PTSD were assigned to treatment and delayed treatment conditions. The children had shown no improvement 3.5 years after the hurricane and a year after the most recent attempts at treatment. Clinical improvements were reported in both groups as measured on the Children's Reaction Inventory, Revised Children's Manifest Anxiety Scale, and Children's Depression Inventory. and these changes remained stable at a six-month follow-up. In addition to the substantial reduction in PTSD symptomatology, a marked reduction in visits to the school nurse in the year following the EMDR treatment, as compared with previous years, was reported.

2. Edmond, T., Rubin, A., & Wambach, K.G. (1999). The effectiveness of EMDR with adult female survivors of childhood sexual abuse. *Social Work Research, 23,* 103–116. Although this study did not involve cases of diagnosed PTSD, the effectiveness of EMDR was tested with adult female survivors of childhood sexual abuse. Fifty-nine women were assigned randomly to one of three groups: (1) individual EMDR; (2) routine individual treatment; or (3) delayed treatment control. In a three-month follow-up, EMDR participants scored significantly better than did routine individual treatment

participants on two of the four measures, with large effect sizes suggestive of clinical significance.

3. Freund, B., & Ironson, G. (in press). A comparison of two treatments for PTSD: A pilot study. *Journal of Clinical Psychology*. A controlled study compared EMDR and prolonged imaginal exposure therapy. Both therapies showed positive effects. The dropout rate was lower in the EMDR group. Further, EMDR proved more efficient: seven of nine clients were successfully treated in the three active sessions of EMDR versus two out of seven for prolonged exposure (i.e., 78% of EMDR versus 29% of prolonged exposure successfully completed treatment in three sessions).

4. Lee, C., & Gavriel, H. (1998). Treatment of post-traumatic stress disorder: A comparison of stress inoculation training with prolonged exposure and eye movement desensitization and reprocessing. *Proceedings of the World Congress of Behavioral and Cognitive Therapies*, Acapulco. Levin, C. (July/August 1993). The effectiveness of EMDR was compared with a combination of stress inoculation therapy and prolonged exposure. The 22 subjects each met DSM-III-R criteria for PTSD and were randomly assigned to one of the treatment conditions. Each subject was also his or her own wait list control. Outcome measures included the IES, MMPI PTSD scale, BDI, and Davidson's Structured Interview for PTSD. Both EMDR and SITPE produced clinically significant improvement posttreatment and these gains were maintained at three months follow-up. EMDR was found to be more efficient than SITE.

5. Marcus, S., Marquis, P., & Sakai, C. (1997). Controlled study of treatment of PTSD using EMDR in an HMO setting. *Psychotherapy, 34*, 307–315, Sixty-seven individuals diagnosed with PTSD were evaluated in a controlled study funded by the Kaiser Permanente Hospital. EMDR was found superior to standard Kaiser care, which consisted of a combination of individual therapy plus group therapy and medication. An independent evaluator assessed participants on the basis of the Symptom Checklist-90, Beck Depression Inventory, Impact of Event Scale, Modified PTSD Scale, Spielberger State-Trait Anxiety Inventory, and SUD. Fidelity was previously judged as high and results indicated twice the effect sizes for EMDR as compared with the control group in half the number of overall sessions.

6. Renfrey, G., & Spates, C.R. (1994). Eye movement desensitization and reprocessing: A partial dismantling procedure. *Journal of Behavior Therapy and Experimental Psychiatry, 25*, 231–239. A controlled component study of 23 PTSD subjects compared EMDR with eye movements initiated by

tracking a clinician's finger, EMDR with eye movements engendered by tracking a light bar, and EMDR using fixed visual attention. All three conditions produced positive changes on the CAPS, SCL-90–R, Impact of Event Scale, and SUD and VOC scales. However, the eye-movement conditions were termed "more efficient." This study was hampered by the small number of subjects (six or seven in each posttest cell), making statistical significance improbable for a component analysis of this kind. No fidelity checks were reported.

7. Rothbaum, B.O. (1997). A controlled study of eye movement desensitization and reprocessing for posttraumatic stress disordered sexual assault victims. *Bulletin of the Menninger Clinic, 61*, 317–334. This controlled study of rape victims found that, after three EMDR treatment sessions, 90% of the participants no longer met the full criteria for PTSD. Results were evaluated on the PTSD Symptom Scale, Impact of Event Scale, Beck Depression Inventory, and Dissociative Experience Scale by an independent assessor. High fidelity to treatment.

8. Scheck, M.M., Schaeffer, J..A., & Gillette, C.S. (1998). Brief psychological intervention with traumatized young women: The efficacy of eye movement desensitization and reprocessing. *Journal of Traumatic Stress, 11*, 25–44. Sixty women ages 16–25 screened for high-risk behavior and traumatic history were randomly assigned to two sessions of either EMDR or active listening. There was substantially greater improvement for EMDR as independently assessed on the Beck Depression Inventory, State-Trait Anxiety Inventory, Penn Inventory for Post-traumatic Stress Disorder, Impact of Event Scale, and Tennessee Self-Concept Scale. Although the treatment was comparatively brief, the EMDR-treated participants came within the first standard deviation as compared with nonpatient norm groups for all five measures. Fidelity to treatment was previously assessed for some of the clinicians in the study.

9. Shapiro, F. (1989). Efficacy of the eye movement desensitization procedure in the treatment of traumatic memories. *Journal of Traumatic Stress, 2*, 199–223. The initial controlled study of 22 rape, molestation, and combat victims compared EMDR and a modified flooding procedure that was used as a placebo to control for exposure to the memory and to the attention of the researcher. Positive treatment effects were obtained for the treatment and delayed treatment conditions on SUDs and behavioral indicators, which were independently corroborated at one– and three–month follow-up sessions. This study was hampered by the lack of standardized measures.

10. Vaughan, K., Armstrong, M. F., Gold, R., O'Connor, N., Jenneke, W., & Tarrier, N. (1994). A trial of eye movement desensitization compared to image habituation training and applied muscle relaxation in post-traumatic stress disorder. *Journal of Behavior Therapy and Experimental Psychiatry, 25,* 283–291. In a controlled comparative study, 36 subjects with PTSD were randomly assigned to treatments of (1) imaginal exposure, (2) applied muscle relaxation, and (3) EMDR. Treatment consisted of four sessions, with 60 and 40 minutes of additional daily homework over a two- to three-week period for the image exposure and muscle relaxation groups, respectively, and no additional homework for the EMDR group. All treatments led to significant decreases in PTSD symptoms for subjects in the treatment groups as compared with those on a waiting list, with a greater reduction in the EMDR group, particularly with respect to intrusive symptoms. No fidelity checks were reported.

11. Wilson, D., Silver, S.M., Covi, W., & Foster, S. (1996). Eye movement desensitization and reprocessing: Effectiveness and autonomic correlates. *Journal of Behavior Therapy and Experimental Psychiatry, 27 ,* 219–229. In a controlled study, 18 subjects suffering from PTSD were randomly assigned to eye-movement, hand-tap, and exposure-only groups. Significant differences were found using physiological measures (including galvanic skin response, skin temperature, and heart rate) and the SUD Scale. The results revealed, with the eye-movement condition only, a one-session desensitization of subject distress and an automatically elicited and seemingly compelled relaxation response, which arose during the eye-movement sets. High fidelity to treatment had been previously assessed.

12. Wilson, S.A., Becker, L.A., & Tinker, R.H. (1995). Eye movement desensitization and reprocessing (EMDR) treatment for psychologically traumatized individuals. *Journal of Consulting and Clinical Psychology, 63,* 928–937. Wilson, S.A., Becker, L.A., & Tinker, R.H. (1997). Fifteen-month follow-up of eye movement desensitization and reprocessing (EMDR) treatment for PTSD and psychological trauma. *Journal of Consulting and Clinical Psychology, 65,* 1047–1056. A controlled study randomly assigned 80 trauma subjects (37 diagnosed with PTSD) to treatment or delayed-treatment EMDR conditions and to one of five trained clinicians. Substantial results were found at 30 and 90 days and 15 months posttreatment on the State-Trait Anxiety Inventory, PTSD Interview, Impact of Event Scale, SCL-90–R, and the SUD and VOC scales. Effects were equally large whether or not the subject was diagnosed with PTSD. High fidelity to treatment had been previously assessed for many of the participating clinicians.

Combat Studies

1. Boudewyns, P.A., Stwertka, S.A., Hyer, L.A., Albrecht, J.W., & Sperr, E.V. (1993). Eye movement desensitization and reprocessing: A pilot study. *Behavior Therapist*, *16*, 30–33. A pilot study randomly assigned 20 chronic inpatient veterans to EMDR, exposure, and group therapy conditions and found significant positive results with EMDR for self-reported distress levels and therapist assessment. No changes were found in standardized and physiological measures, a result attributed by the authors to insufficient treatment time considering the secondary gains of the subjects who were receiving compensation. Results were considered positive enough to warrant further extensive study, which has been funded by the VA. No fidelity check reported for the study.

2. Boudewyns, P.A., & Hyer, L.A. (1996). Eye movement desensitization and reprocessing (EMDR) as treatment for post-traumatic stress disorder (PTSD*). Clinical Psychology and Psychotherapy*, *3*, 185–195. Preliminary reports of the data indicate that EMDR was superior to a group therapy control on some standard psychometric and physiological measures. Both studies were hampered by the insufficient treatment time afforded, which allowed for treating only one or two memories in this multiply traumatized population. In this second study, fidelity to treatment was reported as variable by an external assessor.

3. Carlson, J.G., Chemtob, C.M., Rusnak, K., Hedlund, N.L., & Muraoka, M.Y. (1998). Eye movement desensitization and reprocessing for combat-related posttraumatic stress disorder. *Journal of Traumatic Stress*, *11*, 3–24. The effect of EMDR on chronic combat veterans suffering from PTSD since the Vietnam war was tested. Within 12 sessions, subjects showed substantial clinical improvement, with a number becoming symptom-free. EMDR proved superior to a biofeedback relaxation control group and to a group receiving routine VA clinical care. Results were independently evaluated on CAPS-1, Mississippi Scale for PTSD, IES, PTSD Symptom Scale, Beck Depression Inventory, and STAI. Positive clinical fidelity to treatment was externally assessed and the dropout rate was approximately 3%. This is the only study of combat veterans to achieve acceptable fidelity and to use the number of EMDR sessions suggested for this population by Shapiro (1995).

4. Devilly, G.J., Spence, S.H., & Rapee, R.M. (1998). Statistical and reliable change with eye movement desensitization and reprocessing: Treating trauma within a veteran population. *Behavior Therapy*, *29*, 435–455. The study tested

the effect of EMDR on 51 Vietnam combat veterans, comparing EMDR, an analog treatment without eye movement, and a support control condition. Only one outcome measure showed significant differences at posttest. This study was hampered by having afforded only two sessions of treatment to this multiply traumatized population and fidelity to treatment was questionable based on the described procedures. A 30% dropout rate was reported.

5. Jensen, J. A. (1994). An investigation of eye movement desensitization and reprocessing (EMD/R) as a treatment for posttraumatic stress disorder (PTSD) symptoms of Vietnam combat veterans. *Behavior Therapy, 25*, 311–326. A controlled study of the EMDR treatment of 25 Vietnam combat veterans suffering from PTSD, as compared with a nontreatment control group, found small but statistically significant differences after two sessions for in-session distress levels, as measured on the SUD Scale, but no differences on global measures, such as the Structured Interview for Post-traumatic Stress Disorder. The intern-researchers reported low fidelity checks of adherence to the EMDR protocol and skill of application, which indicated their inability to make effective use of the method to resolve the therapeutic issues of their subjects. The study was also hampered by an insufficient amount of treatment time for these multiply traumatized veterans.

6. Pitman, R.K., Orr, S. P., Altman, B., Longpre, R.E., Poire, R.E., & Macklin, M.L. (1996). Emotional processing during eye-movement desensitization and reprocessing therapy of Vietnam veterans with chronic post-traumatic stress disorder. *Comprehensive Psychiatry, 37*, 419–429. In a controlled component analysis study of 17 chronic outpatient veterans, using a crossover design, subjects were randomly divided into two EMDR groups, one using eye movement and a control group that used a combination of forced eye fixation, hand taps, and hand waving. Six sessions were administered for a single memory in each condition. Both groups showed significant decreases in self-reported distress, intrusion, and avoidance symptoms. Fidelity was judged as variable by an external assessor. The study was hampered by the small sample and the fact that only one to two memories were tested in this multiply traumatized population.

7. Rogers, S., Silver, S., Goss, J., Obenchain, J., Willis, A., & Whitney, R. (1999). A single session, controlled group study of flooding and eye movement desensitization and reprocessing in treating posttraumatic stress disorder among Vietnam war veterans: Preliminary data. *Journal of Anxiety Disorders, 13*, 119–130. Two groups of combat veterans received a single session of exposure

or EMDR focusing on the most disturbing event. Both groups showed improvement on the Impact of Event scale, however, the EMDR treatment resulted in greater positive changes in the level of in-session distress and self-monitored intrusive recollections. This study was designed primarily as a process report to compare both methods. High fidelity to treatment was established.

17

Biopsychosocial Therapy:
Essential Strategies and Tactics

Len Sperry

Introduction

Biopsychosocial therapy is an integrative approach for conceptualizing and implementing treatment when biological factors present along with psychological and social/systemic factors. Biopsychosocial therapy is an integrative approach in two regards: first, it integrates or strategically *combines* various treatment modalities (individual, group, couple, or family, and medication) as well as various methods (dynamic, cognitive-behavioral, systemic, and psychoeducational); and second, it integrates and *tailors* these modalities and methods to the needs, styles, and expectations of the client, be it individual patient, family, or couple.

Biological factors are present in many individuals who present for mental health treatment today, as in depression, bipolar disorder, eating disorders, panic disorder, obsessive-compulsive disorder, and other anxiety disorders. Whenever biological factors are suspected, clinicians—whether they are medical or nonmedical therapists—must formulate the case in biological as well as psychosocial terms. Such biopsychosocial formulations usually lead to treatment plans that combine biological modalities with psychosocial ones. While *biological modalities* usually means psychotropic medication, it also refers to nutrition modification, exercise prescription, and alternative remedies like melatonin and hypericum or St. John's wort, as well as other medical treatments, such as thyroid supplementation and hormone replacement therapy. While utilizing certain biological modalities in psychotherapy may be outside a clinician's scope of practice, effective, ethical treatment requires appropriate referral and collaboration. Increasingly, a nonmedical therapist will begin working with an individual or couple with biological factors, make an appropriate medical or psychiatric referral, and then continue the psychotherapeutic interventions in isolation from the prescribing clinician's intervention. The various providers may never discuss such issues as responsibility for after-hours and vacation coverage, the patient's safety and legal liability, and "splitting." But biopsychosocial therapy emphasizes collaborative clinical practice between and among various providers.

This chapter describes and illustrates the theoretical premises and the essential clinical strategies of biopsychosocial therapy. It also describes and illustrates specific treatment tactics that support these basic strategies. The discussion begins by laying out the theory of the biopsychosocial perspective, then describes the strategies and tactics of focus of biopsychosocial therapy and lists the specific indications for this approach. Finally, two extended case examples are provided to illustrate the application of this approach to individuals and couples.

The Biopsychosocial Perspective

The biopsychosocial model is a holistic and systems perspective for understanding the person and the relationship of the system, both outside and inside the person, that influences both health and illness (Engel, 1977; Sperry, 1988b). The model proposes that a person can be adequately understood only if the therapist considers all levels of the patient's functioning: biological or physical, psychological, and social. *Physical* functioning refers to all peripheral organ system functions, as well as to all autonomic, neuroendocrine, and central nervous system functions that are subcortical—that is, to all processes that are automatic and outside conscious awareness. *Psychological* functioning refers to the self-conscious inner world that directs the patient's information process-ing and communication from and with the outside world. It basically involves cortical structures and conscious awareness. It also includes the internal representation of self, the world, and personal goals, which reflects aspirations, ideals, needs, and the cognitions and strategies that govern behavior. *Social* functioning refers to the person's behavior in rela-tion to family, friends, authorities. peer group, and cultural expectations, as well as community institutions that influence and are influenced by the individual. Some might add that a truly holistic approach would include the spiritual or life-meaning dimension of functioning.

History and Development of Biopsychosocial Therapy

Biopsychosocial therapy is a systematically eclectic approach to thera-peutic intervention that was formally described and articulated by Len Sperry in 1988 (Sperry, 1988a). It is less a uniquely new treatment approach than an articulation and systemization of a way of conceptual-izing treatment planning based on biopsychosocial and teleological prin-ciples. Because of its comprehensive and integrative emphasis, it is particularly appropriate for cases that are termed "difficult" or "treat-ment resistant," or where there is comorbidity of various medical and psychiatric conditions. Evaluating an individual from a biopsychosocial approach oftentimes indicates the reasons for such difficulty and resist-ance.

Biopsychosocial therapy involves three distinct but interrelated stages: evaluation, formulation, and treatment plan (Sperry, 1988b). A biopsy-chosocial *evaluation* includes a systematic review of the presenting com-plaint, the past treatment history, a mental status examination, the social-developmental history, and relevant medical conditions and health habits, as well as family history of emotional dysfunction. A biopsy-chosocial *formulation* should provide an integrative explanation of the individual's current level of functioning in light of present and past antecedents. Biological factors—particularly predispositions, medical conditions, and health habits—are correlated with psychosocial factors. A summary of family-constellation and early-recollections data are reported in the present case. A list of short- and long-term problems, along with a five-axis *DSM-IV* diagnosis, is standard. Finally, the formu-lation suggests treatment focus and speculates on prognosis. A biopsychosocial *treatment plan* specifies the treatment outcomes and, if treatment is likely to proceed in more than one phase, the nature of the treatment contract or contracts. It also indicates decisions about the setting, mode, duration, and treatment strategies and techniques for accomplishing the treatment outcomes.

The question becomes: What is a "treatment-responsive patient," and how can those who are less receptive become "treatment-responsive" so that psychopharmacological treatment can be maximized? This chapter addresses these two questions by describing four treatment strategies that have been shown to maximize treatment outcomes when psychotropic medications are indicated. These overlapping strategies are designed to assist the provider in planning and implementing tailored, focused treatment.

Optimal treatment outcomes presume that a patient is prescribed and utilizes the most efficacious treatment. This presumption is seldom met in clinical practice. Even if the most potent, focused, and tailored treatment is prescribed, the patient may not commit to or cooperate with it over an extended period of time. The treatment-responsive patient is one who is able to make and keep this commitment. The challenge for providers—both those who are prescribers and those who are therapists, if joint treatment is involved—is to expect and facilitate treatment-responsiveness in their patients. Four treatment strategies have been noted to optimize treatment response and outcome (Sperry, 1995, 1996). The four essential strategies are: (1) engage the patient (and other provider[s]) in a collaborative relationship; (2) perform a comprehensive functional assessment; (3) decrease symptomatology and increase functioning; (4) maintain treatment gains and prevent recurrence. These strategies are not unlike the metastrategies or phases of treatment that Beitman (1993) found were common to most Eastern and Western therapy systems and approaches. They have been configured and fashioned to meet the particular needs of patients and couples presenting with a complex of symptoms, functional impairments, or concurrent medical or psychiatric conditions—such as characterological features that undermine or complicate treatment, unresponsiveness to treatment, or the presence of additional clinicians involved with the case.

Three additional treatment tactics that relate to the third strategy are also highlighted: combining treatment modalities, enhancing treatment compliance, and incorporating psychoeducational interventions. Along with the four essential strategies, these three tactics will be discussed and illustrated.

Detailed Description of Biopsychosocial Therapy Strategies

Strategy 1: Engage the Patient (and Other Provider[s]) in a Collaborative Relationship

Premature termination, treatment failure, and partial treatment success are often the resualt of inadequate patient engagement (Sperry, 1995). Usually, these outcomes are due to the clinician's unwarranted assumption that the patient is ready and motivated to collaborate in the change process. Thus, rather than viewing engagement as *the* primary treatment strategy, the clinician proceeds with assessment and change intervention strategies and methods. Research suggests that when patients are not ready or willing to engage in a collaborative treatment process, noncompliance, partial response, and premature termination can be expected (Beitman, 1993).

Involving two or more clinicians in the treatment process can further complicate patient engagement and collaboration. This may occur when one clinician provides individual therapy and another provides another psychosocial modality—such as family or group therapy—or prescribes medication. Collaborating clinicians tend to have different treatment foci and goals, and the duration and frequency of the sessions vary. While the prescribing clinician, for example, may be principally focused on maximizing medication compliance and hopefully increasing a positive placebo response, the nonmedical therapist may be principally focused on enhancing the patient's self-management and interpersonal-relationship functioning. Often the two collaborating clinicians will differ in gender, age, interpersonal style, professional discipline, and attitudes toward somatic and psychosocial therapies. Not surprisingly, the treatment process can be quite complicated, and interactional phenomena such as projective identification and splitting are commonplace.

Active and purposeful collaboration between clinician(s) and patient is

essential not only to facilitate engagement but for overall treatment efficacy. The roles of both clinicians should be clearly distinguished, and frequent discussions about the patient and treatment goals can facilitate
treatment outcomes (Woodward, Duckworth, & Guthiel, 1993). The
quality of clinician-clinician collaboration is crucial for effective treatment and for the necessary mutual respect, trust, and openness. Collaborative communication is useful in sensitizing each other to their concerns.
For instance, the nonprescribing clinician, who sees the patient more frequently, should be able to recognize early signs of hypomania in a patient
who is taking an antimanic medication. Or the prescribing clinician, concerned that a patient's irritability might be a side effect of fluoxetine
(Prozac), can learn from the other clinician that the patient is usually irritable.

Strategy 2: Perform a Comprehensive Functional Assessment

The *functional assessment* should focus on two patient characteristics
that are predictive of treatment-responsiveness and hence a positive treatment outcome. They are treatment readiness and explanatory model
(Beitman, 1993). *Treatment readiness* is the patient's motivation and
capacity to cooperate with treatment. Assessing of treatment readiness
and facilitating the highest level of readiness of which the patient is capable are particularly important when psychotropic agents are the principal
treatment modality

The *explanatory model* is the patient's personal interpretation or
explanation of the disease and symptoms. This model can be fraught with
misinformation or misattribution. But this "explanation" becomes the
basis for patient education and negotiation. For instance, a bipolar
patient who believes that his illness is caused by insomnia and can be
cured by a good night's sleep needs to have his "explanation" corrected
and polarized. Similarly, a patient who explains her experience of generalized anxiety in terms of a single early-life trauma should hear the
provider describe a more complete model of the illness, which also allows
for these particular concerns about the early trauma. The provider must
also elicit and address specific irrational beliefs about illness or treatment.
The delusional belief that the medication being prescribed is poison is one
obvious example. Less obviously, patients with low self-esteem may

ascribe negative meaning to a medication, viewing it as representative of their personal deficiency or worthlessness. Such patients may externalize and dismiss this projected badness by refusing to accept the medication and thus protect themselves from further loss of self-esteem. Helping patients, particularly those seeking a magic pill, understand their illness is best done in a biopsychosocial context. Negotiated explanations that are tailored to the patient's experience are particularly valuable. Such an explanation should be simple, should integrate biological and psychosocial mechanisms, and should incorporate some elements of the patient's explanation. For example, a schizophrenic male may accept that he has a biochemical imbalance that leaves him overly reactive to his environment and other people (the perceptual-filter model of psychosis), resulting in social withdrawal and simple phobia. Or a female patient who insists that hypoglycemia is the basis for her major depressive episode might be offered a treatment plan in which her blood glucose would be checked immediately and reevaluated if a four-week trial of medication is not successful. Finally, patients may perceive medication as both a vehicle and an agent of control: as a chemical means by which the clinician exerts control over their thoughts or actions. Hence noncompliance becomes a means of controlling and defeating the clinician. Similarly, noncompliance may function as a projective identification, as when the patient's feelings of helplessness are projected onto and induced in the clinician.

While the current diagnostic system *(DSM-IV)* may have research and administrative value in specifying diagnoses across a range of patients, it is not clinically useful in evaluating patients for treatment-planning purposes. Not only are the diagnostic categories and criteria somewhat arbitrary, but they do not currently distinguish between symptomatic distress and functional capacity; nor do they address the matter of readiness for change. Clinically speaking, these factors are critical in planning treatment and predicting outcome. An evaluation model that specifies five dimensions is recommended: presentation, pattern, predisposition, perpetuants, and readiness for treatment (Sperry, Gudeman, Blackwell, & Faulkner, 1992; Sperry, 1995).

Presentation is a description of the nature and severity of the individual's psychiatric condition. It can include the type and kind of symptoms (i.e., acute, warning, or persistent), level of life functioning (i.e., self-management, family, intimacy, work, social, and health), past history, and course of the illness.

Pattern is the predictable and consistent style or manner in which a person thinks, feels, acts, copes, and defends the self, in both stressful and nonstressful circumstances. It reflects the individual's baseline functioning. Pattern has physical, psychological, and social features, such as a sedentary and coronary-prone lifestyle, a dependent personality style or disorder, or collusion in a relative's marital problems. Pattern also includes the individual's functional strengths, which counterbalance dysfunction. One way to specify pattern is to use *DSM-IV* Axis II personality traits or disorder terms. Pattern has traditionally been the focus of instrumentation in psychological assessment and the basis for a comprehensive psychiatric interview. Clinicians who can effectively elicit and articulate information on pattern (as distinct but complementary to predisposition, perpetuants, and treatment readiness) are cognitively aided in both case formulation and treatment planning.

Predisposition encompasses all factors that render an individual vulnerable to a disorder. Predisposing factors usually are physical, psychological, and social. *Physical* (or biological) factors include genetic, familial, temperament, or medical patterns, such as family history of a major psychiatric disorder, an organ inferiority, a family history of substance abuse, a difficult or slow-to-warm-up child temperament, or cardiac disease or hypertension. *Psychological* factors might include dysfunctional beliefs or convictions involving inadequacy, perfectionism, or overdependence, which might predispose the individual to a medical disorder, such as coronary artery disease. Psychological factors might also involve social skills, like lack of friendship skills, unassertiveness, or over-aggressiveness. Social factors could include early-childhood losses, an inconsistent parenting style, an overly enmeshed or disengaged family-of-origin, or a family constellation characterized by dogged competitiveness or emotional surveillance. Subcultural, financial, and ethnic factors can be additional social predisposers.

Perpetuants are processes in the patient or the patient's environment that reinforce and confirm the patient's pattern. These processes may be physical, such as impaired immunity or habituation to an addictive substance; psychological, such as loss of hope or fear of the consequences of getting well; or social, such as colluding family members or agencies that foster disordered behavior rather than recovery and growth.

Readiness for treatment is the patient's desire for and capacity to make therapeutic changes. Readiness involves three components: treatment expectations, treatment willingness, and treatment capability (Sperry, 1995). Though related, each of these three is a relatively independent marker of readiness. Patients can have high, low, or ambivalent *expectations* for change, and these expectations may be realistic or unrealistic. Generally speaking, patients with moderate to high realistic expectations do change more than patients with unrealistic or minimal expectations. Treatment *willingness* reflects the patient's potential or likelihood for change. Normative stages or levels of change have been noted in psychotherapy and pharmacotherapy (Beitman, 1993). The stages are precontemplation (denial of the need for treatment), contemplation (acceptance of the need for treatment), decision (agreement to take responsibility for and collaborate with a treatment effort), action (taking responsibility and collaborating in the change effort), and maintenance (continuing the effort and avoiding relapse). Knowledge of a patient's treatment willingness or stage of change is critical in predicting the treatment outcome because patients who have accepted the need for treatment, have decided to cooperate with treatment, and have made efforts to change and maintain change are more likely to have positive outcomes than patients who have not. Treatment *capability* is the degree to which patients are capable of controlling or modulating their affects, cognitions, and impulses. Those who have such capability are psychologically available to collaborate in treatment, in contrast to patients who are continually parasuicidal or engage in treatment sabotage or escape behaviors (Sperry, 1995).

Strategy 3: Decrease Symptomatology and Increase Functioning

Decreasing symptomatology and increasing life functioning are the essential goals of all therapy systems and approaches. Individuals and couples who present for mental health treatment in symptomatic distress are seeking relief from symptoms that they have not be able to reduce by their own efforts. Thus symptom reduction or removal is one of the first goals of treatment. Usually this goal is achieved with medication and/or behavioral interventions. According to phase theory, as patients' symptoms increase, one or more areas of their life functioning decrease; and until symptomatology is decreased, therapeutic efforts to increase functional capacity tend to be thwarted (Sperry, Brill, Howard, & Grissom, 1996). Six areas of life functioning that the Social Security Administration considers in making a determination of health or disability are: self-management, health and grooming, family, social, intimacy, and occupational functioning. Along with levels of symptomatology, these areas of functioning are measured and monitored in current psychotherapy treatment outcome systems (Sperry et al., 1996). Most individuals who present for biopsychosocial therapy have problems with both symptomatic distress and functional impairment, and many of them have only partially responded to previous therapy—usually single-mode, single-approach treatment. Thus it is incumbent on clinicians practicing biopsychosocial therapy to formulate a treatment plan comprehensively and integratively.

The three treatment tactics related to this third strategy can insure and optimize the likelihood of reducing symptoms and increasing functional capacity. They are: combining treatment modalities, enhancing treatment compliance, and incorporating psychoeducational interventions.

Combining treatments means adding treatment modalities to the primary modality. When a patient begins a course of psychotherapy, during which increasing symptoms prevent the patient from adequately functioning in relationships or on the job, medication may be added to the primary modality. When medication is the primary modality but issues of compliance or patient safety become an issue, individual psychotherapy, group psychotherapy, or couple or family therapy is typically added to increase treatment response and outcome. Group or family therapy may simply be combined with individual therapy. Or the three modalities may be combined: individual therapy, family therapy, and medication.

Enhancing treatment compliance is a major challenge facing both prescribing and nonprescribing clinicians. Compliance is affected by patient factors, provider-patient interaction, the treatment regimen itself, and family factors. The placebo effect is the belief and expectation that the patient will positively respond to treatment. It is operative anytime in any clinical situation, specifically when medication is involved. The provider can enhance or trigger the placebo effect in several ways: by spending time with the patient, especially at the outset of treatment; by expressing interest and concern; and by demonstrating a confident, professional manner (Sperry, 1995).

Incorporating psychoeducational interventions is a powerful optimizing tactic in psychopharmacotherapy. Psychoeducation is much more than merely explaining a medication, its dosing schedule, and its side effect profile. It includes drug information sheets, patient education videos, medication groups, self-help organizations, support groups, social skills training, and more. Incoporating psychoeducational strategies and tactics in medication management is almost always essential to ameliorating symptoms, particularly in the long term.

Strategy 4: Maintain Treatment Gains and Prevent Recurrence

Technically, a *relapse* is a continuation of the "original" episode, while a *recurrence* is the instigation of a "new" episode. In this discussion, however, both terms will be used synonymously. In order to prevent relapse, the provider must assess the patient's risk factors and potential for relapse, and incorporate relapse prevention strategies into the treatment process.

Clinical Indications for the Strategies

The clinical indications for the four biopsychosocial therapy strategies just described can be stated in both broad and narrow terms. In *broad* terms, all four strategies are indicated in instances when an adult patient or a couple (1) exhibits significant symptomatic distress and/or considerable functional impairment, particularly when biological factors are implicated, as in most severe Axis I disorders; (2) has a concurrent Axis I, II, or III condition that complicates treatment; (3) has not responded to a single modality or approach treatment; or (4) has more than one clinician providing treatment.

In *narrow* terms, each of the four strategies has more specific indications and contraindications—particularly the three tactics associated with the third strategy. Space precludes detailing them here. The interested reader is referred to *Psychopharmacology and Psychotherapy: Strategies for Maximizing Treatment Outcomes* (Sperry, 1995) for these specific indications.

Clinical Applications with an Individual: Case Example

Jeanne is a 35-year-old never-married, white female clerk-stenographer who presented with a two-week onset of depressed mood. Other symptoms included loss of energy, markedly diminished interest, insomnia, difficulty concentrating, and increasing social isolation. She had not showed up for work for four days, prompting the psychiatric referral. Cutbacks at her office led to her being transferred out of a close-knit secretarial pool where she had been for 16 years—and had been an administrative assistant for 6 years—to a senior administrative assistant position for the new vice-president for sales in the executive annex. Jeanne experienced this transfer as a significant loss, which appears to have triggered her depressive symptoms and social isolation. No personal or family psychiatric or alcohol- and substance-abuse history was reported. She denies current medical problems or the use of prescription or over-the-counter medications. She lives alone in a duplex in a quiet residential neighborhood. She reports having one close female friend at her office and has not been involved in an intimate relationship since college. Jeanne has worked at the same company since graduating from a two-year business college program at the age of 20.

Engaging the Individual in a Collaborative Relationship

As is often the case with shy or avoidant patients, Jeanne showed up late for the initial evaluation. She indicated she had come only at the insistence of the director of human resources, and while she admitted she felt awful, she was not sure she needed treatment. Self-disclosure was clearly difficult for her. She did, however, view her job transfer as a significant loss and tentatively agreed that it might have triggered her depressive symptoms and isolative behavior. Since there was no indication that she was a danger to herself, outpatient treatment seemed possible. In taking the history, the clinician became increasingly aware of Jeanne's longstanding hypersensitivity to criticism. Accordingly, as the formulation of her avoidant personality style emerged, the clinician was notably gentle and supportive both verbally and nonverbally.

Avoidant individuals tend to "test" and provoke clinicians in several ways in early sessions, such as by criticizing them for being late, or for changing or canceling appointments. Accordingly, near the end of the first session, the clinician made a predictive interpretation that Jeanne would probably have a difficult time making and keeping subsequent sessions. Needless to say, the next appointment was made with relative ease, and Jeanne arrived at the second session on time.

Because the clinical picture of patients seeking biopsychosocial therapy is complex, combined treatment is often a consideration. Thus it is incumbent on the clinician to establish collaborative relationships with other possible providers, such as a prescribing psychiatrist, a group or family therapist, or a consulting medical specialist. A patient with avoidant personality dynamics will likely "test" the prescribing physician and group therapist's trustability and criticalness as well. Consequently, the clinician shared and discussed these considerations with collaborating clinicians—a prescribing physician and a group therapist, in this case.

Performing a Comprehensive Functional Assessment

Jeanne's score on the Beck Depression Inventory, given after the initial session, was 26, indicating a moderate-severe level of clinical depression. The profile on Jeanne's MCMI-III suggested the diagnosis of major depression and avoidant personality disorder.

Family-constellation data revealed that Jeanne is the older of two siblings. Her brother, Joe is four years younger, is married with two children, and works as a computer programmer for a pharmaceutical manufacturer. Both parents are alive and relatively healthy. Jeanne's father had worked as a senior accountant until three years ago, when the firm he had been at for 28 years had downsized and forced him into early retirement. Two years ago the parents relocated to a retirement village in Arizona. Jeanne's mother never worked outside the home. Family values included hard work, social conformity, and obedience.

Jeanne thinks she is most like her mother but has had a somewhat distant relationship with her, both as a child and even now. But Jeanne recalls being "fussed over" by her aunt, her mother's older sister, until she died when Jeanne was 7. Jeanne believes her brother was the favorite of both her parents. She recalls having few friends growing up, after her best friend moved away when Jeanne was 8 years old. She also recalls, in junior and senior high school, being ridiculed by others for being somewhat obese and "clumsy." She didn't date in high school but did attend the senior prom. In college she had a few dates with fellow students, which involved a single sexual encounter.

Her earliest childhood recollection involved seeing her infant brother for the first time, when she was 4 years old. Her parents had just returned from the hospital; Jeanne had been frightened staying with her aunt and not knowing where her mother had gone. Her mother lovingly placed her baby brother in Jeanne's old crib, while Jeanne's father said that Joe's birth had been the happiest day of his life. Jeanne was told to stop whining and asking questions about the baby and to go outside to play, or she would be punished. She remembers running outside crying and hiding in her tree fort until it got dark. She felt frightened and confused. Jeanne described intense feelings of humiliation and rejection following her brother's birth. In a second recollection, from when she was about 6 years old, Jeanne was supposed to have been watching Joe in his playpen while their mother went inside to make lunch. Unbeknown to Jeanne, Joe had taken a small plastic toy apart and stuffed a piece of it up his nose, where it lodged. He began screaming. Responding to the crying, the mother spanked Jeanne for being a disobedient and uncaring sister. Jeanne recalled running to her room crying and feeling hurt for being unjustly punished and unloved because her mother gave so much attention to her brother. In short, she experienced her brother's birth and his subsequent spoiling by her parents as nullifying the sense of specialness and nurturance that she had previously enjoyed.

The following diagnostic and clinical formulation was developed. Jeanne's history and mental status exam were consistent with major depressive episode. In addition, she met criteria for avoidant personality disorder. The *diagnostic formulation* included the following five axes of *DSM-IV* diagnosis:

Axis I:	296.22 Major Depressive Disorder, Single Episode, Moderate
	V62.2 Occupational Problem
Axis II:	301.82 Avoidant Personality Disorder
Axis III:	None
Axis IV:	Limited Support System; Job Stressor
Axis V:	GAF=45 (at time of psychiatric evaluation);
	GAF=69:(highest in past 12 months)

The following *clinical formulation* was specified: Jeanne came to believe that the opinions of others were all that counted. She was teased and ridiculed by her peers for her personal appearance, especially her obesity. There were also strong parental injunctions against discussing important matters with "outsiders." Now when she is in unfamiliar or in close interpersonal relations, she typically distances and isolates herself from others. Presumably, she anticipates and fears disapproval and criticism. She views others as critical and harsh and is convinced that others see her as inadequate. Therefore, she is slow to warm up to and trust others, and she "tests" their trustability by being late for, canceling, or missing agreed-upon engagements. Her lack of social skills in relating to new or less-known individuals, and her limited social network—she is a "homebody" who spends much of her time reading romance novels, watching soap operas, or knitting—further contributes to a isolative lifestyle and reinforces her beliefs about self, the world, and others. With the exception of intimacy and social relations, she has functioned above average in the life task of work.

She agreed she was severely depressed and was willing to comply with combined treatment involving medication. It was started and monitored on an outpatient basis, along with time-limited psychotherapy. She did not appear to be particularly psychologically minded and had moderate skill deficits in assertive communication, trust, and friendship skills. Given her avoidant personality structure, it was anticipated that she would have difficulty discussing personal matters with health providers and that she would "test" and provoke them into criticizing her for changing or canceling appointments at the last minute, being late, and the like. Nevertheless, some three and half years after completing a smoking cessation program, she continued to be nicotine abstinent. Her support system includes only minimal contact with an older female cousin and a pet dog.

Decreasing Symptomatology and Increasing Functioning

A biopsychosocial treatment plan was developed that specified a number of treatment targets, including ameliorating symptoms, increasing trustfulness, making workplace accommodations, and returning to work. Table 17-1 lists these treatment targets.

Table 17-1. Biopsychosocial Treatment Targets: Jeanne

Biological Targets:

Reduce/eliminate depressive symptoms

Psychological Targets

Reduce shyness
Increase trustfulness
Increase assertive communication

Social/Relational Targets

Decrease shyness and increase friendship skills
Decrease job stressors through workplace accommodation
Return to work
Enlarge social support system

These goals were designed to facilitate therapeutic outcomes by maximizing therapeutic leverage while minimizing the influence of previous perpetuant and other forms of resistance to change. An initial treatment agreement was established for eight 45–minute individual sessions combining medication and brief psychotherapy. These sessions focused on symptom reduction and returning to work.

First, the clinician addressed the biological target of depressive symptomatology. Elicitation of Jeanne's explanatory model of her illness and her treatment expectations suggested she would be a good candidate for medication. The clinician decided to refer her to her family physician, of whom she was quite fond, rather than to a psychiatrist whom she did not know or have a reasonable level of trust. For someone like Jeanne, who is overly cautious, referral to a trusted provider can easily trigger the placebo effect.

The clinician contacted the family physician, clarified the nature of collaboration, and suggested the need for a medication that would not have the kind of side effects that would easily dissuade Jeanne from compliance. A medication trial was begun, apparently without untoward effects. Within 10 days, Jeanne's sleep and energy had returned to baseline.

Since job-circumstance stressors had triggered Jeanne's disordered response, the goal of reasonably returning Jeanne to work might not be achieved without some workplace accommodation. A hallmark of the Americans for Disability Act is that employers must reasonably accommodate an employee's disability, including the kind of psychiatric disability manifest in Jeanne. This would require some measure of collaboration between the clinician and Jeanne's work supervisor. After getting a signed release from Jeanne, the clinician contacted the work supervisor about issues of work stress, peer support, and possible job accommodation. The supervisor agreed that Jeanne needed a familiar, trusting social support and was able to assign one of her coworkers to the same office to which Jeanne had been moved.

With regard to the some of the other social and psychological targets, the clinician and Jeanne mutually agreed that skill-oriented group therapy was probably the treatment of choice to increase her trustfulness and decrease her social isolation. Aware that Jeanne's pattern of avoidance would make entry into and continuation with the group difficult, individual sessions were to serve as a transition into the group. Then shorter individual sessions would focus on medication management, probably on a monthly and then bimonthly basis.

Individual sessions continued with gradual transition into time-limited group therapy, focused on interpersonal skill development. It was predictable that Jeanne would "test" the prescribing clinician and group therapist's trustworthiness and criticalness. Throughout treatment all the clinicians involved were mindful of her therapeutic leverage (Jeanne's success with nicotine abstinence, her relations with her cousin and her pet, her close-knit typing pool) as well as the perpetuants that would likely hamper treatment. As Jeanne's depressive symptoms ameliorated and a maintenance medication schedule was established, the prescribing clinician began preparing her for transition into the group. Because of her fear and ambivalence concerning the group process, the clinician suggested, and Jeanne agreed, that it might be helpful for her to meet in advance with the therapist who led the interpersonal-skills group. During the fifth individual session, the group therapist was briefly introduced to Jeanne, and they discussed a three-way treatment plan. The three agreed that Jeanne would continue in individual weekly appointments concurrent with weekly group sessions. Assuming things were proceeding well enough, sessions with the prescribing clinician would be reduced to monthly medication checks.

A subsequent two-way discussion between the group therapist and the clinician concluded that projective identification and splitting were unlikely to be issues with Jeanne. Instead, they predicted she would have difficulty maintaining active group participation and following up on "homework" between group sessions. The clinician agreed to encourage and support Jeanne's group involvement in the concurrent individual sessions. After the third group session, the therapist and psychiatrist conferred with the prescribing clinician about the transition from weekly to monthly sessions.

Maintaining Treatment Gains and Preventing Recurrence

Jeanne's progress was sufficient that, after 10 weekly group sessions, she "graduated" from the group. She remained on antidepressants for nearly a year, after which the monthly medication management sessions were discontinued. Because this was her first depressive episode, one that was acute and reactive, and there was no family history of a mood disorder, her chances of a recurrence of major depression is quite unlikely. In a follow-up session 18 months later, Jeanne showed that she continued to work, was asymptomatic, and was functioning well with regard to all the life tasks. At that time her GAF was estimated to be 78. Furthermore, Jeanne was proud to announce that she was engaged to marry a coworker.

Clinical Applications with a Couple:
Case Example

Bill and Janice, who have been married for 13 years and are both 34 years old, presented for couple therapy with both acute symptoms and chronic issues. They have two children, ages 9 and 11. Bill has been unemployed for nearly five months. Previously he was a marketing manager for a *Fortune* 500 corporation, but his division had been dramatically restructured, eliminating his position. After losing his job, he became increasingly quiet and socially inactive. About six weeks ago, full-blown depressive symptoms seemed to erupt. He experienced insomnia, decreased concentration, lack of energy, constant rumination about being a failure, and anhedonia, and not surprisingly, he reported that he had little motivation to search for a job. Two weeks earlier his family doctor started him on an antidepressant, but he did not seem to be responding. Janice complained that Bill seemed to have no sexual desire and had become impotent in the past few weeks. It was increasingly difficult for Bill to get out of bed in the morning. He received a substantial severance package, but his benefits would stop in three weeks, so Janice had recently shifted from part-time to full-time work as an account executive for a telemarketing firm to support the family. She was both worried and angry about this.

For the past three years, Janice had been in psychotherapy for chronic subclinical depression, which was diagnosed as dysthymic disorder. She had worked with two therapists during this period but seemed to make little progress in reducing her sense of being "stuck in a down mood." Her family doctor started her on a low dose of Prozac, but since it had no apparent effect after a week, Janice stopped it. Recently, Janice realized that not only was her own life not improving, but her marriage was quickly deteriorating. Her husband, who had always been a steady and faithful ally, was increasingly depressed and withdrawn, and his sexual impotence has strained their relationship even further. In desperation, Janice had put her individual therapy on hold to seek out couple therapy.

In short, Janice initiated the appointment for couple therapy because of her frustration with Bill's unemployment, his emotionally unavailability, and financial stressors, as well as increasing difficulties with their son Timmy's acting out at school and home. Her frustrations had peaked the week before when she reviewed how bleak their immediate future appeared to be and Bill just shrugged his shoulders. In desperation she gave Bill an ultimatum: "Start doing something about these things, or I'm leaving." Needless to say, Bill agreed reluctantly to couple therapy.

Engaging the Couple in a Collaborative Relationship

The intent of the first session or two is to establish a working relationship that is sufficient to engage the couple in the therapeutic process. A basic premise of biopsychosocial therapy is that the patient or couple will leave sessions—especially initial sessions—with a sense of having derived some tangible benefit. It is often important to leave the couple at the initial interview with a feeling of hope. By providing hope, the clinician often can help them to settle down and begin to benefit from the therapeutic process. Bill and Janice arrived early for the first interview but came in separate cars. Janice initiated contact with the receptionist and clearly dominated the early part of the first session, while Bill seemed pained and preoccupied.

A commonplace tactic in biopsychosocial therapy for engaging the couple is to initiate some clinical interventions in the first session. Unlike high-functioning and minimally distressed individual clients, for whom extended in-depth evaluation typically precedes treatment intervention, clinicians practicing biopsychosocial therapy typically treat individuals and couples who are experiencing acute distress or dysfunctioning and are in need of immediate intervention. Such interventions can range from hospitalization to medication or to some environmental intervention, such as a medical leave from a job or extracation from an abusive or non-supportive living arrangement. The clinician's quick and decisive response engenders a sense of trust and hopefulness in the individual or couple, which usually facilitates engagement. In the early sessions, when such immediacy is present, the strategies of establishing a collaborative relationship, performing a functional assessment, and effecting symptom reduction and increased functioning tend to parallel one another.

It seemed clear that both Janice and Bill wanted and needed help. But because Bill was clinically depressed and so was perceived as a "patient," the clinician thought it necessary and useful to socialize the couple to a systems perspective for the conjoint treatment. He framed that neither of them was "sick" and that each was simply expressing in his or her characteristic style what neither had "permission" or "ability" to verbalize. Both partners responded favorably to this perspective. The clinician also framed that their symptomatic behavior was their attempts to communicate with each other. Not only did the receiving partner not understand the communication, the sending partner was not completely aware of the message. Thus, an important task of treatment was to accept responsibility for sending messages, that is, to acknowledge that messages were being sent, and then to clarify them. Only then could each partner decide how to respond favorably.

Performing a Comprehensive Functional Assessment

In biopsychosocial therapy, assessment and intervention/treatment are closely related and proceed by phases. In couple therapy, of necessity, effective assessment deals with both the marital system and the individ-ual/personal subsystems. For Janice and Bill, formal assessment involved both an individual and a systems measure: the Millon Clinical Multiaxial Inventory (Millon, 1983) and the Marital Inventory (Dinkmeyer & Dinkmeyer, 1983), as well as the Self-Report Inventory (Beavers, Hamp-son, & Hulgus, 1985). After the first session, Bill was asked to complete the Beck Depression Inventory, he scored a 23, confirming the clinician's clinical impression of major depressive episode. The Millon results indi-cated the involvement of significant personality factors in both partners, with compulsive, passive-aggressive, and dependent features in Bill, and histrionic and dependent features in Janice. The Self-Report Inventory results suggested that the marital relationship was characterized by a "mixed" style—that is, enmeshed in some areas and disengaged in oth-ers—while being primarily in the "midrange" level of functioning. The Marital Inventory results confirmed that the couple had notable problems in communication, finances, and child rearing, but it also indicated the presence of significant intimacy issues, which the couple had initially denied when their relationship history was taken.

Developmentally, Bill is the youngest of three children. His father was a real estate broker and his mother an elementary school teacher. Bill's father had been treated for depression in his late thirties and had died at age 45 of a sudden cardiac arrest after exercising. Bill described him as an ambivalent man who had difficulty being a breadwinner. The marriage was highly con-flictual, with frequent bickering and a variety of sexual concerns. Bill's mother was a caregiver who never remarried and continues to spoil her son. Both of Bill's older siblings have professional careers and stable marriages.

Janice is an only child. Her father is a stockbroker and as "steady as the day is long." Her mother is an accountant by profession but has not worked in that capacity for several years because of depression and anxi-ety "attacks." Her mother appears to experience agorophobia, which has essentially kept her homebound for as long as Janice can remember. She apparently has refused treatment of any kind.

Janice and Bill have been married for 13 years and have known each other for more than 19 years, having grown up in the same suburban neighborhood. They met and began dating in high school, and neither had any serious relationships with others. Their early years of marriage were quite uneventful, and their marital satisfaction during those years was described by both as relatively high. Recently, that had all changed. Their

11-year-old son, Timmy, was diagnosed with attention deficit/hyperactivity disorder—which was described more as behavior problems and hyperactivity than as attention deficit—and is currently taking Ritalin (10 mg twice a day). Janice was furious that Bill said that taking medication "is proof that Timmy is just as hysterical as his mother." Timmy had always been closer to Janice than to Bill, and lately Bill has seemed even more removed from Timmy. Janice believes that Timmy is acting out to get Bill's attention.

The following diagnostic and clinical formulation was developed for both spouses. In terms of *DSM-IV* this five-axis *diagnostic formulation* is:

BILL

Axis I:	296.22 Major Depression: Single Episode: Moderate	
	V61.10 Marital Problems	
Axis II:	V71.09 Compulsive and Passive-Aggressive Features	
Axis III:	None	
Axis IV:	Moderate-Severe: Marital Discord, Unemployment	
Axis V:	GAF-39 (current); GAF-68 (highest past year)	

JANICE

Axis I:	300.4 Dysthymic Disorder V61.10 Marital Problems	
Axis II:	301.60 Personality Disorder NOS: Histrionic and Dependent Features	
Axis III:	None	
Axis IV:	Moderate–Severe: Marital Discord, Financial Concerns	
Axis V:	GAF=51 (current); GAF=67 (highest past year)	

Similarly, a *clinical-systemic formulation* was stated: This couple is currently experiencing some acute stressors, which complicate their individual and couple dynamics. Bill's ambivalence—reflecting his compulsive and passive-aggressive personality style—seems to complicate his return to gainful employment, which increases his wife's current distress. She functions in a more histrionic and dependent manner, meaning that she indirectly demands attention from him, but she is frustrated by his relational ambivalence and his sexual and emotional impotence. Timmy appears to be overly identified with Janice, an enmeshment that seems to reinforce Bill's distancing from both his son and his wife. The couple have notable deficits in relational skills, particularly assertiveness, as well as a transgenerational history that predisposes both to maladaptive functioning when under considerable stress. In addition, biological factors (i.e., his clinical depression and, medication-induced impotence and her chronic dysphoria) further exacerbate their problems and concerns.

Nevertheless, they appear to be adequately motivated for treatment, and the prognosis seems to be fair to good. Combined treatment involving systemic, cognitive-behavioral, and psychoeducational interventions seems indicated for the psychological and social factors, and medication and psychoeducational interventions for the biological factors.

Decreasing Symptomatology and Increasing Functioning

A biopsychosocial treatment plan identifies the biological, psychological, and social target areas for intervention. Table 17-2 summarizes these intervention targets delineated by the biopsychosocial assessment.

Table 17-2. Biopsychosocial Treatment Targets:
Janice, Bill, and Timmy

Biological Targets:

Depressive symptoms (Bill)
Medication-induced impotence (Bill)
Chronic dysphoria (Janice)

Psychological Targets

Demandingness and overdependence (Janice)
Pessimism and perfectionism (Bill)
Difficulty with direct expression of feelings (Bill)

Social/Relational Targets

Deficits in intimacy skills (couple)
Limited social activities :(couple)
Deficits in assertive communication (couple)
Triangular relationship among Bill, Janice, and Tim

From a biopsychosocial therapy perspective, the initial focus of treatment typically addresses symptomatic distress. Usually this involves reducing or eliminating acute symptoms. After sufficient symptomatic relief is achieved, treatment can shift to increasing functional capacity, addressing psychological and social/relational targets.

Because of his obvious acute distress, Bill's vegetative symptoms of depression were addressed first. The clinician elicited his explanatory model of his illness and his treatment expectations—including his fantasies about taking medication. He believed that his symptoms were the result of stress (job loss) and biology ("a chemical imbalance in my brain") and should respond to proper medication and therapy. He made no connection between his impotence and the antidepressant he had been prescribed, since no mention had been made of potential sexual side effects. He and the clinician agreed to switch him to another antidepressant (Serzone) that was less likely to induce impotence. Although Bill insisted that the medication trial would "work this time," the clinician, mindful of Bill's ambivalence, made no predictions about the medication's efficacy and actually cautioned Bill not to get his hopes up too high. The medication was begun at a low dose and was increased over the next seven days. By the twelfth day, Bill reported that he was feeling considerably better.

Janice indicated that she wanted to try medication again, convinced that she had previously not given Prozac a sufficient trial. Eliciting her fantasies about medication was quite instructive: She believed that Prozac would not only be a magical solution to her subclinical depression—much as in the case histories reported in the book Listening to Prozac—but she also expected she would lose weight in the process! When neither happened within two weeks, she disappointedly stopped taking it. The clinicians gave her psychoeducation about likely treatment response and discussed it with her sufficiently to dispel her prior notions.

Next the clinician addressed the couple's psychological and social/relational targets, pointing out their interlocking personality dynamics. He reframed Janice's dysthymia as a way of asking to be cared for, and her "moodiness" as her attempt to keep the relationship together. She valued love and the marriage and her family, and she wanted them all to be happy. She was trying to keep them together and to look out for her husband and his health. Bill, for his part, was trying to keep his family together too, and the clinician reframed his perfectionistic manner as his way of showing caring and concern. In effect, their symptoms were serving the same purpose, just in different ways. The challenge for both of them was to communicate their desires in more direct, constructive way.

The clinician then directed their attention to rebalancing their relationship pattern. This proved exceedingly challenging, since power was rather evenly distributed: Bill would manifest his aloofness, perfectionism, and passive-aggressivity until Janice became upset and "hysterical," at which point she would regain power in the relationship. Then Bill would calm the situation by capitulating, which she liked, but he eventually regained power again. She would allow this until she felt he cared more about his needs than her, after which she would grow impatient and become upset, and the cyclic pattern would repeat itself. This cyclic pattern was pointed out to them. Bill immediately grasped it and its ramifications, but Janice found it harder to comprehend.

Issues of boundaries and intimacy were not as easily addressed. A triangle existed, in which their son Timmy oscillated between being a husband-surrogate for his mother when Bill was away from home, to acting like a friend to his father when Bill was home. His presence both fueled the maladaptive cyclic pattern and perpetuated the very problems that, without his presence, might lead to some kind of resolution. The next several weeks of conjoint treatment focused on these issues. While switching to a family therapy mode might have had value at this point, it had inherent dangers as well. Introducing Timmy into the conjoint sessions could perpetuate the very problem he was (inadvertently) helping to maintain: intruding upon the couple's relationship.

Instead, the clinician undertook to strengthen the couple's bond without the son in the session. Psychoeducation, including skills training, was begun. Assertive communication was the first focus of training; the couple built this skill both within and between sessions by role playing and focused practice. To enhance their relational intimacy, the couple made a commitment to arrange a "date" following each conjoint treatment session. In addition, the clinician framed to Bill that his son needed some fatherly "guidance" now that he was moving into adolescence, and that Bill needed to expand his own social network. He framed to Janice that encouraging Timmy to "separate" would strengthen not only her marriage but her son's future. Both agreed, and a "weaning" process began, which was aided by Timmy's increasing involvement in soccer and other team sports at his junior high school. Bill got involved as an "assistant" to the soccer coach. Subsequently, Timmy manifested fewer problems at school and at home, such that their pediatrician was able to lower his Ritalin dose.

Bill's controlling behavior and Janice's emotionality were mutually complementary. She was encouraged to "teach" him to be more passionate, and he was urged to be her consultant on matters of organization, regardless of household duties. They grasped this way of working, and though they still experienced some conflict, they were able to become more affectionate with each other.

Similarly, the clinician introduced a psychoeducational approach to insomnia. By modifying his evening schedule and attending to other aspects of sleep hygiene, Bill's chronic insomnia was gradually replaced with restful sleep within three weeks. His worrisome ruminations were reduced by learning the technique of "productive worry time." The clinician prescribed 30-minute sessions of productive worry—in which Bill would write down his worries in a journal—as daily homework. Finally, after about 10 conjoint sessions, 6 separate individual sessions were scheduled with each spouse. To modify Bill's perfectionism and pessimism, cognitive restructuring was utilized.

The clinician was effectively able to use paradox and reframing to help Janice and Bill continue to do what had to be done. Reframing their patterns of interaction as constructive, rather than destructive, changed the way they related to each other. The clinician also initiated efforts to reverse their pattern of nonproductive dialogue. Both Janice and Bill learned to appreciate each other's parenting strengths (i.e., Bill's silent withdrawal was reframed as "patience"; Janice's demandingness was reframed as "firmness"). In general, as treatment progresses, direct intervention in the presenting marital issues becomes a principal focus, and the relative importance of issues changes over time. Janice, for example, was still discouraged about Bill's lack of employment, but she was much less resentful, since he had been meeting with a career counselor. They communicated more directly with each other, learned to create boundaries, and were able to resolve problems as they occurred. Throughout their couple therapy, the clinician better understood and appreciated how Bill and Janice responded to conflict. They seemed to enjoy conflict as long as it did not get too far out of hand. When it did, Bill tended to shut down, whereas Janice tended to increase her demands and pursuit of him. To help them deal more effectively with conflict, the clinician obtained from them the compromises necessary to secure accommodation and eventually resolution. The couple learned how to resolve their specific issues and, specifically, what each of their roles had to be for effective resolution.

As Janice explored her hurt and resentment about Bill's emotional and sexual distancing, Bill began to understand how his passive-aggressive pattern of withholding intimacy safeguarded his belief that he was still a "perfect" husband-lover because he didn't risk failing at intimacy, but that the price he—and Janice—had to pay was too high. Subsequently, he agreed to begin to initiate and participate in sexual relations and to fulfill more of Janice's expectations.

Maintaining Treatment Gains and Preventing Recurrence

In the twentieth conjoint session, a review of progress revealed that the couple had resolved many of the issues for which they had requested help. As Janice's dysthymia came more under her control, she experienced more satisfaction in her relationship with Bill. He was able to secure a position as a faculty member in an executive MBA program, teaching marketing. He had always wanted to teach but had not done so because his father had insisted that "only those who can't, teach." Not wanting to be perceived by anyone, especially his father, as a failure, Bill had banished the thought of teaching—until now. He gained greater control over his schedule, worked fewer hours more efficiently, and found more pleasure at home.

After 20 conjoint sessions over a period of eight months, the clinician suggested a follow-up session in two months to monitor their progress. Individual therapy would continue with Bill, to focus on his perfectionism and passive-aggressive pattern. Bill and the clinician also arranged for medication monitoring on a three-month basis over the next 12 months, after which it was anticipated that medication could be discontinued. It was mutually agreed that Janice would take a "therapeutic holiday" from individual therapy but would check in with the clinician in six months.

Concluding Summary

Biopsychosocial therapy has been described as an integrative approach for conceptualizing and implementing treatments when biological as well as psychological and social/systemic factors are present. Rather than being a "new" treatment approach, it is a set of systemic strategies for planning and implementing effective treatment interventions within a biopsychosocial perspective. It uses four basic or essential treatment strategies, as well as three specific treatment tactics. While these strategies are not unrelated to meta-strategies common to other therapeutic approaches (Beitman, 1993), biopsychosocial therapy tailors them to the particular needs of patients and couples presenting with a complex of symptoms, functional impairments, or concurrent medical or psychiatric conditions that tend to undermine or complicate treatment. Many experienced clinicians are quite likely already utilizing many or all of these strategies and tactics intuitively or without acknowledging their reliance on the time-honored biopsychosocial perspective.

References

Beavers, W., Hampson, R., & Hulgus, Y. (1985). The Beavers systems approach to family assessment. *Family Process, 24,* 398–405.

Beitman, B. (1993). Pharmacotherapy and the stages of psychotherapeutic change. In J. Oldham, M. Riba, & A. Tasman (Eds.), *American Psychiatric Press review of psychiatry* (Vol. 12, pp. 521–540). Washington, DC: American Psychiatric Press.

Beitman, B., & Klerman, G. (Eds.). (1993). *Integrating pharmacotherapy and psychotherapy.* Washington, DC: American Psychiatric Press.

Dinkmeyer, D., & Dinkmeyer, J. (1983). *Marital inventory.* Coral Springs, FL: CMTI Press.

Engel, C. L. (1977). The need for a new medical model: A challenge to biomedical medicine. *Science, 196,* 129–136.

Millon, T. (1983). *Millon clinical multiaxial inventory.* Minneapolis: National Computer Service.

Sperry, L. (1988a). Biopsychosocial therapy: An integrative approach for tailoring treatment. *Individual Psychology, 44* (2), 225–235.

Sperry, L. (1988b). Designing effective psychiatric interventions. *Journal of Psychiatric Education, 12* (2), 125–128.

Sperry, L. (1995). *Psychopharmacology and psychotherapy: Strategies for maximizing treatment outcomes.* New York: Brunner/Mazel.

Sperry, L., Brill, P., Howard, K. & Grissom, G. (1996). *Treatment outcomes in psychotherapy and psychiatric interventions.* New York: Brunner/Mazel.

Sperry, L., Gudeman, J., Blackwell, B., & Faulkner, L. (1992). *Psychiatric case formulation.* Washington, DC: American Psychiatric Press.

Woodward, B., Duckworth, K., & Guthiel, T. (1993). The pharmacotherapist–psychotherapist collaboration. In J. Oldham, M. Riba, & A. Tasman (Eds.), *American Psychiatric Press review of psychiatry* (Vol. 12, pp. 631–649). Washington, DC: American Psychiatric Press.

Index